U2

The Complete Encyclopedia

Mark Chatterton

FIRE FLY

PUBLISHING

For Wendy and Alex

and all U2 fans everywhere

About the author

Mark Chatterton first saw U2 in 1981. Since then he has followed the band throughout each stage in their career. In the 1990s he edited and published the U2 fanzine, *Silver and Gold*, which was read by U2 fans throughout the world.

He has written for a variety of music publications including *Q*, *Classic Rock*, *Record Collector*, *Blueprint* and *Wondrous Stories*. This is his second book.

Also by Mark Chatterton:

Blowin' Free - 30 years of Wishbone Ash
(with Gary Carter) Firefly publishing

U2

The Complete Encyclopedia

Mark Chatterton

FIRE FLY PUBLISHING

First published in 2001 by Firefly Publishing.
Firefly is an imprint of SAF Publishing Ltd in association
with Helter Skelter Publishing Ltd.

SAF Publishing Ltd
Unit 7, Shaftesbury Centre,
85 Barlby Road, London. W10 6BN
ENGLAND

www.safpublishing.com
www.skelter.demon.co.uk

ISBN 0 946719 41 1

Cover photo credits: Front: Paul Bergen / Redferns

                                  Back: Edge: Rajiv Udani

                                          Larry: Shawn Brand

                                          Adam & Pop Mart: Claire Bolton

In some cases it has not proved possible to ascertain or trace original illustration copyright holders, and the publishers would be grateful to hear from the photographers concerned.

All lyrics quoted are for review, study or critical purposes.

A CIP catalogue record for this book is available from the British Library.

Printed in England by The Cromwell Press, Trowbridge, Wiltshire.

Foreword and Acknowledgements

This book has been a very large undertaking, taking up several years of my life, tucked away in front of my computer night after night, away from my family, listening to thousands of hours of U2 music and reading possibly millions of words written about U2! Thank God it's all over! There are several people who I would like to thank for their support, help, guidance and belief in this project.

Firstly a big thank you to my editor, Sean Body at Helter Skelter for support, encouragement and belief in me. Thanks also to Michael O'Connell and Tracey Bellaries for putting up with my numerous phone calls. Thanks also to Dave Hallbery and Mick Fish at SAF.

Thanks to all these kind, hard working ladies who helped with typing the original manuscript:- Jenny Davy, Jan Hannocks, Jennifer Iddon and Sue Churchman.

Hello and thanks to the various members of the U2 tribute bands, The Doppelgangers and Achtung Baby for reproducing some great U2 music in intimate surroundings. Also to Pete and Tab at Fives, Leigh; Bob at Leigh Record Exchange and Steve, Sheila and Steve at Club Riga, Southend.

Next I would like to thank the various dedicated U2 fans from around the world who helped in various ways by providing information, photographs, newspaper cuttings, tapes, videos and support in general. These are listed country by country:-

Argentina: Linda Wiske

Australia: Mark Bosnich, Martin Curnow, Georgia Everett

Austria: Elisabeth Heinrich, Hans-Jurgen Kuber

Belgium: Bart Moons

Canada: Steve Lewis

France: Patrice Bruhat

Germany: Tom Angermeier, Kay Bauersfeld, Iris Burger, Wiebe and Sieke Feddersen, Peter and Tanya Helmling, Sascha Kremer, Frank Rumpf, Nina Thomsen

Holland: Caroline Van Oosten de Boer

Italy: Paolo Ferranti, Alessandro Rasman

New Zealand: Simon Daniel, Emma Reilly, Mike Verney

Portugal: Ricardo Abrantes

Sweden: Anna Pomeroy

Uruguay: Laura Marchesco

United Kingdom: Vincent Bird, Karl Blain, Paul Brush, Jane Chalmers, Rita Cousins, Clark Denham, Julie Emms, Sue Fell, Diane Fussey, Simon Grayson, Richard Hare, Jackie Harper, Richard Mossop, Yvonne Neville, Mark Richards, Helen and Louise Taylor, Debbie Voisey, Sophie Watson, Deborah Wilson, Alan Workman

USA: Julie Berberich, Shawn Bland, Christine Enedy, Kim and Laura Mancini, Kris Martens, Matt McGee, Fatima Ontiveros, Andy and Pauline Powell, Robbie Robinson, Rajiv Udani, Kristy Voltolini, Sandi Wheeles

To the following people associated with U2 a special thank you for your help.

In Dublin: Steve Averill, Barry Devlin, Dave Fanning and Jim Lockhart at 2FM, Jackie Hayden, Dave Kavanagh, Philomena Lynott, Catherine Rutter at Windmill Lane and a big thank you to Cecilia Coffey at *Propaganda* for her patience and kindness.

In London: Anton Corbijn, Flood, Willie Williams, Martin Wroe and the girls at RMP for their helpfulness in answering my questions - Louise Butterly, Sandra McKay, Amanda Freeman and Regine Moylett

Thanks also to my "Dublin Companion" Paul Daly, who also provided several of the photos in this book.

A very special thank you to U2 super fan, Claire Bolton, who has helped with this project in many ways by providing photographs, books and articles, programmes, as well as helping with typing and proof-reading the manuscript.

Thanks to my son, Alex, whose proof-reading skills and knowledge of U2 helped make sure I avoided some sticky situations.

Lastly, a very big thank you to my wife, Wendy, who has always supported me throughout this project and whose love of U2 has been an inspiration. Thanks for being understanding, patient, kind, etc, etc..... I promise I will pay you back one day!

Mark Chatterton

Introduction

It was twenty five years ago this Autumn at Mount Temple Comprehensive school in Dublin, Ireland that a student called Larry Mullen placed a notice on the school message board asking for people to join the pop group he was starting. Amongst those that responded were Paul Hewson, Dave Evans and Adam Clayton. This was the beginning of a journey that was to take these four teenagers to the giddy heights of rock 'n' roll stardom and see the group U2 take on the mantle of the biggest band in the world. U2 is a now a name that is familiar to music fans the world over.

The four musicians that make up U2 started at the bottom rung of the ladder and through hard work, dedication and self belief, coupled with the guiding hand of manager, Paul McGuinness, they were able to reach the top. It was through playing live that U2 began to build up a following first in Dublin and Ireland, then in London and the rest of Britain, before moving on to conquer Europe, America, and eventually the rest of the world. At the time of writing U2 will have played their thousandth concert somewhere in America in the spring of 2001 - no one knows quite where. Quite an achievement! Millions of people have seen them play live the world over, whilst millions more hear their music daily on the radio or TV. The group have now sold in excess of 100 million records in just over twenty years, making them one of the all time biggest exports from Ireland and biggest selling band in the world.

What is it that makes U2 so special? Several factors come to mind. Longevity is one of them. Most groups are lucky if they can stay together for ten years. Inevitably musical differences, lack of inspiration, family ties, personality clashes and the rock 'n' roll lifestyle all play their part in causing suc-cessful bands to break up. Those that do survive for longer have usually had a gap of several years rest in between albums and touring, or have added new blood over the years. Yet the four members of U2 have been together now for twenty five years and have never split and reformed like some other big bands. As those close to the band have remarked on more than one occasion they are four friends who have stuck together over the years, never quitting when the going gets tough.

Another factor is their creativity, which remains undiminished. They have somehow managed to produce great music in all their years together which has always been contemporary, never sounding dated and which is at the cutting edge of the music scene. Musically they haven't been afraid to re-invent themselves which has helped bring a new generation of fans into the massive U2 fan base. Through their use of promo videos, remixes of their songs, collaborations with other musicians and a willingness to still learn, they have managed to stay fresh and inventive. Unlike some other big name groups and artists they have always been keen to stay in touch with their fans. There seems to be a bond between band and fans which is unique. How many other groups will come and sign autographs or allow themselves to be photographed both before and after a concert? They may be mixing with all sorts of celebrities nowadays from supermodels to sportsmen, from politicians to Popes, but they still recognise the importance of the support they receive from their fans.

Attending a U2 concert is not just going to be entertained for a few hours. For many it can be an emotional event, for some it can even be a spiritual experience. The Christian beliefs of the members of U2 have always influenced their music and whilst lyrically they have hardly ever preached through their songs, many U2 songs show a spiritual side that very few groups would ever use. Apart from their music, U2 have always supported a wide range of human and environmental issues, being promoters of such organisations as Amnesty International and Greenpeace, to the extent of publicising these organisations in their concert programmes and record sleeves. In fact U2 have always attracted a deep thinking sort of fan, who obviously likes the music but who sees the problems of the world around him and who wants to do something about them. It is no coincidence that many of their early gigs were at colleges and universities in both Britain and America where their thought-provoking music struck a chord. The wheel has now come full circle with Bono recently making a speech to the students at Harvard University. The wide variety of U2 web sites around the world show the depth of interest in all things U2 and hopefully this book will both go a long way to satisfying the hunger amongst fans for information.

This book has been written partly through my own interest in U2, including publishing the U2 fanzine, *Silver & Gold* for several years, and partly to give a detailed and accurate picture of the world of U2 that many previous U2 books have failed to do. Some of the myths and even downright mistruths that I came across in my researches have been laughable. Here are a few - Paul McGuinness was the manager of the Stranglers before he became manager of U2, Adam Clayton was born in Africa and "Bad" was a track off *The Joshua Tree*! Whilst this book is about U2, it is not an official book and as such was done without any input from the members of U2 or their management. Therefore certain events known only to the band and those close to them are not covered in as much detail as they might have been.

I have tried to cover every aspect of U2 in this book, hopefully in enough detail to please even hardened fans. Certainly there should be something in here for both the casual and the committed U2 fan. All the songs they've ever played and recorded are included, as well as remixes of these songs. I haven't attempted to explain the meaning behind the lyrics, except in a few cases. For that I would recommend

Niall Stokes' *Into The Heart* or Bill Graham's *Complete Guide To The Songs Of U2*.

Collaborations with other artists both as a group and as individuals are there. Most of the venues they've ever played at are included, though some might have changed their names. For convenience sake these are listed under their new name as a separate entry. Again I haven't attempted to describe what happened or was played at each concert, though certain stand out events are included. Important concerts such as Live Aid and Save The Yuppies are included in more detail along with set lists. (All concerts that U2 have played are listed in the appendix.) For a detailed description of U2's concerts though I would recommend the highly detailed *U2 Live* by Pimm Jal de la Parrra. All the promotional videos, TV specials and other non-musical events that have involved U2 have been included.

Finally there's a lot of people that U2 have come into contact over the years which I have tried to include, such as producers, musicians, writers, politicians and celebrities, as well as behind the scenes people like their road crew and management team who have all been a part of the U2 story. If I have missed you out and you think that you should have been included my apologies. Let me know and I will included in a future edition of the book.

To finish, when you read the book, I would advise you not to read it from cover to cover as that is not how it is meant to be used. Rather, skip about the book. Check the details about a U2 track that you are listening to, or a venue that you attended in the 1980's. There are plenty of cross-references where a subject is interrelated. Hopefully, you will be informed, enlightened, surprised and even entertained when you read this book. Remember though it is the music of U2 that counts. For the music of U2 is the musical soundtrack to our lives as we have grown older. A U2 song might remind us of a birth or death in our family, going out with someone for the first time, moving house, going to college, graduating or getting married. U2 and their music have played a big part in your life and my life. Long may they continue to do so.

Mark Chatterton October 2001

Above: U2: Adam Clayton, Larry Mullen Jr, The Edge, Bono. Wembley Stadium, August, 1997
Below: U2: The Edge, Bono, Larry Mullen Jr, Adam Clayton. Earl's Court, August, 2001
Photos: Claire Bolton

**A&M STUDIOS, HOLLYWOOD, LOS ANGELES, CALI-
FORNIA, USA** This was the studio where two of the
tracks that appeared on the *Rattle and Hum* album
were recorded. They were: "Hawkmoon 269" and
"All I Want Is You". Several other tracks from the
album were also mixed here.

See also: *Rattle & Hum* album

ABBA See: Globe Areana, Stockholm.

ABBEY THEATRE, DUBLIN, IRELAND Bono made his
first solo appearance as a poet/singer here on 30th
April 1989 when he made a special appearance to
raise funds to help save the financially struggling
85-year-old Abbey Theatre. Using a specially prepared backing tape, Bono performed two political
poems by the well-known Irish poet, WB Yeats; "Mad
As The Mist And Snow" and "September 1913".

See also: WB Yeats

ABEYRATNE, SOPHIE & ZAN These two female singers provided backing vocals during the encore with
BB King for the Australian shows of the *Lovetown*
tour of 1989.

ACADIE This was the title of the 1989 album by U2
producer Daniel Lanois, on which Adam and Larry
played. They played on two tracks: "Jolie Louise"
and "Still Water".

ACHESON, ANN Larry Mullen's girlfriend and long-
time partner. Anne first met Larry in Dublin in the
early days of the band and they have been together
ever since. She is the mother of their three children,
Aaron Elvis, Ava and a son born in February 2001.
Although she has not appeared in public with the
band that often, her most memorable appearance was
at the Pontiac Silverdome near Detroit in the USA.
This was on 31st October 1997, Larry's 37th birthday,
when she presented him with a birthday cake on the
B-stage and kissed him in front of the 40,000 fans
present.

ACHTUNG BABY (ALBUM) (U 28 510347-1) After
U2's previous album release, *Rattle & Hum* in 1988,
had received a poor reception from many music critics, the band went away to "re-invent" themselves
for the 1990s. *Achtung Baby* was the result. Much
of it was recorded at Berlin's Hansa Ton Studios
between November 1990 and March 1991, just after
the reunification of the two Germanys. Once again

Brian Eno and Daniel Lanois were in charge of production, (though Eno was not involved until later
in the sessions). For Brian Eno it was a return to
the studio where he had recorded the David Bowie
albums, *Low, Heroes* and *Lodger*.

Halfway through the recording process, demo
recordings purportedly of the new album surfaced
as a bootleg entitled, *The New U2 - Rehearsals and
Full Versions*, a two album set which sported new
titles like "Sugar Cane", "Sick For Love" and "She's
Gonna Blow Your House Down". Paul McGuinness
and Island Records immediately threatened to take
out court injunctions against any record dealer selling
them. The sessions continued in the spring of 1991
back in Dublin at Dog Town, STS and Windmill Lane
studios.

When the album was finally released in November
1991, it received a universal thumbs up from critics
and fans alike. Full of the anguish of broken relationships, perhaps a reflection of The Edge's recent marital breakdown, the album pointed in a new musical
direction for the band. Dominated by Larry's heavy
and prominent drumming, giving a more industrial
sound, the songs gradually evolved into the mainstay
of the *Zoo TV* set which would go round the world
over the next couple of years. U2 had well and truly
achieved their aim of "re-inventing" themselves for
the 1990s.

Opening with the abrupt, yet powerful chords of
"Zoo Station", the listener travels through a myriad
of musical genres, each different and self-contained.
One moment the band would be rocking, as with
"Even Better Than The Real Thing" or "The Fly";
the next they would be going through soul-searching
anguish, as in "One" and "So Cruel". Critics such as
Chris Roberts, writing in *Melody Maker*, declared it
"a robust, a scarlet record... verging on the terrific",
whilst *Q*'s Matt Snow said *Achtung Baby* was "U2's
Blood On The Tracks", referring to the classic Dylan
album of the early 1970s.

Achtung Baby went straight to the number one spot
in the US album charts, following the success of the
single, "The Fly", a few weeks earlier, but was held
off the top spot in the UK by Michael Jackson's *Dangerous* album. *Achtung Baby* was at one stage going
to be called "Adam" after the bass player whose full
frontal nude picture is one of the thirty square pictures
that adorn the front and back cover. Another subject
that made its debut on the *Achtung Baby* cover was
the famous German car – the Trabant, which U2 had
fallen in love with in Berlin. Not only did it appear
on this album cover and several successive single
covers, but it also made it into the lighting and stage
equipment of U2's live shows!

(Ăh/k-tŏŏng Bāy-bi)

INITIAL copies with FREE PRINT while stocks last

The title came from a phrase that Joe O'Herlihy used during the recording sessions.

Complete track list: Zoo Station, Even Better Than The Real Thing, One, Until The End Of The World, Who's Gonna Ride Your Wild Horses? So Cruel, The Fly, Mysterious Ways, Trying To Throw Your Arms Around The World, Ultraviolet (Light My Way), Acrobat, Love Is Blindness

See also: Berlin / Hansa Ton studios / Trabant Car

ACHTUNG BABY THE VIDEOS, THE CAMEOS AND A WHOLE LOT OF INTERFERENCE FROM ZOO TV (085 556-3) (ISLAND/POLYGRAM VIDEO) This was the fourth video collection release of U2 material and contained most of the tracks from *Achtung Baby* in video form interspersed with snippets from *Zoo TV*. The "interference" part was directed by Maurice Linnane and produced by Ned O'Hanlon of Dreamchaser Productions. For details of each video see their individual entries.

Track list: 1) Interference, 2) Even Better Than The Real Thing, 3) Interference, 4) Mysterious Ways, 5) One (version 1), 6) The Fly, 7) Interference, 8) Even Better Than The Real Thing (Dance Mix), 9) One, (Version 2), 10) Even Better Than The Real Thing, 11) One (Version 3), 12) Until The End of the World

ACHTUNG DOG TOWN This was the nickname given to the studio in The Edge's house in Dalkey, south east of Dublin where the final stages of the recording of the *Achtung Baby* album took place.

ACKLAM HALL, ACKLAM ROAD, LONDON, ENGLAND As part of the 1980 "Sounds of Ireland Festival" in London, U2 (along with the Virgin Prunes) played at the Acklam Hall in Acklam Road, West London on 19th March 1980. Admission cost £2 and the headlining act was another Dublin band, Berlin.

ACOSTA, ARNIE The studio engineer who has mastered the following U2 albums: *Rattle & Hum, Achtung Baby, Zooropa, The Best of 1980-1990, All That You Can't Leave Behind.*

"ACROBAT" (*ACHTUNG BABY* ALBUM TRACK) (4.30) The penultimate track on *Achtung Baby* and the only track off that album never to have been played live. The song reflects on a loving relationship that has gone wrong as well as a typical Bono tirade against those who would criticize what he does.

ACURIA, ALEX This musician played percussion on the *Rattle and Hum* track "Hawkmoon 269".

ADAMS, BRYAN The Canadian guitarist and vocalist, who came to prominence in the mid-1980s, shared the bill with U2 on the *Conspiracy Of Hope* tour. His and U2's paths again crossed in 1991, when his song "Everything I Do (I Do It For You)", the theme song from the "Robin Hood – Prince of Thieves" movie, was at the number one spot in the UK singles chart. It had been at number one for a record breaking 16 weeks when U2's new single, "The Fly", finally knocked it off the top of the chart.

ADAMS, ROBBIE The studio engineer who helped with the engineering and mixing of the *Achtung Baby* and *Zooropa* albums.

AEROPORTO DELL' URBE, ROME, ITALY U2 played at this military airfield on the outskirts of Rome on 18th September 1997 during the *Pop Mart* tour of Europe. It was attended by 70,000 fans who sang the Italian song "Volare" during the Karaoke segment. The concert was marred by the death of a male fan, Andrea Gianotti, from a suspected heart attack.

AIDS/AIDS AWARENESS U2 have actively supported the whole AIDS awareness campaign and have promoted the use of safe sex in various ways. They contributed the track "Night & Day" to the *Red Hot & Blue* album in 1990. Then in their *Zoo TV* tour programme they included adverts for the Terrence Higgins Trust, a British based AIDS charity. One of the symbols on the Zoo TV tour was a little condom figure that promoted safe sex, to the extent that special "U2 condoms" were on sale at each venue! He reappeared on the cover of the *Zooropa* album in 1993. Also "One" off *Achtung Baby was* dedicated to David Wojnarowicz, an artist and AIDS sufferer. All proceeds from the single went to AIDS charities.

See also: Terrence Higgins Trust

AIKEN, JIM One of Ireland's foremost concert promoters who helped to bring major international artists to Ireland in the 1960s when he started promoting concerts at Dublin's National Stadium. He was also responsible for putting on concerts at Slane Castle in County Meath, north of Dublin. Artists such as The Rolling Stones, Bruce Springsteen, Bob Dylan, Thin Lizzy and of course U2 have all played there. He was also responsible for promoting the larger concerts that U2 have played in their home country, including the first Dublin Croke Park concert in June 1985.

See also: Slane Castle

"AIN'T ROCK 'N ROLL" The Edge played guitar on this track which comes from the 1992 album by Rolling Stone member Ronnie Wood, called *Slide On This*.

See also: Ronnie Wood

AIR CANADA CENTER, TORONTO, CANADA U2 played two sell out dates at this 20,000 capacity arena on 24th and 25th May 2001 during the *Elevation* tour of North America (first leg). These were the first shows after the tour had taken a week's break whilst Bono went back to Dublin to be present at the birth of his fourth child. The first show coincided with the 60th birthday of Bob Dylan, who the band have known for fifteen years. Snippets of "Mr Tambourine Man" and "Forever Young" were played in his honour.

See also: Bob Dylan

AIRFIELD WIENER NEUSTADT, AUSTRIA U2 played their second ever gig in Austria at this airfield on 16th August 1997 during the *Pop Mart* tour of Europe before 75,000 fans. As it was the 20th anniversary of Elvis Presley's death, the band included some Elvis songs in their set. They were: "His Latest Flame", "Suspicious Minds" and the final number, "Can't Help Falling In Love". Bono also talked about Elvis before "Last Night On Earth" and right at the end of the show he uttered the famous words, "Elvis Is Still In The Building".

See also: Elvis Presley

AIRPORT HOTEL, CROFTON, IRELAND U2 played to just six people at this late 1978 gig which was only their third gig outside Dublin. They also played a series of Sunday night concerts here in June 1979.

"AIR SUSPENSION" Bono sang vocals on this track peformed by Mocean Worker.

"AIRWAVES" Larry played drums on this track from Paul Brady's 1986 album entitled *Back To The Centre*.

AKERLUND, JONAS The Swedish film director who has been responsible for two U2 promo videos – "Beautiful Day" and "Walk On". Prior to U2 he had already worked with several big names in the music world including Madonna, Metallica, Jamiroquai and The Prodigy. He won a Grammy for his video of "Ray of Light" for Madonna and an MTV Best Video award for "Smack My Bitch Up" for The Prodigy.

See also: Beautiful Day promotional video / Walk On promotional video

ALAMODOME SAN ANTONIO TEXAS USA U2 played to 30,000 fans here on 23rd November 1997 during the *Pop Mart* tour. The concert took place the day after the death of INXS singer, Michael Hutchence who Bono mentioned at the start of "I Still Haven't Found What I'm Looking For". He stated, "He was a good friend and one of us." Various pictures of Hutchence were put up on the giant TV screen and as the band left the stage the INXS song, "Never Tear Us Apart" was played.

ALARM, THE The group from North Wales fronted by Mike Peters, famous for hits like "68 Guns", played support to U2 at many of their shows in the mid-1980s. They first appeared on the same bill as U2 during the pre-*War* tour in Europe in 1982. The following year The Alarm again supported U2 on several of their American dates during the *War* tour. At some of the shows, members of the two bands performed together. For example, at the Colorado State University in Boulder, Colorado on 6th June 1983, they joined forces for "A Hard Rain's Gonna Fall". Later in September when The Alarm played at The Ritz in New York City, Bono came on stage for "Knocking On Heaven's Door". The Alarm also supported U2 on several dates of the 1984 *Unforgettable Fire* tour, as well as at the "Homecoming" concert at Croke Park, Dublin on 29th June 1985 and at Cardiff Arms Park on 25th July 1987 during the *Joshua Tree* tour.

See also: "Give Me Back My Job"

ALEX DESCENDS INTO HELL FOR A BOTTLE OF MILK/ KOROVA 1 ("THE FLY" SINGLE TRACK) This was the second track off the "The Fly" single (CID 500) released in November 1991, and has the distinction of having the longest title of any U2 song. Written by Bono and The Edge, this instrumental comes from the score of the Royal Shakespeare Company stage production of *A Clockwork Orange 2004*, performed in London in 1990. It is the only piece of music from the score that Bono and The Edge wrote that made it onto record. As The Edge said in an interview in *Propaganda* at the time, "I wouldn't expect a U2 fan to recognise this music as that of Edge and Bono, except perhaps on a couple of tracks. It is not really to do with U2. It's a different attitude." The title comes from the Korova Milk Bar in *A Clockwork Orange* where Alex and his companions would go to drink milk laced with drugs before starting their sprees of ultra-violence.

See also: A Clockwork Orange 2004

"ALL ALONG THE WATCHTOWER" (LIVE) (*RATTLE & HUM* FILM/ALBUM TRACK) (4.24) U2 played this Bob Dylan song in the film of *Rattle and Hum* although it is probably better known as a 1968 single release for Jimi Hendrix. It also appeared on the soundtrack album of the film. This version comes from the "Save The Yuppies" concert at the Justin Herman Plaza in San Francisco on November 11th 1987. In the film, we see The Edge practising the chords in the trailer just prior to the band going on stage. It was the set opener and only the second time that the band had performed it live, the first time being on 1st February 1981 at the Lyceum London. It was not played live again until the *Lovetown* tour of Australia and Europe in 1989-90, where it became a regular number in their set.

See also: Jimi Hendrix

"ALL I WANT IS YOU" (*RATTLE & HUM* ALBUM TRACK) (6.30) The final track on the *Rattle & Hum* album. It is a simple song played over an acoustic guitar, but ends with the chorus "All I want is you-ou" which is accompanied by a string arrangement, provided by Van Dyke Parks (who had been the arranger on several Beach Boys songs). It is basically a love song from Bono to his wife, Ali. It was produced by Jimmy Iovine and was first performed live at the Perth Entertainment Centre in Australia on 21st September 1989.

"ALL I WANT IS YOU" (SINGLE) (IS 422) (6.30) The fourth single to be released from the *Rattle and Hum* album (in June 1989) reaching number 4 in the UK charts, but only number 83 in the US charts. However, it got to number 1 in the Australian charts where the release was delayed until October 1989 to tie in with the *Lovetown* tour. The single was released in 7 inch format with "Unchained Melody" as the B-side, and in 12 inch and CD format with the extra track of "Everlasting Love". Some 7 inch singles were released in a limited edition film case (U2 ISB 422). This track was also included on the compilation CD, *The Best of 1980-1990*.

"ALL I WANT IS YOU" (LIVE) ("STUCK IN A MOMENT YOU CAN'T GET OUT OF" SINGLE). The only official live version of "All I Want Is You" was recorded at U2's club gig at Man Ray in Paris on 19th October 2000. It was included on the French single release of "Stuck In A Moment You Can't Get Out Of".

"ALL I WANT IS YOU" (PROMOTIONAL VIDEO) The promo video for "All I Want Is You" was directed by Meiert Avis, written by Barry Devlin and was filmed at a circus situated on the coast near Rome in Italy in April 1989. It was more like a film than a promotional video with the members of U2 only making a cameo appearance. It tells the story of a circus dwarf called Jani who is in love with a trapeze artist called Rosa. The trapeze artist in turn is in love with the circus strong man. The dwarf buys her a ring and then climbs up the ladder to the trapeze. You see the dwarf fall and then seemingly fly past everyone. Then a coffin is seen being lowered into the ground. The dwarf is standing over the coffin at the end, adding to the mystery of the video. The closing scenes have caused debate amongst U2 fans about who actually died in the video!

U2 make a cameo appearance walking along the beach. The whole video was shot in black and white and took 4 days to complete. Paolo Rissi played the part of Jani and Paola Rinaldi played the part of Rosa. This promo video was included in *The Best of 1980-1990* video collection.

(THE MAKING OF) "ALL I WANT IS YOU" (DOCUMENTARY FILM) This was a short documentary film shown on Channel 4 in Britain in late 1989, showing the story of how the promo video for "All I Want Is You" was made.

"ALL I WANT IS YOU" (LIVE) (*U2: POP MART LIVE FROM MEXICO CITY* VIDEO TRACK) The eleventh track on the video *U2: Pop Mart Live from Mexico City* and was filmed at the Foro Sol Autodromo, Mexico City on 3rd December 1997.

"ALL IN THE LIGHT" (Also known as "In The Light") An early U2 song that was recorded at a demo session in Dublin around 1978/79.

"ALL OVER YOU" A song that Larry sang on an Australian Radio interview on 14th November 1989 along with "Twist & Shout".

ALL THAT YOU CAN'T LEAVE BEHIND (ALBUM) (CIDU212/548095-2) U2's tenth studio album was released worldwide on 31st October 2000. On its release it reached number 1 in the album charts in a staggering 32 countries, including most European countries, the USA, Australia, Colombia and New Zealand. In the USA, it sold almost half a million copies in the first few weeks of release, whilst in Britain it sold 164,000 copies in its first week alone. It was also U2's eighth number 1 record in Britain putting them equal with Led Zeppelin in terms of number one albums. The album was recorded over a period of two years at the new Windmill Lane studios, as well as Hanover Quay, Westland Studios and Totally Wired in Dublin. Bono's house in the south of France was also used.

U2

ALL I WANT IS YOU

RELEASED MONDAY 12th JUNE

INCLUDES PREVIOUSLY UNRELEASED B-SIDES

7", LIMITED EDITION 12" BOX SET, CASSETTE, PICTURE DISC, C.D.

Initially around forty new songs were put forward for the album; to be eventually whittled down to eleven. After the techno production of their previous album (*Pop*), *All That You Can't Leave Behind* was a conscious attempt by the band to get "back to basics" with more emphasis on songs rather than effects. The Edge called it "a very simple record" and several reviewers referred to a "stripped down sound". James Hunter writing in *Rolling Stone* claimed "the album represents the most uninterrupted collection of strong melodies U2 have ever mounted". *The Times* described the album as reflecting "U2 back to being stylishly precise, and song-based, instead of grimly self-indulgent, and theme-based". The title came from a line in "Walk On", one of the album's stand out tracks, along with "Beautiful Day" and "Elevation".

Once again Daniel Lanois and Brian Eno were the producers. The cover and inside photos were shot at Charles De Gaulle airport near Paris, France, by Anton Corbijn and the design was courtesy of Sean McGrath and Steve Averill from their Four5One design company. The CD booklet contained full lyrics and above each song was a logo indicative of the title. For instance "New York" was complimented with an apple, whilst "Wild Honey" featured a beehive. The cover had the letter/numbers "J 33:3" in the background which referred to chapter 33 verse 3 in the book of Jeremiah in the Old Testament. In the United States the album was released on Interscope Records, a company formed by U2 producer Jimmy Iovine, and included the bonus track, "Always". In several territories the album came in a specially numbered slip case.

Full track list: 1) Beautiful Day, 2) Stuck In A Moment You Can't Get Out Of, 3) Elevation, 4) Walk On, 5) Kite, 6) In A Little While, 7) Wild Honey, 8) Peace On Earth, 9) When I Look at The World, 10) New York, 11) Grace, 12) The Ground Beneath Her Feet (this last track was included as a bonus track on the European and Australian editions of the album), 12) Always (bonus track on North American editions)

ALTERNATIVE NRG (ALBUM) (HOLLYWOOD RECORDS) (HR-61449-2) This was a Greenpeace album that came out in 1994 on which all the tracks had been recorded live in the USA using Greenpeace's revolutionary solar power generator, named "Cyrus". U2 donated the track, "Until The End Of The World" which was recorded live at the Jack Murphy Stadium in San Diego California on the 10th November 1992. The album was co-produced by Dave Wakeling and Kate Karim. Other featured artists included REM, UB40, Annie Lennox and Midnight Oil. The album topped the charts in the USA.

See also: Greenpeace

"ALWAYS" ("BEAUTIFUL DAY" SINGLE TRACK) (3.46) The third track on the "Beautiful Day" single (CD1) and was one of the tracks taken from the *All That You Can't Leave Behind* sessions that didn't make it onto the album. Some of the chord changes are the same as those on "Beautiful Day". It was a bonus track on the American version of the album.

"ALWAYS FOREVER NOW" (*ORIGINAL SOUND-TRACKS 1* ALBUM TRACK) (6.23) This was the fourth track off *Original Soundtracks 1* by the Passengers, which was released in 1995. It featured a sequencer from Des Broadberry and strings provided by Paul Barrett.

"ALWAYS FOREVER NOW" (*HEAT* SOUNDTRACK ALBUM TRACK) A longer version of this track was included on the soundtrack album for the film *Heat* which came out in 1995.

AMNESTY INTERNATIONAL Amnesty International is one of several charities/political pressure groups that U2 have openly supported over the years. Amnesty International was formed when British lawyer, Peter Benenson wrote an article in *The Observer* newspaper dated 28th May 1961. In it he called for people from all walks of life to begin working impartially and peacefully for the release of thousands of men, women and children throughout the world imprisoned for their political or religious beliefs. This was intended as a brief campaign to protect human rights, but within a year "Amnesty International" had grown into an organisation that had taken on over 200 cases of human rights violations.

Today, Amnesty International has well over 1,000,000 members worldwide, who finance the organisation completely with their donations and fund raising efforts. This is because Amnesty International does not receive any government funding whatsoever. As the Amnesty International mandate states, Amnesty "is a world-wide human rights movement which is independent of any government, political faction, ideology, economic interest or religious creed". Based on the Universal Declaration of Human Rights of 1948, the organisation seeks the release of political prisoners of conscience, who have been imprisoned solely for their beliefs, colour, ethnic origin, sex, language or religion – provided they have neither used nor advocated the use of violence. It also seeks an end to torture, the death penalty and other cruel, inhuman or degrading treatment or punishment of all prisoners without reservation; fair and prompt trials for all political prisoners; and an end to extrajudicial executions and "disappearances".

U2 first became publicly involved with Amnesty when they staged a benefit concert for the organisation at Radio City Music Hall in New York in December 1984. U2 had decided to give all the profits from this concert to help finance Amnesty's "Stop Torture Week" campaign. The following year, the executive director of Amnesty International, Jack Healey, approached U2 manager Paul McGuinness to see if U2 would play a series of concerts in the USA to help publicise Amnesty in its 25th anniversary year. The series of concerts under the title of "Conspiracy of Hope" took place in six American cities in June 1986. As a result of this tour, Amnesty

gained 35,000 new members, over 100,000 letters had been sent out to different governments about certain prisoners of conscience, and new donations gave the organisation a much needed boost in funds.

The following year *The Joshua Tree* albumincluded a track called "Mothers of the Disappeared", about the many thousands of people who had mysteriously disappeared from their homes in South and Central America. On the album artwork, immediately after the lyrics of this, the final song on the album, followed details about Amnesty International. This has now become standard practice on all U2 albums and concert programmes. In addition, *Propaganda,* the official U2 fan magazine (as well as many independent U2 fanzines) carries a page or two in each issue about particular prisoners of conscience needing the help of readers, who are asked to write letters to the prisoners' governments.

In 1994 Bono accepted the MTV "Free Your Mind Award" on behalf of Amnesty International. Then in 1998 U2 signed a petition started by Amnesty International in support of the 50th Anniversary of the Universal Declaration of Human Rights. In 2001 the organisation celebrated its fortieth anniversary and, in a kind gesture, U2 donated the song "40" for use in Amnesty's continuing campaign.

Website: www.amnesty.org

See also: Conspiracy of Hope tour / Rene Castro

"AMSTERDAM BLUE (CORTEGE)" (*THE MILLION DOLLAR HOTEL* SOUNDTRACK ALBUM) (9.18) The thirteenth track off *The Million Dollar Hotel* soundtrack album. It is performed by Jon Hassell, Gregg Arreguin, Jamie Muhoberac and Peter Freeman.

ANAHEIM STADIUM, ANAHEIM, CALIFORNIA, USA Not only was this venue the last American venue on the 1992 *Outside Broadcast* tour of America, it was also the 100th concert of the Zoo TV tour and took place on 14th November 1992. Over 40,000 fans packed out this venue near Disneyland to see Bono make one final phone call to President George Bush. As he made his call, Bono mischievously gave out the number of the White House to the audience. When he got through to the operator and was told that the president wasn't available, he said, "What? George isn't available? But it's our last night! Can I leave a message for George? I just want to say that I won't be bothering him anymore from now on. I'm going to be bothering Bill Clinton now!"

"ANARCHY IN THE USA" (*THE MILLION DOLLAR HOTEL* SOUNDTRACK ALBUM) (3.37) This is the final track off *The Million Dollar Hotel* soundtrack album and is performed by Tito Larriva and the MDH Band, as well as Adam and Larry. It is based on the

Sex Pistols song, "Anarchy In The UK", with some of the lyrics adapted by Bono to fit into the American situation.

"AN CAT DUBH" (*BOY* ALBUM TRACK) (4.45) The third track on the *Boy* album. "An Cat Dubh" means "the black cat" in Gaelic and is about a girl that Bono briefly went off with after temporarily splitting from his girlfriend, Alison Stewart. A slowish track, reminiscent of Siouxsie and the Banshees, it segues straight into "Into The Heart" and because of this the track numbers on the CD version are out of sync with the list on the cover.

"AN CAT DUBH" (LIVE) ("SWEETEST THING" SINGLE) This live version of "An Cat Dubh" from Red Rocks Amphitheater in June 1983 was included on the "Sweetest Thing" single released in 1998.

EAMON ANDREWS STUDIO, DUBLIN, IRELAND This was the studio in Dublin where U2 made a third demo tape in February 1979. The songs they recorded were "Twilight", which was put on the B-side of their second Irish single, "Another Day" and probably "The Magic Carpet", "Another Time, Another Place" and "Alone In The Light". According to Bono there was no producer at the session.

ANGEL, NICK One time head of A&R at Island Records in London. Part of his job included responsibility for commissioning various artists to remix some of U2's back catalogue, especially during the 1990s. The result was the *Melon* Remixes CD which was given out free with *Propaganda* magazine at Christmas 1994.

"ANGEL OF HARLEM" (*RATTLE & HUM* ALBUM TRACK) (3.49) The tenth track on the *Rattle & Hum* album. It was a tribute to the black American jazz/blues singer Billie Holiday, as well as American music in general. Bono had been reading a biography of her and was inspired to write the song. The film *Rattle & Hum* features the recording of this song at Sun Studios in Memphis, with accompaniment from the Memphis Horns and Joey Miskulin on organ. Many famous songs had been recorded at the studios over the years, including the classic rock 'n' roll hit by Jerry Lee Lewis, *Great Balls of Fire*. One survivor from that session in the 1950s was Cowboy Jack Clement who happened to be the recording engineer for U2's own recording session that day.

See also: Memphis Horns / Joey Miskulin / Rattle & Hum

"ANGEL OF HARLEM" (SINGLE) (IS 402) (3.42) The second song from the *Rattle & Hum* album to be released as a single. It was released in December 1988 and reached number 9 in the UK and number 14 in the US. It was produced by Jimmy Iovine and

recorded at the Sun Studio sessions that took place in November 1987. Billie Holiday, who is the subject of the song, has her photograph on the back cover of the record sleeve and on the record label. Adam is featured on the front cover of the sleeve. The B-side was "A Room At The Heartbreak Hotel", (continuing the American references), whilst the 12 inch and CD versions had the additional track "Love Rescue Me" which was recorded live at the *Smile Jamaica* concert in London on 16th October 1988. "Angel of Harlem" was included on the 1998 compilation CD, *The Best of 1980-1990*.

"ANGEL OF HARLEM" (PROMOTIONAL VIDEO). This video was directed by Richard Lowenstein in New York City in November 1988. It was the second video he directed for U2, the previous one being "Desire". It shows the various band members of U2 in different New York settings as well as performing the song in an empty theatre.

"ANOTHER DAY" (SINGLE) (CBS 8306) U2's second ever single release coupled with "Twilight". It was released only in Ireland by CBS Ireland in February 1980 and reached number 1 in the Irish charts. It was produced by Chas De Whalley and recorded in London at the CBS Studios in December 1979 during their first ever London dates. "Another Day" was not included on their first album *Boy*. It was a fairly weak effort - "a failed and mistaken effort to emulate the Jam as a singles band" was how Bill Graham put it in his *Hot Press* review.

"ANOTHER TIME, ANOTHER PLACE" (*BOY* ALBUM TRACK) (4.33) The third track on side two of the *Boy* album. It is punctuated by Larry's heavy drumming and Bono sings about heaven, which is "another time" and "another place". Although it was good enough to be a single it was never released as such. It remained a staple of U2's live set from 1978 until 1982.

"ANOTHER TIME, ANOTHER PLACE" (BOOK) (Mandarin Books, 1989) This was the title of a book written about U2 by Bill Graham from *Hot Press* who was the first journalist to write about U2. It concentrated on the band's early days from 1976 right through to their eventual signing by Island Records in 1980. It gives the reader a useful insight into how the band developed and mentions the principal movers in their story. It also includes many rare early black and white photos of the band on and off stage.

See also: Bill Graham

ANTHEM FOR THE '80s (TV DOCUMENTARY FILM) This was the title of a *World In Action* UK TV programme about U2 and in particular their 1987 concerts at Dublin's Croke Park. *World In Action* was a current affairs programme transmitted on the ITV network and this particular episode looked at Ireland's political and economic situation at the time. Both Bono and The Edge were interviewed, as well as Bob Geldof and a group from Ballymun.

The film also included footage of the Irish Prime Minister, Garrett Fitzgerald, speaking about U2. The following songs from the June 1987 Croke Park shows were aired: "Where The Streets Have No Name", "Running To Stand Still", "Bad", "Sunday Bloody Sunday", "Bullet The Blue Sky" and "I Still Haven't Found What I'm Looking For".

ANZ STADIUM, BRISBANE, AUSTRALIA One of the final gigs of the whole *Zoo TV* tour took place here on 20th November 1993. It was a 50,000 sell out and Bono rang the Australian cricket captain, Allan Border from the stage. U2 then returned here to play before 30,000 fans during the *Pop Mart* tour on 25th February 1998.

APOLLO THEATRE, LONDON, ENGLAND See: "The Big One" Concert

APOLLO THEATRE, MANCHESTER, ENGLAND U2 played this important Manchester venue on four occasions in the early 1980s: 2nd December 1982, 19th March 1983, and 9th and 10th November 1984. The first gig here was one of six specially prepared *War* "preview" shows in the UK, which gave the band a chance to try out some of the new *War* album material before a live audience. At this concert U2 played "I Will Follow" twice! They returned in March 1983 as part of the *War* tour proper. The two shows in November 1984 were both sold out and were recorded for possible inclusion in a proposed mini-album that later came out in America under the moniker of *Wide Awake In America*. In the event none of the Manchester recordings were used.

APOLLO 440 A group who have remixed U2 material including "Even Better Than The Real Thing"

and "Mysterious Ways". They had two top 10 hits in the UK with their remixes of the themes from the TV programmes, *Lost in Space* and *Charlie's Angels*.

website: www.apollo440.com

"APRIL THE THIRD" The Edge played guitar on this track from the TV documentary, *Bringing It All Back Home*.

"ARABESQUE" This was a four EP release from April 1986 which included "Pride", "Sunday Bloody Sunday", "Two Hearts Beat As One" and five other tracks.

ARAGON BALLROOM, CHICAGO, ILLINOIS, USA U2 played two concerts at this 5,500 capacity ballroom on two dates – 21st May 1983 and 11th December 1984. This gig was notable in the history of U2, as while they were in Chicago for the first date, the band members visited The Chicago Peace Museum, which inspired them to name their next album, *The Unforgettable Fire* after seeing an exhibition of paintings there.

ARCADIA THEATRE/BALLROOM, CORK, IRELAND U2 played their first gig in Cork here at the Arcadia in the summer of 1978. They returned in October to play their first headline gig outside Dublin. It was an all Dublin affair with the four bands on the bill all coming from the capital city. Apparently there was a crowd of about 2,000 in attendance, but due to technical difficulties U2 didn't come on stage until after midnight, by which time the crowd had dwindled to around 200.

ARENA, ST LOUIS, MISSOURI, USA U2 played this 18,000 capacity arena on 25th October 1987, which happened to be the same night as the local baseball team, the St Louis Cardinals, played the Minnesota Twins in a grudge match. As a gesture to such an important match Bono came out on stage dressed in the Cardinal's red jacket and cap.

ARIZONA STATE UNIVERSITY CENTER, TEMPE, ARIZONA, USA This venue hosted the first two dates of the *Joshua Tree* tour on the 2nd and 4th April 1987. The second show should have taken place on the 3rd, but was put back a day due to Bono having problems with his voice due to the dry desert air, which had affected his singing on the first date. Prior to the band starting their set on the first day, promoter Barry Fey came on stage to read a statement by the band concerning Governor Meechum, the Governor of the State of Arizona, who was trying to abolish the national holiday that Arizona had to honour the birthday of Martin Luther King. It read: "Governor Meechum is an embarrassment to the people of Arizona. We condemn his actions and views as an insult to a great spiritual leader."

The show saw the live concert debut of five songs from *The Joshua Tree*: "I Still Haven't Found What I'm Looking For", "Bullet The Blue Sky", "Running To Stand Still", "In God's Country" and "Exit" – the last two having been performed before a studio audience in Belfast a month earlier. At the second show, after the encore, U2 had their picture taken on stage by a photographer from the American magazine, *Time*, for use on a future cover of the magazine. (In the event this photo was not used, but one from a shot taken prior to the show was used instead.) Both these last two events were filmed and used in the special documentary film, *Outside It's America*.

Joshua Tree tour opening night set list: Where The Streets Have No Name, I Still Haven't Found What I'm Looking For, Gloria, I Will Follow, Bullet The Blue Sky, Running To Stand Still, Exit, In God's Country, A Sort Of Homecoming, Sunday Bloody Sunday, Maggie's Farm, Bad, October, New Year's Day, Pride. Encore: People Get Ready, 40.

See also: The Joshua Tree tour / Outside It's America / Time Magazine

ARLOW SILVER BAND This Yorkshire brass band played on the track "Red Hill Mining Town" on *The Joshua Tree* album.

AMIN FAMILY, THE This family from New Zealand played on the track "One Tree Hill" on *The Joshua Tree* album.

ARMS PARK, CARDIFF, WALES U2 played at the former Welsh national rugby stadium on two occasions. The first was during the *Joshua Tree* tour on 25th July 1987. This date was hastily arranged after a fan had organised a petition of 10,000 signatures pleading for U2 to play this venue. During the show The Edge kicked a rugby ball out into the audience after Bono had said that The Edge's father (Gavin Evans), a Welshman, had predicted that one day his son would play rugby at Cardiff Arms Park!

The second time U2 played here was on 18th August 1993, during the *Zooropa* tour. At the *Zooropa* show, Bono rang up former British Prime Minister, Margaret Thatcher from the stage. He only got through to her secretary, who told him to write her a letter instead! Footage of this concert and a short documentary film about the *Zoo TV* set up was shown on the BBC TV programme *What's That Noise!* in September 1993.

See also: Margaret Thatcher

ARROWHEAD POND, ANAHEIM, CALIFORNIA, USA U2 played here three dates here on 23rd, 24th and 26th April 2001 during the *Elevation* tour of North America. The last date was added after the first two dates sold out. Bono's wife, Ali, was at the second show

and Bono dedicated the final song of the show, "Walk On" to Johnny Cash.

ARROWHEAD STADIUM, KANSAS CITY, MISSOURI, USA U2 played this 40,000 capacity stadium in Kansas City on 18th October 1992 as part of the *Zoo TV* tour, *Outside Broadcast* leg. It was belly dancer Morleigh Steinberg's birthday, so Bono presented her with a cake during "Mysterious Ways". The band also played here during the *Pop Mart* tour on 19th May 1997. In the two days after the show they filmed the promo video for "The Last Night On Earth" in Kansas City.

ARTANE This is the district in North Dublin where Larry Mullen Junior was brought up in a house in Rosemount Avenue. He attended the local national school here.

See also: Dublin

ARTANE BOYS BAND Larry was a member of this Dublin boys' marching band for just a few weeks. In it he played a military style drum, but because of rules about the length of hair, he soon left and joined the Post Office Worker's Union band instead. The Artane Boys Band were also featured in the promotional video of "The Sweetest Thing" as they were one of the things that Bono's wife Ali Hewson liked!

See also: Sweetest Thing promotional video

ARTISTS UNITED AGAINST APARTHEID A collective of musicians set up by Little Steven (Van Zandt), the guitarist in Bruce Springsteen's E Street Band in 1985, in response to the Apartheid laws in South Africa which discriminated heavily against the indigenous black population. In particular, a huge entertainment complex called "Sun City" had been built to entice big name acts to appear in spite of the United Nations embargo on entertainers playing in South Africa. Little Steven had decided to record an album of anti-apartheid songs by artists who were strongly opposed to the South African regime and all that Sun City stood for.

The album was entitled *Sun City* and featured such artists as Bruce Springsteen, Pete Townshend, Lou Reed and Bob Dylan. Bono was invited to join the line up by Little Steven and flew to New York City where he met up with Keith Richards, Mick Jagger and Peter Wolf (of the J. Geils Band). As a result of the meeting he wrote "Silver & Gold" which made it onto the album. He also took part in the recording of the single "Sun City" which was released to promote the album.

See also: Sun City / Little Steven / Lou Reed / The Rolling Stones

ASTORIA THEATRE, LONDON, ENGLAND This "secret" gig, on 7th February 2001, was the third of three between the release of *All That You Can't Leave*

Highly prized ticket for the Astoria gig, 7/2/01

Behind and the start of the *Elevation* tour. U2 had chosen to play three one-off concerts in small capacity venues in New York, Paris and London. The Astoria, with a capacity of under 2,000, was chosen for the London date. The only way to get a ticket was through being a competition winner or by being an invited celebrity. Such was demand that the U2.com website had over sixty thousand entries for just 200 tickets!

As tickets were so scarce for such a unique concert, touts outside were asking in excess of £800 for tickets. There was no support band apart from DJ Jon Carter who played some tracks before U2 came on stage to play a ninety-minute set. Surprisingly, not one track from *The Joshua Tree* was included in the set. Highlights included "40" which hadn't been played for several years, as well as the rarely played live "11 O'clock Tick Tock" and "Desire". In the audience were Mick Jagger, Noel and Liam Gallagher, and Salman Rushdie.

Set List: Until The End Of The World, Beautiful Day, Elevation, Stuck In A Moment You Can't Get Out Of, Gone, Discotheque, Staring At The Sun, New York, 11 O'clock Tick Tock, I Will Follow, Desire, The Ground Beneath Her Feet, Mysterious Ways, One, All I Want Is You, Bad, 40.

ASTRODOME, HOUSTON, TEXAS, USA U2 played to an audience of over 30,000 people at this indoor stadium on 14th October 1992 during the *Zoo TV Outside Broadcast* tour of America. This gig is memorable for the fact that the band played Bob Marley's "Redemption Song" during the acoustic section of the set. U2 returned on 28th November 1997 to present their *Pop Mart* show.

ATRIX, THE A Dublin band who often shared the bill with U2 at their early gigs.

AUNG SAN SUU KYI The Burmese human rights campaigner who returned to her native Burma in 1989

after lecturing and living in Oxford, England for several years, leaving her husband and children behind. As leader of the National League For Democracy she had been elected as leader of Burma in 1989 under free elections held during her exile, but when she returned to Burma she was put under house arrest by the dictatorship. Bono wrote and dedicated "Walk On" to her. On 18th March 2000 she was awarded the Freedom of Dublin in a special ceremony where the members of U2 and Paul McGuinness were also given this honour.

See also: The Burma Campaign / "Walk On"

AUTODROMO, MEXICO CITY, MEXICO U2 played here during the *Pop Mart* tour on 2nd and 3rd December 1997 before crowds of approximately 50,000 people each night. An incident is said to have occurred after the first show which left Adam's security guard, Jerry Meltzer, unconscious and needing stitches to his head after an altercation with security guards accompanying the President of Mexico's son. The second show on 3rd December was broadcast live on MTV and *Showtime* and was brought out as the video *Pop Mart Live From Mexico City*. Part of the show was also used for a special CD given away free to *Propaganda* readers called, *Hasta La Vista Baby! U2 Live From Mexico City*.

AUTOMATIC BABY The name given to a specially formed "supergroup" of members of both U2 and REM, possibly the two biggest groups in the world at the time. The occasion was the MTV Inaugural Rock 'n' Roll Ball in honour of the newly elected president Bill Clinton in the USA. It took place on 20th Janu-

E END OF THE WORLD
2 BEAUTIFUL DAY
1 ELEVATION
5 STUCK IN A MOMENT
B GONE
P DISCOTHEQUE
9 NEW YORK
W 11 O'CLOCK
N FOLLOW
N DESIRE
N GROUND BENEATH
3 MYSTERIOUS WAYS
D ONE
7 ALL I WANT
I BAD
40

Set list for "secret" Astoria gig, 7/2/01

ary 1993. Originally Michael Stipe and Mike Mills of REM were going to perform the U2 song "One", but on meeting Adam and Larry who were also present at the ball they decided to join forces to perform the song together. They chose the name "Automatic Baby" by taking half of the titles of each band's current albums - "Automatic For The People" (REM) and "Achtung Baby" (U2).

See also: Bill Clinton / One / REM

AUTZEN STADIUM, EUGENE, OREGON, USA U2 played one show here before 35,000 fans during the *Pop Mart* tour (first leg) of North America on 6th May 1997. During "Sunday Bloody Sunday" a male fan managed to get past security guards and onto the stage before being caught by the security team. The show, being one of the earlier ones on the first leg, still had some glitches with part of the video screen not working and the lemon getting stuck!

AVERILL, STEVE Steve came to prominence as the vocalist for the Dublin new wave band called The Radiators From Space. In the group he was known as "Steve Rapid" and apart from his group commitments was also a designer at Arrow, one of Dublin's leading advertising agencies. It was Steve who Adam turned to for advice concerning the name of his group The Hype. Steve suggested the name "U2", which was also the name of an American spy plane and a brand name for batteries. It could also mean "you too" or "you two" – it was ambiguous yet memorable. Although Adam was happy with Steve's suggestion it seems that some of the other the members of U2 needed some persuading!

Later, once the name had been accepted, Adam asked him if he would be interested in managing the band, but Steve having other commitments at the time was not interested. His contact with the band however did continue. In 1980 he was asked to design the cover of U2's first album, *Boy*, and from then on he has been involved in designing the cover for each U2 album (apart from *Rattle & Hum*). He has also been involved with designing other products connected with U2 including the book of the film *Rattle & Hum* and each issue of *Propaganda*, the official U2 magazine. His design companies have included "Rapid Exteriors", "Works Associates" and "ABA", with "Four5One" being the current incarnation.

Steve currently works alongside Sean McGrath who has been involved with U2 from *Achtung Baby* onwards. Apart from designing promotional material such as T-shirts, tour programmes and U2 merchandise, Four5One is involved with many different aspects of design for Irish and international companies, as well as musicians such as Elvis Costello.

Steve also produces his own country music-based fanzine called *Lonesome Highway*.

See also: Sean McGrath / The Radiators From Space

AVIS, MEIERT The Irish film maker who has made more U2 promotional videos than anyone else. His first promo video was for "Gloria" (believed to be the first U2 video) shot in October 1981, shortly after the launch of MTV. He went on to direct the next three U2 videos: "A Celebration", "New Year's Day" and "Two Heart's Beat As One". After a break of a couple of years Meiert directed the promo video for "The Unforgettable Fire" in 1985, followed by "In A Lifetime" featuring Bono and Clannad. He also directed "With Or Without You" with Matt Mahurin in February 1987, followed by the Grammy award-winning "Where The Streets Have No Name".

His last promo video for U2 was perhaps his most ambitious: "All I Want Is You". This was more like a film rather than a video, and was based on the relationships between several performers of an Italian circus. Meiert is now based in America where he continues to make both promotional and feature films.

See also: Promo videos for: All I Want Is You / A Celebration / Gloria / In A Lifetime / New Year's Day / Two Hearts Beat As One / The Unforgettable Fire / With Or Without You / Where The Streets Have No Name

AWARDS Over the years U2 have won a vast amount of awards, starting with the Harp Lager/Evening Press contest in Limerick, west Ireland in 1978. In January 1980 they won no less than five categories in the *Hot Press* reader's poll. It wasn't until 1982 that they would win an award for sales of their records, the first of which was a silver disc for sales in excess of 250,000 for the *October* album. Sales were even better for *War* the following year, meriting a gold disc. Since then every album U2 have released has gone at least platinum, with *The Joshua Tree* selling the most records to date. In 1988 *The Joshua Tree* won a coveted Grammy award as "Album of The Year", beating Michael Jackson's *Bad* into second place.

In 2000 they won a Grammy again, this time for "Beautiful Day". In Britain they have been "Best International Band" at the Brit Awards on several occasions and in 2001 they received a special Lifetime Achievement award. Other organisations and publications such as MTV, *Q* magazine, *New Musical Express*, *Hot Press* and *Rolling Stone* magazine have all given awards to U2 for their musical achievements.

See appendix for complete list of awards.

B

"BABYFACE" (*ZOOROPA* ALBUM TRACK) (4.01)
The second track off the *Zooropa* album tells the story
of a man obsessed with a video image of a girl who
he can freeze frame on his TV set and thus 'manipu-
late' her. The song was first performed live at Wembley Stadium, London on 11ᵗʰ August 1993 during
the *Zooropa* tour. Whenever the song was played live
Bono would get a girl on stage and get her to film
him singing the song. "Babyface" was only played at
five *Zooropa* shows before being dropped from the
set.

Bono and friend during "Babyface", Wembley Stadium,
London, 11-8-93. *Photo: Claire Bolton*

"BAD" (*THE UNFORGETTABLE FIRE* ALBUM
TRACK) (6.08) The second track on the second side
of *The Unforgettable Fire* album and an ever popular
live U2 track. It was first performed live on 18ᵗʰ October 1984 at the Espace Tony Garnier in Lyon, France
and has been performed on most U2 tours since, apart
from the *Pop Mart* tour. The band's performance of
the song at 1985's *Live Aid* concert helped to promote
U2 to a world-wide audience.

Bono once told the story of why he wrote "Bad" at
a concert in America: "We come from Dublin City.
This song is written about one particular person, but
it's probably written about many, many more; it's
probably even written about myself. This song is
inspired – on the street where I live a lot of people,
you know, I joined a rock 'n' roll band, they joined
the dole queue, and some of them didn't even get as
far as the dole queue. This is for them; this is for
those of them that fell in love with a very dangerous
lover – that lover was the drug heroin, and this is the
song 'Bad' ". The track was included on the compilation, *The Best of 1980-1990*.

"BAD" (LIVE) (*WIDE AWAKE IN AMERICA* MINI-
ALBUM TRACK) (7.59) This was recorded live at
the National Exhibition Centre, Birmingham, England on 12ᵗʰ November 1984. It was produced by U2
and mixed by Ron St. Germain. As the album version was heavily orchestrated, it was clear that the
guitar parts on the album couldn't be reproduced live,
so a sequencer was used to try and bridge the gap
between studio and live setting. "Bad" has always
been a vehicle for Bono's improvisations, the most
famous performance of the song being at Live Aid in
1985. Among the various songs that he has inserted
into "Bad" are: Lou Reed's "Walk on the Wild Side"
and "Satellite of Love" and the Rolling Stones "Sympathy For the Devil" and "Ruby Tuesday".

"BAD" (LIVE) (*RATTLE & HUM* FILM/VIDEO
TRACK) This black and white film of U2 perform-
ing "Bad" live at the McNichols Arena in Denver,
Colorado on 8ᵗʰ November 1987 was included in the
Rattle & Hum movie, but not on the album sound-
track. A rare audio version of this film segment was
included on the promo album, *Excerpts From Rattle
& Hum*.

"BAD" (LIVE) (*THE BEST OF 1980-1990* VIDEO
COLLECTION) The film version of U2 performing
"Bad" is the same clip of the song from the *Rattle &
Hum* film. Surprisingly this was used as the video for
The Best of 1980-1990 video collection rather than
the Barry Devlin video.

"BAD" (PROMOTIONAL VIDEO) The promo video
of "Bad" was directed by Barry Devlin and was the
first promo video that he directed for U2. It is basically a film of U2 performing the song live in concert
somewhere in Europe. If you look closely at Bono
you can see he is wearing two different shirts during
the song – indicating that the film was shot at two different concerts. The excitement of the video is further
enhanced by scenes of the audience singing along
while the roadies scurry on and off the stage. It was
included in *The Unforgettable Fire Video Collection*.
See also: Barry Devlin

B.A.D.II (BIG AUDIO DYNAMITE) This group supported U2 on several of its shows during the *Zoo TV* tour of 1992-3, and are featured in the *Stop Sellafield* video that Greenpeace made about the then proposed nuclear re-processing plant, called THORP. The video featured clips of the Manchester G-Mex gig of 19th June 1992, where BAD II were one of the support bands. BAD II was led by Mick Jones who used to be in The Clash, one of the bands that inspired U2 in their early days.

See also: The Clash / *Stop Sellafield* video

BAEZ, JOAN The famous American folk singer shared the bill with U2 on the 1986 *Conspiracy of Hope* tour for Amnesty International in the USA.

BAGGOT INN, DUBLIN, IRELAND This was the venue for the infamous gig on 21st August 1979 when two record company A&R men from EMI Records came over from London to see this new up-and-coming Irish band called U2. With the possibility of being signed to EMI the band treated this as a 'make or break' gig, but the A&R men were not impressed and left before the end in order to see The Specials on *The Old Grey Whistle Test* back at their hotel. However, a journalist called Dave McCullogh from *Sounds* music paper was also in the audience. He was impressed enough to publicise U2 in the British music press in the coming months.

BALGRIFFIN CEMETRY, BALGRIFFIN, IRELAND In 1979 U2 used the gatehouse to this cemetery as a place where they could rehearse without fear of interruption. It was nicknamed "The Gingerbread House" and was the place where several of the songs that made it onto the *Boy* album took shape.

BALLYMUN HOUSING ESTATE, DUBLIN, IRELAND This is a notorious Dublin housing estate that was built in the early 1960s in an area of land north of Bono's childhood home in Cedarwood Road. It had several high rise blocks of flats which were immortalised in "Running To Stand Still". Like many housing estates built to re-house people from derelict inner city areas, it soon degenerated into a deprived area with lack of employment and basic facilities, and a drugs and crime problem. Bono often referred to it in interviews. In 1997 it was announced that the flats at Ballymun would be torn down and replaced with over 2,000 residential homes, though at the time of writing this has not yet happened.

BALTARD PAVILLION, PARIS, FRANCE U2's first ever concert in France took place in this venue on 3rd December 1980, supporting Talking Heads.

BALTHUS When this French artist died in February 2001, Bono flew over to Switzerland to attend his funeral in Rossiniere, at which he sang.

BAND AID The brainchild of fellow Irishman, Bob Geldof of Dublin group, The Boomtown Rats. One November evening in 1984, after seeing pictures of starving refugees in Ethiopia on TV, Geldof decided to try and get some musicians together to make a record to raise funds for famine relief. The result was a 'Supergroup' made up of nearly forty musi-

The Baggot Inn, Dublin. *Photo: Paul Daly*

cians called "Band Aid" who recorded the then biggest ever selling single in Britain: "Do They Know It's Christmas?" – co-written by Geldof and Ultravox vocalist Midge Ure.

Both Bono and Adam flew over to London to take part in the recording session which took place at Sarm West Recording Studios one Sunday in November, 1984. Bono got to sing one of the opening lines along with fellow musicians, Sting, Boy George, Tony Hadley and George Michael. As a result of the success of Band Aid, a live concert featuring some of the world's best groups and artists was called for. This became Live Aid.

See also: "Do They Know It's Christmas" / Live Aid

BARNUM, BILLIE One of three singers who provided backing vocals on the track "Hawkmoon 269" which appeared on the *Rattle & Hum* album.

BARRETT, PAUL An engineer and producer who was first involved with U2 when he mixed the track "A Room At The Heartbreak Hotel" and helped in the recording of *Rattle & Hum*. He also played piano on the track "Everlasting Love", which was on the B-side of the 12 inch version of the single "All I Want Is You". In the 1990s he became involved with the remixing and post-production of several U2 releases, including the additional tracks on the "Who's Gonna Ride Your Wild Horses" CD single. He was also one of the "extra" Passengers on the *Original Soundtracks 1* album.

BARROWLANDS, GLASGOW, SCOTLAND U2 played two sold out nights at this 2,500 capacity venue on 6th and 7th November 1984. It is interesting to note that for the second show the Simple Minds guitarist Charlie Burchill came on stage to play guitar on "40", the encore song, whilst the rest of Simple Minds watched the gig from the back of the theatre. At a Simple Minds concert here on 5th January 1985, Bono came on stage to duet with Jim Kerr on "New Gold Dream".

BARSALONA, FRANK The head of Premier Talent, a booking agency based in New York City, who agreed to represent U2 in the USA. Barsalona had a house in the Bahamas near to Island Records head Chris Blackwell, and it was Blackwell who persuaded him to take U2 on. Paul McGuinness flew over to New York City in the autumn of 1980 and the two of them agreed a strategy for U2 to "conquer" America. They were to start with a few gigs in December 1980, followed by a three-month stint in the spring of 1981 to coincide with the release of *Boy* in the USA. After U2's first ever concert in America at New York's The Ritz, Barsalona was so impressed that he came backstage after the gig and congratulated the band, prom-

Ballymun housing estate, Dublin. *Photo: Claire Bolton*

ising to break them in America. The rest, as they say, is history.

"BASS TRAP" ('THE UNFORGETTABLE FIRE' SINGLE B-SIDE) (5.17) This track was available on the B-side of the 12 inch and special double pack versions of "The Unforgettable Fire" single (IS 220). As the title suggests, this is a gentle instrumental, dominated by the bass guitar of Adam Clayton. It was produced by Daniel Lanois and Brian Eno. This track was also included on the compilation CD, *The B-sides*, which was included on early pressings of *The Best of 1980-1990*.

"BATHTUB" (*THE MILLION DOLLAR HOTEL* SOUNDTRACK ALBUM) (1.06) A track off *The Million Dollar Hotel* soundtrack album performed by the MDH Band.

BAY CITY ROLLERS The teeny-bopper group from Edinburgh, Scotland who had several number 1 hit singles in Britain in the mid-1970s. It has been suggested that U2 used to do cover versions of their songs when they were known as Feedback and The Hype. In a 1984 interview Larry put the record straight by saying that they only played a Bay City Rollers' number once "for a laugh".

BAYMOUNT, SLIGO, IRELAND U2 played here on 19th December 1980 on a short tour of Ireland prior to a Christmas break.

BBC RADIO U2 have had their songs played on BBC Radio from early on in their career. The first session they did was in September 1980 when they recorded four numbers for Richard Skinner's Radio Show: "I Will Follow", "The Electric Co.", "An Cat Dubh" and "Into The Heart". The next broadcast was on 3rd October 1981 when a show recorded on 23rd August 1981 was broadcast on the *In Concert* programme. The set consisted of the numbers "11 O'clock Tick Tock", "I Will Follow", "An Cat Dubh", "Into The Heart", "With A Shout", "Twilight", "Out of Control" and "Rejoice". The band then recorded a set for Kid Jensen's Programme on 14th October 1981 when they played four numbers – "Boy-Girl", "With A Shout", "I Threw A Brick Through A Window" and "Scarlet", the last three coming from their recently released *October* album, with this being the only performance of "Scarlet". Since then U2 have had several concerts broadcast on the radio as well as interviews and band histories.

See **appendix** for a list of radio appearances.

BBC STUDIOS, MAIDA VALE, LONDON, ENGLAND U2 recorded their first British radio session here in September 1980 for Richard Skinner's BBC radio programme. The band came back in October 2000 as part of the promotional tour for the *All That You Can't Leave Behind* album, playing songs from the album and being interviewed by DJs Simon Mayo and Jo Whiley.

BBC TELEVISION U2 have made numerous appearances on the BBC over the years. They made their British TV debut on the BBC 2 TV programme *The Old Grey Whistle Test* on 28th February 1981 playing three numbers; "The Ocean", "11 O'clock Tick Tock" and "I Will Follow". Then in August 1981 they made their debut on the long running chart music show 'Top of the Pops' when they performed their latest single "Fire" which had just entered the charts at number 35. Unfortunately it didn't do them any good as the single actually went down the charts the following week! U2 have continued to appear on TOTP over the years. Notable appearances have included having "One" premiered live at the start of the *Zoo TV* tour, and performing "Beautiful Day" live from the roof of the Clarence Hotel in Dublin in September 2000 just prior to its release.

See **appendix** for a list of TV appearances.

BC PLACE STADIUM, VANCOUVER, CANADA U2 have played this stadium on four occasions: 12th November 1987, 3rd and 4th November 1992, and 9th December 1997. The first date in 1987 was set up at the last moment as U2 were meant to play in the nearby American town of Seattle, but things could not be arranged in time. Instead 10,000 tickets were put on sale for fans in Seattle who wanted to see U2 play live in their area. The two shows in 1992 happened to occur in the middle of the US Presidential election, so just before the second show Willie Williams announced to the audience that Bill Clinton had been elected president of the USA. U2 then returned for another date at this stadium as the penultimate date of the second North American leg of the *Pop Mart* tour in December 1997. In spite of having flu, Bono still managed to complete the show, dedicating "One" and "Wake Up Dead Man" to Amnesty International.

"BEACH SEQUENCE" (*ORIGINAL SOUNDTRACKS 1* ALBUM TRACK) (3.31) This is the sixth track off *Original Soundtracks 1* album by Passengers.

THE BEATLES The biggest and most famous group in the world ever. U2 would often acknowledge the influence of The Beatles, playing several of their songs in live sets over the years. Of the Beatles songs played live, only "Helter Skelter" has been recorded on a U2 album, (*Rattle and Hum*). There is a short clip of U2 playing "Help" at the *Conspiracy of Hope* concert at the Giant's Stadium in New Jersey which was put on the John Lennon Tribute video, *Lennon A Tribute*. Other songs by the Beatles that U2 have performed in whole or in part have included "Dear Prudence", "Let It Be", "Hello, Goodbye", "Norwegian Wood" and "Rain" – the latter being a favourite of Bono's for when it rains at a U2 concert. The only Beatles song that U2 have recorded in a studio for release on record has been the "white album" track, "Happiness Is A Warm Gun" which was included on the "Last Night On Earth" single. In 1997 U2 were criticised by former Beatle George Harrison who had said in an interview that the *Pop Mart* tour was "all about big hats, lemons and egos".

See also: John Lennon / Paul McCartney

"BEAUTIFUL DAY" (*ALL THAT YOU CAN'T LEAVE BEHIND* ALBUM TRACK) (4.06) The opening track on the *All That You Can't Leave Behind* album. Starting off quietly the song builds into a large crescendo with its memorable chorus. The sound is reminiscent of earlier U2 material and in a way sets the tone for the rest of the 'back to basics' album. Lyrically there are references to the environment and 'the Flood', though Bono has said the song is about a man who loses everything and then feels better for it. "Beautiful Day" was first performed live on the roof of the Clarence Hotel in Dublin for *Top Of The Pops* on 27th September 2000.

"BEAUTIFUL DAY" (SINGLE) (4.06) The single of "Beautiful Day" was released before the album, *All That You Can't Leave Behind* and reached number 1 in both the UK and US charts. It came in two CD formats. CD1 (CID 766) had the extra tracks "Summer Rain" and "Always" – both recorded at the album sessions. CD2 (CIDX 766) had the extra tracks "Discotheque" and "If You Wear That Velvet Dress", both recorded live at the Foro Sol Autodromo, Mexico City on 3rd December 1997 during the *Pop Mart* tour. "Discotheque" had already been available on the *Propaganda* free CD, *Hasta La Vista Baby*, but "If You Wear That Velvet Dress" was not included on that CD and so was the more worthwhile inclusion.

"BEAUTIFUL DAY" (*THE SUNDAY TIMES* FREE CD) (4.07) This version of "Beautiful Day" was the first track of an exclusive CD given away free with *The Sunday Times* newspaper on 3rd June 2001. It was the same version as that on the album and single.

"BEAUTIFUL DAY" (LIVE) ('STUCK IN A MOMENT YOU CAN'T GET OUT OF' SINGLE TRACK) This live version of "Beautiful Day" was the second track on the "Stuck In A Moment You Can't Get Out Of" CD2 single. It was recorded from the Farmclub.com stage in Universal City, USA on 27th October 2000. It was also included on the Canadian release of the "Walk On" CD1 single (3145728192).

'BEAUTIFUL DAY' (PROMOTIONAL VIDEO) The promo video for "Beautiful Day" was filmed at Charles de Gaulle airport near Paris, France over a weekend in the summer of 2000. The director was Jonas Akerlund who also directed the "Walk On" promo video. The most memorable scene was of U2 performing the song at the end of a runway as planes take off and land on the runway just behind them. Other scenes were shot in Hall F in the airport with the band collecting their luggage and going through the security check.

See also: Jonas Akerlund

"BEAUTIFUL DAY" (VIDEO) (*THE SUNDAY TIMES* FREE CD) (4.05) This video of "Beautiful Day" was on the CD given away free with *The Sunday Times* newspaper in June 2001. It was one of two video tracks on the CD and was filmed by Dreamchaser Productions in the south of France in April 2000. It was different to the one directed by Jonas Akerlund and so soon became a collectors item amongst U2 fans.

'BEAUTIFUL DAY' (QUINCEY AND SONANCE REMIX) (7.56) This remix version of the track "Beautiful Day" was the third track on the "Stuck In A Moment You Can't Get Out Of" CD 1 single. (It was also included on the Canadian release of the "Walk On" CD2 single (3145728202).

BERLIN (CITY) The capital of the reunited Germany has many U2 connections. U2 first played in the then West Berlin in February 1981, gaining inspiration for "Stranger In A Strange Land", on the way through East Germany to Berlin. They came back in November 1981 to play at the Metropol for the German TV programme *Rockpalast* before a meagre audience of 350. U2 had hoped to play a free concert in June 1985 on the Platz der Republik in front of the Reichstag building in the Western sector of the divided city. Although it was listed in the tour programme, this concert never happened due to organizational difficulties.

After a break of nine years and the fall of the Berlin Wall, U2 returned to Berlin to film the promo video of "Night & Day" for the *Red, Hot & Blue* project at director Wim Wenders' house in Berlin in 1990. Shortly afterwards the band set up shop at the Hansa-by-the-Wall studios to record much of their *Achtung Baby* album over the winter of 1990-1991. The opening track on the album, "Zoo Station", refers to a station on the Berlin underground by the famous Berlin Zoo. During the recording of *Achtung Baby*, the band and crew took some time off to visit the zoo - presumably for inspiration for the concept of Zoo TV!

Berlin was also the setting for the promo video of "Stay (Faraway So Close!)" again directed by Wim Wenders. U2 then played to a half empty Olympic Stadium on 15th June 1993. By then U2 had helped bring the East German Trabant car to everyone's attention through its use on the *Achtung Baby* album cover and at *Zoo TV* shows around the world.

See also: "Stay" promo video / Wim Wenders

BERLIN (GROUP) One of the various groups that came out of Ireland at around the same time as U2 were making it big in the early 1980s. U2 supported them at an important early London gig at The Acklam Hall on the 19th March 1980. (Note: This Berlin is different from the Berlin that had a number 1 hit in 1986 with "Take My Breath Away".)

BEST OF 1980-1990 & B SIDES (ALBUM) (CIDDU211/524612-2) Although U2 have said on several occasions that they were not in favour of "best ofs" or "greatest hits" albums, Island Records released *The Best of 1980-1990* compilation in 1998. Although it wasn't a "greatest hits" package as such, ten of its fourteen tracks were still hit singles, plus the specially commissioned former B-side, "Sweetest Thing" was added, which soon became a hit once it was released. The other three tracks were all live favourites – "Sunday Bloody Sunday", "Bad" and the early single, "I Will Follow" (which was not a hit).

In addition to this compilation, Island added a second CD of B-sides from the same era, though the majority of them came from the years 1987-1989. This was a limited edition extra CD which helped initial sales as many fans did not have these B-sides in their collections. The complete package was released on 14th November 1998 in time for the Christmas market that year. It reached number 1 in the UK album charts and number 2 in the American charts. A few weeks later on 5th December, the original double CD was withdrawn and *The Best Of 1980-1990* CD was released solely as a single CD reaching number 4 in the UK album charts and 45 in the US album charts.

Many U2 fans were critical of the whole package though, citing that the early U2 singles like "Out of Control" and "11 O' clock Tick Tock" (which were not chart hits in Britain or the USA) should have been included. These had never been released in a CD format and so their vinyl copies were quite rare. Similarly, the B-sides CD missed out many of the early B-sides such as "Things To Make And Do" and "Touch". Also, the *Best Of* didn't include anything from the *October* album, though on some CDs that album's title track comes in as a "ghost track" after the fade out on "All I Want Is You" (the final listed track).

The album cover featured a picture of Pete Rowan (who had been on the cover of the *Boy* and *War* albums) wearing a soldier's helmet taken at the *War* album cover photo shoot by Ian Finlay in 1983. The booklet featured several previously unpublished photos from 1979 through to 1988, though no song lyrics were included.

The Best of 1980-1990 track list: 1) Pride (In The Name of Love), 2) New Year's Day, 3) With Or Without You, 4) I Still Haven't Found What I'm Looking For, 5) Sunday Bloody Sunday, 6) Bad, 7) Where The Streets Have No Name, 8) I Will Follow, 9) The Unforgettable Fire, 10) Sweetest Thing, 11) Desire, 12) When Love Comes To Town, 13) Angel Of Harlem, 14) All I Want Is You (plus October not listed)

The B-sides track list: 1) The Three Sunrises, 2) Spanish Eyes, 3) Sweetest Thing, 4) Love Comes Tumbling, 5) Bass Trap, 6) Dancing Barefoot, 7) Everlasting Love, 8) Unchained Melody, 9) Walk to The Water, 10) Luminous Times (Hold Onto Love), 11) Hallelujah Here She Comes, 12) Silver And Gold, 13) Endless Deep, 14) A Room At The Heartbreak Hotel, 15) Trash, Trampoline And The Party Girl

THE BEST OF 1980-1990 (VIDEO) This video collection was released early in 1999 after the CD, *The Best of 1980-1990*. It contained exactly the same songs as on the CD in video form with the additional "bonus track" of "One Tree Hill", a video which came from previously unreleased concert footage from the *Rattle & Hum* movie. As an extra incentive, four black and white postcards were included – shots that were included in the CD booklet.

The Best of 1980-1990 video track list: 1) Pride (In The Name of Love), 2) New Year's Day, 3) With Or Without You, 4) I Still Haven't Found What I'm Looking For, 5) Sunday Bloody Sunday, 6) Bad, 7) Where The Streets Have No Name, 8) I Will Follow, 9) The Unforgettable Fire, 10) Sweetest Thing, 11) Desire, 12) When Love Comes To Town, 13) Angel Of Harlem, 14) All I Want Is You, 15) One Tree Hill

"BE THERE" Believed to be an early U2 song from 1981 or 1982 which the band recorded at a session in New York with the producer, Jimmy Destri. The lyrics are concerned with a relationship and many of the lines start with the words, "You don't have to…" It was never released.

See also: Jimmy Destri

BEURSSCHOUWBURG, BRUSSELS, BELGIUM This concert, 10th February 1981, was recorded for the *Rock Follies* Belgian TV programme which was broadcast four days later.

BIBLE AND BIBLE READING In the early 1980s three members of U2 (Bono, The Edge and Larry) were all heavily into Christianity to the extent that they would take their Bibles with them wherever they went, even getting into 'holy huddles' on the tour bus. This led to the three of them getting alienated from Adam and the tour crew at times. It came to a head in late 1981 when The Edge nearly left the band, and the other two went through a period of heart searching as to whether it was right for them as Christians to be playing in a rock 'n' roll band. Thankfully all three of them sorted out their doubts and the band continued, stronger and more united than before.

The Bible however has still played an important part in U2's lyrics over the years, the best known example being "40" off the *War* album with lyrics based on Psalm 40. The songs "Sunday Bloody Sunday", "Drowning Man", "I Still Haven't Found What I'm Looking For" and "Until The End of The World" for instance, all contain images or stories taken from the Bible. On the cover of the *All That You Can't Leave Behind* album, a coded biblical verse is shown: "J 33:3" referring to Jeremiah chapter 33 and verse 3 which talks about untold riches with God.

See also: "40" / "Sunday Bloody Sunday" / "Until The End Of The World"

"BIG GIRLS ARE BEST" ("STUCK IN A MOMENT YOU CAN'T GET OUT OF" SINGLE TRACK) (3.37) The second track on the "Stuck In A Moment You Can't Get Out Of" single (CD1). This industrial sounding track, complete with raunchy lyrics by Bono and The Edge, was produced by Flood and Howie B at the *Pop* sessions. (This track was also included on the Canadian release of the "Walk On" CD2 single (3145728202).

BIG D PIRATE RADIO STATION This was one of a number of pirate radio stations that sprang up in Dublin and other parts of Ireland after the first pirate radio station, Radio Dublin, had been raided by the Garda (Irish Police) in the late 1970s. The Big D radio station had been founded by James Dillon in March 1978. One of its earliest DJs was Dave Fanning who gave the young U2 an early mention on his programme. He was to continue to champion the band when he moved to the new national RTE2 radio station where listeners were invited to choose which of three tracks would be the A-side to the first U2 single, "U2-3".

See also: Dave Fanning

"THE BIG ONE" CONCERT The title of a special concert at London's Apollo Theatre which took place on 18th December 1983. It was organised by CND (Campaign for Nuclear Disarmament) in protest at the siting of nuclear Cruise Missiles at Greenham Common air base in England. U2 were the headline act above The Alarm, The Style Council, Elvis Costello, Ian Dury and Chas Jankel, Mari Wilson and Hazel O'Connor. It would be U2's last show for eight months.

Set List: I Will Follow, 11 O'clock Tick Tock, Seconds, Sunday Bloody Sunday, Knocking On Heaven's Door, New Year's Day, 40.

See also: CND

BIJOU CAFÉ, PHILADELPHIA, PENNSYLVANIA, USA U2's eighth American gig took place here on 15th December 1980. They returned to play another gig here on 4th March 1981 before an audience of 250. This was the date that U2's first album *Boy* entered the US charts at number 135, a point mentioned by Bono during their set which included two plays of "The Ocean" and "I Will Follow".

BIJOU, DALLAS, TEXAS, USA (2nd April 1981) One of the many club dates that U2 played on their second tour of the United States. The band were actually second on the bill to a "Miss Wet T-shirt" competition that night! When U2 played at the Cotton Bowl in Dallas in May 1997 sixteen years later, Bono actually made reference to this gig.

"BILLY BOOLA" (*IN THE NAME OF THE FATHER* SOUNTRACK ALBUM TRACK) (3.45) A track off the *In The Name Of The Father* soundtrack album written by Bono, Gavin Friday and Maurice Seezer.

A pleasant dance song, it was not released as a single despite its potential.

'BILLY BOOLA' (TIM SIMEON MOVIE MIX) This remix of "Billy Boola" was included on Gavin Friday's *You Me And World War Three* CD.

BIRMINGHAM ODEON, ENGLAND U2 have played this 2500 capacity venue on three occasions - 5th December 1982, and 10th and 27th March 1983. During the show on 10th March, it was announced that the *War* album had entered the UK charts at number 1, so a bottle of champagne was brought on stage for the band to celebrate, but no one was able to get it open.

BLACKWELL, CHRIS The founder of Island Records, the label that signed U2. The son of an Anglo-Irish soldier and a Costa Rican mother, he grew up in Jamaica where he developed his entrepreneurial flair. He would rent cars to tourists, teach water skiing and export local Jamaican records to New York and London. Before long he got involved in recording groups and artists. His first major break was with Millie who had a UK number 1 hit in 1964 with "My Boy Lollipop" which gave him the finance to set up Island Records, a small independent label. His big break though was with the discovery of Bob Marley and the Wailers, whose success made Island Records a major force in the record industry.

Although he didn't see U2 play live before they were signed to Island Records, Chris Blackwell had the ethos of backing people who showed long term commitment and potential. This meant trusting the views of Island executives Rob Partridge and Bill Stewart signed U2. In fact it was not until U2's eleventh London gig on March 19th at the Acklam Hall that Chris Blackwell first got to see U2 play live. Blackwell's belief in the band was instrumental in him persuading his neighbour in Jamaica, Frank Barsalona, to sign them to his Premier Talent Booking Agency in the US. During the recording of *The Unforgettable Fire*, Blackwell, after a three month period of negotiations, managed to persuade U2 to stick with Island in a new deal which left U2 and Paul McGuinness financially secure for the rest of their lives, as well as artistically in control of what they produced. In the 1990s when Island Records was in financial difficulty, U2 put forward the money to keep it afloat until it was bought out by Polygram Records. In January 1996, Chris, Bono and Jimmy Buffett were mistaken for drug smugglers in Buffett's plane. As the plane was taking off from Montego Bay in Jamaica, it was shot at by Jamaican police who, acting on a tip off, thought it was being used to smuggle drugs. Although the plane was damaged by the bullets, none of the occupants were hurt. In 2001 Chris Blackwell, in recognition for his services to the music industry was inducted into the Rock 'n' Roll Hall of Fame by Bono.

See also: Island Records / Rock 'n' Roll Hall of Fame

BLACK WIND WHITE LAND - LIVING WITH CHERNOBYL (DOCUMENTARY FILM) A film made by Dreamchaser about the after effects of the Chernobyl Nuclear power station explosion. It was aired in Ireland on RTE in 1995 and then on other TV stations around the world. A team of seven people, including Ali Hewson, spent three weeks in the Chernobyl area making the film, which showed how Belarus had been affected with footage of children who had been born deformed and former farmers now living in high rise blocks of flats. The documentary was shortlisted for the International Monitor Awards.

See also: Children of Chernobyl

BLAKE, LEIGH See: Red, Hot and Blue

"BLUE" Bono co-wrote the lyrics of this song with Zucchero, included on Zucchero's album, *Blue Sugar.*

BLOODY SUNDAY This was the infamous shooting of 13 people by the British Army in the Bogside area of Derry in Northern Ireland on 31st January 1972. Widely condemned, the events of that day were put to song by amongst others, former Beatle John Lennon, who wrote a song called "Sunday Bloody Sunday" which appeared on his *Sometime in New York City* album. U2's song of the same name appeared on the *War* album. Whilst the events of Bloody Sunday were influential in the writing of the song, as Bono said in a statement at the time, it wasn't just about Bloody Sunday: "'Sunday Bloody Sunday' is a day that no Irishman can forget, but should forget, which is what we were saying – 'How long must we sing this song?' When I introduce it I say, 'This isn't a rebel song'. The name comes up all the time and we're saying, 'How long must we have songs called "Sunday Bloody Sunday"?'

See also: "Sunday Bloody Sunday"

BLUE LIGHT PUB, GLENCULLEN, IRELAND On 6th August 1989 Adam Clayton was arrested in this pub car park for possessing 19 grams of cannabis with intent to supply. His arrest put the whole *Lovetown* tour in jeopardy, with a possible jail sentence if he was found guilty. He appeared in court at Dundrum courthouse on 1st September and pleaded guilty to possession of cannabis (the previous charge of intent to supply had been dropped). After half an hour's deliberation between Adam's solicitor and the prosecuting solicitor it was agreed that Adam would be fined and the Probation of Offender's Act would be applied to his case. So Adam was fined £25,000 which was to be donated to the Women's Aid Refuge

Centre in Dublin. The application of the Act meant that he was free to go to Australia as he was able to successfully apply for a visa to travel having no drugs offences on his record.

BLUE MOUNTAIN MUSIC The publishing arm of Island Records to which Paul McGuinness signed U2 in their first contract with Island Records. This deal was renegotiated when U2 signed a new contract with Island in 1984. So all U2 records feature the legend "published by Blue Mountain Music (UK)" on the record label.

BLUES MUSIC U2 have been influenced by American blues music in many ways. One of the first influences arose when the band first toured America and travelled the length and breadth of the country, listening to the various radio stations playing blues, gospel or soul. A big influence on Bono was Keith Richards of the Rolling Stones who Bono first met when he went to New York City in 1985 to contribute to the *Sun City* album. It was Richards who introduced him to some of the traditional blues artists such as Howlin' Wolf, John Lee Hooker and BB King – who U2 enlisted as support artist on the *Lovetown* tour in 1989, having previously recorded "When Love Comes to Town" with him.

See also: BB King / Keith Richards

BOGART'S CLUB, CINCINNATI, OHIO, USA U2's first gig in Cincinnati took place on 17th April 1981 was where "I Fall Down" off the *October* album was first played live.

BOLAND, ANDREW An engineer who originally worked at Keystone Studios in Dublin where U2 recorded their first ever demo tape. He then moved to Windmill Lane studios where he has engineered many albums by various artists over the years. He is now a co-owner of Windmill Lane studios.

BOLAND, TONY One of the initiators of Self Aid, an Irish version of Live Aid aimed at raising funds and, more importantly, jobs for Ireland's unemployed youth.

See also: Self Aid

BOLAND'S MILL, DUBLIN, IRELAND This club owned by Tony Boland was the venue for Adam's 27th birthday party on 13th March 1987. U2 performed "People Get Ready" to the 300 or so guests as a prelude to going to America for the *Joshua Tree* tour, for which they had been rehearsing in that very hall.

BOLTON STREET TECHNICAL COLLEGE, DUBLIN, IRELAND This might have been where The Edge would have gone to college if U2 hadn't taken off. He had agreed with his parents that he would give the group a year of his time. If they didn't take off he would quit and go to this college to study engineer-

The Dublin shop from where Bono got his name. *Photo: Paul Daly*

ing. (It is also called Kevin Street Technical College in some U2 books.)

BONAVOX HEARING AID SHOP, DUBLIN, IRELAND
This famous hearing aid shop is situated in Earl Street North, just off O'Connell Street in the centre of Dublin. It is the place where Paul Hewson got his nickname from – "Bono Vox", the latin for "Good Voice". The shop was originally called "Bonovox" but the name was changed for obvious reasons.

BONNIE, JOE Larry Mullen's drum tutor when he first started drumming lessons. After Joe's death his daughter, Monica, took over.

BONO Paul Hewson was born on 10th May 1960 at the Rotunda Hospital in Dublin, Ireland. He was the second son of Bobby and Iris Hewson whose other son, Norman, had been born several years earlier in 1952. For the first seven weeks of his life the baby Paul lived at the family house in Stillorgan to the south of the River Liffey. Then the whole family moved to a house to the northside of Dublin – 10 Cedarwood Road in Ballymun, which then bordered the countryside on the edge of Dublin.

Paul's parents were in what is termed a 'mixed' marriage, where his father was a Roman Catholic and his mother was a Protestant. This meant that Paul and his brother had to be brought up in either the Catholic or the Protestant church. So each Sunday, his father would go to mass at St. Canice's Roman Catholic Church, while the rest of the family would attend the local Church of Ireland Protestant church. This seemed to work well and continued in the matter of Norman and Paul's education. They attended primary school at Glasnevin National School in Botanic Avenue, Glasnevin (a ten minute bus ride away) although there was a nearer Catholic school in Ballymun.

One of Paul's childhood friends was Derek Rowan who lived in a nearby street. Like Paul he was brought up in the Protestant faith, though in the more extreme Plymouth Brethren denomination. He was later to become a member of the Lypton Village comprising Paul and another friend, Fionan Hanvey, who would be better known as Gavin Friday. In 1971 when he was eleven, Paul left Glasnevin, to move to St. Patrick's Secondary School in the city centre. Here he got involved in the sporting side of school life as well as excelling at chess, but all the travelling each day and the school's stricter regime started to alienate Paul, and as a result of throwing dog excrement at his Spanish teacher when she was having lunch in a nearby park, he was more or less asked to leave. Luckily his parents had heard about Mount Temple, Dublin's first comprehensive, co-educational and, most important of all, non-denominational school.

Paul started at Mount Temple in September 1972. Here he did not have to wear school uniform and the whole ethos of the school made for a more relaxed atmosphere. Some of his friends in his early years at Mount Temple included Reggie Manuel, Cheryl Gillard, Mark Holmes, Shane Fogerty, Zandra Laing and Maeve O'Regan. In the summer of 1974 Paul went to Criccieth in North Wales with the 'Bee Dees' – The Boy's Department of the YMCA whose Bible classes he occasionally attended with Derek Rowan. Fairly soon after his return in September 1974, a major tragedy shattered his life – his mother, Iris, died of a brain haemorrhage. This one event naturally had a disturbing effect on Paul, resulting in him being more rebellious on the one hand and yet seeking out the spiritual side of life on the other.

At Mount Temple, Paul enjoyed the subjects of art, history and drama. He eventually became a member of the school drama group. He also joined the Christian Union at this time and was particularly close to a girl called Maeve O'Reagan, though it was another pupil, the dark-haired Alison Stewart, to whom he would eventually swear his allegiance.

In the autumn term of 1976 he answered the invitation from Larry Mullen Junior, two years his junior, to meet at his house with the intention of forming a band. Although Paul claimed that he could play the guitar, it was his way of organising the group that endeared him to the others. Although he couldn't yet sing to a decent standard, his abilities of being able to communicate easily and write poetry made him a good choice for the role of front-man and songwriter.

As the fledging U2 developed into a half-decent band, another group of people around Paul grew into a distinct group that would be known as The Lypton Village, each with their own individual nickname. Peter Rowan became Guggi and it is he who gave Paul the name Bono, from a hearing aid shop just off O'Connell Street in Dublin, called "Bonovox", (meaning "good voice" in Latin).

From the earliest U2 gigs onwards it would be Bono who would cajole and communicate with the audience in order to gain their attention, if not their acceptance of the band. He even (along with Gavin Friday) took stagecraft lessons to improve his impact upon audiences. In the background he was constantly writing lyrics. Many of these were influenced by his new-found interest in Christianity. Songs such as "Street Mission", "In The Light" and "False Prophet" eventually gave way to more contemporary teenage influences like "Boy-Girl", "Cartoon World" and "Stories For Boys". Like Adam, Bono was keen for U2 to succeed and went as far as going over to London in frustration at the lack of interest from the big London based record companies at the time, in order to stir up some interest in U2. Eventually U2 did "make it" with a record deal from Island Records and the money to make albums and tour foreign lands.

Whenever they played a gig, it would be Bono who was the link between the band and the audience. At times this might be just with words, on other occasions it might be jumping into the audience or walking around the venue. As U2's audiences got bigger, Bono's antics got more and more outrageous. By 1983 Bono would regularly climb scaffolding at the side of the stage to wave a flag or jump up onto the balconies to sing. Things came to a head in Los Angeles in 1983 where Bono had to jump down twenty feet into the audience below to escape getting trapped by fans in the balcony. Even then his clothes got ripped to shreds!

From then on Bono would rely more on the music and the lyrics to unite the band and the audience, though a regular feature of U2 concerts since then has been to bring a member of the audience onto the stage, either a girl fan to dance with, or a male fan in some cases to play guitar. Lyrically, U2's songs grew away from basic spiritual matters and were now concerned with issues such as human rights ("Mothers of the Disappeared"), drugs ("Bad" and "Running To Stand Still"), sexual desire ("With or Without You")

Bono, Wesfalenhalle Dortmund, 1989
Photo: Kay Bauersfeld

and politics ("Sunday Bloody Sunday" and "New Year's Day"). More often than not Bono would use his performance as a way of preaching to his audience about some event or issue that was in the news, such as the Enniskillen bombing speech in the *Rattle & Hum* film. As Bono was more often than not the spokesman for the band off-stage, it was he who started to take the flak as the once pro-U2 music press became disenchanted with the band.

By the time of *Rattle & Hum*, U2 had grown into one of the biggest bands in the world and had more or less achieved what they set out to do as a group. Musically there was still plenty to come, but as Bono said as U2 played one of their final gigs of the 1980s at the Point Depot in Dublin, "It's time to think it up all over again." When the "new" U2 emerged in 1991 it was obvious that they had re-invented themselves, both on a musical and on a visual level. Bono typified this change with a character he created called "the Fly". His hair was much shorter and died black; he wore dark sunglasses like Roy Orbison or Lou Reed and was dressed in a black leather jump suit. He smoked cheroots and swore frequently, painting a picture of a futuristic cyberpunk. From this Zoo TV character metamorphosed other characters – the Mirrorball Man, dressed in silver, was suited to the American audiences, whilst Europe and the Far East got Mr Macphisto, the Devil dressed in a gold lame suit and platform heels, with an English upper-class accent, who liked to ring the rich and famous from the stage of U2 concerts.

Bono himself was now rich and famous, being feted by models, politicians and film stars. He even got to sing with one of his heroes – old Blue Eyes himself – Frank Sinatra! Bono has always been been in demand by other musicians to sing on their records. Amongst his most memorable have been: "Do They Know It's Christmas" (Band Aid), "In A Lifetime" (Clannad), "My Wild Irish Rose" (Bringing It All Back Home), "Hallelujah" (Leonard Cohen) and "New Day" (Wyclef Jean).

At the same time, Bono's humanitarian causes have developed via his Christian beliefs from an interest in human rights, through environmental issues, the AIDS issue, the war in Bosnia, to third world debt. As an ambassador for the Jubilee 2000 "Drop The Debt" campaign and NetAid he would meet such superstars as Muhammed Ali on one side through to Pope John Paul on the other as well as winning several awards for his work.

Apart from song writing, Bono's long-term film screenplay project, *The Million Dollar Hotel*, finally came to fruition in 2000 when it was first shown at the Berlin Film Festival. Bono made a brief cameo appearance in the film as well as in *Entropy*, a film

Bono. *Photo: Claire Bolton*

by *Rattle & Hum* producer, Phil Joanou. Healthwise, Bono has had problems with his voice at several U2 concerts over the years, such as at the 1997 *Pop Mart* concert in Sarajevo. Things came to a head in 1999 when sinus trouble led to an operation. He has since given up smoking.

In all of this madness, Bono has remained married to his teenage sweetheart, Alison Stewart, for almost twenty years. They now have four children: two daughters, Memphis Eve and Jordan, and two sons, Elijah Bob Patricius Guggi Q, and the latest addition, John Abraham, who was born in May 2001.

BOOKS on U2 - See appendix

"BOOMERANG" ('PRIDE' SINGLE B-SIDE) (2.47) The B-side of the "Pride" single (IS 202-B) was an instrumental that reflected the influence of the producer Brian Eno, having a dominant synthesiser sound forming a backdrop to The Edge's funky guitar work.

"BOOMERANG 2" ('PRIDE' 12 INCH SINGLE) (4.51) Only available on the 12 inch single version of the "Pride" single (along with *The Unforgettable Fire* album track "The 4th Of July"). This track is musically the same as "Boomerang", but has vocals added.

BOOMTOWN RATS, THE The Dublin based group fronted by vocalist Bob Geldof were Ireland's most successful group in the late 1970s and early 1980s, riding in on their own brand of punk rock. The line-up was Bob Geldof (vocals), Johnny Fingers (keyboards), Pete Briquette (bass), Gerry Cott (guitar), Garry Roberts (guitar) and Simon Crowe (drums). Their first single, "Looking after Number One" reached number 11 in the UK charts and was followed by the number ones, "Rat Trap" and "I Don't Like Mondays", making them the first Irish group to have a number one in the UK. Their success was an inspiration for the young U2 who wanted to follow in their footsteps.

Bob Geldof was the instigator of Band Aid and later Live Aid where he enlisted U2 to help out with the fund raising events for famine relief. In 1986 at Self Aid, the Boomtown Rats appeared on the bill with U2 as they had done a year before at Live Aid. After their appearance at Live Aid the band got together for one last tour before disbanding in 1986, with Self Aid being their final gig.

See also: Bob Geldof / Self Aid

BOOTLEGS U2, like many other major artists, have had a lot of their concerts (and some of their studio recordings) illicitly taped and then sold as "bootleg" recordings. Although U2 didn't record commercially as such until 1979, it is possible to get bootleg tapes of their early demos and studio recordings. This is also the case with some of their earliest concerts in Ireland, though the quality of the recordings would indicate that they are copies of audience recordings. Since then most U2 concerts have been bootlegged, primarily by fans who trade tapes with each other. U2 have come to accept bootlegs of their concerts as an occupational hazard that goes with the job, even going so far as to encourage fans to record their New Year's Eve concert at The Point Depot in Dublin in 1989, by providing a specially designed cassette cover for the recording of the show.

This was again repeated in 1993. When U2 played the final show of the 1993 *Zooropa* leg of the *Zoo TV* tour at Dublin's RDS Showground, *Hot Press* music paper carried a similar cassette cover. However U2 and their record company have taken legal action where tracks recorded in a studio have been copied without permission. This happened with the tapes of the early *Achtung Baby* sessions, which were stolen from a Berlin hotel room in 1990 and later surfaced as two double albums worth of material under the title, *U2 – New & Unreleased* (or *Salome* in some cases). Any record dealer found selling these albums was warned in a music press advertisement that they would face swift and sudden legal proceedings against them.

It is impossible to say just how many U2 bootlegs there are out there, but a conservative estimate of at least 2,000 is probably not far from the truth. There are at least three books on U2 bootlegs giving details of the bootlegs that are available with track listings and venue details. Even The Edge has admitted in an interview with *JAM! Music* magazine in 2001 that he has over 200 U2 bootlegs! The last word on U2 bootlegs however goes to Bono who said in a 2000 interview in *Propaganda*: "Anyone is welcome to tape our shows and pass them around to their friends. But if you start selling them, we will find out where you park your car and we will pay you a little visit!"

BORDER, ALLAN See: ANZ Stadium

BOTANIC GARDENS, BELFAST, NORTHERN IRELAND U2 played to 40,000 fans here – their biggest audience in Northern Ireland – on 26th August 1997 during the *Pop Mart* tour of Europe. The concert was a last minute addition to the tour, having been arranged just two weeks earlier after it seemed as if the two shows in Dublin might not take place. The Edge dedicated the karaoke song, "Suspicious Minds" to Tony Blair, Mo Mowlam, Gerry Adams, Ian Paisley and everyone involved in Northern Ireland politics. There was even a threat of violence from one of the extreme political groups in Northern Ireland, but this first U2 show in Belfast for ten years passed off peacefully.

BOTTACI, CANDIDA One of the staff at Principle Management Dublin who has been involved with the album production on *Pop*, *The Million Dollar Hotel* and *All That You Can't Leave Behind*.

BOWIE, DAVID The British singer who has enjoyed chart success right through from the early 1970s to the present. The pre-U2 group, The Hype had the same name as one of David Bowie's former backing groups. They used to cover his song, "Suffragette City" in their early sets and were influenced by his music and the persona of Ziggy Stardust, as was Gavin Friday whose Bowie records Bono used to borrow. Bowie's associate, Iggy Pop was also an influence. When U2 played The Agora in Cleveland, Ohio, USA in April 1981, Bono commented during the gig that Cleveland was the American town where David Bowie had started his first major American tour, indicating that he was a fan of Bowie.

In 1985 U2 shared the same bill as Bowie at Wembley Stadium for the Live Aid concert. In 1989 during the *Lovetown* tour of Australia, David Bowie came to their show at the Sydney Entertainment Centre on 17th November 1989 and spent some time with the band afterwards. In June 1990 Bono joined Bowie on stage at his concert at the Richfield Coliseum (coincidentally in Cleveland, Ohio) during Bowie's *Sound & Vision* tour to sing the Them song "Gloria" with him. David Bowie has also been involved in the Jubilee 2000 campaign alongside Bono.

BOY (ALBUM) (ILPS 9680) U2's first album was released in October 1980 in Britain and Ireland on Island Records. It was the culmination of four years work, beginning with the formation of Feedback in autumn 1976 at Mount Temple Comprehensive School, Dublin. After gaining a manager in the form of Trinity College graduate Paul McGuinness, and constant gigging, first in Dublin, then around Ireland and finally in London and the UK, U2 eventually got the record deal that they wanted with Island Records in March 1980.

After first rehearsing the album, the band started recording in August 1980 at Dublin's Windmill Lane studios. The producer was Steve Lillywhite who had enjoyed previous success with Siouxsie and the Banshees, Ultravox, Eddie and The Hot Rods, and Peter Gabriel. Before he agreed to produce *Boy*, Lillywhite and U2 worked together on the recording of their second Island Records single, "A Day Without Me"/"Things To Make And Do" which was recorded in the spring of 1980.

The album features a young and immature, yet fresh and vibrant sound from U2 whose average age then was 20. Most of the music could be loosely described as 'post-punk', though there are subtleties in tracks like "The Ocean" and "An Cat Dubh". The majority of tracks however, such as "I Will Follow" and "Out Of Control" are much more aggressive, both lyrically and musically, with The Edge using the guitar echo effect on several tracks.

On its release, *Boy* got rave reviews from the music press on both sides of the Atlantic. *Melody Maker* went so far as to claim that *Boy* was one of the finest debut albums of all time – up there with the likes of The Rolling Stones, The Velvet Underground and Roxy Music. However, it was not a commercial success mainly because U2 were still relatively unknown outside of their native Ireland, and also because the music scene at the time was dominated by 'The New Romantics' and synthesiser bands such as The Human League and Ultravox. *Boy* did, however, enter the British charts in August 1981 at number 52, following heavy touring in the UK that year, as well as a triumphant gig at the *Rock on The Tyne* festival in August 1981. Also, U2 had made their first appearance on BBC TV's "Top Of The Pops" at the same time, promoting their next single "Fire", which had given them massive exposure to the British nation.

In America *Boy* was not released until March 1981 to tie-in with a massive three month US tour to promote the album. The album's cover (designed by mentor Steve Averill) helped give the band some much needed publicity. It featured a young innocent looking boy ("Radar" – Peter Rowan, the younger brother of Guggi from the Virgin Prunes) but was taken as having a connection with paedophiles. Thus Warner Brothers, the US distributors for Island Records, had to change the cover to a shot of all four band members in a more abstract pose. The album eventually reached number 63 in the US album charts.

Track list: I Will Follow, Twilight, A Cat Dubh, Into The Heat, Out Of Control, Stories For Boys, The Ocean, A Day Without Me, Another Time, Another Place, The Electirc Co., Shadows And Tall Trees.

"BOY-GIRL" (U2-3 SINGLE B-SIDE) The third track that made it onto U2's first ever single "U2-3" (CBS 7591), which also contained the tracks, "Out Of Control" and "Stories For Boys". This single was released in September 1979 and while the other two tracks made it onto the *Boy* album, "Boy-Girl did not, though a live version of this song was put on the B-side of the "I Will Follow" single. U2's Lypton Village friends, The Virgin Prunes, also had a song called "Boy-Girl" which was about "gender-bending", though U2's was more innocently about boy-girl relationships. Whenever the song was played live Bono would use it as a vehicle for his miming skills, where he would take a cigarette from someone in the audience and pretend to smoke it secretly like an adolescent teenager would.

"BOY-GIRL" (LIVE) ('I WILL FOLLOW' SINGLE B-SIDE) This live track was the B-side of the "I Will Follow" single (WIP 6656) released in October 1980. It had been recorded at The Marquee Club in London on 22nd September 1980.

BOY TOUR The *Boy* "tour" as it is known, took place in the autumn of 1980 and the spring of 1981, although it was not actually billed as the tour to promote the *Boy* album. The first leg took place in Britain and Europe throughout September and October 1980. It started at the General Woolfe in Coventry on 6th September 1980 before covering the rest of England and visiting Holland and Belgium for the first time. The first leg ended at the Lyceum in London on 19th October - the day before the album actually came out. This was followed three weeks later by a mainly college and university tour throughout Britain in November. Although U2 went to the USA in December 1980 for their first ever visit, it was not to promote *Boy* as such but rather the band themselves. However when they returned to the States (and Canada) in March 1981, the resulting three month tour was pitched at promoting *Boy*, released stateside in March 1981.

Songs played on the tour were from: A Day Without Me, An Cat Dubh, Another Time Another Place, Boy-Girl, 11 O'clock Tick Tock, Father Is An Elephant,

Fire, I Fall Down, Into The Heart, I Will Follow, Out Of Control, Stories For Boys, The Electric Co. (with Cry), The Ocean, Things To Make And Do, Touch, Twilight

BOYZONE The Irish "Boy Band" were the world leaders of that genre for much of the 1990s. They made a cameo appearance in the promo video for "Sweetest Thing" as they were one of the many things that Ali, Bono's wife, liked.

BRADLEY CENTER, MILWAUKEE, WISCONSIN, USA Surprisingly, this show marked only U2's second gig in Milwaukee, having played there once before twenty years ago in April 1981. This gig took place on 9th May 2001 and was on the first leg of the *Elevation* tour. It was also the day before Bono's 41st birthday – so he sang "Happy Birthday" to himself!

BRADSHAW, ALBERT The music teacher at Mount Temple Comprehensive in Dublin who in the Autumn of 1976 encouraged the young Dave Evans to follow up the notice board request from Larry Mullen Junior for people interested in forming a band to contact him. He also ran the school choir of which Paul Hewson was a member.

BRADY, PAUL The well-known Irish folk and blues singer who released his *Back to the Centre* album in 1986. Larry Mullen played on the track "Airwaves".

BRADY'S, LIVERPOOL, ENGLAND U2's first visit to the city of the Beatles took place on 25th September 1980 when they played a gig at Brady's Club. They returned here again a couple of months later on 22nd November 1980.

BRAGG, BILLY The left-wing singer from Barking, Essex, the town where The Edge was born. He supported U2 at their 1985 Milton Keynes Bowl appearance. At the 1993 Brit Awards he presented U2 with their award for the Best Live group.

"THE BRATS" The name given to the annual awards that the UK music paper *The New Musical Express* holds each year the day before the Brit awards. In 2001 U2 won two awards, voted for by the readers of the paper. These were the Best Rock Act award and the God Like Geniuses award!
    See also: New Musical Express

MAIRE NI BRENNAN (BHRAONAIN) The former vocalist with the Irish band Clannad, well-known for their traditional Irish music and Gaelic lyrics. In 1986 she sang lead vocals with Bono on the Clannad single "In A Lifetime". In July 1993 during the *Zooropa* tour of Europe Macphisto rang her up from the stage at Verona in Italy to wish her a happy birthday. She currently has a successful solo career.
    See also: Clannad / "In A Lifetime".

BRIDGE HOUSE, CANNING TOWN, LONDON, ENGLAND U2 played this famous East End of London pub venue just once on 11th December 1979, on their first visit to Britain. Around this time another band used to play regularly here before they became a major rock act in the 1980s – Iron Maiden.

BRIDGE HOUSE, TULLAMORE, IRELAND This gig was one of a series of dates around Ireland in February 1980, just prior to U2 landing that elusive recording contract with Island Records. U2 played to 650 people that night and their set included several songs that were dropped from their live set soon afterwards including: "Cartoon World", "The Speed Of Life", "The Dream Is Over" and "The Magic Carpet".

BRINGING IT ALL BACK HOME A massive documentary series on Irish music, produced by Irish musician and writer Philip King. It showed to the world Irish music's rich heritage and included contributions from all of Ireland's major musical artists including Van Morrison, Rory Gallagher and U2. Bono sang a song called "My Wild Irish Rose" which he had composed specially for the series. The whole series was eventually released on video.
    See also: "April The Third" / "The Bucks of Oranmore" / "My Wild Irish Rose"

BRITISH NUCLEAR FUELS LIMITED The organisation that took out an injunction against U2 in June 1992, stopping them from holding a protest rally outside the gates of the Sellafield Nuclear Power Station in Cumbria. When U2's presence was discovered, BNFL realised that there could be up to 15,000 demonstrators outside the Nuclear Power Plant and argued that public safety could be compromised.
    See also: Stop Sellafield / Sellafield Nuclear power Station

THE BRITS The annual awards ceremony organised by the British Phonographic Industry is the British equivalent of the Grammy awards. U2 have won the Best International group award several times as well as the Best Live Group award in 1993. In 2001 they were presented with the Outstanding Contribution to Music award for their services to the UK music industry as well as "Best International Act". At the ceremony held at London's Earl's Court the band performed a five-song set of "One", "Beautiful Day", "Until The End of The World", "Mysterious Ways" and "Elevation".
    See appendix for a list of U2's awards at the Brits
    See also: Earl's Court / Jubilee 2000 / The Lemon

BRIXTON ACADEMY, LONDON, ENGLAND U2 played two consecutive nights at this major South London rock venue on 2nd and 3rd November 1984 as part of the *Unforgettable Fire* tour. These were U2's first UK dates for nearly a year and due to the absence of seats

On stage at the Brixton Academy, November 3rd 1984. *Photo: Kay Bauersfeld.*

at this venue, there was a lot of shoving and pushing at the front, which led inevitably to fighting in the crowd. Bono tried to calm the situation by talking to the audience. As there was a large number of music press reporters there, he got a lot of criticism for his speeches, including the *NME* stating that U2 were "the most boring band in the world"!

BROADBERRY, DES A member of U2's road and studio crew who joined the band during the recording of *The Joshua Tree*. By the time of *Achtung Baby* he had been promoted to keyboard and guitar technician. On the *Zooropa* album he was the programming technician and is credited for providing the chimes loop on "Babyface" and loops on "Daddy's Gonna Pay For Your Crashed Car". He was also the keyboards technician for the *Pop Mart* tour.

BROWN, ALEXANDRA She was the singer who provided backing vocals on the track "Desire (Hollywood Remix)."

BROWN THOMAS' FASHION SHOW This fashion show in aid of Children of Chernobyl took place on 14th February 2000 in Dublin. Ali Hewson helped to organise it and Larry was one was of the models along with Christy Turlington, Naomi Campbell, Yasmin Le Bon and Anna Friel.

See also: Naomi Campbell / Children of Chernobyl / Christy Turlington

BROWN UNIVERSITY, PROVIDENCE, RHODE ISLAND, USA U2 appeared here on 30th April 1983 during the *War* tour of the USA. This gig is significant for the live debut of "Party Girl" in the USA.

BRUNEL UNIVERSITY, UXBRIDGE, ENGLAND One of U2's first British gigs took place at the Brunel University in Uxbridge on the outskirts of London on 12th December 1979, where they supported The Photos.

THE B SIDES (CD) see *The Best Of 1980-1990*

BUCKLEY, JEFF Acclaimed singer and son of early seventies cult figure Tim Buckley, who died in a mysterious drowning accident in Memphis in 1997. As a tribute, on 1st June 1997 at the Giants Stadium, New Jersey Bono sang Leonard Cohen's "Hallelujah", a version of which had also appeared on Jeff Buckley's debut album *Grace*. At the end of the concert at Franklin Field in Philadelphia on 8th June 1997 Bono also dedicated "One" to the recently deceased singer.

BUCKLEY, TIM (Known as 'Timmy' so as not to confuse him with the American singer of the same name) One of U2's earliest roadies. He had been first employed by U2's sound engineer, Joe O'Heirly, back in his home town of Cork, where Joe had his own equipment hire shop. When Joe became U2's full-time sound engineer, Timmy was also taken on, and has stayed with the band ever since. He is credited as being in the crew for *The Unforgettable Fire* and *The Joshua Tree* albums.

"THE BUCKS OF ORANMORE" This was a track off the 1991 album *Bringing It All Back Home* which was the soundtrack album of a RTE/BBC TV series on contemporary Irish music. Adam plays bass on this track by The Hughes Band.

BUFFETT, JIMMY The American singer-singer songwriter whose sea plane, the Flying Boat was shot at by Jamaican police in January 1996. Bono, Ali and Chris Blackwell had just disembarked and as the plane was taking off it came under fire as it was thought to be carrying drugs. No one was hurt and the police later apologised.

BUKOWSKI, CHARLES The American writer whose work is said to have influenced Bono and inspired many of the songs on the *Zooropa* album. "Dirty Day" from the *Zooropa* album was dedicated to him. Bono had originally been introduced to Bukowski by actor Sean Penn who had phoned him up from Bono's house. Bukowski had then attended a U2 show in Los Angeles and met the band. He died in March 1994 after a lifetime of alcohol abuse.

See also: Dirty Day

"BULLET THE BLUE SKY" (*THE JOSHUA TREE* ALBUM TRACK) (4.32) The fourth track on side one of *The Joshua Tree* album. The song was written following Bono's visit to the Central American countries of Nicaragua and El Salvador in 1985 as a guest of Amnesty International. In these countries he witnessed the effect of American foreign policy at first hand with civil war causing mayhem to the ordinary people caught in the crossfire.

The song is dominated by The Edge experimenting with slide guitar and according to Bono this is due to the influence of Jimmy Page of Led Zeppelin. Bono had told The Edge to "put El Salvador through your amplifier" and this is the musical result. It is believed that the band were unsure about referring to America in the final line, in view of the controversy it might cause. An alternative ending had been recorded with the words: "of the world". In the end Paul McGuinness gave the go-ahead for the "America" ending. It certainly worked better. The track was produced by Daniel Lanois and Brian Eno.

"BULLET THE BLUE SKY" ("IN GOD'S COUNTRY" SINGLE B-SIDE) The same track as on *The Joshua Tree* album appeared on the B-side of "In God's Country" (S7-99385), which was released only in the USA in November 1987. "Running To Stand Still" was also on the B-side.

"BULLET THE BLUE SKY" ("ONE TREE HILL" SINGLE B-SIDE) "Bullet The Blue Sky" also appeared on the B-side of the "One Tree Hill" single (K338), which was released only in New Zealand in November 1987, in memory of Bono's personal assistant Gregg Carroll who originated from New Zealand and had died tragically the year before.

See also: Gregg Carroll

"BULLET THE BLUE SKY" (LIVE) (*RATTLE & HUM* ALBUM TRACK) (5.37) The first live version of "Bullet the Blue Sky" comes from the soundtrack album of *Rattle & Hum*. It was recorded live at Sun Devil Stadium, Tempe, Arizona on 20th December 1987, the final date of the *Joshua Tree* tour. It was immediately preceded by Jimi Hendrix playing the American National Anthem, "The Star Spangled Banner" at the 1969 Woodstock Festival. This was added to give the song a further sense of irony, as it was about the unacceptable face of America.

"BULLET THE BLUE SKY" (LIVE) ("STAY" LIVE FORMAT SINGLE) (5.36) The second live version of "Bullet The Blue Sky" comes from the "Stay" (live Format) single (CIDX 578), and was recorded on the final date of the *Zooropa* leg of the Zoo TV tour at Dublin's RDS on 28th August 1993. This version is a different arrangement to the one from the *Rattle & Hum* album, with The Edge letting rip with a long slide guitar solo.

"BULLET THE BLUE SKY" (LIVE) (*HASTA LA VISTA BABY! U2 LIVE FROM MEXICO CITY* CD TRACK) (6.11) This live version of "Bullet The Blue Sky" was recorded during the *Pop Mart* tour of 1997 at the Foro Sol Autodromo in Mexico City, Mexico on 3rd December 1997. Again the guitar solo by The Edge has changed with more use of echo apparent.

"BULLET THE BLUE SKY" (LIVE) (*RATTLE & HUM* FILM/VIDEO) The first live film version of "Bullet the Blue Sky" comes from the *Rattle & Hum* film. It was recorded live at Sun Devil Stadium, Tempe, Arizona on 20th December 1987 and is the same version as that on the soundtrack album.

"BULLET THE BLUE SKY" (LIVE) (*ZOO TV LIVE FROM SYDNEY* VIDEO) The second live film version of "Bullet The Blue Sky" is the fourteenth track on the *Zoo TV Live From Sydney* video. It was recorded on the final date of the *Zoomerang* leg of the Zoo TV tour at the Sydney Football Stadium in Australia on 27th November 1993.

"BULLET THE BLUE SKY" (LIVE) (*U2: POP MART LIVE FROM MEXICO CITY* VIDEO) This third film version of "Bullet The Blue Sky" is the fourteenth track on the video *U2: Pop Mart Live from Mexico City* and was filmed at the Foro Sol Autodromo, Mexico City on 3rd December 1997. It is the same version as that on the *Hasta La Vista Baby!* CD.

BUNKER, LARRY The musician who played timpani on the *Rattle & Hum* track "Hawkmoon 269".

THE BURMA CAMPAIGN A campaign aimed at securing the freedom of Aung San Suu Kyi, the elected leaded of Burma who has been under house arrest (in Burma) since 1989.

Website: www.burmacampaign.org.uk

BURNETT, T-BONE The Texan singer-songwriter who was the first musician that Bono joined musical forces with in the summer of 1984. The two had got together through Ellen Darst who looked after T-Bone's career as well as guiding U2 in America. Bono and T-Bone wrote "Having A Wonderful Time, Wish You Were Her" together which ended up on T-Bone's *Beyond The Trap Door* album.

The two of them collaborated again on "Purple Heart" which was included on T-Bone's 1988 album, *Talking To The Animals*, produced by Bono. The following year T-Bone persuaded Bono and The Edge to write "She's A Mystery To Me" for Roy Orbison's comeback album, *Mystery Girl*. T-Bone has also produced several artists with a U2 connection including Elvis Costello, The BoDeans and Los Lobos, all of whom have supported U2.

BURNS, JAKE The leader of the Belfast punk group Stiff Little Fingers noticed U2's early potential. U2 happened to be waiting for the ferry back to Ireland at Fishguard in South Wales after some gigs supporting Talking Heads in December 1980. They had their radio tuned to the Dave Fanning show on Ireland's Radio 2 and heard Fanning interviewing Jake Burns. He said there was very little life on the Irish music scene in general, except for one act, who he thought could be the greatest rock band of all time – U2.

BURROUGHS, WILLIAM An American writer whose work has influenced Bono, as well as a whole myriad of rock stars including David Bowie. He attained considerable notoriety through books such as *The Naked Lunch* and the autobiographical *Junkie*. Burroughs' writing often challenged mainstream attitudes to drugs, sexuality and the very nature of writing itself. Bono had first read *Junkie* as a teenager and had become a fan. On the *Zoo TV* tour footage of Burroughs reading a poem called "Thanksgiving Prayer" which attacked American institutions was used at the start of "Where The Streets Have No Name". In 1997 Burroughs worked with U2 on their "Last Night on Earth" promo video which was set in Kansas City. He died a few months later.

See also: "Last Night On Earth" promotional video

BURST.COM This Internet comunications company, part owned by U2, broadcast the *Pop Mart* Mexico show as a webcast on 8th June 2000. The show was available for three weeks.

BUSHELL, GARY The former *Sounds* music journalist, now entertainment critic. He was the first person in Britain to review U2's "U2-3" single, calling them "another great undiscovered Irish band" adding that the single had "atmospheric sounds with floating dreamy vocals".

See also: U2-3

BURSWOOD DOME, PERTH, AUSTRALIA U2's only visit to this western Australian town was on 17th February 1998 when they played the first gig of the Australian section of the *Pop Mart* tour of the Rest Of The World here. The venue was the smallest on the whole tour so the giant olive and toothpick were not erected for this show. About 18,000 fans attended and Michael Hutchence was remembered by having "One" dedicated to him.

BUSH, GEORGE (SENIOR) The Republican President of the USA from 1988 to 1992. Footage of him making a speech was specially doctored by the Emergency Broadcast Network for use at the beginning of U2's *Outside Broadcast* Zoo TV concerts in America and Canada. It had George Bush saying "We will, we will rock you", imitating the lines from the Queen song. At the end of each show, Bono in the guise of the Mirrorball Man would ring the White House and ask to speak to President George Bush. Each time he would be told that the President was not available. As it was near to the US presidential elections U2 used this to publicise various political issues.

Clearly these phone calls had come to George Bush's attention as in a pre-election speech he mentioned U2, who a few days earlier had spoken to the opposition candidate, Bill Clinton in a radio phone in. "They try to call me every night during the concert!" he said, "but if Clinton is elected you too will have higher inflation, you too will have higher taxes!" in a play on the band's name.

See also: Emergency Broadcast Network / Ananheim Stadium

BYRNE, CIARAN Originally an engineer and producer at Dublin's Windmill Lane studios where he was involved with engineering such artists as The Cranberries, Metallica and U2.

BYRNE, GAY The famous Irish talk show host of the programme "The Late, Late Show". He has interviewed the members of U2 on several occasions on the programme and finally retired as show host on 21st May 1999 after 37 years. As a special leaving present, Bono and Larry presented him with a Harley Davidson motorbike.

See also: The Late Late Show

C

CACTUS WORLD NEWS One of the first signings to U2's Mother Records label. Bono co-produced their first single "The Bridge" with Jon Kelly, as well as the two B-sides, "The Other Extreme" and "Frontiers". It was released in November 1985.

See also: Mother Records

CAIRD HALL, DUNDEE, SCOTLAND U2 played this northern Scottish city on only one occasion on 26th February 1983, the first date of the *War* tour in Britain and Europe. Several new songs were premiered: "Two Hearts Beat As One", "Seconds", "Party Girl" and "Like A Song". It was also the last time that "Fire" was played in concert. "Like A Song" proved difficult to play live and was promptly dropped from the set. The *War* album was released two days after this concert, on 28th February 1983.

CAMPBELL, NAOMI The world famous supermodel was engaged to Adam for most of 1993, with a Valentine's Day wedding scheduled to take place in February 1994. She was initially introduced to Adam at a U2 gig at the Giant's Stadium, New Jersey in August 1992 after he had said in the *Zoo TV* programme that the thing he would most like to do was meet

Naomi Capbell helps Bono with the champagne, Dublin RDS, 28/8/93. *Photo: Zoo Sonic Photography*

Naomi Campbell. The following February they met again at Ellen Darst's farewell dinner in New York and from then on the romance blossomed with Naomi attending several U2 gigs that year (along with fellow supermodel, Christy Turlington).

At the final gig of the *Zooropa* leg of the Zoo TV tour at Dublin's RDS in August 1993, Naomi was the girl who came onto the catwalk to record Bono with the handicam during "Trying To Throw Your Arms Around The World." However, instead of filming Bono, she walked straight past him and began filming Adam instead! A few weeks later, after the British press had published stories about an alleged liason between Adam and several call girls in a London hotel, things began to deteriorate. Although Naomi was quoted in the press as saying that she had forgiven him and still loved him, the couple began to drift apart and by the end of 1993 the press had stories linking her to other men. Naomi's relationship with U2 as a whole did however continue with her attending shows on both the *Pop Mart* and *Elevation* tours. She also organised the Frock and Roll Fashion Show / concert at which Bono performed in June 2001.

CAMP RANDALL STADIUM, MADISON, WISCONSIN, USA U2 played to over 60,000 fans at this stadium in the Wisconsin town of Madison on 13th September 1992, their first concert in this town for over ten years. When the Mirrorball Man rang up the White House from the stage, he said that his name was Elvis. The message he left with the operator for the president was, "I'm alive, and he's dead!" This was the first date on the tour for support bands BAD II and Public Enemy. U2 returned to play at this stadium on 25th June 1997 during the *Pop Mart* tour of the USA. This time the stadium was only half full with many fans being put off by the high ticket prices.

"CAN'T HELP FALLING IN LOVE" This was a number 1 hit for Elvis Presley back in 1962 and was the number that U2 finished many of their *Zoo TV* concerts with. The first occasion of this song being used on the *Zoo TV* tour was at the Robert F. Kennedy Stadium in Washington DC on 15th August 1992, the day before the 15th anniversary of Elvis' death. It was played as the final number of the set, taking over from "Love Is Blindness" and as it worked so well, was used as the final number of the set for nearly every subsequent *Zoo TV* show. It had only previously been played once before on the *Joshua Tree* tour at Murfreesboro, Tennessee on 28th November 1987, as U2 had just visited Elvis' home at nearby Graceland and been inspired by the Elvis legend. A version of the song performed by Bono was included on the soundtrack album of the film, *Honeymoon In Vegas.*

"CAN'T HELP FALLING IN LOVE" (TRIPLE PEAKS REMIX) ("WHO'S GONNA RIDE YOUR WILD HORSES" SINGLE) (4.35) This remix version of "Can't Help Falling In Love" was the fourth track on the limited edition CD of "Who's Gonna Ride Your Wild Horses" (CIDX 550). It was performed by Bono who played all the instruments on the track apart from the Hammond organ, played by Paul Barrett.

"CAN'T HELP FALLING IN LOVE" (LIVE) (*ZOO TV LIVE FROM SYDNEY* VIDEO TRACK) The only live footage of U2 performing the Elvis Presley song, "Can't Help Falling In Love" is on the video, *Zoo TV Live From Sydney.* It is the final song on the video.

CAPITAL CENTER, LANDOVER, MARYLAND, USA U2 played to a crowd of 15,000 fans here as part of the *Unforgettable Fire* tour on 8th April 1985. This concert had problems with over-eager bouncers reacting angrily when people left their seats to dance or move down to the front of the stage. Bono encouraged the fans to move to the front in spite of the bouncers' heavy-handedness. As a result of disturbances between the crowd and the bouncers the police were called and after the show Steve Iredale, the band's production manager, was arrested, as it was he who had signed the contracts for the band and was thus held to be responsible for a breach of the peace.

CAPTIVE (FILM SOUNDTRACK ALBUM) In 1985, after the *Unforgettable Fire* tour had ended (apart from some summer festival appearances) all four members of U2 took a break from touring. The Edge decided that he would like to broaden his composing talents by writing a film score, but initially found access to the film world extremely difficult.

He got his break when British producer David Puttnam introduced him to Don Boyd, who was producing a film called *Captive.* Following another meeting with the film's director, Paul Mayersberg, The Edge was flown to Paris to see the film's rushes. The result was a film soundtrack that featured up-and-coming Irish singer, Sinead O'Connor, (who had previously been associated with In Tua Nua, one of the first signings for Mother Records, U2's own record label). She sang the theme tune "Heroine". The Edge, along with Michael Brook, wrote and produced most of the tracks on the album with both of them playing on every track. Larry Mullen was drafted in to play drums on "Heroine". The album was released in October 1986, but did not make the charts.

Track listing: Rowena's Theme, Heroine (Theme from Captive), One Foot In Heaven, The Strange Party, Hiro's Theme 1, Drift, The Dream Theme, Djinn, Island, Hiro's Them (Reprise)

CARDI'S, DALLAS, TEXAS, USA U2 played this Dallas club on 16th February 1982 as part of the *October* tour. The band played the Neil Young song "Southern Man" for the first time – Bono had heard this anti-redneck song on the radio prior to playing the gig. As he wasn't sure of the words he got a member of the audience to come up on stage to sing the song with him.

See also: "Southern Man"

"CAROLINA CONCERT FOR CHILDREN" This concert took place on 23rd April 1983 at the Kenan Stadium, Chapel Hill, North Carolina, USA. It was a benefit concert for UNICEF (United Nations International Children's Educational Fund). Todd Rundgren topped the bill with U2 second and The Producers third, playing to an audience of about 4,000. As the concert stage was situated in the middle of a large field in front of one of the stadium stands, a large walkway was used to join the stage to the stands. Bono ran along the walkway several times during the concert and this set up is thought to have inspired the group to use a similar mini-stage and catwalk at their *Zoo TV* shows.

CARROLL, GREG Bono's personal assistant for two years from 1984 until 1986 when his life was cut tragically short after he was killed in a motorcycling accident in Dublin. Gregg was born in 1960 of Maori parents in New Zealand, his father being a government minister. As his father's sister was childless, she and her husband had adopted Greg soon after his birth according to Maori tradition. When U2 first visited New Zealand in August 1984, Gregg asked Steve Iredale for his U2 jacket as he walked down an Auckland street. Gregg then helped out with the setting up of the U2 gigs as one of the "local crew".

When the band returned to Auckland after dates in Christchurch and Wellington, Gregg showed Bono the famous One Tree Hill, one of seven volcanic hills that surround Auckland. Through his vibrant personality he made a lasting impression on Bono and Paul McGuinness who took him on as Bono's stage roadie. At their first concert at the Logan Campbell Centre in Auckland Bono told the audience about Greg and thanked him for agreeing to work with U2. Carroll stayed on with U2 as they toured Australia, Europe and then America throughout 1984 and 1985. He can be seen at *Live Aid* jumping off the Wembley Stadium stage after Bono during "Bad" holding Bono's microphone cable. He was also with U2 for their Amnesty International shows in the summer of 1986.

A few days after returning from America, his motorbike collided with a car without lights on More-hampton Road, Dublin. He was taken to St. Vincent's Hospital but died shortly after being admitted. Steve Iredale and Joe O'Herlihy flew back to New Zealand with his body as well as attending his funeral. Bono, Ali, Larry, Ann and Greg's girlfriend, Katie McGuinness also attended Greg's funeral at Wanganui, New Zealand on 10th July 1986. It was a traditional Maori funeral lasting three days and nights. As a tribute to him, U2 wrote and recorded "One Tree Hill". It appeared on the second side of *The Joshua Tree*, an album that was dedicated to his memory. The track was released as a single in New Zealand in March 1988 and whenever U2 have played concerts in that country, "One Tree Hill" has always been sung in his memory.

See also: One Tree Hill

CARTER, BILL The American film maker who first came to U2's attention on the *Zooropa* leg of the *Zoo TV* tour where he met the band at Verona in July 1993 and told them about the plight of the besieged citizens of Sarajevo. As a result Bill Carter went back to the city and provided a link up to several *Zoo TV* shows to show the audiences what life was like in Sarajevo. He produced a film about the citizens of Sarajevo and some of the things they did to forget about the war, such as a beauty contest, giving the title of his film and the subsequent song, "Miss Sarajevo".

See also: Sarajevo / Miss Sarajevo film and promo video

CARTER FINLAY STADIUM, RALEIGH, NORTH CAROLINA, USA The show scheduled to take place here on 29th May 1997 during the *Pop Mart* tour of the USA was cancelled, the reason being a storm a few days earlier which had waterlogged the pixels on the giant TV screen at the show in Washington DC. These needed three days to dry out and rather than playing a show with only part of the equipment available, U2 chose to cancel. The 20,000 fans who had bought tickets were given a refund and despite rumours that the show might be rescheduled for the third leg of the tour in the Autumn of 1997 this never happened.

"CARTOON WORLD" An early U2 song that never made it onto a U2 record. It was a song designed to put some humour into their music as The Edge once explained in an early interview.

CARVER-HAWKEYE ARENA, IOWA CITY, IOWA, USA U2 played a sell out concert here on 20th October 1987 to over 15,000 people. This was the first time for a month that Bono was onstage without a sling, (after dislocating his shoulder in Washington on 20th September) It was also the first night that The BoDeans played in support of U2, as they would for the rest of the tour.

CASH, JOHNNY The American country singer who had his first UK hit in 1965 has the rare honour of singing the lead vocal on a U2 track – "The Wanderer", the final track off the *Zooropa* album. U2 had admired Johnny Cash for several years, attending his live show at Dublin's Olympia Theatre on 11th February 1993, where Bono, Larry and The Edge joined him on stage. After the concert the band invited Johnny down to the studio where he recorded "The Wanderer" with them. In April 1999, U2 took part in an American TV special called *The All Star Tribute To Johnny Cash* where many music greats performed Johnny Cash songs. U2's contribution was "Don't Take Your Guns To Town" which was filmed in Dublin. Johnny Cash returned the favour in 2000 by recording a haunting version of "One" on his album *American Recordings III: Solitary Man*.

See also: The Wanderer / Don't Take Your Guns To Town

CASTLE HALL, OSAKA, JAPAN U2 played three sell out concerts here on 28th and 29th November and 1st December 1989 during the *Lovetown* tour. These were the last shows of the Japanese leg of the tour and on the last night "Slow Dancing" was played for the first time. This song did not appear on a U2 record until it was released on the B-side of the "Stay (Faraway, So Close)" single in November 1993.

CASTLE PARK SCHOOL, DALKEY, IRELAND The preparatory school on the south side of Dublin that the young Adam Clayton was sent to when he was eight years old. Although it was still in Dublin, he lived too far away in Malahide to the north of Dublin for him to travel daily, so he had to board each week from Sunday evening to Friday afternoon. He attended Castle Park from 1968 until 1973, when he left to attend St Columba's College a few miles away to the west.

CASTRO, RENE The Chilean artist and designer who Bono got to know through Amnesty International, who had rescued him from torture in Chile. Bono first met him in San Francisco when the band were playing there as part of the *Conspiracy of Hope* tour. Rene took Bono to the Mission district and showed him a wall mural that he had painted. Bono thought it was beautiful and the following year Rene and a group of artists called Placa joined the band on stage at their Oakland Stadium concert on 15th November 1987. They then spray-painted the stage backdrop with large white doves to promote their message of peace in Central America. It was also a way of showing the mayor of San Francisco, that graffiti art could be constructive after Bono's graffiti act at the "Save The Yuppies" concert a few days earlier. In 1989 Castro was given the job of designing the *Lovetown* stage set and associated merchandise/posters/tickets, etc.

See also: Lovetown tour / Placa / Save The Yuppies concert

"CAVITY SEARCH" The title of the song performed by Weird Al Yankovitch which was a parody of the U2 song "Hold Me, Kiss Me, Kill Me".

CBS RECORDS, IRELAND U2's first record company before they secured a recording deal with Island Records. The band had come to the attention of CBS Ireland when they had won the *Harp Lager/Evening Press* talent contest in Limerick in March 1978. One of the judges was Jackie Hayden, the marketing director of CBS, who donated a recording session at Dublin's Keystone studios to U2. Shortly afterwards Hayden offered the young managerless U2 a recording deal with CBS Ireland which they didn't take up.

After this first demo tape had been rejected by CBS in London it was left in the vaults, but after U2 had gained more experience and a manager, as well as recording more demos, another demo session was arranged with Chas De Whalley from CBS London coming over from London to produce the sessions. The band recorded three tracks, "Boy-Girl", "Stories For Boys" and "Out Of Control", which ended up on U2's first record release.

As a result of this demo tape Paul McGuinness renegotiated a deal for U2 with CBS Ireland whereby in exchange for CBS Ireland releasing "U2-3" as a single in Ireland, CBS Ireland would have the rights in Ireland to all U2 recordings for the next five years. The single was then released only in Ireland as CBS UK had decided not to sign U2. The single, through a clever marketing strategy, such as a numbered 12 inch

Bono's childhood home, 10 Cedarwood Road.
Photo: Claire Bolton

limited edition single and listeners of Dave Fanning's radio show voting for the A-side, went to number 1 in the Irish charts, as did the follow up "Another Day".

See also: CBS Studios / Jackie Hayden / U2-3 / Chas De Whalley

CBS STUDIOS, LONDON, ENGLAND While U2 were undertaking their first visit to London in December 1979, playing several dates in and around the capital, they also fitted in a recording session with Chas De Whalley who had produced their first single, "U2-3". The session gave rise to their second Ireland single release, "Another Day" and several other tracks, thought to include "The Dream Is Over" and "Touch".

CEDAR BALLROOM, BIRMINGHAM, ENGLAND On U2's first tour of the UK (outside London) the band's first visit to England's second city was at this venue on 29th May 1980. They then returned a few months later on 26th September 1980.

10 CEDARWOOD ROAD, DUBLIN, IRELAND The house where Bono lived for much of his life until he became famous with U2. The Hewson family first moved here a few weeks after Paul was born in 1960. When the Hype were formed the group occasionally met at his house as did the Lypton Village. He wrote many of the early U2 songs here including "Out Of Control" on his 18th birthday.

CELAN, PAUL A Romanian artist and poet who killed himself in 1970 after he was unable to reconcile the difficulties he had after many members of his family had been killed in the Auschwitz Concentration camp. His writings are said to have influenced Bono when writing the lyrics to "A Sort of Homecoming", a song reflecting Bono's own doubts about his own faith.

See also: "A Sort of Homecoming"

"A CELEBRATION" (SINGLE) (WIP 6770) U2's sixth single released on Island Records. It was recorded at Dublin's Windmill Lane studios in early 1982 with Steve Lillywhite as producer. It was released in March 1982 and despite the fact that it was not available on the *October* album released in the previous year, it only got to number 47 in the UK singles charts. An uptempo number, the song seems very positive in its outlook with Bono beginning each line with the words: "I believe in..." Some commentators have viewed the song as a statement of assurance after three of the band members (Bono, Larry and The Edge) had doubts about being Christians in a rock band. The B-side, "Trash, Trampoline and The Party Girl" was also not available on a studio album.

"A CELEBRATION" (LIVE) A rare live version of "A Celebration" was included on the cassette single version of "Pride".

"A CELEBRATION" (PROMOTIONAL VIDEO) This video was filmed mainly at Dublin's Kilmainham Gaol in April 1982. The band are seen performing the song in various parts of the jail. Meiert Avis who had already directed the "Gloria" promo video was the director. He would go on to direct the next two U2 promo videos.

See also: Kilmainham Gaol

CELTIC PARK, GLASGOW, SCOTLAND The first British concerts of the 1993 *Zooropa* tour took place at this football stadium, the home of Glasgow Celtic, on 7th and 8th August 1993. The second night was The Edge's 33rd birthday, so after the crowd sang "Happy Birthday", Bono decided to play a trick on him by announcing that The Edge would sing "The Lost Highway", a song he hadn't sung on stage for several years. He managed to sing one verse before stopping. The show also marked the live debuts of "The First Time" (which was slotted in between "Bad" and "Bullet the Blue Sky") and "Zooropa" which was only played at the next three *Zooropa* concerts. On the first night Macphisto phoned Ian Lang, the Secretary of State for Scotland. On the second night he called John Major, the British Prime Minister. Both politicians were not in. When Macphisto said in jest that John Major was doing a marvellous job for Scotland he was loudly booed!

CENTER STAGE, PROVIDENCE, RHODE ISLAND, USA U2 played this venue twice in 1981 the first time being 25th May during the North American *Boy* tour and the second being 17th November during the North American *October* tour.

CENTRAL PARK, NEW YORK CITY, USA During the *Conspiracy of Hope* tour an Anti-Apartheid rally was held in New York's Central Park on 14th June 1986. After speeches by various speakers including the Reverend Jesse Jackson, Peter Gabriel sang his song "Biko". He was then followed by Black Uhuru and Little Steven who started to sing "Sun City", being joined on stage by U2 and some of the other tour artists.

CENTRUM WORCESTER, MASSACHUSETTS, USA This 11,000 capacity American venue near Boston has been visited by U2 on nine occasions, making it the second most popular U2 venue. The first visit was during the *War* tour on 28th June 1983, which was U2's biggest selling gig to date, though the gig was not quite sold out. Steve Wickham, the violinist who played on the studio version of "Sunday Bloody Sunday" made a special appearance to play on that song. U2 next came to the Centrum on 2nd December 1984 during the *Unforgettable Fire* tour, this time easily selling out the venue – the first time in America that they had sold out an arena. The band then returned later in the second leg of the *Unforgettable Fire* tour playing three sold out nights on 16th, 18th and 19th April 1985. On the 16th, the show had to stop suddenly in the middle of "Wire" as a lighting rig was in danger of collapsing. Adam had noticed it at first and then told Bono who stopped the show and made the crowd move back from their seats whilst it was made safe. During the *Joshua Tree* tour of 1987 U2 played three more dates here on 2nd, 3rd and 4th May 1987. The second show was filmed by the Irish TV show "Today Tonight". U2's last visit to the Centrum was during the *Zoo TV* tour on 13th March 1992, the occasion of Adam's 32nd birthday.

CHARISMATIC CHRISTIAN MOVEMENT Three members of U2 – Bono, The Edge, and Larry – were all influenced by this movement during the early years of the band. Through the invitation of a man called Dennis Sheedy, Lypton Village members Pod and Guggi went to a prayer meeting of the Shalom Charismatic Christian group at a house on Dublin's North Circular Road. Soon Bono, Larry and The Edge, as well as other members of the Village, had all joined this group.

Apart from its emphasis on the Bible as God's Word, greater emphasis was placed on the third person of the Trinity, God The Holy Spirit. In particular, the experience of speaking "in tongues" (glossalalia) was seen as part of the experience of being baptised in the Holy Spirit. This experience was central to the tenets of belief of Charismatic Christian groups including the Shalom group. As this group was completely outside the established Catholic and Protestant churches, there was the danger of the weaker personalities in this group being dominated and influenced by the stronger ones. This was probably the main reason why Gavin, then Guggi and finally the members of U2 all left the group.

See also: Shalom Group

CHARLES M MURPHY ATHLETIC CENTER, MURFREESBORO, TENNESSEE, USA This concert on 28th November 1987 was the first time that U2 played the Elvis Presley song, "Can't Help Falling In Love". The number was probably chosen as the venue was near to Presley's home, Graceland, which the band had visited whilst in Tennessee.

CHAPLIN, CHARLIE Bono once paid £35,000 for the outfit worn by Charlie Chaplin in the film *The Great Dictator* at an auction in Sotheby's London. It was put on a Charlie Chaplin figure on display at Mr. Pussy's De Luxe Cafe in Dublin.

See also: Mr Pussy's De Luxe Cafe

CHERNOBYL CHILDREN'S PROJECT A charity that Ali Hewson actively supports. It aims to help the children who have suffered as a result of the nuclear explosion at Chernobyl in the Ukraine in 1986. It is an Irish registered charity, founded in response to a desperate appeal from doctors caring for children in the Chernobyl-affected country of Belarus in 1991. Since then it has brought thousands of affected children to Ireland for summer breaks, as well as organising many life saving operations for children from the region

Website: www.adiccp.org

See also: *Black Wind, White Land*

CHICAGO PEACE MUSEUM, CHICAGO, ILLINOIS, USA This museum, dedicated to the work of the peace movement, was set up in 1981. When U2 visited it in May 1983 during the *War* tour, they were influenced greatly by some of the exhibits. First, they were influenced by an exhibition dedicated to the memory of the black American civil rights leader Martin Luther King, who would be remembered in two U2 songs – "MLK" and "Pride (In The Name Of Love)". Second, they saw an exhibition on loan from Japan, entitled "The Unforgettable Fire", made up of 60 pictures created by survivors of the nuclear explosions of Hiroshima and Nagasaki. It was this exhibition that led to the album and song "The Unforgettable Fire". U2 donated the stage backdrop from the *War* tour (the picture of Peter Rowan and the white flags) and the hand written lyrics to "New Year's Day" to an exhibition entitled "Give Peace A Chance", showing how musicians have helped further the cause of peace.

Website: www.peacemuseum.org

See also: Martin Luther King / The Unforgettable Fire

"CHILDREN OF THE REVOLUTION" (*MOULIN ROUGE* SOUNDTRACK ALBUM TRACK) The old T.Rex top 10 hit from 1972 was revamped by Bono and Gavin Friday for the soundtrack of the film, *Moulin Rouge* in 2001. Previously U2 had performed part of the song live on the *Pop Mart* tour at the Maimarkt in Mannheim, Germany.

CHINA THEATER, LOS ANGELES, CALIFORNIA, USA The venue for the American premiere on 4th November 1988 of the U2 feature film *Rattle & Hum*. The band performed three numbers for the waiting crowd from a small stage in front of the theatre: "When Love Comes to Town", "Stand By Me" and "I Still Haven't Found What I'm Looking For". Some of the footage from this performance was included in the promo video for "Angel Of Harlem".

"CHRISTMAS (BABY, PLEASE COME HOME)" (*A VERY SPECIAL CHRISTMAS* ALBUM TRACK) (A&M CD 3911) U2 sang this Phil Spector song on the 1987 album *A Very Special Christmas*, produced by Jimmy Iovine, who had produced U2's *Under A Blood Red Sky* live album and *Rattle & Hum*. The track had been recorded at the SEC in Glasgow, Scotland during a soundcheck on 30th July 1987. The album was a special charity release in aid of the Special Olympics, and featured contributions from Madonna, Bruce Springsteen and Run DMC. U2 sang the song live on the very last date of the *Joshua Tree* tour at the Sun Devil Stadium in Tempe Arizona, USA on 20th December 1987.

"CHRISTMAS (BABY, PLEASE COME HOME)" (PROMOTIONAL VIDEO) U2 appeared in the promo video for "Christmas (Baby, Please Come Home) which was filmed at the LSU Activity Center in Baton Rouge, Louisiana, USA in November 1987.

CINE GRAN VIA, MADRID, SPAIN The venue for the Spanish premiere, on 29th October 1988, of the film *Rattle & Hum*. Before the film there was a speech on the cinema's stage by the members of U2 about the film and Amnesty International who received the proceeds from this show. Bono and Edge then sang a verse from "I Still Haven't Found What I'm Looking For".

"CITY AT NIGHT" An early song that U2 recorded for a demo tape which was never released on record.

CITY CENTRE, THE The name of a building in Dublin that U2 had set up for up-and-coming bands to rehearse in. It was finally opened in June 1989 but had been years in the planning. The headlining gig that the band played at Croke Park in Dublin on 29th June 1985 had been the springboard for the scheme. All the proceeds from that gig had been dedicated to the project.

CITY HALL, NEWCASTLE-UPON-TYNE, ENGLAND U2 played Newcastle's main rock music venue twice within the month of March 1983 – on the 1st and on the 26th. In between on the 16th they had come back to Newcastle to appear on *The Tube* TV music programme. This "over-exposure" in Newcastle might explain why the second City Hall show was not a sell out.

CITY HALL, SHEFFIELD, ENGLAND U2 played a sell out show here during the *War* tour on 17th March 1983. Bono described the venue as the "best building in England". This was the last concert where "A Celebration" was performed live.

CITY OF ANGELS This was a re-make of the Wim Wenders film, *Wings Of Desire* starring Nicholas Cage. The soundtrack contained the song, "If God Will Send His Angels".

CIVIC ARENA PITTSBURGH PENNSYLVANIA USA U2 played to a full house of 15,000 fans here on 9th April 1985 during the *Unforgettable Fire* tour. Bono dedicated "Pride" to a girl called Beth Lieberman, who would have attended the concert but had died suddenly shortly before.

CIVIC CENTER, HARTFORD, CONNECTICUT, USA U2 have played this 15,000 capacity arena on no less than seven occasions. The first two concerts here were on 20th and 23rd April 1985, with U2 playing a show in Philadelphia in between the two dates because it was not possible to book this venue on two nights running. The next time they played here was for three consecutive nights – 7th, 8th and 9th May 1987. Bono's brother Norman Hewson was said to have attended the first night show. During the *Zoo TV* tour U2 played the Civic Center on 12th March 1992, the show selling out in a record 40 minutes. More recently the band played here on 3rd June 2001 as part of the *Elevation* tour of North America

CIVIC CENTER, LAKELAND, FLORIDA, USA See: Zoo TV Tour

CIVIC CENTER, ST. PAUL, MINNESOTA USA U2 played two sell out shows here during the *Joshua Tree* tour on 3rd and 4th November 1987. For the second show Bono introduced The Edge's guitar technician, Fraser McAllister to the audience as it was his birthday. He was allowed to play the guitar on "People Get Ready" as a present.

See also: Fraser McAllister

CLANNAD The Irish folk-rock group who first came to international prominence when their song "Theme From Harry's Game" from the TV series of that name reached number 5 in the British charts in November 1982. The song won an Ivor Novello award in 1983. U2 used this piece for the ending to their shows for the *War* tour of 1982-3. Clannad, Gaelic for "Family", was originally formed in 1976 when various members of the Brennan family decided to form a group. They were Maire Ni, Paul and Claran Brennan accompanied by Patrick and Noel Duggan. Clannad were originally managed by Fachtna O'Kelly and then Dave Kavanagh. In 1984 they gained an even bigger audience when their *Legend* album provided songs for the TV series, *Robin of Sherwood*. For their next album, *Macalla* in 1985, Maire teamed up with Bono to sing on the hit single "In A Lifetime". In 1986 they appeared alongside U2 at the Self Aid concert in Dublin. The band finally split up in the 1990s, though Maire continues to perform as a solo artist. To date, Bono and Maire have never performed "In A Lifetime" together in concert.

See also: Maire Ni Brennan / "In A Lifetime" / Fachtna O'Kelly / Dave Kavanagh

CLARENCE HOTEL, DUBLIN, IRELAND Situated on Wellington Quay in the Temple Bar district of Dublin on the south bank of the River Liffey, the Clarence Hotel was bought by U2 in 1992. They have since renovated it to fit in with the newly redeveloped area of Temple Bar. Apart from the main hotel site, there is The Kitchen, a night club which opened in February 1994, situated in the hotel basement. When lifelong friend, Gavin Friday got married on 1st October 1993 his wedding reception was held there. At the reception the members of U2 played the old Thin Lizzy song, "The Boys Are Back In Town", and then The Edge, Naomi Campbell and other guests performed some karaoke songs.

U2 bought the hotel partly through "self indulgence – it was a case of rock stars playing with expensive ideas", claimed Bono in a *Propaganda* interview, and partly through sentimental reasons: "In the 1970s the Clarence was one of the few places where punks and eccentric types could get served." On 27th September 2000, on the roof of the hotel, U2 played two new songs from their *All That You Can't Leave Behind* album, "Beautiful Day" and "Elevation". These were for the TV programme *Top Of The Pops*, transmitted on 8th October 2000.

See also: The Kitchen

CLARENDON HOTEL, HAMMERSMITH, LONDON, ENGLAND This pub rock venue was virtually next door to the more famous Hammersmith Odeon. U2 played here on 10th July 1980 to an audience of around 200, many of whom were Island Records executives or music press reporters. *Hot Press*'s Bill Graham reviewed the gig for that paper and reported that by the end of the evening U2 had won over the audience

The Clarence Hotel, on the banks of the Liffey, Dublin.
Photo: Mark Chatterton

The Adam Clayton caricature, Wembley, 11/8/93.
Photo: Claire Bolton

Adam Clayton outside Danesmoat Summer 1994.
Photo: Nina Thomson

and managed to do an encore of "I Will Follow".

CLAYTON, ADAM The first son of Jo and Brian Clayton and U2's bass player was born on 13th March 1960 in the English village of Chinnor in Oxfordshire. The family lived partly in England (where Brian was an RAF pilot) and partly in Africa until 1965, when they moved to Ireland as Adam's father had taken a job as a pilot with Aer Lingus, the Irish airline. The family moved to a house in Yellow Walls Road, Malahide, a small seaside town ten miles north of Dublin. In Malahide Adam attended St Andrew's Primary school, also attended by David Evans. He stayed at St Andrew's until he was eight, when he was moved to Castle Park Preparatory School in Dalkey, south Dublin, where he boarded during the week. He stayed here until 1973, when he was moved to St. Columba's College Rathfarnham, aged thirteen.

Like his Prep School before, Adam resented boarding school life and as he began to grow older would rebel more and more against it. One of his main friends at St. Columba's was a boy called John Lesley, who introduced Adam to some of the main album-orientated groups of the era. John played guitar and persuaded Adam that he would be able to play bass guitar and join the band that he was forming. Adam asked his mother to buy him a bass guitar in return for working harder at school. She paid £52 for the guitar in 1975, but after more misdemeanours including breaking a "gating" order not to leave the school premises and smoking, his parents decided to take him out of the school and send him to a local state school – Mount Temple.

Adam started at Mount Temple in September 1976, but even with its relaxed attitude he continued to break the rules and rebel against authority. Actions such as drinking coffee in class and streaking down the school's main corridor ultimately led to him being asked to leave in March 1978. Although Adam did very little work at Mount Temple, he had come across Larry Mullen and his note asking for people to join his band. Due to the fact that he had a bass guitar and had been in a band already – the Max Quad Band – he got the gig.

After leaving Mount Temple, Adam in many ways stepped into the role of manager for the group, badgering anyone with a connection in the music business for advice, including Bill Graham, Steve Averill and Phil Lynott. Once Paul McGuinness became the band's manager, Adam seemed to move away from the centre of the group, especially when the other three members became committed Christians. On the early tours Adam would tend to spend more time off stage with Paul McGuinness, rather than with the other three who would be studying their bibles. Nevertheless, the fact that he was asked by Bono to be

Adam Clayton plays guitar on "40" at the Astoria, London 7/2/01. *Photo: Wendy Chatterton*

Adam Clayton, Earl's Court, 22/8/01. *Photo: Claire Bolton*

his best man at his wedding to Alison Stewart in 1982 showed that he was still close to the other three. Similarly, he took part in the recording session of the Band Aid single, "Do They Know It's Christmas?" with Bono.

As Adam has admitted, his bass playing at first was not that good – he was completely self taught – but with determination to succeed as a musician and from playing a large number of gigs in the first years of the band's existence, his bass playing improved considerably. Notable musical contributions by Adam to U2 have included "New Year's Day", "With Or Without You" and "Dirty Day".

Adam has had his fair share of publicity. In August 1989, he was arrested in Dublin after being found in possession of a small amount of cannabis. The resulting court case left him with a £25,000 fine – donated to the Dublin Women's Aid Refuge Centre.

Then in 1993 when he became engaged to supermodel Naomi Campbell, it seemed like he was never out of the headlines; more a celebrity than a musician. The messy ending of the engagement as reported in several British Sunday newspapers only served to send Adam further downwards into alcohol dependency. This came to a head in Sydney Australia when, as a result of a massive hangover from an alcoholic binge, he missed playing with the band at their Sydney Football Stadium gig on 26th November 1993. This brought things to a head and from then on he has stayed off the alcohol.

In 1994 he settled in New York City (along with Larry) and started having bass lessons to increase his understanding of the instrument. In the period between the *Zoo TV* and *Pop Mart* tours he branched out musically, working with several other artists away from U2, including Nanci Griffiths (*Flyer)* and Little

Stephen ("Born Again Savage"). 1995's *Original Soundtracks 1* courtesy of The Passengers contained the first recorded vocal by Adam on the track, "Your Blue Room", even if it was spoken! Then in 1996 in collaboration with Larry he had a Top 10 hit in the UK with "Theme From *Mission: Impossible*".

On both *Pop* and *All That You Can't Leave Behind*, Adam has continued to shine musically, on tracks such as "MoFo", "Please", "Beautiful Day" and "Walk On". In recognition of his sterling bass work with U2, Adam won the Bassist of the Year award at the Gibson Guitar Awards ceremony in Los Angeles in February 2000. Adam, or "Sparky" as he is sometimes called, is now more than ever committed to the band that he first pushed and promoted way back in 1978.

CLAYTON, BRIAN Adam Clayton's father was originally a Royal Air Force pilot. Adam was born in Oxfordshire, England, as Brian was stationed at a nearby airfield. Having decided to leave the RAF, he got a job with Aer Lingus, the Irish airline company. As a result the family moved to Ireland in 1965 and settled in Malahide, not far from Dublin airport. As a pilot he would often be away from home – for instance he had to spend some time in Singapore. This was perhaps influential in Adam being sent to boarding school at the age of eight.

CLAYTON, JO Adam's mother was a former air hostess who had met her husband through her work. She gave birth to Adam in March 1960 in the Oxfordshire village of Chinnor, about ten miles north of Oxford. Her daughter, Sara Jane, was born two years after Adam. When the family moved to Malahide she had another son, Sebastian. Always concerned about her children's welfare, she arranged a meeting with Paul McGuinness when she heard that he was to be her son's manager. On several occasions throughout the past twenty years, both Jo and husband Brian have attended U2 concerts.

CLAYTON, SEBASTIAN Adam's younger brother was born in Dublin, after the Clayton family had moved from Oxfordshire in England to Malahide in Ireland. Sebastian has always been keen on computers and runs the Dublin-based computer company Digital:CC. He is now the Internet consultant to the U2.Com website.

CLINTON, BILL Democrat politician, elected President of the USA in November 1992. U2 first spoke to him in August 1992 on an American radio programme called "Rockline", a few months before he won the presidential election. Although the impression was given that Bill Clinton had just happened to call, it was all pre-arranged, partly because of Bono's onstage calls to President George Bush and partly

for political capital. The radio programme mostly involved Bono questioning the soon-to-be President rather than the other way round! Bill Clinton used the programme to praise U2 and their music, saying: "I wanna say as a middle aged man, that I appreciate the fact that you made *The Joshua Tree* and that record "Angel of Harlem" at Sun Studios. You made me feel like I had a place in rock music even at 46!"

When Clinton was inaugurated as president in January 1993, Adam and Larry were present at the MTV inauguration ball, where they joined up with Michael Stipe and Mike Mills of REM to form a new supergroup for the evening, Automatic Baby, performed the U2 song "One" for the new president. Clinton invited all of U2 to the millenium celebrations at the White House on 31st December 1999, though only Bono and his family attended. After Clinton stepped down from office, he visited Ireland in 2001 as part of the ongoing peace process, hosting a gala dinner in Dublin Castle in aid of the Northern Ireland Peace Fund. Both Bono and Bob Geldof attended the £10,000 a table charity dinner.

A CLOCKWORK ORANGE 2004 The Royal Shakespeare Company production of the Anthony Burgess novel, performed on stage in London in 1990. In the spring of 1989, U2 were approached by RSC director Ron Daniels to "collaborate" on the project. After seeing his production of *Macbeth* at Stratford in August 1989, The Edge and Bono decided to "go for it", despite the *Lovetown* tour of Australia looming up. In September they entered a studio in Dublin and prepared some demos for producer Paul Barrett to work on. Immediately after the tour and after extra dates in Holland in January 1990, the two of them, left with only two weeks to go before the show opened, managed to get the score sorted and ready. Phil Daniels, star of such films as *Quadrophenia* and *Breaking Glass* played the lead part of Alex, an ultra violent young man who undergoes special "treatment" to turn him into a model citizen. Although the music was not released, one track, "Alex Descends Into Hell For a Bottle Of Milk/Korova 1" made it onto the B-side of "The Fly" single released in 1991.

CLONGOWES WOOD COLLEGE, IRELAND The boarding school that U2 manager Paul McGuinness attended from the age of ten in 1961 until he left to attend Trinity College in Dublin. Whilst there he became interested in drama and debating. He edited the college's magazine, won the gold medal for being the college's best debater and also directed plays.

CND (CAMPAIGN FOR NUCLEAR DISARMAMENT) This anti-nuclear organisation was started by Bertrand Russell and Canon John Collins in Britain in 1958. It used to hold protest walks and rallies to such places as the Aldermaston Nuclear Weapons establishment west of London. Although CND continued throughout the 1960s and 1970s, it suddenly became popular again in the early 1980s when nuclear cruise missiles were located at Greenham Common air force base in Berkshire to the west of London. In December 1983 a concert called "The Big One", protesting against the cruise missiles was organised by CND with U2 topping the bill.

See also: The Big One

COASTERS, EDINBURGH, SCOTLAND A one-off gig at this venue took place on 31st August 1981 at the end of a summer where U2 had played several festival dates. It was the last time the band played the instrumental "Things to Make and Do" live.

THE COCONUTS The all female backing group of the disco singer Kid Creole who was also signed to Island Records. They were Taryn Haggy, Adriana Kaegi and Cheryl Poirer and sang backing vocals on the *War* album tracks, "Surrender" and "Red Light".

COFFEY, CECILIA A long standing associate of U2 who works in the offices of Principle Management in Dublin. Cecilia is in charge of dealing with the many and varied enquiries that come into *Propaganda* about U2.

COHL, MICHAEL The Canadian promoter whose company (CPI) Concert Promotions International had the huge task of promoting the *Pop Mart* tour.

COLISEUM, CHARLOTTE, NORTH CAROLINA, USA The third date of the American leg of the *Zoo TV* spring tour of 1992. U2 played here on 3rd March 1992 to the biggest crowd of this leg of the *Zoo TV* tour – nearly 23,000. The band then returned here on the *Elevation* tour, again to play the third date of the tour. This time the show very nearly didn't happen as the plane bringing the band to this show was held up by bad weather. In the end, the band arrived just before they were due to go on and so had to play a shorter set than planned.

COLISEUM, HAMPTON, VIRGINIA, USA U2 have played this 10,000 capacity arena on four occasions, the first being 10th April 1985 during the *Unforgettable Fire* tour. They then played two dates here – 11th and 12th December 1987 – during the *Joshua Tree* tour, which were originally scheduled to be the final dates of the whole tour. So the second night was full of surprises with older numbers, "11 O'clock Tick Tock" and "Out Of Control" being played. Then Larry made his vocal debut singing the old Eagles song, "Tequila Sunrise". At the end several roadies came on stage dressed as the Dalton Brothers and started to sing "Lucille" much to Bono's surprise. (Two more dates were added to the tour at the Sun

Devil Stadium in Tempe a week later for the *Rattle & Hum* film). U2 played one more concert here on 7th March 1992 during the *Zoo TV* spring tour.

COLISEUM, NEW HAVEN, CONNECTICUT, USA U2 played this 10,000 capacity arena first on 27th June 1983 during the *War* tour. It was hastily added at the last minute, the band having already played a concert at Yale University in this town only a month earlier. Although over 5,000 fans attended the show, it was not a sell out by any means. U2 then came back to this venue during the *Joshua Tree* tour on 23rd September 1987.

COLISEUM PHOENIX ARIZONA USA U2 played this 13,000 capacity arena on 25th March 1982 as support act to the J. Geils Band. Despite the reputation of the audience being hostile to support bands to the point of throwing bottles at them, U2 managed to play a full set as well as two encores.

COLLINS, STEVE The Irish boxer who appears in the promo video of "Sweetest Thing". He once admitted to listening to U2 music before a big fight in order to put him in the right frame of mind.

COLORADO STATE UNIVERSITY, BOULDER, COLORADO, USA This show took place the day after the famous "Red Rocks" show at Denver on 6th June 1983. It was designated a free show as Paul McGuinness had booked this venue in nearby Boulder in case the Red Rocks show was cancelled or spoilt by heavy rain. At the end of the U2 set, support band The Alarm came on stage to play the Bob Dylan song, "A Hard Rain's Gonna Fall" with U2.

COLSTON HALL, BRISTOL, ENGLAND U2 played a sell out concert here on 7th March 1983 during the *War* tour. In the audience was an escapee from a remand centre in Devon. After the concert he went back to the remand centre and persuaded the Governor to let him and several other remand prisoners attend the next show at Exeter University on 8th March.

"COME OUT TO PLAY" TOUR The name given to a tour of Ireland by U2 in February and March 1980 to promote the second CBS single "Boy-Girl". As a result the single reached number 1 in the Irish singles charts.

COMIC RELIEF The British based charity that was set up by several British comedians in a similar vein to Live Aid as a way of raising funds for suffering people. It is held every two years and shown on TV as a telethon with people all around the country doing silly and comical things to raise money for several charities in Britain and abroad. In 1999 Bono appeared on the programme dressed in drag, then in 2001 he donated his Fly glasses to a charity auction for Comic Relief.

"COMING THRU" This was the first release on Mother Records, the record company that U2 and their management had set up in 1984. It was a 7 inch single released by the Irish group In Tua Nua in July 1984, recorded at Dublin's Windmill Lane studios with Peter Walsh producing and engineering. The B-side was called "Laughing at the Moon".

See also: In Tua Nua

COMMON GROUND (ALBUM) An album put together by Irish producer Donal Lunny featuring traditional Irish songs performed by Irish musicians. Bono was originally going to sing on a Christy Moore track called "The Yellow Bittern" but didn't have enough studio time to complete it. In the end he sang on an updated version of the *October* album track "Tomorrow" with Adam helping out.

See also: Donal Lunny / "Tomorrow"

COMMONWEALTH STADIUM, EDMONTON, CANADA U2 played to over 100,000 fans at two concerts here on 14th and 15th June 1997 during the *Pop Mart* tour of North America. This was the first time U2 had visited this Canadian town and Bono referred to the audience's warmth on the first night: "How come we haven't been here before? They didn't tell us about you. That's why!"

COMMUNITY CENTRE, HOWTH, IRELAND This is believed to be the Hype's farewell concert which took place on 20th March 1978 with The Edge's brother Dik Evans bowing out to join the Virgin Prunes. He played the first half of the concert with the Hype, then as he left the stage the new four piece band continued under the name U2. One of the songs they played that night was Thin Lizzy's "Dancing in the Moonlight".

COMMUNITY CENTER, TUSCON, ARIZONA, USA This was the second town that U2 played on their *Joshua Tree* tour of North America. They played here on 5th April 1987 to a 8,000 sell out audience. The gig marked the live debut of a country song, called "Lucille" that Bono had recently written. It would be played several times on the rest of the tour.

COMPAQ CENTER, HOUSTON, TEXAS, USA U2 played here on 2nd April 2001 during the first leg of the *Elevation* tour of North America. The film of Charlton Heston talking about gun control immediately before "Bullet The Blue Sky" did not go down well with many members the audience who shouted out whilst it was being shown.

See also: Charlton Heston

COMPAQ CENTER, SAN JOSE, CALIFORNIA, USA U2 played two sell out shows at this 20,000 capacity venue on 19th and 20th April during the *Elevation* tour of North America. At the first show, The Edge's par-

Above and below: U2 at Conseco Fieldhouse, Indianapolis, 10/5/01. *Photos: Shawn Bland*

ents were present, whilst at the second show, "Kite" was played live for the first time. Also "Stay (Faraway, So Close!)" was given its American debut, the first time a song from the *Zooropa* album has been played on that continent.

COMPASS POINT/ROSE STUDIOS, NASSAU, THE BAHAMAS The studios where U2 recorded their "Fire" single in April 1981, during a break from their mammoth three month tour of North America. Steve Lillywhite was the producer at these sessions which also saw the recording of the B-side "J. Swallo". The single was released in July 1980 and gave U2 their first UK single chart entry.

See also: "Fire" / "J. Swallo".

COMPTON TERRACE, PHOENIX, ARIZONA, USA This gig drew the largest crowd that U2 had played to as headline artists in their career thus far, with 23,000 fans watching them in an open field on 1st March 1985. This led to problems with people shoving and pushing at the front, so in the middle of "The Unforgettable Fire" Bono stopped the song to intervene in a fight that had developed below him. To try and calm things down, the band played "Pride" early on in the set as well as at the end.

"CONCENTRATION CRAMP" An early U2 song that was never recorded or released. The lyrics can be seen in the Hot Press Music Hall of Fame in Dublin.

CONGRESS CENTRE, HAMBURG, GERMANY U2 played this venue just once – on 28th January 1985, though it was the third time that they had played in Hamburg.

CONSECO FIELDHOUSE, INDIANAPOLIS, INDIANA, USA U2 played here on 10th May 2001 during their *Elevation* tour (first leg) of North America. This was the date of Bono's 41st birthday, so the rest of the band played an excerpt from the Beatles' "Birthday" at the end of "Elevation". To celebrate, Bono allowed around 25 girls to get on the stage with him during the show.

CONSPIRACY OF HOPE TOUR This tour took place in June 1986 in the USA and was a series of concerts designed to raise awareness and funds for Amnesty International, the human rights organisation. The American Director of Amnesty International, Jack Healey, had first approached U2 about taking part in this tour in August 1985, having seen the band play an Amnesty benefit show at New York's Radio City Music Hall the previous year. Paul McGuinness had promised him two weeks of the band's time in 1986. With this promise, Healey went about getting other acts for the line-up, which was eventually to feature Sting, Peter Gabriel, Bryan Adams, Lou Reed, Joan Baez and The Neville Brothers.

There were six shows in all: The Cow Palace, San Francisco (4th June), The Forum, Los Angeles (6th June), McNichols Sports Arena, Denver (8th June), The Omni, Atlanta (11th June), The Rosemont Horizon, Chicago (13th June), and The Giants' Stadium, New Jersey (15th June). U2 headlined the first three shows, but when Sting was reunited with Andy Summers and Stewart Copeland, the reformed Police headlined. The Omni Centre was the first show that the reunited Police played and U2 joined them onstage to sing "Sun City" and "I Shall Be Released".

The day before the final show, there had been a large Anti-Apartheid rally in New York's Central Park attended by 60,000 people. U2, Peter Gabriel and some of the other artists on the Conspiracy tour sang live on stage in support of this cause. The *Conspiracy Of Hope* tour was a huge success, with over $4,000,000 being raised for Amnesty International. The American branch doubled its membership to over 70,000 members. Finally, over 100,000 letters of pro-

Bono and Sting, Conspiracy of Hope Tour.

test were sent out to various governments and heads of state, helping the cases of hundreds of prisoners of conscience.

See also: Amnesty International / Sting / The Police

CONTINENTAL ARENA, EAST RUTHERFORD, NEW JERSEY USA U2 played two gigs here during the *Elevation* tour (first leg) of North America. They were on 21st and 22nd June – the final dates of this leg of the tour. The last date was, as usual for a tour closer, full of surprises. In attendance was the former US President Bill Clinton, as well as the Secretary General of the United Nations, Kofi Annan. "Wild Honey" was played live for the first time (an acoustic version). Daniel Lanois joined the band on stage for "Wild Honey" and "The Ground Beneath Her Feet".

See also: Meadowlands Arena

CONTRACEPTION The Republic of Ireland, being a staunchly Roman Catholic country, had until recently very strict laws on contraception (and abortion). All forms of contraception were banned including the Pill, condoms and the IUD. U2, being against this law, paid the fine levied against The Irish Family Planning Association for selling condoms in Dublin's Virgin Megastore in defiance of Irish law in 1991. Then at their show at the Pairc Ui Chaoimh in Cork, they were banned from selling condoms on their merchandise stalls by the owners of the stadium, the Gaelic Athletics Association. In defiance of this ban, U2 manager, Paul McGuinness gave out free condoms to the crowd. Another U2 connection with contraception occurred in 1994 when Bono's wife paid £200 for a vasectomy at a charity auction in Dublin. She didn't use it for Bono though, but gave it away to a woman called Helen who wanted one for her husband.

See also: Pairc Ui Chaoimh / Irish Family Planning Association

"CONVERSATION ON A BAR STOOL" A song written by Bono and The Edge, sung by Marianne Faithful on the soundtrack of the film *Short Cuts*.

COOTE, CARAGH The person responsible for booking bands for the Project Arts Centre in Dublin in the late 1970s. After Adam's persuading, she booked the Hype for a special St. Patrick's Day Eve concert in March 1978. She was also a friend of Phil Lynott of Thin Lizzy whom Adam was able to contact through her at the hotel he was staying in at Dublin at that time. She also booked the young U2 for several more concerts at the Project, including one as support to the Gamblers on Thursday 25th May 1978, where Paul McGuinness met U2 for the first time.

CORBIJN, ANTON The famous Dutch photographer has been U2's principal photographer since 1982. The band first met him in New Orleans on 11th February 1982 when he had come to America with a reporter from the *New Musical Express* to photograph U2. The band performed a gig on the SS President riverboat as it sailed down the Mississippi and before it sailed Corbijn took the photos. He was then given the job of photographing the band in Sweden in December 1982 for the inner cover of their next album, *War*. From then on he has photographed U2 for all their album covers from *The Unforgettable Fire* right through to the latest *All That You Can't Leave Behind*. In between he has shot thousands of publicity photos of U2 chronicling their career through the 1980s, the 1990s and into the new millennium.

Anton started in 1972 by taking photos of a Dutch band called Solution with his father's camera in Gronningen, Holland. Immediately, he was hooked on photography. After finishing college he went on to become the chief photographer for the Dutch *Oor* magazine from 1977 to 1979. He then went to England to shoot Joy Division, before landing a job with the *NME* where he was principal photographer until

1985. Over the years he has photographed just about every rock star there is, including The Rolling Stones, David Bowie, Nirvana, The Police, The Sex Pistols, Johnny Cash, REM, Nick Cave, Captain Beefheart and Depeche Mode as well as doing the covers for albums such as REM's *Automatic For the People*, John Lee Hooker's *Chill Out* and Depeche Mode's *101*, *Violator* and *Exciter*. He has also produced and directed promotional videos for several artists including U2. He directed the first video of "One" which was set in Berlin and featured Bono's father, Bobby Hewson, and also the video for "Please". It was his idea to use a joshua tree for the cover of the album of the same name and the Trabant car as a symbol for the reinvented U2 of the 1990s.

Werk, a book of pictures taken over the past twenty-five years, was published in 2000. It included photos of many film-stars and directors, models, writers and painters. It even featured a whole chapter devoted to Bono. In April 2000 an exhibition of Anton's photography was opened by Bono in Groningen, Holland. His photographs and other works of art are regularly exhibited at exhibitions all over the world.

website: www.corbijn.co.uk

C.O.R.E. – CUMBRIANS OPPOSED TO A RADIOACTIVE ENRIONMENT This was the local organisation that first proposed a protest rally at the gates of Sellafield Nuclear Power Station in Cumbria, England on 20th June 1992. U2 said they would join in the rally and play, until British Nuclear Fuels stepped in with a High Court injunction banning the event. Instead, U2 played a gig at Manchester's G-Mex Centre the night before the proposed rally would have taken place and then filmed a protest on the beach at Sellafield the next morning.

See also: Stop Sellafield

"CORPSE (These Chains Are Way Too Long)" (*ORIGINAL SOUNTRACKS 1* ALBUM TRACK) (3.34) The tenth track off the Passengers album, *Original Soundtracks 1*. It featured David Herbert on saxophone.

COSTELLO, ELVIS (Real name: Declan McManus) Elvis Costello first came to the public's attention as one of the leading lights in the punk/New Wave explosion in Britain in the late 1970s. With his group the Attractions, he had several top 10 hits in Britain with songs such as "Oliver's Army" and "I Don't Want To Go To Chelsea". U2 first met him when they played on the same bill at the 'Rock On The Tyne' Festival at Gateshead, England in August 1981. He also appeared on the same bill as U2 at 'The Big One' at London's Victoria Apollo in December 1983. A big U2 fan, Elvis appears on the *Joshua Tree* video where he admits to queuing up at midnight to buy *The Joshua Tree* when it came out in 1987.

COUNTRY CLUB, CORK, IRELAND U2 played this venue in February 1980 as part of a small Irish tour prior to their prestigious gig at Dublin's National Stadium later that month in front of Island Records executive Bill Stewart. A journalist from the *New Musical Express* newspaper, Paul Morley, came over to Ireland for this gig and gave it a favourable review.

CLEMENT, COWBOY JACK He was the famous engineer at Sun Studios who had the job of engineering the records of Elvis Presley, Jerry Lee Lewis and Johnny Cash in the 1950s. When U2 did a session at the studios in November 1987, they specifically asked for Cowboy Jack Clement to be there to engineer the session just like in the old days.

See also: Sun Studios

COW PALACE, SAN FRANCISCO, CALIFORNIA, USA U2 have played this 14,500 capacity San Franciscan venue on five occasions. The band first played two nights here on 7th and 8th March 1985 during the *Unforgettable Fire* tour. On the second night there was a possibility that the show might have to be cancelled due to Larry having intense pain in his left hand. After seeing a hospital doctor he was advised to have two weeks rest, but due to the number of gigs that still had to be played, he was given a special plaster to put his hand in when not playing the drums. U2 next played here on 4th June 1986 during the *Conspiracy of Hope* tour. Finally they played two nights here on 24th and 25th April 1987 during the *Joshua Tree* tour. At these shows Bono invited a worker from Amnesty International up on stage to talk about their work. Afterwards many of the audience joined the organisation or signed petitions at the various stands that the organisation had put up in the lobby.

CREATIVE DEPARTMENT LTD, DUBLIN, IRELAND One of U2 designer Steve Averill's former companies.

See also: Steve Averill

CRICKET GROUND, MELBOURNE, AUSTRALIA (12th and 13th November 1993) The opening dates of the *Zoomerang* leg of the *Zoo TV* tour in Australia in the autumn of 1993. U2 played to a total audience of 95,000 on these two dates. They marked the live debuts of three songs from the *Zooropa* album – "Lemon", "Daddy's Gonna Pay For Your Crashed Car" and "Dirty Day". On the second night Macphisto rang up Dame Edna Everage, the famous Australian entertainer.

CROKE PARK, DUBLIN, IRELAND This famous Irish sporting venue has seen three U2 concerts in its history. The first was on 29th June 1985 when U2 played a triumphant homecoming gig in front of 57,000 fans

at the end of the *Unforgettable Fire* tour. At the concert they played the Bruce Springsteen song "My Hometown" – the one and only occasion they have played it live. Steve Wickham, the violin player with support band In Tua Nua played with the band on "Sunday Bloody Sunday" at the venue where the first "Bloody Sunday" had taken place in November 1920. RTE TV made a documentary about the concert called *Wide Awake In Dublin*, which was shown on Irish TV at Christmas 1985. Apparently the day before the gig U2 had been rehearsing and the noise carried over to a nearby secondary school where students were taking some very important exams. The caretaker came over to the stadium to complain and as a result the band immediately stopped playing!

U2 played two more emotional concerts here on 27th and 28th June 1987 during the European leg of the *Joshua Tree* tour. The concerts were filmed for a *World in Action* TV special on the band called *Anthem for The 80s*, which was shown on ITV in the autumn of 1987. Lou Reed was one of the support acts for both nights and on the second night sang "Walk on the Wildside" as a duet with Bono. The previous year Simple Minds had played a concert at this venue and Bono had come on stage to duet with Jim Kerr singing: "Sun City", "Lovesong" and "Dance To The Music".

See also: Anthem For The 80's / Wide Awake In Dublin

"CRY" This was a guitar riff that The Edge first used in November 1980 at a U2 gig in Edinburgh, which led into "The Electric Co.". The riff was then recorded as the opening section to the *October* album track "Is that All". It next appeared on vinyl on the live album *Under A Blood Red Sky* at the beginning to "The Electric Co." but wasn't named "Cry" as such.

CYCLONE STADIUM, AMES, IOWA, USA U2 played to nearly 50,000 fans at this stadium during the *Outside Broadcast* leg of the *Zoo TV* tour on 11th September 1992. This was the last show of the tour for the support band The Disposable Heroes of Hiphoprisy who did a special rap in the confessional booth.

CZUKAY, HOLGER The German musician, best known for his work with the German group Can, collaborated with The Edge on Jah Wobble's *Snake Charmer* EP in 1983. He had previously worked with Jah Wobble on his 1981 EP *How Much Are They*.

See also: Jah Wobble

D

"DADDY'S GONNA PAY FOR YOUR CRASHED CAR" (ZOOROPA ALBUM TRACK) (5.19) This is the first track on the second side of the *Zooropa* album. It starts off with an excerpt from the 'Fanfare' off the Russian album *"Lenin's Favourite Songs"*, and then moves into a very echoey industrial sounding song, complete with harmony loops. The Edge credited Flood with creating the sound on this track: "He is just very good at creating places out of sound. I feel that the track is more of a location than a song." It is believed to be about drug dependence.

"DADDY'S GONNA PAY FOR YOUR CRASHED CAR" (*ZOO TV LIVE FROM SYDNEY* VIDEO TRACK) This song was not played live in full on the *Zooropa* tour, but finally made its live debut on the *Zoomerang* leg in Australia at the Melbourne Cricket Ground on 12th November 1993. This film version comes from the show at Sydney's Football Stadium on 27th November 1993. It is the first song to be sung after the main set has ended and starts off in Bono's dressing room as he transforms himself into Macphisto. The camera follows him as he sings the song starting in the dressing room and ending up on the stage.

DALTON BROTHERS, THE This was the fake group that featured all four members of U2 in disguise, who pretended to be the support band at certain dates on the *Joshua Tree* tour of North America. The name came from one of the legendary Wild West gangs, the other being The Doolins, immortalised on The Eagles' album *Desperado*. U2 first appeared as the Dalton Brothers at the Hoosier Dome in Indianapolis on 1st November 1987. The support band for this gig, Los Lobos, had for some reason failed to show up on time, so U2 (who had been thinking of playing in disguise for some time) decided to use the opportunity to make their live debut. Wearing wigs and cowboy hats, the Dalton Brothers sang two songs, "Lucille" and "The Lost Highway". Bono was called Alton Dalton, Edge was Luke Dalton, Adam was Betty Dalton (complete with skirt!) and Larry was Duke Dalton. Very few fans recognised them in spite of their ludicrous outfits and mock Texan accents. Later on in the show when U2 were back on stage as themselves, Bono sang "Lucille" again and this led to the audience realising that a trick had been played on them.

U2 again appeared on stage as the Dalton Brothers a few weeks later on 18th November at the Memorial Coliseum in Los Angeles as an extra support act in between The BoDeans and The Pretenders. Once again they played the same two songs, though this time most of the audience recognised the band. For what was originally going to be the final date of the *Joshua Tree* tour of America at The Coliseum in Hampton, Virginia, it was the road crew's turn to be the Dalton Brothers. At the end of the gig, Dallas Schoo, The Edge's guitar technician came out on stage dressed as a Dalton Brother. He was followed on stage by three more of the road crew, who were all similarly dressed.

DALYMOUNT FESTIVAL, DUBLIN, IRELAND U2 played at this festival to mark the occasion of the "Dublin Festival 1980" on 28th July 1980.

"DANCING BAREFOOT" ('WHEN LOVES COMES TO TOWN' SINGLE TRACK) (4.13) This Patti Smith and Ivan Kral song was featured on the B-side of the "When Love Comes To Town" 7 inch single (IS 411). It was also featured on the A-side of the 12 inch version (12IS 411). It features a powerful rhythm from an acoustic guitar all the way through and then finishes with a frenzied guitar break from The Edge. It was produced by U2 at STS Studios in Dublin in 1989 with some help from Paul Barrett. To date it has never been performed live. It was also included on *The B-Sides* CD of the *The Best of 1980-1990* collection.

"DANCING BAREFOOT" (*THREESOME* SOUNDTRACK ALBUM TRACK) A longer version of this track is on the soundtrack of the film *Threesome* which features an extra thirty seconds of guitar at the end.

"DANCING IN THE MOONLIGHT" Originally a number 14 hit in the UK for Thin Lizzy in 1977. U2 are said to have played this song at their early gigs.

"DANCING MASTER" (NME 001) An audio cassette that the *New Musical Express* music paper issued by mail order to readers in Britain in 1981. It featured tracks by several artists, including the U2 track "An Cat Dubh", recorded live at the Paradise Theatre, Boston, USA on 6th March 1981.

"DANCIN' SHOES" (*MILLION DOLLAR HOTEL* SOUNDTRACK ALBUM TRACK) (2.06) The twelfth track off *The Million Dollar Hotel* soundtrack album, performed by Bono and the MDH Band. Bono's vocal is very restrained on the track almost sounding like a female voice. The lyrics were written by Bono and Nicholas Klein, whilst the music was written by Bono and Daniel Lanois.

DANDELION MARKET, GAIETY GREEN, DUBLIN, IRELAND This was a disused car park in the centre of Dublin near to the Gaiety Green market. U2 first played here one Saturday afternoon in May 1979, the first of six gigs here over the next few months. The gigs were organised by John Fisher who charged between 50p and £1 entrance, as long as the groups provided their own sound equipment. As it was a public place, many teenagers who couldn't see U2 in Dublin's pubs because they were under 18 were able to see U2 here instead. The first time U2 played here on 11th May, there was a power cut, so Bono did some quick improvisations to keep the crowd's attention. U2 played here five more times during the summer of 1979 with their show on 12th August being their last. As the word spread about U2 playing there the crowd got bigger and bigger each week until the Dublin authorities eventually put a stop to these gatherings on the grounds of public safety.

See also: John Fisher

DANESMOAT STUDIOS, DUBLIN, IRELAND Adam's Dublin home where "Heartland" from *Rattle & Hum* and much of *Zooropa* was recorded.

"THE DARK SPACE FESTIVAL" A festival that took place over the weekend of 17th-18th February 1979 at the Project Arts Centre in Dublin. The Mekons from Leeds were the headline act and the whole event was compered by John Peel. U2 were low down on the bill along with The Virgin Prunes and appeared on the Saturday. The event was reported in the *New Musical Express*, though U2 did not get a mention. Festival line up: The Mekons, Rudi, The Vipers, Terri Hooley and The Good Vibrations, DC Nien, The Blades, The Atrix, The Virgin Prunes and U2.

DARST, ELLEN One of the people responsible for guiding the career of U2 in America from their first visit in December 1980 right through to the *Zoo TV* tour in 1993. She was originally a member of Warner Brothers Artist Development staff in America and part of her job was to oversee each American tour by U2. As a result of her favourable report on U2's first American dates, U2 were given that little bit of extra support from their American record company. By 1983 she had joined the U2 organisation as Paul McGuinness's American number two. She continued to be heavily involved in the day-to-day running of the U2 organisation in America until her departure in 1993. At the *Zoo TV* show at the Hippodrome De Vincennes in Paris, Bono dedicated "Satellite of Love" to her after she had announced that she was leaving.

DAVE-ID (DAVID WATSON) One of the members of The Lypton Village which existed in Dublin in the late 1970s. As a child he caught meningitis which left him with a slowness of speech and movement. This made him look slightly mentally disturbed (although inwardly he was very intelligent) and he would often play on this "madness" to his peers. The way he slowly spoke his name led to his nick-name of "Dave-id". He was later known as Dave-id Busarus Scott. His large record collection was the magnet that drew members of the Village to him. Once the Hype had been formed, the Village formed an alternative group called The Virgin Prunes where Dave-id would be one of the vocalists. **Website:** www.dave-id.com

See also: Lypton Village / The Virgin Prunes

DAVIS, MILES The celebrated jazz musician and trumpeter appeared on the same bill as U2 for the final concert of the 1986 Amnesty tour of America at the Giant's Stadium on 15th June 1986. He also gets a name check in the lyrics for "Angel of Harlem".

"A DAY AT THE RACES" This was the name given to a concert that U2 played at Phoenix Park Racecourse in Dublin on 14th August 1983. It was a triumphant homecoming gig for the band who had just finished the *War* tour and by now had established themselves as one of the best rock bands in the world. The one-day festival was attended by 20,000 fans and was the only gig the band played in Ireland that year. U2 were introduced by one of their champions – DJ Dave Fanning – and during the show Bono dragged his father Bobby onto the stage to his shock and horror! Steve Wickham joined the band on stage for two songs: "Sunday Bloody Sunday" and "I Fall Down". In the

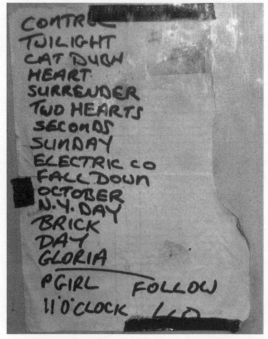

Set list from "A Day At The Races", 1993
Photo: Paul Daly

final number, "40", Annie Lennox from the Eurythmics sang along to the chorus. Apart from The Eurythmics, the festival also featured Simple Minds, Big Country, Steel Pulse and Perfect Crime.

"A Day At The Races" set list: Out of Control, Twilight, An Cat Dubh, Into the Heart, Surrender, Two Hearts Beat As One, Seconds, Sunday Bloody Sunday, The Electric Co., I Fall Down, October, New Year's Day, I Threw A Brick, A Day Without Me, Gloria Encore: Party Girl, 11 O'clock Tick Tock, I Will Follow, 40.

"A DAY WITHOUT ME" (*BOY* ALBUM TRACK) (3.13) The third track on the second side of the *Boy* album and the first U2 track produced by Steve Lillywhite. The song opens with some echoey guitar work from The Edge courtesy of his recently purchased echo unit.

"A DAY WITHOUT ME" (SINGLE) (WIP 6601) U2's second Island Records single, released in August 1980. Like it's predecessor, "11 O'clock Tick Tock" it failed to make the charts. It was the same version as on the *Boy* album. The single cover featured a bridge crossing over a railway line in black and silver colouring.

"A DAY WITHOUT ME" (LIVE) ("NEW YEAR'S DAY" SINGLE) One of the bonus tracks on the 12 inch and 7 inch special double pack version of the "New Year's Day" single (600741), released in January 1983. It was recorded live at the Werchter Festival in Belgium on 4th July 1982 and was the third number of the set. It was recorded and filmed for ID-TV and Film Productions of Amsterdam in Holland for later radio transmission and TV broadcasting. Harry De Winter was the producer and Steve Lillywhite later mixed this and two other tracks that appeared on the single. Although the band played well, Bono's voice was not that strong which detracted from the overall performance.

DE BURGH, CHRIS One of the best-known Irish musicians throughout the world. Having toured widely in the late 1970s and early 1980s, he finally hit the big time with his world wide number one record, "The Lady In Red" in 1986. In May 1986 he took part in the Self Aid concert at the RDS in Dublin alongside U2. During the previous year he had headed the bill at a series of European festivals where U2 were one of the supporting groups.

DEAN, JOHN F See: Driving To Mass In Dublin On Christmas Eve

DEATH VALLEY STADIUM, CLEMSON, SOUTH CARO-LINA, USA U2 played here just once on 26th May 1997 during the first leg of the *Pop Mart* tour of America.

The 80,000 capacity stadium show was attended by 22,000 fans.

THE DECADE, PITTSBURG, PENNSYLVANIA, USA U2's first show in Pittsburgh took place here on 21st April 1981 during U2's first major tour of the USA. This show was their last for a couple of weeks as U2 went to the Bahamas to record their next single, "Fire" under the watchful eye of producer, Steve Lillywhite.

DEENY, MICHAEL One of Paul McGuinness's earliest business associates. Together, after a failed attempt at a mobile discotheque venture, they managed to promote a concert by the folk singer Donovan at the RDS in Dublin. After this Deeny moved into the management of the Irish folk rock band Horslips, who were moderately successful on both sides of the Atlantic. This success inspired Paul McGuinness to follow the same road with his own "baby band" – U2.

See also: Horslips

DENSELOW, ROBIN The journalist who interviewed Bono at the Grand Theatre in Swansea Wales in October 1995 as part of the UK "Year of Literature and Writing 1995". In 1989 he published the critically acclaimed book, *When The Music's Over*, which looked at the relationship between popular music and politics. U2 and Amnesty International were discussed within its pages.

See also: Grand Theatre Swansea

"DESIRE" (*RATTLE & HUM* ALBUM TRACK) (2.58) The third track on side one of the *Rattle & Hum* album. It starts off with a sharp chord from The Edge and then quickly goes into the three-chord riff that dominates the song. The Edge said that the riff came from The Stooges song "1969", which he reworked, though the song's rhythm was influenced by the guitar style of Bo Diddley. The lyrics talk of the desire of a woman, the power of a gun and the drug heroin. The song was first recorded at STS studios in Dublin and then re-recorded at A&M studios in Los Angeles with Jimmy Iovine producing. "Desire" won a Grammy in 1989 for the Best Rock Performance by a Duo or Group with Vocal.

"DESIRE" (SINGLE) (IS400) (2.59) The single version of "Desire" (which was the same recording as the album version) was released in the UK in September 1988 and became U2's first number 1 record in Britain, entering the charts at number 3 before moving up to the number 1 spot the following week. It also did well in the USA where it peaked at number 3. The B-side of the single was "Hallelujah (Here She Comes)", whilst the 12 inch version (12IS400) also included the track "Desire (Hollywood Remix)". "Desire" was first performed live at The Entertainment Centre, Perth, Australia on 21st September 1989, though a live audio version of the song has never officially been released. The song was also included on *The Best of 1980-1990* collection.

"DESIRE" (HOLLYWOOD REMIX) ('DESIRE' SINGLE B-SIDE) (5.23) The extra track included on the B-side of the 12 inch version of the "Desire" single. It was remixed by Louil Silas Junior and Taavi Mote with Jimmy Iovine producing. It starts off with the sound of a car alarm going off, quickly followed by a barrage of sounds from the Hollywood night – not unlike the sounds at the beginning of the live version of "Numb". Bono is accompanied by backing vocalists Alexandra Brown and Edna Wright. It was remixed at Larrabee Sound.

"DESIRE" (*RATTLE & HUM* FILM/VIDEO TRACK) This film version of "Desire" is the third U2 song on the film *Rattle & Hum* directed by Phil Joanou. It shows the band performing the song inside the warehouse in Dublin, which was to become the Point Depot music venue.

"DESIRE" (LIVE) (*U2: POP MART LIVE FROM MEXICO CITY* VIDEO TRACK) The twelfth track on the video *U2: Pop Mart Live from Mexico City* was filmed at the Foro Sol Autodromo, Mexico City on 3rd December 1997. It features both Bono and The Edge on acoustic guitars.

"DESIRE" (PROMOTIONAL VIDEO) The promo video for "Desire" was directed by Richard Lowenstein and shot mainly on location in Los Angeles in September 1988. It features many scenes from the city with all four members of U2 appearing at various times. It was also included on *The Best of 1980-1990* video collection.

"DESIRE" (HOLLYWOOD REMIX) (PROMO-TIONAL VIDEO) Apparently there was also a promotional video of the remix version of "Desire" made, based on footage filmed by the director Richard Lowenstein.

DESMOND, DENNIS An Irish promoter who booked the young U2 on several occasions in the period 1980-1984. Throughout the 1980s and 1990s his promotions company MCD grew into one of the biggest in Europe. In August 1997 Desmond again promoted U2, first at their Botanic Gardens show in Belfast and then at their two Lansdowne Road gigs in Dublin.

See also: Eamon McCann

DESTRI, JIMMY The producer of several Blondie albums, in 1981/2 Destri was a possible contender for the role of producer for U2's third album, *War*, though this never materialised. He is believed to have done a session with U2 in November 1981 at New York's Kingdom Sound Studio where they recorded a song called "Be There".

DEVLIN, BARRY Barry was originally the vocalist and bass player with the Irish folk-rock group Horslips. Through their manager, Michael Deeny, Paul McGuinness had got to know him and asked Barry to help U2 make their first proper demo tape. The recording session took place in December 1978 at the Keystone Studios in Dublin and featured "The Fool", "Shadows And Tall Trees" and "Street Mission". Paul McGuinness then took this tape around several London record companies in the hope of getting U2 signed to one of them.

Devlin then went to produce two albums by the hard rock group Mama's Boys, before moving into video and film production. He was then re-united with U2 in 1984 when Devlin got involved with producing several U2 videos. His first venture with the band was *The Making of The Unforgettable Fire Documentary* which featured film of U2 recording this album at Slane Castle and in Windmill Lane studios. This documentary was part of *The Unforgettable Fire Collection* video which also featured three promo videos all directed by Devlin – "Pride" (Version 2), "Bad" and "A Sort Of Homecoming" – the latter two featuring shots of U2 on the road and in concert in various European cities.

Devlin's next U2 promo video was for "I Still Haven't Found What I'm Looking For" which was shot on the streets of Las Vegas in April 1987. At the same time he also made a documentary film of U2 on the road at the start of the *Joshua Tree* tour in America, entitled *Outside It's America*, shown at Christmas 1987 on BBC TV. This film included two more videos of U2 songs directed by Barry Devlin: "Spanish Eyes" and "In God's Country". Barry also wrote the script for the promo video of "All I Want Is You", which was set in a wintering circus in Italy.

See also: Horslips / The Unforgettable Fire Collection / Bad / Pride (#2) / A Sort Of Homecoming / I Still Haven't Found What I'm Looking For promo videos / *Outside It's America* documentary film / (The Making of) "All I Want Is You".

DIANA, PRINCESS OF WALES Like U2, Diana had supported several charities connected with AIDS and suffering children. In September 1995 she was guest of honour at the concert called *Pavarotti and Friends Together For the Children of Bosnia*. Bono, The Edge and Brian Eno performed "Miss Sarajevo" and "One" that night. Afterwards they all took part in a grand dinner, which lasted most of the night.

When she was tragically killed in a car crash on 31st August 1997, her death was announced on the morning of U2's second Dublin concert at Landsdowne Road. Several times during the concert Bono alluded to her, such as "she's gone... she's gone" and "last night on the river Seine... beautiful girl... big black

Images of Diana, Princess of Wales appear on screen at Landsdowne Road the night after her tragic death in August 1997. *Photo: Claire Bolton*

car... fairytale life... it just went too far". Her image was shown on the giant screen that night and at several subsequent concerts. On the day of her funeral in London, U2 were ironically playing in Paris at the Parc Des Princes and again her image was shown on the screens as U2 performed an emotional version of "MLK". U2 donated the track "Miss Sarajevo" to the Diana Memorial record, which came out shortly after her death.

DICKSON, BARBARA This Scottish singer is one of the first artists to cover a U2 song on record. Her version of "Pride (In The Name of Love)" appeared on her 1987 live album, *After Dark*.

"A DIFFERENT KIND OF BLUE" (*ORIGINAL SOUNDTRACKS 1* ALBUM TRACK) (2.02) The fifth track off the Passengers album *Original Soundtracks 1*, with Brian Eno providing the vocals.

DILLON, JAMES The Irish entrepreneur who started the Irish pirate radio station called "Big-D" which featured U2 champion Dave Fanning on its night slot. It was on this radio station that U2 got their first ever radio airplay.

  See also: Dave Fanning

"DIRTY DAY" (*ZOOROPA* ALBUM TRACK) (5.24) The fourth track on side two of the *Zooropa* album. The bare industrial track is dominated by Adam's bass riff, which holds the song together. This slow lazy song is woken up by the wah wah guitar of The Edge. It has rather depressing lyrics, which add to the mood of the song. It was dedicated to Charles Bukowski, the writer and was recorded in Dublin in early 1993.

  See also: Charles Bukowski

"DIRTY DAY (JUNK DAY)" ("PLEASE" SINGLE) (4.41) This remix was included on the "Please" single released in October 1997. It was produced by Flood, Brian Eno and The Edge. It was mixed by Flood and Robbie adams, as well as having a further remix by Butch Vig and Duke Erikson. It also features Mary Gaines playing cello.

"DIRTY DAY (BITTER KISS)" ("PLEASE" SINGLE) (4.32) This remix was also included on the "Please" single released in October 1997. It was again produced by Flood, Brian Eno and The Edge, and mixed by Flood and Robbie Adams, as well as having a further remix by Butch Vig and Duke Erikson. Mary Gaines plays cello.

"DIRTY DAY" (*ZOO TV LIVE FROM SYDNEY* VIDEO TRACK) The only live film version of "Dirty Day" to have been released is thirteenth track on the video. Bono sings the main part on the B-stage and catwalk at the Sydney Football ground on 27th November 1993. The song had been first performed live two weeks earlier on 12th November at the Cricket Ground, Melbourne, Australia.

"DIRTY OLD TOWN" This song was written by Ewan MacColl about his native Salford, a Northern English industrial town, situated just west of Manchester in England. The song was popularised in Ireland by The Dubliners, and resurrected by the Pogues who included it on their 1985 album, *Rum, Sodomy and The Lash* resulting in it being adopted as an Irish drinking song. U2 have performed the song live several times with Larry taking lead vocals. A verse was first sung at one of the Point Depot shows in Dublin at the end of 1989, but it wasn't until the *Zoo TV* tour in America in 1992 that the song was sung in full. It received its live premiere on St. Patrick's Day 1992 at the Gardens in Boston, Massachusetts, USA.

See also: The Dubliners / Ewan MacColl / The Pogues

DISCO BUS This highly decorated bus was used by U2 during the *Pop Mart* tour and was fitted with the latest hi-tech equipment. In 2000 the band auctioned off the bus for charity.

"DISCOTHEQUE" (*POP* ALBUM TRACK) (5.08) The opening track on the *Pop* album, featuring a powerful opening riff. As "The Fly", on *Achtung Baby*, showed the world that a new form of U2 had been born, so "Discotheque" did with *Pop*. The track features loops and decks by Howie B and even a sample – "Fane" by Freeform. It was the closest that U2 had come to a club sound on track prior to any remix. U2 fans had already heard this track as a single version had been released about a month before the *Pop* album. Even before its official release fans could hear most of it on the Internet after it had illegally been made available. It was officially released to radio stations on 8th January 1997.

"DISCOTHEQUE" (SINGLE) (5.08) This single came in two formats – the single edit with the tracks "Holy Joe (Garage Mix")" and "Holy Joe (Guilty Mix)", and the remix version with four remixes of "Discotheque": the DM Deep Club Mix, the Howie B Hairy B Mix, the Hexidecimal Mix and the DM Tec Radio Mix. On its release in February 1997 it went straight into the UK singles chart at number 1. It also reached the number 1 spot in the US.

"DISCOTHEQUE" (DAVID HOLMES MIX) (6.14) This remix of "Discotheque" by David Holmes was only available on the 12 inch vinyl DJ promo version.

"DISCOTHEQUE" (DM DEEP EXTENDED CLUB MIX) (10.02) This remix of "Discotheque" by David Morales was only available on the US promo CD and 12 inch vinyl DJ promo version.

"DISCOTHEQUE" (DM DEEP BEATS MIX) (3.59) This remix of "Discotheque" by David Morales was only available on the 12 inch vinyl DJ promo version.

"DISCOTHEQUE" (DM DEEP CLUB MIX) (6.58) This remix version of "Discotheque" was remixed by David Morales for Def Mix Productions. This was the first track on the "Discotheque" remixes single. Note: This remix is also known as the DM Deep Instrumental Mix

"DISCOTHEQUE" (DM TEC RADIO MIX) (3.46) This remix version of "Discotheque" was remixed by David Morales for Def Mix productions. This was the fourth track on the "Discotheque" remixes single.

"DISCOTHEQUE" (HOWIE B HAIRY B MIX) (7.40) This remix version of "Discotheque" was remixed by Howie B. This was the second track on the "Discotheque" remixes single.

"DISCOTHEQUE" (HEXIDECIMAL MIX) (7.21) This remix version of "Discotheque" was remixed by Steve Osborne for 140dB. This was the first track on the "Discotheque" remixes single. This was the third track on the "Discotheque" remixes single.

"DISCOTHEQUE" (LIVE) (*HASTA LA VISTA BABY!* CD/ 'BEAUTIFUL DAY' SINGLE) The only officially released live version of "Discotheque" is available on two different U2 releases. The first is on the free CD for *Propaganda* readers, *Hasta La Vista Baby!* issued in summer 2000. The second is on the "Beautiful Day" single (CD 2). The track was recorded live during the *Pop Mart* tour at the Foro Sol Autodromo, Mexico City, Mexico on 3rd December 1997.

"DISCOTHEQUE" (LIVE) (*U2: POP MART LIVE FROM MEXICO CITY* VIDEO TRACK) The eighteenth track on the video *U2: Pop Mart Live from Mexico City* was filmed at the Foro Sol Autodromo, Mexico City on 3rd December 1997.

"DISCOTHEQUE" (PROMOTIONAL VIDEO) The promotional video for "Discotheque" was directed by Stephen Sedenaoui and filmed in London in December 1996. It featured the four members of U2 dressed as Village People characters dancing in a discotheque, as well as doing John Travolta impersonations!

"DISCOTHEQUE" (DAVID MORALES MIX) (PROMOTIONAL VIDEO) There was also a promotional video for "Discotheque" made for one of the David Morales mixes of the song, also directed by Stephen Sedenaoui. This was made in Miami in January 1997.

"DISCOTHEQUE" (STEVE OSBORNE MIX) (PROMOTIONAL VIDEO) There was a further promotional video made for "Discotheque" with the Steve Osborne Hexidecimal mix of the song, also directed by Stephen Sedenaoui. This too was made in Miami in January 1997.

DISPOSABLE HEROES OF HIPHOPRISY This American hip-hop rap act sang the tune, "Television - the Drug of the Nation" which U2 used as the introductory music on the 1992 *Zoo TV* tour. The band was given the support slot on the *Outside Broadcast* leg of American stadia in the late summer and autumn of 1992.

See also: Television - Drug Of The Nation

"DJINN" The only track of the *Captive* film soundtrack album not written by The Edge. He did play on the track though, along with the composer, Michael Brook.

DOCKERS PUB, DUBLIN, IRELAND This famous Dublin pub situated on Sir John Rogerson's Quay just around the corner from the original Windmill Lane studios has been known to be frequented by members of U2 and their crew when they are in Dublin. It did close down but reopened in 2001.

Dockers Pub, Dublin. *Photo: Paul Daly*

DODDS, CAROL One of the video directors for the *Zoo TV* tour having the job of making sure that the right pictures and images went on the screens at the right time.

DODGER STADIUM, LOS ANGELES, CALIFORNIA, USA Surprisingly U2 didn't get to play at this well-known baseball stadium until 1992, when they performed two shows during the *Outside Broadcast* leg of the 1992 *Zoo TV* tour on 30th and 31st October. The second show happened to be the occasion of Larry's 31st birthday and as Bono was zapping through the various TV channels inbetween songs, he came across Elvira, the TV personality, who encouraged the crowd to sing "Happy Birthday" to him. Bono wore a Freddie Kreuger glove (of *Nightmare On Elm Street* fame) for some of the songs.

DOG TOWN STUDIOS, DUBLIN, IRELAND This was the nickname that U2 gave to a house called "Elsinore" in Dalkey to the south of Dublin which they used for part of the *Achtung Baby* album sessions. After the sessions at the Hansa Studios in Berlin were completed, the band moved to these studios to finish off the album. "Even Better Than the Real Thing" was one of several tracks that were completed here.

DOLLY MIXTURES This was the all-girl band who U2 supported on the majority of the band's early London dates in December 1979.

DOMINION THEATRE, LONDON See: Smile Jamaica

DONAU INSEL, VIENNA, AUSTRIA U2's first concert in the country of Austria took place on 24th May 1992 on a narrow strip of land next to the River Danube and its by-pass canal. An estimated crowd of 60,000 watched U2 perform here, making it the largest crowd for the European leg of the 1992 *Zoo TV* tour. In fact it was the first time that U2 had played at an outside concert since November 1989 in New Zealand. As Guns 'N Roses had played at the same venue the night before, the band's lead vocalist, Axl Rose came up on stage to duet with Bono and sing "Knocking On Heaven's Door."

"DON'T FORGET ABOUT ME" A track off Nanci Griffiths' album *Flyer*, which featured the drumming of Larry and the bass of Adam.

"DON'T TAKE YOUR GUNS TO TOWN" The song by Johnny Cash that U2 performed at the special Johnny Cash tribute show that took place in April 1999 under the title *An All Star Tribute To Johnny Cash*. It was filmed in U2's Hanover Quay studio a few days before the broadcast by Dreamchaser Productions.

　　See also: Johnny Cash

"DON'T TAKE YOUR GUNS TO TOWN" (VIDEO) (*THE SUNDAY TIMES* FREE CD) This film of U2 performing "Don't Take Your Guns To Town" for the Johnny Cash tribute show in April 1999 was given away free with *The Sunday Times* newspaper in June 2001.

DOOLEY'S, EAST LANSING, MICHIGAN, USA U2 played at this venue in the small town of Lansing on 7th December 1981 during their tour of America to promote the *October* album.

DOPPELGANGERS, THE They were the U2 lookalike group that were featured in the promo video of "Even Better Than The Real Thing" which was filmed in February 1992. They were again used for the *Zoo TV* special in November 1992. One of the original Doppelgangers, Clark Denham then went on to form a U2 tribute band called The Doppelgangers who toured the UK, Ireland, Europe and the Middle East for most of the 1990s.

　　See also: "Even Better Than The Real Thing" promo video.

"DO THEY KNOW IT'S CHRISTMAS" (BAND AID SINGLE) (Phonogram - FEED 1) The second biggest selling single of all time was recorded at Sarm West Studios in London in November 1984 by a group of musicians collectively known as Band Aid. Both Bono and Adam flew in to London to take part in the recording of this single, co-written by Bob Geldof and Midge Ure. Bono was one of several star vocalists including Sting, Paul Young, Boy George and George Michael who all sang a line of the song.

Bono's line was "Well tonight thank God, it's them instead of you". Adam took part in the singing of the chorus. It was designed to raise funds for famine relief in Africa and eventually sold in excess of 8 million copies and was number 1 for four weeks. The success of "Do They Know It's Christmas" led to the 1985 Live Aid concerts in Britain and America, which helped project U2 to a worldwide audience. The B-side was an instrumental version of "Do They Know It's Christmas?" and had some of the singers each saying a line. Bono says the words: "Well this is Bono here – the singer with U2, wishing you a Happy Christmas and a merry New Year. Is that right?"

See also: Band Aid / Live Aid / Bob Geldof

"DO THEY KNOW IT'S CHRISTMAS?" (PROMO-TIONAL VIDEO) The video that was used to promote the Band Aid single, "Do They Know It's Christmas?" was filmed in its entirety at the Sarm West Studios in London on the day they song was recorded. It showed the various artists arriving, singing their lines, and then the playback. Boy George's contribution was filmed later in the day as he missed the morning recording session. There was also a documentary film made of the day's events.

DOWNING STADIUM, RANDALL'S ISLAND, NEW YORK CITY, USA See: Tibetan Freedom Concert

DOYLE, SUZANNE One of the staff at Principle Management, Dublin who works as Bono's personal assistant. She was also the studio production manager for the *Zooropa* album and assistant tour manager for the *Zoo TV* tour.

"DO YOU FEEL LOVED" (*POP* ALBUM TRACK) (5.07) The second track on the *Pop* album is heavily

The Doppelgangers, before the *Zoo TV* show, November, 1992. *Photo: Clark Denham*

programmed giving it a very techno sound. It was co-produced by Steve Osborne, who also played keyboards on the track. Naked Funk apparently provided "inspiration" for this track.

DRAMMENSHALLE, DRAMMEN, NORWAY U2's second performance in Norway took place at this 7,000 capacity venue on 23rd January 1985 during the *Unforgettable Fire* tour.

DREAMCHASER PRODUCTIONS The company run by Ned O'Hanlon and Ritchie Smyth who have directed and produced several U2 videos. The first was the *Achtung Baby* set *The Videos, The Cameos, And A Whole Lot Of Interference From Zoo TV.* They also directed the *Zoo TV Live From Sydney* video, winning a Grammy award for Best Music Video, The *Pop Mart Live from Mexico City* video and the *Black Wind, White Land* documentary.

See also: Ned O'Hanlon / Ritchie Smythe

"DREAMING WITH TEARS IN MY EYES" A track off the 1996 tribute album to American blues singer Jimmie Rodgers entitled *Jimmie Rodgers A Tribute.* It featured Bono on vocals and Larry on drums.

"DREAMS IN A BOX" This was a poem that Bono had written in 1987, which he donated to the Chicago Peace Museum.

"THE DREAM IS OVER" This was an early U2 song that the band used to perform in early gigs and was probably influenced by the lyric from the John Lennon song "God". It was recorded as a demo track in Dublin in 1979.

"THE DREAM THEME" This piece of music written by The Edge was the seventh track on the *Captive* film soundtrack album.

"DREAM VISION" Supposedly another early U2 track, which was probably "Street Mission".

"DRIFT" The sixth track on the soundtrack album of *Captive* for which The Edge wrote the music.

DRIFTING COWBOYS, A local country and western band who The Edge and Larry might have joined in 1977 if they hadn't decided to go with U2. The two of them, along with Dick Evans, did actually play some gigs with The Drifting Cowboys in Ireland.

"DRINKIN' IN THE DAY" This was a song that Bono co-wrote with Simon Carmody. Appearing on the Ronnie Drew album, *Dirty Rotten Shame.*

"DRIVING TO MIDNIGHT MASS IN DUBLIN ON CHRISTMAS EVE" A poem by John F. Dean which Bono narrated to a background of the U2 songs "New Year's Day" and "Endless Deep".

DRIVING WILD HORSES (DOCUMENTARY) A documentary about the making of the promo video of "Who's Gonna Ride Your Wild Horses?" shown on

British TV in the autumn of 1992 shortly before the *U2 -Zoo TV* documentary was broadcast.

"DROP THE DEBT" The slogan adopted by the Jubilee 2000 campaign aimed at politicians from the world's richest countries who are owed billions of pounds in debts from the world's poorest countries. Bono has been an ambassador for the campaign and has regularly spoken with officials and politicians from several countries asking them to "drop the debt". For instance on 10 June 1999 Bono took part in an on-line Internet session answering questions about the Drop The Debt campaign. A few days later on 19th June, Bono, Ali and The Edge all took part in demonstration at the G8 Summit in Cologne, Germany where protestors joined hands in a human chain around the building where the summit was taking place. A petition of 17 million signatures was handed in to the Summit asking for action to "drop the debt".

See also: Jubilee 2000

"DROWNING MAN" (*WAR* ALBUM TRACK) (4.10) The fifth song on the first side of the *War* album. The song starts off quietly with some beautiful acoustic guitar, before Bono comes in with a strong vocal. The lyrics talk about love, though it isn't clear if it is human or divine love at first. Then towards the end we are told that God's strong love is able to save a drowning man. The track also featured violin courtesy of Steve Wickham. This is one of three songs off the *War* album never to have been played live.

DR RUTH The famous German sex therapist was used by U2 in American adverts to promote the *Achtung Baby* album as it was thought of as a sexy record. In fact the four members of U2 were really sending themselves up.

DUBLIN, IRELAND The capital city of the Republic of Ireland. All four members of U2 were brought up in Dublin and continue to live in and around the city, though only Bono and Larry were actually born there. The Edge and Adam Clayton were both born in England but moved to Dublin at an early age. Dublin, being the capital city (and largest city in Ireland), has always had a flourishing music scene. Groups such as The Dubliners and The Chieftans came to prominence in the 1960s, followed by Thin Lizzy and the Boomtown Rats in the 1970s, then in the 1980s it was U2's turn. There has always been a large number of clubs and small venues for up-and-coming bands to play, including McGonagles, The Project Arts Centre and The Baggott Inn. Larger venues have included the RDS (Royal Dublin Showground), The Olympia and The Point Depot.

Dublin has been immortalised in several U2 songs including "Running To Stand Still" which mentions the "seven towers" of the Ballymun housing estate and "North And South of the River". Several of the band's early promotional videos were also filmed in Dublin including "Gloria" and "Pride" which featured the docks area, and "A Celebration" which featured Kilharmain Gaol. Similarly the band's first few albums were all recorded in Dublin studios, notably Windmill Lane studios but also at STS studios. It is a fitting tribute to the U2 organisation that their management headquarters are based in Dublin and not London or New York. The band have even invested in the city, buying the near derelict Clarence Hotel and transforming it into a fully-refurbished going concern.

The Dublin based *Hot Press* music paper has recently opened a museum dedicated to Irish music and Dublin musicians in particular. Called "The Hot Press Irish Music Hall of Fame" all periods of Irish music are featured. Also there is now a "Rock 'n Roll Stroll" along the streets of Dublin where special plaques have been put onto buildings associated with a particular artist or band. U2 are mentioned on two plaques: at Windmill Lane studios and at Dandelion Market. On 18th March 2000 the city of Dublin finally acknowledged the contribution the four members of U2 have made to their city by giving them (and Paul McGuinness) the Freedom of the City of Dublin.

See also: Hot Press Irish Music Hall of Fame / Rock 'n Roll Stroll / Windmill Lane studios

DUBLINERS, THE This well-known Irish folk group made up of the Kelly brothers and others has influenced several generations of Irish musicians includ-

Dublin Power Station, featured in the promo video for "Pride" and opening shots of the *Rattle and Hum* film.
Photo: Mark Chatterton

ing U2 who used to listen to them on the radio when they were children. U2 took part in a TV special on RTE's "The Late Late Show" to celebrate the group's 25th anniversary. They sang an old Dubliners' standard, "Springhill Mining Disaster", and joined the band (and The Pogues) on the stage at the end.

See also: The Late Late Show / Gay Byrne / The Pogues / Springhill Mining Disaster

DUNCAN, HELEN One of the backing vocalists on "When Love Comes To Town" and the sister of Phyllis. The song was recorded at the Sun Studios in Memphis, Tennessee on the night of 29th/30th November 1988. The other backing vocalist was Becky Evans.

DUNCAN, PHYLLIS One of the backing vocalists of "When Love Comes To Town" and the sister of Helen. The two sisters (and Becky Evans) were called up to Sun Studios by Gary Hardy, the owner, who had been asked to find three female backing singers by Jimmy Iovine, the producer of the *Rattle & Hum* album.

DUNNE, ORLA A friend of Stella McCormick, and the sister of Ivan McCormick who had attended the first practice session for the fledgling U2. Orla and Stella provided backing vocals and flute accompaniment to Feedback's final gig at St Fintan's School, Sutton, on 11th April 1977.

See also: Feedback / Stella McCormick

DUNNES STORE, DUBLIN, IRELAND The shop in Dublin at the centre of a political storm in Ireland in 1986 when it sacked some of its assistants who had refused to handle goods originating from South Africa because of its apartheid policy. Bono took a cassette of the shop assistants saying why they had taken such a stand with him to New York for the *Sun City* project.

See also: Artists United Against Apartheid / Sun City Project

DUNPHY, EAMON The author of the official U2 biography, *Unforgettable Fire*. Originally a professional footballer with Millwall Football Club in London, he went on to to write what is considered to be the definitive book about football, *Only A Game?* After his career as a professional footballer had ended, he returned to Dublin where he became a journalist and in 1986 was asked to write the official U2 biography. Although the book only went as far as 1987 and the *Joshua Tree* tour, it received a mixed reception from U2 fans who were able to read in detail about the members' home backgrounds and learn about how the band had started. It is rumoured that the band were not completely happy with the final product as Dunphy was given editorial control and is said to have included some fictitious episodes in the biography. Neil McCormick, who had been a friend and associate of the band from the early days wrote a scathing attack in *Hot Press* on the book in an article entitled "The Unbelievable Book". He pointed out the mistakes and inaccuracies and tried to set the record straight. In 1993 the book was re-released with an additional epilogue written by Bill Graham taking the U2 story up to *Achtung Baby*.

See also: *Unforgettable Fire* book

DUCHESS NELL CATCHPOLE, THE The musician who played violin and viola on the track "So Cruel" on *Achtung Baby*.

DYLAN, BOB The iconic US singer-songwriter who began as a protest singer, invented modern electric rock and later controversially converted to Christianity. Although this phase did not last there was a common link between him and U2.

Bono first met Bob Dylan in 1984 when Dylan headlined a festival at Slane Castle, north of Dublin. Bono had gone there to interview Dylan for *Hot Press*. In the interview Dylan explained how Irish music and culture had influenced his songwriting. Dylan advised Bono to "reach back" into his Irish roots as well as to look at the work of the American blues singers like Muddy Waters and Howlin' Wolf. "He was the one that sent us on this journey into the past that ended up with *Rattle & Hum*," said Bono several years later. During his set Dylan invited Bono up on stage to sing "Leopard Skin Pillbox Hat" with him. Unfortunately Bono was not too familiar with the lyrics and so messed up some of the words.

Bono then joined Dylan again during the encore number "Blowing In The Wind". U2 repaid the compliment in 1987 when they were playing at the Los Angeles Sports Arena. Dylan joined them on stage on 20th April to perform "Knockin' on Heaven's Door". Later in 1987 Bono and Dylan collaborated on "Love Rescue Me" which was on the *Rattle & Hum* album. Dylan also appeared on "Hawkmoon 269" where he played the organ. When Dylan was playing at the RDS in June 1989 Bono once again came on stage to perform "Knockin' on Heaven's Door" and "Maggie's Farm" with him. In March 1999 Bono joined Dylan on stage at the House of Blues in Las Vegas to perform their favourite collaboration – "Knockin' On Heaven's Door".

U2 have performed the following Bob Dylan songs live: "All Along The Watchtower", "Maggie's Farm", "Knockin' On Heaven's Door" and "A Hard Rain's Gonna Fall" as well as snippets from "Forever Young" and "The Times They Are A-Changing".

See also: All Along The Watchtower / Knockin' On Heaven's Door / Love Rescue Me / Slane Castle

EARL'S COURT ARENA, LONDON, ENGLAND U2 first played Britain's biggest indoor arena (capacity 18,000) on 31st May 1992 during the European leg of the 1992 *Zoo TV* tour. As this was U2's first British date in their own right for five years, there was a heavy demand for tickets, with several hundred fans camping out overnight prior to tickets going on sale. Due to poor crowd control many jumped the queue and bought tickets instead of those who had queued overnight. Bono drew attention to this in the concert, apologising for the cock up. During the show he rang a sex phone line and asked to speak "to his baby".

Earl's Court has also been the venue for the Brit Awards ceremony for several years and in February 2001 U2 played a four song set there after they had been given the Outstanding Contribution to Music award.

U2 then played four nights here on 18th, 19th, 21st and 22nd August as part of the *Elevation* tour. The four shows sold out in less than an hour. This was a paticularly difficult time for Bono as he was flying back to Dublin after each show to be at his father's hospital bedside. Indeed, the final two shows looked like they might be cancelled after the death of Bono's father, Bobby, early on the morning of the 21st, but they went ahead in spite of this. As a sad reminder of his death Bono sang "When Will I See You Again" after "One" at the final two shows.

See also: The Brits

Earl's Court Arena, London. *Photo: Claire Bolton*

ECCLES, NOEL This musician played congas on the U2 track "Night & Day", which was included on the *Red Hot and Blue* album.

ECOLE NATIONAL DES TRAVAUX, LYON, FRANCE This was U2's first headlining show in France, having played just once before as support act to Talking Heads in Paris the previous December. The show took place on 20th February 1981.

EDGE, THE (DAVID EVANS) David was born on 8th August 1961 at Barking Maternity Hospital in east London, England where his Welsh parents, Garvin and Gwenda Evans, were then living. A year later, the Evans family moved over the Irish Sea to settle in Malahide, near Dublin due to his employers, Plessy Engineering, offering Garvin employment there. Dave was the middle of three children, having an older brother, Dick, and a younger sister, Jill. As a child, Dave attended St. Andrew's Church of Ireland School in Malahide, where he briefly came across Adam Clayton before Adam went off to prep school. Dave moved on to secondary school at Mount Temple, but found it hard to be accepted at first, being a naturally reserved child. He was a diligent student who worked hard and was liked by all the teachers. His ambition at that time was to go to university and become a doctor.

At Mount Temple he took an interest in the guitar and piano, following in his father's footsteps. After his mother had bought him an old acoustic guitar at a jumble sale for £1 he soon began playing the instrument regularly. After some prompting by Mount Temple's music teacher Albert Bradshaw, Dave went along with his brother Dick to the audition at Larry Mullen's house, not having seen the note from Larry. Here, after a run through of old Led Zeppelin and Deep Purple standards, he showed the others present that he really could play. Accepted as a member of the group that came to be called Feedback, Dave began to hang around with the other members both in and out of school. He was accepted into the Lypton Village group and christened "Dave Edge" by Bono, partly because he was on the edge of things assessing what was going on and partly because of the shape of his head, which had a straight edge.

The Edge continued his studies at Mount Temple at the same time as pursuing his musical interests in The Hype (as Feedback was now called). When the time came for The Edge to leave school, he told his parents that he would take a year off from his studies, to see what would happen with the band. During this period in the late 1970s, the Hype and then U2 (from March 1978 onwards) began to develop their sound. Although they started off influenced by the bigger groups of the early 1970s, the Punk and New

The Edge. *Photo: Claire Bolton*

Wave movements began to shape the music of U2. Also, some of the American punk/ncw wave acts like the Ramones and Televison began to influence the band and The Edge in a particular. His style of playing developed further when he was able to buy a Gibson Explorer guitar – which he still uses today. Coupled with this, was the purchase of a Memory Man echo unit that was also instrumental in the development of the U2 sound.

As U2 started to grow musically in this period, so did their interest in things spiritual. The Edge was one of three members of the band who joined the Shalom Charismatic Christian group in Dublin. This led to a great deal of soul searching – was it right to be a Christian and in a rock 'n' roll band? This all came to head in 1982. Shortly after Bono had returned from his honeymoon, The Edge told him that he was going to take two weeks leave from U2 in order to sort out whether he wanted to stay in the band or not. After a few days, he made up his mind after listening to Bono's advice to follow his heart; he would stay committed to U2.

In 1983, The Edge married Aislinn O'Sullivan, whom he had met at an early U2 concert. They had three daughters: Holly (1985), Arun (1986), and Blue Angel (1989), but in 1990 they separated, during the recording of *Achtung Baby*. In 1996 they were finally divorced. In 1992 Edge first met Morleigh Steinberg, the belly dancer and choreographer from the *Zoo TV*

tour. They started going out in 1993 and have stayed a couple ever since. They have two children. A daughter called Sian and a son called Levi.

The Edge's contribution to the music of U2 over the years is immeasurable. From the opening notes of "I Will Follow" on the *Boy* album to the graceful chords of "Beautiful Day" on *All That You Can't Leave Behind*, his trademark is there. He tends to avoid the long drawn out solo – the exception being the early composition "Street Mission". Instead he prefers precise, short, memorable riffs, examples being "Rejoice" from *October*, "Bad" from *The Unforgettable Fire* and "Spanish Eyes", an outtake from *The Joshua Tree* sessions. At times his aggression and frustration can be seen in the chords he uses: "Sunday Bloody Sunday", "Pride" and "Bullet The Blue Sky" are prime examples. Yet at other times he can be gentle and melancholic as on "One" and "Please". In 1996 he was deservedly the first recipient of the Rory Gallgaher Rock Musician award.

His ability as a keyboard player is often under-estimated, but this often adds a different quality to the "U2 sound". The tracks "October" and "New Year's Day" come to mind here. Also his vocal contribution to U2 is often overlooked. Songs like "Van Dieman's Land" and "Numb" show his range. His solo rendition of "Sunday Bloody Sunday" on the latter stages of the *Pop Mart* tour was one of the show's highlights. Finally, his role as "musical director" of the band has led to him being given credit for his produc-

The Edge leaves The Lemon.
Photo: Claire Bolton

tion skills. On *Zooropa*, he was so involved with the album, that it he was credited as producer alongside Flood and Brian Eno.

The Edge was the first member of U2 to take a musical sidestep. This was in 1983 when he was asked by former PIL bassist Jah Wobble to play on his album, *Snake Charmer*. In 1986 he wrote most of the soundtrack music for the film *Captive*, which featured a young Sinead O'Connor singing on one of the tracks. This was followed in 1990 with a score (alongside Bono) for the Royal Shakespeare Company production of *A Clockwork Orange 2004* and the song "Goldeneye" for the 1995 James Bond film of the same name.

It is perhaps fitting that in early 2001 he was included in a TV programme titled *The Top Ten Guitar Heroes* on Channel 4 in Britain. He was placed 7th on the list just behind the likes of Jimi Hendrix, Eric Clapton and Hank Marvin, but ahead of greats like Carlos Santana and Ritchie Blackmore.

The Edge celebrateded his 40th birthday during the European leg of the *Elevation* tour, at the Palau Sant Jordi in Barcelona concert on 8th August 2001. A birthday cake was brought out to him during "Mysterious Ways". He is reported to have flown out to Ibiza to party the night away straight after the show.

EINSTÜRZENDE NEUBAUTEN The support act for only one gig on the *Zooropa* tour on May 10th 1993 at the Feyenoord Stadium in Rotterdam. The notorious industrial group from Germany were thrown off the rest of the tour after one of their members threw an iron bar into the crowd, luckily no-one was injured.

ELECTRIC BALLROOM, CAMDEN TOWN, LONDON, ENGLAND Two of U2's early shows in London took place here on 7th and 8th December 1979 on their first visit to the capital. At both shows they were the support act for the Talking Heads and Orchestral Manoeuvres in The Dark. At the shows they saw the tribalism that was creeping into the musical void that punk had left behind. This partly inspired the lyrics of "11 O'clock Tick Tock".

See also: 11 O'clock Tick Tock

"THE ELECTRIC CO." (BOY ALBUM TRACK) (4.47) The fifth track on the second side of U2's first album, *Boy*. It was recorded at Windmill Lane studios in Dublin in 1980 with Steve Lillywhite producing. Featuring some aggressive echoey guitar by The Edge and equally aggressive drumming from Larry, this track soon became a live favourite, and was a regular in the U2 set until 1985. Bono would often climb to the top of the stage scaffolding during the performance of this song. It tells the story of someone that Bono knew in Dublin who underwent Electro-Convulsive Therapy to supposedly make him better, but only succeeded in making him worse.

"THE ELECTRIC CO." (LIVE) ("FIRE" SINGLE) (U WIP 6679) This live version of "The Electric Co." was preceded by a track entitled "Cry" which is the beginning of "Is That All?" off the *October* album. It was recorded at the Paradise Theatre Boston, USA on 6th March 1981 and was available on the second single of the double 7 inch pack of the "Fire" single, released in July 1981.

See also: "Cry"

"THE ELECTRIC CO." (LIVE) (*UNDER A BLOOD RED SKY* ALBUM TRACK) (4.57) The second track on the second side of the live mini-album entitled *Under a Blood Red Sky*. It was not recorded at the Red Rocks Amphitheatre in Denver, USA as many think, but at the Lorelei Ampitheatre in Germany on 20th August. At this and other concerts at the time Bono would sing a few lines of the Stephen Sondheim song, "Send In The Clowns" in the middle section of this song. Early versions of this album had Bono singing such lines, but after a successful lawsuit from Stephen Sondheim, the lines were skilfully removed by producer Jimmy Iovine for later pressings.

"ELEVATION" (*ALL THAT YOU CAN'T LEAVE BEHIND* ALBUM TRACK) (3.46) The third track on the album *All That You Can't Leave Behind* is one of the heavier tracks on the album. Lyrically Bono speaks about being elevated to a higher plain, though with many U2 songs it is ambiguous whether this high is reached through sexual pleasure or through spiritual connections. The song was first performed on the roof of the Clarence Hotel in September 2001 followed by its premiere before an audience at the Man Ray Club in Paris the following month.

"ELEVATION" (SINGLE) (3.46) The "Elevation" single was released in July 2001 in two different formats. CD 1 had "Elevation" (Tomb Raider Mix) as the main track, together with the Escalation Mix and the Influx Mix. The limited edition CD2 also had "Elevation" (Tomb Raider Mix) as its main track, backed with live versions of "Last Night On Earth" and "Don't Take Your Guns To Town". It also contained a double-sided poster of U2 shot by Anton Corbbijn and Andrew Macpherson. Other tracks appeared on various releases around the world.

"ELEVATION" (*TOMB RAIDER* MIX) (3.35) This mix of "Elevation" was also included on the soundtrack of the *Tomb Raider* movie as well as on the single releases.

"ELEVATION" (ESCALATION MIX) (7.04) This version of "Elevation" was remixed by Jon Carter and was on the single release CD1.

"ELEVATION" (INFLUX REMIX) (4.02) This was remixed by Leo Pearson and Johnny Moy and was on CD1 of the "Elevation" single release.

"ELEVATION" (THE BIFFCO MIX) (4.18) This remix of "Elevation" was included on the soundtrack album of *Tomb Raider* and the Australian single.

"ELEVATION" (QUINCEY AND SONANCE REMIX) (6.53) This remix by Richard Rainey was only available on the Australian single version.

"ELEVATION" (DVD) The DVD of "Elevation" contained the *Tomb Raider* Mix, the promo video and interviews with all four members of U2.

"ELEVATION" (PROMOTIONAL VIDEO) The promo video for "Elevation" was shot in Hollywood in April 2001 partly on the set of *Tomb Raider*. It was directed by Joseph Kahn and has a storyline of an evil U2 kidnapping The Edge from a good U2. Bono is told about this when he receives a phone call on his mobile phone. The video features all sorts of high action scenes with Adam stealing a taxi cab and then crashing it and Larry riding a motorbike through the streets. This is interspersed with footage from the *Lara Croft - Tomb Raider* film starring Angelina Jolie as Lara Croft.

See also: Joseph Kahn

ELEVATION TOUR The name of U2's latest world tour. Unlike the previous two outings, it has been an arena as opposed to a stadium tour with U2 playing to between 10-20,000 people a night. Starting off in America with the opening date at the National Car Rental Arena in Fort Lauderdale on 24th March 2001, there followed 48 shows in 32 cities throughout America and Canada, before finishing at the Continental Arena in East Rutherford on 22nd June 2001. It then moved over to Europe for 32 shows in 16 venues starting in Copenhagen Denmark on 6th July 2001 and finishing at Slane Castle north of Dublin with two shows on 25th August and 1st September 2001.

The tour was then scheduled to return to North America for more dates throughout the autumn, with visits to Australia and Japan also rumoured. Although many reviewers commented on the fact that it was on a much smaller scale than the previous *Zoo TV* and *Pop Mart* tours, there was still plenty of technology in evidence with video screens still in use. Most noticeable of all was a heart shape in the middle of each arena, which contained the stage and a lucky first three hundred fans through the doors. This "Into The Heart" area was surrounded by a walkway along which Bono would parade whilst it would light up during the show. Long drapes were dropped down onto the stage during "New York" so Bono could make a silhouette effect behind them. Film of Charlton Heston talking about gun control was shown as a lead in to "Bullet The Blue Sky". Also, at several venues the stage was surrounded by the audience, creating a more intimate setting.

Elevation tour, songs performed so far: A Sort Of Homecoming, All I Want Is You, Angel of Harlem, Bad, Beautiful Day, Bullet the Blue Sky, Dancing In The Moonlight, Desire, Discotheque, Elevation, 11 O'clock Tick Tock, The Fly, 40, Gloria, Gone, The Ground Beneath Her Feet, In A Little While, I Will Follow, Kite, Mysterious Ways, New Year's Day, New York, One, Out of Control, Pride (In The Name of Love), Sunday Bloody Sunday, Sweetest Thing, Staring at the Sun, Stay (Faraway, So Close!), Stuck In A Moment You Can't Get Out Of, Wake Up Dead Man, When Will I See You Again, Where the Streets Have No Name, With or Without You, Until the End of the World, Walk On.

"11 O'CLOCK TICK TOCK" (SINGLE) (CBS 8687/Island WIP 6601 This was U2's debut single on Island Records, released on 23rd May 1980, with Martin Hannet producing. U2 had asked specifically for him for their first Island single, as he had worked

The *Elevation Tour* in Detroit.
Photo: Shawn Bland

on the seminal Joy Division album, *Unknown Pleasures*. "11 O'clock Tick Tock" was previously known as "Silver Lining" and was not included on U2's first album, *Boy*. Sadly, it did not get into the UK charts, despite a UK tour to promote it. The song was reported to have been influenced by U2's first London gigs at The Electric Ballroom in Camden Town, where they played support to Orchestral Manoeuvres in The Dark and Talking Heads, and saw how the music scene after Punk was beginning to disintegrate into a kind of tribalism. The title comes from a note that Gavin Friday pinned to Bono's front door after he had forgotten an appointment with him. The B-side of the single was called "Touch".

"11 O'CLOCK TICK TOCK" (LIVE) (*FIRE* SINGLE) This was the A-side of the second single that was included as a bonus single with the "Fire" 7 inch single (Island U-WIP 6679). It was recorded live at the Paradise Theatre in Boston, USA on 6th March 1981 and was produced by Steve Lillywhite. The "Fire" single was released in July 1981 and became U2's first British hit reaching number 35 in the charts.

"11 O'CLOCK TICK TOCK" (LIVE) (*UNDER A BLOOD RED SKY* ALBUM TRACK) The second track on the first side of the live mini-album called *Under a Blood Red Sky*. It was recorded live at the Orpheum Theatre,

Boston, USA on 6th May 1983 during the *War* tour of North America. It is interesting to see how the song had developed over a period of two years, since the other live version of this track had been recorded.

"11 O'CLOCK TICK TOCK" (LIVE) (TRACK FROM *LIVE AT RED ROCKS* VIDEO) This track was included on the live video of U2's performance at The Red Rocks Amphitheatre near Denver, USA on 5th June 1983.

"11 O'CLOCK TICK TOCK" TOUR SPRING 1980 Following U2's first visit to London in December 1979, they returned to Britain in May 1980 to undertake a tour to promote their first Island single, "11 O'clock Tick Tock". The tour started at The Hope & Anchor pub in Islington, London on 22nd May and continued through to the Half Moon Club in Putney, South London on 8th June. In all, U2 played sixteen English dates including clubs, pubs, universities and the prestigious Marquee club in central London. At each date U2 were supported by Fashion.

Songs played included: A Day Without Me, An Cat Dubh - Into The Heart, Another Day, Boy-Girl, 11 O'clock Tick Tock, I Will Follow, Out Of Control, Stories For Boys.

ELLAND ROAD STADIUM, LEEDS, ENGLAND U2 played a concert at the ground of Leeds United Football Club on 1st July 1987 during *The Joshua Tree* tour of Europe. 30,000 fans attended the concert, which was filmed in part for a later TV broadcast.

"ELLIS ISLAND" A song that Bono wrote for Johnny Cash in 1990.

EL MAOCAMBO, TORONTO, CANADA U2'S first ever concert in Canada took place here on 9th December 1980 during their first visit to North America.

EL SALVADOR The Central American country was visited by Bono in 1986. While he was there a civil war was going on between rebel forces and the US backed government forces. Bono was there as a guest of Amnesty International and was shocked to see the devastation that American foreign policy was bringing to that country. His visit inspired the song, "Bullet The Blue Sky". He had seen US backed government jet fighters flying overhead on their way to firing on the locals and it was this experience that he attempted to get across in the song. Bono and Ali both narrowly missed being shot at when troops opened fire just above their heads. "I just felt sick," was how Bono described the experience.

See also: Bullet The Blue Sky

ELSINORE See: Dog Town Studios

"ELVIS: AMERICAN DAVID" This was a piece that Bono wrote for a guide used for an exhibition of Elvis Presley and Marilyn Monroe pictures entitled *2*

x Immortal: Elvis and Marilyn. It was later published in Issue 22 of *Propaganda* and is said to have influenced the track "Elvis Ate America" on the *Original Soundtracks 1* album.

"ELVIS ATE AMERICA" (*ORIGINAL SOUNDTRACKS 1* ALBUM TRACK) (3.00) This track comes from the Passengers album *Original Soundtracks 1* reflecting Bono's fascination with the King of Rock 'n' Roll. It originated from the poem "Elvis: American David". The lyrics are spoken as a monologue with Howie B providing a vocal echo.

ELVIS FROM THE WAIST UP A VH-1 TV special on the early career of Elvis Presley that Bono provided the narration for at the House of Blues recording studio in Memphis Tennessee in May 1997.

ELVIS PRESLEY See: Presley, Elvis

"ELVIS PRESLEY AND AMERICA" (*THE UNFORGETTABLE FIRE* ALBUM TRACK) (6.22) The fourth track on the second side of the album *The Unforgettable Fire* features Larry's powerful drumming against an acoustic guitar in the background. The title points at Bono's fixation with the King of Rock 'n' Roll, which would resurface with "Can't Help Falling In Love" on the *Zoo TV* tour and "Elvis Ate America" on the *Original Soundtracks 1* album. According to Bono, the song was "recorded in five minutes". All he did was sing some lyrics over a piece of music on the suggestion of producer Brian Eno.

EMERGENCY BROADCAST NETWORK The multimedia performance group that created the film clip of President George Bush saying "We will, we will rock you" used at the start of the *Zoo TV* concerts in 1992. Formed in 1991 in reaction to the biased coverage of the Gulf War, The Emergency Broadcast Network made video montages from news clips, films and TV shows with a techno soundtrack. The two principal figures are Josh Pearson and Gardner Post – both graduates of Rhode Island School of Design. They were joined by computer technician Greg Deo-Campo and DJ Ron O'Donnell. When U2 played at the Yankee Stadium in New York in 1992, they managed to get in without passes or tickets to set up their satellite dish projector on the roof of the mixer tower. They also directed "Numb (Video Remix)" included on the "Numb" video single in 1993.

"ENDLESS DEEP" ("TWO HEARTS BEAT AS ONE" SINGLE B-SIDE) (2.57) The B-side of the 7 inch single "Two Hearts Beat As One" (IS-109). It was produced by U2 and "St. Francis Xavier" and was released in March 1983. It also appeared on the 12 inch version of "Two Hearts Beat As One" (ISD109) which was only released in the UK. It was also on the B-side of the Dutch single, "Sunday Bloody Sunday" (105-330), released in March 1983. Essentially it is an instrumental with all three instruments to the fore, with some one-liners from Bono which are lost in the mix. It was also included in *The B-Sides* CD compilation released in 1998.

ENO, BRIAN A founder member of Roxy Music in 1971 who played on their first two albums, *Roxy Music* (1972) and *For Your Pleasure* (1973) before leaving in 1973 following personal differences. He went on to record albums under his own name, including *No Pussyfooting* (1973) with King Crimson's Robert Fripp, *Here Come The Warm Jets* (1974) and *Taking Tiger Mountain By Strategy* (1974). In 1975 Eno started his own Obscure Records label to release his and other artists' music. In the late 1970s he produced three albums for David Bowie, *Low* and *Heroes* and *Lodger*, which further enhanced his reputation. He also produced albums for Talking Heads, Devo and Ultravox, as well as releasing his own ambient records such as *Music For Films* (1978) and *Music For Airports* (1981).

Brian Eno. *Photo: Nicky J. Sims / Redferns*

After U2 had finished recording *War* in 1983 they had decided that they wanted Eno to produce their fourth studio album. Initially Eno turned U2 down, but after a few meetings, resulting in an agreement to let him bring along Canadian engineer Daniel Lanois, the band and Eno got together at Slane Castle in the spring of 1984 to record *The Unforgettable Fire*. The album overall was not as well received by some critics as its predecessor *War* had been, having a completely different feel, but it did contain the gems, "Pride (In The Name of Love)" and "Bad". Eno and Lanois were invited to produce U2's next and most successful album to date, *The Joshua Tree*.

In the 1990s the Eno/Lanois partnership was again put to use in the production of *Achtung Baby* and its hastily recorded follow up *Zooropa*. Brian Eno almost became a fifth member of U2 on the Passengers album *Original Soundtracks 1* (1995), when he and the band recorded an experimental album of mainly instrumental tracks. It was not wholeheartedly accepted by U2 fans – many saw it as the next U2 album (which it was not) and found it wanting. For their next album, *Pop* in 1997, U2 chose the services of their former engineer Flood, as producer, taking a break from the successful Eno/Lanois partnership. They did however return to the pair for 2000's *All That You Can't Leave Behind*. Outside of producing, recording and other artistic endeavours, Brian Eno has been a patron of the *War Child* charity and was a Passenger along with The Edge and Bono at Luciano Pavarotti's Modena concert in September 1995.

ENTERTAINMENT CENTRE, BRISBANE, AUSTRALIA
U2 played three sell out concerts here on 2nd, 3rd and 4th October 1989 during the *LoveTown* tour of Australia. During the second of the three shows, Bono introduced his daughter Jordan (who was then four months old) to the audience.

ENTERTAINMENT CENTRE, PERTH, AUSTRAILIA
These two shows, on 23rd and 24th September 1984, were the final shows of U2's first Australian tour, which took place in September 1984 as part of the *Unforgettable Fire* tour. The band returned here for three more shows on 21st, 22nd and 23rd September 1989. These were the opening dates of the *Lovetown* tour, U2's first tour since the *Joshua Tree* tour two years earlier. The first show marked the live debut of the *Rattle & Hum* album track "God Part II". For the second encore support artist BB King came out to sing on "When Love Comes to Town" and "Love Rescue Me".

ENTERTAINMENT CENTRE, SYDNEY, AUSTRALIA
This is the venue that U2 have played most times both in Australia and the world, visiting here on 13 separate occasions. The band played their first ever Australian dates here on 4th, 5th, 6th, 8th and 9th September 1984. Such was the euphoria of U2's first visit to Australia that all five shows in this 12,000 capacity arena sold out easily. This was also the first time that U2 had played the same venue on five nights. U2 next visited the Sydney Entertainment Centre in 1989 during the *Lovetown* tour where they played three consecutive nights (27th, 28th and 29th September). During the third concert Bono got Larry to come out to the front of the stage and sing "Stand By Me" with him – the first time that Larry had sung on stage since the *Joshua Tree* tour in 1987. Bono then went behind the drum kit and proceeded to play along on drums until the end of the song.

After dates in Brisbane and Melbourne, U2 returned here to play two more shows on 20th and 21st October 1989. They were meant to play here on the 22nd, 24th and 25th October as well, but these shows were post-poned due to Bono having laryngitis, which forced him to rest his voice for a week. The three shows instead took place on 17th, 18th, and 19th November 1989 after U2 had been to New Zealand. All three shows were filmed by Richard Lowenstein, an Australian film maker, who had directed the promo videos of "Desire" and "Angel of Harlem". They surfaced in a special TV documentary entitled *Lovetown*, which was shown in Australia and Europe at Christmas 1989. As the second show was about to begin, the hall had to be evacuated due to a bomb scare. After a 90-minute delay, the show went ahead without any problems. The show on the 19th was the final Australian show, so during the encore song "Party Girl", Anne-Louise Kelly of the U2 management brought out champagne for everyone.

ENTROPY (FILM) The film made by *Rattle & Hum* director, Phil Joanou about a film director whose marriage and world in general were breaking up around him as he filmed a U2 concert. The concert was at the Greenpoint Stadium in Cape Town, South Africa in March 1998. During the performance of "Mysterious Ways", the scene of the director getting married in Las Vegas was shown on the giant TV screen. Apart from the four members of U2 playing themselves, the film featured the actor Stephen Dorff and the actress Kelly Macdonald in the leading roles.
See also: Greenpoint Stadium / Phil Joanou

ERIKSBERG SHIPYARD, GOTHENBURG, SWEDEN U2 played this unusual venue on 6th June 1987 during the *Joshua Tree* tour of Europe. The concert was meant to have taken place at the 60,000 capacity Ullevi Stadium, but as repairs were still going on, the nearby Eriksberg Shipyard with a capacity of 50,000 was chosen instead.

ESPACE BALLARD, PARIS, FRANCE U2 played this 12,000 circus tent in Paris on 25th October 1984. The show was spoilt by technical problems when heavy rain outside started to come through the roof, coupled with condensation from the crowd which made for a very damp atmosphere inside the tent. As a result, the instruments and PA system were affected with The Edge's guitar going out of tune on one song.

ESPACE TONY GARNIER, LYON, FRANCE U2 have played at this 17,000 capacity venue twice. The first time was on 18th October 1984 when they opened the 1984 *Unforgettable Fire* tour here. Several new songs from the recently released *The Unforgettable Fire* album were played. Unfortunately the majority of the crowd were unfamiliar with them and as the concert ended several members of the audience actually booed, having expected U2 to play material from their previous *War* set. The songs that were played live that night for the first time were "MLK", "Indian

Summer Sky" and "Bad". U2 then returned here on 11th May 1992 during the *Zoo TV* tour of Europe to a better reception.

ESTADIO NACIONAL, SANTIAGO, CHILE U2's one and only gig in the South American country of Chile took place on 11th February 1998 on the final leg of the *Pop Mart* tour. The venue was the stadium that was notorious as the place where political prisoners were taken after they had been arrested under the dictatorship of General Pinochet. As a memorial to what had gone on here several years earlier, U2 had arranged for the local "Mothers of the Disappeared" to come on stage during "One" and "MLK". One by one they came up to the microphone and spoke the names of their lost ones into the microphone. Bono dedicated "One" to the Chilean poet Victor Jara, whose name was on the U2 song "One Tree Hill".

See also: "Mothers Of The Disappeared"

ESTADIO OLIMPIC DE MONTJUICH, BARCELONA, SPAIN U2 played this venue (the site for the 1996 Olympic Games) on 13th September 1997 during the *Pop Mart* tour of Europe before 60,000 fans. For the karaoke section the band performed "Macarana", which was booed loudly as this Spanish song is not at all popular in the Catalonian region! In the end The Edge stopped the song and Paul McGuinness later admitted that playing that song was one of the biggest mistakes of the tour.

ESTADIO SANTIAGO BERNABAU, MADRID, SPAIN U2's first ever concert in Spain did not take place until 15th July 1987 as part of the *Joshua Tree* tour of Europe. However, the crowd of 115,000 at the famous Bernabau football stadium more than made up for the wait. (The capacity was set at 75,000 but the promoter was believed to have illegally sold 40,000 extra tickets!) This was the highest attended show of the whole *Joshua Tree* tour and was only the second time that U2 had played before an audience of over 100,000. Naturally, the Spaniards showed great enthusiasm throughout the whole set, but went crazy when "Spanish Eyes" was played live for the first time.

ETHIOPIA The east African country that became the focus of the world's attention in 1984 when it was struck by a large scale famine. It was scenes of this famine and the resulting death of many millions of people that inspired Bob Geldof to make the Band Aid record that Adam and Bono contributed to. The success of this record led to the 1985 Live Aid concert at which U2 played and gained world wide exposure, leading to them becoming major rock superstars. After Live Aid, Bono and his wife Ali visited Ethiopia in September to see for themselves how the relief effort was going and to help out with other volun-

teers. They were based in Wello for a period of six weeks during which they helped out at a refugee camp and educated children in an orphanage.

EVANS, BECKY One of the three backing singers that took part in U2's session at Sun Studios in Memphis Tennessee in November 1987. Becky was a member of the group Reba and the Portables and joined sisters Phyllis and Helen Duncan for the session at which "When Love Comes To Town" was recorded.

EVANS, DAVID See: The Edge

EVANS, DICK (RICHARD) The older brother of The Edge. He was born in 1959 and attended Mount Temple Comprehensive School two years before his younger brother, David started. He was interested in electronics as a teenager and attempted to build an electric guitar from an article in *Everyday Electronics*. He attended Larry's band audition with his younger brother and stayed with the newly formed Feedback for a couple of years until he left when the band became U2. Instead he had been asked to join the Virgin Prunes as guitarist by Gavin Friday and the other members of the Village who wanted to form an alternative group to the Hype. Dick also became an honorary member of the Village changing his name to Dik. He provided the musical base for the Virgin Prunes, who would often play on the same bill as U2. He stayed with the Prunes until 1984.

See also: The Virgin Prunes

EVANS, GARVIN The Edge's father, Garvin was born in Llanelli, South Wales in the 1930s but moved to London a few years later. When the second world war started he was moved back to Llanelli as an evacuee to live with his grandparents. He attended the local secondary school where he met his wife Gwenda. The two of them both took degrees at University College, London, with Garvin gaining a degree in Engineering. They married soon after graduating, living in London whilst Garvin did his national service in Northern Ireland. In 1962 they moved with their two young sons to Malahide just north of Dublin as Garvin was now working with Plessey Engineering. Eventually, Garvin left Plessey to set up his own engineering business. Aside from his work, Garvin was a founder member of the Dublin Welsh Male Voice Choir and a keen piano player and golfer.

EVANS, GWENDA (NEE RICHARDS) The Edge's mother, Gwenda, was also born in Llanelli, South Wales, but moved with her family to Blaegwynfi as her father had set up a grocery shop there. She met her husband Garvin at secondary school and trained to be a teacher at University College in London, marrying Garvin after graduation. Staying on in London, she gave birth first to Dick and then Dave before the family moved to Malahide in Ireland. She gave birth to a daughter, Jill, in Dublin a couple of years later. Both Gwenda and Garvin have attended various U2 concerts over the years, including the historic performance in Cape Town, South Africa in 1998, the band's first concert in Africa.

EVANS-RUSSELL, REBECCA She provided backing vocals on the track "When Love Comes To Town" off *Rattle & Hum*.

"EVEN BETTER THAN THE REAL THING" (*ACHTUNG BABY* ALBUM TRACK) (3.41) The second track off the first side of the *Achtung Baby* album. One of the most commercial tracks off the album, the song was originally going to be called "The Real Thing", but U2 wanted to make the title sound more catchy, more up-to-date, so they added the "even better than" prefix. The song has a catchy refrain, and rocks along at a fast pace. Bono's voice is double tracked in high and low mode and The Edge's gritty slide guitar juxtaposes the keyboards in the mix. It was first performed live at the Civic Center in Lakeland, Florida on 29th February 1992.

"EVEN BETTER THAN THE REAL THING" (SINGLE) (3.41) The fourth track from *Achtung Baby* to be released as a single. It was released in May 1992 tying in with the *Zoo TV* tour of Europe. The 7 inch version (Island IS 5250) had "Where Did It All Go Wrong" as the B-side, whilst the cassette version (Island CIS 525) had the track "Salome" instead. Both these tracks were featured on the CD single (Island CID 525), as well as the track, "Lady With The Spinning Head UVI" (Extended Dance Mix). The single reached number 12 in the UK charts and number 36 in the US charts.

"EVEN BETTER THAN THE REAL THING" (REMIXES SINGLE) (REAL U2 864 197-1) Following the success of the "Even Better Than The Real Thing" single, Island released this 12 inch single featuring three remixes of the song for use in clubs. The A-side featured the Perfecto Mix, whilst the B-side featured the Trance Mix and the Sexy Dub mix, all remixed by Paul Oakenfold and Steve Osborne. This 12" remix single did even better than the original single reaching number 8 in the UK singles charts in July 1992.

"EVEN BETTER THAN THE REAL THING" (REMIXES CD) (REAL 2 864 197-2) (30.29) This was the CD version of the above 12 inch single and also featured the Apollo 440 Stealth Sonic Remix, the V16 Exit Wound Remix and the A440 vs U2 Instrumental Remix, all mixed by Apollo 440. (The Trance Mix that was on the 12 inch single was not included on this CD.)

"EVEN BETTER THAN THE REAL THING" (APOLLO 440 STEALTH SONIC REMIX) This remix by Apollo 440 was the third track on the CD version of the "Even Better Than The Real Thing" remix single.

"EVEN BETTER THAN THE REAL THING" (A440 VS U2 INSTRUMENTAL REMIX) The fifth track on the "Even Better Than The Real Thing" remixes CD.

"EVEN BETTER THAN THE REAL THING" (PERFECTO MIX) This mix by Paul Oakenfold and Steve Osborne was the A-side of the 12 inch single of "Even Better Than The Real Thing" and was also included on the free Melon CD given to readers of *Propaganda* in December 1994. An organ plus the all-girl chorus were prominent on this remix.

"EVEN BETTER THAN THE REAL THING" (SEXY DUB MIX) This version was remixed by Paul Oakenfold and Steve Osborne. It was the second track on the B-side of the 12 inch vinyl version of the "Even Better Than The Real Thing" remixes single.

"EVEN BETTER THAN THE REAL THING" (V16 EXIT WOUND REMIX) The fourth track on the "Even Better Than The Real Thing" remixes CD. It was remixed by Apollo 440.

"EVEN BETTER THAN THE REAL THING" (LIVE) (THE RADIO 1 FM SESSIONS CASSETTE) The cassette tape called *The Radio 1 FM Sessions* given away free with *Vox* magazine in the UK contains a live recording of the song from U2's show at Dublin's RDS, which was broadcast live around the world on the radio on Saturday 28th August 1993.

"EVEN BETTER THEN THE REAL THING" (LIVE) ("STUCK IN A MOMENT YOU CAN'T GET OUT OF" SINGLE). This rare live version of "Even Better Than The Real Thing" was recorded at U2's club gig

Video shoot for "Even Better Than The Real Thing", Zoo shop, Carnaby Street, London, February 1992.
Photo: Clark Denham

at Man Ray in Paris on 19th October 2000. It was included on the French single release of "Stuck In A Moment You Can't Get Out Of".

"EVEN BETTER THAN THE REAL THING" (LIVE) (*STOP SELLAFIELD* VIDEO) This filmed live version of "Even Better Than The Real Thing" comes from the U2 concert at the G-Mex Centre, Manchester, England on Friday 19th June 1992. It was one of the two U2 songs featured on the special *Stop Sellafield* video, produced by Greenpeace.

"EVEN BETTER THAN THE REAL THING" (LIVE) (*ZOO TV LIVE FROM SYDNEY* VIDEO) This live film version of "Even Better Than The Real Thing" comes from the *Live in Sydney* video. It was filmed at U2's concert at the Football Stadium in Sydney Australia on 27th November 1993.

"EVEN BETTER THAN THE REAL THING" (LIVE) (*POP MART LIVE FROM MEXICO CITY* VIDEO) This live film version of "Even Better Than The Real Thing" comes from the *U2: Pop Mart Live From Mexico City* video. It was filmed at U2's concert at the Foro Sol Autodromo in Mexico City on 3rd December 1997.

"EVEN BETTER THAN THE REAL THING" (PROMOTIONAL VIDEO 1) (3.41) This video was directed by Kevin Godley and featured a specially formed "U2 lookalike" group, who Bono called "The Doppelgangers", who appeared at various times during the video. The shots featuring this group were shot in a shop called Zoo in London's Carnaby Street in February 1992 (since closed down). Other scenes of famous rock stars such as Jimi Hendrix and Prince were filmed just around the corner in a waxworks museum dedicated to rock musicians called "Rock Circus" in Piccadilly Circus. The shots of the band turning full circle were done with a specially constructed revolving camera at Pinewood Studios, near London on 13th February 1992. Finally there were various film clips from satellite TV programmes like MTV and CNN also included. The video was voted Video of the Year in the 1992 MTV awards.

See also: The Dopplegangers / Kevin Godley

"EVEN BETTER THAN THE REAL THING" (PROMOTIONAL VIDEO 2) (3.46) An alternative video of "Even Better Than The Real Thing" directed by Armando Gallo and Kampah. It was filmed in Los Angeles in May 1992 and features all sorts of *Zoo TV* memorabilia and photos. It is available on the *Achtung Baby - The Videos* collection.

"EVEN BETTER THAN THE REAL THING" (DANCE MIX VIDEO) (4.35) The dance mix video of "Even Better Than The Real Thing", set to the Perfecto Remix, was directed by Ritchie Smyth and produced by Ned O'Hanlon of Dreamchaser Productions. It featured some of the street scenes from the "Mysterious Ways" promo video shot in Morocco as well as some shots in the Canary Islands at the festival of Tenerife. It is also featured on the *Achtung Baby - The Videos* collection.

"EVERLASTING LOVE" ("ALL I WANT IS YOU" SINGLE B-SIDE) (3.20) This track was featured on the B-side of the "All I Want Is You" 12 inch single (Island 12IS 422) and CD single (Island CVID 422). Recorded at STS Studios in Dublin and produced by U2, the song was originally a number 1 hit in the UK in 1968 for the Love Affair. Bono sings along to the strumming of a 12 string acoustic guitar. It was also included in the *The B Sides* compilation CD released in 1998.

EXILE ON CLASSICAL STREET This classical music compilation album featured several popular musicians' favourite pieces of classical music. Bono's choice was "String Quartet No.8 In C Minor, Largo" by the Russian composer Shostakovich.

"EXIT" (*JOSHUA TREE* ALBUM TRACK) (4.14) The fifth track on the second side of *The Joshua Tree* Album. It starts off so quietly that you can hardly hear it, but then builds into a crescendo, before dipping again, all the while held together by Adam's bass line. The violence of the music makes this a bit of a black sheep when compared to the other tracks on *The Joshua Tree*, showing that U2 were prepared to explore other areas in their music. The title and lyrics of "Exit" would indicate that the song is about death, but is it about murder or suicide? Such was the bleakness of the song that a man accused of murder in America claimed in his defence that listening to "Exit" had influenced his actions.

"EXIT" (LIVE) (*RATTLE & HUM* FILM/VIDEO) This live version of "Exit", (which was not included on the *Rattle & Hum* soundtrack album) was shot in black and white and shows how U2 had made the *Joshua Tree* song a highlight of their live set. It was recorded at the McNichols Arena, Denver, USA on 8th November 1987 during the *Joshua Tree* tour of America.

EXPO, HANNOVER, GERMANY U2 played at this exhibition site for the Expo 2000 exhibition on 20th August 1997 during the *Pop Mart* tour of Europe. For the final song, the band sang the first verse of "Wake Up Dead Man", the first time the song had been performed live on this tour.

FABRIK, HAMBURG, GERMANY U2 played here on 3rd November 1981 in what was only their fourth German gig. The concert should have also featured the British group The Psychedelic Furs, but they did not play. As a result, several members of the audience who had come to see the Psychedelic Furs were aggressive to U2 to the point of throwing things on stage. This resulted in "Gloria" and "I Will Follow" being stopped while Bono tried to calm things down.

THE FACTORY STUDIOS, DUBLIN, IRELAND The studio where much of the *Zooropa* album was recorded from February to May 1993. It is also where U2 prepare for their live shows.

The Factory Studios, Dublin. *Photo: Mark Chatterton*

"FALSE PROPHET" An early U2 song that never made it onto record.

"FALLING AT YOUR FEET" (*MILLION DOLLAR HOTEL* SOUNDTRACK ALBUM TRACK) (4.54) The fifth track on the soundtrack album *The Million Dollar Hotel* is performed by Bono and Daniel Lanois who had also written the track.

FALLON, BP U2 fans will probably remember BP Fallon as the colourful DJ for the first year of the *Zoo TV* tour, though he has had a long and interesting career in music before that. Fallon originally came to prominence on Irish TV and radio as a DJ before he moved to Britain where he worked in the Beatles' Apple headquarters in London in the late 1960s. He even got to appear alongside John Lennon on *Top Of The Pops* performing "Instant Karma"! He then started working with several big names on the British

music scene including Marc Bolan, Led Zeppelin and Roy Harper.

Keeping in touch with his Irish roots he had a regular column in *Scene* magazine before becoming the publicist for The Boomtown Rats and Ian Dury amongst others. In the 1980s he returned to Ireland and was a DJ for RTE Radio with his "BP Fallon Orchestra" show. He even appeared on stage briefly with U2 at their show at the Punchestown Racecourse in Dublin in July 1982. Bono got him to sing a verse of "Give Peace A Chance" during "11 O'clock Tick Tock". For the first year of the *Zoo TV* tour he was the DJ who would play records between the support act and U2 taking the stage. In the programme he is credited as "Guru, Viber and Disc Jockey".

Fallon also wrote the liner notes for the *Zoo TV* programme. After the *Zoo TV* tour he brought out the book *U2 Faraway, So Close*, which chronicled the ups and downs of life on the *Zoo TV* tour. He has also written books on Boyzone and has worked with Sinead O'Connor as well as regularly appearing on TV as a highly entertaining talk show guest.

FANNING, DAVE The premier Irish DJ who was the first radio DJ in Ireland to play U2 music. He was from the Southside of Dublin and attended Blackrock College as did Bob Geldof. In the 1970s he took over the running of *Scene* magazine from Niall Stokes who went on to found *Hot Press*. He began DJing for pirate radio stations Radio Dublin and Big D, before progressing to the official radio station RTE 2FM in 1978. While he was a DJ on Big D, he interviewed U2 and played tracks from the demo disc they had cut as the prize for winning the Harp Lager talent contest. Then in 1979, after Jackie Hayden had got U2 a recording deal with CBS Ireland for their first single, Fanning got listeners of his RTE show to vote for which of the three tracks should be the A-side.

Many times over the years Fanning has interviewed U2 on his radio programme, often being the first DJ to play tracks off a forthcoming U2 album. Perhaps the most notorious radio interview Fanning conducted with U2 was on 25th June 1987 when the members of U2 stripped off their clothes whilst being interviewed (see In the Nude). He has also introduced U2 on stage at several of their Dublin concerts including the shows at Croke Park in June 1985 and 1987, and at Self Aid in May 1986. Apart from his own radio show, FY1, which includes the live "Fanning Sessions", he has also appeared on the Satellite TV station VH-1's *Rock Stories* and *Music Express* shows where he has interviewed many rock stars.

Website: www.2fm.ie.
See also: U2-3

FARAWAY, SO CLOSE (FILM) The 1993 film directed by Wim Wenders for which U2 were asked to write the title track. The result was "Stay (Faraway, So Close!)" which was also included on the *Zooropa* album. Apart from "Stay"' the film also included the *Zooropa* track "The Wanderer" on its soundtrack.

FARMCLUB.COM An American music TV show for which U2 performed at the Universal Studios in Los Angeles on 27th October 2000. They played: "Beautiful Day", "New York", "Stuck In A Moment You Can't Get Out Of", "Elevation" and "Pride". The first two tracks were included on the singles, "Walk On" and "Stuck In A Moment You Can't Get Out Of".

FAST LANE, ASBURY PARK, NEW JERSEY, USA The final show of U2's first coast-to-coast tour of America took place at this venue on the New Jersey seafront on 31st May 1981. The gig was a sell out and a welcome reward for the band after playing sixty gigs the length and breadth of America and Canada in just under three months.

"THE FATHER AND HIS WIFE THE SPIRIT" (*IN THE NAME OF THE FATHER* FILM) A song from the *In The Name Of The Father* film written by Bono, Gavin Friday and Maurice Seezer and sung by Sinead O'Connor. It was not included on the soundtrack album.

"FATHER IS AN ELEPHANT" Another early U2 song that the band would play in their set in 1980. It was never released. At some concerts Bono would dedicate the song to his father.

FEAR OF FALLING Bono produced a track called "Prodigal" for this group, included on their single "Like a Lion", released in 1983.

FEEDBACK The name the embryonic U2 called themselves when they first formed the band at Mount Temple Comprehensive School in Dublin in the autumn of 1976. Through the efforts of teachers such as Albert Bradshaw and David Moxham the band were allowed to rehearse in the music room and other classrooms during the lunch hour, as well as at Larry's house, 60 Rosemount Avenue. After a few months of rehearsals the band entered a talent contest at the school towards the end of the autumn term. The contest took place in the school's gymnasium before an enthusiastic crowd of pupils. The band were second from last on the bill and performed a cover of Peter Frampton's "Show Me The Way". They didn't win the contest but were inspired to continue the quest for stardom. After their final gig at St. Fintan's School, Sutton, a few months later, they had changed the name of the group to The Hype after deciding the name was too much like the sound they first made.

The Hype was more up-to-date and a record industry buzzword.

See also: 60 Rosemount Avenue / The Hype / Mount Temple Comprehensive School

FELTON, JESSICA One of the singers from Kid Creole's backing group, The Coconuts, who provided backing vocals on some of the tracks on *War*.

FERGUSON, DAVE The engineer who helped out at the famous Sun Studios sessions in November 1987 where U2 recorded several tracks for the *Rattle & Hum* album.

FESTA DELL' UNITA REGGIO, EMILIA, ITALY An estimated 150,000 to 170,000 fans attended this one-day festival in Italy making it the biggest attendance at a U2 concert ever. It also holds the record for the biggest attendance for a single act. The concert took place on 20 September 1997 during the *Pop Mart* tour of Europe. Bono dedicated the event to Andrea Gianotti who had died two days earlier of a heart attack at the band's concert in Rome. At the end of the concert he commented to the crowd "You gave four Irish boys an evening they'll never forget!"

FESTIVAL AGAINST RACISM See: Thalia Theatre Hamburg

FESTIVAL DE PRINTEMPS, BOURGES, FRANCE U2 played at this French festival on 3rd April 1983. The show before 5,000 fans actually took place in a tent and was a one-off appearance in France inbetween British and American tours.

FESTIVAL HALL, OSAKA, JAPAN U2's first ever concert in Japan took place here on 22nd November 1983, the first date of a six date tour of Japan. The concert was sold out, though the audience remained fairly quiet during the show.

FESTWEISE, LEIPZIG, GERMANY U2's first gig in the former East Germany (apart from Berlin) took place here on 29th July 1997 during the *Pop Mart* tour of Europe.

FEY, BARRY The concert promoter from Denver, Colorado who has appeared in two U2 films. In the *Under a Blood Red Sky* he is shown introducing U2 at the Red Rocks Amphitheatre near Denver. Then in the documentary film *Outside It's America*, he is shown reading out a statement about Governor Mechum on behalf of U2 before their show at the State University Activity Center in Tempe, Arizona. He was also a partner in the company set up to film the Red Rocks Concert, "U2 At Red Rocks Associates".

See also: Martin Luther King / Governor Mechum / Red Rocks Amphitheater

FEYENOORD STADIUM, ROTTERDAM, HOLLAND U2 have played this 45,000 capacity football stadium five times. The three opening shows of the 1993 *Zooropa* tour took place here on 9th, 10th and 11th May 1993. U2 had actually played an impromptu show on the 7th as a way of ironing out any last minute technical problems. Several fans were invited in by Bono to watch the rehearsal, which lasted about two and a half hours.

For the first of the three shows proper many reporters from all over Europe were present. As these were the first shows of *Zoo TV* since the *Outside Broadcast* leg in America in 1992, there were several noticeable changes. First, an Irish drama group called Macnas performed on the catwalk and mini stage, with four of the group wearing large U2 look-alike heads. Second, as the usual set opener the Disposable Heroes of Hiphoprisy's "TV - Drug of the Nation" started, the audience saw many images of Europe beamed up on the various TV screens, including the Hitler Youth playing drums before the 1936 Berlin Olympic games (an excerpt from Leni Riefenstahl's Nazi-Propaganda film "The Triumph of the Will"). This climaxed with the music of Beethoven's "Ode to Joy", before Bono rose up on the stage to a backdrop of the European Community flag. Third, the character of Macphisto was introduced to the crowd during the singing of "Desire". As in America a phone call was made, usually to a famous politician or celebrity. On the first night it was just to a local taxi firm to hire a cab!

The second show on 10th May was Bono's 33rd birthday. This time he rang the KLM Dutch Airlines reservation desk to book a flight out of Holland. He spoke to a girl called Monique who didn't know what was going on, but kept the conversation going nonetheless. The last song of the show was not the usual "Can't Help Falling in Love" but another Elvis song "Are You Lonesome Tonight", the first time this song had been played live by U2. After the show, at the group's hotel a very unusual present was waiting for Bono from Gavin Friday – it was a full size Cross lying on his bed with the words, "Hail Bono, King of the Zoos!" on it.

For the third show at the Feyenoord Stadium, Macphisto rang up Queen Beatrix of Holland, but her receptionist put the phone down on him.

Zooropa tour opening night set list: Zoo Station, The Fly, Even Better Than The Real Thing, Mysterious Ways, One/Unchained Melody, Until The End Of The World, New Year's Day, Dirty Old Town, Trying To Throw Your Arms Around The World, Angel Of Harlem, When Love Comes To Town, Satellite of Love, Bad/All I Want Is You, Bullet The Blue Sky, Running To Stand Still, Where The Streets Have No Name, Pride. Encores: Desire, Ultra Violet, With Or Without You, Love Is Blindness, Can't Help Falling In Love.

U2 again used this venue as the site for their opening shows of the European leg of the *Pop Mart* tour. They had a rehearsal show on 17th July 1997, followed by two proper shows on 18th and 19th July. It rained all through the first show and as usually happens when it rains, Bono sang part of the Beatles song "Rain" at the end. The first half hour of this show was broadcast live on the Internet on the U2 *Pop Mart* website, as well as on MTV Europe. Three songs recorded at this show were later released on the *Popheart Live EP*. They were "Please", "Where The Streets Have No Name" and "Staring At The Sun". For the second show The Edge led everyone in the karaoke segment with a version of "Radar Love" by the Dutch group Golden Earring.

See also: Macnas, Disposable Heroes of Hiphoprisy, Leni Reifenstahl, Elvis Presley, Gavin Friday, *Zooropa* tour, *Popheart Live EP*

FINLAY, IAN U2's official photographer before Anton Corbijn, responsible for the photographs on the *Boy* album and the "Two Hearts Beat As One" single.

"FIRE" (*OCTOBER* ALBUM TRACK) (3.51) The fifth track on the first side of the *October* album. It had been recorded specially as a single in the Bahamas a few months before the *October* album had been recorded. With its echoing vocal chorus, it was not unlike some of the material of the then-current British chart topper Adam Ant.

"FIRE" (SINGLE) (WIP 6679) "Fire" was released as a single in Ireland and the UK in June 1981 and became U2's first top 40 hit single reaching number 35. It had been recorded in Nassau in the Bahamas during a ten-day break in U2's gruelling first major tour of the USA in the spring of 1981. Steve Lillywhite was the producer. The B-side was "J. Swallo". The single was also released in the UK in a special double-pack with an extra single featuring the live tracks "Cry-Electric Co", "The Ocean" and "11 O'clock Tick Tock" (U-WIP 6679). The same "Fire" track appeared on the B-side of the single "A Celebration" (7S-69), only released in Japan.

"FIRE" (LIVE) ("NEW YEAR'S DAY" SINGLE B-SIDE) This live recording of the *October* album track, "Fire" appeared as a B-side track on both the 7 inch double pack (EP600417) and 12 inch versions of the "New Year's Day" single (U-WIP 6848). It had been recorded live at the Werchter Festival in Belgium on 3rd July 1982 and was produced by Steve Lillywhite.

FIRST AVENUE, MINNEAPOLIS, MINNESOTA, USA U2 first played at this venue when it was known as "Uncle Sam's" on 9th April 1981 during the *Boy* tour of North America. They then played to a sell out crowd of 1,000 fans here on 21st February 1982 on the *October* tour. During "11 O'clock Tick Tock", Bono danced on stage with a fan whom he had picked out of the audience. This is thought to be one of the first gigs where this happened. It subsequently became a regular occurrence on both the *October* and *War* tours.

"THE FIRST TIME" (*ZOOROPA* ALBUM TRACK) (3.45) The third track on the second side of the *Zooropa* Album. From the opening chords of this quiet song, listeners could be forgiven for thinking that they were hearing "All I Want is You", but then the song develops in a different way, with The Edge coming in on piano as the song progresses. The lyrics were said by Bono to be about the prodigal son and about losing your faith. Some fans have seen them as being autobiographical.

"THE FIRST TIME" (*MILLION DOLLAR HOTEL* SOUNDTRACK ALBUM TRACK) (3.43) The fifth track on the soundtrack album of *The Million Dollar Hotel*. It is the same version as the one on *Zooropa*.

"THE FIRST TIME" (REPRISE) (*MILION DOLLAR HOTEL* SOUNDTRACK ALBUM TRACK) (2.05) This instrumental version of "The First Time" is performed by Daniel Lanois and the MDH Band.

FIRST UNION CENTER, PHILADELPHIA, PENNSYLVANIA, USA U2 played two shows here on 11th and 12th June 2001 as part of the *Elevation* tour (first leg). For the show, Bono sang part of "Night & Day" after "Beautiful Day", and in "Bullet The Blue Sky" he referred to the Oklahoma Bomber, Timothy McVeigh who had been executed earlier in the day. At the second show when a girl's mobile phone started ringing during the encore, Bono answered it and told the girl's mother that she was fine. He also made a speech about guns and gun control during "Bullet The Blue Sky" saying that over the next 20 years, 600,000 Americans would be shot with a bullet.

JOHN FISHER The organiser of the Dandelion Market car park gigs in Gaiety Green Dublin at which U2 played on certain Saturdays in the summer of 1979. The entrance fee was either 50 pence or a £1 and the band playing had to provide their own PA and mixing desk (and lights if they could afford them). These gatherings were eventually stopped by the local authorities.

See also: Dandelion Market

FISHER, MARK A stage designer who has worked with Pink Floyd and the Rolling Stones. He worked on the stage design for the *Outside Broadcast* stadium shows for *Zoo TV* along with Jonathan Park and Willie Williams.

FITZGERALD, FINTAN U2's make up and costume man who is sometimes called "Fighting" Fintan Fitzgerald. He was the head of wardrobe for the *Zoo TV* tour and goes down in history as the man who found the Fly shades for Bono – in a second hand shop to be precise.

FITZGERALD, GARRETT The Prime Minister of Ireland in the 1980s. He had met Bono once at Heathrow Airport when they were both flying to Dublin. The two of them had talked together on the plane, the story being reported in the Irish papers. Later as the *War* album was being recorded, and Garrett was campaigning to get his Fine Gael party elected, he and his wife Joan visited U2 at Windmill Lane studios along with several newspaper cameramen, the resulting pictures boosting his popularity. A week later, Fitzgerald was elected Taoiseach. The connections did not end there as Bono was invited by Fitzgerald to be part of the Select Government Action Committee on Unemployment, though his commitment did not last long due to the "committee language" he had to fight against.

See also: Anthem For The 80s

FITZGERALD, PATRIK U2 were the support act for his two shows at the Project Arts Centre in Dublin on 11th and 12th September 1979. On both nights there was trouble from a group of punks called the "Black Catholics" who disrupted U2's set before they were thrown out of the venue. This was the last time that U2 played at the Project Arts Centre.

FLEET CENTER, BOSTON, MASSACHUSETTS, USA U2 played four sell our shows at this arena on 5th, 6th, 8th and 9th June 2001 on the *Elevation* tour of North America. The first show was filmed by Ned O'Hanlon and recorded by Steve Lillywhite for a planned TV special on the band as well as for DVD release later in 2001. "Where The Streets Have No Name" from the second concert was shown live by NBC at the NBA finals and footage of "Elevation" was also broadcast.

FLOOD (real name: Mark Ellis) The respected record producer and engineer who has worked with U2 on several of their albums. He apparently got his nickname from the large amounts of tea that he would make during recording sessions. He was the engineer responsible for recording *The Joshua Tree*, *Achtung Baby* and *Zooropa* albums, the latter of which he co-produced with Brian Eno and The Edge. In 1996 he was promoted to the role of producer for the *Pop* album. This was the most techno and dance orientated album that U2 had ever done. He has also remixed several U2 songs including "Staring At The Sun". Flood has produced, engineered and remixed many other artists including Depeche Mode, Smash-

"The Fly" at Wembley Stadium, Zoo TV, Zooropa Tour, 11/8/93. *Photo: Claire Bolton*

ing Pumpkins, PJ Harvey, Nick Cave and Nine Inch Nails.

FLUFFY COD TRIO This unusually named group received a mention of thanks on the track "Love Is Blindness" off *Achtung Baby.* Some people think this is the Joshua Trio spoof group.

"THE FLY" (*ACHTUNG BABY* ALBUM TRACK) (4.29) The first track on side two of the *Achtung Baby* album. It features a simple repetitive riff from The Edge, plus some falsetto vocals from Bono in the "Gospel Voice" section. Musically it was as far removed as possible from anything on the their previous album, *Rattle & Hum.* Bono went so far as to say that "The Fly" was "the sound of four men chopping

down *The Joshua Tree*". The lyrics go back to The Fall of Adam and Eve in the Bible. Man is a fallen animal just like the stars that fall from the sky and is like a fly trying to climb back up the wall. The track was produced by Daniel Lanois. "The Fly" was first performed in concert at the Civic Centre, Lakeland in Florida on 29th February 1992. To date, an official audio recording of the "The Fly" performed live has not been released.

"THE FLY" (SINGLE) (4.29) The single of "The Fly" was released in November 1991 with an accompanying video, several weeks before the *Achtung Baby* album came out. The video was premiered on *Top of The Pops* in October 1991. The following week it went straight into the charts at Number 1, knocking the Brian Adams single, "Everything I Do I Do It For you" off the top spot after a record breaking run of 16 weeks. Most U2 fans were shocked by this new incarnation of U2, but this suited the band who wanted to stress how radically U2's music had changed for a new decade.

"The Fly" single came out in four different formats: 7 inch single (IS 500), 12 inch single (12IS 500), Cassette (CIS 500) and CD (CID 500) It was only available in the shops for a period of 4 weeks which partly explained why so many copies were initially sold and why it only stayed on the charts for just five weeks. The B-side was "Alex Descends Into Hell For A Bottle Of Milk/Korova 1" for the 7 inch and cassette versions, whilst the 12 inch and CD versions included the extra track, "The Lounge Fly Mix", a remix version of "The Fly".

See also: The Lounge Fly Mix

"THE FLY" (LIVE) (*STOP SELLAFIELD* VIDEO TRACK) This live film version of "The Fly" was recorded at the G-Mex Centre, Manchester, England on 19th June 1992 appearing on the special *Stop Sellafield* video produced by Greenpeace.

"THE FLY" (LIVE) (*ZOO TV LIVE FROM SYDNEY* VIDEO TRACK) This live film version of "The Fly" was performed at the Sydney Football Stadium on 27th November 1993, and included on the *Zoo TV Live from Sydney* video.

"THE FLY" (PROMOTIONAL VIDEO) The promotional video for "The Fly" single was shot mainly in London during September 1991. Ritchie Smyth was the director, along with John Klein, and Ned O'Hanlon was the producer. One of the scenes involved Bono walking precariously along the edge of the London Pavilion 200 feet above Piccadilly Circus. Another scene was shot in front of a second hand television shop in Walworth Road, South London at midnight with the second hand TVs swapped for state of the art televisions showing U2 clips.

"THE FLY" CHARACTER The Fly was one of Bono's alter-egos used for the *Zoo TV* show, dressed in black leather and PVC with overlarge dark glasses. The Fly was an attempt for Bono to get away from some of the more serious set ups he'd had in the 1980s. Bono explained the persona during the shooting of *The Fly* video: "He's the kind of character who has all the answers – who shot the Kennedys. A barfly; he's made himself a self-appointed expert on the politics of love, a bullshit philosopher who occasionally hits the nail on the head, but more often its his own fingernail he leaves black and blue!"

MANNIX FLYNN A former prisoner who became a successful writer and actor. He once gave acting lessons to Bono and Gavin Friday in an attempt to help them improve their stagecraft.

See also: Boy-Girl

FOG HORN, PORTLAND, OREGON, USA Although U2's concert here on 22nd March 1981 went well, it is believed that someone came backstage after the show and stole Bono's briefcase. In it were all the new lyrics he had written for the next U2 album. As a result, when U2 entered the studio to record the *October* album, Bono had to improvise lyrics on several of the tracks. (Another theory is that this incident happened the following night at Astor Park in Seattle.)

"THE FOOL" This was an early U2 song from their live set of 1978 and 1979, recorded as a demo at their sessions at the Keystone Studios, Dublin with Barry Devlin in 1978. It was also known as "Out Of The Living World" and is said by some to be the first song the band ever wrote. It was never released on record.

FOOTBALL STADIUM, SYDNEY, AUSTRALIA U2's last two shows of the 1993 *Zoomerang* Zoo TV tour of Australia took place at this 50,000 capacity football stadium on 26th and 27th November 1993. The first show is important in U2 history as it was the only U2 show where all four members of U2 did not play together. Adam Clayton stayed in bed that day – officially he had "a virus", which made him miss the sound check and prevented him from playing. He later revealed that the real reason for his absence was a massive hangover from a drinking binge.

U2 could have cancelled the show and rearranged it for a later date, but on this occasion the show needed to go ahead as a TV crew were preparing to film the following evening's show as a live broadcast and so needed to check technical aspects such as camera angles and show timings. Adam's place was taken by his bass guitar technician, Stuart Morgan, who did extremely well to play in front of a 50,000 capacity crowd.

Adam was back for the second show however, which was beamed live to America for Thanksgiving Day. It was also shown in many other countries at a later date. Finally the recording was used for a special video, released in April 1994, entitled *Zoo TV Live from Sydney*.

U2 played again here on 27th February 1998 during the *Pop Mart* tour of the Rest of The World. As this was the city where Michael Hutchence, the late INXS singer, came from, there were rumours that the remaining members of INXS would join U2 on stage to perform a musical tribute. This did not happen but Bono still dedicated "MLK" to Hutchence and his picture was shown on the giant TV screen. The end of the show was blacked out during "One" due to an overhead electrical storm. Fans held their lighters up to illuminate the stadium.

See also: Stuart Morgan

"FORTUNATE SON" ('WHO'S GONNA RIDE YOUR WILD HORSES' SINGLE) (2.39) This song was written by John Fogerty when he was with Creedence Clearwater Revival. It is about how some American males were fortunate to escape having to go to fight in the Vietnam War in the 1960s and is one of three extra tracks featured on the "Who's Gonna Ride Your Wild Horses" single. Some commentators have said that it was supposedly recorded by U2 as a way of informing potential voters in the 1992 Presidential campaign about how vice-president Dan Quayle was one of these "fortunate sons" in the late sixties who managed to escape the Vietnam War draft.

"40" (*WAR* ALBUM TRACK) (2.36) The closing track of the *War* album. In many ways it is designed as a foil for the album's opening track, "Sunday Bloody Sunday". Using lines taken from The Bible's Psalm 40, this gentlest of all U2's songs became the final song of their set for many of their 1980s shows. The refrain was often sung by concert audiences long after the band had left the stage and as a result a live single version with the subtitle "How Long" was released in Germany (see below). "40" was first performed live at the Caird Hall in Dundee, Scotland on 26th February 1983.

"40" (LIVE) (*UNDER A BLOOD RED SKY* ALBUM TRACK) (3.53) "Sing with me! This is 40" announces Bono from the stage at the Lorelei Amphitheatre in Germany on 20th August 1983 as U2 play the only officially released live version of "40". This version was deemed better than the one recorded at Red Rocks and so made it onto the album. This version was also released as a single in Germany with "Two Hearts Beat As One" from the same show on the B-side.

"40" (LIVE) (*UNDER A BLOOD RED SKY* VIDEO) This live version of the Red Rocks final song helped to show the world how special a live band U2 actually were. As the show closes, the band members leave the stage one by one, until finally Larry is just left playing a basic back beat while the whole audience sings the refrain. Whenever the song was played live Adam would play lead guitar and Edge would play bass guitar. The song was always the last number of the U2 set from the *War* tour in 1983 right through to the *Lovetown* tour in 1990. It was played live once again at several of the *Elevation* tour shows.

"THE 4TH OF JULY" (*THE UNFORGETTABLE FIRE* ALBUM TRACK*)* (2.15) The first track on the second side of *The Unforgettable Fire* album is a very quiet instrumental with Adam's bass to the fore, indicating the experimental direction prompted by Brian Eno. It has never been played live, but was used as the introductory music to U2's shows on the *Unforgettable Fire* tour.

"THE 4TH OF JULY" ('PRIDE' SINGLE B-SIDE) The same version of "The 4th Of July" as that on *The Unforgettable Fire* album was put on the B-side of the "Pride" single which was issued in double 7 inch (ISD 202), 12 inch (ISX 202) and cassette (CIS 202) formats. It was also released in Ireland only on the B-side of a "Pride" single (CBS 4727) that made up the 4 pack set entitled "U24U". The track would be used as the opening theme music for U2's first tour of Australia and New Zealand.

FORUM, LOS ANGELES, CALIFORNIA, USA This was one of the venues for the 1986 Amnesty International Concert tour called *Conspiracy of Hope*. U2 played as headliners here on 6th June 1986 on a bill which also featured Tom Petty & The Heartbreakers and Bob Dylan. There were surprise appearances from Bob Geldof, Dave Stewart, Joni Mitchell, Don Henley, Bonnie Rait and Maria McKee who joined the other performers on stage for a rousing version of "I Shall Be Released".

THE FORUM, COPENHAGEN, DENMARK U2 played the first two shows of the European leg of the *Elevation* tour here on 6th and 7th July 2001.

FORUM DI ASSAGO, MILAN, ITALY Originally U2 were scheduled to have played here on 20th and 21st May 1992, but one of the equipment trucks broke down on the way causing the first show to be moved to the 22nd May. The second show marked the live debut of "So Cruel".

FOUNTAIN STREET CHURCH, GRAND RAPIDS, MICHIGAN, USA One of the most unusual venues U2 have played was at the Fountain Street Church in Grand Rapids on 5th December 1981.

FOXBORO STADIUM, BOSTON, MASSACHUSETTS, USA This 50,000 capacity stadium in Boston has seen U2 play here five times. Due to enormous demand, the band played three sell out shows here during the *Outside Broadcast* leg of the *Zoo TV* tour, on 20th, 22nd and 23rd August 1992. At the first show, Larry sang the old Thin Lizzy hit "Whiskey in The Jar", a song that U2 had not performed live before. At the second show, Larry sang another traditional Irish song – "The Wild Rover", again another first for U2. For the third night Larry sang, "Dirty Old Town", which he had first sung a few nights earlier at the show at the Saratoga Raceway.

The band played two more sell out shows here during the *Pop Mart* tour of North America on 1st and 2nd July 1997. These were the final two dates of the first leg of the North American section of the tour and were probably the most highly charged shows of this particular leg. When the band started to play "New Year's Day" the cheer that went up from the crowd was so loud that Bono pretended to faint. On the final night, the support act The Fun Lovin' Criminals came on stage and started teasing The Edge during the karaoke number, "Suspicious Minds". Then when the band emerged from the lemon they could be seen drinking champagne. Finally, as the band ended their set it began to rain. Bono started singing a solo version of the Beatles song "Rain" before the rest of the group came on stage to join in.

FOX THEATER, DETROIT, MICHIGAN, USA U2 played here just once on 8th December 1984 to a sell out crowd of 5,000. Due to the size and enthusiasm of the crowd there were some problems in front of the stage, which led to the band stopping in the middle of "Sunday Bloody Sunday" to calm things down.

FRADLEY, KENNEDY He was the trumpet player with Kid Creole's backing band, The Coconuts, who played trumpet on some of the tracks on *War*.

FRANKLIN, KIRK Bono joined this singer on his version of "Lean On Me" which reached number 79 in the US charts in 1998.

See also: Lean On Me

"FREEDOM FOR MY PEOPLE" (*RATTLE & HUM* ALBUM TRACK) (0.38) The third track on side two of the first album in the double *Rattle & Hum* album set. This snippet of a track was composed by Sterling Magee, Bobby Robinson and Macie Mabins and was performed by Sterling Magee (Guitar/Percussion) and Adam Gussow (harmonica). In the film we are shown the members of U2 watching these two musicians perform the song on 125th Street, Harlem, before they go into a nearby church to try out "I Still Haven't Found What I'm Looking For".

FREE TIBET CAMPAIGN The campaign that the "Tibetan Freedom Concert" supported which U2 appeared at in 1997 in New York. It was organised by Adam Yauch of The Beastie Boys.

Website: www.tibet.org

"FREE YOUR MIND AWARD" An annual award donated by MTV to an individual or organisation that has worked to help mankind through its actions. In November 1994 Amnesty International was given this award, which Bono accepted on their behalf saying, "Free your mind and your ass will follow!" In 1999 Bono himself was given the award in recognition of his work on behalf of Jubilee 2000 and NetAid.

See also: MTV

FRIEDLANDER, LIZ The director of the second promo video for "Walk On", shot in London in 2000.

FRIAR'S, AYLESBURY, ENGLAND U2 played a one-off gig here on 6th June in the summer of 1981.

FRIDAY, GAVIN (real name Fionan Hanvey) Gavin lived not far from Bono's Cedarwood Road home and was well-known in the area as someone who dressed in a camp style after his idols Marc Bolan and David Bowie. He was known locally as "yer man with the handbag". Gavin first became friendly with Bono, who lived near him in Ballymun, and was then a member of The Lypton Village. His name came via

Long-time U2 collaborator, Gavin Friday.
Photo: Mary Scanlon

two routes: Gavin was chosen as it sounded more transatlantic than Irish, and Friday came from the Robinson Crusoe character "Man Friday", as he was good at organising things and other people.

When the early U2 started gigging under the name The Hype, Gavin along with Village members Guggi and Pod formed The Virgin Prunes, with Edge's brother Dick Evans providing the music. The Prunes weren't so much a musical group as more "performance art". Gavin and Guggi were the frontmen on stage. Gavin liked to perform his song "Art Fuck 2" – a song that attacked Irish stereotypes of masculinity and other pillars of the Irish way of life.

As The Hype/U2 became more well known, The Virgin Prunes would support U2 at their gigs, even making it to England in 1980 at the Acklam Hall in London. Although The Virgin Prunes disbanded in 1986, Gavin has continued to record and perform. He has released three albums - *Each Man Kills The Thing He Loves* (1989) *Adam and Eve* (1992) and *Shag Tobacco* (1995), which he has promoted in both Europe and America. Gavin has kept in close contact with Bono over the years and can be seen briefly in the film *Rattle & Hum* walking down the street in Harlem next to Bono.

In 1993 Gavin was U2's stage advisor for the *Zooropa* tour. He collaborated with Bono (and his pianist Maurice Seezer) on the *In The Name Of The Father* film soundtrack in 1993 and on the *Moulin Rouge* soundtrack song "Children of The Revolution" in 2001. For the 1997 *Pop Mart* tour Gavin was "Consultant Popmartician", whilst on the latest *Elevation* tour he has the role of "Flight Consultant".

Website: www.gavinfriday.com

See also: Lypton Village / Virgin Prunes

FROCK 'N' ROLL FASHION SHOW/CONCERT The charity fashion show and benefit concert in aid of the Nelson Mandela Children's Fund, organised by Naomi Campbell. It took place at the Paulo Saint Jordi in Barcelona, Spain on 30th June 2001. The show included several top fashion models including Kate Moss and Elle McPherson. Bono was one of the musical performers along with Macy Gray and Wyclef Jean. He performed a solo acoustic version of the Bob Dylan song "I Shall Be Released" as well as "One" and "Sunday Bloody Sunday" with the Wyclef Jean Band. At the end he sang "Redemption Song" with Wyclef Jean.

"FUNNY FACE" This is the eleventh track on *the Million Dollar Hotel* soundtrack album and is performed by the MDH Band.

FUTURAMA FESTIVAL, LEEDS – See: Queen's Hall Leeds

G

GABRIEL, PETER A founder member of Genesis, now a renowned solo artist in his own right. He has also benefitted from the production skills of U2 collaborators Steve Lillywhite (*Peter Gabriel*, 1980) and Daniel Lanois (*So*, 1986). Gabriel first crossed paths with U2 when he took part in the *Sun City* project alongside Bono in 1985. He toured with U2 on the 1986 *Conspiracy of Hope* tour of America. Like U2 he holds passionate beliefs about human rights, including anti-apartheid (as evidenced in his well-known song "Biko") and ecology (being a committed supporter of Greenpeace). He accompanied The Edge on a visit to Russia in 1989 to publicise Greenpeace. In the 1992 MTV awards ceremony both he and Annie Lennox presented U2 with their award for the Best Group video. His subsequent *Steam* tour of 1994 utilised some of the stage props that U2 had used on their *Zoo TV* tour.

GAIETY GREEN, DUBLIN - See Dandelion Car Park

GALAVAN, BARBARA Barbara was originally one of the main members of staff at Principle Management Dublin. She stepped down to help with the setting up of the Celtic Heartbeat label, which is co-owned by Paul McGuinness. She now runs U2's Mother Publishing and McGuinness-Whelan Music Publishing companies.

GALLAGHER, JULIAN He was one of the assistant producers on *All That You Can't Leave Behind*.

GALLAGHER, LIAM - See OASIS

GALLAGHER, NOEL - See OASIS

GALLAGHER, RORY The famous Irish rock-blues guitarist from Cork who was one of the first Irish pop/rock musicians to make it big in Britain, Europe and America. Although he started his musical life playing in various small time bands, he subsequently toured with the Fontana Showband. His interest in blues music led to him forming his own rock-blues group, Taste, in the late 1960s. After a triumphant appearance at the 1970 Isle of Wight festival Rory split the band in 1971 to go solo and tour with his own backing band.

His high calibre guitar playing led to large commercial success in the 1970s with best selling albums such as *Deuce* (1972), *Blueprint* (1973) and *Against the Grain* (1975). He continued to record and tour throughout the 1980s and into the 1990s, but died in 1995 after a liver transplant. Both Bono and Adam attended his funeral. U2 sound engineer Joe O'Herlihy used to be his sound engineer before he joined U2. The Edge and Adam were both inspired by Rory to "want to learn guitar and play in a band". In fact, The Edge saw Rory play at Macroom when he was 15, which he later admitted was a big inspiration.

Certainly the fact that Rory Gallagher was able to make it big outside his native Ireland was an inspiration for many Irish musicians. A special "Rory Gallagher Musician Award" was set up soon after his death to recognise the special talents of Irish musicians. The Edge was the first recipient of this award in March 1996, which was presented at the annual Hot Press/Heinekin awards. The following year in February 1997 Larry won the award.

GALLO, ARMANDO Photographer, biographer of rock band Genesis and co-director of the second "Even Better Than The Real Thing" promo video along with Kampah.

GARAGE, THE The name of a bar that used to be in the basement of the Clarence Hotel which U2 bought and refurbished in the 1990s.

GARDEN OF EDEN CLUB, TULLERMENY, IRELAND U2 played here on Sunday 5th February 1980, shortly before their breakthrough gig at the National Boxing Stadium in Dublin which led to them being signed by Island Records. This was an unusual gig for U2 in that they played as support act to the Tony Steven's Showband, which meant an audience indifferent to their music. The gig was reviewed by Paul Morley in the *NME* who commented, "the performance hardly captures the depth of U2". After the gig, Bono admitted that the band had blown the gig: "Tonight we could have shown what rock 'n' roll can do, but we failed."

See also: Paul Morley

GARDENS, BOSTON, MASSACHUSETTS, USA U2 have played three concerts at this well-known Boston venue. They played two concerts here during the *Joshua Tree* tour on 17th and 18th September 1987. On the first night the spotlights on the lighting rig failed, so the band continued to play with the house lights on whilst the problem was solved. U2 then played here again during the *Zoo TV* tour on 17th March 1992 – a show specially timed for St. Patrick's Day (Boston has a large Irish community). Before the show there was chaos in the roads outside the venue and the atmosphere inside caused Bono to refer to Boston as "a home away from home". Larry sang "Dirty Old Town" for the first time on the tour and The Edge sang "Van Dieman's Land".

GARDENS LOUISVILLE, KENTUCKY, USA U2 played at this 7,000 capacity arena on 13th March 1982 as support act to the J. Geils Band. Bono jumped into the audience during "I Will Follow" and as a result had his shirt ripped off him.

GAUMONT THEATRE, ISPWICH, ENGLAND U2 have only played in this East Anglian town on one occasion – on 15th March 1983 during the *War* tour of Europe.

GAYE, MARVIN The famous soul singer who was tragically killed by his own father in April 1984. He had tremendous success with Tamla Motown in the 1960s with such hits as "I Heard It Through The Grapevine" and "Abraham, Martin And John". After his death, Bono recorded Gaye's song "Inner City Blues" for the 1995 tribute album "Save The Children". Bono has also sung parts of Gaye's "Sexual Healing" on stage at several U2 concerts.

J. GEILS BAND One of America's biggest groups on the arena circuit in the early 1980s. They had formed in the Boston area of the USA in 1967 and had gained a solid reputation as a first class rock band in the 1970s. Their greatest success came in 1981 with the release of their *Freeze-Frame* album, which hit the number 1 spot in America, as did the single off the album, "Centrefold". U2 were given the support slot to them for fourteen dates during March 1982, playing to potentially hostile J. Geils Band fans in arenas of up to 15,000 capacity. The idea was to expose U2 to an even larger audience and hopefully sell more records. Also it would give them valuable experience in playing in larger arenas. U2 survived the tour without any major incidents and did gain some new fans on the way.

The lead singer of the J. Geils Band, Peter Wolf, met up with Bono some four years later when they were both involved with the recording of the "Artists United Against Apartheid" album and single in New York. It was Wolf who introduced Bono to The Rolling Stones who were in town recording their *Dirty Work* album. As a result of this session U2 looked into the blues musical heritage of America, which came out on the *Rattle & Hum* album.

GELDOF, BOB Fellow Irishman and Southside Dubliner, Bob Geldof found fame and fortune a few years earlier than U2 in his punk band The Boomtown Rats. Like DJ Dave Fanning he had been to Blackrock College. U2 were inspired to follow the path that the Rats had laid. Although U2 didn't actually play support to any Boomtown Rats gigs they did get to know Bob Geldof as their popularity grew.

In 1984 Geldof enlisted the help of Bono and Adam for the Band Aid single and Live Aid concert, playing on the same bill as the Rats. A year later in Dublin's RDS both U2 and The Boomtown Rats played at the Self Aid concert. As a tribute to Phil Lynott, who had died earlier that year, they played a set with Bob Geldof helping out on vocals backed by the remaining members of Thin Lizzie.

See also: The Boomtown Rats

GELEEN HOLLAND (8th June 1981) **See:** The Pink Pop Festival

GELREDOME, ARNHEM, HOLLAND U2 played at this revolutionary soccer stadium with a movable roof and pitch as part of the European leg of the *Elevation* tour on 31st July, 1st and 3rd of August 2001. Around 30,000 fans attended each night. At the first show, Bono mentioned his father Bob Hewson, who was ill in a Dublin hospital with cancer. He dedicated the song, "Kite" to him. Bono also sang "When I Get Home" by the Dutch artist Herman Brood, who had recently committed suicide. At the second show, he got the crowd to sing "Happy Birthday" to a girl called Anna. Then at the final show Bono brought several photographers onto the stage to shoot photos of the band during "Until The End of The World".

GENERATION 80 A Belgian TV programme on which U2 performed "I Fall Down" and "Gloria". It was broadcast live on 25th October 1981 by the TV station RTBF 1.

GEORGIA DOME, ATLANTA, GEORGIA, USA U2 played to a capacity crowd of over 50,000 here on 25th September 1992 on the *Outside Broadcast* leg of the *Zoo TV* tour. The stadium had only been open for a month when U2 became the first rock band to play there. The band then played here during the autumn leg of the *Pop Mart* tour on 26th November 1997. This show was memorable for the fact that "40" was played for the first time since the *Lovetown* tour of 1988-9.

GET SET FOR SUMMER A British TV Show on which U2 appeared in May 1982. They performed three songs: "Rejoice", "Gloria" and "A Celebration".

GIANT'S STADIUM, EAST RUTHERFORD, NEW JERSEY, USA This 50,000 capacity baseball/football stadium first saw U2 play here during the *Conspiracy of Hope* tour on 15th June 1986. It was the final concert of the tour and was broadcast live on MTV. The climax of the show was the appearance on stage of many prisoners of conscience who had been freed by the work of Amnesty International.

U2 then played here on 14th September 1987 during the *Joshua Tree* tour. Finally, they played two shows here on 12th and 13th August 1992. These two shows were planned to be the opening shows of the *Outside Broadcast* leg of the 1992 *Zoo TV* tour of America but an extra show at Hershey Park Stadium was fitted in on 7th August. The 12th August show sold out in a record 23 minutes. It was memorable for the fact that Lou Red appeared on stage to sing "Satellite of Love" with Bono. U2 then returned here for three shows during the opening leg of the *Pop Mart* tour on 31st May, 1st and 3rd June 1997. The first two shows were sold out but the third show was not.

Bono also performed here on the 9th October 1999 at Net Aid along with such artists as Wyclef Jean, Sting and Jimmy Page.

GIBSON, MEL The Australian actor who has appeared in such films as *Braveheart* and *Lethal Weapon*. His film company, Icon Productions, were the sponsors who put up the money for *The Million Dollar Hotel* in which he starred as Skinner, an FBI agent. His picture appears in the CD booklet for the film soundtrack album.

See also: Million Dollar Hotel

GIBSON, WILLIAM A writer of Science fiction novels. His most well-known novel is *Neuromancer* (1984) which sees the future in terms of a complete breakdown in law and order with computer networks (cyberspace) calling the shots. In an interview in 1993 Bono said that a lot of the *Zooropa* album was influenced by reading Gibson's novels.

GINGERBREAD HOUSE, THE The nickname given to the gatehouse of the Balgriffin Cemetery situated near Dublin Airport where U2 would rehearse and practice their material during 1979.

GINSBERG, ALLEN The beat poet who came to public attention with the publication of his poem "Howl". Along with Jack Kerouac, Ginsberg was one of the leading lights of the beat movement. He was hugely influential on the whole counter-culture scene of the sixties that culminated in the "summer of love" in San Francisco in 1967. Ginsberg was no stranger to the world of pop, having appeared in Bob Dylan's promotional film for "Subterranean Homesick Blues" and appearing on The Clash's triple LP *Sandanista*.

Ginsberg is shown in the documentary *A Year In Pop* reading the lyrics of "Miami" as U2 perform the song in the background. In May 1997 he appeared in the promo video of "The Last Night On Earth", filmed in Kansas City, along with his old friend, William Burroughs. In it he is pictured pushing a shopping trolley containing a spotlight.

See also: "The Last Night On Earth" promo video

"GIVE ME BACK MY JOB" A song written by the Alarm's Dave Sharp which was covered by Bono with Johnny Cash, Tom Petty and Willie Nelson for the album *Common Sense*, recorded to raise funds for the World Foundation for Children. Bob Johnson was the producer. It was also on the Carl Perkins album *Go Cat Go* released in 1996.

"GLAD TO SEE YOU GO" A song by the Ramones that the early U2 used to play as an encore.

See also: The Ramones

GLASNEVIN NATIONAL PRIMARY SCHOOL, DUBLIN The primary school in Dublin that Bono attended from the age of five until eleven. It was Bono's first school.

Gasnevin National Primary School, Dublin.
Photo: Mark Chatterton

GLASTONBURY FESTIVAL, SOMERSET, ENGLAND Although U2 have been rumoured to be playing Britain's longest running annual rock music festival on more than one occasion, they have never done so. However, in 1989 Adam did appear on stage with the Irish band Hothouse Flowers, playing bass on "Feet on the Ground".

GLEN HELEN REGIONAL PARK, DEVORE, CALIFORNIA, USA See: The US Festival

THE GLOBE ARENA, STOCKHOLM, SWEDEN U2 played two shows here on 10th and 11th June 1992 during the *Zoo TV* tour of Europe. For the second show the winner of an MTV contest, John Harris, had the show beamed live into his front room of his house in Nottinghamshire, England. Bono spoke to him after "The Fly" and after "Even Better Than The Real Thing".

When the MTV European Music Awards took place here on 16th November 2000, U2 performed "Beautiful Day". U2 then returned here to play two shows during the European leg of the *Elevation* tour on 9th and 10th July 2001. At the second show a rare live version of "out Of Control" was played.

See also: MTV / Abba

GLOBO STUDIOS, RIO DE JANIERO, BRAZIL U2 took part in a special broadcast here for Brazilian TV as part of their promotional tour for *All That You Can't Leave Behind*. They performed "Beautiful Day", "Stuck In A Moment You Can't Get Out Of",

"Elevation" and "Ground Beneath Her Feet" for a small audience.

"GLORIA" (*OCTOBER* ALBUM TRACK) (4.11) The first track on the first side of the *October* album. It starts off with some grandiose drumming from Larry and, after Bono shouts "2,3,4!", goes off at a blistering pace. As Bono's briefcase with lyrics for this album had been stolen whilst on tour in America, Bono came into the recording session at Windmill Lane studios with very few prepared words, so he was forced to improvise. The theme was influenced by Paul McGuinness playing some records of Gregorian chants, hence the Latin lyrics. It was also the first time that The Edge had used slide guitar on a U2 track.

"GLORIA" (SINGLE) (WIP 6733) The single taken from the *October* album track was released in October 1981. It was U2's second chart entry in the UK, albeit at the lowly position of 55. It remained in the chart for 4 weeks. The B-Side was a live version of "I Will Follow" recorded at the Paradise Theatre in Boston on 6th March 1981.

"GLORIA" (*I WILL FOLLOW* SINGLE B-SIDE) The album track of "Gloria" was also released on the B-side of the single "I Will Follow" (104-525), released only in Holland. The A-side had been recorded live at 'T Hattem in Holland on 14th May 1982.

"GLORIA" (LIVE) (*UNDER A BLOOD RED SKY* ALBUM TRACK) (4.44) This live recording of "Gloria" opens side one of the *Under A Blood Red Sky* mini-album, released in November 1983. It was recorded at the Red Rocks show on 5th June 1983. For the majority of U2 shows in 1982 and 1983, "Gloria" was the opener, though at Red Rocks it was moved to the end of the set.

"GLORIA" LIVE (*UNDER A BLOOD RED SKY* VIDEO) The video film of "Gloria" is the same version that made it onto the *Under A Blood Red Sky* mini LP. It is the eighth song on the video, though in the actual show it was the fifteenth song.

"GLORIA" (PROMOTIONAL VIDEO) One of U2's earliest promotional videos, filmed on a barge in the docks of Dublin in October 1981. It was directed by Meiert Avis who went on to direct several more U2 videos.

"GLORIA" (ALTERNATIVE SONG) The original song "Gloria" was originally written and performed by the Northern Irish group Them, which included vocalist Van Morrison. It was the B-side of their first UK top ten hit "Baby Please Don't Go" in January 1965. Since then it has become a live favourite for many bands including U2, who have often performed the song live either in whole or in part. There is a version on the *Rattle & Hum* video filmed at their concert at the McNichols Arena in Denver on 8th November 1987.

GM PLACE, VANCOUVER, CANADA U2 played a sell out show at this arena on 13th April during the *Elevation* tour of North America (first leg). At the end Bono thanked Greenpeace for their work in saving the Great Bear Rainforest, the natural habitat of the bear population of British Columbia.

See also: Greenpeace

"GOD" A John Lennon song that appeared on his *John Lennon/Plastic Ono Band* album. It was basically a list of things that he didn't believe in any more including God, Jesus and The Beatles. He concludes that he just believes in himself and Yoko. It was written by Lennon as a reaction to fellow Beatle George Harrison's belief in religion. The words influenced Bono to write "God Part II" as a continuation of this theme.

"GOD PART II" (*RATTLE & HUM* ALBUM TRACK) (3.15) The first track on side four of the *Rattle & Hum* album. It was recorded at Ocean Way studios in Los Angeles by David Tickle and produced by Jimmy Iovine. It was written as a reaction to the John Lennon song, "God". Bono, like Lennon, lists a plethora of things that have affected him, including the writer Albert Goldman, who wrote a controversial biography of John Lennon. In the end Bono concludes that love is the only answer. Musically it was the most aggressive track on the *Rattle & Hum* album with a powerful rhythm provided by Adam and Larry. Yoko Ono is reported to have told Bono that he did "a nice cover version" of John's song! The track was first performed live at the Perth Entertainment Centre, Australia on 21st September 1989.

"GOD PART II" (THE HARD METAL DANCE MIX) ("WHEN LOVE COMES TO TOWN" SINGLE B-SIDE) (4.46) "We are still determined to use the weapon of love" is how this remix of God Part II starts off. These words of Martin Luther King were included in this remix by Louil Silas Junior. After Bono sings the second verse of this song through what sounds like a megaphone, this version sticks pretty much to the original album version.

"GOD PART III" The title of a song by the Gospel singer Larry Norman, who had originally written a song called "God Part II" as an alternative to John Lennon's "God" When he found out that U2 had written and published "God Part II" he changed his song title to "God Part III". In his version he concludes each verse with the lines, "I believe in God".

The Edge and Bono, co-writers of "Golden Eye", the theme for the Bond film of the same name.
Photo: Kay Bauersfeld

GODLEY, KEVIN The former member of the British rock group 10cc has directed several videos for U2. The first was "Even Better Than The Real Thing" in February 1992 which won awards for Best Group Video and Best Special Effects Video at the 1992 MTV Video awards. In June 1993 he flew over to Berlin to direct the "Numb" promo video. His most difficult video shoot was for "I've Got You Under My Skin" featuring Bono and Frank Sinatra in the autumn of 1993, where Sinatra walked away from the shoot with only a few minutes of footage in the can.

In 1996 Godley directed the video for Adam and Larry's "Theme From Mission: Impossible". This was followed a year later by another U2 promo video for "Sweetest Thing" shot in a Dublin street. Finally, Kevin directed the promo video for "Stuck In A Moment You Can't Get Out Of".

See also: Promo videos for: "Even Better Than The Real Thing", "Numb", "I've Got You Under My Skin", "Theme From Mission: Impossible", "Sweetest Thing" and "Stuck In A Moment You Can't Get Out Of".

"GOLDEN EYE" The theme song from the James Bond film of the same name, written by Bono and The Edge. It was performed by Tina Turner.

GOLDMAN, ALBERT The infamous muck-raking biographer of Elvis Presley and John Lennon who wrote many pernicious things about his subjects. In return, Bono hit back at him in "God Part II".

"GONE" (*POP* ALBUM TRACK) (4.26) The seventh track on the *Pop* album. It is dominated by the feedback of The Edge's guitar juxtaposed with some low-key piano. Lyrically the song is about leaving home and moving away. In the *Pop Mart* tour programme Bono revealed that "Gone" is "a goodbye song of some kind. I feel like walking away from being in a band sometimes. For some people it might be like walking away from a relationship. Sometimes you feel like walking away from life itself." "Gone" was first performed live at The Sam Boyd Stadium, Las Vegas, USA on 25th April 1997, the first night of the *Pop Mart* tour.

"GONE" (LIVE) (*HASTA LA VISTA BABY!* ALBUM TRACK) The only official live recording of "Gone" can found on the free CD given out to *Propaganda* readers in summer 2000.

"GONE" (LIVE) (*U2: POP MART LIVE FROM MEXICO CITY* VIDEO) The fourth track on the video *U2: Pop Mart Live From Mexico City*, filmed at the Foro Sol Autodromo in Mexico City on 3rd December 1997.

GOOD EARTH STUDIOS The name given to the mobile recording studio manned by Kevin Killen that recorded U2 shows at Birmingham, Manchester, Wembley Arena and Brussels in November 1994. Two songs recorded at these shows were eventually released: "A Sort Of Homecoming" and "Bad" both on the *Wide Awake In America* EP.

"A GOOD MAN" Bono provided backing vocals to this track off the *Cookies Fortune* soundtrack album.

"GRACE" (*ALL THAT YOU CAN'T LEAVE BEHIND* ALBUM TRACK) (5.31) The eleventh track on the *All That You Can't Leave Behind* album. It is a very laid back song with Bono exploring the idea of Grace both as a person and as a Christian concept. To date it has not been performed live.

GRACELAND The home of Elvis Presley in Memphis, Tennessee, USA. The four members of U2 visited Graceland in Memphis while they were in the area playing a gig at the Charles M. Murphy Athletic Center in Murfreesboro on 28th November 1987. Footage of the band visiting Graceland was used in the film of *Rattle & Hum*. Larry was seen being pictured on one of Elvis's motorbikes and looking at his grave. Later on in the day the band visited Sun Studios in Memphis where Elvis recorded many of his early records.
See also: Elvis Presley / Sun Studios

GRAHAM, BILL (PROMOTER) The legendary American entrepreneur who first came to prominence as the promoter of concerts at San Francisco's Fillmore West venue. Such were the success of his concerts that soon there was a Fillmore East in New York. In 1985 Bob Geldof managed to get him to help set up the American side of Live Aid in Philadelphia. The next year he was responsible for arranging the 1986 *Conspiracy of Hope* tour of America on which U2 took part. Bono personally thanked him for his efforts whilst on stage at the Forum in Los Angeles in June 1986. A year later in November 1987 Graham helped U2 set up their free "Save The Yuppies" concert in the financial district of San Francisco on 11th November 1997 at a day's notice. Bill Graham died in 1994.
See also: Save The Yuppies Concert

GRAHAM, BILL (WRITER) The Irish rock journalist was an old friend of U2 manager, Paul McGuinness. Like him, he had attended Trinity College, Dublin and was writing for the Dublin magazine *Scene* when McGuinness took him on the road with the group he was then managing – Spud. Graham had first been contacted by Adam as a possible ally in U2's desire to get to the top. By 1978 he was writing for the new Dublin rock journal *Hot Press*, and after a series of phone calls from Adam to his home, agreed to meet the band in April 1978. Graham was immediately impressed with their honesty and desire to find out more about the music business. In the 28th April edition of *Hot Press* Bill Graham wrote the first ever piece on U2 entitled "Yep! It's U2". It described how they had won the Harp Lager talent contest in Limerick a month earlier and how they were still at school. Graham also suggested to his friend Paul McGuinness that U2 might be the baby band that he was looking for and eventually persuaded him to go along to see them.

Bill continued to write about U2 in *Hot Press* at regular intervals over the years, seeing at first hand their gradual rise to greatness. In 1989 he brought out a book on U2's early years entitled *Another Time, Another Place*. In 1995 his guide to the music of U2 was published. Sadly, he died after a heart attack on 11th May 1996. At his funeral in Howth on 15th May, Bono sang the Leonard Cohen song "Tower of Song" and helped carry his coffin. Gavin Friday and Maire Ni Brennan also sang at the funeral.
See also: *Hot Press*

GRAHAM, NICKY The A&R man for CBS Records in London who came over to Dublin in 1979, on the recommendation of CBS Ireland's Jackie Hayden, to watch the early U2 at a couple of gigs. As a result of his visit he arranged for record producer Chas De Whalley to make a demo with the band, which evolved into U2's first Irish record, "U2-3".

GRAMMY AWARDS U2 have won several Grammy awards over the years, the first being for *The Joshua Tree* album which was voted "Album of the Year" for 1987 in the 1988 awards. The group also won the award for the "Best Rock Performance" for *The Joshua Tree*. Other successes have included Grammy awards for "Desire", *Achtung Baby*, *Zooropa* and "Beautiful Day" amongst others.

The most controversial award ceremony as far as U2 were concerned took place in 1994 when the band received an award for *Zooropa* as the "Best Alternative Music Album". Bono made the acceptance speech saying that they would "continue to abuse our position and fuck up the mainstream!" At the 2001 award ceremony at the Staples centre in Los Angeles, U2 played live for the first time here, performing "Beautiful Day" which had won the "Song of The Year" award. They also won the "Record of the Year" for *All That You Can't Leave Behind* and the Best Performance by a Rock Group or Duet award.
See appendix: for list of awards.

GRAND THEATRE, SWANSEA, WALES Bono made a rare public appearance here on 1st October 1995 in his role as a patron of the UK "Year of Literature and Writing 1995". He was interviewed by journalist

Robin Denselow and answered questions from members of the audience.

See also: Robin Denselow

GRAPEVINE ARTS CENTRE, DUBLIN, IRELAND The venue for a joint exhibition in June 1985 of original paintings from the "Unforgettable Fire" and of exhibits entitled "Martin Luther King - Peacemaker".

See also: Unforgettable Fire exhibition / Martin Luther King

GRAY, HOWARD The artist who remixed two versions of "Mysterious Ways" with his brother Trevor. They were the "Solar Plexus Club Mix" and the "Solar Plexus Extended Club Mix".

GRAY, TREVOR See: above

GREEDY BASTARDS (AKA THE GREEDIES) A group formed by Thin Lizzy frontman, Phil Lynott that included ex-Sex Pistols Steve Jones and Paul Cook. They played a concert at the Stardust Club in Dublin in December 1978 with U2 as support band. The story goes that Steve Jones' guitar was not working properly, so he asked The Edge if he could borrow his precious Gibson Explorer. The Edge nervously agreed, so he could say that his guitar had been played by a Sex Pistol.

See also: Phil Lynott

GREENBELT FESTIVAL, ODEL, BEDFORDSHIRE, ENGLAND This was a Christian Arts and Music festival that had started in 1975 as an alternative festival for Christians to celebrate their music and culture. By 1981 it had become an annual event with upwards of 20,000 people attending. Although U2 were not announced in the programme as appearing at Greenbelt that year, they nevertheless made a surprise appearance on 24th August 1981, the day after recording a radio session for the BBC in London. It was here that the band first met their lighting designer, Willie Williams, who was one of the DJs at the festival. Bono was so impressed with the whole festival set up that he came back the following year and helped out as a steward.

See also: Willie Williams

GREENPOINT STADIUM, CAPE TOWN, SOUTH AFRICA U2's first appearance not just in South Africa but in the whole of the African continent took place here on 16th March 1998 during the *Pop Mart* tour. In fact it was one of just two shows that U2 have played in the continent of Africa and was the penultimate one of the whole tour. The show was attended by Garvin and Gwenda Evans, The Edge's parents. Phil Joanou who had directed the *Rattle & Hum* film was there filming another movie called *Entropy*, about a director making a film of U2 while his personal life collapses all round him. "Staring at the Sun" was dedicated to Kadar Asmal, the South African Minister of Water Affairs, who had got to know Paul McGuinness and U2 when he was in exile in Dublin. It was also Adam's 38th birthday and so naturally everyone sang "Happy Birthday" to him.

See also: *Entropy* / Phil Joanou

GREENPEACE The environmental pressure group that U2 has supported since the late 1980s. It was founded in 1971 as an international organisation dedicated to the protection of the world's natural environment. It began when a group of concerned individuals set sail for Amchitka Island off Alaska to protest against United States nuclear weapons testing. As a result of this protest the test site was subsequently closed and Amchitka became a wildlife sanctuary. From this beginning Greenpeace has steadfastly maintained three fundamental principles from which it has not strayed: non-violence, no government or corporate funding, and no endorsement of any political party.

Today Greenpeace has over five million members worldwide in 150 countries, dedicated to the protection of our natural environment. Among its many and varied campaigns Greenpeace is concerned with such issues as nuclear and toxic pollution; the deforestation of rainforests and temperate forests; the testing and proliferation of nuclear weapons; and the destruction of marine resources through indiscriminate fishing methods.

U2 first began to publicise the work of Greenpeace in Issue 11 of their fan club magazine *Propaganda*, when it carried a report on The Edge visiting Russia along with other rock musicians to publicise the release of the Greenpeace album *Rainbow Warriors*. The album was conceived as a way of raising awareness of environmental issues in the former Soviet Union, with all proceeds from its sale helping the work of Greenpeace. The album contained songs donated by various rock artists including U2 who donated the track "Pride"(live) to the album.

U2 have continued to donate their songs to Greenpeace albums including "I Still Haven't Found What I'm Looking For" to the *Earthwise* album and "Until The End of The World"(live) to the *Alternative NRG* album in 1994. In 1992 U2 supported Greenpeace's "Stop Sellafield" protest by agreeing to play a free concert outside the gates of the nuclear power station in Cumbria, northern England in June 1992. Unfortunately a high court injunction prevented this and a proposed march from happening. Instead U2 played the concert at Manchester's G-Mex Centre, the nearest available large scale venue and donated the proceeds from the concert to the campaign. After the concert had finished they travelled to Cumbria and sailed to Sellafield arriving at dawn on the Saturday morning accompanied by the world's press. Landing below the high water mark (so as not to break the terms of the injunction), the four members of U2 posed for photographs dressed in special suits next to barrels of 'nuclear waste'. In this way the message of protest still received plenty of publicity.

U2 continue to promote the activities of Greenpeace through their magazine *Propaganda*, through their concerts where there is always a Greenpeace stand and in their tour programmes.

Website: www.greenpeace.org

See also: Stop Sellafield

GRIFFITH, NANCI Critically acclaimed singer/ songwriter from Austin, Texas who became associated with the new country movement that included Dwight Yoakem and Lyle Lovett. Her *Lone Star State Of Mind* and *Little Love Affair* saw Griffith become popular in Britain and particularly Ireland, where she enjoyed a number of hit albums.

Griffith spent a lot of time in Ireland and wrote a number of songs about the country. She used U2's rhythm section for four songs on her *Flyer* album, including her song "On Grafton Street".

"THE GROUND BENEATH HER FEET" (*ALL THAT YOU CAN'T LEAVE BEHIND* ALBUM TRACK) (3.43) The final track on the European and Australian versions of the album *All That you Can't Leave Behind*. This was a special bonus track, which appeared on European and Australian releases only. The lyrics were written by Salman Rushdie and come from his book of the same title. This is the first time that U2 have used the words of another writer with their music. The track was originally included on the soundtrack of *The Million Dollar Hotel*. The song was first performed live by U2 at the Man Ray club in Paris France on 19th October 2000. Bono and Edge previously performed the track on several TV talk shows in 1999 such as *TFI Friday* on Channel 4.

"THE GROUND BENEATH HER FEET" (*MILLION DOLLAR HOTEL* ALBUM SOUNDTRACK) (3.43) The opening track on the soundtrack album of *the Million Dollar Hotel*, credited as being performed by U2 with guest Daniel Lanois on pedal steel.

"THE GROUND BENEATH HER FEET" (*THE SUNDAY TIMES* FREE CD) This version of "The Ground Beneath her Feet" was the same version as the opening track on the soundtrack album of *the Million Dollar Hotel*. It was on the CD given away free with *The Sunday Times* newspaper in June 2001.

"THE GROUND BENEATH HER FEET" (PROMO VIDEO) This was directed by Wim Wenders in Cologne, Germany in April 2000.

GUGGI (DEREK ROWAN) One of the founder members of The Virgin Prunes sharing vocals with Gavin

Friday. He was one of eleven children and lived near the childhood home of Paul Hewson in Cedarwood Road. The two of them would often play together as well as spending time drawing and painting. Their friendship continued through school and then they formed the Lypton Village. He was given the name Guggi due to the way his lower lip stuck out like a baby's. He in turn christened Paul Hewson with the name Bono Vox after a hearing aid shop in Dublin. Guggi's brother Trevor (Strongman) was also a member of the Virgin Prunes. For a few weeks in 1978 when Larry had got into the habit of being late for rehearsals, Guggi would be his stand in. He also became a member of the Shalom Christian group for a short time before being one of the first to leave.

Guggi stayed with the Prunes until 1984 when he left, having become fed up with the music industry. From an early age he showed a talent for painting and this is what he has concentrated on over the years. He has had his work exhibited on several occasions at galleries in both Europe and America.

Website: www.guggi.com

See also: Bonavox Hearing Aid Shop / The Virgin Prunes

GUND ARENA, CLEVELAND, OHIO, USA U2 played at this arena on the *Elevation* tour of North America on 3rd May 2001. Bono dedicated "Kite" to all the old fans who had seen the band play at the Agora in Cleveland twenty years ago.

GUSSON, ADAM He played harmonica on "Freedom For My People" as featured in the film *Rattle & Hum*. This track was also featured on the album of the film soundtrack.

GUTHRIE, WOODY The famous America folk singer who inspired the likes of Bob Dylan and Joan Baez. His song "Jesus Christ" was recorded by U2 at Sun Studios in Memphis in 1987 and used on the Woody Guthrie tribute album *A Vision Shared*, released in 1988. Bono and Edge also played on "This Land Is Your Land".

See also: Jesus Christ

Larry Mullen, Hammersmith Palais, 29/3/83
Photo: Kay Bauersfeld

HAGGY, TARYN A singer from Kid Creole's backing troupe, The Coconuts, who helped with the backing vocals on the tracks "Surrender" and "Red Light" on the *War* album.

HALF MOON CLUB, PUTNEY, LONDON, ENGLAND U2 played at this well-known South London club on three occasions in 1980: 8th June, 11th July and 5th October. The second date is a landmark in U2 history – the first time they managed to sell out a venue in the United Kingdom.

HALL, MS BOBBYE One of the musicians who played percussion on the single "When Love Comes To Town", recorded in Sun Studios, Memphis in November 1987.

"HALLELUJAH" The Leonard Cohen song that Bono sang on the Leonard Cohen tribute album *Tower of Song*, released in 1995. Several times on the 1997 *Pop Mart* tour, Bono sang this song as the final number of the set.

"HALLELUJAH (HERE SHE COMES)" ("DESIRE" SINGLE) (4.12) This track was on the B-side of the "Desire" single (ISG 100). Written by U2 and produced by Jimmy Iovine, it is notable for featuring Billy Preston on vocals and Hammond organ. Billy is best known as a session musician who played with Beatles ("Get Back") and The Rolling Stones amongst others. It was also a track on the compilation CD *The B-Sides*, which accompanied *The Best of 1980-1990*.

HALLENSTADION, ZURICH, SWITZERLAND U2 played this 10,000 capacity stadium in Switzerland on several occasions. The first time was on 8th February 1985 as part of the *Unforgettable Fire* tour. The set was plagued by Bono losing his voice during "Sunday Bloody Sunday". This meant there was a twenty-minute break while Bono rested his voice. When the band came back on stage, they resumed with "Sunday Bloody Sunday" – the only time it has been played twice in one set. The second time U2 played this venue was on 27th May 1992 as part of the European leg of *Zoo TV* tour. This time there were no problems, apart from a mickey-take by the show designer, Willie Williams. When Bono was zapping the TV screens to see what channels were on the *Zoo TV* station, there was an ad for 'U2's Greatest Hits',

which had been put together by U2 technicians. U2 played two more dates here on 23rd and 24th July during the *Elevation* tour of Europe. At the first show Bono invited a male fan on stage to play "People Get Ready" - a stunt that regularly took place on the *Joshua Tree* tour. At the second show, the band played "Who's Gonna ride Your Wild Horses" for the only time on the tour.

HAMLYN, MICHAEL The producer of the film *Rattle & Hum*. Michael's face is probably best known to U2 fans from the video of "Where The Streets Have No Name" where he is seen arguing with an L.A. cop and nearly getting arrested in the process. He began working as assistant film director in London during the 1970s. Since then he has worked on video productions for a wide variety of musicians including Bruce Springsteen, The Rolling Stones, INXS and Pete Townsend. He has produced several U2 videos including "Angel Of Harlem", "Bad", "With Or Without You" and, of course, "Where The Streets Have No Name".

HAMMERSMITH ODEON, LONDON, ENGLAND (Now renamed the Hammersmith Apollo) This famous London rock venue has for many years been a major rock music venue in London. Immortalised in the title of the Motorhead live album *No Sleep 'til Hammersmith*, it is one of London's biggest theatres with a capacity of approximately 4,000. U2 first played there early on in their career, when they landed the support slot for Talking Heads on 1st December 1980. U2 then returned as headlining artists on 14th March 1983 during the tour to promote the newly released *War* album. They came back just a week later on 21st March; this time they were joined by Steve Wickham, the violinist who played with the band on "Tomorrow" and "Sunday Bloody Sunday".

HAMMERSMITH PALAIS, LONDON, ENGLAND Just down the road from the Odeon is the Hammersmith Palais, a ballroom that was used for rock concerts in the 1970s and 1980s. U2 played at this venue on no less than five occasions between 1980 and 1983. The first time was as support to Talking Heads on 2nd December 1980. The second time they played here, 9th June 1981, the band were watched from the wings by Bruce Springsteen, who had delayed returning to America in order to watch U2 play live. When they next played here on 6th December 1982 the show was recorded for broadcast on the radio. The final visits here were on 22nd and 29th March during the *War* tour.

HANNETT, MARTIN The producer of U2's first single for Island Records – "11 O'clock Tick Tock", which was recorded at Windmill Lane studios, Dublin during Easter 1980. Martin was already well known as a producer of groups such as Joy Division and the Teardrop Explodes. U2 had specifically asked Martin to be their producer because they had admired his production work on Joy Division's *Unknown Pleasures* album. He was also pencilled in for recording U2's debut album, but pulled out on the death of Joy Division's Ian Curtis. Martin Hannett died suddenly in April 1991 at his home in Manchester after undergoing treatment for a chest infection. "11 O'clock Tick Tock was included in a special tribute album *Martin* that came out after his death.

HANOVER QUAY STUDIOS, DUBLIN, IRELAND (AKA "HQ") These studios are situated near the original Windmill Lane studios in Dublin and have become one of the main studios which U2 use to do their recordings. A lot of *Pop* and most of *All That You Can't Leave Behind* was recorded here. Live webcasts of the recording sessions were also broadcast from these studios.

Hanover Quay Studios, Dublin.
Photo: Mark Chatterton

HANSA TON STUDIOS, BERLIN, GERMANY The studios where much of the *Achtung Baby* album was recorded during 1990 and 1991. Also known as the 'By The Wall' studio, the studios were situated in the former East Berlin and have been host to several well-known musicians, including Iggy Pop, Nick Cave, David Byrne and David Bowie (who had recorded his *Low* and *Heroes* albums there). Formerly a Nazi ballroom, the studios shut down soon after U2 had finished recording there. In an interview with MTV, Bono explained the reasons for choosing this particular studio: "It's a great rock 'n' roll room. It's one of those great old studios where the emphasis is on the sound and not the actual hardware and we were looking for a big room which would just be great to play in, and do the records like they used to – just sitting around in a circle playing the songs. It was an old SS ballroom which is kind of a bad vibe really, but it's kind of odd. It seems like the music has driven those demons out because there were no bad vibes there when we were there – only The Edge's smelly feet!"

Although a fair proportion of *Achtung Baby* was recorded there, the band decided that they weren't completely happy with the results, so they moved back to Dublin in the early months of 1991 to finish the album at Dog Town studios in Dalkey.

See also: Achtung Baby

"HAPPINESS IS A WARM GUN" (THE DANNY SABER MIX) (4.51) This is a cover of the Beatles song from their double white album and was the first time that a Beatles song was covered by U2 in a studio setting. The song was played several times as the karaoke number during the *Pop Mart* tour. This remix is the third track on the "Last Night On Earth" alternative single (CIDX 664/572 055-2). It was remixed by Danny Saber with "discipline and perversion" provided by John X.

"HAPPINESS IS A WARM GUN" (THE GUN MIX) (4.45) The fourth track on the "Last Night On Earth" CD single (CID 664/752 051-2).

HARBOUR YARD THESSALONIKI GREECE U2's one and only show in Greece took place on 26th September 1997 during the *Pop Mart* tour of Europe. The show very nearly didn't happen as the trucks bringing the stage equipment in were held up at the border due to a strike. In the end special dispensation was given to U2 so that show could go ahead.

"A HARD RAIN'S GONNA FALL" One of several Bob Dylan songs that U2 have performed live over the years. This song from Dylan's second album *The Freewheelin' Bob Dylan* deals with the subject of a nuclear holocaust, a theme reflected in several U2 songs. U2 first played the song live with their support group, The Alarm, at the Colorado State University, in Boulder, Colorado on 6th June 1983. It was an appropriate choice as the day before at the show at Red Rocks Amphitheatre it had rained virtually all day.

See also: Bob Dylan

HARDY, GARY The owner of Sun Studios in Memphis, Tennessee which was used by U2 on the night of 29th/30th November 1987 to record some songs which would eventually appear of the *Rattle & Hum* album. Gary's version of the events surrounding that session can be found in the book on the *Rattle & Hum* film by Willie Williams and Steve Turner.

See also: Sun Studios

HARING, KEITH The artist who painted the "Radiant Baby" logo on one of the Trabants used on the *Zoo TV* tour. His artwork was also used on the giant video screen for several sequences during the *Pop Mart* tour.

See also: Trabant

HARP LAGER/EVENING PRESS TALENT CONTEST, LIMERICK, IRELAND This was one of U2's earliest breaks. Larry had seen a newspaper advert for a talent contest being sponsored by Harp Lager and the *Evening Press* newspaper and persuaded the others to enter. The first prize was £500 plus a recording session for a demo tape. The concert was to take place on St Patrick's Day 1978 in Limerick in the West of Ireland. The band went to Limerick along with their supporters from the Village and found their opposition was made up mainly of show bands. Originally entered under the name of The Hype, the band had decided to make the change to U2 by the time they arrived in Limerick.

After coming through the preliminary heats before the judging panel (which included Jackie Hayden, the marketing manager for CBS Ireland), U2 had to compete in the finals that evening in front of an audience. Their three song set (one of which was sung in Gaelic) convinced the judges who awarded them first prize in preference to the more musically accomplished East Coast Angels. As a result of winning the contest, not only did U2 get the opportunity to record a demo tape, but it also led to them getting their first mention in *Hot Press*, courtesy of writer Bill Graham and most important of all, being introduced to their future manager, Paul McGuinness.

See also: Jackie Hayden / CBS Records

HARPO'S, DETROIT, MICHIGAN, USA U2's first visit to Detroit took place on 18th April 1981, where they nearly managed to sell out this 1,500 capacity club.

HARVARD UNIVERSITY, CAMBRIDGE, MASSACHU-SETTS, USA Bono gave a speech to the students at the Class Day here on June 6th 2001. The speech was broadcast live on the college radio Harvard Radio, WHRB 95.3 FM.

HASTA LA VISTA BABY! U2 LIVE FROM MEXICO CITY (CD) A special limited edition CD given out free to the readers of *Propaganda* magazine (Volume 2, issue 1) in July 2000. It contained fourteen tracks recorded live at U2's *Pop Mart* show at the Foro Sol Autodromo, Mexico City. Although other tracks from other gigs on the *Pop Mart* tour have made it onto U2 single releases, this is the only official live concert recording from a *Pop Mart* concert released on CD. Most of the show had already been made available on the video, *Pop Mart Live From Mexico City*.

Track List: 1) Pop Muzik, 2) Mofo, 3) I Will Follow, 4) Gone, 5) New Year's Day, 6) Staring At The Sun, 7) Bullet The Blue Sky, 8) Please, 9) Where The Streets Have No Name, 10) Lemon (Perfecto Mix), 11) Discotheque, 12) With Or Without You, 13) Hold Me, Thrill Me, Kiss Me, Kill Me, 14) One

See also: *Pop Mart Live from Mexico City* video

"HAVING A WONDERFUL TIME: WISH YOU WERE HER" This is a song off the 1984 T-Bone Burnett album, *Beyond The Trap Door* on which Bono sang. This was the first time Bono had sung on someone else's record.

See also: T-Bone Burnett

"HAWKMOON 269" (*RATTLE & HUM* ALBUM TRACK) (6.22) This song was recorded at A&M studios Los Angeles in the summer of 1988, along with "All I Want Is You". Bono's lyrics deal with all the things in life that won't function by themselves but need something else to stimulate them, such as a town needing a name or a blind man needing a cane. The words are said to have been influenced by American writer Sam Shepard. Bob Dylan plays Hammond Organ on this track. The 269 apparently comes from the number of mixes the song needed before it was good enough to be included on the finished album. Hawkmoon is a place in Rapid City, Dakota, USA.

HAYDEN, JACKIE The CBS marketing manager who gave U2 their first record deal. He first started working for Polydor Records in 1967 before moving on to CBS Ireland, where he became their Marketing Manager. In 1978 when U2 won the Harp Lager/*Evening Press* Talent Contest, Jackie Hayden was one of the judges. As a result of what he saw, Hayden gave the young U2 the opportunity to record a demo tape at the Keystone Studios in Dublin, which they entered in April 1978. Hayden produced the session which provided a rough set of songs, but CBS in London were not impressed. In spite of being rejected by CBS in London, Jackie still offered them a recording contract for Ireland which the band declined to take up. However they did keep in contact with Jackie Hayden who remembers them visiting his office from time to time with lists of questions about the music business for him to answer.

When Paul McGuinness became U2's manager, a new contract with CBS Ireland was negotiated and as Jackie Hayden was marketing manager of CBS Ireland he became personally involved with the release of U2's first single, "U2-3". He personally numbered all one thousand copies of the 12 inch version! Since his involvement with the early U2, Jackie Hayden moved on to write for and become general manager of *Hot Press* magazine. He has also been involved in writing several books including *My Boy - The Philip Lynott Story* with Philomena Lynott, *The Need To Know Guide To Careers In Music* and *The Winner in Me*, the story of Don Baker whom Bono once described as the best harmonica player in the world.

See also: Harp Lager/*Evening Press* Talent Contest / Keystone Studios / CBS Records / U2-3

HEALEY, JACK The executive director of Amnesty International, the human rights organisation that U2 had started to publicly support in the mid-1980s after they had given the proceeds from their December 1984 Radio City Music Hall show in New York to Amnesty's 'Stop Torture Week' campaign. Healey had the idea of having a massive publicity campaign for Amnesty International in 1986 in America, to coincide with its 25th anniversary. He approached U2 and Paul McGuinness in August 1985 and they promised two weeks of their time in 1986 for this campaign. The result was the 1986 *Conspiracy Of Hope* tour in June 1986, which saw not only U2, but also the likes of Bryan Adams, Joan Baez, Peter Gabriel, Lou Reed, Sting and the Neville Brothers take part in six shows across America.

See also: Amnesty International / Conspiracy of Hope tour.

"HEARTLAND" (*RATTLE & HUM* ALBUM TRACK) (5.02) This track was originally written in 1986 for *The Joshua Tree* sessions but did not make it onto that album, being given the push to make way for "Trip Through Your Wires". It had been recorded at Danesmoat Studios in Adam's house in 1986 and featured Brian Eno playing keyboards. The song is a picture of America as seen through Bono's eyes. The images reflect the America that U2 had witnessed over the previous few years whilst touring in that land. In the film of *Rattle & Hum* the song is shown with the band sitting by the side of the great Mississippi river. It is interesting to note that in the CD version of the album the lyrics to "Heartland" are printed on the first page of the insert booklet that accompanies the CD, as well as with the other song lyrics further on

in the book. It is the only song from *Rattle & Hum* never to have been played live.

"HELTER SKELTER" (*RATTLE & HUM* ALBUM TRACK) (3.07) This Beatles song originally appearing on the 'White Album'. The album opener for the double album of *Rattle & Hum*, was recorded live at the McNichols Arena, Denver, Colorado on 8th November 1987, and was the first song from the concert to feature in the film of *Rattle & Hum*, although it was actually performed midway through their set. Bono prefaces it with the famous words: "This is a song that Charles Manson stole from the Beatles. We're stealing it back!" This refers to the Sharon Tate murder case in America in the late 1960s where Charles Manson and his followers were reportedly influenced by the words of the song before carrying out their murderous assaults.

"HELP" One of several Beatles songs that U2 have played live over the years. It was first sung at the *Conspiracy Of Hope* Amnesty shows in America in 1986 and then at most of the *Joshua Tree* and *Lovetown* shows. Although never released on a U2 record, a live version of U2 performing the song at one of the *Conspiracy of Hope* shows was included on the John Lennon Tribute video, *Lennon - A Tribute*.

See also: The Beatles

HENDRIX, JIMI The legendary guitarist who died in 1970 is one of the few musicians to appear in their own right on a U2 album. His version of the US National Anthem, "The Star Spangled Banner" (taken from 1969's Woodstock Festival) is played for 43 seconds before The Edge takes over for a live version of "Bullet The Blue Sky" on the *Rattle & Hum* album. It is interesting to note that The Edge's style on this track is very reminiscent of Jimi Hendrix's playing – both using a Fender Stratocaster guitar. U2 have also played "All Along The Watchtower" at several shows – a Bob Dylan song that Jimi made popular after releasing it as a single in 1968.

HENRY, COLM One of the first photographers to photograph U2. He first shot them at their Dandelion Car park gigs in 1979 and then went on to photograph them several times over the years. Colm's pictures were used on the albums *Rattle & Hum* and the *Best of 1980-1990*. In 1996 he had an exhibition of his work on display at the Temple Bar Music Centre in Dublin. These included (apart from U2) Sting, Bob Marley, Phil Lynott and Bob Geldof.

HERBERT, DAVID He has worked with U2 as a production assistant on the *Pop Mart* and *Elevation* shows.

"HEROINE" (THEME FROM "CAPTIVE") The second track on the film soundtrack album of *Cap-*

tive, composed by The Edge and Sinead O'Connor who sings the vocal. Both The Edge and Larry Mullen played on this track. It was released as a single but failed to make the charts.

HERSHEY PARK STADIUM, HERSHEY, PENNSYLVA-NIA, USA U2 played the first night of the *Outside Broadcast* leg of the *Zoo TV* tour at this 25,000 capacity stadium in the small Pennsylvanian town of Hershey on 7th August 1992. This was an extra gig set up as a last minute addition. U2 were originally using this venue as a start-of-tour base, setting up camp here several days earlier in order to practise putting up such a complicated stage set as well as to try out new songs for the coming tour. U2 rehearsed various songs each evening, including the Beatles "She Loves You" and "Dear Prudence", the soon to be released "Slow Dancing", plus an acoustic version of "Acrobat", the only song off "Achtung Baby" never to be performed live. The word soon got out that U2 were in town, so many local and not-so-local U2 fans would gather each night to listen to the rehearsals. Daily reports even appeared in the local newspapers. Inevitably rumours were rife of a practice concert and on the 5th August tickets bearing the words 'Outside Rehearsal' went on sale at just $15 each for a concert on 7th August.

The concert itself differed from the following dates of the tour in that the set started with three old numbers – "Sunday Bloody Sunday", "New Year's Day" and "Pride", the former not having been played live for nearly five years. After these three songs, George Bush, the then US President, appeared on the giant TV screens introducing the show. The set then continued its usual course with "Zoo Station".

Outside Broadcast opening night set: Sunday Bloody Sunday, New Year's Day, Pride, Zoo Station, The Fly, Even Better Than The Real Thing, Mysterious Ways, One/Unchained Melody, Until The End Of The World, Who's Gonna Ride Your Wild Horses, Van Diemen's Land, Trying To Throw Your Arms Around The World, Angel Of Harlem, When Love Comes To Town, All I Want Is You, Bullet The Blue Sky, Running To Stand Still, Where The Streets Have No Name, Pride. Encores: Desire, Ultra Violet, With Or Without You, Love Is Blindness.

HESTON, CHARLTON The American actor who has appeared in many well-known films over the years including *The Ten Commandments* and *Ben Hur*. As President of the National Rifle Association, which is in favour of Americans having the right to carry guns, Heston has come in for criticism from those who are opposed to this freedom. During the *Elevation* tour of North America (first leg), footage of him talking about his views on firearms was used as an introduc-

tion to "Bullet The Blue Sky". Heston's comments were set against an anti-gun film segment that featured footage of war and gun violence, displayed on video screens behind the band while they performed this song. In the segment, Heston says: "There are no good guns. There are no bad guns. Any gun in the hands of a bad man is a bad thing. Any gun in the hands of a good person is no threat to anybody, except bad people."

HEWSON, ALI See: Alison Stewart

HEWSON, IRIS (NEE RANKIN) Bono's mother, the second of eight children, left school at sixteen and after a short spell at Premier Dairies, she worked as a book keeper at Kelmac Knitwear in Dublin. She first met her husband to be, Bobby Hewson, when he was nineteen at a dance at the Catholic Young Men's Society. They were married at St John the Baptist Church of Ireland in Drumcondra on 6th August 1950. Although it was a mixed marriage – Iris was a Protestant and Bobby was a Roman Catholic – the marriage was later blessed by a Catholic priest.

Two years after the wedding, their first son, Norman, was born. In 1960, their second child, Paul, was born. Soon after his birth, the family moved to 10 Cedarwood Road in north Dublin, which would be the Hewson home for the next twenty or so years. Sadly, Iris died as the result of a brain haemorrhage in September 1974 following her father's funeral. Several songs that Bono has written the lyrics for have references to his mother, notably "I Will Follow", "Tomorrow" and "Mofo".

HEWSON, PAUL See: Bono

HEWSON, NORMAN Bono's brother was born in 1952 in Dublin, when the Hewson family lived in Stillorgan to the south of Dublin. It wasn't until he was seven that his younger brother, Paul, was born, so naturally the age gap meant that the two brothers were not initially that close. By the time Bono was eighteen, Norman had married his girlfriend Geraldine and was living away from the family house in Cedarwood Road. After starting to train as an accountant, Norman then went into computing. Then for several years he ran a successful Italian restaurant in Dublin called "Tosca". This closed down in 2000, but instead next door he opened a new cafe called "Nude" on the site of the former Mr. Pussy's Cafe De Luxe.

HEWSON, ROBERT (BOBBY) Bono's father was born and bred in Dublin in the Oxmantown Road area of the city. When he left school aged fourteen, he followed his father's footsteps by working for the Post Office as a clerk. In his spare time, he would listen to the music of the day, be it Bing Crosby and Al Johnson, or the opera music of people such as Mario

Lanza and Tiro Gobbi. He was also a keen golfer and enjoyed painting as well as being a member of the Post Office drama group.

Keeping a close eye on his rock 'n' roll star son, Bobby Hewson has often been at U2 concerts around the world. For instance, when U2 headlined at Phoenix Park in Dublin in 1983, Bobby was persuaded by his son to come out on stage and dance with him. Then at a U2 concert at the Omni in Atlanta, Georgia, USA, Bono arranged to have the spotlight pick him out when he introduced him from the stage. The only problem was that Bobby stuck his middle finger up at Bono for doing this! Bobby even made a cameo appearance in the promotional video of "One" which was directed by Anton Corbijn. A tenor singer, he was able to meet Luciano Pavarotti when his son performed with him at his concert for the children of Bosnia in Modena, Italy in September 1995.

In August 2001, Bobby Hewson died after a long struggle against cancer in a Dublin hospital.

See also: Earl's Court / Slane Castle

TERRENCE HIGGINS TRUST One of the charities that U2 supported during the *Zoo TV* tour. It was named after Terrence Higgins who died of AIDS in 1983, when very little was known about the illness. The organisation aims to educate the public about HIV and AIDS and to give help and advice to those affected by the virus. **website:** www.tht.org.uk

See also: AIDS / AIDS Awareness

HIPPODROME DE VINCENNES, PARIS, FRANCE U2 played at this famous horse racing track in Paris on two occasions. The first, on 4th July 1987, was a 70,000 sell out – the highest attendance for a rock concert in France up to this point. As part of Island Records 25th anniversary celebrations several of the songs were broadcast live on British TV. The set was marred by crowd problems though, with fans being crushed and others fainting in the heat. This was made worse by a tear gas canister going off near the stage which caused "With or Without You" to be stopped while the smoke cleared. For the band's second visit, on 26th June 1993, the attendance was 75,000 despite the fact that U2 were initially going to play two nights with a limit of 40,000 on each night. Once again, there was a lot of pushing and shoving at the front with many people fainting in the hot conditions.

"HIRO'S THEME 1" This piece of music comes form the soundtrack album of *Captive*. It was composed and performed by The Edge and released in 1986.

"HIRO'S THEME" (Reprise) The final track on the soundtrack album of *Captive*. It was composed and performed by The Edge.

"HOLD ME, THRILL ME, KISS ME, KILL ME" (SINGLE) (4.47) This single was released on 5th June 1995 on Island/Atlantic in the UK, with some 7 inch copies coming in red vinyl (A7131). The song had originally been recorded at the *Zooropa* sessions and was about being a celebrity. After some changes it was used on the soundtrack of *Batman Forever* which was the first time a U2 song had been used for a film soundtrack. It reached number 2 in the UK singles charts and 16 in the US singles charts. Although Batman was not mentioned in the lyrics, Jesus was, which some said was blasphemous. The title incidentally was the same as the single by Muriel Smith that reached number 3 in 1953. Bono, The Edge and Nellee Hooper were the producers.

"HOLD ME, THRILL ME, KISS ME, KILL ME" (LIVE) *(HASTA LA VISTA BABY!* CD TRACK) The only official live version of the song to be released on CD was on the CD given out free to *Propaganda* readers in July 2000, called *Hasta La Vista Baby! U2 Live From Mexico City*. It was taken from the band's concert at the Foro Sol Autodromo in Mexico City on 3rd December 1997.

"HOLD ME, THRILL ME, KISS ME, KILL ME" (LIVE) (*U2: POP MART LIVE FROM MEXICO CITY* VIDEO) The twenty-first track on the video *U2: Pop Mart Live from Mexico City*.

"HOLD ME, THRILL ME, KISS ME, KILL ME" (PROMOTIONAL VIDEO) The promo video for "Hold Me, Thrill Me, Kiss Me, Kill Me was directed by Maurice Linnane and Kevin Godley. It was a completely different type of video for U2 with the band being portrayed as cartoon characters in a fast moving video. Bono changes from The Fly to Macphisto to Batman and back again. Elsewhere you see Bono coming out of Mr. Pussy's and then getting run over by Elvis! Scenes from the film were also included as well as some of the cuts that didn't make it onto the final film.

"HOLD ONTO YOUR DREAMS" A track off Jah Wobble's 1983 album *Snake Charmer* on which The Edge played guitar and provided "atmospherics".

HOLI The Japanese singer who features on the track "Ito Okashi", a track she co-wrote on the *Original Soundtracks 1* album. She also provided the voice on the track "One Minute Warning".

HOLIDAY, BILLIE The legendary American blues singer was the subject of the U2 song "Angel Of Harlem". Her picture is featured on the back cover of the record sleeve and on the record label.

"HOLY JOE" (GARAGE MIX) (*DISCOTHEQUE* SINGLE) (4.21) This song is based on the story of Holy Joe, a soldier in Vietnam – a Christian who stands up for his beliefs. His superior sends him on a dangerous mission where he gets killed, but as a result he too repents and turns to God. This mix of the song is the second track on the "Discotheque" single, featuring Des Broadberry on keyboards. Bono and The Edge wrote the lyrics.

"HOLY JOE" (GUILTY MIX) (*DISCOTHEQUE* SINGLE) (5.09) The third track on the "Discotheque" single. Marius De Vries plays keyboards.

"HOLY JOE" (LIVE) U2 performed the only live version of "Holy Joe" at the press conference at the K Mart store in Greenwich Village, New York City on 12th February 1997.

HOLZER, JENNY The artist whose use of maxims on large billboards helped to inspire their use on the lyrics of "The Fly". They were then used on the *Zoo TV* tour on all the various TV screens on the stage when "The Fly" was performed. Slogans like: "Watch More TV" and "Everything You Know Is Wrong" and single words like "Pussy" and "Whore" were flashed so quickly on the screen that you could almost miss them.

HOOPER, NELLEE Nellee had first been involved with U2 when he had co-produced with Bono and The Edge the "Hold Me, Thrill Me, Kiss Me. Kill Me" single. Then some of his photos appeared in the *Pop* album booklet. He also produced "Two Shots of Happy, One Shot of Sad" which was on the "If God Will Send His Angels" single.

HOOSIER DOME, INDIANAPOLIS, INDIANA, USA This concert on 1st November 1987 will go down in history as the one in which U2's alter-egos, The Dalton Brothers, first came to light. In between support acts from The BoDeans and Los Lobos, U2 came on stage in disguise to play a set under the name of The Dalton Brothers. They played two numbers, "Lucille" and "The Lost Highway", before leaving the stage, having fooled the majority of the audience. Later on in the normal U2 set, Bono introduced "Lucille" again and this time most of the audience laughed as they realised they had been fooled.
See also: The Dalton Brothers.

THE HOPE & ANCHOR PUB, ISLINGTON, LONDON ENGLAND Contrary to other U2 histories, this was not the first venue that U2 played in London or the UK. That honour goes to The Moonlight Club in West Hampstead, where U2 played on 1st December 1979. The Hope and Anchor was famous as one of the venues where the musical phenomenon "Pub Rock" had originated. Groups such as Ducks De Luxe, Brinsley Schwarz and Dr Feelgood had all played here regularly in the mid-1970s. This was an important gig in U2's early history as, despite the fact that only nine paying customers turned up to see the band, several more record company and music journalists came to

see this new Irish band. Rumour has it that U2 only played half a set as they were so nervous playing in front of all these important media types. When The Edge broke a string half way through the set and left the stage to get another one, the rest of the band followed him into the dressing room never to return! U2 did however come back the following year on 22nd May 1980.

HORSLIPS The Irish folk-rock group consisted of: Charles O'Connor (violin, mandolin and vocals), Jim Lochart (keyboards, flute and pipes), Barry Devlin (bass and vocals), Eamon Carr (drums) and Johnny Fean (guitar, banjo and flute). They were one of the few major Irish rock bands of the 1970s who managed to have commercial success outside of Ireland. Managed by Michael Deeny, a contemporary of Paul McGuinness at Trinity College, Dublin, they achieved enough success to inspire Paul McGuinness to think seriously about managing his own rock band. This he did, first with Spud and then with U2. In 1978 Horslips played at London's Wembley Arena with Thin Lizzy on a special Irish double bill. Paul McGuinness, who had recently started to manage U2, took Adam to the concert and introduced him to Barry Devlin, Horslips' vocalist and bass player. This led to Devlin helping with the production of U2's second demo. After the session, Devlin told Paul McGuinness that he would certainly "have a major British success with them". Barry Devlin went on to produce several of U2's promotional videos, including "A Sort Of Homecoming" and "I Still Haven't Found What I'm Looking For".
See also: Michael Deeney / Barry Devlin

HOTHOUSE FLOWERS One of the first signings to U2's Mother Records label. The Irish band gave Mother Records their first single success in Ireland with "Love Don't Work This Way" in 1987. The band went onto commercial success in Britain, Europe and America in the late 1980s. When they played at the Glastonbury Festival in England in 1989, Adam joined them on stage to play bass on the number, "Feet On The Ground".

HOT PRESS The famous Dublin based Irish Music journal started in 1977 and was the first music paper to pick up on U2. In U2's early years much of their early publicity was due to *Hot Press*. It was founded by Niall Stokes who had previously worked with his bother Dermott on a magazine called *Scene,* which also had Bill Graham as one of its writers. *Hot Press* was the first publication to mention U2. This was their triumph at the Harp Lager contest in Limerick in 1978. It was also the first publication to include a feature on U2. This was written by Bill Graham, entitled "Yep! It's U2" and featured in *Hot Press* 23.

Later on in January 1980, U2 won five categories in the annual *Hot Press* readers' poll, indicating that U2 were about to make it big. In 1984, when Bob Dylan played at Slane Castle, Bono was dispatched by *Hot Press* to interview Bob for the magazine. All the *Hot Press* articles on U2 up to 1985 were published in *The U2 File - A Hot Press History*. A follow-up book, *Three Chords And The Truth,* taking in the years 1985–1989, was published in 1989. *Hot Press* opened a museum dedicated to Ireland's musical heritage in 1999 called The Hot Press Irish Music Hall of Fame.

See also: Bill Graham / Niall Stokes

HOT PRESS IRISH MUSIC HALL OF FAME, DUBLIN, IRELAND This unique museum was the brainchild of *Hot Press* editor Niall Stokes and was opened on 2nd September 1999. The museum is dedicated to Ireland's popular music heroes and includes exhibits on artists such as Van Morrison, Thin Lizzy, Rory Gallagher and of course U2. Some of the U2 exhibits include Macphisto's gold suit and boots, early U2 records, tickets and posters, and some of the original hand-written lyrics to songs including "Concentration Cramp" and "Cartoon World". Larry's hands have been plaster casted in a special section devoted to drummers.

HOULIHAN'S STADIUM, TAMPA, FLORIDA, USA This show, on 10th November 1997, was believed to be the lowest attended concert on the whole of the *Pop Mart* tour of 1997-8 with a figure of just over 17,000 in attendance.

HOWIE B The Scottish DJ and remix artist first came across U2 when he was asked by Nick Angel of Island Records to remix the track "Hallelujah" which Bono had recorded for the Leonard Cohen tribute album, *Tower Of Song*. He also remixed the Gavin Friday *Shag Tobacco* album track "Angel" before being invited by Gavin to host a session at the Kitchen in Dublin. He met U2 here and was then invited onto the Passengers sessions in 1995, where he added different parts and mixed some of the tracks. He contributed a vocal to the track "Elvis Ate America", which he co-wrote with Bono. He was then invited by Flood to join the band in the role as "vibes man" whilst they were working on the *Pop* album. He contributed tape loops as well as helping with the remixing of various tracks.

For the *Pop Mart* tour he was the DJ for both the first and second legs playing his choice of music after the support bands had finished and before U2 came on stage. He always finished his stint with the "Theme From Mission: Impossible". He stayed on the tour until the first dates of the third leg of the tour at the Skydome in Toronto, but as he later admitted in

Bono model from the *Hot Press* Music Hall of Fame, Dublin. *Photo: Gill Sullivan*

an interview with *NME* he was caught in possession of marijuana at the airport. This meant that his work permit was revoked and as result he did not take part in the rest of the tour. Apart from U2 he has worked with Bjork, Tricky, New Order and Soul II Soul. He has his own record label called Pussyfoot. The 'B' in his name stands for Bernstein.

HUMAN RIGHTS NOW The Coliseum in Los Angeles was the venue for a show on 21st September, 1988 on the Amnesty International tour called "Human Rights Now", featuring Peter Gabriel, Sting and Bruce Springsteen. Although U2 didn't take part in this tour, Bono made a surprise appearance on the Bob Dylan song, "Chimes Of Freedom" which he sang with the rest of the artists at the end of the show.

HUBERT H HUMPHREY METRODOME, MINNEAPOLIS, MINNESOTA, USA U2 played here on 29th October 1997 during the *Pop Mart* tour of North America. Bono told the crowd that this was the town where he wrote two songs that were included on the *October* album. These were "Stranger In A Strange Land" and "I Threw A Brick Through A Window".

HUME, JOHN The Northern Ireland politician who has been heavily involved in the Peace process in Northern Ireland. He is one of four Northern Ireland politicians whose face is pictured on the sleeve for the "Please" single. He is leader of the Democratic Party and was one of the two politicians whose arms Bono lifted aloft at the "Yes Vote" concert in Belfast on 19th May 1998 (the other was David Trimble).

When John Hume appeared on the *Late Late Show* after he had been told that he had won the Nobel Peace Prize for his efforts for bringing about peace in Northern Ireland, Bono rang the programme to publicly congratulate him. A few days later he and his wife were guests of honour at Bono's house for a special dinner also attended by the other members of U2 and other notables. When John Hume and David Trimble went to Oslo on 10th December 1998 to receive their awards, The Edge and Paul McGuinness attended the award ceremony, whilst Bono sent a taped message.

HUTCHENCE, MICHAEL The lead singer of the Australian group INXS who died tragically in 1997. Michael had become a close friend of Bono and they had recorded "Slide Away" together. This was released on Michael's posthumous solo album *Michael Hutchence* in 1999. The news of Michael's death broke while U2 were on the *Pop Mart* tour in North America. At the Alamodome San Antonio Texas on 23rd November 1997, the day after Hutchence death, Bono stated at the start of "I Still Haven't Found What I'm Looking For", "He was a good friend and one of us." Various pictures of Hutchence were put up on the giant TV screen and as the band left the stage the INXS song, "Never Tear Us Apart" was played. Bono subsequently dedicated "One" to him at several of the shows, whilst his image was beamed on the giant TV screen.

When the *Pop Mart* tour finally reached Australia in February 1998, each show there featured a tribute to him. There were rumours that the remaining members of INXS would appear on stage with U2 at their Sydney Football Stadium gig on 27th February but this did not happen, though they were in the audience for the show. Bono also wrote "Stuck In A Moment You Can't Get Out Of" for Michael and dedicated it to him at each of the *Elevation* tour shows where it was performed.

See also: Slide Away / Stuck In A Moment You Can't Get Out Of

HYNDE, CHRISSIE The lead singer with The Pretenders pop group who are best remembered for their hits "Brass in Pocket" and "I'll Stand By You". Chrissie provided backing vocals to the track "Pride (In The Name of Love)" whilst it was being recorded in Windmill Lane studios in the summer of 1984. She was credited on *The Unforgettable Fire* as Mrs Christine Kerr as she was the wife of Jim Kerr of Simple Minds at the time. She also appeared in conversation

with Bono in a UK Channel 4 programme about The Pretenders on 17th October 1995.

See also: The Pretenders

HYPE, THE Interim name of the group, initially called Feedback, before they became U2. After just a few gigs as Feedback, including Mount Temple Comprehensive and St Fintan's School in north Dublin the name had been changed to The Hype. This was because the band felt that the name "Feedback" was not hip and up-to-date enough. "The Hype" sounded cooler and more relevant to those Punk influenced times. Apart from the four members of U2 – Bono, Adam, Larry and The Edge – The Hype consisted of The Edge's brother, Dik Evans, also on guitar.

Over the next year the Hype played several concerts around Dublin, gaining more and more experience and a small, but loyal, following. On the advice of Steve Averill, The Hype decided to change their name to U2. At their last gig at Howth Community Centre in March 1978. The five-piece Hype played the first half of the gig before Dik Evans left the stage and the band. Then for the second half they were now known as U2. At one time Adam was acting as manager of The Hype/U2 and to try and get people interested in the band, he placed this advert in a local newspaper in January 1978: "Manager seeks the whereabouts of The Hype after amazing Howth gig. Please ring Brian 450822 (Malahide, Dublin)".

Bono and Chrissie Hynde, Cologne, Germany, 1987
Photo: Kay Baursfeld

"I DON'T WANNA GO" This was the title of an early U2 song, never released on record.

"I FALL DOWN" (*OCTOBER* ALBUM TRACK) (3.39) The second track on the first side of the *October* album. It was recorded at Windmill Lane studios with Steve Lillywhite producing. It was a radical change to the music U2 had produced so far, featuring The Edge on electric piano and acoustic guitar. The song was autobiographical in that U2 were still learning and quite often made mistakes – they would fall down but then get up again and get on with the task in hand. The song was first performed live at Bogart's club in Cincinnati, USA on 17th April 1981 and was one of the first songs to feature Bono playing guitar on stage.

"I REMEMBER YOU" (LIVE) (*THE SUNDAY TIMES* FREE CD) (1.28) This live version of the Ramones song "I Remember You" came from U2's concert at New York's Irving Plaza on 5th December 2000. It was one of three tracks from that concert on the CD given away free with copies of the *Sunday Times* newspaper and was also on the Australian release of "Elevation".

"I STILL HAVEN'T FOUND WHAT I'M LOOKING FOR" (*JOSHUA TREE* ALBUM TRACK) (4.38) The second song on the first side of *The Joshua Tree* album. The title comes from a phrase spoken by The Edge and the song shows how the band's religious beliefs had developed since the *Boy* album. Bono can sing about all the experiences he's tasted, but he's still not reached his goal. Musically the track is laid back with acoustic guitar and bongos from Larry. The song was first performed live at the State University Activity Center in Tempe, Arizona on the opening night of the *Joshua Tree* tour on 2nd April 1987.

"I STILL HAVEN'T FOUND WHAT I'M LOOKING FOR" (SINGLE) (IS 328) (4.38) The second single to be taken from *The Joshua Tree* album was released in May 1987. It reached number 1 in the American singles charts, making it U2's second American number 1 that year. In the British charts it only reached number 6. It was also included on *The Best of 1980-1990* compilation CD.

"I STILL HAVEN'T FOUND WHAT I'M LOOKING FOR" (LIVE) (*RATTLE & HUM* ALBUM TRACK) (5.53)

This live version of "I Still Haven't Found What I'm Looking For" was recorded live at U2's show at Madison Square Gardens, New York City on 28th September 1987. It differed from the studio version in that it had a gospel arrangement courtesy of The New Voices of Freedom Choir from Harlem. This version is different to the one shown in the film.

"I STILL HAVEN'T FOUND WHAT I'M LOOKING FOR" (LIVE) (*POP MART LIVE FROM MEXICO CITY* VIDEO*)* The tenth track on the video *U2 Pop Mart: Live From Mexico City*, released in 1998. It was filmed at the Foro Sol Stadium, Mexico City on 3rd December 1997.

"I STILL HAVEN'T FOUND WHAT I'M LOOKING FOR" (*RATTLE & HUM* FILM) This version of "I Still Haven't Found What I'm Looking For" was filmed and recorded in the Harlem church in New York City where the New Voices of Freedom Choir are based. We see U2 meeting the choir and watching them singing a gospel version of "I Still Haven't Found What I'm Looking For", after Bono and The Edge have started the song. The choir was conducted by Dennis Bell and the soloists were George Pendergrass and Dorothy Terrell. The actual performance of the song by the choir and U2 at New York's Madison Square Gardens was recorded for *The Rattle & Hum* album.

"I STILL HAVEN'T FOUND WHAT I'M LOOKING FOR" (PROMOTIONAL VIDEO) The promotional video for "I Still Haven't Found What I'm Looking For" was filmed on the streets of Las Vegas, Nevada on 12th April 1987, straight after U2's concert at the Thomas & Mack Arena in Las Vegas. In it the four members of U2 walk down the brightly lit streets of Las Vegas with Bono singing the song to several passers by. Even Larry and Adam join in as The Edge plays acoustic guitar. Barry Devlin was the director.

"I THREW A BRICK THROUGH A WINDOW" (*OCTOBER* ALBUM TRACK) (4.53) The third track on side one of the *October* album. Larry's heavy drumming dominates this track, which is also notable for the slide guitar from The Edge. The song seems to be self accusing, with Bono looking at the things he's done in anger and with violence, then returning to God and the Bible. The song was premiered at U2's appearance at Slane Castle on 16th August 1981, where the band supported Thin Lizzy.

"I THREW A BRICK THROUGH A WINDOW" (LIVE) ("NEW YEAR'S DAY" SINGLE B-SIDE) This live version of "I Threw a Brick Through a Window" was recorded at the U2 concert at the Werchter Festival on 3rd July 1982. It was only available on the double 7 inch single (UWIP 6848) and the 12 inch single (12WIP 6848) versions of "New Year's Day".

"I WILL FOLLOW" (*BOY* ALBUM TRACK) (3.36) The opening track on side one of U2's first album, *Boy*. It was produced by Steve Lillywhite and recorded at Dublin's Windmill Lane studios. The opening riff from The Edge remains one of the most memorable in U2's music. The unusual thing about this track is the use of the xylophone as well as milk bottles in the middle section. A stormer of an opening track for an album, "I Will Follow" was destined to become a live favourite. The title and refrain "I will follow", like many U2 lyrics, is ambiguous. Is Bono talking about following his mother, or is it God? For the 1997 *Pop Mart* tour the lyrics were changed to include references to Bono's mother leaving a hole in his life. The track is believed to have been first performed live in 1980, either at the Acklam Hall in London in March or on the first date of the *11 O'clock Tick Tock* tour at the Hope & Anchor in London in May. "I Will Follow" holds the record for the number of live versions that have been officially released (see below).

"I WILL FOLLOW" (SINGLE) (3.36) (WIP 6656) U2's third Island single was released on 7 inch only, being the same as the album version. The B-side was a live version of "Boy-Girl" (recorded at London's Marquee club in September 1980). It was released in October 1980 at the same time as the *Boy* album, but despite its strong musical content failed to get into the British charts. It also featured on the compilation *The Best of 1980-1990*.

"I WILL FOLLOW" (LIVE) (DUTCH SINGLE) (104-525) In Holland, Island Records released a live version of "I Will Follow" recorded at T Heem, Hattem in Holland on 14th May 1982. It was released in June 1982 with "Gloria" as the B-side.

"I WILL FOLLOW" (LIVE) (US SINGLE) (7-99789) This live version of "I Will Follow" was released as a single in the USA in January 1984. It was taken from the *Under A Blood Red Sky* album. The B-side featured a remixed version of "Two Hearts Beat as One".

"I WILL FOLLOW" (LIVE) ("GLORIA" SINGLE B-SIDE) This version of "I Will Follow" appeared on the "Gloria" single which was released in Ireland, the UK, Holland and Australia. It was recorded live at the Paradise Theatre, Boston on 6th March 1981

"I WILL FOLLOW" (LIVE) ("PRIDE" SINGLE B-SIDE) (7-94976) The same *Under A Blood Red Sky* version of "I Will Follow" was put on the B-side of the "Pride" single released in America in 1985 as part of the "Revival of The Fittest" series.

"I WILL FOLLOW" (LIVE) (*UNDER A BLOOD RED SKY* ALBUM TRACK) (3.47) This live version of "I Will Follow" was recorded at the Lorelei Amphitheatre in Germany on 20th August 1983. It was produced by Jimmy Iovine and is the third track on the first side of the album.

"I WILL FOLLOW" (LIVE) (*1 AND ONLY* ALBUM TRACK) A rare recording of U2 performing the song at the BBC's Maida Vale Studios in London on 8th September 1980. It was included on the BBC album, *1 And Only – 25 Years of Radio 1*, released in 1996.

"I WILL FOLLOW" (LIVE) (*HASTA LA VISTA BABY!* ALBUM TRACK) (2.50) This live version of "I Will Follow" was recorded at the Foro Sol Stadium, Mexico City on 3rd December 1997 during the *Pop Mart* tour. It was on the free CD given away to *Propaganda* readers in July 2000.

"I WILL FOLLOW" (LIVE) (*THE SUNDAY TIMES* FREE CD) One of three live tracks on a CD given away free with The Sunday Times Newspaper on

3rd June 2001. It was recorded at U2's concert at the Irving Plaza in New York City on 5th December 2000.

"I WILL FOLLOW" (LIVE) (*UNDER A BLOOD RED SKY VIDEO*) The live version of "I Will Follow", as filmed at Red Rocks, Denver on 6th June 1983, is the eleventh track on the video. On the day it was actually the eighteenth song they played and was part of the encore.

"I WILL FOLLOW" (LIVE) (*POP MART: LIVE FORM MEXICO CITY* VIDEO) The third track on the video *U2 Pop Mart: Live From Mexico City*, released in 1998. It was the version filmed at the Foro Sol Stadium, Mexico City on 3rd December 1997.

"I WILL FOLLOW" (PROMOTIONAL VIDEO #1) The main promotional video for "I Will Follow" showed the band playing the song in a London studio with a completely white background in September 1980. Although some people have suggested that Meiert Avis was the director, this has never been established.

"I WILL FOLLOW" (PROMOTIONAL VIDEO #2) There are rumours of a second and possibly even a third promo video of "I Will Follow". One was meant to have been shot whilst the band were on tour in the United States in the first few months of 1981. This is said to consist of concert scenes shot at a show in New York during the spring of 1981. As the single of "I Will Follow" was not released in the USA, this video was used to publicise the group rather than the single.

"I WILL FOLLOW" (PROMOTIONAL VIDEO #3) A third promotional video for "I Will Follow" was rumoured to have been shot at a concert in Holland in 1980 or 1981. Again this is unsubstantiated.

"IF GOD WILL SEND HIS ANGELS" (*POP* ALBUM TRACK) (5.22) The fourth track on the *Pop* album is one of the tracks recorded at the *Zooropa* sessions, but which didn't make it onto that album. In it Bono is looking at the world and seeking a solution to all the evil by looking to God to send help in the form of his angels. It was produced by Flood and Howie B and was first performed live at the Sam Boyd Stadium in Las Vegas on 25th April 1997.

"IF GOD WILL SEND HIS ANGELS" (SINGLE) (4.32) (CID 684/572189) (4.32) The single version of "If God Will Send His Angels" was released in December 1997 and reached number 12 in the UK singles charts. It was a different version to the one on the album, opening with some quiet wah-wah guitar from The Edge. The single also featured the tracks: "Slow Dancing", "Two Shots Of Happy, One Shot of Sad" and "Sunday Bloody Sunday" (live from Sarajevo).

The song was also featured on the soundtrack album of the film *City Of Angels*.

"IF GOD WILL SEND HIS ANGELS" (THE GRAND JURY MIX) (5.40) ('MOFO REMIXES' SINGLE) (CIDX 684/572191-2) This remix of "If God Will Send His Angels" was the third track on the "Mofo Remixes" single. It was remixed by Gerald Baillergeau who according to the credits is also known as Big Yam and by Victor Merritt aka Vino.

"IF GOD WILL SEND HIS ANGELS" (PROMOTIONAL VIDEO) The promo video for "If God Will Send His Angels" was directed by Phil Joanou in Chicago in October 1997. It is an unusual video showing Bono singing from a seat in a cafe as various groups of people come in, sit down, talk and then leave. They sit next to him and opposite him, but don't notice him as he is an angel. The screen is split into two halves with Bono in the top half and those opposite him in the bottom half. At one point the other three members of U2 come in. Edge sits next to Bono, and Larry and Adam sit opposite him.

"IF YOU WEAR THAT VELVET DRESS" (*POP* ALBUM TRACK) (5.15) The tenth track on the *Pop* album is a slow song which builds up into a climax in a similar

Bono performs "If You Wear That Velvet Dress", Jacksonville, USA, 12/11/97. *Photo: L. Wiske*

way to "With Or Without You". It was produced by Flood and features Marius De Vries on keyboards. It was first performed live at the Sam Boyd Stadium in Las Vegas on 25th April 1997, the opening night of the *Pop Mart* tour.

"IF YOU WEAR THAT VELVET DRESS" (LIVE) (BEAU-TIFUL DAY SINGLE) (2.43) The only live version of this track to have been officially released is on the "Beautiful Day" single (CD2) (CIDX 766/562 946-2) released in October 2000. It was recorded live at the Foro Sol Autodromo in Mexico City, Mexico on 3rd December 1997 during the *Pop Mart* tour. This track was not included on the *Hasta La Vista Baby!* free CD for *Propaganda* subscribers that featured most of this concert.

"IF YOU WEAR THAT VELVET DRESS" (LIVE) (*U2: POP MART LIVE FROM MEXCIO CITY* VIDEO) The nineteenth track on the video *U2 Pop Mart: Live From Mexico City)*, released in 1998. It was the same version as the one above filmed at the Foro Sol Stadium, Mexico City on 3rd December 1997.

"I'M NOT YOUR BABY" This song performed by U2 and Sinead O'Connor was included on the sound-track album of the film, *The End of Violence.*

"I'M NOT YOUR BABY" (SKYSPLITTER DUB) (PLEASE SINGLE) (5.47) The fourth track on the "Please" CD single (CID 673/572129-2). The lyrics were written by Bono and The Edge.

"IN A LIFETIME" (CLANNAD SINGLE & ALBUM TRACK) Bono was the guest vocalist on this Clan-nad album track (from the *Macalla* album), released as a single in late 1985. Bono duets with Clannad singer Maire Ni Brennan. The single reached number 20 in the UK singles charts in January 1986. It was re-released in June 1989 reaching number 17. The song has never been performed live with both Bono and Maire together.

See also: Maire Ni Brennan / Clannad

"IN A LIFETIME" (PROMOTIONAL VIDEO) The promotional video for "In A Lifetime" featured a bearded Bono singing lead vocals with Maire ni Bren-nan. It was filmed in and around the Irish village of Gweedore, County Donegal where Clannad were based. Meiert Avis was the director and at the end Bono can be seen driving a hearse!

"IN A LITTLE WHILE" (*ALL THAT YOU CAN'T LEAVE BEHIND* ALBUM) (3.37) The sixth track on the *All That You Can't Leave Behind* album was dedi-cated to Joey Ramone by Bono at several concerts on the *Elevation* tour. It was first performed live at The National Car Rental Center in Fort Lauderdale, Florida on 24th March 2001 at the start of the *Eleva-tion* tour.

"IN COLD BLOOD" A poem that Bono wrote as a reac-tion to the events of Sarajevo and the war in Bosnia in 1993. He did consider reading it from the stage on the *Zooropa* tour and including it on the album, but in the end this did not happen. The lyrics, which speak of a child being raped by soldiers, were published in *Hot Press* and the *NME.*

"INDIAN SUMMER SKY" (*THE UNFORGETTABLE FIRE* ALBUM) (4.16) The third track on side two of *The Unforgettable Fire* album. Adam's bass is very prominent in the song and is the guiding force throughout. The Edge once described this song as being "autobiographical" of U2, without pin-pointing exactly what he meant. It was first performed live on the opening night of the *Unforgettable Fire* tour at Espace Tony Garnier in Lyon, France on 18th October 1984.

INFINITE GUITAR A specially made guitar created by Michael Brook with whom The Edge had collabo-rated on the soundtrack album of *Captive.* It works by giving instant feedback as soon as a string is pressed. The guitar has been used by The Edge on such tracks as "With or Without You" and "Night & Day".

See also: Night & Day

"IN GOD'S COUNTRY" (*THE JOSHUA TREE* ALBUM TRACK) (3.37) The second track on side two of *The Joshua Tree* album. It is about America (a theme that runs throughout the album) though it is the opposite to the America of "Bullet The Blue Sky". Here the theme of the desert, also mentioned in "Where The Streets Have No Name", is prominent. The rivers – the people's dreams – have now run dry. We need dreams for the future, as it was the dreams of the past immigrants that made America what it is. The song is an up-tempo number with a beat reminis-cent of a train travelling across this vast country. The use of acoustic guitars here helps to give it a unique feel not found anywhere else on the album. The song was first performed at Balmoral TV studios in Bel-fast when U2 made a special appearance to preview some of the new songs from *The Joshua Tree* album.

"IN GOD'S COUNTRY" (SINGLE) (S7-99385) A single released only in the United States in Novem-ber 1987 with "Bullet The Blue Sky" and "Running to Stand Still" on its B-side. It reached number 44 in the US singles charts in January 1988 and number 48 in the UK charts on import.

"IN GOD'S COUNTRY" (VIDEO) The documentary film *Outside It's America* featured a specially made video of "In God's Country". It showed mainly black and white film images of men working in factories and woman doing their laundry. Bono was the only member of U2 to feature. It was directed by Barry Devlin.

"IN GOD'S COUNTRY" (*RATTLE & HUM* FILM/ VIDEO) U2's performance of this song at the McNichols Arena in Denver on 8th November 1987 was included in *Rattle & Hum*. The rare audio version of this film footage was one of three live tracks included on the promo album, "Excerpts from Rattle & Hum".

"INSIDE OUT" A song that the young U2 used to play in their set around 1978 to 1979.

INTERNATIONAL STADIUM, GATESHEAD See: Rock On The Tyne Festival

INTERSCOPE RECORDS U2's American record company was set up by Jimmy Iovine. *All That You Can't Leave Behind* was the first release by U2 on Interscope Records in the US.

IN THE NAME OF THE FATHER (FILM) The 1994 film made by Dublin film maker Jim Sheridan, who had directed the award winning *My Left Foot*. It tells the story of The Guildford Four who were wrongly imprisoned in 1974 on the charge of planting a bomb in that English town. It starred Daniel Day-Lewis, Emma Thompson and Pete Postlethwaite. The original songs used in the film were co-written by Bono, Gavin Friday and Maurice Seezer, who performed on several of them - see below.

IN THE NAME OF THE FATHER (FILM SOUND-TRACK ALBUM) (Island CID 8026) The film sound-track album from the *In The Name of The Father* film featured some original songs (co-written by Bono, Gavin Friday and Maurice Seezer), alongside some "standards" from the 1960s and 1970s, as well as some incidental film music by Trevor Jones. Full track list: "In The Name of The Father", "Voodoo Chile" (Slight Return), "Billy Boola", "Dedicated Follower of Fashion", "Interrogation", "Is This Love", "Walking The Circle", "Whiskey in the Jar", "Passage of Time", "You Made Me The Thief of Your Heart".

"IN THE NAME OF THE FATHER" (SINGLE) (CID 593) (5.42) The title track from the film of *In The Name of the Father* was co-written by Bono, Gavin Friday and Maurice Seezer. It was released in March 1994 and peaked at number 46 in the UK charts. The lyrical theme is one of tribalism, be it drugs, football, religion, etc. The music has an Indian rather than an Irish feel, which is enhanced by Maurice Seezer's distorted accordion. The CD single also contained three remixes of the song: the Unidare Mix, the Beats Mix and an instrumental mix.

"IN THE NAME OF THE FATHER" (PROMOTIONAL VIDEO) The promo video for "In The Name of The Father" was directed by Jim Sheridan and featured scenes of Bono and Gavin Friday singing the song interspersed with clips from the feature film.

"IN THE NUDE INTERVIEW" The name given to an interview that U2 did live on the Dave Fanning Radio Show on the 25th June 1987 during a break in the *Joshua Tree* tour. As Fanning was playing Iggy Pop's "Lust For Life", which has the line "He's gonna do another striptease" in it, the story goes that the four members of U2 instinctively took off their clothes and sat around the studio for the interview in the nude. Bono also reportedly went into the studio next door and interrupted the news bulletin.
See also: Dave Fanning

"INTO THE HEART" (*BOY* ALBUM TRACK) The fourth track on side one of the *Boy* album, seguing from the previous track, "An Cat Dubh". When played live, it was always preceded by "An Cat Dubh". The song was first played live on the "11 O'clock Tick Tock" tour of England in the spring of 1980.

"INTO THE HEART" (LIVE) ("SWEETEST THING" SINGLE) The only live version of "Into The Heart" comes form the "Sweetest Thing" single released in 1998. The track was recorded at Red Rocks Amphitheater in June 1983.

IN TUA NUA Irish group who became the first signing to Mother Records, the record label that U2 set up to help up-and-coming musicians get a foothold in the music business. Their first single entitled "Coming Thru" was released in 1984. In Tua Nua included Leslie Dowdall, Brian O'Briaian, Martin Colncy, Vincent Kilduff, Paul Byrne and Steve Wickham.

In 1986 Wickham left to join the Waterboys. He was replaced on violin by Angela De Burca. The group had a hit in 1989 with "Only All I Wanted". In Tua Nua drummer, Paul Byrne is said to have discovered Sinead O'Connor when she was singing at a wedding. Together they wrote the song, "Take My Hand", which was the group's first single on Island Records.

See also: Vincent Kilduff / Mother Records / Sinead O'Connor / Steve Wickham

"IN YOUR HAND" An early U2 song from 1978 that was never released on record.

IOVINE, JIMMY The well-known producer of artists such as Bruce Springsteen and Patti Smith. With U2 he has produced the live albums *Under A Blood Red Sky* and *Rattle & Hum* as well as the charity album *A Very Special Christmas* which featured a contribution by U2. Based in Los Angeles, he had also worked with Patti Smith, Stevie Nicks, Tom Petty and John Lennon before he worked with U2. Having heard the *War* album, he flew with his engineer Shelly Yakus to Dublin to try and negotiate a deal to produce the band's next studio album. Impressed with Iovine's enthusiasm, they gave him and his partner a set of live tapes from Red Rocks and some European festivals to mix in stereo. As a result Iovine and Yakus were given the producer/engineering roles for the *Under A Blood Red Sky* album and the video of the Red Rocks show.

In 1987 Iovine got U2 to record a song called "Christmas (Baby Please Come Home) for *A Very Special Christmas* compilation album in support of the Special Olympics. Then in 1988, after the *Joshua Tree* tour had finally ended, Iovine got the job of producing the soundtrack album of *Rattle & Hum* as well as the movie soundtrack itself. This included the recording of a few new songs including "All I Want Is You". In the 1990s he set up his own record label, Interscope Records, releasing *All That You Can't Leave Behind* in America.

See also: Interscope Records / *Under A Blood Red Sky*

IREDALE, STEVE U2's chief production manager originates from Kiltimagh in County Mayo, Steve Iredale had been a roadie with Horslips, before joining U2 as a roadie in 1981. At his first gig where U2 were supporting Thin Lizzy at Slane Castle no one told him that the guitars were always tuned a semi-tone down to fit in with Bono's vocals! In spite of this start, from then on he became part of U2's permanent road crew,

staying with the band during the recording of *October*. The following summer just before the *War* album sessions, he decided he'd had enough and quit. After a long chat with Bono and The Edge he was brought back in, being given the position of stage manager for the *War* tour. This involved making sure that all members of the band had the right equipment at the right time as well as keeping an eye on Bono if he decided to move off the stage to climb up the scaffolding or move out into the audience. Bono would often do this during "The Electric Co." and more often than not Steve (or Dennis Sheehan) would have to make sure that he got back to the stage safely. From the 1984 *Unforgettable Fire* tour of Australia and New Zealand onwards Steve has been U2's Production Director. This requires making sure that nothing goes wrong at each show and being on hand to sort out any musical problems.

IRISH FAMILY PLANNING ASSOCIATION This organisation was found guilty of selling condoms in the Virgin Megastore in February 1991. Their fine of £500 was paid by U2 who felt that condoms should be on sale in Ireland, not only because of the need for contraception, but also for protection against the AIDS virus.

See also: AIDS / Contraception

IRVING PLAZA, NEW YORK CITY, USA U2 performed a free show for 1,000 people here on 5th December 2000 as part of the build up to the 2001 *Elevation* tour. It was presented by the New York radio station 92.3 FM K-ROCK and was broadcast across the country. The concert was memorable for the inclusion of two covers: the Ramones' "I Remember You" and The Who's "Won't Get Fooled Again" which finished the show. It also included the early U2 song, "11 O'clock Tick Tock". Three of the songs from the concert were included on the CD given away with The Sunday Times in June 2001. They were: "I Will Follow", "New York" and "I Remember You". Set list: Beautiful Day, Elevation, Stuck In a Moment You Can't Get Out Of, I Remember You, New York, I Will Follow, Desire, The Ground Beneath Her Feet, Mysterious Ways (Sexual Healing), One (Walk On), All I Want Is You, Bad (Ruby Tuesday), 11 O'clock Tick Tock, Won't Get Fooled Again

"ISLAND" The ninth track on the *Captive* film soundtrack album was composed by The Edge.

ISLAND RECORDS U2's record label. Island Records was founded by Chris Blackwell in 1964 after the chart success of Millie's "My Boy Lollipop", which provided him with the funds to set up his independent record label. With the signing and success of Bob Marley and The Wailers, Island's future was secured so that by the end of the 1970s Island Records was one of the biggest and most influential independent labels. Included on its roster were such names as Emerson Lake and Palmer, Cat Stevens and Traffic. It was its ethos that attracted U2 and Paul McGuinness to the label: U2 would be given time to develop and not be expected to have three hits singles in the first year, as most major record companies demanded.

Their five year contract, which was secured largely due to the efforts of Rob Partridge and Bill Stewart, gave U2 £50,000 to begin with, which was spent on recording, and another £50,000 for setting up tours. U2 were initially signed for four albums. The band also secured a publishing deal with Blue Mountain Music, also owned by Chris Blackwell. By the time this first deal came up for renewal in 1984, U2 were in a much stronger negotiating position, having been voted Band of the Year for 1983 by *Rolling Stone* magazine.

In the new deal that Paul McGuinness negotiated with help from Ossie Kilkenny and Owen Epstein, U2 were to receive a $2,000,000 dollar advance for their next four albums and their royalty rate would be doubled. They would be allowed to appoint their chosen producer and Island would have to accept the album in its finished state. Each album would be promoted by at least three videos and, best of all, U2 were able to have the publishing rights to their songs back in their control. This meant that the band were now financially secure for the rest of their lives.

In 1989 Chris Blackwell sold Island to Polygram for £200 million, which led to Polygram distributing U2's records worldwide, although the Island name would remain on U2 records. The band's contract was again renewed in 1993 with Island acquiring the worldwide rights to U2's next six albums for reportedly $60 million dollars and a generous 25% royalty rate.

See also: Chris Blackwell / Polygram Records

"IS THAT ALL?" (*OCTOBER* ALBUM TRACK) (2.59) The final track on the *October* album. It starts off with the riff that would later become known as "Cry" and would be the introduction for "The Electric. Co." when played live. The title "Is That All?" has been suggested as meaning is that all God wants from him – to be a singer in a rock 'n' roll band? It is one of two tracks from *October* never to have been performed live.

"ITO OKASHI" (*ORIGINAL SOUNDTRACKS 1* ALBUM) (3.24) The eighth track from the album, *Original Soundtracks 1*, released in November 1995. It was co-written by Japanese singer, Holi, who also sang on the track. It is credited as coming from "Ito Okashi" (Something Beautiful) written by performance artist, Rita Takashina.

See also: Holi

"I'VE GOT YOU UNDER MY SKIN" (TRACK OFF *DUETS* ALBUM) (3.32) Frank Sinatra recorded an album of some of his greatest hits in 1994, the only difference to these and the originals was that they were all duets with various guest vocalists, including Aretha Franklin, Tony Bennett and Bono. The track that Bono duetted on was "I've Got You Under My Skin". Bono recorded his half of the duet at a Dublin studio in September 1993, immediately after the end of the *Zooropa* tour. Phil Ramone was the producer.

"I'VE GOT YOU UNDER MY SKIN" (BONO & FRANK SINATRA / "STAY" SWING FORMAT SINGLE) (3.31) This track was lifted from the *Duets* album by Frank Sinatra and guests. It was issued as a double A-side with "Stay (Faraway So Close)" "Swing format" and appeared in several formats: 7 inch single (IS 578), cassette (CIS 578) and CD (CID 578). It was released (with accompanying promotional video) in November 1993. It reached number 4 in the UK charts in December 1993.

"I'VE GOT YOU UNDER MY SKIN" (PROMOTIONAL VIDEO) The promo video was filmed partly in the back of a limousine on the way from the airport to a bar in Palm Springs California. The rest of the video was shot in one take with Bono and Sinatra talking, but when Anton Corbijn took a photo of the two singers, Sinatra just walked out. Kevin Godley, the director then had the job of putting a promo video together with the little film that had been shot, adding snippets of Sinatra performing the song from past shows and Bono performing it separately.

"JACK IN THE BOX" This was an early U2 song that the group used to play in their set circa late 1979/early 1980. The song was was never released.

JACK MURPHY STADIUM, SAN DIEGO, CALIFORNIA, USA This was the venue for one of the last dates of the *Outside Broadcast* leg of the *Zoo TV* tour, taking place on 10th October 1992. It is memorable for being the concert where a couple who had just got married came onto the catwalk to be paraded in front of the crowd. The attendance at the gig was disappointing – 33,000 from a possible 55,000 capacity. The performance of "Until The End of the World" from this show was included on the Greenpeace "Alternative NRG" release. U2 played again here on 28th April 1997 on the second night of the *Pop Mart* tour. As it was still an early show on the tour, there were several technical problems: "If God Will Send His Angels" had to be cut short and Adam broke a string on his bass at the start of "Pride".

JACKSON, MICHAEL The renowned singer has been at times a major rival to U2 over the years. Although both camps would probably deny it, there have been several instances when both would seem to be trying to outdo each other. U2 (*The Joshua Tree*) and Michael Jackson (*Bad*) were the main runners for the album of the year award at the 1988 Grammy awards. U2 beat Michael Jackson into second place. Michael Jackson released his *Dangerous* album shortly after U2 released *Achtung Baby* in 1991, causing the latter to be knocked off the number 1 spot in several album charts around the world. In 1992-93 both U2 and Michael Jackson seemed to be in battle as to who could be on tour the longest with their *Zoo TV* and *Dangerous* tours, both of which lasted for nearly two years.

However it has not just been rivalry between the two camps. For instance in 1993 when the furore broke over Michael Jackson being accused of child sex, Bono at the final concert of the *Zooropa* tour (Dublin, 28th August 1993) dedicated the U2 song "Bad" to Michael Jackson saying, "I don't think you're Bad." Then in "The Playboy Mansion", about the excesses of America, Michael Jackson gets a name check. Later on when Michael Jackson was playing New York's Madison Square Garden, U2 were asked

to come and see him backstage after the gig, the whole event being filmed by Jackson's aides.

JAGGER, MICK The vocalist with the Rolling Stones first met Bono when he was in New York in 1985 taking part in the "Sun City" project. They were introduced by Peter Wolf of the J.Geils Band. Mick has a house in the south of France near to Bono's and in July 1999, for Mick's 56th birthday, Bono came along and joined in an all-star jam with Mick, Ron Wood and Elton John. Mick and his daughter Lizzy then joined in the session for "Stuck In A Moment You Can't Get Out Of" in Dublin in 2000, adding backing vocals. That take wasn't used though, as it was thought that it sounded too much like the Rolling Stones!

See also: The Rolling Stones

"JAH LOVE" This track was written by Bono and appeared on the 1990 album *The Brother's Keeper* by The Neville Brothers.

JAH WOBBLE (real name JOHN WARDLE aka DAN MACARTHUR) The bass player with Public Image Limited, the group formed by former Sex Pistols singer Johnny Rotten (John Lydon). The Edge played guitar on two tracks on Jah Wobble's 1983 *Snake*

Original poster for "The Jingle Balls" gigs, on display at the Irish Music Hall of Fame.
Photo: Wendy Chatterton

Charmer album with Holgar Czukay. The tracks were "Snake Charmer" and "Hold Onto Your Dreams".

JAMMIES, OKLAHOMA CITY, OKLAHOMA, USA U2's second visit to Oklahoma City was during the tour to promote the *October* album and took place on 17th February 1982. During the show someone gave Bono a pair of earplugs, an incident he would remember the following year when the band returned to Oklahoma.

JARA, VICTOR The Chilean poet who was killed for his political beliefs. He was mentioned in the lyrics of "One Tree Hill". When U2 played in Santiago, Chile on 11th February 1998, Bono dedicated "One" to him.

See also: Rene Castro

J.B. SCOTT'S, ALBANY, NEW YORK STATE USA U2 played this small club twice in the same tour – the *Boy* tour of North America – in the spring of 1981. The first time was on 5th March and the second time was on 23rd May, the only time they played a venue twice on the whole tour. They then returned to play here once again in 1981, on 13th November, during the *October* tour.

"JESUS CHRIST" This was the title of a track written and performed by U2 for the Woody Guthrie/Leadbelly tribute album called *Folkways - A Vision Shared*, released in 1988. The full song title is "When They Lay Jesus Christ In His Grave" and the song was recorded at Sun Studios in Memphis, Tennessee on the night of 29th/30th November 1987. Apparently U2 were so pleased with this recording that they stayed on to record "Angel of Harlem", "Love Rescue Me", "When Love Comes To Town" and "She's A Mystery To Me"

See also: Sun Studios

JINGLE BALLS, THE A series of Thursday night U2 concerts at McGonagles club in Dublin during the month of June 1979. Basically it was designed to draw attention to U2 by pretending it was Christmas even though it was June. To this end the stage was decorated with Christmas decorations, with the legend "Christmas in June" put on the publicity posters.

See also: McGonagles

JOANOU, PHIL The young director of the film *Rattle & Hum*. Joanou had little previous experience of film making – directing two episodes of Stephen Speilberg's "Amazing Stories" and making a film called *Three O'clock High*. Joanou had first been introduced to the band after a show at Hartford, Connecticut, USA in April 1985. After initial discussions he was invited to come over to Dublin to continue negotiations, where his unorthodox ideas, such as filming in both colour and black and white endeared him to U2.

Joanou got the job instead of first choice Jonathon Demme, but the making of *Rattle & Hum* was not always straightforward. For instance at the concert in Arizona, a downpour put paid to filming in colour as had been planned. At one point in the tour when Bono slipped on stage and hurt his shoulder, Joanou filmed Bono at the hospital and had to be told in no uncertain terms to stop filming!

Film of BB King meeting U2 was included in the promo video for "When Love Comes To Town". In 1992 Joanou was U2's choice as director for *The Million Dollar Hotel* film, but in the end Wim Wenders got the job. He did get to make the third promo video for "One" however. U2 and Joanou again met up in 1997 when Joanou directed the promo video for "If God Will Send His Angels". The following year Joanou made a film called *Entropy* about a director making a documentary on U2 as his personal life explodes around him. For a scene from the film he filmed part of U2's concert at the Greenpoint Stadium in Cape Town South Africa in March 1998.

See also: *Entropy* film / *Rattle & Hum* film

JOHANNESBURG STADIUM, JOHANNESBURG, SOUTH AFRICA U2's second concert in South Afirca took place here on 21st March 1998, the final show of the *Pop Mart* tour. As the band emerged from the lemon they were drinking champagne and were surrounded by streamers and balloons. Bono reminded the audience "to be united – to be 'One' – is a great thing. But to be tolerant, to respect differences is maybe even a greater thing."

JOHN F KENNEDY STADIUM, PHILADELPHIA, PENNSYLVANIA, USA U2 played this venue, famous as the American venue for Live Aid, on 25th September 1987. This date saw the biggest attendance for the whole of the *Joshua Tree* tour in 1987 with 86,145 people in the stadium. A second date had originally been put in the programme for the next day, 26th September, but this never took place. During the encore U2 were joined on stage by Bruce Springsteen who played guitar and sang along to the Ben E King song, "Stand By Me".

"JOLIE LOUISE" The title of a track off Daniel Lanois' 1989 album entitled *Acadie*. It featured Adam and Larry playing bass and drums respectively.

JONES, BUSTA Busta played with Talking Heads amongst others, who U2 had supported in December 1980. When U2 were playing at the Palladium in New York in May 1982, Busta joined U2 on stage for their final number, "11 O'clock Tick Tock". He died in 1995.

See also: The Palladium, New York

JONES, QUINCY The world famous record producer, arranger and composer who has worked with Michael

Jackson, Aretha Franklin, BB King, Little Richard and Frank Sinatra amongst many others. He has also had a successful career as a musician in his own right, playing trumpet in jazz and soul combos. He appeared with Bono at the NetAid concert and conducted the orchestra backing him singing "One". Qunicy then invited Bono to "America's Millennium Gala" in Washington where Bono once again performed "One", though this time he was accompanied by Daniel Lanois. Bono once described him as the coolest person he had ever met.

JORDAN, NEIL The Irish film director of *Interview With The Vampire* and *The Crying Game*. In 1987 he directed the promotional video of *The Joshua Tree* track, "Red Hill Mining Town" as it was mooted as a potential single. However, the video was never released to the general public as it is believed that U2 were unhappy with the finished product. Consequently "Red Hill Mining Town" was never released as a single.

See also: Red Hill Mining Town promotional video

JOSHUA TREE (CLASSIC ALBUMS SERIES - VIDEO) (ILC 0184) This documentary film about the making of U2's *The Joshua Tree* was originally shown in the TV series, *Classic Albums*. The four members of U2 and Paul McGuinness were all interviewed as well as producers, Brian Eno and Daniel Lanois, Steve Lillywhite and Flood. The documentary shows how tracks such as "Where The Streets Have No Name", "I Still Haven't Found What I'm Looking For" and "With Or Without You" were put together. The video also shows film of U2 performing "Mother's of the Disappeared" live at the Estadio Nacional in Santiago, Chile during the *Pop Mart* tour. The film also explains how the outtake song, "Sweetest Thing" came to be written and shows the promo video. Running Time: 60 minutes

THE JOSHUA TREE (ALBUM) (U26/CID 26) *The Joshua Tree* was released world-wide on March 9th 1987. *The Joshua Tree* has been U2's biggest album to date, selling in excess of 16 million copies. Preparations for the album first began in the summer of 1986 after U2 had made their only European appearance of that year at May's *Self Aid* concert in Croke Park, Dublin. U2 then went to America for a few weeks in June to take part in the *Conspiracy of Hope* tour in aid of Amnesty International, and then returned to set about recording the new album. The band had agreed that the songs on this album should be more straightforward than on its predecessor, *The Unforgettable Fire*. Brian Eno and Daniel Lanois were asked to produce the album, though original U2 producer, Steve Lillywhite, ended up remixing three

of the tracks. The album was once again recorded at Dublin's Windmill Lane studios, with STS Studios also being used. Some commentators argue that it was originally planned as a double album, not least because of the number of tracks that subsequently made it onto the B-sides of single releases from the album.

The album was dedicated to the memory of New Zealander Greg Carroll (Bono's personal assistant), who had been killed in a motorcycle accident in Dublin in 1986 shortly after the band had returned from the Amnesty tour. The song, "One Tree Hill" is a eulogy to him. The album title came from a small town of that name in California's Death Valley. The gatefold sleeve cover, photographed by Anton Corbijn, was shot in the Californian desert where the Joshua tree variety is found. It was called U2's "American album" by many critics, not least for its love/hate relationship with America evidenced by songs such as "In God's Country" and "Bullet The Blue Sky". Though it could also be argued that other areas of the world had influenced some of the album's subject matter, such as the 1984 British miner's strike for "Red Hill Mining Town" and the mysterious disappearances of political opponents under the regimes of certain South American countries for "Mothers of The Disappeared".

Within days of its release, *The Joshua Tree* had become the fastest selling album in British music history, entering the album charts at number 1 and achieving platinum status after only two days. Tower Records in London's Piccadilly Circus arranged to start selling the album at midnight on the day of its release in anticipation of public demand – this would again happen with each subsequent U2 album release. In the USA the album reached the number 1 spot on 25th March and stayed there for the next nine weeks.

Music critics on both sides of the Atlantic were unanimous in their praise for *The Joshua Tree*. Steve Pond writing in *Rolling Stone* called the album "unforgettable", whilst *NME*'s Adrian Thrills called *The Joshua Tree* "the strongest and most complete album they have ever released". The album elevated U2 to the premier league of rock groups alongside the likes of the Beatles and The Rolling Stones. The album also produced no less than five singles. In the USA the band achieved their first number 1 hit single with the track "With or Without You". This feat was then repeated with "I Still Haven't Found What I'm Looking For". In the UK these singles did not achieve the same success with number 4 being the highest position of any of the single releases. The following year, *The Joshua Tree* won countless awards including "Album of the Year" in *Rolling Stone* magazine and a prestigious Grammy for the best album.

Bono and Adam, the *Joshua Tree* tour, Wembley Stadium, England, June 12th 1987.
Photo: Kay Bauersfeld

Track List: Where The Streets Have No Name, I Still Haven't Found What I'm Looking For, With Or Without You, Bullet The Blue Sky, Running To Stand Still, Red Hill Mining Town, In God's Country, Trip Through Your Wires, One Tree Hill, Exit, Mothers Of The Disappeared.

JOSHUA TREE TOUR, THE The tour to promote the album was divided into three separate stages. The first leg took place in America in the spring of 1987, starting at Arizona State University Activity Centre, Tempe, Arizona on 2nd April and finishing at the Meadowlands Arena, East Rutherford, New Jersey on 16th May. The second leg took place in Europe during the summer of 1987, starting at the Comunale Braglia in Modena, Italy on 29th May, and ran on until 8th August finishing at the Pairc Ui Chaoimh, Cork, Ireland.

The band then went back to the United States for the third and final leg, which started at Nassau Veteran's Memorial Coliseum in Uniondale, New York on 10th September. The tour finally finished on 20th December 1987 at the Sun Devil Stadium, Tempe, Arizona, in the same town that the tour had started in nine months earlier. The venues that U2 played on this tour ranged from smaller arenas like Birmingham's NEC to large stadiums such as London's Wembley Stadium, showing that U2 had now become "a stadium band". It was the third biggest tour that U2 have ever undertaken, resulting in over 3 million people seeing U2 play live that year.

Apart from the numerous bootleg recordings from virtually every show on the tour, several shows were officially recorded. Songs from these would appear on the album *Rattle & Hum*. Parts of the tour were also filmed for the U2 movie *Rattle & Hum* directed by Phil Joanou, as well as for the documentary film *Outside It's America*, directed by Barry Devlin.

See appendix for complete list of *The Joshua Tree* tour dates.

Songs played on tour:

A Sort Of Homecoming, Bad, Bullet The Blue Sky (with Star Spangled Banner intro), Christmas (Baby Please Come Home), C'Mon Everybody, 11 O'clock Tick Tock, Exit, 40, Gloria, Knocking On Heaven's Door, Help, Helter Skelter, In God's Country, I Shall Be Released, I Still Haven't Found What I'm Looking For, I Will Follow, Lucille, Maggie's Farm, MLK, Mothers Of The Disappeared, New Year's Day, October, One Tree Hill, Out of Control, Party Girl, People Get Ready, Pride (In The Name Of Love), Running to Stand Still, Silver And Gold, Southern Man, Spanish Eyes, Springhill Mining Disaster, Stand By Be, Sunday Bloody Sunday, The Electric Co, Tequilla Sunrise, The Unforgettable Fire, Trip Through Your

The Welsh leg of the *Joshua Tree* Tour

Wires, When Love Comes To Town, Where the Streets Have No Name, With Or Without You

JOSHUA TRIO, THE This Dublin group were one of the first U2 "tribute" bands, though their set was more comical than serious. The Joshua Trio were originally three Dublin based musicians led by Paul Wonderful who had a dream one night where Bono told him to "go and spread the message of U2". Joined by two others they formed the Joshua Trio. Their mission in life was to spread the word about U2. When Adam was aquitted of his drugs charge in 1989, Paul is said to have freed 25,000 white butterflies in celebration. They even performed for The Edge's 30th birthday bash alongside the likes of David Bowie and Van Morrison. When one of them left to become a missionary, they recruited two new members. This line up consisted of Paul Wonderful (vocals), Keiran Matthews (bass), John Connolly (guitar) and Keith Connolly (drums). Wearing angel wings and shiny silvery dresses they would entertain U2 fans at their gigs. They also once played to crowds in Dublin waiting to buy the *Achtung Baby* album in 1991. They tended to re-work U2 standards to fit their own style. For example, "The Fly" was played as a country and western number!

"J. SWALLO" (FIRE SINGLE B-SIDE) (U WIP 6679 1B) This track was the B-side of the "Fire" single, released in July 1981. It was produced by Steve Lillywhite and recorded at Compass Point Studios in Nassau, the Bahamas. The song starts off with some military style drumming from Larry, before the bass and guitar kick in, quickly followed by a continuous shout from Bono. It is a slow and somewhat dreary number that has never been played live and barely lasts more than two minutes. The J. Swallo in the title refers to "Johnny Swallow", a member of the Lypton Village, whose real name was Reggie Manuel.

JUBILEE 2000 CAMPAIGN Jubilee 2000 is an international movement whose objective was to campaign for the cancellation of the unpayable debts owed by the world's poorest countries to the world's richest countries by the end of 2000. Although that deadline has passed the campaign continues with various protests, petitions and public events around the world. Bono is a major supporter of the campaign and first drew attention to the issue at the Brit Awards in London in February 1999.

As part of his role as roving ambassador for the campaign he has visited the United Nations' Headquarters in New York, the White House in Washington, 10 Downing Street in London and The Vatican in Rome.

Website: www.jubilee2000uk.org
See also: Drop The Debt

JUDITH/LIFE ON A DISTANT PLANET Thought by some reviewers to be the title of a U2 song, but in fact both titles come from "The Magic Carpet", an early U2 song which had been dropped from their live set by the middle of 1980.

JUST FOR KICKS This is believed to be Ireland's first ever rock compilation album, released in January 1980. It was the brainchild of Deke O'Brien, who had previously been in Bluesville in the 1960s and Bees Make Honey in the 1970s. In 1978 he started an independent label called Scoff Records, which released this album containing tracks by up-and-coming Irish bands such as The Atrix, The Teen Commandments and U2. U2's track was "Out Of Control" from the CBS Ireland only single.

JUSTIN HERMAN PLAZA, SAN FRANCISCO, CALIFORNIA, USA U2 played here on 11th November 1987

See also: Save The Yuppie Concert

KAEGI, ADRIANA She was one of the members of The Cocounts, who backed the singer Kid Creole. She provided backing vocals on three of the tracks on the *War* album.

KAHN, JOSEPH The director of the "Elevation" promo video, shot on the Tomb Raider set in Los Angeles in April 2001.

See also: Elevation promo video

KALVOYA FESTIVAL, OSLO, NORWAY U2 played a set in at this Norweigan festival on 21st August 1983. This was the last concert on European soil where U2 played the *War* set.

KAMPAH The co-director of the promo video #2 of "Even Better Than The Real Thing" along with Armando Gallo.

KANTKINO, BERLIN, GERMANY U2's first concert in Berlin and second show in Germany took place here on 17th February 1981. It was one of three dates they played in Germany.

KAPLAN, KERYN Keryn was for many years the deputy to Ellen Darst at New York's Principle Management offices. When Ellen left, Keryn took over as Director.

KAVANAGH, DAVID Originally Dave Kavanagh had been responsible for organising gigs at University College in Dublin where he was Entertainments Officer. He started his own promotions company in the late 1970s and through his friendship with Paul McGuinness became U2's booking agent. The two of them would drive the band around from gig to gig in their early days. After the band's success in the 1979 *Hot Press* Poll, David and Paul decided to book the band to play the National Stadium in Dublin in a special gig to show the popularity of U2 to visiting Island Records executives.

Dave went on to manage Clannad for fourteen years in all, ensuring that they became another international success, following in the footsteps of U2. After leaving his management role with Clannad he joined forces with Paul McGuinnness and Barbara Galavan to set up the Celtic Heartbeat label, scoring a huge worldwide triumph with *Riverdance*. In 1996 he became the chief executive of Claddagh Records.

KEARNEY, CONAL A protegy of Marcel Marceau, the great mime artist. Through sessions with him and another actor called Mannix Flynn, both Bono and Gavin Friday learned some basic stagecraft.

KELLY, ANNE-LOUISE For many years she was second in command to Paul McGuinness in the U2 organisation. Anne-Louise joined U2 as Paul's personal assistant in 1983 after graduating at Dublin's College of Communications. Her first job was to sort out the U2 office, which then was in the spare room of Paul's house in Ranelagh. Soon after, the U2 organisation moved into an office in Windmill Lane studios, where Anne-Louise had a staff of five working under her. One of her major triumphs in the 1980s was to help bring to fruition the 1986 Amnesty International *Conspiracy of Hope* tour. It was through her persuasion that the likes of Sting, Peter Gabriel and Brian Adams agreed to take part in the tour. By 1987 she had become Director of Principle Management, second only to Paul McGuinness, having helped build up the organisation into an international company. She left Principle in 1997 and retired temporarily from the music business before returning to manage Gavin Friday and Paul Brady.

See also: Gavin Friday

KEENAN STADIUM, CHAPEL HILL, NORTH CAROLINA, USA See: The Carolina Concert For Children

KENNEDY, JOHN One of the original road crew who worked with U2 on the *Boy* tour.

KENNELY, BRENDAN This Irish poet is probably best known for his "Book of Judas". His line, "the best way to serve an age is to betray it" was used as an adage for the whole concept of *Zoo TV* by U2. In fact Bono reviewed the book in 1991 for the *Irish Times*. Several years earlier, Brendan Kennelly as Junior Dean of Trinity College, Dublin imposed a fine of £50 on Paul McGuinness, then editor of the college magazine, after it printed an article that was deemed to be libellous.

KENNY, PAT He interviewed U2 on the *Zoo TV* special in November 1992, which was broadcast all over the world. This was where the "U2" playing in the studio are not the real U2 but in fact the Dopplegangers!

KEROUAC, JACK Writer of *On The Road*, the defining novel of the "beat generation", Kerouac's stream of consciousness prose was an attempt to mirror the improvisation of Bebop jazz saxophonists. Influential on a whole generation of artists and writers, Kerouac himself died from alcohol abuse in 1969. *On The Road* remains a highly quoted and seminal piece of prose. Bono would often read extracts from the book on the *Joshua Tree* tour before the band performed "Where The Streets Have No Name".

KERR, MRS CHRISTINE The name given to singer Chrissie Hynde on *The Unforgettable Fire* album as a dedication for her backing vocals on the track "Pride (in The Name of Love)". She was married to Jim Kerr, the lead singer with Simple Minds, at the time.
  See also: Chrissie Hynde

KEVORKIAN, FRANCOIS The DJ from New York who was the first person to remix a U2 song. It was on the suggestion of Chris Blackwell, the head of Island Records that Kevorkian, a respected New York DJ, was invited to remix the track "Two Hearts Beat As One" from the *War* album. This was to try and get U2 music across to those in the clubs of Europe and America. Kevorkian also remixed the track "New Year's Day". The tracks appeared on a special 12 inch single which was pressed intitially for DJs to play in clubs.

KEYSTONE STUDIOS, DUBLIN, IRELAND The studios where U2 recorded their first demo tape. The session took place in April 1978 shortly after they had won the Harp Lager talent contest in Limerick on 17ᵗʰ March 1978. The band recorded three songs at the session under the guidance of Jackie Hayden, but the session had to be cut short when Larry Mullen Senior arrived to take his son home as he had to get up early the next day to go to school! Unfortunately no one seems to remember what songs were actually put down at that session.

U2 came back to these studios in November 1978 to record a second demo tape, this time with Barry Devlin, the former bass player with Horslips. The songs were: "Street Mission", "Shadows And Tall Trees", Strories For Boys" and "The Fool".

See aslo: Barry Devlin / Jackie Hayden

KILDUFF, VINCENT A member of In Tua Nua who played the uilliean pipes on the track "Tomorrow" off the *October* album. He also appeared on stage with U2 performing that song live for the very first time at The Royal Dublin Society Hall on 26ᵗʰ January 1982. He then played again with U2 during their three night stint at the SFX Centre in Dublin on 22ⁿᵈ, 23ʳᵈ and 24ᵗʰ December 1982.
  See also: In Tua Nua / RDS / SFX Centre

KILMAINHAM GAOL, DUBLIN, IRELAND This former prison, situated in west Dublin, was the setting for the promo video of "A Celebration". The band were filmed performing the song in various parts of the gaol, which was also used for the film, *In The Name of the Father* and was the setting for much of the promo video.

Kilmainham Gaol, Dublin. *Photo: Claire Bolton*

See also: A Celebration / In The Name of the Father

KILKENNY, OSSIE U2's accountant for many years. Ossie was educated at Gormanstown College near Dublin and then at University College Dublin, where he graduated as an accountant. He also played in a band called the Chosen Few. Apart from U2 his clients have included other notable Irish rock musicians including Van Morrison, Bob Geldof, Sinead O'Connor and Chris de Burgh. Kilkenny also helped Paul McGuinness to renegotiate U2's Island Records contract in 1984. In 1994 he was given the job of looking after the accounts for the 25th Anniversary of the Woodstock festival.

KILLEN, KEVIN An engineer who worked on several U2 recordings in the 1980s, being the assistant to Steve Lillywhite on *War* and to Brian Eno/Daniel Lanois on *The Unforgettable Fire*, both of which he mixed. He was also responsible for the recording of the track "Heartland" at Danesmoat in 1986. The track was left off *The Joshua Tree* album but was included on *Rattle & Hum*. He also worked with Daniel Lanois on Peter Gabriel's best selling album *So*, which led to him moving to New York. Here he worked with Patti Smith, Kate Bush and Brian Ferry. The artist he has worked most with has been Elvis Costello – five albums, including *The Juliet Letters*, *Kojak Variety* and *Painted From Memory*.

KING, BB ("Blues Boy" King) The world famous blues musician has recorded over fifty albums in his long and highly productive career. He was born

Bono and blues legend BB King onstage at the Westfalenhalle, Dortmund, Germany, 1989
Photo: Kay Bauersfeld

in Indianola, Mississippi in 1925 and has played with many musicians from all musical backgrounds, including The Rolling Stones and The Crusaders. U2 first saw BB King play at a concert in Dublin and invited him and his band to support them on some dates on the third leg of the *Joshua Tree* tour in the USA.

Their first meeting was at a soundcheck at the Tarrant County Convention Center in Fort Worth in Texas on 24th November 1987. The event was filmed for inclusion in the film *Rattle & Hum*, showing Bono giving BB the lyrics of "When Love Comes To Town". BB King opened for U2 that night and then joined the band for their encore singing "When Love Comes To Town" live for the first time. U2 then recorded the song at Sun Studios in Memphis a few days afterwards, with BB adding his guitar parts later. The song was included in the *Rattle and Hum* film soundtrack and released as single in April 1989 shortly after BB King had played a gig at the National Stadium in Dublin on 11th March 1989. At this show, Bono and The Edge joined BB on stage to play "When Love Comes To Town" and "Lucille". BB King was then the support act for U2 for the *Lovetown* tour of Australia and Europe in 1989-90. In October 1998, The Edge presented BB with a Lifetime Achievement Award at the Music of Black Origin (MOBO) Awards ceremony in London.

See also: "When Love Come To Town" / *Lovetown* tour

BB KING'S BLUES CLUB MEMPHIS TENNESSEE The members of U2 visited this club the day after their Liberty Bowl concert in Memphis on 14th May 1997. The Edge got up on stage to play with house band The King Beez, performing "Stand By Me".

KING, MARTIN LUTHER The black American preacher and civil rights leader who was assassinated in 1968 has been a big inspiration for both Bono and the other members of U2. Bono first mentioned King when he was talking about "Sunday Bloody Sunday", saying how he hoped that someone like him would come forth out of the troubles of Northern Ireland to bring about peace.

The band were futher inspired by a visit to the Chicago Peace Museum in May 1983. The museum features a major section dedicated to King's life and work. Their next album, *The Unforgettable Fire*, contained two songs dedicated to him – "MLK" and "Pride (In The Name of Love)". When the *Joshua Tree* tour was about to start in America on 2nd April 1987 at the State University Activity Center in Tempe Arizona, the band asked promoter Barry Fey to read out a statement. This concerned the fact that a public holiday in honour of Martin Luther King's birthday (15th January) was likely to be scrapped by the then Governor of Arizona, Evan Mecham.

The statement said: "Governor Meechum is an embarrassment to the people of Arizona. We condemn his actions and views as an insult to a great spiritual leader." Unlike some other groups, such as The Doobie Brothers who boycotted playing gigs in

Martin Luther King appears on screen on the Pop Mart Tour *Photo: Claire Bolton*

Arizona altogether, U2 chose to play there and draw attention to the issue. This speech and part of the gig were shown in the documentary film *Outside It's America* made by Barry Devlin in 1987. Martin Luther King was again to the fore with U2 on their *Zoo TV* tour. Whenever "Pride (In The Name of Love)" was performed, film of Martin Luther King making his famous "Promised Land" speech, was screened mid-way through the song. He was also shown on the screen for the *Pop Mart* tour during "Pride".

See also: Governor Mechum / MLK / Pride (In The Name of Love)

KINGDOM SOUND STUDIO, LONG ISLAND, NEW YORK, USA During the *October* tour of America, the band spent a couple of days at these studios in November 1981. It is thought that the producer at the session was Jimmy Destri of Blondie fame. The song they recorded is believed to be called "Be There" but it was never released, as the band were not happy with the outcome.

See also: Be There / Jimmy Destri

KINGDOME SEATTLE, WASHINGTON STATE, USA U2 played their last concert of the *Pop Mart* tour (North American leg) here on 12th December 1997. As it was the final show of the tour and near Christmas, a Christmas tree had been placed at the top of the giant arch on the stage and Bono entered the venue in a red and white gown in the guise of Santa Claus. During "Even Better Than The Real Thing" several of the roadies came on stage wearing muscle man shirts, like Bono had worn at the start of the show. During "If You Wear That Velvet Dress" the "girl" that Bono danced with turned out to be bass technician Stuart Morgan dressed as a woman. He even squeezed Bono's bottom! At one point Bono briefly put on a Santa hat that a fan had thrown onto the catwalk. The song "One" was dedicated to Kurt Cobain who was from Seattle. As the show ended, Larry and Adam left the stage but Bono and Edge stayed and sang "40" for the first time since 1990. Bono finished with the words: "The next time you see us, things will be different. I don't think we can afford to do this kind of thing anymore."

KING'S HALL, BELFAST, NORTHERN IRELAND The one and only time U2 played at this large Belfast venue, and their first gig in Belfast for almost five years, took place on 24th June 1987 during the *Joshua Tree* tour to a capacity crowd of 8,000.

"THE KING'S NEW CLOTHES" An early U2 song played in their live shows, but which never made it on to vinyl.

KIRWAN, ROB One of the engineers on the *Zooropa* and *Pop* albums.

The entrance to the Kitchen, U2's Dublin nightcub.
Photo: Mark Chatterton

KISS AMC A rap group from Manchester, England who sampled some of the U2 track, "New Year's Day" for their 1989 single entitled "A Bit of U2".

KITCHEN, THE The name of the club in the basement of the Clarence Hotel in Dublin that was set up by U2 opening in February 1994. It is a serious dance club and was the brainchild of U2 after they had experienced other dance clubs around the world during the *Zoo TV* tour. The site is the old kitchens of the Clarence Hotel, hence the name. The refit cost an estimated £300,000.

Website: www.the-kitchen.co.ie
See also: the Clarence Hotel

KITCHEN RECORDS An underground record label specialising in dance acts that was set up by U2 in 1998. It is run by Reggie Manuel who is also its A&R man.

"KITE" (*ALL THAT YOU CAN'T LEAVE BEHIND* ALBUM TRACK) (4.23) The fifth track on the *All That You Can't Leave Behind* album. This is apparently a song about the new millenium looking back from the year 2030. It was first peformed live at the San Jose Arena on 20th April 2001 during the *Elevation* tour (first leg) of America.

KLARICK, BRUSSELS, BELGIUM U2's first concert in Belgium took place here on 18th October 1980.

KLEIN, JON The co-director of "The Fly" promo video alongside Ritchie Smythe.

KLEIN, NICHOLAS The writer of the script of *The Million Dollar Hotel* for which he and Bono had written the original story line.

See aslo: Million Dollar Hotel

K-MART STORE, GREENWICH VILLAGE, NEW YORK CITY, USA This was the venue for the press conference that announced the *Pop Mart* tour. The conference was held in a section called "Pop Group" which was right next door to the lingerie department. After answering questions from the world's media, U2 performed "Holy Joe" for the one and only time to date.

See also: Holy Joe / *Pop Mart* tour

"KNOCKIN' ON HEAVEN'S DOOR" U2 have performed this Bob Dylan many times at their shows over the years. The band used it at some shows on their *Unforgettable Fire* tour as a way of inviting a member of the audience up on stage to play along with the band. Also, Bono has actually performed the song with its writer, Bob Dylan, on several occasions.

See also: Bob Dylan

KNOX, DON See - SPUD

KOBAYASHI, IWAKICHI He was the person who founded "The Unforgettable Fire" exhibition.

KOHL, HELMUT U2 played at the other Olympic stadium in Germany, the site of the 1972 Olympic Games in Munich, to a capacity crowd of 56,000 fans on 4th June 1993. Macphisto rang the German Chancellor, Helmut Kohl from the stage and left the message, "I'm back!"

KONSERTHUSET, STOCKHOLM, SWEDEN U2 played just one concert here on 15th December 1982. Prior to the show the group went out into the hills surrounding Stockholm to shoot scenes for the promo video of "New Year's Day".

KOSEVO STADIUM, SARAJEVO, BOSNIA HERZEGOVINA This special gig in Sarajevo took place on 23rd September 1997 during the *Pop Mart* tour of Europe. Sarajevo was a place dear to the hearts of U2 and nightly on their previous tour (the *Zooropa/Zoo TV* tour) they had communicated with the beseiged inhabitants by satellite, drawing attention to the plight of those trapped there. Soon after the war finished in 1995 Bono visited as a guest of the mayor to Sajarevo for New Year celebrations in 1996.

A year later U2 were at last able to play in Sarajevo. Tickets for the show were three times cheaper than for the other European *Pop Mart* shows and special buses and trains were laid on to bring fans from other areas of Bosnia-Herzogivina. This included trains running for the first time since the war had ended from Mostar in the south and Maglaj in the north.

At the start of the concert Bono said, "Viva Sarajevo! Fuck the past! Kiss the Future! Viva Sarajevo!" to the 45,000 fans present. Although Bono had problems with his voice for much of the set, the crowd joined in and sang for him on many numbers. There were two highlights in the show. The first was The Edge singing "Sunday Bloody Sunday" by himself, the first time in the tour that this song was performed. The second highlight was the first live performance by all of U2 of "Miss Sarajevo". The band were joined by Brian Eno, whilst Pavarotti's section was played over the speakers. All proceeds from the show went to the War Child charity.

Set list: Mojo, I Will Follow, Gone, Even Better Than The Real Thing, Last Night On Earth, Until The End Of The World, New Year's Day, Pride, I Still Haven't Found What I'm Looking For (Stand By Me/ All I Want Is You), Staring At The Sun, Sunday Bloody Sunday, Bullet The Blue Sky, Please, Where The Streets Have No Name, Lemon, Discotheque, If You Wear That Velvet Dress, With Or Without You, Miss Sarajevo, Hold Me Thrill Me Kiss Me Kill Me, Mysterious Ways, One (Unchained Melody).

See also: Sarajevo/Miss Sarajevo

KOZ, DAVID He played saxophone on the "When Love Comes To Town" (Kingdom Mix).

KRAFTWERK The German synthesizer band, who had a number one hit in the UK with "The Model", were one of the support bands who played at the "Stop Sellefield" protest gig at the Manchester G-Mex centre on 19th June 1992. They were also featured in the video of the concert entitled *Stop Sellafield - The Concert*.

The previous month, when U2 played to a sell out crowd of 10,000 at the Festhalle in Frankfurt on 28th May 1992, Kraftwerk were in the audience that night and Bono dedicated "Satellite of Love" to them.

See also: Stop Sellafield concert and video

KRO STUDIOS, HILVERSUM, HOLLAND U2's first show in Holland and in Europe took place at this radio station on 14th October 1980. The show was recorded and transmitted the next day, prior to the group playing their first Dutch gig at Amsterdam's The Milkyway.

KUTI, FELA Controversial Nigerian band leader who created a unique style of music called "Afro-Beat". He was one of the guests who appeared on stage at the final show of the *Conspiracy of Hope* tour of America in 1986. He was there as he had served 20 months in prison for his political beliefs, but through the efforts of Amnesty International members Kuti had been released.

See also: Amnesty International

L

"LADY WITH THE SPINNING HEAD (UVI)" ("ONE" SINGLE) (3.54) This song was featured as one of the tracks on the "One" single released in February 1992. It was included in all three single formats and was produced by Paul Barrett. It seems to be an amalgamation of "The Fly" and "Ultra Violet", though which came first is open to question.

"LADY WITH THE SPINNING HEAD (UV1) (EXTENDED DANCE MIX)" ("EVEN BETTER THAN THE REAL THING" SINGLE) (6.08) Alan Moulder was responsible for remixing this track, which had originally appeared on the "One" single.

LANCASTER PARK, CHRISTCHURCH, NEW ZEALAND U2 have played this New Zealand rugby stadium twice. The first time was on 4th November 1989 during the *Lovetown* tour. This was the biggest concert ever to be held in Christchurch, with over 40,000 fans attending. U2 then returned here with the *Zoo TV* show, playing a concert on 1st December 1993. This time there were only 25,000 fans watching U2 on a bitterly cold day. At both shows, "One Tree Hill", the song dedicated to New Zealander Greg Carroll, was played.

LANOIS, DANIEL The French-Canadian record producer. He was first brought into the U2 camp when he came along with Brian Eno to help with the produc-

Daniel Lanois *Photo: David Redfern / Redferns*

tion of U2's fourth album, *The Unforgettable Fire*, in 1984. As a result of that collaboration, Lanois was asked to work with Peter Gabriel on the soundtrack album *Birdy* (1984) and then the albums *So* (1986) and *Us* (1992). He also worked with Robbie Robertson of The Band on his solo album in 1987, and with Bob Dylan on his 1989 *Oh Mercy* album.

Already a musician and producer in his own right, Lanois had set up his own studio in his native Canada called Grant Avenue Studio in the 1970s. In 1979 Brian Eno used Lanois' studio. They both hit it off and when Eno was asked by U2 to produce their fourth album, he insisted on having Daniel Lanois to work with him. Initially taking the role as engineer, Lanois gradually spread his influence on such tracks as "Elvis Presley & America" and "The 4th Of July", both of which convey a particular atmosphere rather than a sound. He and Eno then worked with U2 on *The Joshua Tree* and *Achtung Baby*, with Lanois being the main producer on the latter. He won a Grammy award for his production work on both albums.

In 1999-2000 Lanois was once again producing a U2 album with Brian Eno – *All That You Can't Leave Behind*. In addition to producing, Daniel has also contributed his own skills as a musician to several U2 tracks including "With or Without You" (tambourine) and "Zoo Station" (guitar). On *All That You Can't Leave Behind* he plays additional guitar and sings on several of the tracks. On 27th August 1992, during the *Outside Broadcast* leg of the *Zoo TV* tour, he appeared onstage with U2 at the Olympic Stadium in Montreal Canada. He played guitar and sang along to an acoustic version of "I Still Haven't Found What I'm Looking For". Lanois has released two albums himself: 1989's *Acadia* (which featured the services of Adam and Larry) and 1993's *For The Beauty of Wynona*.

LANSDOWNE ROAD STADIUM, DUBLIN, IRELAND U2 played two sell out shows at this Irish Rugby Union stadium on 30th and 31st August 1997 during the *Pop Mart* tour of Europe. For several months before, it was touch and go whether they would take place at all. This was due to opposition from some local residents who were concerned about noise and other problems a concert of this size would bring. In the end the whole affair had to be settled in the Irish Courts with promoters MCD eventually winning the right to stage the concerts at a hearing on 1st August. It was rumoured that U2 paid for local residents to go away on holiday for the weekend, or if they chose to stay, they received free tickets.

During the first night Bono made amusing references to the neighbours who had brought the court case, such as "Hey Missus, can I have my ball back please?" and "Keep the noise down – I don't want to get us thrown out of here!" to the 42,000 capacity crowd. At the end of "Pride" Bono added the old Irish song, "Molly Malone" and for the karaoke The Edge played Dana's "All Kinds of Everything" which he introduced as a future Irish National Anthem. The song "One" was dedicated to Bill Graham, an old friend of U2's and a former champion of the band.

The second show was overshadowed by the death of Princess Diana and Dodi Al Fayed in Paris earlier that day. Images of Diana were displayed on the TV screen and Bono dedicated "MLK" to her saying, "I was surprised how much that affected me: we're a lot the same, the English and the Irish". As the audience left the stadium "Candle In The Wind" was played over the speakers. The band included "Dirty Old Town" and "Whiskey In The Jar" in their set.

See also: Diana, Princess of Wales

LARK BY THE LEE FESTIVAL, CORK, IRELAND U2 made a surprise appearance here on 25th August 1985, their first live concert after *Live Aid*. The band played an hour long set, this being the final show based around *The Unforgettable Fire* album. The band then played just one concert over the next eighteen months (at *Self Aid* in May 1986) as they were recording *The Joshua Tree* album.

"LAST NIGHT ON EARTH" (*POP* ALBUM TRACK) (4.45) The sixth track on the *Pop* album. With a catchy hook line, it describes a woman who is living life at a pace so fast, it is as if the end of the world was about to happen. The song contains excerpts from "Trayra Boia". It was first performed live at the Sam Boyd Stadium in Las Vegas, Nevada on the opening night of the *Pop Mart* tour on 25th April 1987.

"LAST NIGHT ON EARTH" (SINGLE) (CID 664/572 051-2) (4.14) The single version of this *Pop* album track was released in July 1997 in the US where it could only reach a lowly number 57. In the UK it was released in August 1997 during the middle of the *Pop Mart* tour of Europe and reached a more respectable number 10 on the UK singles chart. The CD single also included the tracks "Pop Muzik" (Pop Mart Mix) and "Happiness Is a Warm Gun" (The Gun Mix).

"LAST NIGHT ON EARTH" (FIRST NIGHT IN HELL MIX) (5.50) This remix version of "Last Night On Earth" was released as a separate single (CIDX 664/572-2) to the standard version. As well as this track it contained "Numb" (the Soul Assassins Mix), "Happiness Is a Warm Gun" (The Danny Sauber Mix) and "Pop Muzik" (Pop Mart Mix).

"LAST NIGHT ON EARTH" (LIVE) (ELEVATION SINGLE) (6.20) This live version was recorded at

the Foro Sol Autodromo, Mexico City, on the 3rd December 1997

"LAST NIGHT ON EARTH" (LIVE) (*POP MART LIVE FROM MEXICO CITY* VIDEO) The sixth track on the video *Pop Mart Live From Mexico City* was filmed at the band's concert at the Foro Sol Autodromo, Mexico City, Mexico on 3rd December 1997.

"LAST NIGHT ON EARTH" (PROMOTIONAL VIDEO) The promotional video for the single "Last Night on Earth" was shot in Kansas City, Missouri, USA on 19th and 20th May. The video shoot is probably best remembered by the residents of Kansas City for the fact that it caused traffic jams on all the main roads in the region including Interstate Highways 35, 70 and 670. The latter highway was closed completely on one stretch showing U2 driving a car along this deserted highway with the Kansas City skyline in the background.

The idea behind the video was that of an airborne virus killing all forms of life and U2 being the only survivors – a type of spoof of the Sci-Fi films that were popular in the 1950s and 60s. The poet Allen Ginsberg was shown at the end of the video pushing a shopping trolley with a spotlight in it. The director was William Burroughs who died not long after.

See also: William Burroughs / Allen Ginsberg

THE LATE LATE SHOW The longest running show on Irish TV. This chat show was for many years hosted

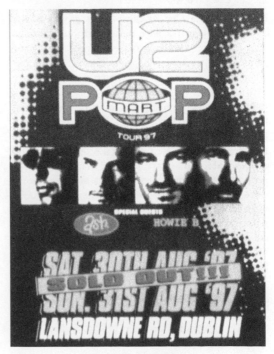

Photo: Wendy Chatterton

by Gay Byrne. U2 first appeared on 15th January 1980 when they performed "Stories For Boys" live. On 16th March 1987 they took part in a special show, which celebrated the 25th anniversary of one of Ireland's most popular groups, the Dubliners. U2 sang "Springhill Mining Disaster" and joined the Dubliners and The Pogues at the end of the show.

When the politician John Hume appeared on the programme in October 1998 after he was named as co-winner of the Nobel Peace Prize 1998 with David Trimble, Bono rang the programme to offer his congratulations. A few weeks later U2 appeared on the show – a special edition to remember the victims of the Omagh bomb. U2 played "North And South Of The River" for the first time and "All I Want Is You". On 21st May 1999, Bono and Larry appeared on the programme to give presenter Gay Byrne a special leaving present – a Harley Davidson motorbike!

See also: Gay Byrne / The Dubliners / The Pogues / Springhill Mining Disaster

LEAN ON ME The Bill Withers song recorded by Kirk Franklin in 1998 with backing from Bono, Mary J Blige, R Kelly, Crystal Lewis and The Family. It reached number 79 in the US charts. There was also a promo video made which featured all the singers, including Bono.

"THE LEAP" The name of a bronze sculpture created in Ireland that had been inspired by Bono's leap from the stage at Live Aid.

LED ZEPPELIN One of the biggest groups of the 1970s. Although U2 have never performed onstage with any of the members of Led Zeppelin, U2 have connections with Led Zeppelin through their tour manager Dennis Sheehan who had been tour manager with Led Zeppelin throughout the 1970s. Rumour has it that after one English gig in the Birmingham area, Dennis took U2 to Robert Plant's house to meet him. Also U2's guru and DJ for the 1992 Zoo TV tour, BP Fallon, had been Led Zeppelin's press officer. The early U2 are said to have included the odd Led Zeppelin number in their sets and on a couple of occasions The Edge has played segments of the band's most famous song "Stairway to Heaven" on stage. Also, "Whole Lotta Love" was played at several of the Pop Mart shows. The Edge actually got to play with Jimmy Page in 1991, when he inducted the Yardbirds into the Rock 'n' Roll Hall of Fame.

See also: BP Fallon / Dennis Sheehan

LEE COUNTY ARENA, FORT MYERS, FLORIDA, USA The first date that U2 played as support act to the J Geils Band tour of America in 1982 took place on 3rd March 1982. It was the first time that they had played in an arena as opposed to halls and theatres, but the 6,000 crowd did not seem to intimidate the band who played a shortened set of about 45 minutes.

LEGION FIELD, BIRMINGHAM, ALABAMA USA U2 did not manage to sell out their first ever show in the state of Alabama, selling 35,000 out of the 40,000 tickets available. They played here on 7th October 1992 as part of the Zoo TV *Outside Broadcast* tour.

LEISURELAND, GALWAY, IRELAND U2 have played three concerts in this west of Ireland town. The first, on 18th December 1980, was their first date in Ireland after returning from their maiden visit to America. They played here again on 23rd January 1982 on a three date Irish tour to promote the *October* album. Their last visit here was also in 1982, on 19th December during the pre-*War* tour of Europe.

LEIXLIP CASTLE, DUBLIN, IRELAND The audience of 15,000 present at this Festival on 27th July 1980 was the biggest crowd that U2 had played to so far in their career. It was part of the "Dublin Festival 1980" with The Police being the headlining band. It was also the first time that U2 had played at an outdoor festival.

"LEMON" (*ZOOROPA* ALBUM TRACK) (6.56) The fourth track on side one of the *Zooropa* album. The most prominent feature of the track is Bono's falsetto vocal. It also featured The Edge and Brian Eno on backing vocals. This disco number was one of the strongest tracks off *Zooropa* but was only released as a single in Australia, though the track was remixed extensively for club DJs. To date "Lemon" has been the U2 single remixed the most times.

"LEMON" (SINGLE EDIT) (4.42) The single of "Lemon" was released in Australia to tie in with the visit of U2 in the Autumn of 1993 for the *Zoomerang* tour. The CD format (858 115-2) featured the following tracks. "Lemon" (Edit), "Lemon" (Oakenfold EP Mix), "Lemon" (Album Version) and "Lemon" (Morales BYC Version Dub).

"LEMON" (PROMOTIONAL RELEASES) "Lemon" was released in a limited edition of 1,000 copies in the UK as a promo for DJs in September 1993. This was released as both a double 12 inch pack (12LEM DJ1 & DJ2) and as single 12 inch. DJ1 contained the following remixes of Lemon: Bad Yard Club Mix, Momo Beats, Version Dub and Serious Def Dub, whilst DJ2 contained The Perfecto Mix and The Trance Mix. In the USA, there was a promo 12 inch and CD of Lemon which contained the Lemon track off the *Zooropa* album coupled with The Lemonade Mix. There were also 10 inch and 12 inch vinyl promos (422826 957-1). The 10 inch contained the Bad Yard Club Mix and the Serious Def Dub, whilst the 12 inch contained the Bad Yard Club Mix, the Version Dub, the Perfecto Mix, the Jeep Mix and

Momo's Reprise mix. All the remixes of "Lemon" are shown below.

"LEMON" (BAD YARD CLUB MIX) (5.19) This remix version of "Lemon" by David Morales was featured on the Swing format version of the "Stay (Faraway So Close!)" single, as well as on the *Melon* CD given away free by *Propaganda* magazine. It was also the first track on the special DJ 12 inch promo that was limited to a 1,000 copies only in the UK.

"LEMON" (LEMONADE MIX) This remix of "Lemon" was on a US only promo release (PRCD 6800-2).

"LEMON" (MOMO BEATS MIX) This remix of "Lemon" by David Morales was only available on the special DJ 12 inch copy of the "Lemon" remixes (12 LEM DJ1).

"LEMON" (MOMO'S REPRISE) This version of "Lemon" was only available on the 12 inch vinyl version, released as a promo record in the USA.

"LEMON" (MORALES VERSION DUB) (6.36) This mix of "Lemon" by David Morales can be found on the Australian single release of "Lemon" and on the 12 inch DJ promo of "Lemon".

"LEMON" (PERFECTO MIX) (8.57) This remix version of "Lemon" was the first track on the *Melon* CD given away free by *Propaganda* magazine. It was remixed by Paul Oakenfold and Steve Osbourne and featured a female vocalist. It was also a track on the "Stay" (Swing Format) single.

"LEMON" (OAKENFOLD JEEP MIX) (5.32) This remix of "Lemon" was only available on the 12 inch vinyl version of "Lemon" that was released as a promo in the USA and on the Australian single release of "Lemon".

"LEMON" (SERIOUS DEF DUB) This mix of "Lemon" was available on the 12 inch UK DJ promo and 10 inch US promo versions of "Lemon". It was remixed by David Morales.

"LEMON" (TRANCE MIX) This remix of "Lemon" was only available on the DJ 12 inch UK promo version of "Lemon".

"LEMON" (PERFECTO MIX) (LIVE) (*HASTA LA VISTA BABY!* ALBUM TRACK) This live version of the Perfecto Mix of "Lemon" was taken from the U2 concert at the Foro Sol Autodromo in Mexico City, Mexico on 3rd December 1997 during the *Pop Mart* tour. It was the number played over the PA as the lemon containing U2 came down onto the stage. It was on the CD that was given away free to *Propaganda* readers in the summer of 2000.

"LEMON" (LIVE) (*ZOO TV LIVE FROM SYDNEY* VIDEO TRACK) This live version of "Lemon" comes

The Lemon, Dublin, 31/8/01. *Photo: Claire Bolton*

on the *Live from Sydney* video which was filmed and recorded at the Cricket Ground, Sydney, Australia on 27th November 1993.

"LEMON" (PROMOTIONAL VIDEO) The promotional video of "Lemon" was directed by Mark Neal in London and was released to promote the *Zooropa* album. It was filmed in both colour and black and white and was released in September 1993. This is the only promo video to feature the Macphisto character in person. The time-lapse techniques used in the film were reminiscent of the motion studies by Edward Muybridge, a Victorian film maker.

"LEMON" (BAD YARD CLUB MIX) (PROMOTIONAL VIDEO) The Bad Yard Club Mix of "Lemon" promo video was also directed by Mark Neale in London and was released in October 1993.

THE LEMON The giant lemon stage prop used on the *Pop Mart* tour (1997-8). For most of the show it would be sitting by the stage wrapped in a yellow cover, but once the main set was over it would come into action. The cover would be removed revealing a mirrored lemon moving slowly down towards the walkway to the B-stage with the perfecto mix of "Lemon" playing. In clouds of smoke it would start to open and the four members of U2 would be revealed inside, standing motionless. One by one they would walk down a special staircase and start performing "Discotheque".

At the show in Oslo Norway on 6th August 1997, the lemon would not open properly so the hysterical members of U2 had to climb out at the back! Then in February 1998 Bono accepted the Brit award for best international group from inside the lemon during a recording transmitted to the ceremony in London. For the final show of the whole tour in Johannesburg, South Africa in March 1998, the band were revealed drinking champagne surrounded by balloons and streamers.

See also: Valle Hovin, Oslo / Johannesburg Stadium

LENNON, JOHN When ex-Beatle John Lennon was assassinated on 8th December 1980, U2 had been playing their first North American dates. Their date in New York at the Ritz, took place just three days before his assassination. Always a hero to Bono, U2 dedicated their song "God Part II" to him as he had written the original "God" on his solo *Plastic Ono Band* album. John Lennon also recorded a song called "Sunday Bloody Sunday" which was on his 1972 album *Sometime In New York City*. Several Beatles songs have been covered by U2 including "Happiness Is A Warm Gun" and "She Loves You". At Self Aid in 1986 the band very nearly performed Lennon's "Working Class Hero" but at the last minute decided on "Maggie's Farm", to which Bono added some of "Cold Turkey", another Lennon song. At the band's gig at The Omni, Atlanta, on 8th December 1987, Bono dedicated "40" to John as it was the seventh anniversary of his death.

See also: The Beatles / God Part II

LE PALACE PARIS FRANCE U2 played their second show in Paris here on 21st February 1981. This was their first headlining show in Paris – at their previous Paris show they had supported Talking Heads.

LESLEY, JOHN He was a fellow student of Adam's at St. Columba's College in the 1970s. John introduced Adam to some of the more "album-oriented" bands around at the time such as Crosby, Stills, Nash and Young and The Grateful Dead. He played guitar and it was through John's persuasion that Adam bought a bass guitar and so became a member of his group. Both John and Adam started writing simple songs together, but their musical dreams were broken when Adam had to leave St Columba's.

"LET'S MAKE IT WORK" The single by the Self Aid band that included Larry. The song was specially written by Paul Moran for Self Aid.

See also: Self Aid

"LET THE GOOD TIMES ROLL" The track that Bono recorded with Stevie Wonder and Ray Charles for the Quincy Jones album, *Le Q's Jook Joint.*

See also: Quincy Jones

LIBERTY HALL, DUBLIN, IRELAND U2 played a benefit gig here on 11th August 1978 in aid of the Contraceptive Action Campaign. This was a campaign against Irish laws on contraception, forbidding the selling of condoms.

See also: Contraception

LICHTENSTEIN, ROY The comic book artist whose pictures of fighter planes were used on the big screen for "Bullet The Blue Sky" on the *Pop Mart* tour. He died in 1997 aged 73.

See also: Catherine Owens

"LIFE ON A DISTANT PLANET" See: THE MAGIC CARPET

"LIKE A SONG" (*WAR* ALBUM TRACK) (4.47) The fourth track on side one of the *War* album. It is an aggressive track driven along by Larry's dominant drumming. As on "11 O'clock Tick Tock", Bono makes a plea to the young not to argue amongst themselves about which so-called fashion is best, but to make a new start. It was first performed live at the Caird Hall in Dundee, Scotland on 26th February 1983, but didn't stay in the set long, due to its difficult time signatures.

LILLIE'S BORDELLO A Dublin night club, often frequented by U2.

LILLYWHITE, STEVE The producer of the first three albums by U2: *Boy*, *October* and *War*. He had previously worked on the production of artists such as Penetration, Ultravox, Siouxsie & The Banshees and Peter Gabriel. First of all with U2, he produced their second Island single – "A Day Without Me"/ "Things To Make & Do", to see how he and the band got on. He was then asked to produce the first album, *Boy*, which was critically accepted as a promising debut from the band. Lillywhite then went onto produce its follow up, *October*, which was probably the hardest of the three, not least as the lyrics that Bono had prepared for this album had been stolen in America.

Originally Steve was not going to produce U2's third album as he had a policy of two albums maximum per band, so U2 began looking for another producer for *War*. In the end they couldn't find anyone suitable and so Steve agreed to produce *War,* which in many ways came to be the band's breakthrough album, helping to establish the band in Britain and Europe. For the fourth album U2 had decided to try a different producer and so he was not asked to produce a U2 album again. He did however mix some of the tracks off *The Joshua Tree* album, notably "Where The Streets Have No Name", "With Or Without You" and "Bullet The Blue Sky". On 2000's *All That You Can't Leave Behind* he helped out with some of the production duties. He was for many years married to the singer Kirsty MacColl, who was tragically killed in December 2000.

LIMERICK Ireland's third city. The only time that U2 are known to have played here was when they won the Harp Lager talent contest in 1978, though they may well have played here on the "Come Out To Play" tour of Ireland in early 1980.

LIMIT CLUB, SHEFFIELD, ENGLAND U2's first two concerts in the town of Sheffield took place here within two months of each other – on 23rd September and 13th November 1980.

LINANE, MAURICE The director of the U2 video collection known as *Achtung Baby - The Videos, The Cameos And A Whole Lot Of Interference From Zoo TV*. He went onto to co-direct the promo video for "Hold Me, Thrill Me, Kiss Me, Kill Me" with Kevin Godley. He also directed a live video of "Please", shot at a *Pop Mart* concert in Europe in August 1997.

LIQUOR STORE ROOFTOP AT 7TH AVENUE AND MAIN STREET, LOS ANGELES CALIFORNIA USA The roof of this store in downtown Los Angeles was the scene for the video shoot of "Where The Streets Have No Name". It took place on 27th March 1987 and caused traffic chaos when a crowd of a thousand or more assembled on the streets outside. If you look closely in the video you can see the neon sign for the original Million Dollar Hotel on the other side of the building. Some people say this was put up especially for the video shoot.

"LITTLE BLACK DRESS" This was a track off the Gavin Friday album *Shag Tobacco*, to which Bono and The Edge added backing vocals.

LITTLE RICHARD The legendary rock 'n' roll singer provided the sermon which was used on the track "When Love Comes to Town" (Live From The Kingdom Mix).

LITTLE STEVEN - (AKA MIAMI STEVE) (Real name: Steven Van Zandt). A member of Bruce Springsteen's E Street Band who formed the musical collective known as "Artists United Against Apartheid". They produced the "Sun City" single and album that included Bono, Bruce Springsteen and Bob Dylan. His band, Little Steven and The Disciples of Soul, supported U2 on several of their *Joshua Tree* tour dates in the Autumn of 1987. In 1994 Adam played on Little Steven's album, *Born Again Savage*.

See also: Artists United Against Apartheid / Sun City

LIVE AID The name of the concert that took place simultaneously at London's Wembley Stadium and Philadelphia's JFK Stadium on Saturday 13th July 1985. It was the culmination of events that had started the previous autumn in England when Bob Geldof of the Boomtown Rats had been watching a news report on BBC TV about the famine in Ethiopia.

He decided to do something about it and arranged for several musicians, including Adam and Bono to record the charity single, "Do They Know It's Christmas?" under the moniker "Band Aid".

Such was the success of the single that in January 1985 several American artists calling themselves "USA For Africa" followed suit and recorded the single "We Are The World". Both singles topped the charts around the world raising millions of pounds for famine relief. Many people felt that all these musicians donating their services for free shouldn't be a "one-off" and so demands for a concert featuring some of these artists grew. Bob Geldof, with the help of the highly regarded American promoter Bill Graham, set to work to bring the concert to reality. U2 were one of the twenty two groups and artists who had agreed to appear at the Wembley end. That summer they had already played at eight European festival shows in the weeks preceding Live Aid and so were in good form.

U2 were introduced by Jack Nicholson from the stage in Philadelphia via satellite as they took the stage at 5.20 pm London time. Bono said the words "Sunday Bloody Sunday" and the band started their set. The crowd who had been fairly subdued up until this point suddenly came to life with several U2 flags sprouting up. As The Edge was performing his solo, Bono pulled the stage cameraman towards him and pointed him to the crowd as he jumped down to the photographer's platform. The next song, "Bad", was introduced by Bono with these words: "We come from Dublin city, Ireland. Like all cities, it has its good and it has its bad. This is a song called 'Bad'". Straightaway Bono started to improvise, singing a snippet from Lou Reed's "Satellite of Love" in recognition of the event being beamed around the world by satellite.

Once again Bono jumped off the stage onto the photographer's platform and after looking into the crowd beckoned to the security men to lift a girl with blonde hair out of the crowd. As the men were struggling to pull her free, Bono suddenly jumped a full ten feet onto the platform below. In the confusion another girl was pulled out for Bono to dance with before the original girl and her sister (Melanie and Elaine Hills) were finally united with Bono. He also sang snippets from the Rolling Stones' "Sympathy For The Devil" and "Ruby Tuesday", as well as another Lou Reed song, "Walk on the Wild Side". From the latter he sang the improvisation, "Holly came from Miami FLA, hitchhiked all the way across the USA. She could hear the satellite coming down, pretty soon she was in London Town... Wembley Stadium! And all the people went Do-do-do-do..." Apart from those at the front, most of the audience could not see what was going on, but for those watching on the TV it was a very real act of artist reaching out to the audience, something Bono had done at countless previous shows.

Eventually Bono got back to the stage with the band still playing "Bad". He then picked up a towel and walked off looking upset as U2 were faded from the TV screen and the Beach Boys in Philadelphia started their set. U2 had planned to play "Pride" as their final number but as "Bad" had gone on too long, the song had to be dropped. At the time Bono thought that he had overstepped the mark and spoilt the impression that U2 could have made at Live Aid. But weeks later after meeting a sculptor who was creating a statue called "The Leap" about the singer's plunge into the audience, Bono was convinced that it had been right. Bono was later interviewed after the set and U2 also issued a statement about their involvement in Live Aid:

"U2 are involved in Live Aid because it's more than money, it's music; but it's also a demonstration to the politicians and policy-makers that men, women and children as they lie, bellies swollen, starving to death for the sake of a cup of grain and water. For the price of Star Wars, the MX missile offensive-defence budgets, the deserts of Africa could be turned into fertile lands. The technology is with us. The technocrats are not. Are we part of a civilisation that protects itself by investing in life... or investing in death?"

After sets by The Who, Dire Straits, Queen, Elton John and Paul McCartney, there was a star-studded grand finale of "Do They Know It's Christmas". Bono shared Paul McCartney's microphone and sang his line from the song, adding "Tell them Springtime is here!" While the concert wound up in Wembley it continued for another six hours in Philadelphia. Press reports proclaimed U2, along with Queen, as the stars of the Wembley show. The concert helped to raise

U2's profile to a worldwide audience and their next world tour saw them making the jump from arenas to stadiums, making them one of the biggest rock acts in the world.

See also: Band Aid / "Do They Know It's Christmas?" / Bob Geldof / The Leap / Jack Nicholson / Wembley Stadium

"LIVE MY LIFE TONIGHT" A song that the early U2 recorded onto a demo tape, but was never released on record.

LIVE FOR IRELAND (ALBUM) This was the 1987 album release of the 1986 *Self Aid* concert which featured all the main artists who took part including The Boomtown Rats, Rory Gallagher, Van Morrison and The Pogues. U2 are included singing the Bob Dylan song "Maggie's Farm".

LLOYD NOBEL CENTER, NORMAN, OAKLAHOMA, USA This was one venue where the promoter made a big mistake by booking U2 into a venue they were not yet ready to play. Only 2,000 of the 13,000 seats were sold for the show on 10th June 1983. However, the gig did still go ahead with the audience moving forward to seats nearer the stage. Not surprisingly, this was the last show to date that U2 have played in the state of Oklahoma.

LOGAN CAMPBELL CENTRE, AUCKLAND, NEW ZEALAND U2 played two shows here on 1st and 2nd September 1984 – the first time U2 had played in New Zealand's capital city. On the second night, U2 premiered the song "The Unforgettable Fire" which had yet to be released. These shows are also memorable for the fact that this was the town where Greg Carroll, Bono's personal roadie, was first hired. He then stayed with the band for two years until he was killed in a motorcycle accident in Dublin.

See also: Greg Caroll

LONDON, ENGLAND After Dublin, London was the most important place for the young U2 to conquer. As capital of England it was the home of many important record labels who might one day sign U2, as well as the home of several important music journals including the *New Musical Express*, *Melody Maker* and *Sounds* all of whom could give the band much-needed publicity. Although U2 had to raise £3,000 to play their first gigs outside of Ireland in December 1979, both Bono and Paul McGuinness had already visited London earlier in the year. Paul had gone in the spring of 1979 armed with the demo tape they had recorded in Dublin with Barry Devlin.

Not much happened on this first trip, but after U2 had reached number 1 in the Irish charts with U2-3, Bono had gone to London himself, taking Ali and his friend, Andrew Whiteway with him. He had delivered copies of the single to every music journal in

London in the hope of igniting some interest in U2. When the band did eventually play in the capital at Islington's Hope & Anchor pub, things went wrong when a string on The Edge's guitar broke and their set was hastily abandoned in front of several record company talent scouts. However the band managed to start a London U2 following through playing ten London venues during this visit. The following year, in September 1980, the track "Boy-Girl", recorded at the Marquee in central London, was put on the B-side of their "I Will Follow" single.

Gradually the band made its way up through the different sized London rock venues – the Marquee, Hammersmith Odeon, Wembley Arena and eventually to the prestigious Wembley stadium where they first played in July 1985 at Live Aid. Since then they have gone on to play at Wembley in their own right on eight occasions. Apart from playing in London, U2 have also recorded several of their promo videos there, either in studios or on street locations, such as "Even Better Than The Real Thing" (Carnaby Street) and "The Fly" (Piccadilly Circus). In 2001 London was one of three cities around the world where U2 played "secret" warm-up gigs prior to the *Elevation* tour. The London venue they chose was the Astoria where they played on 7th February. At their most recent concerts at Earl's Court in August 2001, Bono mentioned most of the London venues they had played at during the song "I Will Follow" and referred to the fact that they had lived in London during 1980.

See also: The Astoria / Earl's Court / *Even Better Than The Real Thing* promo video / *The Fly* promo video / The Marquee / Wembley Stadium

LONDON SCHOOL OF ECONOMICS, LONDON, ENGLAND U2 played this educational establishment,

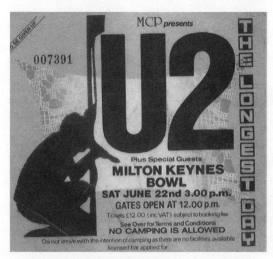

The Longest Day, Milton Keynes, 22/6/85

famous for its student protests in the 1960s, on 4th October 1980 on the UK leg of the *Boy* tour

LONE JUSTICE A four-piece rock band from Los Angeles who were given the support slot to U2 on their *Unforgettable Fire* tour through America in 1985. They also supported U2 at several American dates on the 1987 *Joshua Tree* tour. Their female vocalist, Maria McKee, had a very powerful voice and was invited on stage to sing with Bono on several occasions. Bono provided guest vocals on her 1999 album, *This World Is Not My Home*.

See also: Maria McKee

"THE LONG BLACK VEIL" Bono added backing vocals to this track by The Chieftains, the title track of their *The Long Black Veil* album.

LONGEST DAY CONCERT, MILTON KEYNES BOWL, MILTON KEYNES ENGLAND U2 headlined this one day festival at the Milton Keynes Bowl entitled 'The Longest Day' on 22nd June 1985. There was a crowd of 50,000 in attendance and U2 were supported by R.E.M, The Ramones, Billy Bragg, Spear of Destiny and The Faith Brothers. This was the band's biggest UK audience to date and the first time they had played in Britain that year. Despite the fact that it rained the crowd still showed a lot of enthusiasm. U2 even sang some of the Beatles song, "Rain" in their set when the sequencer broke down at the star of "Bad".

LORELEI AMPHITHEATRE, ST. GOARSHUSEN, GERMANY U2 played before an audience of 20,000 at the "Lorelei Festival" on 20th August 1983. Others on the bill included Joe Cocker, Steve Miller, The Stray Cats and Dave Edmunds. The whole festival was broadcast live on German TV and radio for the TV programme *Rockpalast*. This was the first time that U2 had played live on television and Bono's performance betrayed his nervousness. However the band played a good set, so much so that five of the songs they played were included on the live mini-album, *Under A Blood Red Sky*: "Cry"/"The Electric Co", "Sunday Bloody Sunday", "I Will Follow", "New Year's Day" and "40" (which was released as a single in Germany).

"THE LOST HIGHWAY" This Hank Williams song was one which Bono and The Edge sang live on the American leg of the *Joshua Tree* tour, both as U2 and as The Dalton Brothers. The band are shown playing the song in a Houston Texas night-club in the film *Outside It's America*. It was also performed specially for the final edition of the UK TV programme *The Tube*.

LOUISIANA STATE UNIVERSITY ASSEMBLY CENTER, BATON ROUGE, LOUISIANA, USA U2 played to a capacity crowd of 15,000 fans here on 26th November 1987 during the *Joshua Tree* tour of America. The show was filmed in part by Phil Joanou but none of the footage made it onto the film of *Rattle & Hum*.

"THE LOUNGE FLY MIX" ("THE FLY" SINGLE) (6.28) This remix of "The Fly" was produced by Daniel Lanois and engineered by Flood, who also did the remix. It was available as an extra track on the 12 inch and CD versions of "The Fly" single.

"LOVE COMES TUMBLING" ("THE UNFORGETTA-BLE FIRE" SINGLE B-SIDE) (4.40) This track was available on the 12 inch and double 7 inch versions of "The Unforgettable Fire" single. It was also included on the compilation CD *The B-Sides* which was part of *The Best of 1980-1990* package.

"LOVE COMES TUMBLING" (*WIDE AWAKE IN AMERICA* EP TRACK) (4.45) The same version of "Love Comes Tumbling" as above is also available on the American mini-album which was originally released in May 1987.

"LOVE FROM A SHORT DISTANCE" A poem that Bono wrote for the people of East Timor in November 1995, that appeared on a benefit album to raise funds for that nation.

"LOVE IS BLINDNESS" (*ACHTUNG BABY* ALBUM TRACK) (4.23) The final track on the *Achtung Baby* album. As the title suggests the song is about the despair that love can bring. It is an emotional song that is uplifted by Edge's guitar break and Bono's wailing at the end. The song was used as one of the encores on the *Zoo TV* tour. It was first performed live at the Civic Centre in Lakeland, Florida on 29th February 1992, the opening night of the *Zoo TV* tour.

"LOVE IS BLINDNESS" (LIVE) ("STAY" SINGLE) (5.58) This live version of "Love is Blindness" was included on the Live format version of the "Stay (Faraway So Close)" single, released in November 1993. It was recorded live at the Yankee Stadium, New York on 30th August 1992 and is one of only four live tracks from the *Zoo TV* tour that have been officially released.

"LOVE IS BLINDNESS" (LIVE) (*ZOO TV LIVE FROM SYDNEY* VIDEO TRACK) The only live footage of this song is available on the *Live from Sydney* video filmed at the Cricket Ground, Sydney on 27th November 1993. As was customary during this song, a girl was chosen from the audience to come up on stage and dance with Bono.

"LOVE IS BLINDNESS" (NUMB VIDEO SINGLE) (4.23) "Love Is Blindness" was included as the third track on the "Numb" video single. It was directed by Matt Mahurin, who was also responsible for the camera work and editing. He had previously taken the photos on the cover of the *Wide Awake In America* mini-album. The video shows live clips of this

The Edge on The Lovetown Tour.
Photo: Emma Reilly

sad song interspersed with scenes of children, dolphins, streets and clouds.

"LOVE RESCUE ME" (*RATTLE & HUM* ALBUM TRACK) (6.23) The second track on the third side of the *Rattle & Hum* album. The lyrics were jointly written by Bono and Bob Dylan in November 1987. Bono was staying in a rented house in the Beverley Hills district of Los Angeles. After Bono had a dream about Bob Dylan singing a song, Dylan rang him and invited him over to his place. Although Bono had started writing the lyrics, it was Dylan who helped finish them off. There is a lot of Biblical imagery in the song and it is interesting to note that Dylan went through a born again Christian phase in the late 1970s and early 1980s. From the lyrics it would seem that this had now been rejected for a more open view of religion and life in general. The song was recorded at Sun Studios, Memphis on the night of 29th/30th November 1987, though Dylan's backing vocals were added at a later date.

See also: Bob Dylan / Sun Studios

"LOVE RESCUE ME" (LIVE) ("ANGEL OF HARLEM" SINGLE B-SIDE) This live version of "Love Rescue Me" was recorded live at the *Smile Jamaica* concert at the Dominion Theatre in London on 16th October 1988. It included Keith Richards on guitar and Ziggy Marley and the Melody Makers on backing vocals, as well as The Rumour horn section. It was included on the B-side of the 12 inch and CD versions of the "Angel of Harlem" single.

See also: Smile Jamaica Concert

LOVETOWN TOUR The tour that U2 made at the end of 1989, initially of Australia, New Zealand and Japan. Later dates were added in Ireland, France, Holland and Germany. The tour was originally planned to finish at the Point Depot in Dublin on 31st December 1989 but due to problems with Bono losing his voice at a show in Amsterdam on 18th December 1989, four extra shows were added in Rotterdam on 5th, 6th, 9th and 10th January 1990.

This was U2's first tour in nearly two years since the end of the *Joshua Tree* tour. It was also the first time that they had played Australia and New Zealand since 1984 and in Japan since 1983 so demand for tickets was very high. As it was the first tour since the release of the *Rattle & Hum* album, the set consisted of several songs from that album including "All I Want Is You", "Angel of Harlem", "Love Rescue Me", "God Part II" and "Van Diemen's Land". As U2 were playing at the same venue several nights running and as many fans had brought tickets for more than one show, U2 had a selection of 35 songs that they would chose from, playing around 20 each show, but varying the set so that it was different each night. All the dates on the tour sold out and a documentary film was made of the Australian leg entitled *Lovetown*, directed by Richard Lowenstein.

The stage set was designed by Rene Castro from Chile, the mural artist who had appeared onstage at the *Conspiracy of Hope* tour. BB King and his band, who had played a few dates as support act in America in 1987, were the support act for the whole tour and would join U2 during encores. For the Australian shows, two female backing vocalists were featured, Sherine and Zan Abeyratne. For the European shows they were replaced by two singers called Claudia and Sophia. Three of the shows scheduled to take place at the Sydney Entertainment Centre on 22nd, 25th and 26th October had to be postponed and rescheduled due to Bono having problems with his voice. They took place on 17th, 18th and 19th November instead.

See appendix for a complete list of venues .

Songs performed on the tour: All Along The Watchtower, All I Want Is You, Angel Of Harlem, Bad, Bullet The Blue Sky, Desire, 11 O'clock Tick Tock, Exit, 40, Hawkmoon 269, Help, Gloria, God Part II, In God's Country, I Will Follow, I Still Haven't Found What I'm Looking For, Knockin' On Heaven's Door, Love Rescue Me, MLK, October, One Tree Hill, New Year's Day, Out Of Control, Party Girl, People Get Ready, Pride, Running To Stand Still, She's A

Mystery To Me, Slow Dancing, Stand By Me, The Unforgettable Fire, Two Hearts Beat As One, Van Diemen's Land, When Love Comes To Town, Where The Streets Have No Name, With Or Without You.

LOVETOWN (FILM) A film documentary of the band's *Lovetown* tour of Australia directed by Richard Lowenstein who had made the promo videos for "Desire" and "Angel of Harlem". It was shown on BBC2 in Britain in December 1990 and in several other countries around the world. The film shows a young Australian girl reporter interviewing each member of the band asking them what they think is the difference between love and sex. Several members of the public are also interviewed. It also features several songs from the final three dates in Australia at the Sydney Entertainment Centre, including "When Love Comes To Town", "Desire", "All I Want Is You" (which was number 1 in the Australian charts for much of the tour), "God Part II", "Hawkmoon 269", "All Along The Watchtower" and "Love Rescue Me".

LOWENSTEIN, RICHARD The Australian film maker who has directed several U2 promo videos as well as making the documentary film *Lovetown*, about U2's 1989 Australian tour. The first video that he directed for U2 was "Desire" filmed in Los Angeles in September 1988. This was followed by "Angel Of Harlem" filmed in New York City in November 1989. The *Lovetown* documentary was made soon after.

See also: Angel of Harlem / Desire promo videos / Lovetown documentary

"LUCILLE" This was a country song that Bono wrote at the start of the *Joshua Tree* tour in the USA. It was about BB King's legendary guitar called "Lucille". It was first played live at the Community Centre in

Tucson, Arizona on 5th April 1987 and performed at several other shows on the *Joshua Tree* tour, but has never been released on record.

See also: BB King

"LUMINOUS TIMES (HOLD ONTO LOVE)" ("WITH OR WITHOUT YOU" SINGLE B SIDE) (4.35) Co-written by Brian Eno and U2, this song is said to be about Ali, Bono's wife. It was one of two songs on the B-side of the "With or Without You" single. It was also on *The B-sides* CD of *The Best of 1980-1990* double CD.

LUNNY, DONAL The Irish producer who put together the *Common Ground* album – a collection of traditional Irish music performed by Irish musicians. A new version of the *October* track "Tomorrow" was included in this collection. Donal had originally been in traditional folk bands Emmet Spiceland and We 4, before moving onto Planxty, The Bothy Band and Moving Hearts.

See also: Tomorrow

LYCEUM THEATRE, LONDON, ENGLAND U2 have played this central London 1500 capacity venue on six occasions. They first played here on 7th September 1980 as one of the support acts to Echo & the Bunnymen. The audience response to U2 at this gig was minimal and the band were disappointed. However, Lynden Barber from *Melody Maker* was very impressed with the band and claimed that U2 had blown the headliners off the stage. For the next visit here, on 19th October 1980, they supported the 1970s glam-rock band Slade, who by then were playing in a more heavy metal style. Once again they failed to win over the audience.

However, when the band returned on 1st February 1981, U2 were the headlining act, the hall was sold out and over 700 fans were shut outside. The band played the Bob Dylan song "All Along the Watchtower" live for the first time that evening. U2 then played two further concerts here on 20th and 21st December, which were again sold out. It was "the gig of 1981" according to Gill Pringle writing in *Record Mirror* about the second show. The band made their final concert appearance at the Lyceum on 5th December 1982.

LYNN, TODD The designer of the leather jackets that Bono wore on the *Elevation* tour, as well as in the "Beautiful Day" video.

LYPTON VILLAGE The group of teenagers from the Northside of Dublin to which Bono belonged in the mid to late 1970s. "The Village" as it was known, began as a reaction to the other groups of young people that hung around the streets of North Dublin. They were rebelling against the social norms – that

The Edge and Bono, Lyceum, London, 1/2/81
Photo: Kay Bauersfeld

you went to school, got a job, got married, had children, worked for forty years, retired and then died. They felt that the was more to life than this and openly challenged these values, often wearing make up and dresses, trying to show that it was OK to be different.

Although they did not have a leader as such, Paul Hewson, Derek Rowan, and Fionan Hanvey were perhaps the most influential members. They would meet at each other's houses to discuss the issues of the day such as music, school, education and Catholic morals. They gave each other nicknames to show aspects of their particular character. Paul Hewson became Bono, Fionan Hanvey became Gavin Friday, Derek Rowan became Guggi. The other members included Dave-id, Sir Poddington, Bad Dog, Strongman, and Pompous Holmes. The other three members of The Hype were not members although Dave Evans was christened with a Village name: The Edge. Adam and Larry weren't actual members though they did hang around together, especially when several of The Village formed their own alternative group called "The Virgin Prunes". The Edge's brother, Dick became the musical leader of the group and became an honorary member of The Village having his name changed to Dik.

See also: Bono / Dave-id / The Edge / Dik Evans / Gavin Friday / Guggi / Strongman / The Virgin Prunes

MacCOLL, EWAN The English folk singer from Salford near Manchester who wrote "Dirty Old Town", covered by U2 on several occasions. His second wife was Peggy Seeger, whose song "Springhill Mining Disaster" U2 performed live during the *Joshua Tree* tour. He was also the father of the singer, Kirsty MacColl.

MacCOLL, KIRSTY The English singer who died tragically in December 2000 in a boating accident. She was the daughter of the folk singer, Ewan MacColl, and had married U2 producer Steve Lillywhite in 1984 and knew all the members of U2 closely. She is said to have suggested the track order for *The Joshua Tree* album. She had her own successful career as a solo singer with such hits as "A New England" and "Days" as well as the song with one of the most unusual titles ever: "There's A Guy Works Down The Chip Shop Swears He's Elvis". Her biggest hit was a collaboration with the Pogues in 1987, "Fairytale of New York". Bono attended her funeral.

McALISTER, FRASER One of the U2 crew from 1988 to 2000, working with the band from the *Rattle & Hum* album through to *All That You Can't Leave Behind*. During this time he was Bono's guitar technician. At the Civic Center St. Paul Minnesota during the *Joshua Tree* tour on 4th November 1987, Bono introduced McAlister to the audience as it was his birthday. He was allowed to play the guitar on "People Get Ready".

McALISTER, RAB A member of U2's studio and road crew since the *Zooropa* album. In the studio he is a studio technician, and on the road he is the tour technician.

McCANN, EAMON A promoter from Northern Ireland who set up the MCD promotions company with Denis Desmond. Together they have made MCD one of the largest promotions companies in Europe, promoting many large acts including U2 at the Botanic Gardens in Dublin in 1997.
See also: Dennis Desmond

McCANN, EAMONN The journalist who wrote for the magazine *In Dublin*. He wrote the infamous article in that magazine entitled 'Self Aid Makes it Worse', a pun on the 'Self Aid Makes it Work' slogan used for the 1986 Self Aid concert. This was reprinted as an appendix at the back of Eamon Dunphy's *Unforgettable Fire* U2 biography. At the time, U2 were said to be upset by McCann's view that the concert would take away responsibility from the politicians for making jobs.
See also: Self Aid

McCARTNEY, SIR PAUL As a member of the Beatles, Paul McCartney's compositions had an early influence on the young members of U2. Their use of his song, "Helter Skelter" on the *Joshua Tree* tour was more than a nod to his influence in their music. Other McCartney Beatles songs they have covered live have included "Let It Be" and "Hello Goodbye". Although there has never been any musical collaboration between U2 and Paul McCartney, they did play on the same bill at the Live Aid concert in 1985, with Bono managing to share the microphone with Paul during the concert's climax.
See also: The Beatles / Live Aid

McCORMICK, IVAN One of the people who turned up at Larry's house for the audition for the band he was starting in 1976. Ivan was a fellow pupil at Mount Temple Comprehensive School and, at fourteen, was a couple of years younger than the others at the audition. He attended a few rehearsals before being given the push.

McCORMICK, NEIL Neil attended Mount Temple Comprehensive in Dublin at the same time as U2 and later became a journalist for *Hot Press* Magazine. In Eamon Dunphy's *Unforgettable Fire* biography, Neil was mistaken for his brother Ivan, as one of the group of pupils who attended that first get together at Larry's house. Neil was however present at Feedback's first gig in the gym of Mount Temple school in the autumn term of 1976. In 1988, after the *Unforgettable Fire* biography had came out, McCormick wrote a critique of the book in *Hot Press* entitled 'The Unbelievable Book', which proceeded to highlight the mistakes and inaccuracies in Eamon Dunphy's book. On several occasions he has interviewed U2 and written about the band. He now writes freelance for several publications including *The Daily Telegraph* newspaper in London.

McCORMICK, STELLA The sister of Ivan and Neil McCormick. She, with her friend Orla Dunne, provided backing vocals at Feedback's final gig at St Fintan's School in Dublin, on the 11th April 1976.
See also: The Hype / Orla Dunne

McGONAGLE'S, DUBLIN, IRELAND U2 played this famous Dublin club in Anne Street South, just off Grafton Street, on seven separate occasions in the late 1970s. The first time was in the early months of 1978 when they supported Revolver, one of the leading groups in Dublin at that time. They next played here on 11th April 1978, followed by an appearance on 31st July, when U2 were bottom of the bill to the Modern Heirs and Revolver. This was the first gig that U2 played with Paul McGuinness as manager. He is said to have argued that U2 should not play at the bottom of the bill. Although this did not succeed, he did manage to get the start delayed until there were some people in the venue.

U2's next visit here was on 3rd January 1979, where they played to a full house and were watched by Chas De Whalley, who was then working as an A&R executive for CBS records. He recalls U2 as being "second-rate punk", though he thought that "Bono was brilliant" and that "he could become either a new Alex Harvey or a new Bowie". Chas De Whalley would then go on to to produce the band's first single "U2-3". U2 then played a lunchtime slot a month later on 3rd February 1979 before going off to play at Trinity College in the evening. The group then played a series of four Thursday night gigs on the 7th, 14th, 21st and 28th June 1979. These gigs were called "The Jingle Balls" with the stage lavished with Christmas decorations to give the idea of being "Christmas in June" as the publicity posters promised.

See also: The Jingle Balls / Chas De Whalley

McGRATH, SHAUGHN A colleague of Steve Averill and a designer who works alongside Steve at Four5One in Dublin. He began his working relationship with U2 by helping to design the cover of *Achtung Baby*. Since then he has designed the covers of *Pop* and *All That You Can't Leave Behind*. He has also been involved with designing *Propaganda*, the U2 fan club magazine, and various pieces of U2 merchandise.

McGUINNESS, HUGO A Dublin based photographer who shot the early U2. He was responsible for the back photo on *Boy* as well as providing several early photographs of the band for Bill Graham's U2 book, *Another Time, Another Place*. After his work with U2, he moved to Scandinavia in 1982, before returning to Ireland in 1988 to work as a music publicist as well as a photographer.

McGUINNESS, PAUL The manager of U2. He is the first son of Philip and Sheila McGuinness and was born on 16th June 1951 in Rintein, near Hanover, West Germany where his father was stationed in the RAF. The family would move to a different RAF base every few years, so Paul lived in Thorney Island, Hampshire, then Cosford, near Wolverhampton, before going abroad to Malta. Then it was back to England and Poole in Dorset, before Paul was sent to boarding school at Clongowes Wood College in Kildare, Ireland. He was there for six years and emerged as the editor of the school magazine, as well

as having directed two school plays. He was also the school's best debater.

In 1968 he went to Trinity College, Dublin to read philosophy and psychology. At Trinity he met several friends who would play a part in the U2 story, including his wife Kathy Gilfillan and Michael Deeny, who went on to manage Horslips and Chris de Burgh. In his third year, he got sent down from Trinity after it was discovered that he hadn't attended enough lectures to be able to sit his third year exams. He returned to live with his parents in Dorset and enrolled at Southampton University, but only stayed two weeks before going up to London. He worked as a taxi driver before becoming a tour guide in Lourdes in France where he earned enough money to pay for his return to Trinity College. But he didn't finish his degree. Instead he landed the job of location manager on the film *Zardoz* starring Sean Connery.

He next became manager of a folk-rock band called Spud, which he stayed with for a year, managing to secure them a recording and publishing deal. He then went back to film production for a while though it is said that he always had at the back of his mind the idea of discovering a "baby band" and taking them to the top. It was through meeting and chatting with *Scene* magazine's Bill Graham, an old friend from Trinity College, that Paul McGuinness heard about the fledgling U2. This eventually led to him watching and then meeting the band at the Project Arts Centre in Dublin on 25th May 1978. After being impressed with their desire to learn and succeed, as well as their honesty and ambition, he decided to become the manager of U2, initially for a provisional six months.

He first raised the band's profile by getting them more gigs so that they would be seen by a wider audience, outside their own close circle of friends and family. This included support slots to the Stranglers at the Top Hat Ballroom in Dun Laoghaire in September 1978 and to Phil Lynott's Greedy Bastards at the Stardust in December 1978. The next year U2 were able to reach a younger audience by playing six Saturday afternoon gigs at the Dandelion Car Park in Dublin. Having built a reputation for U2 in Dublin, McGuinness then started to court the British press with a view to enticing a major record company into signing U2. The first step was to get a professional demo tape of the band recorded, for which he enlisted the services of Barry Devlin. Once this had been made in 1978, Paul started the hard slog of trying to get a major record company interested.

In the meantime Jackie Hayden had persuaded CBS in England to send someone over to check out U2. This turned out to be Chas De Whalley who recorded a third demo with them in Dublin. CBS in London were not interested, but Paul managed to negotiate a

A pivotal figure in the U2 story, Paul McGuinness
Photo: Claire Bolton

contract with CBS Ireland to release the demo tape as a single in Ireland in return for the rights to all U2's recorded material for the next five years. The single was a number 1 hit in Ireland, helped by clever marketing of a 12 inch limited edition single. This gave Paul the ammunition to push U2 to the major record companies again, who returned to see U2 in the autumn of 1979. This included A&R men from such companies as EMI, CBS, A&M, Stiff and Island, though nothing concrete came from these visits. A series of London club and pub dates in December 1979 was next on Paul's agenda.

Although the gigs were not particularly successful they did lead to various London based music journalists taking an interest in U2. Finally in February 1980 at a specially organised "make or break" gig at the National Boxing Stadium in Dublin in front of two and a half thousand fans, family and friends, U2 were able to convince an A&R scout from Island Records, Bill Stewart. A few weeks later U2 signed with Island Records and their career began in earnest. In 1984 Paul renegotiated their deal with Island, making the band financially secure for their rest of their lives. He has renegotiated U2's position several more times since, with both Polygram and Universal Music, making sure that U2's status as the world's biggest band has remained strong and guaranteed.

Over the years Paul has built up the U2 empire through thoughtful planning, making sure that U2 grew gradually and increased their audience through the right balance of live shows, TV and radio appearances, and recorded material. He made sure they played at some of the biggest festivals on their way to the top including the US Festival, the Werchter Festival in Belgium and Live Aid in 1985.

He set up U2's management company, Principle Management, in the 1980s, so-called because of his belief in honesty and sound ethics in an industry that has a reputation for putting financial gain before the artist's individual needs. Rather than locating his offices in London at the heart of the European Music industry, he chose to stay in Dublin (with a second office in New York) with a highly skilled and devoted team of predominantly female staff. Apart from his managerial commitment to U2 he has set up the "Celtic Heartbeat" label with Dave Kavanagh and Barbara Galavan as well as the publishing company McGuinness-Whelan Publishing, which looks after Bill Whelan's publishing deals. Like the four members of U2 he was made a freeman of the City of Dublin in 2000, though he hasn't yet taken up his option to graze sheep on St Steven's Green!

See also: Michael Deeny / Island Records / Spud / Principle Management

McGUINNESS, KATHY The wife of Paul McGuinness. Born Kathy Gilfillan, she came from Eglinton in Northern Ireland. Kathy attended Limavady Grammar School before moving to Dublin and Trinity College. She first came across Paul in The Players drama group, where he was directing. After graduating, she worked in London for Blackman Harvey, an art brokers, before returning to Dublin and Paul in 1975. They married in 1977, moving into a flat in Waterloo Road, Ballsbridge, Dublin. She was with Paul when he first went to see U2 play live at the Project Arts Centre on Thursday 25th May 1978 and through her work was able to support Paul until U2 became established.

McKEE, MARIA Lead singer with the group Lone Justice who toured as support band for U2 on their *Unforgettable Fire* and *Joshua Tree* tours of America. Maria joined Bono on stage at the Spectrum Arena in Philadelphia on 24th April 1985 to sing "40" with him. At the Sports Arena in San Diego, California, in April 1987 Maria duetted on stage with Bono singing the Bob Dylan song "I Shall Be Released". In June 1989 Adam joined Maria on stage to play along on a few songs at her concert at Mother Redcap's in Dublin.

See also: Lone Justice

McKNIGHT, MICHAEL A member of U2's road crew. On the *Elevation* tour he was a programmer and in charge of "extra keyboards".

McNICHOLS SPORTS ARENA, DENVER, COLORADO, USA U2 have played four concerts in this 17,000 capacity arena. The band first played here on 17th

March 1985 during *the Unforgettable Fire* tour of North America. It was U2's first concert in Denver since their famous show at Red Rocks Amphitheatre, so during the show Bono mentioned this fact and thanked promoter Barry Fey. This concert took place on St Patrick's Day, and as the show began the hymn "Amazing Grace" was played by three kilted pipers.

U2 next played here on 8th June 1986 during the *Conspiracy of Hope* tour. For this show, U2 shared the bill with Sting, Peter Gabriel, Bryan Adams, Lou Reed, Joan Baez and The Neville Brothers. Surprisingly, this show was not sold out. U2 returned here during *the Joshua Tree* tour to play two dates on the 7th and 8th November 1987. Both shows were filmed for the *Rattle and Hum* film (black and white section) but it was only songs from the second night that made it into the film and onto the album. The songs used in both the film and on the album were "Helter Skelter", "Pride" and "Silver and Gold". The songs that were used in the film but not on the album were "Bad", "In God's Country", "Exit" and "Sunday Bloody Sunday", the latter containing Bono's outburst at the Enniskillen bomb outrage.

See also: *Rattle & Hum* / Barry Fey

McPHERSON, ANDREW A photographer whose shots of U2 have been featured in several books and articles on the band.

McVEIGH, TIMOTHY See: The First Union Center, Philadelphia

MABINS, MACIE Co-writer of "Freedom For My People" which appears on the film and album of *Rattle and Hum*.

MACNAS The Irish drama group from Galway, Ireland who performed thought-provoking playletts at the *Zooropa* shows of the *Zoo TV* tour. These included sketches with a giant vacuum cleaner and giant fish. They also had four characters with giant size heads of Bono, Edge, Adam and Larry. These four characters were included in the promo video for "Sweetest Thing". They have also had a regular spot on the Channel 4 programme *TFI Friday*.

MACPHISTO The stage character that Bono created for the 1993 *Zooropa* and *Zoomerang* tours. For the encore of the 1992 *Zoo TV* shows, Bono had came out as the "Mirror Ball Man", a loud American character dressed in a silver lame outfit who threw Zoo money bills into the crowd. For the 1993 *Zoo TV* tour this character developed into Macphisto - a modern alter-ego of Mephistopheles - who sold his soul to the devil and Macdonalds, part of the throw-away society. Instead of silver, he would be dressed in gold and would have 1970s style platform boots. Originally he was going to be called "Mr Gold", then somebody

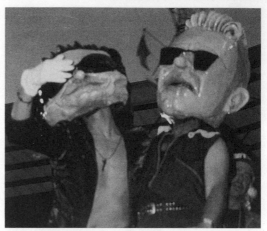
Macnas' Bono and Adam bigheads.
Photo: Claire Bolton

gave him a pair of horns at the last minute and Macphisto was born.

Macphisto was, in essence, the Devil (complete with red horns). He had a refined English accent and white stage make up. Each night, during the encore he would telephone a well-known celebrity (in most cases) from the stage. Usually the celebrity lived in the country where the show was taking place. In a piece of well-staged publicity he was filmed outside the Vatican whilst the band were in Italy. By the *Zoomerang* shows, he would be sitting in the dressing room as the encore began. A camera would show him finishing off putting on his make-up and would then follow him out onto the stage as he sang, Daddy's Gonna Pay For Your Crashed Car". When asked about him in 1995, Bono said, "I think dressing up as the Devil was great!"

See also: *Zooropa* tour / *Zoo TV Live From Sydney*

MADISON SQUARE GARDEN, NEW YORK CITY, USA U2 have played this prestigious New York venue six times. Their first visit on 1st April 1985 was seen as a major triumph by the U2 organisation, who flew over the band's families and friends, as well as several Irish reporters. They next played here on 28th and 29th September 1987 during the *Joshua Tree* tour of North America. During the encore of the first show, The New Voices of Freedom, a black Gospel choir from Harlem, came onstage to sing their gospel version of "I Still Haven't Found What I'm Looking For". The song ended up on the album soundtrack of *Rattle and Hum*, though in the film, footage of the choir and U2 in their church was used. U2 next played here on the 20th March 1992 during their *Zoo TV* tour of America. On the 2001 *Elevation* tour the band played here for two nights on 17th and 19th June. On the first night Bono wished Paul McGuinness a belated happy 50th birthday for the day before. On the second night Daniel Lanois made a guest appearance, joining the band to play guitar on "Stuck In A Moment You Can't Get Out Of". All six visits here were sold out.

MAGEE, STERLING The street musician who co-wrote and recorded "Freedom For My People" on the film and album of *Rattle and Hum*.

"MAGGIES FARM" This Bob Dylan song has been sung live on several occasions by U2, the first time being at the Self Aid concert in Dublin in May 1986, where the words resonated with the contemporary problems of Margaret Thatcher's Britain. The song was also played at every U2 concert on the *Conspiracy of Hope* tour in 1986, as well as on some of the *Joshua Tree* tour dates. The live recording of the song at Self Aid was included on the 1987 release of *Live For Ireland*.

See also: Bob Dylan / Margaret Thatcher

"THE MAGIC CARPET" This was an early U2 song that the band played in the years 1978 to 1980. It was never recorded. Several people thought the song's title was "Lost On a Distant Planet", the first line of the song, or "Judith", a name that crops up in the lyrics. There is a very old film of U2 performing this song on TV in Ireland, which was used as an early publicity "video".

MAGNET BAR, DUBLIN, IRELAND U2 played a benefit gig here in the autumn of 1978 in support of "Rock Against Sexism."

Bono as Macphisto. *Photo: Bart Moons*

MAHURIN, MATT Matt was first involved with U2 when he provided "additional footage" for the promo video for "With Or Without You" with Meiert Avis in 1987. In 1993 he was director and editor of the promo video of "Love Is Blindness", included on the "Numb" video single.

MAIMANKT MANNHEIM GERMANY U2 played here on 31st July 1997 during the European leg of the *Pop Mart* tour. The concert is memorable for the band playing part of the T.Rex hit, "Children of the Revolution" at the end of the encore number, "Hold Me, Thrill Me, Kiss Me, Kill Me".

MALIBU BEACH NIGHT CLUB, LIDO BEACH, NEW YORK, USA This was the last show of U2's 1981 North American tour to promote the *October* album. It took place on 13th December 1981 and was recorded by the local radio station, WLIR Radio.

MALLET, DAVID The director of the *Zoo TV Live From Sydney* video which won a Grammy for the "Best Music Video: Long Form" in 1994. He then went on to direct the *Pop Mart Live From Mexico City* video, released in 1998.

See also: Zoo TV Live From Sydney / Pop Mart Live From Mexico City

MANDAGSBORSEN SWEDISH TV PROGRAMME U2's first public appearance in Sweden was a two song set, consisting of "I Will Follow" and "11 O'clock Tick Tock" for the Swedish TV programme *Mandagsborsen* on 9th February 1981.

MANDELA, NELSON The black South African anti-apartheid leader who was eventually freed in 1990 after spending 27 years in prison for his political activities. He became the first President of the new democratic government in 1993. U2 played two shows in South Africa in March 1998 but weren't able to meet Nelson Mandela due to illness. Bono did get to meet him in May 2000 in Monaco at the Laureus Sports Awards, which both men attended. In 2001 Bono announced that he would like to appear on the Oprah Winfrey show with Mandela to get across to the American people the problems of Third World debt.

MAN RAY CLUB, PARIS, FRANCE U2 performed a special low-key gig here on 19th October 2000 as part of a series of "secret" gigs prior to the 2001 *Elevation* tour. The club held about 600 fans and invited guests. This was the first time that "New York" and "Stuck In A Moment You Can't Get Out Of" were performed live.

Set list: Elevation, New York, Stuck In a Moment You Can't Get Out Of, Beautiful Day, Mysterious Ways, All I Want Is You, Even Better Than the Real Thing, The Ground Beneath Her Feet, Bad.

MANSON, CHARLES The notorious serial killer involved in the Sharon Tate murders in Los Angeles in 1968/9. Bono referred to him in the film (and on the album) of *Rattle and Hum*, when he introduced the Beatles song "Helter Skelter" with the immortal lines: *"This is a song Charles Manson stole from the Beatles. We're stealing it back."* It was the words of this song (and others from the "White Album") that supposedly influenced Manson and his followers to commit the murders.

See also: Helter Skelter

MANUEL, REGGIE A former schoolfreind of Bono's who is also A&R man for Kitchen Records, the underground dance label that U2 set up in 1998.

MARACANA STADIUM, RIO DE JANEIRO, BRAZIL U2 were scheduled to play the first date of their *Pop Mart* tour (final leg) here on 27th January 1998, but at the last minute the venue was changed to the Nelson Piquet Stadium apparently on the orders of the tour sponsors SKOL beer.

See also: Nelson Piquet Stadium

"THE MARGARUITA SUITE" Adam played bass on this track from the 1991 album *Sharon Shannon* by Sharon Shannon.

MARLEY, BOB The Jamaican reggae singer who was signed to Island Records in 1972 and with his group The Wailers had huge worldwide success with songs such as "No Woman No Cry" and "Jammin". Although U2 have never used reggae in their music they have often sung parts of Marley's songs on stage, including "Three Little Birds", "Redemption Song", "Exodus" and "Get Up, Stand Up". Bono was responsible for the speech inducting Bob Marley into the Rock 'n' Roll Hall of Fame in New York in January 1994, where he admitted that he had got into Bob's music through the likes of The Clash and Eric Clapton. Bob Marley died of cancer in 1981.

MARLEY, ZIGGY Bob Marley's son Ziggy performed with U2 at the *Smile Jamaica* concert at the Dominion Theatre in London on 16th October 1988. They sang the track "Love Rescue Me" and this was put on the B-side of the "Angel Of Harlem" single, with all proceeds going to the *Smile Jamaica* Fund.

MARQUEE CLUB, LONDON, ENGLAND U2 have played at this famous London club on eight separate occasions, all in the year 1980, the first time being on 7th June. They next played here on 13th July as support to the Photos. They then had a weekly residency when they played four consecutive Monday night shows on 8th, 15th, 22nd and 29th September. It was from a recording of the show on 22nd September that "Boy-Girl", was taken for the B-side of the "I Will Follow" single. Finally, they played two more nights here on 26th and 27th November (admission £2).

See also: "Boy-Girl"(live)

MARTIN, PETER One of the people who responded to Larry's advert on the notice board at Mount Temple Comprehensive in Dublin in 1976. He came along to the first meeting. It is said that despite the fact that he had a guitar and an amplifier, he was unable to play.

MASTERSON, BRIAN One of the founders of Windmill Lane studios, where U2 recorded their first three albums. When the original site closed down, Brian was instrumental in ensuring that the name of Windmill Lane was kept alive when moving to the new location in Ringsend Road, Dublin. The new studios have been used by The Corrs and the Rolling Stones as well as by U2.

See also: Windmill Lane studios

MAYSFIELD LEISURE CENTRE, BELFAST, NORTHERN IRELAND U2 played to 3,000 people here on 20th December 1982 during the *War* tour. This was the venue where U2 first played "Sunday Bloody Sunday" to a Belfast audience. Bono explained to the audience before playing the song, that it was written especially for them and if they didn't like it they would never play it in Belfast again. However, the audience reaction to the song was very positive and proved that U2 had created the right balance in the lyrics.

MCI CENTRE, WASHINGTON DC, USA U2 played two sold out dates here on 14th and 15th June 2001 before 20,000 fans during the *Elevation* tour (first leg) of North America. On the second night during "Bullet The Blue Sky" a fan came up on stage and recited some of the words with Bono.

MEADOWLANDS ARENA, EAST RUTHERFORD, NEW JERSEY USA U2 have played nine concerts at this 20,000 capacity arena under its original name. They first played three concerts here during the *Unforgettable Fire* tour on 12th, 13th and 14th February 1985. From the first show, "Wire" was shown in a special report on the band on the BBC TV programme *The Old Grey Whistle Test*. U2 next played five shows here between 11th and 16th May 1987 on the *Joshua Tree* tour. On the second of the five nights, The Edge's daughter, Holly, was present – Bono dedicated "People Get Ready" to her. The fourth show was recorded by producer Jimmy Iovine for possible inclusion on U2's next album. This may help to explain why U2 played "Trip Through Your Wires" twice at this concert. Finally, U2 played one more concert here on 18th March 1992 during the *Zoo TV* tour of America. The arena changed its name to the Continental Arena in the 1990s.

See also: Continental Arena.

MECHUM, GOVERNOR EVAN The governor of Arizona, who in 1987 put forward the idea of scrapping in Arizona the public holiday that commemorates the birthday of Martin Luther King. Several artists, including Stevie Wonder and The Doobie Brothers, decided to cancel their shows in Arizona in protest, but U2 chose instead to play and then have the promoter Barry Fey read out a statement condemning the Govenor's actions before their shows at Tempe. They also donated $5,000 to the Mechum Watchdog Committee, which was aimed to oust him from public office. He was later removed from office by impeachment.

See also: Barry Fey / Martin Luther King

MELODY MAKER Before its demise, one of the UK's leading weekly music journals first published in the 1920s. Bono had courted this and other London based publications in 1979. But it wasn't until the release of *Boy* that *Melody Maker* gave U2 its full approval. Through the campaigning of staff writer Adam Sweeting, U2 continued to gain favourable reviews.

MELODY MAKERS, THE Ziggy Marley's backing group who provided the backing vocals for "Love Rescue Me".

MELON (REMIXES CD) (MELONCD1) The specially produced CD of remixed U2 songs was given away free with *Propaganda* Issue 21 in January 1995. Island Records head of A&R, Nick Angel, the executive producer, thought up the whole concept. He commissioned several remix artists to rework several 1990s U2 songs. Soon after it was made available, some record dealers were asking as much as £100 for a copy.

Full track list – "Lemon" (The Perfecto Mix), "Salome" (Zooromancer remix), "Numb" (Gimmie Some More Dignity Mix), "Mysterious Ways" (The Perfecto Mix), "Stay" (Underdog Mix), "Numb" (The Soul Assassins Mix), "Mysterious Ways" (Remixed by Massive Attack), "Even Better Than the Real Thing" (The Perfecto Mix), "Lemon" (Bad Yard Club Mix).

See also: Nick Angel

MEMORIAL COLISEUM, JACKSONVILLE, FLORIDA, USA U2 played just one concert here on 20th April 1985 to 9,000 fans during the *Unforgettable Fire* tour. During "Party Girl", Bono invited a girl onto the stage to open a bottle of champagne to help celebrate the fact that at this concert the band had now played to half a million fans in their career.

MEMORIAL COLISEUM, LOS ANGELES, CALIFORNIA, USA U2 played two dates here on 17th and 18th November 1987 during the *Joshua Tree* tour of America, playing to over 60,000 fans each night. This was

the venue where the 1984 Olympic Games had taken place so the Olympic Flame was lit for the two shows. For the second night, U2 appeared in disguise as an extra act called The Dalton Brothers, a scam they had previously tried at the Hoosier Dome in Indianapolis on 1st November. They performed two songs, "Lucille" and "The Lost Highway" before going off stage and reappearing as U2 later. The band also played another sell out concert here during the *Pop Mart* tour of the USA on 21st June 1997. The show was memorable for the appearance on stage of Davey Jones, one of the original Monkees, who took over from The Edge singing the Monkees' song "Daydream Believer" during the karaoke section.

MEMORY MAN DELUXE ECHO UNIT This was the gadget that The Edge used on his guitar in the early days of the band to enhance their sound. It was first used on U2's second Island Records' single, "A Day Without Me" in 1980 and subsequently on the *Boy* and *October* albums. In many ways it helped to define U2's unique sound.

MEMPHIS HORNS, THE Comprising Wayne Jackson and Andrew Love, they have played on over 300 different hit singles by such artists as Elvis Presley - "Suspicious Minds", Otis Redding - "Dock of the Bay", Al Green - "Let's Stay Together" and Aretha Franklin - "Respect". In November 1987 they formed the brass section that played on the "Angel of Harlem" recording session at Sun Studios in Memphis.

Web site: www.memphishorns.com

MERCURY, FREDDIE See: Oakland Coliseum / Queen

METROPOL, BERLIN, GERMANY U2 played here on 4th November 1981 for the German Rock Music TV programme *Rockpalast*. It was subsequently shown on WDR TV on 6th March 1982.

See also: Berlin

"MIAMI" (*POP* ALBUM TRACK) (4.52) As the title suggests this is about the town of Miami in Florida, which has close associations with U2. In fact some of the *Pop* album was recorded at Miami's South Beach studios. The song was first performed live at the Sam Boyd Stadium in Las Vegas, Nevada on 25th April 1997. When performing the song, Bono would open and close a multicoloured stars and stripes umbrella.

MIAMI ARENA, MIAMI, FLORIDA, USA U2 played the second show of the 1992 *Zoo TV* tour here on 1st March 1992. This show marked the debut of the belly dancer Christina Petro who danced on stage during "Mysterious Ways". She had surprised the band by dancing during the afternoon sound check – a scam set up by the production team. The band then decided to let her do it for real in the evening show. However she didn't appear again at a *Zoo TV* show until 17th March at the Boston Gardens. From then on she appeared every night on the first American leg of the *Zoo TV* tour.

See also: Christina Petro

"MIAMI STEVE" See: Little Steven

A MIDSUMMER NIGHT'S TUBE SPECIAL The TV programme that gave British U2 fans the first chance to see the Red Rocks show of 5th June. It was aired on Channel 4 in June 1983 and featured nine of the songs from the show. The fuller thirteen song version of the show was released as *U2 Live At Red Rocks: Under a Blood Red Sky* in November 1983.

See also: Red Rocks Ampitheater / *The Tube* / *Under A Blood Red Sky* video

MILE HIGH STADIUM, DENVER, COLORADO, USA U2 have played here on two separate occasions. The first time was on 21st October 1992 during the *Outside Broadcast* leg of the *Zoo TV* tour. The show was a sell out with over 50,000 fans attending. The band returned to play one show here during the first leg of the *Pop Mart* tour of America on 1st May 1997. This time there were only 30,000 fans in attendance, with many fans not making the journey out to this venue because of snow being forecast for the day of the concert.

MILKY WAY, AMSTERDAM, HOLLAND U2's second ever show in Holland took place here before about 500 fans on the 15th October 1980.

THE MILLION DOLLAR HOTEL (FILM) A story written by Bono and Nicholas Klein that developed into a full-scale film directed by Wim Wenders. It was filmed in Dublin and Los Angeles and was based around an old run down hotel where rock stars stay when in town. The film starred Mel Gibson as FBI agent Skinner, who was investigating the murder of the hotel's benefactor, Izzy. In the film he interviews the somewhat unusual guests at the hotel in order to find the culprit. These include Tom Tom (Jeremy Davies), Eloise (Milla Jovovich), Vivien (Amanda Plummer), Shorty (Bud Cort), Geronimo (Jimmy Smits) and Dixie (Peter Stormare). The theme of Tom Tom's love for Eloise runs as an undercurrent to the whole film and "The Ground Beneath Her Feet" is used to illustrate this. *The Million Dollar Hotel* won the Silver Eagle prize at the 50th Berlin Film Festival in 2000 and whilst it was not a major box office smash it still gained many positive reviews.

Website: www.milliondollarhotel.com

See also: Mel Gibson / Nicholas Klein / Wim Wenders

THE MILLION DOLLAR HOTEL (FILM SOUND-TRACK ALBUM) (CID 8094/542 395-2) The sound-track album to *The Million Dollar Hotel* film was released on Island Records in April 2000. It contained 16 tracks, six of which were performed by either Bono or all of U2. Most of the other tracks were performed by The Million Dollar Hotel Band, which included Bono, Daniel Lanois and Brian Eno, amongst others. Several of the songs had been written by Bono and Daniel Lanois. The highlight track was "The Ground Beneath Her Feet", performed by U2. This was the first time U2 had used lyrics written by someone outside the band – Salman Rushdie, Booker Prize winning writer and author of a novel of the same title. The *Zooropa* track, "The First Time" was resurrected for the album and the Lou Reed song "Satellite of Love" was also included. The album was recorded at Hanover Quay in Dublin and was produced by Hal Wilner.

Track list – The Ground Beneath Her Feet, Never Let Me Go, Stateless, Satellite of Love, Falling At Your Feet, Tom Tom's dream, The First Time, Bathtub, The First Time (Reprise), Tom Tom's Room, Funny Face, Dancin' Shoes, Amsterdam Blue (Cortege), Satellite of Love (Reprise), Satellite of Love (Danny Saber Remix), Anarchy In The USA.

See also: Hal Wilner

MIRROR BALL MAN The character that Bono played on the 1992 *Zoo TV* tour dates in both Europe and North America. He was dressed in a gold/sliver lame suit and wore a cowboy hat. He appeared at the start of the encore for "Desire" and looked into a mirror and said, "You know something? You're fucking beautiful!" The idea was to personify the Las Vegas mentality of "trash and transcendence". For many of the US shows he would ring up the White House and ask to speak to President George Bush, leaving him the message, "Watch More TV!" For the 1993 *Zoo TV* shows he was replaced by the Macphisto character.

See also: George Bush / Macphisto / Zoo money

"MISERERE" A song written by Bono in 1992 and recorded by the Italian singer Zucchero, appearing on his album *Miserere*.

MISKULIN, JOEY Renowned musician and producer who came to prominence through his accordion playing. He went on to record and produce several Grammy award winning albums, working with many high profile musicians including Johnny Cash, Garth Brooks and Paul McCartney. In 1987 he played organ on the "Angel of Harlem" single, recorded at the Sun Studios in Memphis.

Website: www.musicwagon.com

MISSION: IMPOSSIBLE See: THEME FROM *MISSION: IMPOSSIBLE*

"MISS SARAJEVO" (*ORIGINAL SOUNDTRACKS 1* ALBUM TRACK) (5.40) The seventh track on the *Original Soundtracks Volume 1* album. It was inspired by the film of the same name about life in the besieged Bosnian capital made by Bill Carter. The film showed how the young people of Sarajevo kept going despite the constant shelling of the city. They would listen to rock music, including U2, Sonic Youth and East 17, in an underground shelter, hence the line "Is there a time for East 17?" They even had a beauty contest and the contestant held up a banner, proclaiming "Don't Let Them Kill Us". This image would be used on the cover of the single.

"MISS SARAJEVO" (SINGLE) (5.20) The first single to be taken off the *Original Soundtracks 1* was released on 20th November 1995, and featured Pavarotti. It entered the UK chart at number 6. The single was released in three formats: 7 inch vinyl, CD and cassette. The vinyl single had a free poster of the beauty queen contestants. The B-side was a live version of "One" recorded at the Modena concert on 12th September 1995. The CD included the extra tracks "Bottoms" and "Viva Davidoff". All proceeds from the single went to the War Child charity.

See also: War Child / Pavarotti

"MISS SARAJEVO" (LIVE) (*TOGETHER FOR THE CHILDREN OF BOSNIA* ALBUM) (DECCA 452 100-2) The live version of the "Miss Sarajevo" track was performed at the concert in Modena by Bono, The Edge, Brian Eno and Pavarotti. It was the first time the song had been performed live and included a full orchestra playing. The album also contains a live version of "One".

See also: One (live) / Together For The Children of Bosnia album & video

MISS SARAJEVO (LIVE) (*TOGETHER FOR THE CHILDREN OF BOSNIA* VIDEO) The film of the live version of "Miss Sarajevo" performed by Bono, The Edge, Brian Eno and Pavarotti at the concert in Modena in aid of the War Child children's charity was included on a special video commemorating the event. It also featured performances by Michael Bolton, Meat Loaf and Zucchero. All proceeds went to the War Child charity.

MISS SARAJEVO (PROMOTIONAL VIDEO) The promo video of "Miss Sarajevo" was based on the film of the same name by Bill Carter about the siege Bosnian capital of Sarajevo. It showed various scenes of what life was like in a besieged town, including the beauty contest that inspired the song.

MISS SARAJEVO (DOCUMENTARY FILM) A 26 minute documentary film, directed by Bill Carter and co-produced by Bono and Ned O'Hanlon. It showed the citizens of Sarajevo living under siege and how they tried to go about their daily lives. At the 1994 International Monitor Awards it won the "Best Achievement in a Documentary" award.

See also: Bill Carter / Sarajevo

"MLK" (*THE UNFORGETTABLE FIRE* ALBUM TRACK) (2.32) The last track on *The Unforgettable Fire* album. It is a simple and quiet album closer dedicated to the memory of Martin Luther King, the American civil rights campaigner. The song was first played live at the Espace Tony Garnier in Lyon France on 18th October 1984. It was the opening number of the show but didn't quite work as an opener with the crowd expecting a more familiar rocker. It stayed in the U2 live set until 1990, but was reintroduced for the European section of the *Pop Mart* tour.

"MLK" (*RATTLE & HUM* FILM/VIDEO) Film of U2 performing MLK at the Sun Devil Stadium in Tempe, Arizona on 20th December 1987 was included in the film of *Rattle & Hum*. It was not included on the soundtrack album.

"MOFO" (*POP* ALBUM) (5.49) The third track on the *Pop* album is probably the heaviest song on the whole album with its techno beat and keyboards courtesy of Steve Osborne. The title has been suggested as being an abbreviation for the expletive "Mother Fucker". The lyrics do suggest a relationship between a son and a mother. In the *Pop Mart* tour programme Bono explained some of the thinking behind the lyrics: "If I could put my whole life into one song, it'd be something close to that." The song was first performed live at the Sam Boyd Stadium in Las Vegas, USA on 25th April 1997.

"MOFO REMIXES" (SINGLE) This three track CD single was released in 1997 and featured the tracks: "Mofo" (Phunk Phorce Mix), "Mofo" (Mother's Mix) and "If God Will Send His Angels" (The Grand Jury Mix).

"MOFO" (BLACK HOLE DUB) This remix of Mofo was included on the 12 inch vinyl UK release of "Mofo Remixes" (12 IS684).

"MOFO" (HOUSE FLAVOUR MIX) This remix of Mofo was included on the 12 inch vinyl UK promo (12 MOFO 2) and the 12 inch "Mofo remixes" single.

"MOFO" (MATTHEW ROBERTS EXPLICIT REMIX) This remix of Mofo was included on the limited edition (200 copies) one-sided 12 inch vinyl UK promo (12 MOFO 3).

"MOFO" (MOTHER'S MIX) (8.56) This remix of "Mofo" was done by Roni Size and is the second track on the "Mofo Remixes" CD single.

"MOFO" (PHUNK PHORCE MIX) (8.43) This remix of "Mofo" was done by Matthew Roberts and is the first track on the "Mofo Remixes" CD single.

"MOFO" (ROMIN MIX) This remix of Mofo was included on the 12 inch vinyl UK promo (12 MOFO 1) as well as the 12 inch "Mofo" remixes single.

"MOFO" (LIVE) (*HASTA LA VISTA BABY* ALBUM TRACK) The only official live audio recording of "Mofo" can be found on the *Hasta La Vista Baby! U2 Live From Mexico City* CD which was given away free with Issue 1 Volume 2 of *Propaganda* magazine.

"MOFO" (LIVE) (*U2: POP MART LIVE FROM MEXICO CITY* VIDEO) This film of U2 performing "Mofo" is the second song on the video *Pop Mart Live from Mexico City*. It was filmed at the Foro Sol Autodromo, Mexico City on 3rd December 1997.

MOLSON CENTER, MONTREAL, CANADA On the *Elevation* tour of North America U2 played two consecutive nights here on 27th and 28th May 2001. On the second night Bono had problems with his voice, so two songs were cut from the set list set list – "Ground Beneath Her Feet" and "With Or Without You".

MOONLIGHT CLUB, WEST HAMPSTEAD, LONDON, ENGLAND U2's first gig in Britain took place here on the 1st December 1979. The gig was given a favourable review by David McCullough in *Sounds*: "there's a kind of naive, young refreshing feeling about their music". It was also reviewed by Paul Morley in the *NME*. The band then returned for three more gigs here in 1980, on 23rd May, 12th July and 9th November. The July 12th show was the second night running that they had sold out a venue in the UK. As a reward, Paul McGuinness bought the band a bottle of champagne.
See also: *New Musical Express / Sounds*

MOORE, CHRISTY The well-known Irish folk singer who had also played in two of Ireland's most influential bands; Planxty and Moving Hearts. In February 1995 he recorded "North and South of the River" with Bono and The Edge at Windmill Lane studios in Dublin.
See also: North And South of the River

MORALES, CHRISTY The artist responsible for remixing several U2 tracks in his own style, including "Lemon" (Bad Yard Club Mix Edit) on the *Melon* CD.

MORGAN, STUART Stuart has been Adam's bass technician since the *Zoo TV* tour. He has the honour of being the only other person to have played as part of U2. This happened at the football stadium, Sydney, Australia on 26th November 1993 when Adam couldn't make the gig. Rather than cancel, it was decided to go ahead with Stuart taking Adam's place, playing bass.
See also: Football Stadium, Sydney

MORLEY, PAUL Music journalist and media personality, Morley championed U2 in their early days as a staff writer for the *New Musical Express*. He reviewed their first ever London gig at the Moonlight Club on 1st December 1979, published in the 12th January 1980 edition. He then propelled the band to their first *NME* cover story after he had travelled to Ireland to review U2 in concert at the Garden of Eden Club in Tullermeny in February 1980.
See also: Garden of Eden Club / Moonlight Club / *NME*

BRYAN MORRISON MUSIC Paul McGuinness negotiated a publishing deal for U2's music with this company in 1979. From the advance of £3,000, the band would be able to finance their first visit to London in December of that year. But a few days before the trip the publisher is believed to have rung Paul McGuinness to change the terms of the deal, to which McGuinness and U2 could not agree, so the deal was off. The band and their families however managed to raise enough money for the London trip to go ahead.

MORRISON, JIM See: Palais des Omnisports

MORRISON, VAN The Irish singer who came to prominence with the group Them in the 1960s. He was one of the first Irish artists to have major success outside Ireland, especially in the United States where he first had a top ten hit in 1967 with "Brown Eyed Girl". Albums such as *Astral Weeks* (1968), *Hard Nose The Highway* (1973) and *Beautiful Vision* (1982) have shown him to be a gifted vocalist and an influential songwriter and visionary. U2 appeared on the same bill as Van at 1986's Self Aid in Dublin's RDS Showground. A few years later, on the 6th May 1993, Bono joined Van Morrison on stage at the Point Depot in Dublin to sing "Moondance" and "Gloria". Van became the first inductee into the Irish Music Hall of Fame in Dublin when it opened in September 1999. Surprisingly, Morrison and U2 have never collaborated on record.
See also: Gloria

MORUMBI, SAO PAULO, BRAZIL U2's second and third dates in Brazil took place here on 30th and 31st January 1998 during the *Pop Mart* tour of the Rest of the World. Each night they played to approximately 100,000 people in the world's second biggest stadium. At the first show, The Edge reminded the audience that it was 26 years to the day since "Bloody Sunday" as he introduced the song "Sunday Bloody Sunday". Also, "Bad" was played live for the first time since the *Zoo TV* tour in 1993. At the second show "40" was played as the final number.

"THE MOTHER OF GOD" Bono recited this poem by William Butler Yeats in both English and Spanish on an Argentinian release entitled *20 Anos-Ni Un Paso Atras*.

MOTHER RECORDS The record label that U2 set up in 1984 in Dublin with the aim of giving up-and-coming musicians a step up onto the first rung of the music industry ladder, so that they could hopefully get a decent recording contract. It was not meant to be a record label per se, but more of a bridge between the musicians and the larger record companies. The bands and artists would have a one or two single record deal with the chance to record a single in a studio with a decent producer. The first signing to Mother Records was In Tua Nua, who released their first two records on the Mother Records label: "Coming Thru" and "Laughing At The Moon".

Other artists who got their first break with Mother Records were Cactus World News, Tuesday Blue, Operating Theatre, The Painted Word, The Subterraneans, Hothouse Flowers, Engine Alley and Golden Horde. The label was initially managed by Fachtna O'Kelly, (the former manager of The Boomtown Rats and Clannad) until 1987 when Rusty Egan took over responsibility. He was followed by Dave Pennefather who eventually moved on to Universal Music. A subsidiary company, Son Records, was founded in 1990 for one-off non-rock bands such as the Irish Football team's song, "Put 'Em Under Pressure".

Although Mother Records finally ceased its operations in the 1990s, it did achieve its objective of helping some of its artists to secure recording contracts with the majors including, In Tua Nua (Virgin), Hot House Flowers (London) and Cactus World News (RCA). The Mother Publishing company is still in operation.

See also: Cactus World News / Hot House Flowers / In Tua Nua / Fachtna O'Kelly / Son Records

MOTHER REDCAPS, DUBLIN, IRELAND Adam made a surprise appearance here on 23rd June 1989 when singer Maria McKee performed at this Dublin club.

See also: Maria McKee

"MOTHERS OF THE DISAPPEARED" (*THE JOSHUA TREE* ALBUM TRACK) (5.14) The final track on *The Joshua Tree* album. Inspired by Bono's visit to Nicaragua and El Salvador in 1986, the song continues the tradition set by *War* of using a quiet track as an album closer. The song refers to the mothers that Bono had met whose children had been taken away in the night by the authorities never to be seen again. It is no coincidence that on the album artwork, immediately after the printed lyrics, there are details of the human rights organisation Amnesty International. The song was first performed on the *Joshua Tree* tour at the Sports Arena in San Diego, USA on 14th April 1987.

"MOTHERS OF THE DISAPPEARED" (LIVE) Live footage of this song being performed at the Estadio Nacional in Santiago, Chile on 10th February 1998 can be found on the video of *Joshua Tree* from the "Classic Albums" TV series. At this show, U2 arranged for women who had lost their sons during the dictatorship of General Pinochet to stand on the stage whilst the song was being performed.

See also: Estadio Nacional, Santiago

MOUNT TEMPLE COMPREHENSIVE SCHOOL, DUBLIN, IRELAND The secondary school attended by all four members of U2 in the mid-1970s. It was the place where U2 was first born after Larry Mullen,

Mount Temple Comprehensive School, Dublin. *Photo: Paul Daly*

who was looking for musicians interested in forming a band, put a message on the school's notice board. The resulting group was called Feedback, who then changed their name to The Hype and subsequently U2. The school was a revolutionary establishment becoming the first non-denominational comprehensive school in Ireland when it opened in 1971. This meant that it was not tied to the teachings of either the Roman Catholic or the Protestant church, and as a result was more relaxed in its approach to discipline. Both Adam Clayton and Paul Hewson were sent here after having had to leave their previous secondary schools. Also, the school's ethos was more concerned with individual development than pure academic success.

The music teacher, Albert Bradshaw, openly encouraged the group, giving them rooms in which to rehearse at lunch times. Near the end of the autumn term of 1976, the embryonic U2 made their live debut in the school gymnasium, playing the Peter Frampton song "Show Me The Way". Bono later admitted that the gig was "one of the best concerts of our lives".

See also: Albert Bradshaw / Feedback

MOUNTCHARLES, LORD HENRY The owner of Slane Castle who agreed to let U2 use Slane to record *The Unforgettable Fire*. He had previously allowed the grounds of Slane Castle to be used for major rock concerts in the 1980s, including those headlined by Thin Lizzy, Bruce Springsteen and Bob Dylan. In 1992, parts of Slane Castle burnt down, but has since been restored. In recent years, Lord Henry has once again allowed Slane to be used as a site for major rock concerts with appearances by Oasis and The Manic Street Preachers. U2's first headlining appearances were on 25th August and 1st September 2001.

See also: Slane Castle / Slane Castle Festival

MOXHAM, DAVID A teacher at Mount Temple Comprehensive School in Dublin who encouraged the young Feedback group to rehearse in a classroom at the school.

MOYDRUM CASTLE, WEST MEATH, IRELAND The castle that appears on the cover of U2's *The Unforgettable Fire* album.

MOYLETT, REGINE Regine is best known as U2's publicist, though she has a musical background herself playing keyboards in the new wave band, The New Versions and Max in the late 1970s. With her sister, Susan, she also helped set up a shop called "No Romance" which claimed to be Dublin's first punk clothes shop. In 1983 she moved to London, joining Island Records' press office. She was given the job of publicising several Island Records acts including Frankie Goes To Hollywood and U2 (from 1987 onwards). Eventually she left Island to set up

her own publicity company – RMP (Regine Moylett Publicity), which over the years has publicised artists such as Keith Richards, Marianne Faithfull and Massive Attack. At present RMP publicises the activities of U2 as well as Sting, The Corrs, Blur, PJ Harvey and Gorillaz.

See also: RMP

MR. PUSSY'S CAFE DE LUXE A club that was jointly owned by Bono, Gavin Friday and Jim Sheridan. It was named after the host, "Mr. Pussy", who was a well-known Dublin drag queen. U2 often frequented the club as it stayed open for most of the night. It eventually closed down and was taken over by Norman Hewson, who reopened it as an all day cafe named "Nude".

See also: Nude

MTV (MUSIC TELEVISION) The TV station broadcasting popular music 24 hours a day began in America in 1981 and was part of Sky's satellite package in the UK. It was instrumental in the promotional video explosion of the 1980s as any band that wanted to promote their latest single would need a video which could be shown on MTV to maximize its chance of success. U2 were featured on MTV early on in their career and from "Pride" onwards their videos were shown as soon as they came out.

MTV has always given generous airtime to U2 as well as holding many U2 competitions over the years. For instance in 1992, John Harris, an MTV competition winner from Nottingham, had the U2 concert from Stockholm on June 11th beamed live into his living room. Later that year the MTV awards ceremony went live to U2's concert at the Pontiac Silverdome where they were performing "Even Better Than The Real Thing". The band were presented with the award for the best video, in their dressing room after the show, by Peter Gabriel and Annie Lennox.

U2 have won several MTV awards over the years, as well as appearing at various award ceremonies such as in 1993 when The Edge performed "Numb" solo. In 1995 Bono caused uproar at the European Awards ceremony when, during his acceptance speech he showed his disgust for recent nuclear tests in the Pacific Ocean, by referring to the French president Jaques Chirac as "a wanker". At the 1997 European Music Awards in Rotterdam, U2 performed "Mofo" at the ceremony, and Bono sang a song entitled "Port of Rotterdam" whilst accepting the award for best live act.

As part of a promotional tour for the *All That You Can't Leave Behind* album U2 played a special gig on the roof of the MTV studios in New York City on 30th October 2000 which was transmitted on the TRL programme. The set list was: "Elevation", "Beautiful

Day", "New York", "Elevation" (again) and "Happy Birthday" (for Larry). A few weeks later, U2 performed "Beautiful Day" live at the MTV European Music Awards ceremony at the Globe arena in Stockholm on 16th November 2000. For a full list of MTV awards and appearances see appendix.

MUHAMMAD ALI World famous heavyweight boxer. He had first met U2 on the Conspiracy of Hope Tour in 1986. In February 1999 at the 18th Brit Awards in London, Bono presented him with the Freddie Mercury Award for his work with the Jubilee 2000 coalition, an award that Bono had himself just accepted on behalf of Jubilee 2000.

MULLALLY, TOM Larry's drum technician for most of the 1980s having joined the band for the *War* album onwards.

MULLEN, LARRY JUNIOR The only son of Maureen and Larry Mullen was born on 31st October 1961 in Harmonstown, Dublin, the middle child of three. As a child he attended his local school for one year before going to the Scoil Colmcille in Marlborough Street where Gaelic was the primary language. Larry began to learn the piano when he was eight but after a year decided that he would prefer to to play the drums. His sister, Cecilia, bought him his first drum kit in 1973 for £17. He was taught at first by Joe Bonnie and later by Joe's daughter, Monica. By 1974 he had joined the Artane Boys Band but due to their rules about length of hair he didn't stay long. Through the efforts of his father, he got a place in the Post Office Workers Union Band which meant playing at concerts and fairs all over the country.

It was at his seconary school, Mount Temple Comprehensive, that he decided that he would like to play in his own pop group just like the ones he watched on *Top of The Pops* each Thursday evening. This is when he put the famous note on the notice board at Mount Temple asking for musicians who were interested in forming a band to come to his house after school. David Evans and his brother Dick, Adam Clayton, Paul Hewson, Peter Martin and Ivan McCormick all took up the invitation. The last two were gradually eased out. Dick Evans stayed in the band initially called Feedback and then the Hype until 1978 before joining the Virgin Prunes. Although being in Feedback was enjoyable – the band took part in a talent contest at the school – progress was slow at first and Larry took a job as a messenger. This led to the others having to wait around for him at practice times and him almost being fired before he quit his daytime job.

Gradually the "Larry Mullen Band" (as Larry has often called his group!) gained more experience and started to flourish, gaining a following in Dublin,

then London and eventually a recording contract with Island Records. Like Bono and The Edge, Larry joined the Shalom Christian Group and was the only one of U2 who came from a conventional Catholic background.

As the drummer in the band, Larry has not been without his problems. Before a show in San Francisco in March 1985, Larry was rushed to hospital with acute pain in his left hand. He was diagnosed as having tendonitis, which should have stopped him from playing for a few weeks. But instead, he wore a special plaster and took pain killers for the rest of the tour. He now uses specially designed drumsticks to counteract this problem.

Larry is a big fan of country & western music and this influence can be seen in the *Joshua Tree* documentary *Outside It's America.* He is also a big Elvis Presley fan as shown in the film *Rattle & Hum*, where he visits Graceland and sits astride one of Elvis' motorbikes – another of his loves. He once rode over 10,000 miles on his beloved Harley Davidson between dates on the *Zoo TV* tour and received a special award for doing so from the road crew. Another special award he won was the Rory Gallagher Musician Award at the Irish Rock Music Awards in Dublin in 1997.

Within the U2 organisation Larry has a special interest in the merchandising side, personally over-

Larry Mullen Junior. *Photo: Emma Reilly*

The Edge and Larry Mullen, Wembley Stadium, June 12th 1987. *Photo: Kay Bauersfeld*

seeing what items should be sold on a particular tour. His no-nonsense approach is well known both within and outside the U2 organisation. Whilst he might be the most private of the four members of the U2, he still enjoys a spot of karaoke and playing the odd trick on unsuspecting members of the road crew. He has remained committed to his long-time partner, Ann Acheson, since the early 1980s. They have a son called Elvis Aaron Mullen born in 1995, a daughter called Ava born in 1998, and another son born in February 2001.

MULLEN, LARRY SENIOR Larry's father was born in North Dublin in 1923. One of seven children, he nearly became a priest but instead became a civil servant in the Department of Health and Environment. He married Larry's mother, Maureen Gaffney, in 1956 and had they three children, Cecilia, Larry and Mary.

MULLEN, MAUREEN (NEE GAFFNEY) Larry's mother Maureen was born in 1922 in Anna in the west of Ireland. She was brought up by her mother's grandmother after her mother died giving birth to her. When she was eleven she was moved to Dublin where she attended the Sacred Heart convent school and then Alexandra College. She met Larry senior in the 1950s and they married in 1956 living in Harmonstown

Road in north Dublin. Sadly she died in a road accident in 1978.

MUNGERSDORFER STADIUM, COLOGNE, GERMANY U2 have played this German stadium on two occasions. The first time was on 17th June 1987 during the *Joshua Tree* tour. There was a lot of aggravation at this show before a crowd of 67,000 people. Rather than receiving tickets, fans had been given vouchers to exchange outside the stadium for tickets before the show. The problem was that there was only one ticket booth and "identification papers" were also required, so many fans missed seeing the support acts due to all the bureaucracy. The show itself was spoilt by a poor sound system and bad feelings all around. U2 returned here during the *Zooropa* tour on the 12th June 1993 without any problems.

MURRAYFIELD STADIUM, EDINBURGH, SCOTLAND U2 played this Scottish rugby stadium on 1st August 1987 to a capacity crowd of 58,000 fans during the *Joshua Tree* tour of Europe. They came back ten years later during the *Pop Mart* tour to play here on 2nd September 1997. As in Dublin two days earlier, Bono dedicated "MLK" to Princess Diana, who had recently died, while her image was shown on the TV screen.

MUSIC TELEVISION See: MTV

MUSIQUE VS U2 The American dance act that remixed the U2 song "New Year's Day" into "New Year's Dub", released in May 2001.

See also: New Years's Dub

"MYSTERIOUS WAYS" (*ACHTUNG BABY* ALBUM TRACK) (4.04) The second song on the *Achtung Baby* album. It starts with some heavy chords from The Edge, which dominate the track. When played live, the song featured a belly dancer, as in the promotional video, shot in Morocco. The song was first performed live on the opening night of the *Zoo TV* tour at the Lakeland Arena, Lakeland, Florida, on 29th February 1992. Whilst there might be eight remixes of "Mysterious Ways", to date there has been no official release of a live audio recording.

"MYSTERIOUS WAYS" (SINGLE) The single of "Mysterious Ways" was released in December 1991 and reached number 13 in the UK charts and number 9 in the US. It was the second track to be lifted off *Achtung Baby*. All the B-sides were remixes of the A-side, the first time a U2 single contained different versions of the same song. The B-side of the 7 inch version (IS 509) was "Mysterious Ways" (Solar Plexus Magic Hour Remix). The 12 inch (12IS 5098) had the main single track, the Perfecto Mix, the Apollo Magic Hour Remix and the Solar Plexus Extended Club Mix. The CD however contained the original album track plus the Solar Plexus Extended Club Mix, the Apollo 440 Magic Hour Remix, the Tabla Motown remix and the Solar Plexus Club Mix. There was an alternative 12 inch release (12ISX 509) which had the Ultimatum Mix included, adding to the confusion!

"MYSTERIOUS WAYS" (APOLLO 440 MAGIC HOUR REMIX) (4.25) This remix was on both the 12-inch and CD versions of the "Mysterious Ways" single.

"MYSTERIOUS WAYS" (MASSIVE ATTACK MIX) (4.50) This mix of "Mysterious Ways" only appears on the free *Melon* CD

"MYSTERIOUS WAYS" (PERFECTO MIX) (7.11) This was mixed by Paul Oakenfold and Steve Osbourne in 1991. It appeared as the main track on the 12-inch single version of "Mysterious Ways" and also on the *Melon* CD.

"MYSTERIOUS WAYS" (SOLAR PLEXUS CLUB MIX) (4.10) This mix was available only on the CD version of the "Mysterious Ways" single. Additional production and remixing was by Howard Gray, Trevor Gray and Steve Lillywhite.

"MYSTERIOUS WAYS" (SOLAR PLEXUS EXTENDED CLUB MIX) (7.01) This mix of "Mysterious Ways" was released in both the 12-inch and CD versions of the single. Howard and Trevor Gray along with Steve Lillywhite were responsible for the remix and additional production.

"MYSTERIOUS WAYS" (SOLAR PLEXUS MAGIC HOUR REMIX) This remix appears only on the 7-inch version of the "Mysterious Ways" single.

"MYSTERIOUS WAYS" (TABLA MOTOWN REMIX) (4.27) This mistakenly spelt title – it should have read Tamla Motown – was only available on the CD version of the single.

"MYSTERIOUS WAYS" (ULTIMATUM MIX) (4.05) The only version of this remix of "Mysterious Ways" can be found on the alternative 12 inch release (IS12X 509).

"MYSTERIOUS WAYS" (LIVE) (*ZOO TV LIVE FROM SYDNEY* VIDEO) This live version of "Mysterious Ways" was filmed and recorded at U2's second concert at the Cricket Ground, Sydney, Australia on Saturday 17th November 1993.

"MYSTERIOUS WAYS" (LIVE) (*POP MART LIVE FROM MEXICO CITY* VIDEO) The twenty-second track on the video *U2: Pop Mart Live from Mexico City* was filmed at the Foro Sol Autodromo, Mexico City on 3rd December 1997.

"MYSTERIOUS WAYS" (PROMOTIONAL VIDEO) (4.02) The promotional video of "Mysterious Ways" was directed by Stephane Sednaoui and produced by Phillipe Dupuis-Mendel. It was filmed in Morocco in October 1991 and featured buildings from the old city as well as a belly dancer. When the song was performed live on the *Zoo TV* tour, a belly dancer would come on stage.

"MY WILD IRISH ROSE" The title of a ballad that Bono wrote for the BBC/RTE series called *Bringing It All Back Home*. The Edge played guitar on the track and Donal Lunny helped out on the tin whistle. The song was not included on the album of the series but was included on the video.

NAPSTER U2 fans were able to download free from Napster all the tracks from U2's album, *All That You Can't Leave Behind*, almost two weeks before the official release of the album in October 2000.

NASHVILLE ROOMS, EARL'S COURT, LONDON, ENGLAND U2's second gig in Britain took place in this west London venue on 2nd December 1979 when they played as support act to the Mod revival group, Secret Affair. They returned to play another gig here on 30th May 1980, this time as the headline group.

NASSAU VETERAN'S MEMORIAL COLISEUM, UNIONDALE, NEW YORK, USA U2 have played this 17,000 capacity arena on four occasions. Their first visit, on 3rd April 1985, took place during the *Unforgettable Fire* tour of America. Their next visit was for two dates on 10th and 11th September 1987 – the first two dates of the third leg of the *Joshua Tree* tour. The Beatles song "Helter Skelter" was played live for the first time here, as was the song about U2 roadie, Greg Carroll, "One Tree Hill". Finally U2 played here on 9th March 1992 during the first leg of the *Zoo TV* tour of America.

NATIONAL BOXING STADIUM, DUBLIN, IRELAND This venue goes down in U2 history as the place where U2 finally convinced Island Records executive, Bill Stewart that U2 were worth signing to the label. With the help of many friends and relatives U2 managed to sell out this two and a half thousand capacity boxing venue on 26th February 1980, making it the largest audience that the band had played to at this point in their career. The show was recorded by RTE Radio and broadcast later on in the year. Nine years later, on 11th March 1989, BB King played a gig here and was joined on stage by Bono and The Edge for a version of "When Love Comes To Town", followed by the Little Richard rocker, "Lucille".

See also: BB King / Bill Stewart

NATIONAL CAR RENTAL CENTER, FORT LAUDERDALE, FLORIDA, USA These two dates were the opening shows of the *Elevation* tour. They took place at the 19,000 capacity National Car Rental Center in Fort Lauderdale near Miami, Florida on 24th and 26th March 2001. Both shows were sold out. Many celebrities were present on the first night including Christy Turlington, Daniel Lanois, Elvis Costello, Howie B and Lenny Kravitz. For the first time, Bono played

the piano on stage for "Sweetest Thing" and during "The Fly" he dived into the audience, though some present thought that he had fallen off the stage. For the second night, Bono recited some of Psalm 116 before "Where The Streets Have No Name" and forgot the words to some of "Angel of Harlem". For both shows The Corrs were the support group, as the scheduled opening act PJ Harvey was ill.

Opening night of tour set list: Elevation, Beautiful Day, Until the End of the World, New Year's Day, Stuck In A Moment, Gone, Discotheque, Staring at the Sun, New York, I Will Follow, Sunday Bloody Sunday (Get Up Stand Up), Sweetest Thing, In A Little While, The Ground Beneath Her Feet, Bad, Where the Streets Have No Name, Mysterious Ways, The Fly. Encores: Bullet the Blue Sky, With or Without You, One, Walk On.

NATIONAL TENNIS CENTRE, MELBOURNE, AUSTRALIA U2 played a series of seven sold out shows at this 16,000 capacity venue on 7th, 8th, 9th, 12th, 13th, 14th and 16th October 1989 during the *Lovetown*

beatles - sgt. Peppers 1.55
intro trippy elevation mix
elevation
beautiful day
end of the world
discotheque / staring at the sun
kite
new york
out of control
sunday bloody sunday
wake up dead man (b&e)
stuck in a moment
sweetest thing
in a little while
ground beneath
all I want
streets
mysterious ways
pride
charlton heston
bullet
with or without
****
one
walk on

Birmingham (2) 15th August

Set list, NEC Birmingham, 15/8/01

tour of Australia. (An eighth show on 17th October was pencilled in but did not take place). The third show marked the live debut of the *Rattle & Hum* track, "Van Diemen's Land", featuring The Edge on vocals.

NBC ARENA (NEAL BLAISDELL CENTER), HONO-LULU, HAWAII, USA On route to their first concerts in Japan, the band stopped off in Honolulu in Hawaii for a short break and a one-off concert on 16th November 1983. It was at the sound check for this concert that the first musical ideas for "Pride" began to take shape. The band then returned here on 11th March 1985 during the *Unforgettable Fire* tour of North America.

NBC STUDIOS, NEW YORK CITY, USA U2 performed "Beautiful Day" and "Elevation" here for their first appearance on *Saturday Night Live* on 9th December 2000.

NEALE, MARK The director who made the promo videos for "Lemon" and "Lemon (Bad Yard Club)".

NEC (NATIONAL EXHIBITION CENTRE), BIRMING-HAM, ENGLAND To date U2 have played this 11,000 capacity venue in England's second city on seven occasions. Their first visit on, 12th November 1984, was during the *Unforgettable Fire* tour. This performance was recorded and "Bad" appeared on the EP *Wide Awake In America*. They next played here in 1987 during the *Joshua Tree* tour of Europe – 3rd June, and 3rd and 4th August. The show on 3rd August began with the recording of Jimi Hendrix playing "The Star Spangled Banner" at the 1969 Woodstock festival – the first time this piece of music was used at a U2 concert. The show also featured the live premiere of "Silver & Gold", which the band had just released as the B-side to the "Where The Streets Have No Name" single. U2 next played a show here during the *Zoo TV* tour of Europe on 1st June 1992. At the end of the show Bono recited some lines of the WB Yeats poem "September 1913" straight after "Love Is Blindness". The band played two nights here on 14th and 15th August 2001 as part of the *Elevation* tour of Europe.

See also: Bad / Wide Awake In America

NECKARSTDION, STUTTGART, GERMANY U2 played at this German festival on 26th May 1985. They were second on the bill to fellow Irishman, Chris de Burgh. During their set Bono jumped into the audience during "The Electric Co." and as a result had the shirt he was wearing torn to shreds.

NEGATIVLAND An American underground group, Negativland released a record in September 1991, shortly before U2 were due to release their *Achtung Baby* album. The cover had the characters "U2" across

Bono, *Elevation Tour*, NEC Birmingham, 14/8/01
Photo: Claire Bolton

the front with a spy plane silhouette and the group's name "Negativland" in very small letters printed at the bottom – so there was the possibility that U2 fans might think that it was the next U2 record. The actual track was a remixed, sampled and layered version of "I Still Haven't Found What I'm Looking For". It also included comments by Bono and Casey Kasem, an American DJ, slating U2.

The main problem with the release was that Negativland's record label, SST Records, had not secured the rights to the recording of this song. This resulted in Warner Chapel (U2's publishing company in America) and Island Records taking out an injunction to stop the sale, distribution and promotion of the CD. An out of court settlement was soon reached under which SST agreed to pay a fine and all the legal fees involved. This was not the end of the matter however as SST issued a statement saying that the issue was freedom of speech and that, as it was a satirical recording, they did not need permission to parody the work they were using. They even started a "Kill Bono" campaign!

The press seized upon this story and made matters worse by portraying U2 as the villains of the affair. In fact U2 had asked Chris Blackwell not to press for payment. During the course of events Negativland and SST Records parted company in December 1991, with SST insisting that Negativland should pay 100% of the costs and not 50% as originally agreed. Negativland thus lost out on any royalties due to them, so to raise money they published a magazine in August 1992 filled with all the legal paper work and press reports on the case.

It was called "The letter U and the numeral 2" and contained a CD of someone talking about the US Copyright Act. Once again Negativland were sued for breach of copyright, though at some stage it is believed that U2 and Island Records gave permission for Negativland to re-release the CD. However, this did not happen as Casey Kasem would not give permission for his sample to be used. A thicker 270 page re-issue of the book was then published with even more letters and legal documents in the spring of 1995.

NELSON, WILLIE The famous American country & western singer was born in Texas in 1933. He first came to public attention in the 1960s when he recorded several best selling albums as well as writing several hits for country artists such as Patsy Cline and Faron Young. In the 1980s he collaborated with Bob Dylan, Kris Kristofferson and Waylon Jennings as the Highwaymen. Following on from Bob Geldof, he helped launch the first "Farm Aid" concert to raise funds for America's struggling farmers. This became an annual event. Bono and Larry had been fans of Willie for some time and in 1989 Bono wrote a song for him called "Slow Dancing". U2 recorded their version in 1993, but Willie was finally able to record his version with the band in 1997. It was included on the "If God Will Send His Angels" single.

See also: Slow Dancing

NELSON PIQUET STADIUM, RIO DE JANEIRO, BRAZIL U2's first ever concert in South America took place here on 27th January 1998, the first date of the final leg of the *Pop Mart* tour. It was originally scheduled for the Maracana Stadium, the biggest stadium in the world, but at the last minute the venue was changed, allegedly without the band's knowledge. Many fans missed the start of the concert due to traffic jams on the way to the stadium. Approximately 65,000 fans attended and the band were joined on stage by a samba group of 30 musicians. When they appeared in the lemon, all four members of U2 were wearing the shirts of the Brazilian national soccer team.

See also: Maracana Stadium.

NEP STADION, BUDAPEST, HUNGARY U2's sole concert in the former communist country took place here on 23rd July 1993 during the *Zooropa* tour before a capacity crowd of 60,000. There had been plans to take in several former communist countries during the *Zoo TV* tour including Poland and Czechoslovakia, but in the end only Hungary made it onto the schedule.

"NESSUN DORMA" (*TOGETHER FOR THE CHILDREN OF BOSNIA* ALBUM TRACK) (2.54) The final track on the album *Together For The Children of Bosnia* features Luciano Pavarotti and all the guests at the concert in Modena on 12th September 1995, including Bono, The Edge and Brian Eno.

See also: Together For The Children Of Bosnia

NET AID A special charity event which took place simultaneously in three countries – the USA, the UK and Switzerland – on 9th October 1999, in aid of the NetAid organisation. The American segment took place at a half empty Giant's Stadium in New Jersey, where the likes of Sting, Jimmy Page, The Black Crowes, Puff Daddy, Mary J, Blige, Sheryl Crow, the Counting Crows and Bono all performed. The UK segment took place at a sold out Wembley Stadium and featured Robbie Williams, The Eurythmics, The Corrs, the Stereophonics and David Bowie. The third segment took place in Geneva, Switzerland before an invited audience which included UN Secretary Kofi Annan. Bryan Ferry and Texas performed amongst others.

Net Aid was originally the idea of Dianne Merrick of Cisco Systems, whose company sponsored the event. The event was broadcast live on various TV stations around the world as well as by webcast over the Internet. At the American part of NetAid, the show started off with many of the artists taking part (including Bono) joining Wyclef Jean on stage to perform "New Day". This was broadcast simultaneously at Wembley and Geneva. Bono then performed "One" with Zucchero and an orchestra conducted by Quincy Jones.

The NetAid site was set up to raise awareness amongst Internet users of worldwide problems. It offers information on volunteer efforts and business development initiatives as well as an e-mail petition where users can support Bono's Jubilee 2000 plan to eradicate Third World debt.

Website: www.netaid.org

See also: Wyclef Jean / Quincy Jones / Zucchero / "New Day"

"NEVER LET ME GO" (*THE MILLION DOLLAR HOTEL SOUNDTRACK ALBUM*) (5.35) The second track on *The Million Dollar Hotel* soundtrack album is performed by Bono and The MDH Band. Bono had written the lyrics with scriptwriter, Nicholas Klein.

NEVILLE BROTHERS, THE Highly respected New Orleans soul and R&B group fronted by Aaron Neville, along with his three brothers. Their career began in the fifties and has encompassed several platinum albums. They supported U2 on the 1986 *Conspiracy of Hope* tour. Subsequently, Bono wrote "Jah Love" for their 1990 album, *The Brother's Keeper*.

"NEW DAY" The song that Bono recorded in July 1999 with Wyclef Jean, the former Fugee, in Wyclef's studio in New Jersey. It was used as the theme song for the NetAid concert on 9th October 1999 in New York City. There was also a "Pop" version and a "Hip Hop Clean" version, as well as a promo video of the song.
See also: Net Aid / Wyclef Jean

NEW MUSICAL EXPRESS (NME) This British Music paper has been published weekly since the 1950s. It was the last of the big three UK music journals to write about U2 when they first arrived in Britain in 1979 (the other two being *Sounds* and *Melody Maker*). Surprisingly though, The Hype got a mention in January 1978 when Adam placed an advert in its pages from an "Irish Manager" by the name of Brian who wanted to know more about this up-and-coming band. U2's first mention was from Paul Morley in the January 12th 1980 edition, reviewing their Moonlight Club gig in London the previous month – the band's first gig outside Ireland.

Other favourable mentions were made throughout 1980 until the 27th September edition when the band were reviewed supporting Echo & The Bunnymen at the London Lyceum. This was not a favourable review and from then on a love-hate relationship between the *NME* and U2 has continued on and off over the years, depending on who writes about the band. For instance, in November 1982 David Quantick described them as "the most boring band in the world".

Perhaps the weirdest story was in the summer of 1993 when *NME* ran a article about the *Zoo TV* tour entitled "EMP TV" attacking the whole concept. Prior to the story the *NME* had faxed several questions over to the U2 headquarters in Dublin to which Bono had replied by sending two axes, ready for the reporter to do a "hatchet job" on the band! By the start of the new millennium it seemed that U2 could do no wrong

at the *NME*. At the magazine's 2001 "Brat Awards" held in London, U2 won the Best Rock Act award and the award for being "God Like Geniuses".
See also: The Hype / Paul Morley

NEW VOICES OF FREEDOM CHOIR This choir from Harlem, New York featuring the soloists Dorothy Tennell and George Pendergrass, sang on "I Still Haven't Found What I'm Looking For" on stage at Madison Square Garden with U2 on 28th September 1987. This unique version was included on the *Rattle & Hum* album, though the concert sequence wasn't included in the film. Instead the choir are shown singing in their church with the band joining them.
See also: I Still Haven't Found What I'm Looking For / Rattle & Hum

"NEW YEAR'S DAY" (*WAR* ALBUM TRACK) (5.38) The third track on side one of the *War* album. It begins with The Edge on electric piano – a welcome change of style on a U2 song. The song is ostensibly about the Solidarity Movement in Poland, which was involved in a struggle for free Trades Unions at the time. To counteract this growing popular movement, a state of martial law had been imposed by the Polish authorities – which was later lifted on New Year's Day 1983. As with "11 O'clock Tick Tock" there also seem to be allusions to the end of the world. The song was first performed live at Tiffany's in Glasgow, Scotland on 1st December 1982, though the performance had to be cut short due to problems with The Edge's guitar. It became U2's first top 10 hit single in the UK and has become a permanent fixture in their live shows over the years.
See also: Lech Walesa / Solidarity

"NEW YEAR'S DAY" (SINGLE) (4.17) The single version of "New Year's Day" was released in the UK and several other countries around the world in January 1983. To maximise its selling power the single was released in three formats: the normal 7 inch single format (WIP 6848), a special double 7 inch single pack (VWIP 6848) and a 12 inch single (12WIP 6848). The single reached number 10 in the UK charts and number 53 in the US charts. The B-side was entitled "Treasure (Whatever Happened To Pete The Chop)". The double 7 inch and 12 inch versions had the extra tracks of "Fire", "I Threw A Brick Through A Window" and "A Day Without Me" which had all been recorded at the Werchter Festival in Belgium on 3rd July 1982. (The Japanese 7 inch single version (Island 7S-86) featured a different recording of "New Year's Day"). There was also an EP version (EP 600741). The single version was also included on the compilation *The Best of 1980-1990*, released in 1998.

"NEW YEAR'S DAY" (REMIX VERSION) ("TWO HEARTS BEAT AS ONE" 12 INCH SINGLE) This extended version of "New Year's Day" was remixed by Francois Kevorkian, a New York DJ, who had been introduced to the band by Chris Blackwell, the head of Island Records. Blackwell had thought that it would be an "interesting experiment" to remix one of U2's songs for a club audience. This was the first time that a U2 track had been given the remix treatment, a practice that would be used again and again with U2's music.

"NEW YEAR'S DAY" (LIVE) (*UNDER A BLOOD RED SKY* ALBUM) (4.36) The third track on side two of the *Live Under A Blood Red Sky* mini LP, released in November 1983. The track was recorded at the Lorelei Festival in Germany on 20th August 1983, and was produced by Jimmy Iovine.

"NEW YEAR'S DAY" (LIVE) (*HASTA LA VISTA BABY! U2 LIVE FROM MEXICO CITY* ALBUM TRACK) One of the tracks on the CD given away free to *Propaganda* readers in July 2000. It was recorded live at the Foro Sol Autodromo, Mexico City, Mexico on 3rd December 1997 during the *Pop Mart* tour of North America.

"NEW YEAR'S DAY" (LIVE) (*UNDER A BLOOD RED SKY* VIDEO). The film version of "New Year's Day" that appears on this video was recorded and filmed at Denver's Red Rocks Amphitheatre on 5th June 1983. It is the fifth track on the video, but on the actual night was performed as the twelfth song of the set.

"NEW YEAR'S DAY" (LIVE) (*U2 ZOO TV LIVE FROM SYDNEY* VIDEO) This film version of "New Year's Day" was recorded live at the Sydney Cricket Ground, Australia on 27th November 1993.

"NEW YEAR'S DAY" (LIVE) (*POP MART LIVE FROM MEXICO CITY* VIDEO) The eighth track on the video *U2: Pop Mart Live From Mexico City*. It was recorded live at the Foro Sol Autodromo, Mexico City, Mexico on 3rd December 1997 during the *Pop Mart* tour of North America. "New Year's Day" is the only U2 song that has been included in all three official concert videos.

"NEW YEAR'S DAY" (PROMOTIONAL VIDEO) The promo video for "New Year's Day" was filmed in Sweden in December 1982, during a break from concerts in that country. The director was Meiert Avis and this was the third video in a row that he had directed for U2. The video shows U2 walking and riding horses in the snow. In fact The Edge had problems with his horse misbehaving so in the end a girl stand-in took his place for the video shoot.

"NEW YEAR'S DUB" This was a special single that was released in May 2001 by 'Musique Vs U2' on

Serious Records featuring samples of The Edge's piano and guitar lines from "New Year's Day". It had been premiered in March 2001 at the Miami Winter Music Conference, which was held at the same time as U2's opening *Elevation* tour dates in nearby Fort Lauderdale. Apparently U2 were suitably impressed and allowed the single to be released. It featured five remixes by the following artists: DJ Elite, Hybrid, Mauro Picotto, Skynet and Steve Lawler. There was also a promo video for this track.

See also: Musique Vs U2

"NEW YORK" (*ALL THAT YOU CAN'T LEAVE BEHIND* ALBUM TRACK) (5.28) The tenth track on the album *All That You Can't Leave Behind*, released in November 2000. In the lyrics Bono explores his fascination with this vibrant city that has always held a special place in U2's heart (see below). The song was first performed live at the Man Ray Club in Paris on 19th October 2000.

"NEW YORK" (LIVE FROM FARMCLUB.COM) (6.00) This live version of "New York" was recorded at Universal City Studios, Los Angeles on 27th October 2000. It was included on two U2 singles: first on the "Stuck In A Moment You Can't Get Out Of" single released in the UK and second on the "Walk On" single released in Canada.

"NEW YORK" (LIVE) (THE SUNDAY TIMES FREE CD) (5.42) This live version of U2 performing "New York" was recorded appropriately enough in New York City at the Irving Plaza on 5th December 2000. It was one of three tracks from that concert included on an exclusive CD given away free with *The Sunday Times* newspaper.

NEW YORK CITY, USA This bustling American city has always had a close connection with U2 as it was here where they first entered the USA on 5th December 1980. Their first American date was in New York at the Ritz, just a few days before John Lennon was shot dead in the same city. The band returned to New York to play at various venues over the next few years, including Radio City Music Hall and the Palladium, but a major triumph for them was being able to play a sell out show at Madison Square Gardens on 1st April 1985. Since then they have played even bigger venues in and around New York including the Yankee Stadium and the Giant's Stadium. At the other end of the scale, in December 2000 the band played a small intimate gig at the Irving Plaza as a special warm up show for the *Elevation* tour.

It was in New York City that Bono wrote "Silver & Gold" when he was in town to record the "Sun City" single and album. Promo videos of "Angel of Harlem", "One" and "Save The Children" have all been shot in New York City. After the *Zoo TV* tour had ended in 1993, both Larry and Adam bought apartments in New York as alternative homes to Dublin. Bono has also recently purchased a house in New York. Both The Edge and Bono have been guests of honour at the New York Waldorf Astoria Hotel for the Rock 'n' Roll Hall of Fame ceremony where they have made speeches to induct such artists as Bob Marley and The Yardbirds. Finally, the band recorded the track "New York" on their album *All That You Can't Leave Behind* as a tribute to the city.

See also: Giant's Stadium / Madison Square Gardens / Palladium / Radio City Music Hall / Yankee Stadium

NEW ZOOLAND TOUR This was the name given to the two dates U2 played in New Zealand as part of the 1993 *Zoo TV* tour in December 1993. The dates were Lancaster Park in Christchurch on 1st December and Western Springs Stadium, Auckland on 4th December. Neither of the two shows sold out.

NICE JAZZ FESTIVAL, FRANCE Van Morrison performed at this festival in the south of France on 16th July 1999; he was joined on stage by Bono who sang the old Them hit, "Gloria" with him.

NICHOLSON, JACK The famous American actor introduced U2 on stage at Wembley Stadium for Live Aid in July 1985. The introduction was via satellite from the JFK Stadium in Philadelphia.

NICHOLSON, TIM U2's first tour manager who travelled with them on the *Boy* tour of the UK and Europe in 1980. He is believed to have left the band because of ill health.

"NIGHT & DAY" (*RED HOT AND BLUE* ALBUM TRACK) (5.21) The Cole Porter song that was specially recorded by U2 for the AIDS Awareness album, *Red, Hot & Blue*. They chose this particular Cole

Porter song for "its elements of obsession, love, drivenness, the idea of desperation and isolation". It was notable for the inclusion of The Edge's "infinite guitar" and was recorded at STS Studios in Dublin. It was not released as a single, but there was a DJ promo version. Steve Lillywhite was the producer. "Night & Day" was the only new song released by U2 inbetween 1988's *Rattle & Hum* and 1991's *Achtung Baby*.

See also: AIDS / Infinite Guitar

"NIGHT & DAY" (STEEL STRING REMIX) ("ONE" SINGLE) (7.00) This remix of the Cole Porter song "Night & Day" was only available on the CD version of the "One" single (CIS 550). It was remixed by Youth and produced by The Edge and Paul Barrett.

"NIGHT & DAY" (PROMOTIONAL VIDEO) The promo video of "Night & Day" was the first collaboration between U2 and German film producer Wim Wenders. The video was first shown on TV on the first AIDS Awareness Day on 1st December 1990, when all the tracks/videos from the *Red, Hot & Blue* project were transmitted. It was filmed in Wim Wenders house in Berlin.

See also: Berlin / Wim Wenders

NITE CLUB, EDINBURGH, SCOTLAND U2's first gig in Scotland took place here on 21st November 1981 before a capacity crowd of 400 fans. "The Cry" (the introduction to "The Electric Co.") was first played live here.

NME - See: New Musical Express

NME FREE SINGLE (GIV - 1B) A 7 inch single that was given away free with the *New Musical Express* in June 1985. U2 were one of four artists on the single. Their track was "Wire" (Dub mix) which was (and still is) only available on this single making it a very rare piece of U2 music. The other artists and tracks were Bronski Beat, "Hard Rain"; The Cocteau Twins, "Two"; and The Smiths, "What She Said"(Live).

NOBEL PEACE PRIZE The 1998 award was given jointly to John Hume and David Trimble – the two Northern Ireland politicians who had worked for peace in this region. At the award ceremony in Oslo, a video of Bono congratulating the two men was shown, whilst The Edge and Paul McGuinness were in the audience.

See also: John Hume / David Trimble

"NO MAN'S LAND" A song that the young U2 recorded as a demo which never made it onto record.

"NORTH AND SOUTH OF THE RIVER" (*CELTIC HEARTBEAT VOLUME 2* ALBUM TRACK) The original recording of this song by Christy Moore, Bono and The Edge was included on the compilation album called, *Celtic Heartbeat Volume 2*.

"NORTH AND SOUTH OF THE RIVER" ("STARING AT THE SUN" SINGLE) (4.37) The song about Dublin that Bono and The Edge had written with Irish folk singer, Christy Moore. It had originally started out as a possible track for the *Achtung Baby* album but was not recorded properly until 1995. It was later released as one of the tracks on the two "Staring At The Sun" singles in 1997. U2 performed the song at a special edition of the *Late Late Show* on 20th November 1998, in aid of the Omagh bomb victims.

NORTH HILL AUDITORIUM, MEMPHIS, TENNESSEE, USA U2 played to over 3,000 fans here on 12th March 1982. After the show the band went off to a local club, Miller's Cave, where they celebrated Adam's 22nd birthday by joining the resident group, The Miller's Band, on stage.

"NO TOMORROW LIKE TODAY" A song that U2 recorded with Bob Geldof in 1986 for possible release on his next album. In the end it was shelved and remains in the vaults.

NOVI SAD PARK, MODENA, ITALY The venue where Bono, The Edge and Brian Eno joined Luciano Pavarotti on stage at his annual charity benefit concert. The concert took place on 12th September 1995 in the presence of Princess Diana and was in aid of the War Child charity with the specific aim of raising enough funds to build a music therapy centre in Mostar, Bosnia. The four musicians performed "One", "Miss Sarajevo" and "Nessun Dorma" before a crowd of 15,000. Other artists on the bill included Simon Le Bon, Dolores of the Cranberries, the Chieftans and Zucchero.

See also: Diana, Princess of Wales / Pavarotti / *Together For The Children of Bosnia* / War Child

NRJ AWARDS At the ceremony in Cannes, France on 22nd January 2000 Bono won the award for "Man of the Year" for his role in the work of the Jubilee 2000 campaign.

NUDE The all day cafe owned and run by Norman Hewson in Suffolk Street Dublin. It is on the site of the former Mr. Pussy's Cafe De Luxe.

"NUMB" (*ZOOROPA* ALBUM TRACK) (4.18) The third track on the first side of the *Zooropa* album. It was written by The Edge and sung by him as a rap with a lot of industrial sounding noise in the background. Apparently it was a track left over from the *Achtung Baby* recording sessions with the original title of "Down All The Days". It was first performed live on the *Zooropa* tour at the Stadio Flaminio in Rome, Italy on 7th July 1993.

"NUMB" (THE VIDEO SINGLE) (Polygram/Island Video - 088 162 3) The track "Numb" was released as a "video single" in the UK in August 1993. It did not enter the UK singles' charts presumably because it was not released in CD, vinyl or cassette format, though it still received a lot of plays on MTV. The video contained three video tracks: "Numb", "Numb" (Video Remix) and "Love is Blindness".

"NUMB" (PROMOTIONAL VIDEO) (4.18) The first version of "Numb" which appeared on the "Numb Video Single" was directed by Kevin Godley and produced by Iain Brown. It was filmed in Berlin in June 1993, the day before U2 played at the Olympia Stadium. It featured The Edge sitting in a chair singing the song, whilst various people came up behind him, whispering in his ear, shouting at him, kissing him and tying him up. In addition to the other three members of U2, manager Paul McGuinness also made a rare video appearance. It was banned in Japan because the section showing some feet caressing was considered to be pornographic.

See also: Kevin Godley

"NUMB" (VIDEO REMIX) (NUMB VIDEO SINGLE) (4.52) This remixed video of Numb was created by the Emergency Broadcast Network (Josh Pearson and Gardner Post). It featured several old newsreels of factory workers and natives dancing, as well as harsher pictures such as an animal having its head cut off and a gun being held to a child's head. This video was used as background film during the performance of the song on the *Zooropa* dates.

See also: Emergency Broadcast Network

"NUMB" (GIMMIE SOME MORE DIGNITY MIX) (*MELON* CD TRACK) (8.47) This remix version of "Numb" was the third track on the free *Melon* CD, released in December 1994. The remix was by Rollo and Rob D and was previously unavailable. It starts off with a sample of Jimi Hendrix playing "The Star Spangled Banner".

"NUMB" (PERFECTO MIX) This remix by Paul Oakenfold was only released on a US Promotional CD (PRCD 6795-2) making it one of the rarest U2 remix tracks.

"NUMB" (THE SOUL ASSASINS MIX) (*MELON* CD) (3.57) The sixth track on the *Melon* CD. It was remixed by the Soul Assassins.

NURBURGRING See: Rock Am Ring Festival

OAKENFOLD, PAUL Paul Oakenfold is perhaps the most influential British DJ ever. Amongst his achievements have been introducing the Ibiza sound to Britain which started the acid-house movement in the 1988 "Summer of Love". He was also influential in introducing American hip-hop to the British dance scene. He has been named DJ of the year on three different occasions and he was the first ever DJ to feature on the main stage at the Glastonbury Festival.

Oakenfold was invited to be the DJ on the European leg of the 1993 *Zooropa* tour following his successful remixes of several U2 songs including "Even Better Than The Real Thing" and "Mysterious Ways". His own album, *Perfecto*, was released in the autumn of 1994 and featured remixes of U2 tracks as well as other artists such as Simply Red and New Order. He also wrote the music for the *Big Brother* TV show.

OAKLAND COLISEUM, OAKLAND, CALIFORNIA, USA
U2 played a sell out concert here on 18th April 1992 during the *Zoo TV* tour of America. The whole show was recorded for possible use at the Freddie Mercury Tribute concert at London's Wembley Stadium on 20th April as U2's contribution to that event. Only "Until The End of the World" was transmitted on the day, though throughout the show Bono kept mentioning Freddie Mercury. For instance he referred to him as being "a very cool guy". This show was also memorable for being the first one where the Mirrorball Man rang the Whitehouse to speak to President George Bush. Although he wasn't there, Bono left the same message he would leave each time he rang: "Tell the President to watch more TV!"

See also: Queen

OAKLAND STADIUM, OAKLAND, CALIFORNIA, USA
U2 returned to Oakland in the autumn of 1992 with the *Outside Broadcast* version of the *Zoo TV* tour to play a sold out show at the 60,000 capacity Oakland Stadium on 7th November. Bono dedicated "I Still Haven't Found What I'm Looking For" to the promoter Bill Graham who had just died, as he had promoted U2 in this area on several occasions. The band played two more concerts here on 18th and 19th June 1997 during the first North American leg of the *Pop Mart* tour.

The support band for these two shows was the British Indie band Oasis, who by then had become one of the biggest acts in Britain and Europe but were relatively unknown in the USA. Here they received only a luke-warm reception. Whilst the first night show had been a sell out with 42,500 fans present, less than 25,000 fans attended the second night. For the karaoke number, The Edge sang "If You're Going To San Francisco" in view of the location. In a prearranged stunt many female fans near the B-stage had been given flowers to wear in their hair for this song.

See also: Oasis /Bill Graham (Promoter)

OASIS The British group led by Noel and Liam Gallagher. With their albums, *Definitely, Maybe* (1994) and *(What's The Story), Morning Glory?* (1995), they had quickly risen to the top of rock's premier league. Bono attended their concert at the Point Depot in Dublin on 22nd March 1996 and was pictured afterwards in an open mouth kiss with the tabloids favourite bad lad, Liam Gallagher, in a photograph which was published all over the world. This was actually a bet from Liam who had a guitar pick in his mouth to see if Bono could get it out! A few months later in August 1996, Bono and a bus load of friends attended their concert in Cork. Then in June 1997, Oasis were given the support slots to U2 at the Oakland Stadium in California where they were watched by the members of the band. Whilst Oasis were one of the biggest acts in Britain and Europe, they received only a lukewarm reception. After the show on the second night, "the world's greatest band and the world's next greatest band" (according to Noel Gallagher) went off together to party the night away at the Tosca Cafe.

"THE OCEAN" (*BOY* ALBUM TRACK) (1.35) The second track on side two of the *Boy* album, it is the shortest, running at less than two minutes in length. It is a quiet track where Bono reads from Oscar Wilde over a sparse musical accompaniment. One verse is printed on the *Boy* album sleeve though this is not sung by Bono. The song was first performed live in September 1980 during the *Boy* tour of England. It usually started their set immediately before "11 O'clock Tick Tock" and would be the set opener until it was moved to set closer in the summer of 1981.

"THE OCEAN" (LIVE) ("FIRE" SINGLE B-SIDE) This live version of "The Ocean" was recorded at the Paradise Theatre, Boston, USA, on 6th March 1981. It appears on the second 7 inch single in the limited edition double-pack of the "Fire" single (UWIP 6679). (This double pack was released on CD in 1992.)

OCEAN WAY STUDIOS, LOS ANGELES, CALIFORNIA, USA The song "God Part II" from *Rattle & Hum* was recorded here.

O'CONNOR, FLANNERY The writer whose books about the American Deep South were said to have influenced Bono's lyrics at the time of *The Joshua Tree.*

O'CONNOR, SINEAD Born 8th December 1966 in Glenageary, Ireland, after a troubled childhood Sinead was spotted singing at a wedding by Paul Byrne of In Tua Nua. She co-wrote In Tua Nua's first single for Island Records, "Take My Hand", released in July 1984. As a result of these connections, in 1986 she was asked by The Edge to contribute vocals to the film soundtrack of *The Captive* for which he wrote much of the music. She then moved to London (against the advice of Bono) to work and record for Ensign Records with Fachtna O'Kelly as her manager. Her breakthrough single was "Mandinka" which reached number 17 in the UK charts in 1988. Her biggest selling record was the Prince written follow up, "Nothing Compares 2 U" which hit the number 1 spot in January 1990. On more than one occasion she has spoken out against U2, saying they were "full of bullshit" and "manipulative". By the *Zoo TV* tour of 1992 the rift had healed and Sinead came to U2's concert at Earl's Court. The following year she was then invited to sing on the *In The Name of The Father* soundtrack album song "You Made Me The Thief Of Your Heart" written by Bono, Gavin Friday and Maurice Seezer.

See also: Fachtna O' Kelly

OCTOBER (ALBUM) (ILPS 9680): U2's second album, originally titled *Scarlet,* was released in October 1981 after being recorded at Dublin's Windmill Lane studios during July and August of that year. Steve Lillywhite was once again the producer.

It has often been dubbed "U2's Christian Album" as it is the album that most overtly speaks about their Christian beliefs. Interestingly enough, this is the only U2 album not to feature any of the lyrics on its sleeve.

In the previous year, the band had toured Britain, Europe and America extensively, as well as (with the exception of Adam) getting seriously involved with a Dublin charismatic Christian Group called 'Shalom'. This led to Bono, Larry and The Edge constantly questioning themselves about whether they could be Christians and still play in a rock 'n' roll band. Also, in March 1981 whilst on tour in the USA, Bono had a briefcase stolen containing money and his notebook with lyrics to new songs. It was against this uncertain and highly pressurised background that *October* was recorded. As Bono said at the time: "I remember writing lyrics on the microphone, and at £50 per hour, that's quite a pressure!"

The album, despite its haphazard recording process and many U2 fans citing it as their least favourite U2 album, still contained some musical gems, such as the opening track "Gloria", "Tomorrow" (a lament for Bono's late mother) and the title track, "October", which featured The Edge playing piano on a U2 track for the first time. The track "Fire", which became U2's first UK top 40 hit, had been recorded the previous April in the Bahamas, with Steve Lillywhite again producing. *October* actually reached number 11 in the UK album charts, selling in excess of 250,000 copies, thus gaining U2 their first ever silver disc. The UK music press were on the whole fairly favourable in their reviews. For instance, Ian Cranna in *Smash Hits* when comparing *October* to *Boy,* wrote that while the first U2 album was magic, *October* "is sorcery". The album failed to make the US album top 100. Despite a long US promotional tour, it stalled at number 104.

Track list: Gloria, I Fall Down, I Threw A Brick Through A Window, Rejoice, Fire, Tomorrow, October, With A Shout, Stranger in a Strange Land, Scarlet, Is That All?

"OCTOBER" (*OCTOBER* ALBUM TRACK) (2.20) The second track on side two of the *October* album is a quiet yet emotional track, which features The Edge playing piano (he had recently learnt the rudiments of this instrument and was keen to show this on the album). The lyrics refer to the way that the leaves fall off the trees in October, indicating that everything will one day die, yet God's love will not die, but go on forever. It was first performed live at Slane Castle on 16th August 1981, when U2 were supporting the last major Irish gig by Thin Lizzy.

"OCTOBER" (*THE BEST OF 1980-1990* ALBUM TRACK) Although it is not printed on the track list on the back cover, *The Best Of 1980-1990,* the final track, "All I Want Is You" is followed by the track "October" as a ghost track.

"OCTOBER" (*THEY CALL IT AN ACCIDENT* SOUNDTRACK ALBUM TRACK) (1.25) There is an instrumental version of "October" on the soundtrack album to the film *They Call It An Accident.*

"OCTOBER" (*THEY CALL IT AN ACCIDENT* SOUNDTRACK ALBUM TRACK) (2.30) A remix version of "October" by Frenchman Will Bordarau is included on this soundtrack album - the first time a U2 song appeared on a soundtrack.

OCTOBER TOUR (AUTUMN 1981 to SPRING 1982) The tour to promote the *October* album was split up into three sections. The first section took place in Britain and Europe in the autumn of 1981. It started at the University of East Anglia, Norwich, England on 1st October playing at twenty-eight venues up to the final date on 4th November at the Metropol in Berlin, Germany. The second section took place in the USA in November and December 1981. It started at J.B. Scott's in Albany, New York State on 13th November and continued through to 13th December at the Malibu Beach Night Club in Lido Beach, New York, playing twenty-one dates in all.

After a Christmas break the third section took off in the USA in the winter/spring of 1982 and started on 11th February 1982 on a riverboat on the Mississippi – the SS President Riverboat based at New Orleans, Louisiana. After thirty-two more gigs (including fourteen dates supporting the J. Geils Band), the tour came to an end at the Civic Center in San Francisco, California on 30th March 1982.

October tour set list taken from: A Celebration, A Day Without Me, An Cat Dubh, Another Time Another Place, Cry-The Electric Co., 11 O'clock Tick Tock, Fire, Gloria, I Fall Down, Into The Heart, I Threw A Brick Through A Window, I Will Follow, October, Out Of Control, Rejoice, Southern Man, Stories For Boys, The Ocean, Tomorrow, Twilight, With A Shout.

O'HANLON, NED Ned is the brains behind Dreamchaser Productions, responsible for several documentaries on U2 including *Outside It's America*, *LoveTown* and *The Trabant Land*. Ned has also filmed concerts by The Rolling Stones, Britney Spears and The Cranberries amongst others. He also filmed U2 performing "Beautiful Day" on the roof of the Clarence Hotel for *Top Of The Pops* in September 2000.

O'HERLIHY, JOE Born in St. Anne's Park, Montenotte, Ireland, Joe has been U2's chief sound engineer for almost all of the band's career. He started out as a roadie for Cork band Sleepy Hollow. They were taken to England as support act for Rory Gallagher in 1973 where Joe was taken on by Gallagher after one of his own roadies burst an appendix. From 1974 to 1978 Joe toured all around the world with Rory Gallagher, starting off as "back-line man", setting the instruments up on stage, moving on to monitor engineer and finally sound engineer.

In September 1978, he set up a business in Cork, "Stage Sound Systems", based on two high quality sound systems he'd built up over the years on the road. These would then be hired out to the various bands that visited Cork. When U2 played The Arcadia in Cork in October 1978, they were so impressed by the quality of the sound that Paul McGuinness was keen to hire Joe to do the sound for U2's gigs. Unfortunately U2 couldn't afford his rates. However, when U2 faced a sudden crisis during some important gigs in London, Joe flew over at short notice to take over. He then stayed with the band for a short Irish tour in early 1980, but couldn't be persuaded to come back for the UK summer tour.

For U2's first visit to the USA in December 1980, Joe and his sound system were again hired and from then on he became U2's permanent sound engineer touring all around the world with them right up until the *Elevation* tour. Apart from his work with U2, he has also worked with REM and in 1994 was in charge of the sound for the 25th Anniversary Woodstock concert.

OHIO STADIUM, COLUMBUS, OHIO, USA U2 played to over 43,000 fans here on 24th May 1997 during the first leg of the *Pop Mart* tour in America. At the show, someone was wearing a T-shirt bearing the words "Kill Bono!" Bono saw it and managed to get it from the person so that he could wear it himself. In "Bullet The Blue Sky" he referred to it in the rap: "so this guy comes up to me wearing a 'Kill Bono' T-shirt..."

"OH NO" An early U2 song which was recorded as a demo but did not get any further.

O'KELLY, FACHTNA (O'CEALLAIGH) Fachtna was originally a journalist with the Dublin newspaper *The Evening Press* before moving on to management with Clannad and then The Boomtown Rats. Under his management The Boomtown Rats had success in both Britain and the continent including two number 1 singles. After the demise of the Boomtown Rats, Fachtna was asked to take over the running of U2's new label Mother Records, but after disagreements over how the label was being run, he quit. He then took over the management of Sinead O'Connor and had another number 1 success with her "Nothing Compares 2U" single. The two of them parted company and he returned to Ireland maintaining a relatively low profile.

See also: The Boomtown Rats / Clannad / Mother Records / Sinead O'Connor

OLD GREY WHISTLE TEST, THE (TV PROGRAMME) This BBC2 music TV show began broadcasting in 1971 and was a regular feature on the BBC for almost twenty years. U2 first appeared on this show on 28th February 1981 performing "The Ocean", "11 O'clock Tick Tock" and "I Will Follow". Their next appearance was in December 1984 when they performed songs from *The Unforgettable Fire* album. They appeared next on 11th March 1987 performing before a small audience Curtis Mayfield's "People Get Ready", Neil Young's "Southern Man", "Trip Through Your Wires", "Exit", "In God's Country" and "Pride". The Barry Devlin directed mini-documentary of the beginning of the *Joshua Tree* tour of America, *Outside It's America*, was premiered on a New Year's Day *Old Grey Whistle Test* special on 1st January 1988.

See also: *Outside It's America*

OLYMPIA THEATRE, DUBLIN, IRELAND Bono, Larry and The Edge, joined Johnny Cash and Kris Kristofferson onstage during their concert here on 11th February 1993. This was the start of the collaboration between U2 and Johnny Cash that led to the recording of "The Wanderer".

Olympia Theatre, Dublin. *Photo: Paul Daly*

OLYMPIA STADIUM, BERLIN, GERMANY U2 played to a crowd of 40,000 fans at this 76,000 capacity stadium, which was used for the 1936 Olympic Games, on 15th June 1993 during the *Zooropa* tour of Europe. This was U2's first concert in Berlin since the reunification of Germany, the band having previously played here in 1981. The opening film sequence to the show included parts of the Nazi propaganda film *Triumph of the Will*, which was actually shot in this stadium in 1936. Apparently U2 took a risk by showing the burning swastikas on the TV screens during "Bullet The Blue Sky" as the swastika symbol was banned in Germany, but they got away with it.
See also: Berlin

OLYMPIC STADIUM, HELSINKI, FINLAND U2 played their first concert in Finland since 1982 when they played a show here on 9th August 1997 during the *Pop Mart* tour of Europe. The concert was a sell out with over 50,000 fans attending. At this show, The Edge's girlfriend, Morleigh Steinberg, danced on stage as the belly dancer once more in celebration of his 36th birthday the previous day.
See also: Morleigh Steinberg

OLYMPIC STADIUM, MONTREAL, CANADA U2 have performed at this venue on three separate occasions. Their first visit on 1st October 1987 was during the *Joshua Tree* tour of North America. The 27th August 1992 show during the *Outside Broadcast* leg of the *Zoo TV* tour was memorable for the appearance of U2 producer Daniel Lanois, who joined the group on the B-stage to sing "I Still Haven't Found What I'm Looking For". Footage of this performance was included in the video *Joshua Tree*. The band then played here during the *Pop Mart* tour of North America on 2nd November 1997 before a crowd of around 60,000 fans. During "With Or Without You" Bono brought a girl up on the stage and rather than dance with her, he sat her on his lap and sang to her.
See also: Daniel Lanois

THE OMNI, ATLANTA, GEORGIA, USA U2 have played this 12,000 capacity venue on three separate occasions. Their first visit took place on 29th April 1985 during the *Unforgettable Fire* tour. The show was watched by Bono's Father, Bobby Henson, who had been specially flown over. Bono embarrassed him by introducing him to the audience. U2's next visit here was during the 1986 *Conspiracy of Hope* tour on 11th November 1986. This was the first show that the reunited Police played at on this tour. U2 joined them onstage to sing "Sun City" and "I Shall Be Released". U2's final show here was on 5th March 1992 during the *Zoo TV* spring tour of America.
See also: Bobby Hewson

"ONE" (*ACHTUNG BABY* ALBUM TRACK) (4.36) The third track on the first side of the *Achtung Baby* album, is a slow, haunting song that has become a favourite amongst U2 fans. Bono's lyrics describe the breakdown of a relationship between two people who should really be united and "one". Some commentators have seen this to be between a young man dying of AIDS and his father who cannot accept the way of life that brought about this life-threatening situation. The track was produced by Brian Eno and Daniel Lanois. It was first performed live on the opening night of the *Zoo TV* tour at the Civic Center, Lakeland, Florida on 29th February 1992, though it had been performed at a rehearsal two days earlier for BBC TV's *Top Of The Pops*.

"ONE" (SINGLE) (4.26) The third track from the *Achtung Baby* album to be released as a single – on 24th February 1992. It was released in three formats: 7 inch, 12 inch and CD. All three formats contained the track "Lady With the Spinning Head" (UVI), whilst the 12 inch and CD versions contained the extra tracks of "Satellite of Love" and "Night & Day" (Steel String Remix). Three days after the single's release, U2 played the song live on BBC TV's *Top*

Of The Pops programme via satellite from the Civic Center in Florida, two days before the start of the *Zoo TV* tour of the USA.

The "One" single reached number 7 in the UK singles chart and number 10 in the US singles chart. The cover photo depicting buffalo hurtling to their deaths over a cliff face was taken by an American artist called David Wojnarowicz who was infected with the AIDS virus and who saw in the photograph a link between AIDS sufferers and the buffalo – both being pushed over the edge "by forces we cannot control or even understand". The royalties from the single were donated to AIDS Research.

See also: David Wojnarowicz

"ONE" (AUTOMATIC BABY VERSION) The version of "One" performed by "Automatic Baby" (Adam Clayton with Larry Mullen of U2 and Michael Stipe with Mike Mills of REM) was included on the *Childline* charity album, released in 1997. It was recorded at the MTV inaugural ball for the new US President, Bill Clinton, on 20th January 1993.

See also: Automatic Baby

"ONE" (LIVE) ("MISS SARAJEVO" SINGLE & *TOGETHER FOR THE CHILDREN OF BOSNIA* ALBUM TRACK) (4.55) This live version of "One" was recorded at Luciano Pavarotti's annual charity concert at Modena in Italy on 12th September 1995 and was included on the album of the concert. It was performed by three of the 'Passengers', namely Brian Eno, The Edge and Bono, and featured an orchestra in the background. It was also on the single of "Miss Sarajevo".

"ONE" (LIVE) (*HASTA LA VISTA BABY! U2 LIVE FROM MEXICO CITY* ALBUM TRACK) (6.07) This live audio version of "One" was recorded at Foro Sol Autodromo, Mexico City, Mexico on 3rd December 1997 and was the final track on the *Propaganda* free CD.

"ONE" (LIVE) (*TIBETAN FREEDOM CONCERT* ALBUM) (EMI 859 9110) The live version of "One" performed by U2 at the Tibetan Freedom Concert in New York is on this 3-CD set of the concert. There is also a short interview with Bono on the CD-Rom.

"ONE" (LIVE) (*ZOO TV LIVE FROM SYDNEY* VIDEO) The first video version of U2 performing "One" live was filmed at the Cricket Ground, Sydney, Australia, on 27th November 1993 for the *Zoo TV Live From Sydney* video.

"ONE" (LIVE) (*PAVAROTTI & FRIENDS TOGETHER FOR THE CHILDREN OF BOSNIA* VIDEO) The film version of Pavarotti, Brian Eno, The Edge and Bono performing "One" at the Modena concert in Italy was included on the video of the show – *Pavarotti and Friends Together For The Children of Bosnia.*

"ONE" (LIVE) (*POP MART LIVE FROM MEXICO CITY* VIDEO) This film of "One" comes from the video *Pop Mart Live From Mexico City* and was recorded live at Foro Sol Autodromo, Mexico City, Mexico on 3rd December 1997. It is the penultimate track on the video as, for the *Pop Mart* tour, "One" was now an encore number.

"ONE" (PROMOTIONAL VIDEO) (VERSION ONE) The first promotional video of "One" was directed by Anton Corbijn, produced by Richard Bell, and was filmed in Berlin in February 1992. It was filmed in black and white and featured the four members of U2 dressed in drag, driving Trabants around the streets of Berlin. It also featured Bono's father, Bobby Hewson, in one of the scenes. Later, it was felt that the video subject matter did not really fit with the song's lyrics, so a second promo video of "One" was made. See below.

"ONE" (PROMOTIONAL VIDEO) (VERSION TWO) This version, known as the 'Buffalo' version was the main promotional video used to promote the "One" single. As well as featuring the buffalo running backwards (and forwards over the cliff edge), there is also a flower and the words "one" in several different languages. The video was directed by Mark Pellington and made in New York in February 1992.

"ONE" (PROMOTIONAL VIDEO) (VERSION THREE) This third video version of "One" was directed by Phil Joanou who had directed the film *Rattle & Hum*. It was filmed in New York in March 1992 and featured Bono singing the song in a New York club.

"ONE" (PROMOTIONAL VIDEO) (VERSION FOUR) It is rumoured that there is a fourth promo video of "One". This is probably an alternative version of version 2 with added shots of the heads of the band.

100 CLUB, LONDON, ENGLAND The venue for U2's third gig in Britain, on 3rd December 1979.

"ONE FOOT IN HEAVEN" (*CAPTIVE* SOUNDTRACK ALBUM TRACK) The third track on the soundtrack album of the film *Captive*, for which The Edge wrote the music.

"ONE MINUTE WARNING" (*ORIGINAL SOUNDTRACKS 1* ALBUM TRACK) (4.39) The ninth track on the *Original Soundtracks 1* album by Passengers comes from the Japanese film *Ghost in the Shell* by Mamoru Oshii.

"ONE TREE HILL" (*THE JOSHUA TREE* ALBUM TRACK) (5.24) The fourth track on the second side of *The Joshua Tree* album is named after the smallest of the five volcanic mounds that surround the city of Auckland in New Zealand, the place where U2 first met Greg Caroll, who was to become Bono's personal assistant. Caroll was killed in Dublin in 1986 after his motorbike collided with a car. After Bono and Larry had travelled to his funeral in Wahganui, New Zealand, Bono wrote this song. The song was first performed live at the Nassau Veterans' Memorial Coliseum in Uniondale, USA on 10th September 1987, the first date of the third leg of the *Joshua Tree* tour. Whenever U2 have played in New Zealand, they have always included this song.

See also: Greg Caroll / One Tree Hill Auckland

"ONE TREE HILL" (SINGLE) (K 338) This single version of "One Tree Hill" was a special New Zealand only release in March 1988. The B-side contained the tracks "Running To Stand Still" and "Bullet The Blue Sky".

"ONE TREE HILL" (VIDEO) The video for "One Tree Hill" was included as a bonus track on the video collection *The Best of 1980-1990*. It consisted of footage shot at the Sun Devil Stadium at Tempe, Arizona in December 1987 by Phil Joanou for *Rattle & Hum*, which was not included in the original cut.

ONE TREE HILL, AUCKLAND, NEW ZEALAND The site of One Tree Hill is the smallest of six volcanic mounds that surround the town of Auckland. It was traditionally a Maori burial ground. Sadly the tree standing at the top of the hill had to be removed when it was deemed to be unsafe, after it had been vandalised by someone with a chainsaw.

"ON GRAFTON STREET" Adam provided bass and Larry drums to this track about Dublin's famous main thoroughfare from the album *Flyer* by Nanci Griffith, released in 1994.

See also: Nanci Griffith

OPERA HOUSE, CORK, IRELAND U2's second appearance on Irish TV was recorded at this venue in Cork on 5th October 1979. The set included several songs that would never make it onto vinyl, including "Cartoon World", "The Speed of Life" and "Inside Out". According to The Edge, the band had played two Ramones numbers in the audition for this programme and when asked by the producer if they were their own songs, they said "yes"!

ORBISON, ROY The American singer remembered for his 1962 hit "Pretty Woman". Bono and The Edge wrote "She's A Mystery To Me" and he included it on his 1989 comeback album, *Mystery Girl*.

O'REAGAN, MAEVE One of the school friends of Bono and The Edge at Mount Temple Comprehensive in Dublin in the mid-seventies. She became very

One Tree Hill *Photo: Mike Verney*

close to Bono during 1974 and after the death of his mother, he would confide in her. Together they would attend the Christian Union meetings at the school. After leaving Mount Temple, Maeve O'Reagan went into full time Christian Service.

See also: Mount Temple School

O'REILLY, JOHN BOYLE The song, "Van Dieman's Land" from *Rattle & Hum* was dedicated to this Irishman, who had been deported to Australia "because of his poetry". He wasn born in Drogheda, Ireland in 1844 and had worked in printing before joining the Tenth Hussars of the British Army. At this time he secretly joined the outlawed Fenian movement, which was seeking to free Ireland of British rule, but he was betrayed and subsequently court-martialled. He should have received a life-sentence for his crime but because he was so young was deported to Australia to serve twenty years "penal servitude". In 1869 he managed to escape from Australia and settled in Boston, Massachusetts, USA. There he became editor of the *The Pilot*, a local newspaper, as well as writing several novels and volumes of poetry. He married Mary Murphy in 1872 and they had four daughters. He died in the USA in 1890.

See also: Van Diemen's Land

ORIGINAL SOUNDTRACKS 1 (ALBUM) (CID 8043 524 166-2) The name given to the album by the Passengers (Brian Eno and the four members of U2), released in November 1995. It featured contributions from: Luciano Pavarotti, Howie B, Holi, Craig Armstrong, Paul Barrett, David Herbert, Des Broadberry and Holger Zschenderlin. The album was initially recorded over a period of two weeks at the end of November 1994, at Westside Studios in London, when U2 and Brian Eno got together a year after the end of the *Zoo TV* tour. The idea was to put down some experimental tracks and take it from there, a concept that had come to fruition after an experiment during the *Zooropa* sessions at Brian Eno's suggestion.

The basic tracks were then worked on and mixed at Hanover Quay Studios in Dublin during the spring and summer of 1995. Each of the fourteen tracks was then "auctioned off to the highest bidder from the film world" to be used on "film soundtracks". The sleeve notes were written by "Ben O'Rian" (an anagram for Brian Eno) and "C.S.J.Bofop" (also Brian Eno using each letter after the letters of his name). For astute U2 fans, all sorts of anagrams and twisted meanings can be found in the descriptions of the films, indicating that they weren't really used for films in the first place, the exception being "Miss Sarajevo".

The album was finally released in November 1995 with the proviso that it was not the next U2 album but rather the four members of U2 working with their long-time producer in the studio. The album was critically acclaimed, though most critics did see it as a U2 album. In *Hot Press*, Bill Graham called the album "their most relaxed and their most playful", whilst *Q* referred to it as "U2's third album in five years" and "a fine, atmospheric work". The fans however did not buy it in large quantities. After entering the UK album charts at number 8, it then dropped into the twenties by the third week before dropping out of the charts altogether by Christmas 1995. In the US it could only manage a peak of number 76.

Track Listing: 1) United Colours, 2) Slug, 3) Your Blue Room, 4) Always Forever Now, 5) A Different Kind of Blue, 6) Beach Sequence, 7) Miss Sarajevo, 8) Ito Okashi, 9) One Minute Warning, 10) Corpse (These Chains Are Much Too Long), 11) Elvis Ate America, 12) Plot 180, 13) Theme From The Swan, 14) Theme From Let's Go Native.

ORPHEUM THEATRE, BOSTON, MASSACHUSETTS, USA U2 have played three times at this 2,800 capacity theatre in Boston. Their first visit was on 14th November 1981 during the *October* tour of America. The show was broadcast live on WBCN Radio and became one of the first U2 concerts in America to be bootlegged. The band then returned for two more sell out shows here on 5th and 6th May 1983, the second

of which was recorded for the local radio station. "11 O'clock Tick Tock" was included on the *Under A Blood Red Sky* mini LP.

OSAKA DOME, OSAKA, JAPAN U2 were one of the first bands to play at this newly built venue on 12th March 1998 during the final leg of the *Pop Mart* tour of the Far East. The Bee Gees "Staying Alive" was the karaoke number.

OSBORNE, STEVE One of the DJs who remixed "Even Better Than The Real Thing". He was also assistant producer of *Pop*.

O'SULLIVAN, AISLINN The Edge's girlfriend from the late seventies, whom he married in 1983. They had first met at a U2 gig, but didn't go out together for several weeks. She had joined and then left the Shalom Group with The Edge. They married on 14th July 1983, and had three children, Hollie, Arran and Blue Angel. The couple were later to divorce – a lot of this marital breakdown is said to manifest itself in the lyrics of *Achtung Baby*.

O'SULLIVAN, SAM He joined U2 as part of the road crew for the *Joshua Tree* tour and by the 1990s was Larry's drum technician, a post he has held ever since.

"OUT OF CONTROL" (*BOY* ALBUM TRACK) (4.13) The fifth track on the first side of the *Boy* album. It had already been released as a single in Ireland, but this version is different. It was produced by Steve Lillywhite and is more polished then the single version. The song was written by Bono on his eighteenth birthday and speaks of the mixed emotions of changing from a boy into a man. It was first performed live sometime in the summer of 1978, possibly at the Project Arts Centre gig on 25th May where U2 first met Paul McGuinness, but more likely at McGonagles on 31st July.

"OUT OF CONTROL" (SINGLE) (CBS 7951) The A-side of the 'U2-3' single, U2's first single in Ireland, released in both 7 and 12 inch formats, the latter being limited to 1000 hand numbered copies. The listeners of Dave Fanning's RTE 2 radio programme had voted this track as the A-side for the single. The B-side contained the tracks "Stories for Boys" and "Boy-Girl". It was produced by Chas De Whalley at Windmill Lane studios in Dublin as a demo track, but was deemed good enough for general release. The single reached number 1 in the Irish singles charts.

See also: Chas De Whalley / Jackie Hayden / U2-3

"OUT OF CONTROL" (LIVE) ("I WILL FOLLOW" SINGLE B-SIDE) (4.25) Originally recorded live at the Paradise Theater in Boston USA on 6th March 1981 for a radio broadcast by Radio WBCN, some of the songs from this radio show had been used as B-sides for the U2 singles of "Fire" and "Gloria". This particular track was originally put on the B-side of the American single, "I Will Follow". It was then resurrected (along with "Stories For Boys") for "The Sweetest Thing" single, released in 1998.

"OUT OF THE LIVING WORLD" An early U2 song, recorded as a demo but which never got any further.

OUTSIDE BROADCAST (*ZOO TV* TOUR) The name given to the third leg of the *Zoo TV* tour which took place in America from August to November 1992. The venues were mainly stadiums across America and Canada, whereas the first leg of the *Zoo TV* tour had consisted of indoor arenas. This time around, U2 had gone "mega" to quote Bono, and the whole stage set had been redesigned by Willie Williams along with Jonathan Park and Mark Fisher, so that it would be suitable for a stadium set up.

There were four giant TV screens so those at the back could see, as well as countless TV screens dotted around the stage, all receiving satellite signals from several radio masts on the stage. Three Trabants were hung just above the stage, while a further nine were situated in and around the stadium. The shows began with footage of the US President saying the words of

the Queen song "We will, we will, rock you!" while Bono was lifted up onto the back of the stage by a hydraulic lift to start singing "Zoo Station".

Another addition was the "Video Confessional" booth where members of the audience could make a confession lasting no longer than 20 seconds, and broadcast just before the encore if it was considered controversial or amusing. The first date of the tour was at the Giant's Stadium in New Jersey on 12th August 1992, though a "dress rehearsal" show took place at the Hershey Stadium in Pennsylvania on 7th August. The tour then continued at mainly sold out stadiums throughout America up to its final show at Anaheim in California on 14th November.

Almost 2 million fans saw this leg of the *Zoo TV* tour with gate receipts of over $50,000,000. The band then played four shows in Mexico City a week later in an indoor arena, their first shows in Mexico. (For a complete list of dates see appendix.)

See also: Mark Fisher / Jonathan Park / Willie Williams / Zoo TV tour.

OUTSIDE IT'S AMERICA (DOCUMENTARY FILM) A documentary film made about the early part of the *Joshua Tree* tour of America. It was shown on an *Old Grey Whistle Test* special, just after midnight on New Year's Day morning in 1988. The producer was Barry Devlin who had already directed several U2 promo videos. Apart from showing various snippets of concerts, it also showed U2 buying boots in a Texas shoe shop, singing and playing pool in a bar and driving along the freeway. The film also contained promotional videos of the tracks "Where The Streets Have No Name", "I Still Haven't Found What I'm Looking For", "In God's Country" and "Spanish Eyes", as well as part of "Bullet The Blue Sky" in concert.

See also: Barry Devlin

OWENS, CATHERINE The Irish artist who painted the designs on the Trabant cars for the *Zoo TV* shows. Since then she has gone on to work with U2 on the *Pop Mart* shows where she was "curator of screen imagery". This involved finding the right images to show on the screen during certain songs, such as the pictures by Roy Lichtenstein during "Bullet The Blue Sky". In August 1998, her *Pop Mart* film was shown at the Edinburgh Festival in Scotland. For the *Elevation* tour she created the gun control film shown during "Bullet The Blue Sky".

See also: Roy Lichtenstein

PAARD VAN TROJE, THE HAGUE, HOLLAND 500 Dutch U2 fans watched the band play here on 12th February 1981. The show was recorded for transmission on Dutch TV and radio.

"PAINT IT BLACK" ("WHO'S GONNA RIDE YOUR WILD HORSES" SINGLE) (3.22) U2 put this cover version of the Rolling Stones 1966 number 1 hit on the B-side of their "Who's Gonna Ride Your Wild Horses" single, which was released in November 1992. It was produced by U2 and Paul Barrett, who also played keyboards on the track.

See also: The Rolling Stones

PAIRC UI CHAOMH, CORK, IRELAND U2 have played twice at this Irish Stadium. The band first played here on 8th August 1987, making it the final show of the *Joshua Tree* tour of Europe. It also happened to be The Edge's 26th birthday, so during "Party Girl", a large birthday cake was wheeled onto the stage. Inside was The Edge's wife, Aisling, who jumped out with a bottle of champagne, which she sprayed over everyone on the stage. The gig is also memorable for the fact that they played "Out of Control" here, a song they hadn't played live at all on the tour. Finally at the end of "40" when the other three members of U2 had left the stage, Larry was showered with hundreds of table tennis balls by the road crew as an end of tour trick.

U2 played one of the last concerts of the *Zooropa* tour here on 24th August 1993, not without controversy. All through the tour, in an effort to promote safe sex, special U2 *Achtung Baby* condoms had been on sale. The Gaelic Athletics Association, the owners of the Park, did not agree with condoms being sold on their land and so banned their sale. This led to U2 manager, Paul McGuinness giving out hundreds of free condoms to the fans at the concert. During the show, Bono in his Macphisto character criticised Frank Murphy, the secretary of the GAA for banning their sale and tried to ring him up, but he was actually in the stadium watching the show.

PALACE OF AUBURN HILLS, DETROIT, MICHIGAN, USA. This quaintly named 21,000 all seater venue in Detroit was first visited by U2 on 27th March 1992 during the spring *Zoo TV* tour of America. This show is famous as being the one where Bono ordered 10,000 pizzas after seeing an advert for a pizza take

away on the screen whilst zapping channels after "Even Better Than The Real Thing". Whilst most people had forgotten about the phone call, the pizza shop was busy frantically preparing dozens of pizzas during the show. They duly arrived at the Palace just before the encore and were distributed amongst the audience. The shop had managed to make about 100 pepperoni pizzas in total. Bono even gave the delivery boys $50 each. U2 played here again on 30th May 2001 during the *Elevation* tour of North America (first leg). At this show Bono sang a snippet of the Beatles "In My Life" at the start of "Stuck In A Moment You Can't Get Out Of".

PALACIO DE CONGRESOS, MADRID, SPAIN U2 attended the Amigo Awards here on 13th November when they performed "Beautiful Day".

PALACIO DE LOS DEPORTES, MEXICO CITY, MEXICO U2 played four shows here a week after the *Outside Broadcast* leg of the *Zoo TV* tour had finished in North America. The dates were the 21st, 22nd, 24th and 25th November 1992. All the shows were sold out and took place in an indoor arena with a capacity of 21,000. This was the first time that U2 had played in Mexico.

PALAIS DES OMNISPORTS DE BERCY, PARIS, FRANCE U2 have played this 16,000 capacity arena in Paris on four occasions to date. Their first visit here was on 10th February 1985. It was the final date of the *Unforgettable Fire* tour of Europe and was completely sold out. They next played here during the *Lovetown* tour of Europe on 11th and 12th December 1989. These two shows marked the debut of two female backing singers: Claudia and Sophia, who would sing on some of the songs in this and subsequent shows. U2's next visit to Bercy was on the 7th May 1992, the opening date of the 1992 *Zoo TV* tour of Europe. This was the show where Bono told the audience that he had met legendary Doors singer Jim Morrison (buried in the Pere Lachaise cemetery in Paris), who told Bono to pass on the massage to "buy as many U2 albums as you can afford and the world will be a better place". U2 played two more shows here on 17th and 18th July 2001 as part of the *Elevation* tour of Europe.

PALAU SANT JORDI, BARCELONA, SPAIN U2 played two dates here during the 1992 *Zoo TV* tour of Europe on 16th and 18th May 1992. On the first night Bono got drenched by water whilst he was singing on the B-stage. This happened again on the second night on two occasions, but this time he threw some water back into the crowd in revenge. After the show the Elvis Presley Song, "Can't Help Falling In Love" was played over the PA as the crowd left the building. This was then repeated for every other *Zoo TV* show on the tour. For some of the *Outside Broadcast* shows and all the 1993 *Zoo TV* dates Bono would finish the show by singing it himself.

During the European leg of the *Elevation* tour, U2 played one concert here on 8th August 2001. As it was the Edge's 40th birthday, a birthday cake was brought out to him during "Mysterious Ways". He is reported to have flown out to Ibiza to party the night away straight after the show.

See also: Elvis Presley

THE PALLADIUM, NEW YORK CITY, USA U2 have played this well-known 3,400 capacity New York venue twice. Their first show here on 29th May 1981 was a complete sell out, making it the biggest place they had played in America up to that time. During the show someone threw a box of white mice onto the stage, which caused some moments of mayhem before they either died or ran off! The band were joined onstage by Busta Jones, a bass player who played with Talking Heads when U2 supported them in London and Paris. U2 played there again on 11th May 1983 during the *War* tour of America to another full house with some disturbances from people pushing and shoving.

ROBERT PALMER The English singer, who is best remembered for the song and video of "Addicted To Love", provided backing vocals on Bono's version of "Silver & Gold" recorded for the *Sun City* album.

PAN AMERICAN CENTER, LAS CRUCES, NEW MEXICO, USA U2 played this small town not far from the Mexican border on 10th April 1987, with a sell out crowd of 12,500 in attendance. It was a last minute show as U2 were originally going to play in El Paso or Albuquerque but these shows never happened. It is the only time that U2 have played a gig in the state of New Mexico.

PARADISE THEATRE, BOSTON, MASSACHUSETTS, USA This small theatre in Boston was where U2 made their first American breakthrough on 13th December 1980. Although only 150 people came to watch, U2 were called back for two encores despite the fact that they were the support band for headliners Barooga. U2 returned here to play two sell out shows both on 6th March 1981; largely due to the publicity generated by DJ Carter Alan and his WBCN radio station. The first of two shows was recorded by Warner Brothers (America) who produced a promotional record, *Two Sides Live*, which was distributed amongst American disc jockeys in order to get more airplay and publicity for U2.

Several of the songs recorded were also used as B-sides on various U2 records. "I Will Follow" was used on the B-side of the "Gloria" single (released October 1981), whilst "Out of Control" appeared on the B-side of the American single of "I Will Follow" (released April 1981). Finally "Cry-The Electric Co." and "11 O' clock Tick Tock" were given away as free singles with the UK release of the single "Fire/J. Swallow", whilst "The Ocean" and "11 O' clock Tick Tock" appeared on the B-side of the 12 inch version of "Fire" (released in July 1981). Finally, in 1998 when the single "The Sweetest Thing" was released, "Stories For Boys" and "Out Of Control" were included on one of the versions. In 1987, on 21st September, during a break from the *Joshua Tree* tour, U2 held a special press conference here for U2 fanzine editors from North America. Owing to the vastness of the continent, the conference was only attended by around 25 people from 7 different fanzines. The whole event was filmed by Phil Joanou for possible inclusion in the film *Rattle & Hum* but was not used in the final cut.

See also: Two Sides Live

PARADISO, AMSTERDAM, HOLLAND U2 played at this famous Amsterdam rock venue twice in 1981. On their first visit on 11th February they played to a half full venue, but by their second visit on 30th October the venue was full. As the show came to an end around midnight, Bono made an announcement from the stage: "Tonight is very special because the last teenager, our drummer, has just become 20 years old!" as it was Larry's 20th birthday. The show was recorded for transmission by Dutch radio. On 9th January 1987, a U2 fan convention organised by the Dutch U2 fan club was held here. Adam Clayton was the guest of honour and received a gold record for Dutch record sales from Annelies de Haan, the fan club president. Adam then played onstage with the Mother Records band Tuesday Blue, before signing autographs and chatting to fans.

PARAMOUNT THEATER, SEATTLE, WASHINGTON STATE, USA The night before U2 played at Portland, they played at this venue in Seattle on 26th May 1983. An unusual incident happened here. Half way through "I Fall Down" Bono told the audience about someone ringing him up before the show to tell him about his band. He then invited the caller up on stage to play drums on an extra drum kit.

PARC DES PRINCES, PARIS, FRANCE U2 played to a capacity crowd of over 53,000 fans at this well-known French rugby stadium on 6th September 1997 during the *Pop Mart* tour of Europe. As it was also the date of Princess Diana's funeral and only a week after she had died in the city of Paris, the concert was very emotional with pictures of her beamed up on the giant screen during "MLK". It was also the birthday of U2's stage designer Willie Williams, so Bono said

"Happy Birthday" to him and thanked him for *Pop Mart*.

See also: Diana, Princess of Wales

PARIS CINEMA STUDIO, LONDON U2 played a special set here for the BBC Radio *In Concert* programme on 23rd August 1981. The show was broadcast in the UK on 3rd October 1981. The set was: 11 O'clock Tick Tock, I Will Follow, An Cat Dubh, Into the Heart, With A Shout, Twilight, Out Of Control, Rejoice.

See also: BBC Radio

PARK, JONATHAN One of the stage designers of the *Zoo TV* tour along with Willie Williams and Mark Fisher. He had previously worked with Pink Floyd (*The Wall*) and The Rolling Stones (*Steel Wheels*).

See also: Outside Broadcast / Zoo TV

PARKER, TONY Author of a book about "Red Hill", a town in England which was about to have its mine closed down after the 1984 miners' strike. The book is said to have influenced U2 to write "Red Hill Mining Town".

See also: Red Hill Mining Town

PARKYN, GEOFF The founder and editor of the U2 Information Service, which produced the *U2 Maga-zine*, the first official U2 fan club magazine. This was taken over by *Propaganda* in 1987, which he distrib-uted. He was also the author of *Touch The Flame*, an illustrated documentary about U2.

See also: U2 Magazine / Propaganda

PARTRIDGE, ROB Chief press officer at Island Records in the late 1970s and one of the earliest supporters of U2, taking much of the credit for getting U2 signed to Island Records early in 1980. He was a former *Melody Maker* journalist and had heard about U2 through reports in *Sounds* and *Record Mirror*. He then saw them play live in London in December 1979 and persuaded Island's head of A&R, Bill Stewart, that he should sign the band. However, it took a visit to a U2 gig at the Queen's University in Belfast and the Dublin Stadium gig (both in February 1980) before Island were totally convinced.

"PARTY GIRL" ("A CELEBRATION" SINGLE B-SIDE) See: - TRASH, TRAMPOLINE & THE PARTY GIRL

"PARTY GIRL" (LIVE) (*UNDER A BLOOD RED SKY* ALBUM TRACK) (2.52) The fourth track on the first side of the *Live Under A Blood Red Sky* mini-album. It was the same version as that on the Red Rocks video and one of only two tracks from the Red Rocks concert, (the other being "Gloria"), that made it onto the album.

"PARTY GIRL" LIVE (*UNDER A BLOOD RED SKY* VIDEO TRACK) By the time that the *War* album had been released, the B-side of the "A Celebration"

single had been shortened to plain "Party Girl". The version featured on the *Red Rocks* video is one of the highlights of the show, complete with naff acous-tic guitar solo from The Edge. This was to show that U2 were humans and could make mistakes just like anyone else. The song was performed at the Red Rocks Amphitheatre near Denver in the USA 5th June 1983.

PASSENGERS The name given to the collaboration between the members of U2 and Brian Eno who spent a couple of weeks in Westside Studios in London in November 1994 putting down some musical ideas. The resulting recordings appeared on an album enti-tled *Original Soundtracks 1*, which was a collection of "film soundtracks". The album was mixed at Hano-ver Quay studios in Dublin during the spring and summer of 1995 and various contributions from the likes of Luciano Pavarotti, Holi and Howie B were added. At the time of its release U2 were quick to stress that this was not U2's next album, but rather an experiment that they had been wanting to do for some time.

See also: *Original Soundtracks 1*

"PATROL CAR BLUES" The Edge plays guitar on this track from the 1999 soundtrack album to the film *Cookies Fortune*.

PAVAROTTI, LUCIANO The world-famous Italian opera singer, Luciano Pavarotti first came into the U2 spot-light when Macphisto rang him from the concert at Bologna on 17th July 1993. Unlike most recipients of the phone call he actually spoke with Bono. He then apparently kept ringing Bono at his home in Dublin asking him to write a song for him. This finally mate-rialised in 1995 when he sang with U2 and Brian Eno on the track, "Miss Sarajevo" which was on the *Orig-inal Soundtracks 1* album by Passengers, released in November 1995.

A couple of months earlier he had invited Bono, The Edge and Brian Eno to perform onstage with him in his home town of Modena at one of his annual char-ity concerts in the Novi Sad Park. This took place on 12th September 1995 before a crowd of 15,000 people where the foursome sang "One" and "Miss Sarajevo". The whole concert was filmed and recorded and was released on CD, cassette and video in March 1996 under the title *Together For the Children of Bosnia*. The proceeds from the sales of these and the concert went to the War Child charity so that a music therapy school in the Bosnian town of Mostar could be built. The building was called the Pavarotti Music Centre and was finally opened in December 1997, with both Bono and Pavarotti present.

See also: Together For The Children of Bosnia / War Child

PEACE MUSEUM See: Chicago Peace Museum

"PEACE ON EARTH" (*ALL THAT YOU CAN'T LEAVE BEHIND* ALBUM TRACK) (4.46) The eighth track on the *All That You Can't Leave Behind* album is a plea by Bono for peace in the world and was written shortly after the Omagh bomb atrocity of 15th August 1998. There is a line remembering five of the victims: Sean McLaughlin, Julia Hughes, Gareth Conway, Anne McCombe, and Breda Devin. To date the song has not been performed live.

PEACE TOGETHER (ALBUM) (ISLAND CID 8018/518) This 1993 album featured U2 playing a live version of "Satellite of Love" in Dallas on the *Zoo TV* tour. It was created specially to raise funds for the youth of Northern Ireland, to get them involved in community projects. It featured tracks by several popular Irish artists including, Sinead O' Connor, Therapy? and My Bloody Valentine as well as Blur and Rolf Harris.

PEARLMAN, SANDY Producer of albums by The Clash (*Give 'Em Enough Rope*) and Blue Oyster Cult, he was at one time suggested as a possible producer for U2's third album.

PEARSON, JOSH One half of the Emergency Broadcast Network who directed the "Numb" (Video Remix).
   See also: Emergency Broadcast Network

PELLINGTON, MARK The American film maker who directed the second "One" promotional video which featured the buffalo and the flowers.
   See also: "One" promo video

PENNEFATHER, DAVE Dave was at one time in charge of running U2's Mother Records label. He also helped with the careers of Chris Rea, Nancy Griffiths and Garth Brooks.

See also: Mother Records

"PEOPLE GET READY" This Curtis Mayfield song was used by U2 as a chance to bring someone up on stage to play guitar with the band during the *Joshua Tree* tour. They had first played the song on 8th March 1987 in Belfast for a TV show. They then played it on the second date of the *Joshua Tree* tour in Tempe. The band were posing for photographs for *Time* magazine and invited someone onto the stage to play guitar. He chose to play "People Get Ready" and as soon as the photographer had finished, the band joined in. U2 then repeated this at many of their subsequent shows. On the *Elevation* tour (first leg) a fan called Glen Goland attending their Boston Fleet Centre show on 8th June 2001, was given the opportunity to repeat this tradition.

"PERFECT DAY" (SINGLE) A new version of this song written by Lou Reed for his *Transformer* album was released as a charity record to raise funds for the BBC *Children In Need* charity in 1998. It featured various well-known artists including David Bowie, Annie Lennox and Bono each singing a line of the song. Lou Reed even made a brief appearance singing the opening line. It reached number 1 in the UK singles charts.
   See also: Lou Reed

PERFORMING RIGHTS SOCIETY (PRS) This British based royalty collection organisation was sued by U2 in the British High Court in 1994 over inefficiency in paying them their royalties from other artists performing their songs. The matter was eventually settled in March 1996 when the PRS agreed to pay U2 £400,000.

PETRO, CHRISTINE The original belly dancer who performed during "Mysterious Ways" on the 1992 *Zoo TV* tour of America and Europe. She first appeared at the band's gig at the Miami Arena on 1st March 1992 after persuading the band that she could perform in "Mysterious Ways" just as in the promo video. She had practised in the dress rehearsal at the Civic Centre in Lakeland, and should have made her debut at the first gig there, but when she was due to go on she was trapped by the B-stage and couldn't get free in time. She did make the next show in Miami though, but didn't become a permanent member of the tour until the gig in Boston on 17th March. Her place was taken by Morleigh Steinberg for the *Outside Broadcast* leg and the 1993 *Zoo TV* dates.

PHILIPS ARENA, ATLANTA, GEORGIA, USA U2 played one show here during the *Elevation* tour of America (first leg) on 30th March 2001. In fact, the band only just made it to the show as their plane was delayed by bad weather and they arrived at the arena with just minutes to spare. Two members of REM were in the audience and Bono acknowledged their presence by singing snippets of "Losing My Religion" and "Everybody Hurts" in the middle of "One".

PHOENIX PARK RACECOURSE, DUBLIN, IRELAND
See: A Day At The Races

PIER 84, NEW YORK, USA U2's final show of the 1983 *War* tour of North America took place in this car park by the docks on 29th June 1983 (bringing back memories of their Dandelion car park gigs in Dublin in 1979). The show was filmed for a TV news item.

PINK ELEPHANT NIGHTCLUB, DUBLIN, IRELAND
Former Virgin Prune and soul-mate of Bono, Gavin Friday held a party here on 27th April 1989 to launch his solo album *Each Man Kills The Thing He Loves.* Bono joined him onstage to sing "My Way" and "We Are The Champions".
    See also: Gavin Friday

PINK POP FESTIVAL, SPORTPARK, GELEEN, HOLLAND U2 played this festival on 8th June 1981 before a crowd of 50,000, the largest audience they had played to up to this date. U2 were the second-from-bottom of a bill which included Fischer Z, Madness, Michael Schenker Group, The Pretenders and Ian Dury and The Blockheads. The show was recorded by Dutch radio and broadcast a few days later.

PLACA The group of graffiti artists led by Reno Castro from Chile who came on stage at the U2 show at the Oakland Stadium in California on 15th November 1987 to spray-paint the stage backdrop.

"THE PLAYBOY MANSION" (*POP* ALBUM TRACK) (4.40) The song is about heaven juxtaposed with all the excesses of America. It contains excerpts from "You Showed Me" written by Roger McGuinn and Gene Clark of the Byrds. It also had kits and loops from Larry and inspirational decks from Howie B who co-produced the record with Flood.

"PLEASE" (*POP* ALBUM TRACK) (5.02) The eleventh track off the *Pop* album has The Edge playing organ and Flood providing keyboards and builds slowly to a musical climax only to come down again. The lyrics suggest a relationship where one partner is being selfish and wants to be right all the time. It was first performed live at the Sam Boyd Stadium in Las Vegas on 25th April 1997 on the opening night of the tour.

"PLEASE" (SINGLE) (CID 673/572129) (5.36) The single of "Please" is a different version to that on the album *Pop* featuring a shorter introduction and an orchestral arrangement with extra guitar from The Edge. It was recorded during a break in the *Pop Mart* tour of Europe in July 1997 at Wisseloord Studios in

Hilversum, Holland, with Howie B producing. The single also contained the tracks "Dirty Day" (Junk Day), "Dirty Day" (Bitter Kiss) and "I'm Not Your Baby" (Skysplitter Dub). The cover, a parody of the *Pop* album cover, showed four politicians who were heavily involved with the Peace Process in Northern Ireland. They were: Top left (green face) – Gerry Adams (the leader of Sinn Fein); Top right (yellow face) – David Trimble (moderate unionist party); Bottom left (blue face) – John Hume (moderate democratic party); bottom right (red face) – Ian Paisley (radical unionist party). The single was released in October 1997 and reached number 10 in the UK singles chart.

"PLEASE" ("POPHEART LIVE" EP) (CID 673/572 123-2) The other single of "Please", released in October 1997, it featured four tracks all recorded live on the *Pop Mart* tour. They were "Please" (live from Rotterdam), "Where The Streets Have No Name" (Live from Rotterdam), "With Or Without You" (Live from Edmonton) and "Staring At The Sun" (live from Rotterdam). This was the first time that the two *Joshua Tree* tracks had been made officially available in a live format on a CD.

"PLEASE" (LIVE FROM ROTTERDAM) (*POPHEART* LIVE CD TRACK) (7.11) This live version of "Please" was recorded at Feyenoord Stadium in Rotterdam, Holland on 18th July 1997 during the *Pop Mart* tour of Europe.

"PLEASE" (LIVE) (*HASTA LA VISTA BABY! U2 LIVE FROM MEXICO CITY* ALBUM TRACK) (6.58) This live version of "Please" comes from the live CD, *Hasta La Vista Baby* given free to *Propaganda* readers in July 2000. It was recorded at the Foro Sol Autodromo, Mexico City on 3rd December 1997.

"PLEASE" (LIVE) (*POP MART LIVE FROM MEXICO CITY* VIDEO) This live footage of "Please" comes from the video *Pop Mart Live From Mexico City*. It was recorded at the Foro Sol Autodromo, Mexico City on 3rd December 1997.

"PLEASE" (PROMOTIONAL VIDEO) The promo video for "Please" was directed by Anton Corbijn in the summer of 1997 in Holland. It featured various characters on their knees shuffling past a beggar who has a sign saying "please" hanging from his neck. At the end he "dies" and flies off to heaven and a little girl puts on his sign.

"PLOT 180" (*ORIGINAL SOUNDTRACKS 1* ALBUM TRACK) (3.40) The music was "used" in the film "Hypnotise (Love Me 'til Dawn)" which was directed by Peter Sedgeley.

POD Real name: Anthony Murphy. A member of the Lypton Village and drummer with the Virgin Prunes, who was also U2's main roadie in the early days. He was the next-door neighbour to the Rowens (Guggi and Strongman) and was given the nickname of "Pod" after the character of Sir Poddington in King Arthur, the bravest knight of all, as he was the sort of person who was not afraid of a fight.

Like the rest of the Village he joined the Shalom group in 1979, being the one that leader Dennis Sheedy had met in McDonald's in Grafton Street, Dublin. When Guggi and Gavin left the group it was Pod who remained faithful. When U2 first toured Britain in 1979 and 1980, Pod was there to help move and set up the equipment. Whilst Pod was in the Virgin Prunes from their early days, he left them when he went on the road with U2. He rejoined the Virgin Prunes in 1984 as drummer until the band folded, on the eve of an American tour in 1987.

See also: The Virgin Prunes/The Village

PoD This night club in Harcourt Street Dublin is where the single "Hold Me, Thrill Me, Kiss Me, Kill Me" had its first play. Bono also joined Prince on stage here in 1995 to sing the track "The Cross" with him.

See also: Prince

POGUES, THE The band formed by Shane MacGowan and Spider Stacy in London in 1982 provided a unique mixture of traditional Irish music tinged with punk attitudes. Although to date none of its members have recorded with U2, they have appeared on the same stage. Most notably both bands played at the 1986 Self Aid Festival in Dublin. In March 1987 the two bands appeared on Ireland's *Late Late Show* together as part of an all-star tribute to the Dubliners. Then in 1987 the Pogues supported at U2's Wembley Stadium and Croke Park shows. For a time Bono let Shane MacGowan and his girlfriend Vicki live in his house at Bray, just south of Dublin.

See also: Elvis Costello / Kirsty MacColl

POINT DEPOT, DUBLIN, IRELAND The interview scene with U2 at the start of the *Rattle and Hum* film was filmed in the Point Depot, a derelict locomotive warehouse by the docks in Dublin, in 1988. By the following year, The Point had been restored and transformed into a 5,000 capacity music venue, where U2 decided to hold a series of end of the decade shows in December 1989. When the dates were announced in September 1989, the ticket prices were given as being "£20.50 for standing and £22.50 for reserved seating".

Following a public outcry in Ireland about the prices and the venue not being able to cope with the demand for tickets, Paul McGuinness sent a fax from Australia for publication in *Hot Press* explaining U2's position. In it he mentioned the criticism

that U2 have had in the past for playing in stadia and admitted that "supply could never meet demand", but that U2 had wanted it to be "an opportunity for our hometown audience to see U2 in an intimate setting". As to the criticism of high ticket prices he said: "It seems we have made a mistake. We will therefore be dropping the ticket prices to £16 standing and £18 seating." In conclusion, he in turn criticised the critics who had initially complained about the ticket prices by asking the question of whether this "coalition of priests and other commentators" could also influence "more essential pricing issues of the day like petrol, butter, coal and interest rates!"

The Point Depot, Dublin. *Photo: Paul Daly*

A few days before the tickets went on sale, the promoter announced that the show proposed for the 29th December would be cancelled. This was to give Bono's voice a rest during the residency, after two shows in Amsterdam on 19th and 20th December had to be cancelled due to problems with Bono's voice.

The first show on the 26th featured Bono giving a short homily on Irish writer Samuel Beckett who had died a few days earlier. At the second show on the 27th Bono was joined by Maria McKee on stage to sing and play guitar on "People Get Ready". He also talked about "going away for a little bit", which both fans in the hall and Irish newspaper reporters mistook as a warning that U2 would soon be splitting up.

After a break of two days U2 played at the Point again on 30th December, a show regarded by many fans as their best ever Irish show. The group performed the song they wrote for Roy Orbison "She's A Mystery To Me" for the first time. They also included "11 O'clock Tick Tock", a song they hadn't performed live for over two years. There was a possibility of the final show on 31st December being broadcast live on television, but instead it was broadcast live on the radio to over 20 European countries. For this final show, U2 had special cardboard cutouts included with *Hot Press*, *Q* and *OOR* magazines so that fans could use these as labels when they recorded the show off the radio. There were even rumours that

Bruce Springsteen or Bob Dylan would appear at such a special show, but these were just rumours. Just before midnight some of the ticketless fans waiting outside in the rain, were let in as a special gesture.

Then DJ Dave Fanning led the audience in counting down to midnight, before the band took the stage for an emotional reception with hundreds of balloons being dropped onto the crowd. After singing some of "Auld Lang Syne" Bono wished everyone "Happy Christmas and Happy New Year to you all" before going on to sing "Where The Streets Have No Name". In "Bullet The Blue Sky" he mentioned the fact that the show was not being broadcast live to America, but instead welcomed listeners in Russia, East Germany, Yugoslavia and Romania "and God knows where else they've got their tape recorders turned on!"

A few years later, when Van Morrison played at the Point depot on 6th February 1993, he was joined onstage by Bono who sang "Gloria" and "Moondance" with him. The pair were then joined by Bob Dylan, Stevie Winwood, Elvis Costello, Chrissie Hynde and Kris Kristofferson.

Finally, on 11th November 1999, the Point was the venue for the 1999 MTV European Music Awards where Bono received the "Free Your Mind" award. This was given for his work on behalf of the Jubilee 2000 campaign and for his work with NetAid.

See also: Jubilee 2000 / Maria McKee / Van Morrison / MTV / Net Aid

POIRIER, CHERYL Member of Kid Creole's backing group, The Coconuts, who provided backing vocals on some of the tracks on *War*.

POLYGRAM MUSIC/RECORDS The parent company of Island Records who brought Island Records in 1993. In June 1993 it was announced that U2 had signed a new record deal worth several million dollars. U2 signed another record deal with Polygram in 1998, which included the stipulation that U2 would release three "Best Of" records during the duration of the contract. *The Best of 1980-1990* was the first release under this deal. Then in 1999 Polygram merged with Universal Music when their parent company Seagram bought them out.

Website: www.polygram.org

See also: Island Records / Universal Music

POP (ALBUM) (CIDU210 524 166-2) U2's ninth studio album was released worldwide in March 1997. It was recorded in Dublin at Hanover Quay, Windmill Lane and The Works, and in Miami USA at South Beach Studios throughout 1996. The producer was Flood who had previously worked with U2 on their past three albums, though both Howie B and Steve Osborne were assistant producers. The whole album marked another change in musical direction for U2 with emphasis on a heavier production utilising tape loops, programming and sampling, leading to accusations of U2 having gone "techno" or "jungle"!

Certainly the pre-album release single, "Discotheque" indicated yet another change in musical direction, but the album's overall sound was not all disco orientated, with the acoustic "Staring At The Sun" and "Wake Up Dead Man" showing that U2 were investigating other musical avenues. Critically, the album received mainly favourable reviews. *Rolling Stone* stated that "they've defied the odds and made some of the greatest music of their lives", whilst *Mojo* called it "a cracking record".

Some fans were not so convinced though and sales were not as high as for some of the earlier albums. It was first played on Dave Fanning's 2FM radio show on 20th February 1997. It entered the UK, US and many other charts at number 1, though in several countries its time in the charts was limited.

Track listing: "Discotheque", "Do You Feel Loved", "Mofo", "If God Will Send His Angels", "Staring At The Sun", "Last Night On Earth", "Gone", "Miami", "The Playboy Mansion", "If You Wear That Velvet Dress", "Please", "Wake Up Dead Man".

POPE JOHN PAUL II In 1993 on the *Zooropa* tour of Europe, Bono in his role as Macphisto had rung the Vatican to try and speak to the Pope, but John Paul II had not been there. Then a few days later when the band were playing in Rome, Macphisto had gone along to St Peter's Square to have his photo taken.

Finally on 23rd September 1999 Bono had an audience with Pope John Paul II at the Pope's summer home near Rome, along with other representatives of Jubilee 2000. Bono gave the Pope a book of poetry by the Irish Poet Seamus Heaney as well as a pair of

Pop Mart aftermath, Lansdowne Road, Dublin .
Photo: Claire Bolton

The Pop Mart giant screen. *Photo: Claire Bolton*

his Fly shades, which the Pope is reported to have put on off camera. In return the Pope gave Bono a rosary, which Bono was seen carrying on several occasions afterwards. Bono commented afterwards that the Pope is the world's "first funky Pontiff"!

"THE POP MART TOUR" The *Pop Mart* tour was announced at a special press conference at a K-Mart store in Manhattan's East Village, New York on 12th February 1997. The tour would take in 62 shows in 20 different countries including Greece, Israel, South Africa, Brazil, Argentina and Chile for the first time. It would, like *Zoo TV,* last the best part of eighteen months, and in some ways operate on an even grander scale than the previous tour. For instance the world's largest video screen, measuring 50 feet by 150 feet, would dominate the stage. There would be other gigantic props like a large yellow loop (not unlike the McDonald's "M") towering over the stage, a giant cocktail stick and, most spectacular of all, a large moving Mirrorball lemon.

The tour would be split up into four legs. The first leg of the *Pop Mart* tour opened in Las Vegas, Nevada, USA on 25th March 1997 at the Sam Boyd Stadium. It then played thirty more shows throughout America and Canada, before ending at the Foxboro Stadium, near Boston on 2nd July. For the second leg, the tour moved to Europe, starting at the Feynoord Stadium in Rotterdam, Holland on 18th July. Thirty-two dates later this section of the tour would end at the Ramat Gan Stadium in Tel Aviv, Israel. The third leg then moved back to North America, beginning at the Skydome in Toronto Canada on 26th October. It ended eighteen shows later at the Kingdome in Seattle, USA on 12th December. (This section of the tour grossed $80 million and was watched by 1.7 million

fans.) The final leg of the *Pop Mart* tour then commenced on 27th January 1998 at the Nelson Piquet Stadium in Rio De Janeiro, Brazil and ran through to the Johannesburg Stadium in Johannesburg, South Africa on 21st March 1998.

The *Pop Mart* show was the most colourful U2 show ever with the giant video screen showing hundreds of images from both videos and stills as well as the members of the group in close-up. The show began like a large-scale boxing match with the group walking to the stage through the crowd surrounded by an army of security guards. Adam was dressed as a factory worker with a protective mask on his face for the start of the set. Larry was dressed in army fatigues, whilst The Edge had grown a droopy moustache and wore a cowboy hat. Bono came in as the boxer in a blue silk dressing gown and hood and then removed this to reveal a muscle bound character. The catwalk from *Zoo TV* was again used, as was the B-Stage, but the highlight of the props side was the moving giant lemon which appeared after the main set had ended. It moved from the main stage to the start of the catwalk and got lower and lower until it stopped and split open to reveal the four members of U2 all changed. A staircase descended and down they came, one by one, to start "Discotheque". Other features of the show included a karaoke segment where the audience would sing along to a well-known pop song and Bono once again dancing on the catwalk with a girl member of the audience.

The tour had been promoted by Michael Cohl of Concert Promotions International as opposed to individual promoters in an effort to reduce the risk of staging such an expensive undertaking. It even made the *Guinness Book of Records* as having the biggest video screen and having the largest ever audience for a tour – 2.9 million people at 93 shows.

In hindsight, the *Pop Mart* tour seemed to be U2 trying to outdo the excesses of the *Zoo TV* tour with perhaps too much emphasis on the visual aspect of the show and not enough on the music. As a result, the next tour, the 2001 *Elevation* tour, went back to smaller venues and less gimmicks with more emphasis on the music.

Songs performed on the *Pop Mart* tour included: All I Want Is You, Bullet The Blue Sky, Desire, Discotheque, Do You Feel Loved?, Even Better Than The Real Thing, Gone, 40, Hold Me Thrill Me Kiss Me Kill Me, If God Will Send His Angels, If You Wear That Velvet Dress, I Still Haven't Found What I'm Looking For, I Will Follow, Last Night On Earth, Miami, Miss Sarajevo, MLK, Mofo, Mysterious Ways, New Year's Day, One, Please, Pop Muzik, Pride (In The Name Of Love), Rain, She's a Mystery To Me, Staring At The Sun, Sunday Bloody Sunday, Unchained Melody, Until The End Of The World, Wake Up Dead Man, Where The Streets Have No Name, Whole Lotta Love, With Or Without You.

POP MART (FILM) This film was premiered at the 1998 Edinburgh Festival in Scotland on 9th August where Catherine Owens hosted the presentation.

See also: Catherine Owens

POP MART LIVE FROM MEXICO CITY VIDEO (ISLAND VVL VIDEO) The video of the *Pop Mart* tour, *Pop Mart Live from Mexico City*, was filmed at the Foro Sol Autodromo on 3rd December 1997. This

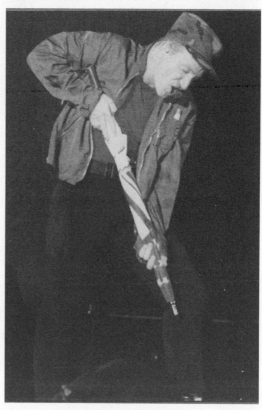

Bono in Miama, Pop Mart tour.
Photo: Claire Bolton

was the second of two shows the band played in the capital of Mexico and the second time the band had visited the city. The show that was filmed was originally scheduled to be the final date of the year but two shows in Vancouver and Seattle were added after this. The video was directed by David Mallett and produced by Ned O'Hanlon of Dreamchaser Productions.

Complete track listing: 1) Pop Muzik, 2) Mofo, 3) I Will Follow, 4) Gone, 5) Even Better Than The Real Thing, 6) Last Night On Earth, 7) Until The End of The World, 8) New Year's Day, 9) Pride (In The Name of Love), 10) I Still Haven't Found What I'm Looking For, 11) All I Want Is You, 12) Desire, 13) Staring At The Sun, 14) Sunday Bloody Sunday, 15) Bullet The Blue Sky, 16) Please, 17) Where The

Streets Have No Name, 18) Discotheque, 19) If You Wear That Velvet Dress, 20) With Or Without You, 21) Hold Me, Thrill Me, Kiss Me, Kill Me, 22) Mysterious Ways, 23) One, 24) Wake Up Dead Man.

"POP MUZIK" This was the title of a single originally released by the British group "M" led by Robin Scott in 1979. The single with its repetitive hook line of "talk about pop music" reached number 2 in the UK singles charts. U2 then adopted it (in a remixed form – see below) as the opening music for the *Pop Mart* tour, for when the band walked through the audience to the stage.

"POP MUZIK" (LIVE) (*HASTA LA VISTA BABY! U2 LIVE FROM MEXICO CITY* ALBUM TRACK) (3.08) The only audio recording of this music from a U2 show is on the free *Propaganda* CD *Hasta La Vista Baby!* recorded live at the Sol Autodromo in Mexico City on 3rd December 1997 during the *Pop Mart* tour of North America. This version is a remix of the original single version but does feature the Robin Scott vocal.

"POP MUZIK" (LIVE) (*POP MART LIVE FROM MEXICO CITY* VIDEO) The only official film of this music from a U2 *Pop Mart* show is on the video *Pop Mart Live From Mexico City*, recorded live at the Sol Autodromo in Mexico City on 3rd December 1997 during the *Pop Mart* tour of North America. This version is the "Pop Mart" remix of the original single version and includes the original Robin Scott vocal as opposed to Bono's vocal.

"POP MUZIK" (POP MART MIX) ("LAST NIGHT ON EARTH" SINGLE) (8.50) This version of the "Pop Muzik" track was a remix version from Steve Osborne and featured Bono on vocals as opposed to Robin Scott. This was the second track on the "Last Night On Earth" single.

PORTER, COLE One of the most influential songwriters of the twentieth century. Porter was born in Indiana, USA in 1891 and showed a musical talent from an early age. He attended Yale University as a Law student but maintained his interest in music by writing many musicals and Yale "fighting songs".

Following Yale, he wrote several Broadway musicals, spending his time in both Paris and Hollywood. Many of his songs became classics including, "Let's Do It (Let's Fall In Love)" and "Night And Day", the latter being covered by U2 on the AIDS charity album, *Red, Hot and Blue* released in 1990.

Web site: www.coleporter.org

See also: Red, Hot & Blue

"PORT OF ROTTERDAM" The song that Bono sang at the 1997 MTV European Awards ceremony in Rotterdam whilst accepting the award for "Best Live Act".

Its proper title was "Port of Amsterdam", but Bono had changed it as they were in Rotterdam. It was dedicated to the Dutch painter and singer Herman Brood whom they had recently met.

POST, GARDNER One half of the Emergency Broadcast Network who directed the promo video of "Numb (Video Remix)" on the "Numb" 3 track video single.

See also: Emergency Broadcast Network

POST OFFICE WORKERS UNION BAND After the efforts of his father, Larry Mullen Senior, Larry Junior played as a member of this Dublin band for a few years before forming Feedback. The band was well known all over Ireland, playing a wide range of musical styles. Larry's debut was on 17th March 1975 for the St. Patrick's Day parade in Dublin.

PREMIER TALENT AGENCY, NEW YORK, USA The booking agency run by Frank Barsalona that booked U2's first dates in the USA. On Barsalona's advice U2 were booked for a short 10 day visit in December 1980, followed by a three month trek across America in the spring of 1981. Premier Talent had been recommended to Paul McGuinness by Chris Blackwell, whose home in the Bahamas was near to Frank's. Premier Talent were not the biggest US booking agency, but they did have both The Who and Bruce Springsteen on their books.

See also: Frank Barsalona

PREMIERSHIP, THE (TV PROGRAMME) U2's song "Beautiful Day" is used as the theme music for this Saturday evening British football programme on the ITV network, which has replaced the BBC's *Match Of The Day*. A competition for musicians to write the theme music was held and U2 beat off opposition from such artists as Robbie Williams, Moby and Badly Drawn Boy.

See also: Beautiful Day

SS PRESIDENT RIVERBOAT, NEW ORLEANS, USA This must rank as one of U2's most unusual gigs – on a Mississippi Riverboat cruising up and down this famous American river. This happened on 11th February 1982, the first date of their spring 1982 tour of America to promote the *October* album. The British Music newspaper the *New Musical Express* had sent over one of its reporters to review the show. They also sent a young Dutch photographer called Anton Corbijn. He first shot the band on this day and from then he became U2's main photographer.

See also: Anton Corbijn

ELVIS AARON PRESLEY: THE TRIBUTE This was an all-star tribute concert to The King held at the Pyramid Arena, Memphis, Tennessee on 8th October 1994. Bono appeared (on video) performing the Elvis song "Can't Help Falling In Love".

PRESLEY, ELVIS The King of Rock 'n' Roll has been a U2 icon, especially for Bono and Larry, for several years. The connection between U2 and Elvis Presley goes back to a track on *The Unforgettable Fire* album, "Elvis Presley And America". The band were shown in the film *Rattle & Hum* visiting Graceland, his home in Memphis and also playing at Sun Studios where Elvis made his first records. It is believed that they didn't perform an Elvis song in their set until the gig at the Charles M Murphy Athletic Center near Memphis in November 1987. This was "Can't Help Falling In Love" which became the set closer for many gigs on the *Zoo TV* tour of 1992-3. Other Elvis songs featured in U2 live sets include "Suspicious Minds", "Are You Lonesome Tonight" and "His Latest Flame".

See also: "Can't Help Falling In Love" / Elvis Presley And America / Elvis: American David / Elvis Ate America / Airfield Wiener Neustadt Austria

PRESTON, BILLY The famous session musician who had previously played with The Beatles and The Rolling Stones provided additional vocals and Hammond organ on the track "Hallelujah Here She Comes".

PRETENDERS, THE This post-punk pop outfit fronted by Chrissie Hynde was formed in England in 1978 and went onto to have several top ten hits on both sides of the Atlantic including the number 1 "Brass In Pocket" and "I Go To Sleep". Chrissie went on to marry Simple Minds vocalist Jim Kerr and get a credit as his wife on *The Unforgettable Fire* album. For the 1987 *Joshua Tree* tour (European leg), the Pretenders were one of the support groups.

See also: Chrissie Hynde / Pride

"PRIDE (IN THE NAME OF LOVE)" (*THE UNFORGETTABLE FIRE* ALBUM TRACK) (3.48) This has become one of U2's most popular songs, being the closer for their live set on several tours, starting in 1984 right through to 1993. The song was recorded at Slane Castle and Windmill Lane studios from May through to July 1984. The lyrics were inspired by Martin Luther King, who had been the subject of a special exhibition at the Chicago Peace Museum that U2 had visited in 1983. The main riff originated at a sound check in the NBC Arena in Honolulu in Hawaii on 16th November 1983. At the recording session for "Pride" "Mrs Christine Kerr (Chrissie Hynde) and BP Fallon are said to have added backing vocals. "Pride" is believed to have been first performed live at the Town Hall in Christchurch, New Zealand on 29th August 1984.

See also: BP Fallon / Chrissie Hynde / Martin Luther King

"PRIDE (IN THE NAME OF LOVE)" (SINGLE) (3.48) The "Pride" single was released in Europe in Sep-

tember 1984 and in the USA and Canada a month later. It was U2's first top 3 hit in the UK, but only reached 33 in the US charts. The B-side of the 7 inch single (IS 202) was "Boomerang II", but the single was also released in a double 7 inch pack (ISD 202) and 12 inch (ISX 202). These two formats contained the extra tracks of "Boomerang I" and "The 4th Of July". "Pride" was a track on the *Best of 1980-1990* compilation CD released in 1998.

"PRIDE (IN THE NAME OF LOVE)" (LIVE) (*RATTLE AND HUM* ALBUM TRACK) (4.27) The live version of "Pride" features on the second side of the *Rattle & Hum* album. It was recorded live at the McNichols Arena in Denver, USA on 8th November 1987. This version was also used in the film.

"PRIDE (IN THE NAME OF LOVE)" (LIVE) (*LIVE FROM SYDNEY* VIDEO) The *Zoo TV* version of "Pride" was filmed at the Cricket Ground, Sydney, Australia on 27th November 1993, and featured on the *Zoo TV Live from Sydney* video.

"PRIDE (IN THE NAME OF LOVE)" (LIVE) (*POP MART LIVE FROM MEXICO CITY* VIDEO) The *Pop Mart* version of "Pride" was filmed at the Sol Autodromo in Mexico City on 3rd December 1997.

"PRIDE (IN THE NAME OF LOVE)" (PROMOTIONAL VIDEO #1) This first promo video of "Pride" was directed by Donald Cammell and produced by James Morris, being filmed in the St. Francis Xavier (SFX) Hall in Dublin in August 1984. It showed the band playing the song on stage before a small yet distinctive audience in a battered hall. The video was featured in full on *The Unforgettable Fire Collection* video and *The Best of 1980-1990* video collection.

"PRIDE (IN THE NAME OF LOVE)" (PROMOTIONAL VIDEO #2) The second promotional video of "Pride" was directed by Barry Devlin and produced by James Morris and showed the band playing the song at Slane Castle in July 1984. This too was featured on *The Unforgettable Fire Collection* video.

"PRIDE (IN THE NAME OF LOVE)" (PROMOTIONAL VIDEO #3) The third promotional video of "Pride" was directed by Anton Corbijn in London during August 1984. Like the video for "Red Hill Mining Town" it is thought that it has never been shown due to the band not being happy with it.

PRINCE In many ways the careers of U2 and Prince have been almost parallel. Coming to prominence around the same time, both are noted for lavish live shows, excursions into the move-making business and a huge following leading to massive album sales and chart success.

However, the only time the two have collaborated is when Bono joined Prince on stage at the Dublin club called PoD on 30th March 1995 to sing parts of a song called "The Cross".

See also: PoD

PRINCIPLE MANAGEMENT The management company set up by Paul McGuinness to deal with the day-to-day running of the U2 organisation. It has offices in Dublin and New York.

PRODIGAL Bono is said to have produced this track by the group Fear Of Falling off their single "Like a Lion".

PROJECT ARTS CENTRE, DUBLIN, IRELAND This theatre in the Temple Bar district of Dublin was one of the first places in Dublin where the early U2 were able to play gigs. It was run by future film director Jim Sheridan and his brother Patrick, with Caragh Coote in charge of booking the bands. U2's first gig here on 16th March 1978 was as the Hype (with Dik Evans in the band) and took place the day before the band travelled to Limerick to take part in the Harp Talent contest which they won. As U2, they then played here again on 2nd May, 1978, the very first time that their manager to be, Paul McGuinness, saw them play live. Their next visit was on 18th September 1978 when U2 were joined on the bill by their friends, The Virgin Prunes. On 17th and 18th February 1979, the *Dark Space Festival* was held here with U2 playing on the first day. The festival was reported in the British press but U2 did not get a mention. U2 later appeared here when they played two shows on 11th and 12th September 1979 supporting Patrik Fitzgerald.

See also: Caragh Coote / Patrik Fitzgerald / Jim Sheridan

"PROMENADE" (*THE UNFORGETTABLE FIRE* ALBUM TRACK) (2.32) A monologue from Bono spoken over a quiet musical background. The images he speaks about are thought to be those of the promenade at Bray, a seaside town to the south of Dublin where Bono and Ali first lived. It has never been performed live.

PROPAGANDA The name of the official U2 fan club that also publishes a magazine of the same name (which has now surpassed 30 issues). It was first published, at the invitation of the band, by Willie Williams (who still writes for the magazine) and Martin Wroe, who has been on the editorial team for fifteen years. It is usually issued two or three times a year depending on band activity and has a circulation in excess of 30,000. As well as interviews with band members and those associated with U2 projects, *Propaganda* has focussed on campaigning organisations such as Amnesty International, as well as putting fans in touch with each other (before the Internet became

popular). It has been designed by Steve Averill ever since its inception. Two fan-only CDs, *Melon* and *Hasta La Vista Baby!* have been issued through *Propaganda* and subscribers often get the early opportunity to buy tour tickets.

Website: www.propaganda.com

See also: Willie Williams / Martin Wroe

PSALMS, THE A collection of songs in the Old Testament of the Bible, the majority of which are credited to King David, the leader of the tribe of Israel. Bono has often referred to the psalms as being the Bible's version of the blues. U2 used some of the words of Psalm 40 in their song "40", the last track on the *War* album. In 1999 a new book of the Psalms, *The Canongate Pocket Book of the Psalms,* was published featuring an introduction by Bono.

The Project Arts Centre, Dublin.
Photo: Mark Chatterton

PUNCHESTOWN RACECOURSE, DUBLIN, IRELAND This music festival was organised by Irish Music paper *Hot Press* to celebrate five years of its existence. It took place at the Punchestown Racecourse in Dublin on Sunday 18th July 1982, with Rory Gallagher top of the bill. U2 were next on the bill and played an impressive set. BP Fallon was pulled on stage near the end to duet with Bono on "Give Peace A Chance". Bono's fiancee, Alison Stewart, also came on stage at the end of the set.

See also: BP Fallon / Alison Stewart

"PURPLE HEART" A track off the 1988 T-Bone Burnett album *The Talking Animals* which featured Bono on backing vocals.

See also: T-Bone Burnett

"PUT 'EM UNDER PRESSURE (OLE OLE OLE)" The song that Larry Mullen wrote and produced for the 1990 Irish World Cup Squad, released on Mother Records' subsidiary label, One Records.

Q MAGAZINE This highly respected British-based music magazine has often featured U2 in its pages, with interviews, features and reviews, in fact U2 have appeared on the cover more times than any other artist. In November 1996, U2 received the inspiration award at the *Q* Awards at London's Park Lane Hotel in recognition of their contribution to contemporary music.

THE MAX QUAD BAND Adam's band before he joined U2. It had been formed at St Columba's and included George Sweeny who would go on to become the guitarist in another Dublin new wave band, The Vipers.

QUEEN One of Britain's most successful rock groups ever. The only time U2 and Queen played on the same bill was at Live Aid in 1985, with many commentators saying that these two groups were the best of the bunch on the day. Queen guitarist Brian May is reported to have told Bono after their set, "You've got a great guitarist in your band. Give my regards to the Hedge"!

When Freddie Mercury died in 1991 and the remaining members of Queen started to organise a tribute concert, U2 offered their services. As they were on the *Zoo TV* tour in America at the time, they recorded some of their concert at the Oakland Coliseum for broadcast at the "Freddie Aid" gig two days later. Also, the words of the Queen song, "we will rock you" were used for the George Bush opening segment on the *Outside Broadcast* tour. Finally, it was Bono who presented the Freddie Mercury award to Muhammad Ali at the 1999 Brit Awards ceremony in London.

See also: Oakland Coliseum

QUEEN ELISABETH THEATER, VANCOUVER, CANADA U2 played a sell out concert at this Canadian theatre on 25th May 1983 as part of the North American tour to promote the *War* album. It was only one of two dates that they played in Canada on this tour.

QUEEN'S HALL, LEEDS, ENGLAND U2 played here to a 4,000 strong audience on 13th September 1980 as part of the "Futurama Festival", that featured several groups who were filling the musical void that punk rock had left. Included in the line-up were Soft Cell, Altered Images and Simple Minds, who along with U2 were all soon to taste chart success.

QUEEN'S UNIVERSITY, BELFAST, NORTHERN IRELAND U2 played this university on two occasions in the early 1980s. The first, in February 1980, was their first ever gig in Northern Ireland. It was here that Rob Partridge, the chief press officer at Island Records brought along the head of Island Records A&R Department, Bill Stewart, to see U2 in concert for the first time. The second time they played here, in January 1981, U2 were now signed to Island Records. The gig was recorded for a BBC Northern Ireland TV special, which also featured Stiff Little Fingers. This programme was not broadcast until 12th August 1981 and only featured four of U2's songs from that night.

QUINCEY AND SONANCE See: Richard Rainey

RADAR See: Peter Rowan

RADD STRINGS, THE They provided the orchestral arrangements on "One Tree Hill" on *The Joshua Tree* album

RADIATORS FROM SPACE, THE The punk/new wave group that Steve Averill, U2's mentor and designer, was a member of during the late 1970s. Like all punk bands each member had a special nickname. His was Steve Rapid and he was the vocalist. They were the main new wave group in Dublin after the Boomtown Rats at that time. Their rise to fame was cut short in the summer of 1977, at their gig at University College in Dublin, when a fan was stabbed. He died on the way to hospital and as a result The Radiators could not get any more gigs in Dublin.

Phil Lynott tried to help the band by giving them the support slot to Thin Lizzy on their *Johnny The Fox* tour in the autumn of 1977, but their punk music did not exactly gel with the hard-rock audience of Lizzy. The band split in 1978, but not before Steve had met Adam Clayton and given the name U2 to his band. Steve went on to form another Dublin-based band called the Modern Heirs who U2 supported at McGonagles on 31st July 1978.

See also: Steve Averill

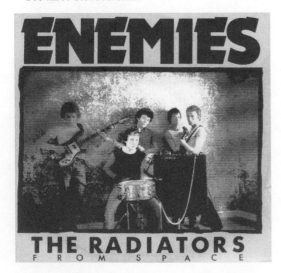

The Radiators From Space 1977 single "Enemies".
(Note: Steve Averill second from right in photo)

RADIO CITY MUSIC HALL, NEW YORK CITY, USA
One of U2's gigs where fan mania got a little too much and spoilt the show, took place on 3rd December 1984 and was part of the winter tour of the USA promoting *The Unforgettable Fire* album. The show sold out in a record 18 minutes and all proceeds were given to Amnesty International's "Stop Torture Week". This meant that many representatives from Amnesty were present as well as several influential reporters from New York based publications.

The moment U2 hit the stage, there was pandemonium with fans rushing down to the front to get a better view of their heroes, or standing on their seats. This prompted a heavy-handed reaction from the bouncers. During "I Will Follow", a fan was beaten up and both Larry and The Edge stopped playing to save him. Then in the encore number of "Gloria" the crush was so bad at the front that several fans jumped up onto the stage for their own safety.

The house manager decided to call a halt to the concert there and then and turned on the house lights. Several bouncers came onto the stage as well to clear the fans away but after an impassioned plea from Bono, most of the crowd did move back so the concert continued for a few minutes more. In 1997, in the middle of the *Pop Mart* tour of Europe, the band flew over to New York to perform "Please" here on 4th September at the MTV Video Music Awards ceremony.

See also: Amnesty International

RAI EUROPA HALL, AMSTERDAM, HOLLAND U2 only played one concert here – on 18th December 1989 – to a crowd of 16,000 during the *Lovetown* tour of Europe. They should have played two more nights here on 19th and 20th but these had to be cancelled due to Bono's voice being in a bad way. All through the concert he had struggled to sing, often getting the crowd to sing along so his voice could rest a little. By the end of the set Bono's voice was so completely shattered that the planned appearance of BB King was postponed.

After this, the promoter came out onstage and told the audience to hold onto their ticket stubs. The next day it was announced that the other two shows at the RAI were cancelled but U2 would play four shows in Rotterdam in January 1990 instead. Those who had tickets for the cancelled shows were guaranteed tickets for the new shows but those who went to the show on the 18th had to apply via a lottery to see if they could get one of the remaining 6,000 tickets available.

See also: Lovetown tour

RAINBOW MUSIC HALL, DENVER, COLORADO, USA
U2's first show in Denver took place here on 28th

March 1981. It was a sell out with over 1,400 fans in attendance. The promoter, Chuck Morris, was so impressed that he booked U2 for a return gig on 11th May 1981, just six weeks later. This show was also sold out, as was their third visit here on 27th February 1982. The next time they would play in Denver would be at the famous Red Rocks Amphitheatre that Chuck Norris had shown the band the day after their first Denver gig.

RAINBOW WARRIORS (GREENPEACE ALBUM) (PL74065) A benefit album jointly released by Mother Records, BMG and RCA in 1989 in aid of Greenpeace. U2 donated the live version of the track "Pride (In The Name of Love)" from *Rattle & Hum* to the album. This marked the first time that a U2 record had been on sale in Russia.

RAINEY, RICHARD The studio engineer who first worked with U2 on their *Pop* album in 1996 at Windmill Lane studios. He was then involved in engineering *All That You Can't Leave Behind*, as well as mixing the tracks "Wild Honey" and "Kite". He received a Grammy award for his work on "Beautiful Day". He was then responsible for club remixes of "Beautiful Day" and "Elevation" under the pseudonym of "Quincey & Sonance", included on the "Stuck In A Moment You Can't Get Out Of" single. He has also worked with the Corrs and Clannad amongst several other Irish artists.

See also: Beautiful Day (Quincey & Sonance Remix)

RAINFORD, STEVE The Edge's guitar technician during the early 1980s.

RAMAT-GAN NATIONAL STADIUM, TEL AVIV, ISRAEL U2's only appearance in Israel took place here on 30th September 1997 during the European leg of the *Pop Mart* tour. It was the final concert of this section of the tour and was a 31,000 sell out. Bono dedicated "One" and "MLK" to the former Israeli Prime Minister, Yitzhak Rabin, who had been murdered two years earlier. Before "New Year's Day" he said "Happy New Year" to the audience as the next day was Rosh Hashana, the Jewish New Year. His plea for the release from imprisonment of nuclear secrets traitor Mordechai Vanunu however did not meet with approval from most of the audience.

RAMONES, THE U2 have been fans of the leather-jacketed New York punk band responsible for three-chord anthems like "Sheena Is A Punk Rocker" and "Beat On The Brat" since their early days when they used to include a cover of the Ramones song "Glad To See You Go" in their set. In fact The Edge has admitted they once played two Ramones songs in an audition for an Irish TV programme and lied to the producer that they were their own songs. The Ramones were the support act for some of the 1993 *Zooropa* shows. In April 2001 when Joey Ramone died of cancer, he is said to have been listening to the U2 track "In A Little While" just before he passed away. At several concerts following his death U2 played the Ramones song "I Remember You" as a tribute.

RAPHAEL, MICKEY He played harmonica on the version of "Slow Dancing" that featured Willie Nelson on lead vocals. It was included on the "If God Will Send His Angels" single.

See also: Willie Nelson / Slow Dancing

RAPID, STEVE See: Steve Averill

RAPID EXTERIOR'S (RX) Steve Averill's design company, credited with the artwork for the cover of the *Boy* album.

RATTLE & HUM (ALBUM) (U27/CID 27) The *Rattle & Hum* album was both the soundtrack album to the feature film of *Rattle & Hum* as well as a collection of new songs that U2 had recorded during and after the *Joshua Tree* tour. The title came from a line in "Bullet The Blue Sky". It was produced by Jimmy Iovine who had produced U2's other live album, *Under a Blood Red Sky*. The album was released worldwide on 10th October 1988. It made the number 1 spot in both the UK and US album charts, but received a mixed reaction from the music press, not least because of the all the hype prior to the release of the film.

The album had originally been intended as a "scrapbook record" showing different facets of America that the band had discovered having toured there every year since 1981. The album was deliberately sequenced to follow the soundtrack of the film, but instead of being one live album and one studio album, it is a hotch potch of studio cuts interspersed with live recordings. Whilst *Rattle & Hum* did not generate the critical response that its predecessor had done, it still sold over 14 million copies worldwide. Although there was never a *Rattle & Hum* tour to promote the album, U2 did play many of the new songs on *Rattle & Hum* during the *Lovetown* tour of Australia and Europe in the autumn of 1989.

Complete album track list: Helter Skelter (live), Van Diemen's Land, Desire, Hawkmoon 269, All Along The Watchtower (live), I Still Haven't Found What I'm Looking For (live), Freedom For My People, Silver & Gold (live), Pride (In The Name Of Love) (live), Angel of Harlem, Love Rescue Me, When Love Comes To Town, Heartland, God Part II, The Star Spangled Banner, Bullet The Blue Sky (live), All I Want Is You.

RATTLE & HUM (FEATURE FILM/VIDEO): The film of *Rattle & Hum* was directed by the then unknown Phil Joanou and produced by Michael Hamlyn. The idea for *Rattle & Hum* came essentially from Paul McGuinness who thought it was time for a replacement of the *Red Rocks* video which had shown the band at an earlier stage in their career. Also, it was felt that the music of U2 was now suitable for a full-scale feature film which would document the band on tour and show the audience how U2 had progressed musically. At one time several of the big Hollywood movie studios were mooted as possible backers for the film, with Paramount Pictures contributing some of the cost, but in the end each member of the group and Paul McGuinness put up most of the money themselves so that artistic control could be guaranteed.

Rattle & Hum was conceived as a documentary of U2's *Joshua Tree* tour of America, taking in some of their heroes such as Elvis Presley, Bob Dylan, Jimi Hendrix and BB King along the way – a kind of celebration of the American rock 'n' roll dream. Unfortunately, after all the hype proceeding the film, some critics saw it as U2 trying to set themselves up as equals to these rock 'n' roll heroes. *Rattle & Hum* was primarily concerned with the music of U2 and thus the film is dominated by the band playing live. There was room, however, for shots of the band visiting Graceland, Elvis Presley's house; playing a session in Sun Studios; sitting by the side of the Mississippi; and visiting a Harlem church.

Joanou followed the band through the third leg of the *Joshua Tree* tour in America shooting over 250 hours of film during the period September to December 1987. The first half was all in black and white with both documentary and concert footage, whilst the second half was shot mainly in colour and was filmed at the final concert of the tour at the Sun Devil Stadium, Tempe, Arizona on 20th December 1987. The black and white film concert clips were filmed at the McNichols Arena in Denver, Colorado on 8th November, the Justin Herman Plaza in San Francisco on 11th November and at the Tarrant County Convention Center on 24th November 1987.

The film was premiered in Dublin on 27th October 1988, followed by premieres in Madrid, London and Los Angeles. The British premiere of the film *Rattle & Hum* took place at the Odeon Leicester Square in London on 31st October 1988. All four members of U2 attended but were unable to perform an inpromptu set as they had done in Dublin, due to police concerns about crowd safety.

Although interest in the film was high in the first few weeks after its release, by Christmas it was out of most American cinemas. A video version of the film was released in 1989 (with a 15 certificate) followed by a DVD in 2000, featuring some extra scenes. The film version contained some extra tracks that were not included on the album soundtrack. These are asterisked * below.

The Best of 1980-1990 video collection, released in 1998, includes an outtake from the film that shows the band performing "One Tree Hill" at the Sun Devil stadium in Tempe.

Songs in the film/video: Helter Skelter, Van Diemen's Land, Desire, *Exit, *Gloria, I Still Haven't Found What I'm Looking For, Silver And Gold, Angel Of Harlem, All Along The Watchtower, *In God's Country, When Love Comes To Town, Heartland, *Bad, *Where The Streets Have No Name, *MLK, *With Or Without You, Bullet The Blue Sky, *Running To Stand Still, *Sunday Bloody Sunday, Pride (In The Name Of Love), All I Want Is You.

See also: Phil Joanou / Gracelands / Sun City / McNichols Arena /Sun Devil Stadium / BB King / Save The Yuppies Concert / Tarrant County Convention Center

RDS See: Royal Dublin Showground

REAGAN, RONALD Former Hollywood B-movie star who was President of the USA from 1980 to 1988. Although U2 never publically ridiculed Reagan as they did his successor, George Bush, they still made a stand against some of his policies, such as in Central America through "Bullet The Blue Sky" and "Pride", which Bono has said was originally written with him in mind. "It was originally meant as the sort of pride that won't back down that wants to build nuclear arsenals. But… I was giving Reagan too much importance. I thought, Martin Luther King, there's a man."

RECORD MIRROR One of the leading British music journals of the late 1970s and early 1980s. Through one of its journalists, Chris Westwood, who Bono had visited in 1979, U2 were given their first cover story outside Ireland. He interviewed Bono, describing the band as "a breath of fresh Eire".

"RED HILL MINING TOWN" (*THE JOSHUA TREE* ALBUM TRACK) (4.51) The first track on side two of *The Joshua Tree* album was inspired by the 1984-85 miners strike in Britain. Many miners lost their jobs when the pits were shut down after the strike ended. In a lot of cases this also meant the death of whole towns and communities. Journalist Tony Parker wrote a book called *Red Hill* on one such mining town, that looked at the way relationships between husbands and wives had been shattered as a result. Bono had read the book and was inspired to write the song. It was at one time seen as a future U2 single, so the band asked Neil Jordan to produce a promotional video for the track. (see below) The song is the only one from *The Joshua Tree* never to have been performed live.

"RED HILL MINING TOWN" (PROMOTIONAL VIDEO) A promotional video of "Red Hill Mining Town" was made in London on 11th February 1987, with Neil Jordan as director. It is extremely rare, never having been released commercially. It is thought that U2 were not happy with the finished video (having appeared in the video wearing miner's outfits) and so changed their minds about its release. Another theory is that Bono found some of the vocals too high to sing in concert – this might explain why the song has never been performed live.

RED HOT & BLUE PROJECT The brainchild of Leigh Blake who managed to get various musicians to record tracks and videos for a special film of the music of Cole Porter. It was shown on TV around the world on Saturday 1st December 1990 – "World AIDS Day". Blake and John Carlin were co-producers of the film featuring U2 playing the Cole Porter song "Night & Day". The video was directed by German film director Wim Wenders. Other film makers involved in directing videos for the project included Jim Jarmusch, Neil Jordan, Alex Cox and Jonathan Demme.
    See also: AIDS / Wim Wenders

RED HOT & BLUE CD (CHRYSALIS CCD 1977): A CD of the *Red Hot & Blue* project was released at the same time as the film was shown and featured various artists singing their interpretations of Cole Porter songs. These included The Neville Brothers, Sinead O'Connor, Debbie Harry & Iggy Pop, Kirsty Mac-Coll & The Pogues, KD Lang, Erasure, Lisa Stansfield, as well as U2 performing "Night & Day".
    See also: Night & Day

"RED, HOT AND DANCE" A benefit concert organised to take place on World AIDS Day on 1st December 1991. U2 were present at the show.

"RED LIGHT" (*WAR* ALBUM TRACK): (3.45) The trumpet of Kenny Fradley from Kid Creole's band adds a different angle to this song. The Coconuts, Kid Creole's backing singers (Cheryl Poirer, Adriana Keagi, Taryn Hagey and Jessica Felton), were also featured on this track. It has never been performed live.

RED ROCKS AMPHITHEATER, DENVER, COLORADO, USA This was the legendary U2 gig of 25th June 1983, filmed for the *Under A Blood Red Sky* video, as well as for transmission on the British Channel 4 TV programme, *The Tube*. The 9,000 capacity amphitheatre was chosen as the venue to shoot a promotional video of U2 in concert. The natural amphitheatre, situated near Denver, two miles up in the Rocky Mountains, was the perfect place to film the band in a concert setting. The only problem was that for several days before the show there was persistent rain, which did not look like easing. On the morning of the show, promoter Barry Fey was calling for the filming to be cancelled, but the band and Paul McGuinness stuck to their plan. The fans still came despite the weather, and just as the band were due to go onstage, the rain stopped and both the show and filming were able to go ahead. Not all of the show ended up on the video – "I Fall Down", "Two Hearts Beat As One", "An Cat Dubh", "Twilight", "Out of Control" and "Into the Heart" were not used. However, the remaining songs that did make it onto the video show U2 at their peak for their first stage of their career. This show was listed as 40th in a list of the "100 Greatest Moments in Rock" by the US Magazine *Entertainment Weekly* in May 1999.
    See also: U2 Live At Red Rocks video

REED, LOU Lou Reed has had a successful career both as a solo artist and earlier as a founder member of hugely influential band, The Velvet Underground. Bono first met Lou Reed in New York in 1985 when the two were involved in the *Sun City* project. U2 and Lou Reed first played together on the 1986 *Conspiracy of Hope* tour of America. His comments to Bono about him having a great gift and not to "give it away" are said to have inspired some of "With Or Without You". The following year when U2 played two triumphant nights at Croke Park in June, Lou Reed was one of the support acts.
    At the second show he joined Bono onstage to duet on "Walk On The Wild Side", which was slotted into "Bad". On the 1991 *Achtung Baby* album, Lou and Sylvia Reed get a special thank you in the credits for "Acrobat". For the *Zoo TV* tour, U2 performed Lou Reed's "Satellite of Love" on the mini-stage. U2's cover version of this song was then included on the single of "One". For the final show of the European leg of the 1992 *Zoo TV* tour at the G-Mex Centre in Manchester on 19th June, Lou Reed actually appeared

in person to duet with U2 on this number. This was then repeated on the first date of the *Outside Broadcast* leg of the *Zoo TV* at the Giant's Stadium in New York on 12th August 1992.

For the show at the Yankee Stadium on 30th August 1992 a video image of Lou Reed singing the song was first shown. This would be repeated on every show of the remaining dates of the *Zoo TV* tour. On the 1993 *Zooropa* tour of Europe the re-formed Velvet Underground supported U2 on several shows. In 1998 both Lou and Bono sang on the charity single version of "Perfect Day", a song, like "Satellite of Love", off Lou's *Transformer* album. Finally Bono's "Fly" character is said by some commentators to be based partly on Lou Reed.

See also: Conspiracy of Hope tour / Satellite of Love / With Or Without You

"THE REFUGEE" (*WAR* ALBUM TRACK) (3.41) The opening track on side two of the *War* album. The song was originally a demo that U2 had recorded before the *War* album sessions, with Bill Whelan producing. Steve Lillywhite, as producer of *War*, managed to take this demo and remix it successfully for inclusion on the album. The song describes a refugee going to the promised land of America – a theme that would resurface on *The Joshua Tree* song "In God's Country". Like "Red Light" off the *War* album, it too has not been performed live.

See also: Bill Whelan

"REJOICE" (*OCTOBER* ALBUM TRACK) (3.38) The fourth track on side one of U2's *October* album. It is one of U2's most aggressive songs, beginning with a powerful opening riff from The Edge. The song shows some of the confusion that the Christian members of the band were going through during the recording of the *October* album. Bono concludes that whatever happens you should be grateful for what you've got. It was first perfomed live at Slane Castle in Ireland on 16th August 1981.

REM The American group from Athens Georgia, who supported U2 in 1985 during the *Unforgettable Fire* tour of Europe. By the 1990s, through multi-platinum albums such as *Out Of Time* and *Automatic For The People* had become almost as big as U2.

In January 1993 at President Clinton's inaugural ball, two members of REM, Michael Stipe and Mick Mills, joined Larry and Adam, to make the group Automatic Baby (the name taken from REM's *Automatic For The People* and U2's *Achtung Baby* albums) to perform the U2 song "One". On more than one occasion the various members of REM have attended U2 shows and vice-versa.

At the Philips Arena in Atlanta Georgia, during the *Elevation* tour of America (first leg) on 30th March 2001 the band only just made it to the show as their plane was delayed by bad weather and they arrived at the arena with just minutes to spare. Two members of REM were in the audience and Bono acknowledged their presence by singing snippets of "Losing My Religion" and "Everybody Hurts" in the middle of "One".

U2's lighting director Willie Williams and sound enginer Joe O'Herlihy have worked in the same capacity for REM.

REUNION ARENA, DALLAS, TEXAS, USA U2 have played this 18,000 capacity arena on three occasions. The first time was on 25th February 1985, the opening date of the 1985 *Unforgettable Fire* tour of North America. Quite a few people jumped up on stage during this concert without any problems, but during the encore a serious situation was narrowly averted. It was believed that a man at the front of the arena pulled out a gun and pointed it at Bono, but security guards quickly overpowered him. U2 returned to this venue during the *Zoo TV* tour of 1992 to play here on 5th April 1992 without any major incidents. More recently U2 played here on the first leg of the *Elevation* tour of North America on 3rd April 2001, with "Desire" being added to the set that night.

RICE STADIUM, SALT LAKE CITY, UTAH, USA U2 played a sell out show here to 30,000 fans on the first leg of the *Pop Mart* tour on 3rd May 1997. Before the show some fans had drawn a 50 foot high "U2" on one of the hills overlooking Salt Lake City. Bono referred to this in the show, saying, "It's a good job we're not called The Red Hot Chilli Peppers!" The show was temporarily halted shortly after the introductory music of "Pop Muzik" had begun playing, apparently because of a bomb scare which turned out to be a false alarm.

RICHARDS, KEITH Founder member of the Rolling Stones. He first met Bono in New York in 1985 when Peter Wolf of the J.Geils Band took Bono to the recording studio where the Rolling Stones were recording their *Dirty Work* album. Richards is reported to have introduced Bono to a variety of blues artists of whom Bono had no previous knowledge. Bono is said to have written "Silver & Gold" after their meeting. Allegedly Keith asked Bono to play one of his songs. Bono realised, without The Edge, he couldn't and wrote "Silver and Gold" on acoustic guitar with solo performance in mind. Richards, along with fellow Rolling Stone Ronnie Wood, played on the recording of the song. In October 1988 at the Smile Jamaica Concert, Keith joined U2 on stage to play "When Love Comes To Town" and "Love Rescue Me". The Edge and Keith also played together in the all-star jam at the Waldorf Astoria

Hotel in New York City after after the induction of the Yardbirds into the Rock 'n' Roll Hall of Fame.

See also: Rolling Stones / Smile Jamaica / Sun City / Waldorf Astoria Hotel

RIEFENSTAHL, LENI A German filmmaker for ever associated with Adolf Hitler's Nazi regime. Riefenstahl is a hugely controversial figure, admired for her ground-breaking technique but castigated for promulgating Nazi propaganda in her films about the Nuremburg rallies and the 1936 Olympic Games. A scene from the Olympics film *Triumph of the Will* was used as an opening sequence for the 1993 *Zooropa Zoo TV* shows.

See also: Triumph of the Will

RIGHT TO REMARRY CAMPAIGN A campaign in Ireland in 1995 concerned with a referendum on whether to allow divorce in the Republic of Ireland and thus the right to remarry. All four members of U2 signed a petiton in support of this campaign with Bono, Ali, Van Morrison and Gavin Friday all taking part in a rally in Dublin a few days before the vote took place.

THE RITZ, NEW YORK CITY, USA This was the venue for U2's first ever-American gig, which took place on 6th December 1980. As fate would have it, they should have made their American dcbut at The Penny Arcade in Rochester, New York State the previous night, but this show was cancelled. Present at the gig was U2's US agent Frank Barsalona, who had put U2 on his Premier Talent Agency's books. He was impressed with the audience's reaction to the band and went straight to the dressing room afterwards to congratulate them. U2 then made a welcome return to the Ritz, just three months later on 7th March 1981. Finally, the band played a 'residency' here in November 1981, when they played three consecutive nights on the 20th, 21st and 22nd. All three shows were sold out.

See also: Frank Barsalona

RIVER PLATE STADIUM, BUENOS AIRES, ARGENTINA U2's only appearances in Argentina to date have been three consecutive nights at the 70,000 capacity River Plate stadium on 5th, 6th and 7th February 1998 during the final leg of the *Pop Mart* tour. At the show on the first night, a group of women from the Madres De Plazo de Mayo (Mothers of the Seat Of May) came on stage during "One". This was a human rights group of women (similar to the Mothers of the Disappeared in El Salvador) who had lost their children or husbands under the previous military dictatorship in Argentina and who had campaigned daily ouside the Plazo de Mayo in Buenos Aires. Most of them came to the microphone and said the names of a lost one to

the audience as the show finished with "Mothers of the Disappeared".

On the second night the band were all wearing the shirts of the Argentinian national soccer team as they emerged from the lemon. For the third night, "Bad" was played for the first time in full since the *Zooropa* tour in 1993. Also played after a long break was "Slow Dancing." "One" was dedicated to Jose Luis Cabezas, a journalist who had been murdered a year previously. At this point Bono told Willie Williams to turn off all the lights in the stadium so that the light from people's cigarette lighters provided a magical end to the concert.

RMP (REGINE MOYLETT PUBLICITY) The company in charge of publicity for U2, based in London and run by Regine Moylett who has known the band since the early days. RMP also look after the publicity for Sting, The Corrs, PJ Harvey and The Proclaimers.

See also: Regine Moylett

ROBERT F. KENNEDY STADIUM WASHINGTON DC USA U2 first played here on 20th September 1987 during the *Joshua Tree* tour of America to a crowd of over 50,000. Unfortunately it was raining during the concert making the stage wet and slippery. During "Exit", Bono slipped and fell badly on his left shoulder. He was taken to hospital straight after the show, where it was diagnosed that he had dislocated his shoulder. As a result Bono had to wear a sling onstage for the next twelve concerts. U2 then played two dates here during the *Outside Broadcast* leg of the *Zoo TV* tour on 15th and 16th August 1992. As it was the eve of the anniversary of Elvis Presley's death, Bono tried singing "Can't Help Falling in Love". The song was well received, so it was used from then on at the end of each *Zoo TV* Show.

U2 last played here during the *Pop Mart* tour (first leg) of North America on 26th May 1997. Again the weather affected the show and a huge thunder storm and incessant rain damaged some of the panels on the giant TV screen. As a result a whole section was blacked out during the show. U2 had been to see President Clinton at the White House the day before and had spoken to him about the imprisoned native American Indian, Leonard Peltier. Bono dedicated "Please" to him.

ROBERTSON, ROBBIE The guitarist with The Band, formerly The Hawks, Bob Dylan's backing group, who redefined late-sixties rock with albums such as *Music From The Big Pink* (1968) and *The Band* (1970). He first met the members of U2 through fellow Canadian Daniel Lanois. Robbie then enlisted the help of U2 on his 1987 eponymous solo debut. Two of the tracks, "Testimony" and "Sweet Fire of Love", were recorded in Dublin in August 1986 with

Bono at the Rock am Ring festival, Germany 25/5/85
Photo: Kay Bauersfeld

U2 as they were starting to record the *The Joshua Tree*.

ROBINSON, BOBBIE He co-wrote "Freedom For My People", the song performed on a New York street corner by Sterling Magee and Adan Gussow in the film *Rattle & Hum*.

ROCHE, SHIELA She works at Principle Management in Dublin and is is charge of the office. She did spend some time running the New York office of Principle but returned to Dublin in the early 1990s and has taken over as number two behind Paul McGuinness.

ROCK AM RING FESTIVAL U2 played at the "Rock am Ring Festival" at the Nurburgring motor racing circuit near Koblenz in Germany on 25th May 1985. They were second on the bill to Chris de Burgh and played to a large crowd of over 70,000 fans – the largest number of fans they had played to in Europe up to that date. The response to U2's set was far from enthusiastic so Bono climbed the lighting rig to get everyone's attention. This was the first of ten festivals that U2 were scheduled to play that summer, including Live Aid.

ROCK & ROLL HALL OF FAME, CLEVELAND, OHIO, USA This world famous museum was opened on 1st September 1995. It contains memorabilia from many

different artists. U2 are well represented with four Trabants from the *Zoo TV* tour hanging in the lobby of the museum. Also included are letters of rejection from record companies, Bono's Fly suit, hand written lyrics for "The Ocean" and "11 O'clock Tick Tock", and early U2 posters. U2 have their own exhibit section, put together under the guidance of Larry.

ROCK & ROLL HALL OF FAME INDUCTION CEREMONY An annual event which takes place every winter in New York's Waldorf Astoria Hotel. Both Bono and The Edge have been involved in inducting several artists over the years: The Who inducted by Bono in 1990, The Yardbirds inducted by The Edge in 1992, Bob Marley inducted by Bono in 1994, Bruce Springsteen inducted by Bono in 2000, and Chris Blackwell of Island Records inducted by Bono in 2001. At the 2000 ceremony Bono joined all the inductees at the end to sing "People Get Ready".
  See also: Chris Blackwell / Bob Marley / Bruce Springsteen / The Who / The Yardbirds

THE ROCK GARDEN, COVENT GARDEN, LONDON, ENGLAND This was one of the first places that U2 played in London during their first visit in December 1979. They played here on the 5th December 1979 though they were billed as "V2". The show was reviewed in *Record Mirror* by the editor Alf Martin, who said "their confidence, energy and damn good music got to us all". U2 then returned to this venue on 27th May 1980.

"ROCK 'N' ROLL, STOP THE TRAFFIC" These were the words that Bono spray painted on a sculpture by Armand Vaillancourt, during the famous "Save The Yuppies" concert at the Justin Herman Plaza in San Francisco, on 11th November 1987. As a result he was given a misdemeanour charge by the San Francisco police department and told to appear in court on 16th December 1987. After Bono made a public apology for and paid for the sculpture to be cleaned up, the charges were dropped. The act of painting the words on the sculpture can be seen in the film *Rattle & Hum*.
  See also: Save The Yuppies concert

ROCK 'N' STROLL WALK, DUBLIN, IRELAND The guide published by the Irish Tourist Board accompanying a walk that visitors to Dublin can make. There are various plaques located on buildings around the city which are connected with prominent Irish groups or musicians. U2 have two plaques associated with them, one at Windmill Lane Studios and the other at the Dandelion Market. Similar plaques commemorate other well-known Irish artists like Phil Lynott, Bob Geldof and Sinead O' Connor.

ROCK ON THE TYNE FESTIVAL This was a two-day festival that took place at the Gateshead International

Stadium in Newcastle Upon Tyne, England on 28th and 29th August 1981. U2 were third on the bill to Elvis Costello and Ian Dury. A dissapointing crowd of around 7,500 turned up each day to watch the bands – the organisers were hoping for a crowd of more than double that figure. It was also a somewhat disappointing U2 show with Bono forgetting some of the lines to the songs. The following year U2 played here again on Saturday 31st July. This time they were second on the bill to the Police. The show was filmed by the TV programme *The Tube* and some of the songs from the show were shown on that programme. When The Police performed "Invisible Sun", Bono joined them on stage.

See also: Elvis Costello

ROCKPALAST (German TV Programme) The name of the famous German Rock Music TV programme that specialises in broadcasting live concerts. U2 were featured on this programme when their set at the Lorelei Festival on 20th August 1983 was broadcast live on WDR TV and radio. Five of the tracks from their set – "New Year's Day", "Sunday Bloody Sunday", "I Will Follow", "Cry/The Electric Co" and "40" – were used on the mini-album *Under A Blood Red Sky* in preference to those recorded at the Red Rocks show in Denver. After the U2's set, Bono was interviewed by Alan Bangs, the presenter of *Rockpalast*.

See also: Lorelei Festival

ROCK-POP IN CONCERT See: Westfallenhalle

ROCK THE VOTE An MTV campaign prior to the 1992 US Presidential election with the aim of getting the young people of America to actually use their vote in the democratic election process. U2 were involved in this campaign through appearing on one of the MTV public information films in the Autumn of 1992 about the forthcoming election and the issues involved. U2

U2 feature prominently on Dublin's "Rock 'n' Stroll" tour. *Photo: Claire Bolton*

also had their own campaign going with the "Vote baby!" slogan.

See also: MTV

ROLLING STONE The leading and most influential American rock magazine. It first began reporting on U2 in February 1981 with an article entitled "U2: here comes The Next Big Thing". Each album release has since then been reviewed and interviews with the band have been regularly published. By 1985 U2 were hailed by *Rolling Stone* as "our choice for the 'Band of the 80s'". That year they won a category in the readers' poll for "Band of the Year" as well as "Best Performance at Live Aid". From then on U2 would regularly win categories in the annual *Rolling Stone* readers' polls. In 1994, a collection of all *Rolling Stone*'s articles, reviews and news reports on U2 was published called *U2- The Rolling Stone Files*.

ROLLING STONES, THE The world's greatest rock 'n' roll band – according to some. Bono first met the Stones in New York in 1985 during the recording of their *Dirty Work* album (which was being produced by Steve Lillywhite). Bono was there to take part in the "Artists United Against Apartheid" album organised by Little Steven of Bruce Springsteen's E-Street Band. In the studio the Stones went through the Everly Brothers back catalogue and also introduced Bono to blues artists such as John Lee Hooker and Muddy Waters. As a result of this session Bono went back to his hotel room and wrote "Silver and Gold" which he recorded with Keith Richards and Ronnie Wood. This was included on the *Sun City* album. Prior to that, Bono had often included a few lines of two Stones songs in "Bad" – "Sympathy For The Devil" and "Ruby Tuesday".

In 1988 Keith Richards played with U2 at the "Smile Jamaica" concert in London. In 1992 U2 included a cover of the Stones' number 1 hit "Paint It Black" on the "Who's Gonna Ride Your Wild Horses" single, the only time the band have covered a Rolling Stones track on record. The two bands have never played together on the same bill, though Bono did sing at Mick Jagger's 56th birthday party at his house in the south of France in July 1999. The following year Mick and his daughter Lizzy came and sang at the sessions for *All That You Can't Leave Behind* on the track "Stuck In A Moment You Can't Get Out Of".

See also: Paint It Black / Mick Jagger / Keith Richards / Stuck In A Moment / Ronnie Wood

ROMAN CATHOLIC CHURCH The biggest and most influential church group in Ireland. U2 have often disagreed with the Roman Catholic church's teaching on birth control and abortion, especially in the light of the AIDS threat. Larry was born a Roman Catholic as was Bono's father, though Bono used to worship each Sunday at the local Protestant church with his mother. In 1995 all four members of U2 joined in the campaign for a "yes vote" in the campaign to allow divorce in Ireland (the Catholic church was against such a change).

In 1999 Bono had an audience with Pope John Paul II in connection with his work for Jubilee 2000, gaining the support of the Pontiff for this campaign.

See also: Contraception / Pope John Paul II

"A ROOM AT THE HEARTBREAK HOTEL" (ANGEL OF HARLEM B-SIDE) (5.29) The track that was featured on the B-side of the "Angel of Harlem" 7 and 12 inch singles. "Heartbreak Hotel" was Elvis Presley's first big hit and it is no coincidence that Elvis' picture appears on the B-side record label in the centre of the single. The track was produced by Jimmy Iovine and features backing vocals from Edna Wright, Maxine Waters and Julia Waters, who help give the song a Gospel feel. There is also a brass section, arranged by Paul Barrett, prominent at the end of the track.

See also: Elvis Presley

ROSE, AXL The lead singer of Guns & Roses. He became a big fan of U2 after the release of *Achtung Baby* and was especially moved by the song "One". When U2 performed at the Donau Unsel in Vienna, Austria in May 1992, Bono dedicated "One" "to the men and boys of Guns & Roses" as the band had played at the same venue the previous night. Later on in the set Axl came on stage and sang "Knocking on Heaven's Door" in a duet with Bono.

ROSEBERRY, ANNIE She was the deputy to Bill Stewart, head of A&R at Island Records. In February 1980, she flew over to Northern Ireland to watch U2 at Queen's University in Belfast along with Bill Stewart and two executives from Blue Mountain Music. After the show, when she and the band were celebrating at the Europa Hotel, Adam is said to have spilt some of his drink over her.

THE ROSE GARDEN, PORTLAND, OREGON, USA U2 played here during the *Elevation* tour of North America on 15th April 2001. Bono dedicated "One" to Joey Ramone who had died earlier that day and as tribute, the band also played the Ramones song "I Remember You". Bono also referred to Portland as the place where his brief case was stolen 20 years ago that week.

ROSEMONT HORIZON, CHICAGO, ILLINOIS, USA U2 first played this 16,000 capacity arena on 13th June 1986 during the *Conspiracy of Hope* tour. During the Police's set, Bono joined them on stage to sing 'Invisible Sun'. The following year U2 played four

concerts here. The first was on 29th April 1987 on the first leg of the American section of the *Joshua Tree* tour. The band then returned for three consecutive nights – 28th, 29th and 30th October 1987, which were all sold out. On the last night, during "Party Girl", Bono sang "Happy Birthday" to Larry, as his 26th birthday was the next day.

Finally U2 played here on 31st March 1992 during the *Zoo TV* tour. After the band had played their section on the mini-stage, Larry tripped on some equipment as he was walking back to the main stage. One female fan grabbed his leg and wouldn't let go. Other fans followed suit, but luckily a security guard came to his rescue.

60 ROSEMOUNT AVENUE, ARTANE, DUBLIN, IRELAND This was the boyhood home of Larry Mullen Junior. The kitchen was the venue where the first "audition" of the soon to be formed "Feedback" group took place. Apart from Larry, Paul Hewson, David Evans and Adam Clayton, there were also Dick Evans (David's older brother), Ivan McCormick and Peter Martin in attendance. Later on the newly formed group would rehearse in the back garden or the garden shed.

Birthplace of U2, childhood home of Larry Mullen.
Photo: Mark Chatterton

ROSKILDE FESTIVAL, DENMARK U2 have played this famous Danish festival on just one occasion – on 2nd July 1982 before a crowd of 25,000. The show was recorded by Danish TV.

ROTUNDA HOSPITAL, PARNELL SQUARE, DUBLIN, IRELAND Paul Hewson was born at this Dublin Maternity hospital on 10th May, 1960.

ROUNDHAY PARK, LEEDS, ENGLAND U2 have played in this suburban park in Leeds on two occasions. The first time was on 14th August 1993 – U2's biggest selling concert on the 1993 *Zooropa* tour with a crowd of around 80,000 witnessing the show. As this concert was the nearest one to the Sellafield Nuclear Power station, McPhisto rang John Selwyn Gummer, the British Secretary of State for the Environment, but he was not in.

A second show for the next day was originally planned, but this was cancelled. The band returned here for another concert on 28th August 1997 during the *Pop Mart* tour of Europe playing to over 50,000 fans. During the show, Bono made a few jibes at George Harrison, the former Beatle as in an interview George had criticised the whole *Pop Mart* tour commenting on it being "all about big hats, lemons and egos". "This is for you, George," said Bono raising his middle finger half way through the show.

See also: The Beatles

ROWEN, DEREK See: Guggi

ROWEN, PETER (AKA "RADAR") The younger brother of Guggi appeared on the cover of the *Boy* album and then the *War* album a few years later. Bono said that he was chosen as a way to show how things change. His photograph on *Boy* shows innonence whilst that on *War* shows fear and pain in his eyes as well as a split lip. Pictures of him from the *War* photo session wearing a soldier's helmet were also used on the front and back cover of *the Best Of 1980-1990* compliation album, released in 1998. He was also on the cover of the "U2-3" and "I Will Follow" singles.

See also: Boy / War / U2-3

ROWEN, TREVOR See: Strongman

"ROWENA'S THEME" The opening track off the soundtrack album of *The Captive*. This instrumental piece of music was composed by The Edge and consists mainly of acoustic guitar.

ROYAL DUBLIN SOCIETY HALL, (SIMMONS COURT) DUBLIN, IRELAND U2 played this 5,000 capacity venue on 26th January 1982, the first time a rock concert had been held here. The show marked the live debut of "Tomorrow" from the *October* album. Vincent Kilduff played with the band on the song (as he did on the album). When Bryan Ferry appeared here in November 1988, The Edge made a guest appearance during the show. Then when Bob Dylan played a show here on 4th June 1989 Bono joined him on stage to sing "Knockin' on Heaven's Door" and "Maggie's Farm".

See also: Bob Dylan

ROYAL DUBLIN SOCIETY SHOWGROUNDS, (RDS) DUBLIN, IRELAND This South Dublin venue is more used to horses jumping over fences than rock groups, yet on 17th May 1986 it became the venue for the Self Aid festival which was aimed at promoting jobs

Zooropa '93 at the RDS, Dublin

for Ireland's unemployed youth. U2 were one of the main headlining acts along with Van Morrison, Rory Gallagher and Chris De Burgh. U2 then chose this showground as the venue for the last two dates of the 1993 *Zooropa* Zoo TV tour, which actually finished in Dublin on 27th and 28th August 1993. The 27th August date was U2's first show in Dublin since they had played at the Point in December 1989. For the phone call, Macphisto rang his own home, where his daughter Jordan had left a message for him on the answer-phone: "Daddy, if that's you, we're not coming home until you take your horns off."

For the second night, the final show of the whole tour, the band were a lot more relaxed, despite the

Rotunda Hospital, Dublin. *Photo: Wendy Chatterton*

fact that the show was being broadcast live on the radio to an estimated audience of 400 million listeners. During "Trying To Throw Your Arms Around The World" Bono took a surprise female onto the catwalk to dance with him. It was Naomi Campbell, the then fiancée of bassist Adam Clayton. She didn't film Bono on the camcorder as was traditional in the show, but went over to film Adam. For the final phone call, Macphisto rang the United Nations, but a pre-recorded message said they were "out for lunch".

See also: Self Aid

"ROYAL STATION 4/16" Bono plays harmonica on this track taken from the 1989 album by Melissa Etheridge, *Brave & Crazy*. He appeared under the pseudonym of "Sonny Boy Hewson".

RTE 2 The Irish Radio station based in Dublin. Dave Fanning got a job here after being a pirate DJ and has stayed ever since. Over the years RTE 2 has had the privilege of being the first radio station in the world to play U2 records including *Achtung Baby* and *Pop*.

See also: Dave Fanning

RUISROCK FESTIVAL, TURKU, FINLAND U2's first ever show in Finland took place on 7th August 1982 at the Ruisrock Festival. It was their last performance of the summer, before they returned to the studio to work on the *War* album.

RUMOUR HORN SECTION, THE The horn section on the live version of "Love Rescue Me" at The *Smile Jamaica* concert in London on 16th October 1988.

See also: Smile Jamaica

"RUNNING TO STAND STILL" (*THE JOSHUA TREE* ALBUM TRACK) (4.20) The final track on side one of *The Joshua Tree* album. It starts off quietly with slide guitar from The Edge, followed by some distinctive piano. Like "Bad" it is about Dublin's heroin problem, the "seven towers" referring to the tower blocks of the Ballymun Estate, which backed onto Bono's childhood home. When it was performed on the *Zoo TV* tour, Bono would act out the junkie injecting the heroin into his arm. It was first perfomed live at the State University Activity Center in Tempe, USA on 2nd April 1987 – the first date of the *Joshua Tree* tour. To date an official live audio recording has never been released.

See also: Ballymun Flats.

"RUNNING TO STAND STILL" (LIVE) (*RATTLE & HUM* FILM/VIDEO) This live film version of "Running to Stand Still" was recorded at the Sun Devil Stadium, Tempe, Arizona, USA, on 20th December 1987. It was not included on the *Rattle & Hum* film soundtrack album.

"RUNNING TO STAND STILL" (LIVE) (*ZOO TV LIVE FROM SYDNEY* VIDEO) The fifteenth song on the

video of U2's second Sydney show on 27th November 1993. As the song developed, Bono would dress up in his "army" uniform complete with microphone attached to his hat. He then sang this song from the catwalk/mini-stage acting out injection the of heroin into his arm.

RUSHDIE, SALMAN The critically acclaimed Booker prize-winning novelist who has been a close friend of U2 since the early 1990s. He was actually in Nicaragua in 1986 at the same time as Bono but didn't get to meet him. In 1988 the publication of his book *The Satanic Verses* caused consternation amongst Muslims and led to a "Fatwa" or death sentence being put on him. As a result he had to keep out of the public eye for several years. He did go to see U2 at Earl's Court in London in May 1992 and met the band afterwards. Then in August 1993 he was the recipient of a phone call from Macphisto on stage at Wembley Stadium, London and then suddenly appeared at the back of the stage.

Rushdie was also present a few weeks later at U2's final *Zooropa* show at the RDS showground in Dublin on 28th August. Several times he has been a house guest at Bono's home in Killiney though newspaper reports said that he had actually lived there in secret for several years. U2 and Rushdie then collaborated on the soundtrack to *The Million Dollar Hotel* film, on the track "The Ground Beneath Her Feet" for which Rushdie wrote the lyrics – the first time U2 have recorded a song with lyrics written by someone else. This was a bonus track on the European release of the *All That You Can't Leave Behind* album.

RUSSELL, REBECCA EVANS One of the singers who provided backing vocals on "When Love Comes to Town" recorded at Sun Studios in Memphis in 1987.

RX See: Rapid Exteriors

SABER, DANNY The producer of albums by such artists as the Rolling Stones, David Bowie and Black Grape who, in 1997, remixed U2's cover of the Beatles' song "Happiness Is A Warm Gun".

SAINT ANDREW'S CHURCH OF IRELAND SCHOOL, MALAHIDE, IRELAND The primary school that Adam Clayton first attended in Malahide after he had moved to Ireland from Oxfordshire in 1965. In 1968 he left to go to the Castle Park Prep School in Dalkey where he would become a boarder. David Evans also attended this school from 1966 to 1971.

St. Andrew's School, Malahide.
Photo: Mark Chatterton

SAINT COLUMBA'S COLLEGE, RATHFARNHAM, DUBLIN, IRELAND This was the private secondary school on the southern edge of Dublin that Adam Clayton attended after he left Castle Park School and before he attended Mount Temple Comprehensive. He was a pupil from 1973 up until 1976 when he was taken out by his parents after breaking the rules on several occasions. It was here that he first started playing bass guitar and joined a group through the influence of his friend, John Lesley.

See also: John Lesley

SAINT DAVID'S HALL, CARDIFF, WALES When U2 played here on 11th March 1983, well into their career, it was only the second time that they had played a gig in the Welsh capital. The concert was watched by a full house of 3,000 fans and at the end Bono got a girl on stage to sing "Land of My Fathers" to The Edge, as his parents came from Wales.

SAINT FINTAN'S NATIONAL SCHOOL, DUBLIN, IRELAND Feedback's final live appearance took place here before they became The Hype. They were accom-

panied by Stella McCormick, Ivan's Sister, and her friend Stella Dunne, who contributed backing vocals and flute. The gig took place on 11th April 1977 and included a version of the Moody Blues' "Nights In White Satin".

See also: The Hype

SAINT FRANCIS XAVIER HALL See: SFX Centre, Dublin

SAINT JAKOB'S FUSSBALL STADION, BASEL, SWITZERLAND U2 have played this Swiss football stadium on three occasions. The first time (1st June 1985) was at the *Rock In Basel* festival, which was attended by 40,000 fans. Also on the bill were Gianna Nannini, The Alarm, Rick Springfield, Joe Cocker and headlining act Chris De Burgh. U2 were second on the bill. U2 next played here during the European leg of the *Joshua Tree* tour on 21st June 1987 with The Pretenders and Lou Reed supporting them. Finally, the band played here on 30th June 1993 during the *Zooropa* leg of the *Zoo TV* tour with the Velvet Underground as the support act.

SAINT PATRICK'S SECONDARY SCHOOL, DUBLIN, IRELAND The secondary school that Bono attended once he had left Glasnevin National School in Drumcondra. He left by "mutual agreement" after he had thrown some dog droppings at his Spanish teacher.

SAINT STEPHEN'S GREEN DUBLIN IRELAND The park south of the city centre of Dublin at the end of Grafton Street, near to the Dandelion Green car park where U2 played six times in 1979. It was also the place where on 19th March 2000, Bono and The Edge grazed some sheep as part of their right as Freemen of the City of Dublin.

"SALOME" ("EVEN BETTER THAN THE REAL THING" SINGLE) (4.32) This song was included on the "Even Better Than The Real thing" single, released in June 1992. It was recorded at STS studios in Dublin and produced by Paul Barrett and U2. Salome is the name of the dancer in the court of King Herod who is said to have asked for the head of John The Baptist on a plate.

"SALOME" (ZOOROMANCER REMIX) ("WHO'S GONNA RIDE YOUR WILD HORSES" SINGLE / *MELON* CD): This remix appeared on the fan club remixes CD called *Melon*, as well as the limited edition CD of "Who's Gonna Ride Your Wild Horses". It was remixed by Pete Heller and Terry Farley.

SAM BOYD SILVER BOWL / SAM BOYD STADIUM, LAS VEGAS, NEVADA, USA The first time U2 played here, on 12th November 1992, it was to a half full stadium during the *Outside Broadcast Zoo TV* tour of North America (second leg). At the show Bono remarked that Las Vegas "is even more Zoo TV than

Zoo TV!" which is probably why the venue was chosen as the opening date of the *Pop Mart* which began here on 25th April 1997. In fact this show was U2's first live show since Tokyo in Japan on 10th December 1993, a gap of well over three years, the longest break in live U2 shows ever.

On the days leading up to this concert the band had been rehearsing and the stage crew had been constantly checking the equipment. This included erecting and dismantling the giant props that came with the show. During the testing of the lights, local residents rang the emergency services to say they had seen a UFO in the vicinity.

The first night show was a 38,000 sell-out with several celebrities in the audience including Christian Slater, Mel Gibson and Pamela Anderson, as well as the world's media. The show did suffer from some first night problems including a stop-start version of "Staring At The Sun", which the press picked up on, but overall the feeling was one of amazement at such a colourful and exciting spectacle. The following songs were performed live for the first time: Mofo, Do You Feel Loved, Last Night On Earth, Gone, If God Will Send His Angels, Staring At The Sun, Miami, Please, Discotheque, If You Wear That Velvet Dress, Hold Me Thrill Me Kiss Me Kill Me.

Pop Mart tour opening night set: Mofo, I Will Follow, Even Better Than The Real Thing, Do You Feel Loved, Pride (In The Name of Love), I Still Haven't Found What I'm Looking For, Last Night On Earth, Gone, Until The End of The World, If God Will Send His Angels, Staring At The Sun, Daydream Believer, Miami, Bullet The Blue Sky, Please, Where The Streets Have No Name. Encores: Discotheque, If You Wear That Velvet Dress, With Or Without You, Hold Me Thrill Me Kiss Me Kill Me, Mysterious Ways, One.

See also: *Pop Mart* tour

SAMPSON, JOHN One of the security team who has special responsibility for Bono.

SAN REMO FESTIVAL, ITALY At the 2000 festival on 26th February, Bono and The Edge performed "All I Want Is You" and "The Ground Beneath Her Feet", the first time the latter song had been played live. Bono spoke to the crowd in Italian and publicly thanked the Pope and the Italian Prime Minister, Massimo D'Alema, for helping to ease the burden of third world debt.

SARAJEVO This was the city in the former republic of Yugoslavia with which U2 set up a satellite link during the *Zooropa* leg of the Zoo TV tour. The idea first came to Bono when he was interviewed by American film maker Bill Carter, before the show in Verona, Italy on 3rd July 1993. He told Bono that

he was working in a relief camp in Sarajevo, a city which was besieged in the Bosnian war, and mentioned that there was a dance club under the buildings where the young people play rock music as loudly as possible to drown out the noise of the bombs going off.

After the show, Bill Carter told Bono and The Edge more about the situation there. They then decided that they had to do something about Sarajevo. At first Bono had the idea of taking all of U2 through the battlelines and into the besieged city to play a concert there. He managed to persuade the other members of U2 and Paul McGuinness, but in the end Bill Carter convinced Bono that this was not the best thing to do and a satellite link-up would probably create just as much publicity. As a result a transmitter was taken into the besieged city and starting with the gig at Bologna on 17th July, there was a live satellite link-up in the middle of the show where various inhabitants were able to tell the crowd what conditions were like for them. This continued for each successive *Zooropa* show until the 12th August show at Wembley Stadium when the last satellite link-up was made. Naturally the link-up with Sarajevo provoked a lot of criticism from the British press who said that a rock 'n' roll show was not the place for politics – but the link-up did give the besieged citizens of Sarajevo some much needed publicity about their plight.

Bono watches the Sarajevo sattelite link on the giant screen, Wembley Stadium, 12/8/93
Photo: Claire Bolton

The *Passengers* album featured a song called "Miss Sarajevo" which was inspired by the beauty contests held during the siege, and was used in the film of the same name by Bill Carter. Later, after the *Zoo TV* tour had ended, Bono, The Edge and Brian Eno performed the song at a special concert which had been set up by Luciano Pavarotti in Modena, Italy in aid of the War Child charity. As the war in Bosnia finally came to an end in 1995 and the siege of Sarajevo was lifted, Bono and Ali were able to spend New Year of 1996 in Sarajevo as guests of the new government.

Then on 23rd September 1997 U2 finally got to play in Sarajevo as a date on the *Pop Mart* tour had been specially put aside for the city. Before the concert all the members of U2 met the President of Bosnia-Herzegovina, President Izetbegovic. As Bono said in an interview before the show, "Sarajevo was a very sophisticated city. Before the war, music was everything to them. After the war, it's going to be the same." In August 2000, Bono again visited Sarajevo, this time with his family, when he took part in the Sarajevo Film Festival promoting *The Million Dollar Hotel* film.

See also: Bill Carter / Kosevo Stadium / Miss Sarajevo / Wembley Stadium

SARATOGA RACEWAY, SARATOGA SPRINGS, NEW YORK STATE, USA U2 played to a 30,000 crowd here on 18th August 1992 during the *Outside Broadcast* leg of the *Zoo TV* tour. This was the first of several shows on this leg of the tour that did not sell out.

"SATELLITE OF LOVE" ("ONE" SINGLE) (4.00) This Lou Reed composition was originally on his *Transformer* album. Bono had sung snippets of it as early as 1985, during "Bad" at *Live Aid* for instance. U2 chose it for their *Zoo TV* shows as it tied in with the theme of satellites beaming out TV signals. It became a regular live favourite during the *Zoo TV* tour, being one of the songs that U2 sang acoustically from the B-stage. A Trabant over the stage was illuminated like a satellite during the song.

The studio version was recorded at STS studios with The Edge and Paul Barrett producing. It appeared on the B-side of the 12-inch/CD version of the "One" single (12IS515), released in February 1992. Three other versions were included in the film of *The Million Dollar Hotel*. It was first played live on the opening date of the *Zoo TV* tour at the Lakeland Arena, Florida, USA on 29th February 1992.

"SATELLITE OF LOVE" (*THE MILLION DOLLAR HOTEL* SOUNDTRACK ALBUM) (4.11) This version of "Satellite of Love" was performed by Milla Jovovich with the MDH Band.

"SATELLITE OF LOVE" (REPRISE) (1.06) (*THE MILLION DOLLAR HOTEL* SOUNDTRACK ALBUM) This version was performed by the MDH Band featuring Daniel Lanois, Bill Frisell and Greg Cohen.

"SATELLITE OF LOVE" (DANNY SABER REMIX) (*THE MILLION DOLLAR HOTEL* SOUNDTRACK ALBUM) (5.13) This remix version of "Satellite of Love" was performed by Milla Jovovich with Jon Hassell and Danny Saber.

"SATELLITE OF LOVE" (LIVE) ("PEACE TOGETHER" ALBUM TRACK) This live version was recorded on 16th October 1992 at the Texas Stadium, Dallas, USA and featured U2 at the gig and Lou Reed on the video screen in a pre-recorded segment. It was released in July 1993 on the *Peace Together* album, an album featuring a mixture of Irish and British artists, who sang songs about peace to raise funds for cross community projects for the youth of Northern Ireland.

SATURDAY NIGHT LIVE U2 appeared on this famous American TV show on Saturday 9th December 2000. They performed "Beautiful Day" and "Elevation".

"SAVE THE CHILDREN" The song that Bono recorded "electronically" with the late Marvin Gaye in 1995. It was taken from the album *Inner City Blues - The Music of Marvin Gaye* and a single release reached 106 in the US charts.

See also: Marvin Gaye

"SAVE THE CHILDREN" (PROMOTIONAL VIDEO) A promotional video of this song featuring Bono and Marvin Gaye was made in 1995.

SAVE THE YUPPIE CONCERT, SAN FRANCISCO CALIFORNIA, USA This famous U2 free concert took place towards the end of the American leg of the *Joshua Tree* tour on 11th November 1987, at the Justin Herman Plaza in San Francisco's financial district. This was a few weeks after the "Black Friday" stock market crash which had repercussions for the financial world for many months afterwards. It was this tenuous connection and the situation of the concert that prompted Bono to quip at the start of the show that it was a "Save The Yuppies" concert. The concert was only announced on the morning of the show, just two hours before it was due to start. It was organised by legendary concert promoter Bill Graham, who had put on some of the many free concerts that had taken place in San Francisco during the "Summer of Love" twenty years earlier.

The concert was filmed by Phil Joanou and recorded by Jimmy Iovine. Only part of it was actually shown in the film *Rattle & Hum*. This was the band rehearsing "All Along the Watchtower", just before they hit the stage, the singing of that opening song, and the infamous spray-painting of the statue at the Vaillancourt Fountain, with the words "Rock & Roll Stop the Traffic". For this act of "vandalism" Bono was given a misdemeanour charge for "malicious mischief", which could have resulted in a $1,000 dollar fine or one year in jail. Bono claimed that he was just an artist expressing himself, and Mayor Feinstein of San Francisco agreed that U2's free gig was sufficient penalty for what he had done. Bono then paid for the statue to be cleaned up and after the sculptor said that what Bono did was in keeping with the spirit of his work, the police dropped the charges. Around 20,000 people attended this concert. The set list was: All Along the Watchtower, Sunday Bloody Sunday, Out of Control, People Get Ready, Trip Through Your Wires, Silver & Gold, Helter Skelter, Help and Pride.

See also: Bill Graham / Rock 'n' Roll Stops the Traffic / Armand Vaillancourt

SAVOY CINEMA, DUBLIN, IRELAND This was the cinema in Dublin's O'Connell Street where the world premiere of *Rattle & Hum* took place on 27th October 1988. Tickets for the premiere cost £40, with the proceeds being given to a homeless charity called "People in Need". Around 5,000 fans gathered outside the cinema in Dublin's main street. Shortly before arriving at the cinema, U2 played two songs for the crowd on a specially constructed stage. They were "When Love comes to Town" and "I Still Haven't Found What I'm Looking For". After the film had been shown, U2 came out and played "Angel of Harlem" and "Stand By Me". This scenario was repeated at the premieres that took place in Madrid and Los Angeles, but not in London, where the police refused to grant permission.

SCANNELL, DONAL A journalist and TV broadcaster who has worked on RTE's *Late Late Show*. His multimedia company 33:45 were responsible for the documentary about the making of the "Beautiful Day" video.

See also: Beautiful Day

"SCARLET" (*OCTOBER* ALBUM TRACK) (2.20) Before the album was released, "Scarlet" had been mooted as a possible title for the *October* album, although it is one of the weaker tracks – Bono just sings the lyric 'rejoice' all the way through the song, which is dominated by Larry's loud drum sound. The song has never been played live apart from on a BBC Radio session for the Kid Jensen programme on 14th October 1981.

SCHOO, DALLAS The Edge's guitar technician who has also worked with Prince and The Eagles. He has been with the band since the *Joshua Tree* tour, during which he once appeared on stage dressed as a Dalton Brother at the Coliseum in Hampton, Virginia on 12th December 1987.

See also: Coliseum Hampton

SCOIL COLMCILLE, DUBLIN, IRELAND This was the school that Larry attended in Marlborough Street, Dublin where Gaelic was the main language spoken in lessons. This was as a preparation for University where Irish was a pre-requisite to gain entry. He attended here between the ages of six and eleven before moving to Mount Temple.

SCOTT, JAKE The American film maker who directed version 1 of the promo video for "Staring At the Sun".

SEC (SCOTTISH EXHIBITION CENTRE), GLASGOW, SCOTLAND U2 have played the Scottish Exhibition Centre on five occasions. They first came here during the *Joshua Tree* tour on 29th and 30th July 1987. At the first show a roadie rushed on stage to tell Bono that their single "I Still Haven't Found What I'm Looking For" had just gone to number 1 in the American charts, so Bono immediately told the audience to loud cheers. During the sound check for the second show, the band recorded "Christmas, (Baby Please Come Home)" for the 'Special Olympics' benefit album, which was being put together by producer Jimmy Iovine.

With a mobile recording unit at the venue, the second gig was recorded but none of the resulting tracks have ever seen the light of day. U2 then played this 10,000 capacity venue during the *Zoo TV* tour on

The Edge's long-serving guitar-tech, Dallas Schoo, February 2001. *Photo: Claire Bolton*

18th June 1992. This was to have been the final date of the European leg of the *Zoo TV* tour, but due to the cancellation of the Stop Sellafield demonstration, the Manchester G-Mex show took its place. During "Mysterious Ways" when the belly dancer got up to dance on the mini stage, several roadies joined in dressed up in wigs and skirts.

Two last minute additions to the European leg of the *Elevation Tour* took place here on the 27th and 28th August, in between the two concerts at Slane Castle.

"SECONDS" (*WAR* ALBUM TRACK) (3.11) The second track on the first side of the *War* album is dominated by The Edge's acoustic guitar and Adam's hypnotic bass line. The lyrics talk about how easy it is to die – especially when a bomb goes off, be it terrorist bomb (as in Northern Ireland) or nuclear device, both of which were in the headlines when this song was written. Halfway through the song there is a short break when an excerpt from the film *Soldier Girls* is played and female soldiers can be heard singing. The song made its live debut on 26th February 1983 at the Caird Hall, Dundee, Scotland on the first date of the European leg of the *War* tour.

See also: Soldier Girls documentary

SEDNAOUI, STEPHANE This film maker directed two U2 promo videos. His first was for "Mysterious Ways", shot in Morocco in October 1991 and featuring a belly dancer. This eventually led to a belly dancer getting up on stage to dance on most of the shows on the *Zoo TV* tour. His second promo video was for "Discotheque" in 1997 featuring the band dessed as The Village People. There were also two remix versions of this video covering the David Morales and the Steve Osborne mix.

See also: "Discotheque" and "Mysterious Ways" promo videos

SEEZER, MAURICE Maurice Seezer is a pianist who has often accompanied Gavin Friday at his one-man shows. Along with Bono and Gavin Friday, he co-wrote the soundtrack of the film *In The Name Of The Father*.

SEISCOM DELTA The oil exploration company that had offices in Dublin. Larry worked briefly as a messenger here on leaving Mount Temple Comprehensive before U2 took off. Whilst he worked during the day the other members of the band would rehearse until he could join them. At one stage the other three were considering getting another drummer for the band as they were not able to practice as much as they wished. In the end Larry gave up his job with Seiscom Delta.

SELF-AID The concert that took place at the RDS showground in Dublin on 17th May 1986. It was inspired by *Live Aid* a year earlier and was designed to help the young unemployed of Ireland. Virtually all the big Irish bands (and a few from England) played for free at the festival including U2, Clannad, The Chieftains, Van Morrison, The Pogues, The Boomtown Rats, Rory Gallagher and Chris de Burgh. All the money raised would go to help Ireland's unemployed which at the time had reached nearly a quarter of a million people.

As with *Live Aid* there was a strict 15 minute slot for all the twenty-seven bands and artists performing on the revolving stage. The show started at noon with and went on throughout the afternoon and evening with this running order: Brush Shields, Bagatelle, Blue In Heaven, Stockton's Wing, In Tua Nua, Clannad, Big Self, Les Enfants, The Chieftains, Chris Rea, Freddie White, Those Nervous Animals, The Pogues, Cactus World News, Scullion, De Dannann, The Fountainhead, Paul Brady, The Boomtown Rats (their final gig), Auto de Fe, Moving Hearts, Rory Gallagher, Christy Moore, Elvis Costello, Chris De Burgh, Van Morrison, U2.

U2's set was as follows: C'Mon Everybody, Pride (In The Name Of Love), Sunday Bloody Sunday, Maggie's Farm, Bad. Straight after U2 had finished, the remaining members of Thin Lizzy came on stage to play as a tribute to Phil Lynott who had died earlier in the year. They played several Lizzy songs with various artists from the day singing the vocals. Bono sang along on "Whiskey In The Jar". Finally the show finished with everyone who had taken part singing the Self Aid anthem "Let's Make It Work".

The whole event was broadcast live on RTE TV and Radio, attracting a lot of criticism from the Irish press and some opposition political groups, who felt that it was the government's responsibility to help the unemployed of Ireland and not the musicians. They argued that with 50 people chasing every job that was going, *Self Aid* would not do much to help. Thus the slogan 'Self Aid makes it work' became corrupted to 'Self Aid makes it worse!' In particular, on the eve of the show a magazine called *In Dublin* printed a critique of Self Aid written by Eamonn McCann. (This was later reprinted as an appendix in the *Unforgettable Fire* book by Eamon Dunphy.) The magazine cover featured a picture of Bono and the headlines "The Great Self-Aid Farce" and "Rock Against the People".

Clearly this upset many of those involved in Self Aid and in particular, Bono, who hit back in "Bad" during U2's set, by adapting a line from Elton John's "Candle In The Wind": "They crawl out of the woodwork onto the pages of cheap Dublin magazines." However, as a result of Self Aid over 1300 jobs were created and over half a million pounds worth of donations were collected.

See also: Royal Dublin Showground / Boomtown Rats / Thin Lizzy

SELF AID BAND The group of Irish musicians who got together in much the same way as Band Aid to record a song written by Paul Doran called "Let's Make It Work" for the *Self Aid* cause. Larry represented U2 on the single. The song was performed as the finale at the *Self Aid* concert.

SELLAFIELD NUCLEAR POWER STATION, CUMBRIA, ENGLAND This major British nuclear power station was built in the 1950s and was originally called Calder Hall. It had been subject to a number of "leaks" over the years, as well as discharging "waste" into the Irish Sea. In the 1990s a second power station, THORP, was being built to take in nuclear waste from all over the world thus making it "the nuclear dustbin of the world". U2 were due to protest against the building of THORP on Saturday 20th June 1992, but BNFL took out an injunction against them and Greenpeace to prevent them from holding the rally. Instead, U2 played a special "Stop Sellafield" show at Manchester's G-Mex Centre on 19th June and then early on the morning of 20th June, U2 and several journalists came ashore below the low-water mark on the beach in front of Sellafield to make their protest.

See also: G-Mex Centre / Stop Sellafield / Greenpeace

"SEND IN THE CLOWNS" A song written by Stephen Sondheim that Judy Collins had taken into the UK top ten in 1975. Bono would insert lines from this song in the live version of "The Electric Co." during the U2 set of the early 1980s. Because lines of this song were included in "The Electric Co" version on the *Under A Blood Red Sky* album, a court case resulted for infringement of copyright. In the out of court settlement, it is believed that U2 had to pay $50,000 compensation. Subsequent copies of the album had the offending lines removed.

See also: The Electric Co (Live)

"SENSE OF IRELAND FESTIVAL" A four-night festival held from 16th to 19th March 1980 in various London venues. It was called *The Sounds of Ireland* and was set up by an organisation called "The Sense of Ireland". U2 played on the final night – 19th March 1980 – at the Acklam Hall in West London along with the Virgin Prunes as support to Berlin. Other Irish artists included Rory Gallagher and The Atrix.

See also: Acklam Hall

SEPTEMBER 1913 A poem by WB Yeats that Bono has recited on stage at U2 concerts. He first used this poem at the Abbey Theatre in Dublin in 1989.

See also: Abbey Theatre / WB Yeats

SFX CENTRE, DUBLIN, IRELAND The SFX Centre is also known as the St. Francis Xavier Centre and was the venue where most of the scenes for the promo video of "Pride" (version 1) were shot in 1984. Before that U2 had played three nights at this 1,200 capacity venue on 22nd, 23rd and 24th December 1982 as the final dates of pre-*War* tour of 1982. At the shows, U2 were joined on stage by Steve Wickham, who had played violin on "Sunday Bloody Sunday" on *War* and Vincent Kilduff, who had played uillean pipes on "Tomorrow" on *October*.

The SFX Centre, Dublin. *Photo: Mark Chatterton*

"SHADOWS & TALL TREES" (*BOY* ALBUM TRACK) (4.36) The final track on side two of the *Boy* album. The title was taken from a chapter in William Golding's novel *Lord of the Flies*, though the image is said to have come from the tall electricity pylons near Bono's house in Cedarwood Road. The "Mrs Brown" and her washing in the song referred to a neighbour called Mrs Byrne, who was Iris Hewson's best friend. The song was one of the first songs the band recorded, being first recorded in November 1978 for their second demo at Keystone Studios in Dublin with Barry Devlin producing. This album version features The Edge on acoustic guitar for the only time on the album, giving the track a more polished sound when compared with the more basic rock/punk tracks on the album. The producer was Steve Lillywhite. It was a regular song in the early U2 set from 1978 onwards.

SHALOM GROUP The Charismatic Christian Group led by Dennis Sheedy that used to meet in a house on the North Circular Road in Dublin. Bono, The Edge, Larry and most of the Village had all become members. The term Shalom was Hebrew for "Peace". It was Village members Pod and Guggi who first encountered Dennis Sheedy in McDonalds in Grafton Street, Dublin. He invited them to his bible study and prayer meeting. They were followed by Bono, then Larry and The Edge, Ali, Aislinn, Gavin, and Maeve O'Regan. After a time the group moved to a new meeting place in Templeogue, South Dublin, where they would meet twice a week for a meeting lasting anything up to three hours. They would sing hymns and modern choruses, study the Bible and pray out loud if they felt moved enough. Some even spoke in tongues – a practice that dated back to the New Testament times.

Eventually Bono and The Edge were baptised in the sea by full immersion. In time the pull of the Shalom group started to cause tension within the band especially over the question of whether it was right for Christians to be in a rock 'n' roll band (playing the music of the devil). This tension came to a head around the time of the recording of the *October* album. Earlier in the year there had been strain on tour when the three members of U2 who were in Shalom would sit in a "holy huddle" reading the bible and praying whilst the rest of the entourage was shut out from their lives. One by one, The Edge, Larry and Bono had to make a decision – which came first? U2 or Shalom?

Guggi left first, followed by Gavin and his girlfriend Rene, who felt that the group was taking over people's lives – it was OK to join in but they were being criticised for what they wore and the music they (The Virgin Prunes) played. Larry was the first member of U2 to leave, citing the group's bigotry as his main reason for going. The Edge went the other way deciding that God must come first and so he told Bono that he was leaving the band. About a week later he relented. Bono also had grave doubts about being in a rock 'n' roll band, but eventually he left Shalom like the others putting his energies into wider causes like human rights via Amnesty International and the environment via Greenpeace.

See also: Charismatic Christianity

SHEEHAN, DENNIS Over the years Dennis Sheehan has been in many ways U2's chief roadie. He has been with the band on every tour from 1982 onwards. Dennis was born in the South East of Ireland in County Waterford and brought up by his grandparents as his parents had gone to England to work during the war. When he was a teenager, he joined his parents in London. Eventually he joined a group called the Carnivals who had moderate success touring Britain as a support act to some the bigger names of the 1960s. When the band split up, he got the job of tour manager for Jimmy James and the Vagabonds, followed by Stone the Crows (featuring Maggie Bell).

Then he was taken on as Led Zeppelin's advance man, which meant organising the hotels, travel and equipment arrangements for the band on the road. After several years working with Led Zeppelin, Dennis worked as tour manager for several other bands before he and Paul McGuinness met to discuss the possibility of him working with U2. He joined the band at the beginning of the 1980s and has been their tour manager ever since. It is his responsibility to check out all aspects of a U2 tour before it has even started. This includes checking out every venue, each hotel and all the travel arrangements not only for the band and the crew but also for the many other people who are part of the U2 entourage, such as the caterers and drivers.

Dennis has also had to look after Bono on stage in the early 1980s (along with Steve Iredale) which meant following his every move, such as climbing up lighting rigs and onto balconies. Once this went disastrously wrong at the Sports Arena in Los Angeles, ending in both Bono and Dennis jumping into the crowd below. Dennis can be seen in action on the videos *Under A Blood Red Sky* and *Rattle & Hum*.

See also: Sports Arena, Los Angeles / Led Zeppelin

SHERIDAN, JIM The Irish film director who came to international prominence with his film *My Left Foot*. U2 first came across Jim and his brother Peter at the Project Arts Centre in Dublin, a venue which put on the occasional rock concert in addition to its regular plays.

Jim Sheridan also directed the film *In The Name of The Father*, which was about the case of the "Guildford Four", four Irishmen wrongly imprisoned for bombing that English town. Bono, along with Gavin Friday and Maurice Seezer wrote three of the songs that were used in the film's soundtrack. These were "In The Name of The Father", "Billy Boola" and "You Made Me The Thief Of Your Heart".

See also: In The Name of the Father / Project Arts Centre

"SHE'S A MYSTERY TO ME" A song on the 1989 Roy Orbison album *Mystery Girl* which was written for Roy by Bono and The Edge. The song was originally written in 1986 and was recorded as a possible U2 release at the Sun Studios session in November 1987. Bono plays guitar and sings on the Roy Orbison version. It is said to have been inspired by the film *Blue Velvet* in which Roy sings "In Dreams".

See also: Roy Orbison

SHIRLEY, SOPHIE The Religious Education teacher at Mount Temple Comprehensive in Dublin who taught Paul Hewson. She also ran the school's Christian Union, which Bono started attending after his mother's death in 1974.

SHORTALL, NIALL U2's sound engineer in the early days. He was eventually replaced by Joe O'Hehirly.

"SHOW ME THE WAY" The top 10 hit by Peter Frampton was the song that Feedback played at the talent contest at Mount Temple School in the autumn of

1976. As the Hype, the early U2 continued to play it at their gigs until their own compositions led to it being dropped from the set.

SHRINE AUDITORIUM, LOS ANGELES, CALIFORNIA, USA U2 performed "Beautiful Day" here at the "My VH-1 Awards" show on 30th November 2000.

SIGHTINGS OF BONO (FILM) A short seven minute film made in Dublin in September 2000 for the Internet website allirelandmusic.com. The film tells the story of a girl called Ellen (played by Marcella Plunkett) who sees Bono everywhere until she eventually meets him in the shop where she works in Dublin. The film was adapted by Kathy Gilfillan from an original story by Gerry Beirne and was produced by Parallel Films. **Website:** www.allirelandmusic.com.

SILAS, LOUIL JUNIOR The artist who remixed the following U2 tracks: "When Love Comes To Town" (Kingdom Mix), "God Part II" (Hard Metal Dance Mix) and "Desire" (Hollywood Remix).

"SILVER & GOLD" ("WHERE THE STREETS HAVE NO NAME" SINGLE B-SIDE) (4.36) This track is on the B-side of the 7 inch and 12 inch versions of the "Where The Streets Have No Name" singles. The 12 inch and CD version also include the tracks "Sweetest Thing" and "Race Against Time". This version was recorded at STS studios in Dublin in June 1987 in between shows on the *Joshua Tree* tour. It was produced by U2, the first time the whole band had been credited with production duties. It was also included on the B-sides CD that came with early releases of *The Best of 1980-1990*. The song was first performed live at the NEC in Birmingham, England on 3rd August 1987.

"SILVER & GOLD" (*SUN CITY* ALBUM TRACK) Bono had flown to New York City in August 1985 to take part in the "Artists United Against Apartheid" project, ostensibly to add vocals to the "Sun City" track, but he ended up going to see the Rolling Stones in the studio at the invitation of former J. Geils band member, Peter Wolf. After hearing Richards and Jagger going through some old blues numbers and Everly Brothers standards, Bono was asked to play one of 'his songs'.

Not having the rest of U2 with him, Bono felt that he didn't have anything suitable, always relying on the music that the other three members made to blend in his vocals. He went back to his hotel room, and in a mixture of rage and worthlessness wrote "Silver & Gold" and "This I've Got to Stop". He then went back to the studio and recorded "Silver & Gold" with Keith Richards, Ronnie Wood and Robert Palmer backing him. This late edition to the *Sun City* album was written as an anti-apartheid song through the eyes of a black man imprisoned for his colour.

See also: Artists United Against Apartheid / Little Steven

"SILVER & GOLD" (LIVE) (*RATTLE & HUM* ALBUM TRACK) (5.50) This live version of "Silver & Gold" is the fourth track on the second side of Disc One of the *Rattle & Hum* soundtrack album. It was recorded live at the McNichol's Arena, Denver, Colorado on 8th November 1987. It is memorable for the "speech" that Bono makes in the song about South Africa and the immortal line, "Am I Bugging ya? I don't mean to bug ya! OK Edge. Play the blues!"

"SILVER & GOLD": (LIVE) (*RATTLE & HUM* FILM/VIDEO) The film version of "Silver & Gold" was shot at the McNichol's Arena, Denver, Colorado on 8th November 1987. It was filmed in black and white and shows the band in aggressive form, in particular Bono, who throws his microphone to the floor straight after his anti-apartheid speech.

SILVERDOME, PONTIAC, MICHIGAN, USA U2 have played this 50,000 capacity indoor stadium near Detroit on three occasions. The first, on 30th April 1987, was their first ever stadium show as headlining artists. In fact this was the only stadium date on the first American leg of the *Joshua Tree* tour and several journalists were sceptical that U2 could pull it off in a venue of this size. Their concerns were unfounded though as the critics concluded that it was a resounding success, especially in the aspect of the band reaching out to the audience.

U2 returned to this Detroit venue during the *Outside Broadcast* leg of the *Zoo TV* tour on 9th September 1992. For this show, the MTV cameras were present as the show was on at the same time as the annual MTV awards ceremony taking place in Los Angeles. After the end of "The Fly", the two shows were linked by satellite with Garth of *Wayne's World* fame being the compere in L.A. After some small talk, Garth played along on drums to "Even Better Than The Real Thing". Later, the MTV cameras entered U2's dressing room where it was announced that they had won the award for the Best Group Video for "Even Better Than The Real Thing".

The band then made another appearance here on 31st October 1997 during the *Pop Mart* tour of North America (second leg). As it was Larry's 36th birthday the audience sang "Happy Birthday" to him, not once but twice. The second time was as the karaoke number and when Larry arrived at the B-stage there was a birthday cake waiting for him, carried by his long-time partner, Anne Acheson. As it was Halloween, many fans were dressed in costumes. Bono invited some of them up onto the stage to dance during "Mysterious Ways".

See also: MTV

"SILVER LINING" An early U2 song that evolved into "11 O'clock Tick Tock".

SIMPLE MINDS The Scottish rock group who came to prominence in the early 1980s at the same time as U2. They shared the same bill as U2 on several occasions including the Punchestown Racecourse in Dublin on 18th July 1982 and Werchter Festival on 3rd July 1983. At this latter festival, Jim Kerr, the lead singer with Simple Minds, came on stage to sing with Bono their song, "Someone, Somewhere, In Summertime". Then he introduced the members of U2 to the audience. In January 1985 at a Simple Minds gig at Barrowlands in Glasgow, Scotland, Bono appeared on stage with the group to sing "Take Me To The River" and "Light My Fire".

See also: Mrs Christine Kerr

SIMPSONS, THE U2 made a special appearance in this popular cartoon show as cartoon characters of themselves. They appeared in the 200th episode entitled "Trash of the Titans" and were seen performing their *Pop Mart* show in Springfield and drinking in Moe's bar. They had been asked by Homer Simpson to help support him in his campaign to become Sanitation Commissioner for Springfield. It was first shown on American TV on 26th April 1998 and then on other TV stations around the world. The band members even did their own voice-overs, where they sang some lines from "The Garbageman's Song".

Paul McGuinness was also featured saying the line, "Where the hell have you been?" The U2 song used was the version of "Pride" from *Rattle & Hum*. Right at the end there was a small scene where Adam's famous "spoon collection" was mentioned. The episode was released on the video *The Simpson's Greatest Hits*, which was given a 12 certificate, presumably because The Edge said "Fuck" on it. "The Garbageman's Song" can be found on the album *Go Simpsononic*.

SINATRA, FRANK Remembered as being one of the biggest entertainers of the twentieth century, Sinatra's baritone voice and unique vocal delivery led to a career stretching from the 1940s right through to the 1990s. Not only did he record such hits as "Young At Heart", "Witchcraft" and "Strangers In The Night", but he also had a parallel career in films, winning an Oscar in *From Here To Eternity* in 1953.

Although his music might seem world's apart from that of U2, the connection came in 1993 when Bono was invited to take part the *Duets* album project in 1993, recording his part for "I've Got You Under My Skin" at STS Studios in Dublin in September. A few months later, in November, Bono flew over to meet Frank in Palm Springs, California, where he lived, for a video shoot for the song. This only took a few

minutes as Sinatra is said to have walked out after having his photograph taken. Bono had written a song for Frank called "Two Shots of Happy, One Shot of Sad" which he sang for him at Frank's house, though Sinatra never got to record it.

Bono also gave the introductory speech to Frank at the 1994 Grammy Awards in New York where Frank received the "Living Legend" award. The speech and Bono's own musings on Frank as a particular hero of his were published in a book called *Idle Worship*. The following year U2 performed "Two Shots of Happy, One Shot of Sad" on film, at a television tribute to celebrate Frank's 80th birthday. They then recorded the song in 1997: it was included on the single of "If God Will Send His Angels". Frank Sinatra died in 1998.

See also: Grammys / I've Got You Under My Skin / Two Shots of Happy, One Shot of Sad

"SIXTY SECONDS IN KINGDOM COME" ("THE UNFORGETTABLE FIRE" SINGLE B-SIDE) (3.15) This instrumental track is one of those rare U2 tracks that is only available on one particular record, namely the double 7 inch pack of the single, "The Unforgettable Fire" (ISD 220).

SKYDOME, TORONTO, CANADA U2 played two sell out dates to over 50,000 fans each night on 26th and 27th October 1997 during the *Pop Mart* tour of North America. The first show was the first date of the third leg of the tour taking in Canada, Mexico and the USA. The second show marked the final appearance of Howie B on the DJ rostrum as after the show he was caught at the airport with some marijuana on him and was immediately deported back to the UK.

SLANE CASTLE, SLANE, COUNTY MEATH, IRELAND This was the setting where much of *The Unforgettable Fire* album was recorded in May 1984, utilising the ballroom which had a unique sound. Situated in County Meath, by the banks of the River Boyne about 30 miles north of Dublin, Slane Castle is owned by Lord Henry Mountcharles. This is where, in May 1984, U2 recorded much of their *The Unforgettable Fire* album, Approximately two thirds of the castle was destroyed by fire on 21st November 1991, though the famous ballroom where U2 did much of their recording was saved. Much of the inside of the castle can be seen in the U2 video *The Unforgettable Fire Collection*. The castle has since been restored to its former glory.

See also: Lord Henry Mountcharles

SLANE CASTLE FESTIVAL, COUNTY MEATH, IRELAND The grounds of Slane Castle form a natural amphitheatre making it highly suitable for rock concerts. Thus in the 1980s Lord Charles decided to hold an annual rock festival there with acts such as

Thin Lizzy (who U2 supported in 1981), The Rolling Stones, Bob Dylan and Bruce Springsteen playing to crowds of around 70,000. U2 played this annual festival as second on the bill to Thin Lizzy on 16th August 1981. As the band had recently finished recording their second album, *October*, several numbers from this album were played live for the first time. They were "Rejoice", "With A Shout", "I Threw A Brick Through A Window", "Gloria", "Fire" and "October". At the end of U2's set there was a giant fireworks display, which apparently didn't go down too well in the Lizzy camp.

On 8th July 1984 it was Bob Dylan's turn to headline this festival and as U2 had recently finished recording their *Unforgettable Fire* album here, they were backstage. Bono had been given the job of interviewing Bob Dylan for *Hot Press* prior to Dylan going on stage. Dylan then invited Bono up on stage to sing "Leopard Skin Pillbox" with him after Bono had assured him that he knew the words to it. On stage he fluffed the song, perhaps being overawed by the occasion. However, Bono was invited back for the encore of "Blowin' in the Wind", again making a mess of things by singing a verse that Dylan had already sung, and then making up one of his own, which didn't go down too well with Dylan's fans.

U2 finally got the chance to play as headliners at Slane in 2001 on 25th August and 1st September, the final two concerts of the *Elevation* tour. When tick-

ets for the first show were announced the previous March, the whole show had sold out within an hour. Many Irish fans who had queued out over night to buy them personally at Dublin's HMV shop and other outlets missed out to the thousands who had bought them on the Internet via credit card. As a result U2 came in for much criticism from fans accusing them of creating a two-tier system for fans who have credit cards and web access and those who do not. Bowing to pressure after several months of legal hassles, the band announced a second show at Slane a week later on 1st September 2001.

These two concerts were the biggest rock concerts in Ireland in 2001 with a combined attendance of over 160,000 fans. They drew several celebrities including racing drivers, Eddie Irvine and David Coulthard, politician Mo Mowlam, and fellow musicians, Bob Geldof and Iggy Pop. The first concert was especially poignant as Bono's father, Bobby had died a few days before. His picture was shown on the screens during "One" and Bono commented, "I want to thank God for taking my old man away from his sickness and his tired old body and giving him a new one". As it was twenty years since U2 had played Slane as support to Thin Lizzy, they played some of the Lizzy hit, "Dancing In The Moonlight" and Bono referred to the proposed statue of Phil planned for erection in Dublin, and welcomed Phil's mother, Philomena to the concert. The band also performed a rare live version of "A Sort of Homecoming".

At the second concert Bono read out the names of all the victims of the Omagh bomb blast and referred to the Troubles in Northern Ireland. Both shows finished with a memorable fireworks display as "The Unforgettable Fire" was played over the PA - something they had done twenty years earlier.

See also: Phi Lynott / Thin Lizzy

"SLIDE AWAY" Bono sings vocals on this track from the 1999 album *Michael Hutchence*.

See also: Michael Hutchence

"SLOW DANCING" ("STAY (FARAWAY SO CLOSE)" SINGLE) (3.19) This beautiful acoustic song was on the B-side of the "Stay (Faraway So Close)" single (Live Format) (CIDX578). Credited as being written by Bono and The Edge, it features some nice harmonies, and shows a more mellow side of U2. It was first performed before an audience as long ago as 21st October 1989 on an Australian Radio show called *The Midnight Show*. Bono dedicated it to Willie Nelson and said that he'd only written one verse. It resurfaced as a full version on 21st April 1992 when U2 performed it live at the Tacoma Dome in Tacoma, Washington State, USA.

Slane Castle, County Meath, 25/8/01. *Photo: Claire bolton*

"SLOW DANCING" (4.00) ("IF GOD WILL SEND HIS ANGELS" SINGLE) This version of "Slow Dancing" was the second song on the single of "If God Will Send His Angels". This version features Willie Nelson on lead vocals and Mickey Raphael on Harmonica.

See also: Willie Nelson

SMILE JAMAICA This was the name of an appeal that was started after the Caribbean Island of Jamaica was hit by Hurricane Gilbert in autumn 1988. On Sunday 16th October 1988 in Britain, both ITV and Channel 4 held special programmes to raise funds for the appeal. One of these was the live broadcast of the *Smile Jamaica* concert at London's Dominion Theatre, featuring U2, The Christians, Robert Palmer, Chris Rea, Womack & Womack and Ziggy Marley. "Love Rescue Me" from the show was put on the B-side of the "Angel of Harlem" single and all profits from the single were donated to the *Smile Jamaica* fund, whose address was put on the record sleeve.

See also: Ziggy Marley / The Melody Makers / Dominion Theatre

SMITH, PATTI The influential poet and songwriter who was instrumental in the New York punk scene of the 1970s. Her 1974 independently released single, "Hey Joe" / "Piss Factory" and first album, *Horses*, established her as a major artist. Her influence on U2 is apparent on their cover of her song, "Dancing Barefoot" on the B-side of "When Love Comes To Town". At the 1997 *Q Awards* ceremony in London

Bono, in his speech presenting Patti Smith with her Inspiration Award, said that he would like to take her home to bed. Smith responded with "Fuck you, Bono."

SMITH, SUSAN One of the staff at Principle Management Dublin. She originally started with the U2 organisation in America, working with the band on the road there. She is now looking after the career of Paddy Casey.

SMITHFIELD CIVIC PLAZA, DUBLIN, IRELAND This was the place in Dublin where on 18th March 2000 U2 and Paul McGuinness received the Freedom of Dublin from the Mayor of Dublin, Mary Freehill. They received the honour in recognition of the work they have done over the years in promoting the city. Bono said to the crowd: "It's still moving to come home and see the amount of goodwill towards us." After the ceremony, U2 performed a four song set: "All I Want Is You", "Desire", "The Sweetest Thing" and "One." It was the first time the band had performed "The Sweetest Thing" live. Also at the ceremony, the Burmese human rights campaigner, Aung San Suu Kyi, was honoured. Her award was accepted by her son, Kim Aris.

See also: Aung San Suu Kyi

SMYTH, RITCHIE The director of three U2 promo videos. His first was for "The Fly" in 1991 which featured Bono for the first time as his "Fly" character. Shortly afterwards he directed the videos for "Until The End Of The World" and "Even Better Than The

Real Thing (Dance Mix)". All three were included on the video collection entitled *Achtung Baby - The Videos, The Cameos And A Whole Lot Of Interference From Zoo TV.*

See also: "Even Better Than The Real Thing (Dance Mix)", "The Fly" and "Until The End Of The World" promo videos

"SNAKE CHARMER" The Edge played slide guitar on this the title track of Jah Wobble's 1983 mini-album. This was the first "non-U2" activity by any of the members of the band.

See also: Hold Onto Your Dreams

"SO CRUEL" (*ACHTUNG BABY* ALBUM TRACK) (5.49) The final track on the first side of the *Achtung Baby* album. It talks about cruel love – someone whose love has been spurned by the person he still loves. The laid back atmosphere is partly due to the arrangement by Flood. It was not performed live that often, but made its live debut at the Forum Di Assago in Milan, Italy on 22nd May 1992.

SOLDIER FIELD, CHICAGO, ILLINOIS, USA U2 played three consecutive concerts here during the *Pop Mart* tour on 27th, 28th and 29th June 1997. The first two shows were sell outs with 42,500 attending each night, though on the third night the attendance was just over 30,000. For the second night, the old favourite "New Year's Day" was re-introduced into the set, whilst on the third night, "MLK" was played for the first time on the tour. Also on the second night a female fan gave Bono a puppet of a nun wearing boxing gloves, which he played with during "If You Wear That Velvet Dress". This also happened on the third night: the puppet came to be christened "Sister Mofo" by American U2 fans.

SOLDIER GIRLS (TV DOCUMENTARY) A documentary on women in the US army, shown on American TV in 1982. U2 used part of this documentary in "Seconds" off the *War* album. Halfway through the track it stops abruptly and the women can be heard singing: "I'm going to be an airborne ranger, I'm going to live the life of danger." In a BBC 1 interview Bono talked about how the documentary had made him see how easy it was to turn people into killing machines.

See also: Seconds

SOLIDARITY MOVEMENT The human rights movement that started in 1980 at the shipyards in the Polish town of Gdansk, under the leadership of Lech Walesa, a trade union leader. After several strikes and political unrest, Solidarity was outlawed by the head of the Polish Communist Party, General Jaruzelski, in December 1981. A state of martial law was imposed and Lech Walesa and other leaders were arrested.

Martial law was eventually lifted on New Year's Day 1983 and after Lech Walesa was freed, he rose to become Prime Minister of Poland. The freedom that the movement brought about was celebrated in "New Year's Day" on the *War* album.

See also: New Year's Day / Lech Walesa

"SOMEBODY ELSE" This is a track from the 1992 album, *Slide On This* by Ronnie Wood which features The Edge on guitar.

"SOME DAYS ARE BETTER THAN OTHERS" (*ZOOROPA* ALBUM TRACK) (4.15) The second track on the second side of the *Zooropa* album is a fairly laid back song, in which Bono reminisces about the way some days are good and some days are not so good – referring in part to the way in which the whole *Zooropa* album had been recorded. It is one of two songs from *Zooropa* never to have been played live – the other being "The Wanderer".

SOMETHING ELSE A British TV programme, on which U2 appeared. It was recorded on 15th May 1982 in London. U2 performed three songs: "Gloria", "A Celebration" and "With A Shout". It was the last time that "With A Shout" was played live before an audience. The programme was broadcast a week later on ITV.

SOME KIND OF WONDERFUL A Dublin based early '80s soul band whose brass section U2 used on "With A Shout" off the *October* album.

See also: With A Shout

SON RECORDS A subsidiary label of Mother Records which released records of non-rock artists, such as the Irish National Football team's "Put 'Em Under Pressure".

See also: Mother Records

"A SORT OF HOMECOMING" (*THE UNFORGETTABLE FIRE* ALBUM TRACK) (5.29) The opening track on *The Unforgettable Fire* album was the only song to have its lyrics printed on the album sleeve. It is a gentle ballad, and its lyrics tie in with the idea of "The Unforgettable Fire" – that of a nuclear holocaust and its aftermath. It was recorded at Slane Castle, County Meath, Ireland with Brian Eno producing. The live debut of "A Sort of Homecoming" was in Australia at the Sports And Entertainment Centre in Melbourne on 17th September 1984.

"A SORT OF HOMECOMING" (LIVE) ("THE UNFORGETTABLE FIRE" SINGLE B-SIDE) (4.04) This live version comes on the B-side of "The Unforgettable Fire" single (IS 220-B) and was recorded at a sound check at Wembley Arena, London, prior to U2's show there on 15th November 1984. The audience applause was later added at Good Earth Studios, which explains why it says on the sleeve of the single that it was recorded "live at Wembley and Good Earth Studios". This track also appeared on the mini-album *Wide Awake In America* (90279-1-A), which was originally released only in America in May 1985, but subsequently released worldwide on CD (CIDU 22) in 1987. The track was produced by Tony Visconti, who had previously worked with Marc Bolan and T.Rex, David Bowie and Thin Lizzy (*Live And Dangerous)* in the 1970s.

"A SORT OF HOMECOMING" (PROMOTIONAL VIDEO) Although "A Sort of Homecoming" was not released as a single, it still had a promo video which featured on *The Unforgettable Fire Collection*. Barry Devlin directed the film which contained scenes of the band on the road in Europe with shots filmed in London, Glasgow, Paris, Rotterdam and Brussels.

SOUNDS This was one of the three main music papers in Britain in the 1970s and 1980s that championed the early U2. *Sounds* reporter Dave McCullough reviewed U2's first ever British date at the Moonlight Club in London's West Hampstead, becoming one of their early champions in the British music press. He went on to review both *Boy* and *October* positively.

"SOUTHERN MAN" A Neil Young song written about the bigotry of the "redneck" in the southern states of the USA. Bono heard the song on the radio while the band were in Texas, and sang it on stage at Cardi's Dallas, Texas on 16th February 1982, with some help from a member of the audience. U2 then performed the song several times more on that tour and several times on the *Joshua Tree* tour.

"SPANISH EYES" ("I STILL HAVEN'T FOUND WHAT I'M LOOKING FOR" SINGLE B-SIDE) (3.14) The B-side of the "I Still Haven't Found What I'm Looking For" single (IS 328). It is one of the most popular B-sides with U2 fans throughout the world, and surprisingly did not make it onto *The Joshua Tree* album. The song is an up-tempo number, which starts off with some simple guitar chords by The Edge and then builds up into a strong rocker with a sudden ending. It was first performed live during the *Joshua Tree* tour at the Bernabau Stadium in Madrid on 15th July 1987 (U2's first ever concert in Spain) and was fully appreciated by the Spanish audience. It has only been played live on rare occasions since – usually at Spanish venues. The track was also included on *The B-sides* CD given away with *The Best of 1980-1990* compilation.

"SPANISH EYES" (PROMOTIONAL VIDEO) The song was featured in the documentary film *Outside It's America*, having its own video. It begins by showing a train approaching with cars and people rushing across the track just before the train passes. The action

then moves to the freeways of the USA showing band members driving along – rather like the Tears For Fears "Everybody Wants to Rule The World" video. It ends with illegal Mexican immigrants trying to enter America by crossing the Rio Grande at El Paso. The video was directed by Barry Devlin.

"THE SPEED OF LIFE" An early U2 song that was played live in the late 1970s but never made it onto record.

SPECTRUM ARENA, PHILADELPHIA, PENNSYLVANIA, USA U2 have played three sell-out shows at this 18,000 capacity venue. They played here first during the *Unforgettable Fire* tour on 22nd and 24th April 1985. (They were not able to play on consecutive nights, as the arena was already booked.) The second night was the final date for support band Lone Justice, so Bono invited their vocalist Maria McKee up on stage to sing the final song "40". U2 then played here again during the *Joshua Tree* tour, on 12th September 1987.

See also: Maria McKee

SPITTING IMAGE Popular satyrical British TV puppet show that flourished in the 1980s, notorious for its scathing caricatures of poiticians and The Royal Family. U2 managed to get lampooned on *Spitting Image* when four puppets sang a song called "I Still Haven't Got A Clue What I'm Going On About" in a parody of "I Still Haven't Found What I'm Looking For".

SPORT PALAIS, ANTWERP, BELGIUM U2 played Antwerp for the first time with two sell out shows on 5th and 6th August 2001 during the *Elevation* tour of Europe. At the first show Bono sang part of "Two Shots of Happy, One Shot of Sad" after a request from a fan. At the second show they sang part of "She's A Mystery To Me" in honour of Roy Orbison who played his final concert at this venue. Also fans present were intrigued to hear U2 perform a new song, dubbed "We Love You" during the encore - something which hasn't been done by U2 since their early days. These shows also marked the first ever U2 shows in Antwerp.

SPORT PALEIS, AHOY, ROTTERDAM, HOLLAND U2 have played this popular Dutch venue on no less than seven occasions. They first played here on 30th and 31st October 1984 during the *Unforgettable Fire* tour. They then returned to play a residency of four dates on 5th, 6th, 9th and 10th January 1990. These dates were U2's first of the 1990s but were were the bands last concerts for a period of two years, after which they went back out on the road with the *Zoo TV* tour. These dates had been hastily rescheduled after two shows at the RAI Hall in Amsterdam on 19th and 20th December had to be cancelled due to Bono having serious problems with his voice. They were all sold out, and featured the band in good form. It was also the last time that BB King played as support. U2 last played here on 15th June 1992 during the *Zoo TV* tour.

SPORTS AND ENTERTAINMENT CENTRE, MELBOURNE, AUSTRALIA U2 played a whole week of concerts here on 13th, 14th, 15th, 17th and 18th September 1984 during the *Under Australian Skies* tour. All the dates immediately sold out. These dates saw the live premieres of two songs from the soon to be released *The Unforgettable Fire* album; "Wire" and "A Sort of Homecoming". The Edge played acoustic guitar for the introduction to the second track.

SPORTS ARENA, LOS ANGELES, CALIFORNIA, USA This Californian arena holds the record for the number of times U2 have played a venue – no less than 12 times between 1982 and 1992. The first time they visited this 12,000 capacity venue, on 27th March 1982, the band were supporting the J. Geils Band and had not yet broken through in America. On their second visit, 15 months later on 17th June 1983, they were the headline artists, this being one of the biggest arenas they had played as top of the bill. They didn't quite manage to sell out the venue (being 2,000 short) but it did indicate that U2 were almost there. Certainly, the hysteria of the crowd at this concert was such that Bono was very nearly injured by fans wanting to touch him.

During "The Electric Co.", he did his usual stunt of climbing onto the balcony with a white flag. Many people got hold of him and wouldn't let go. When he did eventually free himself he tried running back to the stage, but was held back by the crowd. When the song had finished, Bono was still on the balcony and a fight had broken out. The rest of the band went on to play "I Fall Down" and, in order to get back to the stage, Bono jumped off the balcony onto people in the stalls a full twenty feet below. Luckily, the crowd below broke his fall, but they too grabbed and jostled him as he tried to make his way back to the stage. Dennis Sheehan, who had been shadowing Bono all this time, managed to tug Bono free from the hands of the crowd but not before both of them had their clothes torn to shreds. As a result of this and other similar incidents Bono stopped his travels from the stage.

When U2 returned to this venue in 1985 for three nights on 2nd, 4th and 5th March, all the shows were sold out. For the last of these dates there was a "food drive" where the concert goers could bring their unwanted food and leave it in bags, so that it could be distributed to the poor of the city. Their next visit to the L.A. Sports's Arena was during the *Joshua Tree* tour when they played a series of five

concerts – 17th, 18th, 20th, 21st and 22nd April 1987. These were again all sold out with ticket touts outside the venue doing a roaring trade and celebrities such as Madonna and Mickey Rourke attending.

For the 20th April show U2 were joined onstage by Bob Dylan who sang "I Shall Be Released" and "Knocking on Heaven's Door" with Bono. For the concert on the 22nd, the band played "The Electric Co.", the first time it had been played for nearly two years, and one of the last occasions it was played live. U2 then played two more dates here on 12th and 13th April 1992 during the first leg of the *Zoo TV* tour. The second show featured, for the first time, some of the Abba song "Dancing Queen".

SPORTS ARENA, SAN DIEGO, CALIFORNIA, USA U2 have played this 13,500 capacity arena on five occasions, the first being as support act to the J. Geils Band on 26th March 1982. They then played two shows during the *Joshua Tree* tour on 13th and 14th April 1987. During "Pride" in the first show, a woman from the audience came up onto the stage and started to use sign language to interpret the words that Bono was singing. For the 14th April show Maria McKee, the singer of the support band Lone Justice, joined Bono in singing "I Shall Be Released".

On this date *The Joshua Tree* reached number 1 in the album charts and Bono made this fact known to the audience during the show. U2 next played at this venue on 15th April 1992 during the *Zoo TV* tour. Finally U2 played here on the *Elevation* tour (North American leg) on 17th April 2001 with the Ramones number "I Remember You" being included in the set as a tribute to the recently deceased Joey Ramone.

See also: Maria McKee

"SPRINGHILL MINING DISASTER" This was the song written by Peggy Seeger that U2 sang on the *Late Late Show* on Irish TV, a special edition to celebrate 25 years of The Dubliners. The song remembers the victims of a mining disaster at Springhill, Novia Scotia in Canada, who, although trapped underground after the shaft had collapsed, kept on singing. Film of the performance was included on a special video to commemorate the 25th Anniversary of The Dubliners. The song was performed by U2 on several dates during the *Joshua Tree* tour.

See also: Ewan MacColl / Late Late Show

SPRINGSTEEN, BRUCE The famous American singer has been a fan of U2 from very early on in their career. He specially delayed returning to America after his *River* tour of 1981 so that he could see U2 play the Hammersmith Palais in London on 9th June. After the show he met the band in their dressing room. Bono then sang with Bruce on the "Sun City" single and video in 1985. This was followed by a guest appearance by Bruce at their show at the John F Kennedy Stadium in Philadelphia on 25th September 1987.

Finally, in March 1999, Bono inducted Bruce into the Rock 'n' Roll Hall of Fame at New York's Waldorf Astoria Hotel with the words, "He was the end of long hair, brown rice and bell bottoms. He was the end of the 20-minute drum solo. It was good night Haight Ashbury, hello Asbury Park." At the end, in the all-star jam session, Bono, Bruce and other guests sang Curtis Mayfield's "People Get Ready".

See also: John F Kennedy Stadium Philadelphia / Sun City

SPUD The Irish group managed by Paul McGuinness in 1976-1977 before he managed U2. He was asked to manage the band by one of the group, Don Knox, who he had known at Trinity College. Agreeing to do this for a year initially, Paul managed to get them a recording contract with Sonet Records, a Scandinavian Record company, as well as much needed publicity in *Scene* magazine through Bill Graham. Originally a folk group, Spud had turned "electric" and due to disagreements within the band as to what musical direction they should take, Paul decided that after a year, managing Spud was not for him.

SST The America independent record label sued by Island Records in 1992 after their band Negativland had infringed copyrights of some of U2's songs.

See also: Negativland

STADE DE LA MEINAU, STRASBURG, FRANCE Another French city visited during the *Zooropa* tour was Strasbourg on 23rd June 1993. As Strasbourg was the location for a European political summit meeting, Macphisto phoned the hotel where the politicians were staying hoping to speak to the French National Front leader, Jean Marie Le Pen, but he wasn't there. Nor was Helmut Kohl, the German Chancellor. This was the first date where the reformed Velvet Underground (including Lou Reed) played as support band to U2.

STADIO BENTEGODI, VERONA, ITALY U2 played two nights at this 45,000 capacity stadium on 2nd and 3rd July 1993. The first night was the start of a run of eight Italian shows. In this show Macphisto phoned Clannad singer Maire Ni Bhraonain, who had sung with Bono on the "In A Lifetime" single. As it was her birthday, he sang 'Happy Birthday' to her over the phone. On the second night, Macphisto tried to phone the Pope, John Paul II, but was unable to get through to the Vatican. Both before and after the show, Bono and The Edge spoke to the American film maker Bill Carter, about his work amongst the people of Sarajevo. As a result of this, a satellite link-up with Sarajevo was introduced into several of the remaining *Zooropa* shows, from 17th July onwards.

See also: Bill Carter

STADIO COMUNALE, BOLOGNA, ITALY U2 played two sell out nights here on 17th and 18th July 1993, during the *Zooropa* tour of Europe. At the first show Bono rang the famous Italian opera singer, Luciano Pavarotti, who was quite pleasant to Macphisto, even when he asked him to sing a song. At the second show, he rang Allessandro Mussolini, the granddaughter of the Italian Dictator and left a message on her answerphone. At both shows, American film maker Bill Carter was contacted by satellite live from Sarajevo in the middle of the show where he was able to describe what conditions were like in the beseiged town. This was to be a regular feature of the *Zooropa* shows from these shows onwards.

See also: Pavarotti

STADIO DELLE ALPI, TURIN, ITALY U2 visited this northern Italian city on 12th July 1993 during the *Zooropa* tour. After a dispute with the stadium manager, there was no official U2 merchandise on sale inside the stadium, so illegal traders outside did very well. The band also played a one off stadium gig here before 80,000 fans during the *Elevation* tour of Europe on 21st July 2001 after a proposed gig at Imola was cancelled. Such was the enthusiasm of the Italian crowd that the band performed two extra encores - "Pride (In The Name of Love) and "Out of Control".

STADIO FLAMINIO, ROME, ITALY U2 have played this stadium in the Italian capital on three occasions. They first came here on 27th May 1987 during the *Joshua Tree* tour. This show was the opening date of the European leg of the tour and the first of many open-air shows during that summer. There was a 35,000 capacity crowd on hand to see this show. U2 then returned here for two shows during the *Zooropa* tour – 6th and 7th July 1993. At the second show "Numb" was played live for the first time, with The Edge singing the words from a sheet in front of him. As he sang, film from the "Numb" video remix was shown on the TV screens. Both shows were oversold by 14,000 due to the promoter exceeding the agreed 35,000 tickets per show.

See also: "Numb" (video remix)

"STAND BY ME" This Ben E. King song was used by U2 as the introductory music for their *Joshua Tree* shows. They also used to sing their own version as the opening number on some of the shows.

STANNARD, RICHARD He was one of the original producers on the *All That You Can't Leave Behind* album.

STAPLES CENTER, LOS ANGELES, CALIFORNIA, USA The venue where the 2001 Grammy Awards ceremony was held. U2 performed winner of the "Song of the Year" award "Beautiful Day" live. *All That You Can't Leave Behind* won the "Record of the Year" award and "Best Performance by a Rock act or Duo".

See also: Grammy Awards

THE STARDUST CLUB, DUBLIN, IRELAND This was an important early gig for U2, on 11th December 1978, where they were the support act to the Greedy Bastards, a band made up of Thin Lizzy members Phil Lynott and Gary Moore, with ex-Sex Pistols Steve Jones and Paul Cook.

See also: The Greedy Bastards

"STARING AT THE SUN" (*POP* ALBUM TRACK) (4.36) The fifth track on the *Pop* album. Unlike most of this album, it is predominantly an acoustic song. It was produced by Flood and also included Steve Osborne on keyboards. It was first performed live at the Sam Boyd Stadium, Las Vagas on 25th April 1997, the opening night of the *Pop Mart* tour.

"STARING AT THE SUN" (SINGLE) (4.36) The single for "Staring At The Sun" was released in April 1997 and reached number 3 in the UK and number 26 in the US. The CD version had the extra tracks of "North And South Of The River" and "Your Blue Room" on it. There was also a remixes version featuring three mixes of "Staring At The Sun" plus "North And South Of The River".

"STARING AT THE SUN" (LAB RAT MIX) (SINGLE) (5.07) The fourth track on the "Staring At The Sun" single, remixed by the Sonic Morticians.

"STARING AT THE SUN" (MONSTER TRUCK MIX) (5.07) The first track on the "Staring At The Sun" single, remixed by The Sonic Morticians

"STARING AT THE SUN" (SAD BASTARDS MIX) (6.20) The second track on the "Staring At The Sun" single, remixed by Flood and Rob Kirwan.

"STARING AT THE SUN" (LIVE) (*HASTA LA VSITA BABY! U2 LIVE FROM MEXICO CITY* ALBUM TRACK) (4.31) This live version was included on the CD given away free to *Propaganda* readers in July 2000. It was recorded at the Foro Sol Autodromo Mexico City on 3rd December 1997 during the *Pop Mart* tour and featured Bono and The Edge singing the song on the B-stage.

"STARING AT THE SUN" (LIVE FROM ROTTERDAM) (POPHEART LIVE EP TRACK) (5.33) This live version of "Staring At The Sun" was recorded at The Feyenoord Stadium, Rotterdam, Holland on 18th July 1997. It was included as the fourth track on the "Please" (PopHeart Live) EP.

"STARING AT THE SUN" (LIVE) (*POP MART LIVE FROM MEXICO CITY* VIDEO) This film version of "Staring At The Sun" was on the video *Pop Mart Live From Mexico City*. It was filmed at the Foro Sol Autodromo Mexico City on 3rd December 1997 during the *Pop Mart* tour.

"STARING AT THE SUN" (PROMOTIONAL VIDEO) (VERSION 1) The first promo video of "Staring at The Sun" was directed by Jake Scott in April 1997.

"STARING AT THE SUN" (PROMOTIONAL VIDEO) (VERSION 2) The second promo video of "Staring at The Sun" was directed by Morleigh Steinberg in May 1997 and was filmed on the streets of Miami, hence its name of the "Miami Version".

"THE STAR SPANGLED BANNER" The American National anthem was played on electric guitar by Jimi Hendrix at the 1969 Woodstock Festival. U2 first used this version as an introduction to "Bullet the Blue Sky" at their *Joshua Tree* show at the NEC in Birmimgham, England on 3rd August 1987. It was then included at every show on the rest of the tour as well as on the *Lovetown* tour. It was also included on the film soundtrack of *Rattle & Hum*, the version in the film coming from the show at the Sun Devil Stadium in Tempe, USA on 20th December 1987.

STATE COLLEGE AUDITORIUM, SAN JOSE, CALIFORNIA, USA The U2 show here on 18th March 1981 was one of the first where such was the demand to see the band that more people attended than was officially allowed – nearly 2000 in this 1000 capacity auditorium.

"STATELESS" (*THE MILLION DOLLAR HOTEL* SOUNDTRACK ALBUM) (4.05) The third track on the soundtrack album for *The Million Dollar Hotel* is one of only two tracks on the album performed and written by the four members of U2.

"STAY (FARAWAY SO CLOSE!)" (*ZOOROPA* ALBUM TRACK) (4.58) The fifth track of the *Zooropa* album, released on 5th July 1993. It was recorded in Dublin in the spring of 1993. One of the outstanding tracks on the *Zooropa* album, it features excellent lyrics and vocals from Bono, and The Edge's acoustic guitar impart a very laid back feel. The song had been commissioned by German film director Wim Wenders (who directed the "Red, Hot & Blue" U2 video) as the title track for his next movie, *Faraway So Close*. During the *Zooropa* tour, the song would be performed on the mini-stage, being the highlight of that section of the show. The live premiere of the song took place at the Stockholm Stadium in Sweden on 31st July 1993.

"STAY (FARAWAY, SO CLOSE!)" (SINGLE - SWING FORMAT) (IS578) (4.58) The song "Stay (Faraway, So Close)" was released as a single on 22nd November 1993. It camc in two formats: the "swing" format

Morleigh Steinberg dances for Bono, Cardiff, 18/9/93. *Photo: Georgia Everett*

and the "live" format. The "swing" format was so named as it featured Bono and Frank Sinatra singing "I've Got You Under My Skin". The 12 inch and CD versions (CID579 858 077-2), also featured two remixes of the track "Lemon" – The Bad Yard Mix and The Perfecto Mix. The single version was exactly the same as the album version.

"STAY (FARAWAY, SO CLOSE!)" (SINGLE - LIVE FORMAT) (CID578) (4.58) The "live" format of the "Stay (Faraway, So Close)" single was released in the UK a week after the "swing" format on 29th November 1993. It featured live versions of "Bullet The Blue Sky" and "Love Is Blindness". It also featured a previously unreleased song called "Slow Dancing", a soft acoustic number co-written by Bono and The Edge, which had first been played live on a Sydney Radio show back in September 1989. The packaging for the CD consisted of a folder with space for the two different formats of the Stay CD single. It was hoped that if U2 fans bought both versions "Stay" would make the Christmas 1993 number 1 spot, but with stiff opposition from Take That, Mr Blobby and East 17, it stalled at number 6 in the charts.

See also: Slow Dancing

"STAY (FARAWAY, SO CLOSE!)" (*FARAWAY, SO CLOSE!* SOUNDTRACK ALBUM) (Island 8 27216 2) There was also a film version of "Stay (Faraway, So Close!)" used in the Wim Wenders film *Faraway, So Close*. It had a slightly different mix to the original version.

See also: Faraway, So Close! / The Wanderer / Wim Wenders

"STAY (FARAWAY, SO CLOSE!)" (UNDERDOG MIX) (*MELON* CD) (6.45) This was one of the tracks on the free *Melon* CD, given away with the U2 fan magazine *Propaganda* in December 1994. It was remixed by "Underdog" and was perhaps an unusual choice for a remix.

"STAY (FARAWAY, SO CLOSE!)" (PROMO VIDEO) The promo video for "Stay (Faraway So Close!)" was directed by Wim Wenders, who had previously directed U2 in their "Night & Day" video. It was shot mainly in Berlin around the famous Siegessaule Statue and in a club. The idea of the video was that Bono and the rest of U2 were playing the parts of angels who have come down to earth, as in Wenders' movie, *Faraway So Close*. The video has the unusal scene where a group are playing, with a female vocalist singing Bono's part whilst Bono looks on. Then right at the end Bono "falls" from the sky and lands in the middle of a busy Berlin road.

STEINBERG, MORLEIGH The second belly dancer who danced onstage during "Mysterious Ways" in the *Zoo TV* tour from the *Outside Broadcast* leg onwards, taking over from the original belly dancer, Christine Petro. Morleigh was originally the choreographer for the show. She is the now the partner of The Edge and the mother of two of his children, Sian and Levi. She also directed the promo video for "Staring At The Sun" (Miami version).

STEWART, ALISON Bono's wife, often called "Ali", was born in Dublin in 1961 and attended Mount Temple Comprehensive School where she came across the young and fun-loving Paul Hewson. As time went on their relationship became steady. She joined the Shalom Group with Bono and supported the band through the hard early days, often not seeing Bono for months on end. They were married on 21st August 1982 at the Church of Ireland Church in Raheny. Their first daughter, Jordan, was born on Bono's 29th birthday on 10th May 1989, at Dublin's Mount Carmel Hospital. Their second daughter, Memphis Eve, was born on 7th July 1991, their third child, a son, Elijah Bob Patricius Guggi Q, was born on 11th August 1999 and their fourth child, John Abraham, was born on 20th May 2001.

Ali has developed her own career over the long periods of time that Bono is away from home. For instance she went to Chernobyl to film the TV documentary *Black Wind, White Land*. She now spends a lot of her spare time publicising the Chernobyl Children's charity. In 1996 she brought three children back from Belarus who needed medical treatment. One of them, Lena, was adopted by a couple from Cork. Ali is now a godmother to another child, Anna Gabriel, who was also brought back from Belarus and adopted by an Irish couple. "Sweetest Thing" was written for her after Bono forgot her birthday during the recording of *The Joshua Tree*. In the resulting promo video she appeared briefly at the start. In February 2000 she helped to organise the Brown Thomas Fashion Show in Dublin in aid of the Children of Chernobyl charity, one of several she has helped organise in the past few years.

See also: Black Wind, White Land / Children of Chernobyl / Sweetest Thing promo video

STEWART, BILL The A&R man at Island Records who along with Rob Partridge was responsible for signing U2 to the Island record label. It was Partridge who persuaded Stewart to see U2 play live in Dublin. The gig he attended was a specially arranged one at the National Boxing Stadium in February 1980, which was attended by approximately 2,000 fans, friends and relations of the band. After the gig, Stewart offered them a contract with Island, which after further negotiations was signed in London in March.

See also: Island Records

"STILL WATER" A track from the 1989 Daniel Lanois album *Acadie*' which features Adam on bass and Larry on drums.

STING (Real name – Gordon Sumner) Originally the lead singer and bass player with The Police, he later went solo. Sting first performed on the same bill as U2 in July 1980 when The Police were headlining the Dublin Festival 1980 at Leixlip Castle just outside Dublin. Two years later U2 played with the Police at the Gateshead International Stadium in Newcastle in July 1982. The Police were the headlining act with U2 next on the bill. During the Police's set, Bono joined Sting onstage to sing "Invisible Sun" with him. Both he and Bono then sang lead vocals on the 1984 Band Aid single "Do They Know It's Christmas?"

In 1986, both U2 and Sting were on the same bill for the *Conspiracy of Hope* tour of the USA in support of Amnesty International. For the first three shows of the tour Sting performed solo, then for the final three shows he performed as The Police with Andy Summers and Stewart Copeland. For the last two shows Bono joined The Police on stage to sing "Invisible Sun". Sting, like U2, has a concern for environmental issues and human rights, supporting both Amnesty International and the Rainforest Foundation which he helped to set up.

STOCKHOLM STADIUM, STOCKHOLM, SWEDEN U2 played to a sell-out crowd of over 33,000 here on 31st July 1993 during the *Zooropa* tour of Europe. This show marked the live premiere of "Stay (Faraway, So Close!)" which was sung from the mini-stage.

STOKES, NIALL Niall was the founder of *Hot Press* magazine in 1977. Before this he was in several Dublin bands including Eyeless (along with his brother Dermot) where he played guitar. As a student at University College Dublin, he started publishing a magazine called *Buck Out* with partner David McKenna. From there he went on to write for a magazine called *Scene* before starting *Hot Press*, which was the first serious Irish journal that concentrated on the contemporary Irish music scene. It also had Bill Graham as one of its writers, and it was he who first gave U2 their first feature in the pages of *Hot Press*.

From then on the magazine has wholeheartedly supported U2 at each stage of their career. Apart from being editor and guiding light of *Hot Press*, Niall was also for many years Chairperson on the Independent Radio and Television Commission in Ireland, helping to get contemporary Irish music played more on the radio. His own book on the stories behind each U2 song, *Into the Heart*, was published in 1997. More recently he has seen his brainchild, the Hot Press Irish Music Hall of Fame come to fruition. His latest book is based on the six-part history of Irish music called *From A Whisper To A Scream*.

See also: *Hot Press* / *Hot Press* Irish Music Hall of Fame

STOP SELLAFIELD CONCERT, G-MEX CENTRE, MANCHESTER, ENGLAND U2 played here on 19th June 1992, the final concert of the 1992 *Zoo TV* tour of Europe. The concert was meant to have taken place in Manchester's Heaton Park the following day – Saturday 20th June 1992 – as a special "Stop Sellafield" concert, as this was the nearest town to the Sellafield Nuclear Power Station that U2 were playing on this tour. The tickets were priced at £10 and had already gone on sale when the local council cancelled the concert on the grounds of the potential damage that a crowd of 50,000 might do to the park. Instead the 9,000 capacity G-Mex Centre was used as the venue and the concert was designated a "Stop Sellafield" show.

The whole concert was filmed by Greenpeace and "Even Better Than The Real Thing" and "The Fly" were used in the video, entitled *Stop Sellafield*. Songs by the support acts Kraftwerk, Public Enemy and Big Audio Dynamite II were also used in the video. Greenpeace tried to organise a rally outside the gates of Sellafield in Cumbria but were stopped from doing so by a High Court injunction issued on behalf of British Nuclear Fuels who owned the power station. Bono mentioned the whole affair in a short speech after "The Fly".

"We were going to invite you all down to the gates at Sellafield tomorrow. We have personal invitations. I guess when they found out that you were coming, they didn't like it very much – I wonder what they've got to hide. They've cancelled a peaceful demonstration because they said they were worried about 'public safety'! These people are responsible for the deaths of innocent children for God's sake – public safety doesn't come near them. Anyway the whole farce has backfired on them. In the last week they've given Greenpeace more publicity than they could ever want."

The concert featured a surprise appearance from Lou Reed who sang live with Bono on "Satellite of Love" and towards the end of the show, Bono tried to get through to John Major, the British Prime Minister, on the phone. He spoke to the receptionist and left a message for him "to watch more TV" – a message that he would leave for the American President, George Bush, at each of the *Outside Broadcast* shows in the Autumn of 1992. After the show, U2 actually went to the Sellafield Nuclear Power Station travelling on a special Greenpeace boat so they were able to arrive at dawn on the beach in front of Sellafield. As they were on the section between the high and low tide marks they were not in contempt of any court ruling. They were then photographed by the world's press and so got their message across.

See also: *Stop Sellafield* video/ Sellafield / THORP

STOP SELLAFIELD (VIDEO) A special video produced by Greenpeace which drew attention to the proposed building of a second nuclear reactor called THORP at Sellfield nuclear power station in Cumbria. The video featured interviews with local residents expressing their concerns about the power station, as well as footage from the concert showing U2, Kraftwerk, BAD II and Public Enemy.

"STORIES FOR BOYS" (*BOY* ALBUM TRACK) (3.02) The first track on the second side of U2's first album, *Boy*. It was originally one of the three tracks on U2's first single, "U2-3", though the version used here is different. This version was produced by Steve Lillywhite. It was ostensibly about comic book characters that boys read about when growing up, though some others saw gay references in the lyrics. It was perfomed live from 1978 onwards.

"STORIES FOR BOYS" (U2-3 SINGLE) (CBS 7951) This was one of three tracks that U2 fans voted to be included on the "U2-3" single, U2's first ever release. It was released only in Ireland on CBS Records in both 7 inch and 12 inch versions and is now a much sought after collector's item.

"STORIES FOR BOYS" (REMIX VERSION) (KICK KK1) A remix version of "Stories For Boys" was included on Ireland's first rock compilation album *Just For Kicks*.

See also: Just For Kicks

"STORIES FOR BOYS" (LIVE) (LIVE FROM BOSTON) ("SWEETEST THING" SINGLE) (3.02) This live version of "Stories For Boys" was recorded at The Paradise Theater in Boston, USA on 6th March 1981. It was included on the "Sweetest Thing" single release in 1998. The whole show had originally been recorded for the local radio station WBCN, which later came out as a special promotional album for radio stations.

See also: Paradise Theater, Boston

STRAHOV STADIUM, PRAGUE, CZECH REPUBLIC U2's one and only appeance in the Czech Republic took place here on 14th August during the *Pop Mart* tour of Europe. At the concert Bono dedicated "Pride" to the preisdent of the Czech Republic, Vaclav Havel. Bono also uttered the immortal lines: "The Russians came with tanks, but we Irish came with a lemon!"

"THE STRANGE PARTY" The fourth track on the soundtrack album of *The Captive*. It was composed by The Edge.

"STRANGER IN A STRANGE LAND" (*OCTOBER* ALBUM TRACK) (3.57) Bono has said that the song was written about an East German border guard checking their passports when they were on their way to a gig in West Berlin. He has also said that the track was written about being in Minneapolis during the band's first coast-to-coast tour of America. The song has never been performed live.

STRANGLERS, THE One of the first groups that achieved commercial success in the wake of the Sex Pistols. Although their sound was slightly different to most punk groups with keyboards being prominent, they managed to achieve three top 10 hit singles in 1977. In September 1978, they played a gig in Dublin at the Top Hat Ballroom, in Dun Laoghaire and U2 managed to get the support slot. Contrary to the story in the *Unforgettable Fire* book, Bono did not burst into their dressing room and barrack them for failing to live up to punk's ideals, but merely tried to persuade Hugh Cornwell to wear a U2 badge on stage.

"STREET MISSION" An early U2 song that the band used to close their early shows. It was one of the songs recorded for their second demo tape at Keystone studios in Dublin in November 1978 with Barry Devlin producing. It talks about a person seeking God, reflecting the group's Christian beliefs. The song contains what is probably the longest guitar solo The Edge has ever played.

"A STRING OF PEARLS" The name of a photographic exhibition which took place in Dublin in February 1988. It contained photos that Bono had taken while he was working in a relief camp in Ethiopia in 1985. The exhibition was set up by Gavin Friday, Guggi and Charlie Whisker.

STRONGMAN (AKA TREVOR ROWAN) One of the members of the Lypton Village and The Virgin Prunes. Trevor is the brother of Guggi (Derek) and Radar (Peter). In the Virgin Prunes he played bass guitar. Today Trevor is manager of Pelvis, a Dublin band featuring another Rowan – Johnny on lead vocals.

See also: The Lypton Village / The Virgin Prunes

STS RECORDING STUDIOS, DUBLIN, IRELAND Whilst most U2 fans associate Windmill Lane studios as the place where all U2's material has been recorded over the years, STS has been used by U2 on several occasions. For instance, some of *The Joshua Tree*, *Rattle & Hum*, *Achtung Baby* and several B-sides have all been recorded here. The studios closed down in 1999.

"STUCK IN A MOMENT YOU CAN'T GET OUT OF" (*ALL THAT YOU CAN'T LEAVE BEHIND* ALBUM TRACK) (4.32) The second track on the *All That You Can't Leave Behind* album. It was written about Michael Hutchence of INXS who died - either by suicide or by accident - whilst the album was being written and recorded. Apparently Mick Jagger and his daughter Lizzy added backing vocals to the track but this version wasn't used on the album. It was first performed live at the May Ray club in Paris, France on 19th October 2000.

"STUCK IN A MOMENT YOU CAN'T GET OUT OF" (SINGLE) (4.32) The single version of "Stuck In A Moment You Can't Get Out Of" was released in two formats. CD1 (CIDX 770) has the extra tracks of "Big

Girls Are Best" and "Beautiful Day" (Quincey And Sinance Remix). CD2 (CID 770) has the extra tracks of "Beautiful Day" and "New York" both recorded live at FarmClub.com in Universal City on 27th October 2000. The single reached number 2 in the UK singles charts.

"STUCK IN A MOMENT YOU CAN'T GET OUT OF" (PROMOTIONAL VIDEO) The promo video for "Stuck In A Moment You Can't Get Out Of" was directed by Kevin Godley and filmed in the Alameda Fruit Market in Los Angeles in November 2000. It shows Bono being thrown from a van and singing the song on the ground. Then the scene keeps repeating itself. Apparently he is trying to escape from this situation and the other three members of U2 are trying to rescue him.

SULLIVAN STADIUM, FOXBORO, MASSACHUSETTS, USA U2 played to over 55,000 fans here on 22nd September 1987 during the *Joshua Tree* tour of America. It was the first show that U2 had played since Bono dislocated his left shoulder and was the first concert that Bono would have to wear a sling on stage.

"SUMMER RAIN" ("BEAUTIFUL DAY" SINGLE) (4.06) The second track on the "Beautiful Day" single (CD1) was written by U2 with Bono and The Edge coming up with the lyrics.

SUMMIT, HOUSTON, TEXAS, USA U2 first played this 14,000 capacity arena on 27th February 1985 during the *Unforgettable Fire* tour of America. They played two more sell out dates here on 7th and 8th April 1987 during the *Joshua Tree* tour. At the first show, an extra encore of "Trip Through Your Wires" and "Southern Man" was added after enthusiastic calling from the audience. After the second show the members of U2 went to a club and the sequence of them singing three songs was featured in the video documentary *Outside It's America*.

SUN BOWL, EL PASO, TEXAS, USA U2 have played just one show at this 40,000 capacity stadium in El Paso, not far from the Mexican border. This was on 27th October 1992 during the *Zoo TV Outside Broadcast* tour and was the first time in 20 years that this venue had been used for a rock concert – Elton John being the last artist to play previously. The show was broadcast live to the house of a girl called Sherry in California – the prize for winning an MTV competition.

SUN CITY: ARTISTS UNITED AGAINST APARTHEID (ALBUM) This was a record put together by Little Stevie Van Zandt of Bruce Springsteen's E Street Band to draw awareness to South Africa's policy of apartheid. The album featured such artists as The Rolling Stones, Bruce Springsteen and Pete Townshend. Bono contributed the track "Silver & Gold" to the album and also sang on the title track, which was released as a single.

See also: Artists United Against Apartheid / Little Steven / "Silver & Gold"

"SUN CITY" (SINGLE) The single of "Sun City" was performed by "Artists United Against Apartheid" and reached number 21 in the UK and 38 in the US singles charts in November 1985.

"SUN CITY" (PROMOTIONAL VIDEO) The promo video for "Sun City was made in 1985 and featured some of the singers from the single including Bruce Springsteen and Bono singing the chorus together with film clips of rioting in South Africa.

"SUNDAY BLOODY SUNDAY" (*WAR* ALBUM TRACK) (4.40) The opening track of the *War* album is one of U2's most powerful and poignant songs. The guitar riff is said to have been written by The Edge as a result of the inner turmoil he was feeling over the question of being a Christian and being in a rock 'n' roll band. Bono's lyrics rate as some of the best that he has ever written, moving from the events of "Bloody Sunday" on 30th January 1972, when the "troubles" of Northern Ireland came to a head with the shooting of 13 Irish citizens, through to the Sunday when Jesus rose from the dead. The track was also included on *The Best of 1980-1990* compilation CD. The song was first performed live at Tiffany's in Glasgow, Scotland, on 1st December, 1982, the opening date of the winter 1982 tour to preview the *War* album.

"SUNDAY BLOODY SUNDAY" (LIVE) (*UNDER A BLOOD RED SKY* ALBUM TRACK) (5.27) The fifth track on the *Under A Blood Red Sky* mini-album (IMA3/CID1113) Contrary to popular belief, this live version of "Sunday Bloody Sunday" was not recorded at Red Rocks, Denver, but at the Lorelei Amphitheaatre at St Goarshausen in Germany on 20th August 1983.

"SUNDAY BLOODY SUNDAY" (LIVE FROM SARAJEVO) (IF GOD WILL SEND HIS ANGELS SINGLE) (3.50) The fourth track on the "If God Will Send His Angels" single was recorded live at the Kosevo Stadium, Sarajevo, in Bosnia-Herzegovina on 23rd September 1997 during the *Pop Mart* tour of Europe. It is a very moving version with Edge singing solo backed by his guitar.

"SUNDAY BLOODY SUNDAY" (LIVE) (*RATTLE & HUM* FILM/VIDEO TRACK). This live version of "Sunday Bloody Sunday" was filmed at the McNichols Arena in Denver, Colorado, USA on Sunday 8th November 1987. This version has the quieter introduction which U2 had introduced on the *Joshua Tree*

tour, but is still full of emotion, especially from Bono. This is because U2 had just heard about the Remembrance Day atrocity at Enniskillen in Northern Ireland where 13 people had been killed by an IRA bomb.

Halfway through the song, Bono unleashed a vitriolic tirade against "Irish Americans" who support the "Revolution" in Northern Ireland: "I've had enough of Irish Americans who haven't been back to their country in 20 or 30 years. Who come up to me and talk about the Resistance – The Revolution back home, and the glory of the revolution and the glory of dying for the revolution. Fuck the Revolution! They don't talk about the glory of killing for the revolution. Where's the glory in taking a man from his bed and gunning him down in front of his wife and children? Where's the glory in that? Where's the glory in bombing a Remembrance Day Parade of old age pensioners – their medals taken out and polished up for the day? Where's the glory in that? To leave them dying or crippled for life or dead under the rubble of a revolution that the majority of the people in my country don't want. No More!"

"SUNDAY BLOODY SUNDAY" (LIVE) (PROMO VIDEO FROM *LIVE AT RED ROCKS*) "This is not a rebel song – this is Sunday Bloody Sunday" is how Bono introduces this song from the *Red Rocks* video. Although the video is not a promotional video per se, this track was released as a single in several countries including Germany and Holland and is a fine example of the early U2 at the *War* stage in their career. It was also included on the *Best Of 1980-1990* video collection.

"SUNDAY BLOODY SUNDAY" (LIVE) (*POP MART LIVE FROM MEXICO CITY* VIDEO) The fourteenth track on the video *Pop Mart Live From Mexico City*. It was recorded live at the Foro Sol Autodromo, Mexico City on 3rd December 1997 during the *Pop Mart* tour.

SUN DEVIL STADIUM, TEMPE, ARIZONA, USA U2 have played this stadium near Phoenix on four occasions during their career. The first two times that they played here, on 19th and 20th December 1987, marked the final two shows of the *Joshua Tree* tour, not only in America but also in the world. Coincidentally the *Joshua Tree* tour had opened in the same Texan town of Tempe at the State University back on 2nd April. These two shows were also significant in that they were filmed for the colour sequences of *Rattle & Hum*.

Originally, Buenos Aires in Argentina was to have been the place where this would have been filmed, but the high cost of shipping out U2's equipment put paid to this idea. In the end, director Phil Joanou used

"Running to Stand Still", "Bullet The Blue Sky", "Where The Streets Have No Name", "MLK" and "With or Without You" for the film. All of these came from the second show. Footage of the band performing "One Tree Hill" from the first concert was included as a bonus "video" in *The Best of 1980-1990* video collection. It is thought that "Mothers of The Disappeared" very nearly made it into the final cut of the show as the lyrics to this song are included in the offiicial book of the film written by Steve Turner and Willie Williams. To make sure these two shows sold out, the price for tickets was fixed at $5. In all, over 110,000 fans attended the two shows.

U2 returned here during the Zoo TV *Outside Broadcast* tour on 24th October 1992. This time only 35,000 fans attended the show. Here Bono sang the Elvis Presley song "Suspicious Minds" for the only time on this tour. U2 played once more here during the *Pop Mart* tour of North America (first leg) on 9th May 1997 to a two-thirds full stadium.

See also: *Rattle & Hum* film and album

SUN PLAZA HALL, TOKYO, JAPAN U2's first ever concerts in Tokyo, the capital of Japan took place on 26th, 27th, 28th and 29th November 1983. All of them were sold out prior to U2 arriving in the country. During "I Fall Down", Bono invited a member of the audience on stage to play guitar with him as a way of breaking down the traditional reserve of a Japanese audience. This had the desired effect as afterwards the crowd clapped, shouted and screamed just like any Western audience.

SUN RECORDING STUDIOS, MEMPHIS, TENNESSEE, USA The famous recording studio in Memphis founded by Sam C Phillips, where Elvis Presley recorded his first records in the mid-1950s. In 1952 Sam, with his Brother Judd, set up his own record label, Sun Records, and studios at 706 Union Avenue, which over the years went on to record other famous artists including Johnny Cash, Roy Orbison, Jerry Lee Lewis and Carl Perkins.

By 1987 the studio was owned by Gary Hardy and in November of that year U2 took some time off from their *Joshua Tree* tour to record several tracks here, most of which would appear on the *Rattle & Hum* album. They chose this historic recording studio not only for its history but also for its unique sound. As Gary Hardy explained, "They wanted to come here for the magic of the room. The only effect they wanted was that unique tape slap-back echo off the studio floor." The band's arrival at Sun Studios and some of the session was captured for the *Rattle & Hum* film. They are shown recording "Angel of Harlem" in a session that lasted over five hours. In all they recorded five songs: "Angel of Harlem", "When Love

Comes To Town", "She's A Mystery To Me", "Love Rescue Me" and "Jesus Christ" – the last song being the reason they came to Sun in the first place.

The band arrived at the studio at 7.30pm, having been filmed earlier visiting Elvis Presley's house, Graceland, and stayed until nearly 3.00am. As they didn't have their own equipment with them, Gary had to arrange for instruments to be hired in acordance with a list that tour manager Dennis Sheehan had supplied. They included at 1954 Gibson ES295 guitar and a 1953 Fender Telecaster bass, as well as the old WHBQ microphone that Dewey Phillips had used in radio broadcasts from the 1950s. Several other musicians took part in the session, including Tony Thomas (keyboards), Phyllis and Helen Duncan, Becky Evans (backing vocals), Joey Miskulin (organ) and the Memphis Horns.

Film of the band perfoming "Angel of Harlem" was included in the *Rattle & Hum* film, whilst parts of "When Love Comes To Town" were included in the promo video for this song. The session was, according to Gary, "a true historic happening". As Bono said when he first entered the studio, "There would be no U2, there would have been no Elvis, if there hadn't been a Sun."

"SURRENDER" (*WAR* ALBUM TRACK) (5.34) The fourth track on the second side of the *War* album. It tells the story of "Sadie" who is cracking up from all the pressures of living in the city. The title may also be linked to the Christian idea of surrendering one's life to God. Bono said that the idea of "Surrender" was linked to the theme of the whole album. It was first performed at Tiffany's in Glasgow, Scotland on 1st December 1982.

SWEENY, GEORGE The guitarist with the Vipers and a member of the Max Quad Band with Adam.

"SWEETEST THING" (*"WHERE THE STREETS HAVE NO NAME"* SINGLE B-SIDE) (3.03) This song was originally the B-side of the "Where The Streets Have No Name" single (IS340), released in 1987. The song was written by Bono about his wife Ali as a result of forgetting her birthday due to the pressures and commitments of recording *The Joshua Tree* album.

The song was then "rescued" from relative obscurity by being issued as a new single to promote *The Best of 1980-1990* singles collection, although the single was actually released in 1998. The extra album of B-sides that was released with the first copies also included the "Sweetest Thing", though this was the original B-side track, running in at three seconds longer.

"SWEETEST THING" (THE SINGLE MIX) (3.00) (ISLAND CID 727 572 464-2/466-2) This single came in two different formats. One included the tracks

Video shoot for "Sweetest Thing" promotional video, Dublin, 20/9/98. *Photo: Sue Fell*

"Stories For Boys" and "Out of Control". These were old live recordings from the band's gig at the Paradise Theater in Boston, USA on 6th March 1981. The other version had two tracks from the band's memorable gig at Red Rocks stadium near Denver, which had taken place on 5th June 1983. These were "Twilight" and "An Cat Dubh/Into the Heart". The single was released in October 1998 and reached number 3 in the UK singles charts. In the USA it only reached number 63.

"SWEETEST THING" (PROMOTIONAL VIDEO). The whole shoot for the promo video was completed in Fitzwilliam Street, Dublin on 20th September 1998. Kevin Godley was the director and the video was based on Bono being driven down the street in a carriage (not singing). The street was heavily decorated and banners stetching across it with the words "I'm sorry", "I'm really sorry" and "I'm really, really sorry". In the background were various things that Ali liked, as Bono had said, "What the woman wants, the woman gets!" This included an elephant, the Artane Boys Band, a classical ensemble, hunky firemen, the Macnas Drama group, the boxer Steve Collins, traditional Irish dancers from *Riverdance* and the group Boyzone. Ali herself appeared at the beginning. The whole video was included in the documentary film *The Joshua Tree* from the TV series *Classic Albums* and on the *Best of 1980-1990 Video Collection*.

See also: Artane Boys Band / Boyzone / Kevin Godley

"SWEET FIRE OF LOVE" A song written and performed by U2 and Robbie Robertson of The Band on his 1987 album, *Robbie Robertson*. It had been recorded in Dublin in August 1986 just as U2 were beginning work on *The Joshua Tree*.

See also: Robbie Robertson / Testimony

SWEET JANE (LIVE) Bono sang vocals on this track from the 1999 Lone Justice album, *The World Is Not My Home*.

TACOMA DOME, TOCOMA, WISCONSIN, USA U2 played two sell out concerts at this 22,000 capacity venue on 20th and 21st April 1992 during the *Zoo TV* tour of America. During the interval of the first show, parts of the Freddie Mercury tribute concert at Wembley Stadium were broadcast live to the audience. The second show was added after a proposed show in Portland, Oregon failed to materialise.

The second show marked a turning point in the *Zoo TV* tour as two new songs were added to the set: "Unchained Melody" and "Slow Dancing". Also an acoustic version of "When Love Comes To Town" was played for the first time from the B-stage. The band also played here once during the *Elevation* tour on 12th April 2001. For this show The Edge's parents and children were in attendance and Bono danced on stage with two of The Edge's daughters.

TALKING HEADS The American "new wave" band fronted by David Byrne. On U2's first visit to London in December 1979, they were lucky enough to support Talking Heads at the Electric Ballroom in Camden Town (7th and 8th December). A year later U2 managed to get a support slot on three gigs that Talking Heads were playing in London (Hammersmith Odeon and Hammersmith Palais) and Paris (Baltard Pavilion) in December 1980, on the eve of U2's first ever visit to America. The Edge had often cited Talking Heads as one of his musical influences and so was especially pleased for U2 to be playing with them.

Another connection between Talking Heads and U2 was Brian Eno, who had produced the Talking Heads' albums *More Songs About Buildings and Food* (1978), *Fear Of Music* (1979) and *Remain In Light* (1980). This eventually led to Brian Eno being asked to produce U2's fourth album, *The Unforgettable Fire*, in 1984 and most of their subsequent albums.

TAMPA STADIUM, TAMPA, FLORIDA, USA U2 have played this Tampa venue three times. Their first appearance here was during the *Joshua Tree* tour on 4th December 1987 when they played to nearly 60,000 fans. They then played here again during the *Zoo TV Outside Broadcast* tour on 10th October 1992. The show was memorable for the fact that a male fan managed to get onto the stage straight after the band had finished playing "Pride" and was allowed to stay on stage whilst the band went to their dressing rooms. Before the band returned for the encore, the man borrowed one of The Edge's guitars and sang his song, "An Eye For An Eye Makes The Whole World Blind". The band returned here during the *Pop Mart* tour of North America on 10th November 1997.

TARGET CENTER MINNEAPOLIS, MINNESOTA, USA U2 played two sell out shows at this 18,000 capacity venue on two occasions. The first was on 30th March 1992 during the *Zoo TV* tour of America. The second was on 1st May 2001 during the *Elevation* tour of North America. Bono dedicated "Kite" to Uncle Sam's, a small venue near the Target Center where U2 had first played in Minneapolis twenty years earlier. In "With Or Without You" Bono sang down a fan's mobile phone to her friend at the other end of the line.

TARRANT COUNTY CONVENTION CENTER, FORT WORTH, TEXAS, USA During the *Joshua Tree* tour of the USA, U2 played two shows here – on 23rd and 24th November 1987. The second show marked the beginning of a special relationship between U2 and renowned blues singer/guitarist BB King, who was the support act. During the sound check U2 and BB King rehearsed a new song that Bono had specially written for him called "When Love Comes To Town". This song was then performed live in the show during the encore. The rehearsal and performance were filmed and included in the film *Rattle & Hum*.

TAYLOR, GAVIN The director of the U2 video *Under A Blood Red Sky*. As part of the production team for the Channel 4 music programme *The Tube*, Gavin flew out to Red Rocks to direct the film, a joint venture between *The Tube* and U2.

See also: *The Tube, Under A Blood Red Sky*

"TELEVISION - DRUG OF THE NATION" This song by American rap group The Disposable Heroes of Hiphoprisy was used as the introductory music to U2's *Zoo TV* shows in 1992. It was chosen as it fitted in with the idea of *Zoo TV* and the notion of television taking over people's lives. The single of this song reached number 57 in the UK charts when it was first released in March 1992. It was re-issued in December 1992 when it reached number 44. It failed to chart in the US. BP Fallon was the person who "discovered" it. Apparently he tried to play it to the group whilst they were watching the Oscars on TV. Their first reaction was, "Could you turn that down. We're trying to watch TV!"

TENCH, BENMONT Long-time Tom Petty collaborator who played keyboards on "All I Want Is You".

"TEQUILA SUNRISE" The Eagles' song that Larry Mullen performed on stage at the Coliseum, Hampton USA, on 12th December 1987, making his public vocal debut.

"TESTIMONY" A track co-written by the former Band member Robbie Robertson and U2. It was included on his 1987 *Robbie Robertson* solo album.

THALIA THEATRE, HAMBURG, GERMANY This was the venue for an anti-Nazi conference that took place on 30th and 31st January 1993. Bono and The Edge made a special guest appearance here, joining over 50 musicians, actors, scientists, historians, writers and artists who were all concerned about the rise of fascism in the recently re-united Germany. Bono made an impassioned speech where he called for everyone involved to fight to preserve democracy against fascism. On the second day, Bono and The Edge, together with Jo Shankar on violin and Stefan Rager (of the German group Jeremy Days) on percussion, performed "One" as a climax to the conference. This was then followed by the band and others singing "We Will Never Forget". All proceeds from the event went to UNICEF.

THATCHER, MARGARET The Prime Minister of Great Britain from 1979 through the 1980s until her sudden downfall in 1990. Several times her government's policies came under fire from Bono for causing hardship amongst the youth of Britain and Ireland. At the 1986 Self Aid concert at Dublin's RDS Showground, U2 performed the Bob Dylan song "Maggie's Farm" as a protest at the large number of Irish youth who had to leave Ireland in search of work abroad. On *The Joshua Tree* album, "Red Hill Mining Town" looked at the way in which the closing of a mine led to the death of a community and the disintegration of relationships on a more personal level – a throwback from the 1984 miners' strike in Britain which resulted in many mines being closed down as a direct result of government policy.

In 1987 during the *Joshua Tree* tour, at several British shows Bono would change the end of "Bullet The Blue Sky" to include the words "running... into the arms of Margaret Thatcher". During the *Zooropa* tour of 1993, Macphisto tried ringing her from the stage of Cardiff Arms Park in Wales, but could only speak to her secretary.

T'HEEM HATTEM HOLLAND U2 recorded a special programme here for Dutch TV entitled *Countdown in Concert* on 14th May 1982. This was the last time that "Another Time, Another Place" was played live in concert. Another of the songs recorded for the show, "I Will Follow", was released as a single in Holland a few weeks later and reached number 12 in the Dutch charts.

"THEME FROM HARRY'S GAME" This haunting piece of music by Clannad, written for as TV drama about a British soldier going undercover amongst the IRA in Belfast, was used by U2 as the closing music to their *War* shows throughout 1983. It was also included on the video *Live At Red Rocks*.

"THEME FROM LET'S GO NATIVE" (*ORIGINAL SOUNDTRACKS 1* ALBUM TRACK) (3.07) The final track from *The Original Soundtracks 1* album by Passengers. The music was said to have been used in the "banned" South African film *Let's Go Native*, directed by Rodgher Vuijkers.

"THEME FROM MISSION: IMPOSSIBLE" (*MISSION: IMPOSSIBLE* SOUNDTRACK ALBUM) The title track from the soundtrack album to the film *Mission: Impossible*. The music, composed by Lalo Schifrin, was updated by Adam and Larry for the film.

"THEME FROM MISSION: IMPOSSIBLE" (SINGLE 1) The single of "Theme from Mission: Impossible" reached number 7 in both the UK and US charts in June 1996. This version contained the "Theme from Mission: Impossible" main version plus the following: "Mission: Impossible Theme (Mission Accomplished)", "Theme from Mission: Impossible" (Guru Mix), "Theme from Mission: Impossible" (Junior's Hard Mix), "Mission: Impossible Theme" (Dave Clark Remix).

"THEME FROM MISSION: IMPOSSIBLE" (SINGLE 2) This alternative single was released in Germany, Australia and Japan. It contained the following tracks: "Theme from Mission: Impossible", "Theme from Mission: Impossible" (Junior's Hard Mix Edit), "Mission: Impossible Theme (Mission Accomplished)", "Mission: Impossible Theme (Mission Accomplished)" (Cut the Red not the Blue), "Mission: Impossible Theme (Mission Accomplished)" (Dave Clarke Remix).

"THEME FROM MISSION: IMPOSSIBLE" (ALTERNATIVE REMIXES) In addition to the above remixes of the Theme from Mission Impossible, the following remixes were also released: "Theme from Mission: Impossible" (Howie B. Mix), "Theme from Mission: Impossible" (Remix by Goldie & Rob Playford), "Theme from Mission: Impossible" (Junior's Tribal Beats), "Theme from Mission: Impossible" (Junior's Hard Dub I), "Theme from Mission: Impossible" (Junior's Hard Dub II).

"THEME FROM MISSION: IMPOSSIBLE" (PROMOTIONAL VIDEO) The promo video for the Theme from Mission Impossible was directed by the band's old friend Kevin Godley, who by this time had already directed the promo videos for "Even Better Than the Real Thing" and "Numb". The video shows scenes from the film as well as the faces of Adam and Larry on TV monitors.

"THEME FROM THE SWAN" (*ORIGINAL SOUND-TRACKS 1* ALBUM TRACK) (3.24) This piece was "used" in the Hungarian film, "The Swan" directed by Joseph Mamet.

"THESE DAYS AN OPEN BOOK" Both Adam and Larry played on this track by Nanci Griffiths, included on her 1994 album, *Flyer*.

"THINGS TO MAKE AND DO" (A DAY WITHOUT ME SINGLE B-SIDE) A straightforward instrumental that U2 put on the B-side of their second Island single release "A Day Without Me" in August 1980. It was not however included on their first album, *Boy*, released a couple of months later. It is the only instrumental the group have ever performed live.

THIN LIZZY One of the most successful groups to come out of Ireland in the 1970s. Comprising Phil Lynott (bass and vocals), Brian Downey (drums) and Eric Bell (guitar), they first broke into the UK charts with a reworking of a traditional Irish ballad "Whiskey In The Jar" in 1973. After Bell left in 1974, he was replaced by Gary Moore, who was himself replaced by two new guitarists – Scotsman Brian Robertson and American Scott Gorham.

For much of the second half of the 1970s this line-up tasted success on both sides of the Atlantic with their *Live And Dangerous* album being remembered as one of the classic live rock albums. One of U2's earliest gigs was supporting Phil Lynott's "other" band, The Greedy Bastards, on 11th December 1978 at the Stardust Club in Dublin. In August 1981 U2 supported Thin Lizzy at their Slane Castle Festival appearance. U2 had grown in popularity so much by then that they were second on the bill. When Phil Lynott died in 1986, Bono, Adam, Larry and Paul McGuinness all attended his funeral.

See also: Phil Lynott / Self Aid

"THIS HEART" Larry played drums on this song off Nanci Griffiths' 1994 album, *Flyer*.

"THIS I'VE GOT TO STOP" A song that Bono wrote in his hotel room in New York City in 1986 along with "Silver & Gold". He was in New York to take part in the Artists United Against Apartheid session, which give rise to "Sun City" under the leadership of Little Steven Van Zandt. "This I've Got To Stop" was never released.

THOMAS, CHRIS He was at one time considered as a possible producer for U2's third album. He had previously worked with The Pretenders and the Sex Pistols.

THOMAS, PAUL The engineer who has been involved with the recording of many of the tracks on U2's first three albums – *Boy*, *October* and *War*. He went on to produce the Clannad album, *Sirius*. He still produces, mainly younger up-and-coming bands rather than the big names.

THOMAS, TONY A keyboard player with the Bluebeats. He played on the track "Jesus Christ" recorded at the Sun Studios in Memphis, Tennessee on the night of 29th/30th November 1987.

THOMAS AND MACK ARENA, LAS VEGAS, NEVADA, USA The first time that U2 played in Las Vegas, the gambling capital of the world, was here on 12th April 1987 during the *Joshua Tree* tour. After the show the band walked around the streets of Las Vegas filming themselves singing for the promo video of "I Still Haven't Found What I'm Looking For".

THORP was the name given to a "Thermal Oxide Reprocessing Plant" at Sellafield in Cumbria, England. It was the subject of a large scale protest by U2 and Greenpeace in 1992. U2 were to have played a free concert outside the gates of the Sellafield Nuclear Power plant in June 1992, but were prevented by a High Court injunction. Instead they landed on the beach outside the nuclear power station early in the morning and made their protest in front of dozens of reporters. Despite a heavily publicised campaign against the THORP plant, the British government gave the go-ahead for THORP 2 in 1993.

See also: Sellafield / Stop Sellafield

THREE RIVERS STADIUM, PITTSBURG, PENNSYLVANIA, USA U2 have played three times at this 40,000 capacity stadium in Pittsburgh. The first time was on 13th October 1987 during the *Joshua Tree* tour. The second time was on 25th August 1992, on the *Outside Leg* section of the *Zoo TV* tour. Before this show started the lead singer of the support band, the Disposable Heroes of Hiphoprisy, brought out a cake for the DJ, BP Fallon, whose birthday it was. Both shows were sold out, but when the band played here as part of the first leg for the *Pop Mart* tour on 22nd May 1997, the stadium was only three-quarters full.

"THE THREE SUNRISES" ("THE UNFORGETTABLE FIRE" SINGLE B-SIDE) (3.52) This track was included on the 12 inch and double 7 inch pack version of "The Unforgettable Fire" single, but was not available on the B-side of the 7 inch single. It was perhaps too light-hearted a track to be included on the album, but was still worthy nonetheless. It was also included on *the B-Sides* CD given away with *The Best Of 1980-1990* compilation CD.

"THE THREE SUNRISES" ("WIDE AWAKE IN AMERICA" EP) (3.46) The same version of *The Three Sunrises* as above was the third track on the mini-album "Wide Awake in America", released only in the US in 1985.

"TIBETAN FREEDOM CONCERT", DOWNING STADIUM, RANDALL'S ISLAND, NEW YORK, USA This charity event took place on 7th and 8th June 1997 during the *Pop Mart* tour of North America. It was in aid of the Freedom for Tibet campaign and was organised by Adam Yauch of the Beastie Boys to raise awareness of the suffering of the Tibetan people. U2 played a five song set on the first day without all their *Pop Mart* staging. Also on the bill were Patti Smith, Radiohead, Noel Gallagher of Oasis and Sonic Youth. Set List: Gone, Mysterious Ways, Until The End Of The World, One, Please.

TIFFANY'S, GLASGOW, SCOTLAND U2 have played three sell out concerts at this 1500 capacity venue. They first played here on 4th October 1981 during the *October* album tour. Their next visit on 1st December 1982 marked the start of the winter 1982 tour of Britain and Europe which was designed to give the band a chance to try out new material from their forthcoming *War* album in a live setting. So "Surrender", "New Year's Day" and "Sunday Bloody Sunday" were played live for the first time at this concert. U2 made their final appearance here on 24th March 1983 during the *War* tour. Most of the show was recorded for later transmission on Radio Clyde.

TIFFANY'S, LEEDS, ENGLAND U2 played this venue just once on 20th October 1981 during the *October* tour of Britain. When U2 played Leeds Roundhay Park on the *Pop Mart* tour on 28th August 1997, Bono reminisced from the stage about this early gig in Leeds complete with the plastic palm trees.

TIME MAGAZINE U2 appeared on the front cover of this famous American magazine for its issue of 27th April 1987 under the headline "U2: Rock's Hottest Ticket". They were only the third group to have this honour, the other two being The Beatles and The Who.

TOAD'S PLACE, NEWHAVEN, CONNECTICUT, USA This club was one of the first places that U2 played in America, on 14th December 1980. They obviously went down well as they returned for two more gigs on 27th May and 15th November 1981, both of which were sold out. At the May gig, the new single "Fire" was played live for the first time.

TOGETHER FOR THE CHILDREN OF BOSNIA (CONCERT VIDEO AND ALBUM) This was the release on video, cassette and CD of Luciano Pavarotti's 4th annual concert at Modena in Italy. It took place on 12th September 1995 before an audience of 12,000 fans and invited guests including Princess Diana. Bono, The Edge and Brian Eno performed "Miss Sarajevo" with Pavarotti and then later on in the concert, the three of them performed "One". Other artists were: Zucchero, Nenad Bach, Gam Gam, Dolores O'Riordan, Simon Le Bon, Meat Loaf, Jovanotti, Michael Bolton and The Chieftains. The concert finished with all the singers on stage performing "The Bridge Is Broken" and "Nessun Dorma". All proceeds from the concert and sale of the recordings went to the War Child charity to raise funds to build a music therapy centre in Mostar in Bosnia. This was finally opened in December 1997.

See also: Luciano Pavarotti / Pavarotti Music Centre / Miss Sarajevo / War Child

TOKYO DOME, TOKYO, JAPAN U2 have played this well-known Japanese indoor stadium five times. Their first shows were on 25th and 26th November 1989 during the *Lovetown* tour. They then played two shows at the very end of the *Zoo TV* tour on 9th and 10th December 1993 under the title *Zoo TV - Japan*. For these two dates there was a lot of behind the scenes activity as it is believed that Madonna wanted to play a block of dates here at the same time. U2's promoter had already booked the two U2 dates and refused to budge when asked to move them so Madonna could play consecutive nights without a break. Rumour has it that he even threatened a curse on the other promoter who he vowed to "kill" if he didn't get his way!

In the end U2 got their dates and Madonna even came to watch the second show. Macphisto tried to ring her from the stage but couldn't get through. Members of the group Deep Purple were also watching the gig. Unfortunately whilst the final show on the 10th was a sell out, the first show was not, with about 10,000 empty seats. U2 returned here for one date during the *Pop Mart* tour, on 5th March 1998 with many of the fans sitting quietly in their seats to watch the show.

TOMII, SATOSHI The musician/engineer responsible for some of the keyboard programming on U2's work during the 1990s.

"TOM TOM'S DREAM" (*THE MILLION DOLLAR HOTEL* SOUNDTRACK ALBUM TRACK) (1.52) Performed by The MDH Band.

"TOM TOM'S ROOM" (*THE MILLION DOLLAR HOTEL* SOUNDTRACK ALBUM TRACK) (2.24) Performed by Brad Mehldau with Bill Frisell.

"TOMORROW" (*OCTOBER* ALBUM TRACK) (4.39) The opening track on side two of the *October* album and one of the strongest on the album. The track looks back to the funeral of Bono's mother, Iris, in its reference to a black car, and also forward to the second coming of Christ. The song has a haunting

Larry, The Edge and Bono at the Torhout Festival, July 2nd 1983.. *Photo: Kay Baursfeld*

melody, made even stronger by the introduction of Vincent Kilduff's uillean pipes. The song had its live premiere at the Royal Dublin Society Hall on 26th January 1982. Vincent Kilduff was present with the band to play his uileann pipes on this and several other numbers. The Edge also played tin whistle during live performances of this song.

See also: Vincent Kilduff

"TOMORROW" (*COMMON GROUND* ALBUM TRACK) This new version of the *October* album track was specially recorded for the *Common Ground* album, a collection of tracks by Irish musicians, put together by Donal Lunny, a former member of Planxty and Moving Hearts. Both Adam and Bono contributed fresh parts to this reworking of "Tomorrow".

See also: Donal Lunny

"THE TOMORROW SHOW" (US TELEVISION SHOW) U2 made their first major appearance on American TV on this show on 30th May 1981 right at the end of their mammoth 60 concert first major tour of America. They performed "Twilight" and "I Will Follow".

"TOP HAT BALLROOM, DUBLIN, IRELAND" One of U2's most important early gigs in Dublin took place on 9th September 1978 when they played as support act to The Stranglers at The Top Hat Ballroom in Dun Laoghaire.

See also: The Stranglers

TOP OF THE POPS (UK TELEVISION SHOW) U2 have appeared on this long running British popular music show many times in their career. Their first

appearance took place in August 1981 when they performed their new single "Fire". As Bono commented, "We must have been the only band who appeared on *Top Of The Pops* whose single actually went down the following week!" Their next appearance was in January 1983 playing "New Year's Day".

A few months later they appeared on 31st March 1983 singing their next single "Two Hearts Beat As One". During this performance Bono climbed onto the balcony and improvised the words "let's twist again". By then the promotional video was making its mark on the music scene and U2's videos for a time were used on the programme instead of the group playing live. However given their status by the early 1990s, U2 had several single releases premiered to a large audience on *Top Of The Pops* just prior to their release, including "The Fly", "One", "Hold Me, Thrill Me, Kiss Me, Kill Me", "Discotheque" and "Last Night On Earth". Their performance of "One" beamed from the Zoo TV show rehearsals at the Civic Centre in Lakeland, Florida was performed exclusively for *Top of The Pops*. In October 2000 they were shown on the programme performing the single "Beautiful Day" on the top of the Clarence Hotel in Dublin. A month later, the band performed at the *Top Of The Pops* studio "Stuck In A Moment You Can't Get Out Of", "Beautiful Day" and "Elevation".

See appendix for complete list of TV appearances

TOP RANK, BRIGHTON, ENGLAND U2 have played this 2,000 capacity club in Brighton on two occasions: 12th October 1981 and 13th March 1983. The second date was Adam's 23rd birthday, so a cake and champagne, as well as several presents, were brought out to him on the stage. The show also marked the first time that U2 played the Bob Dylan song "Knocking On Heaven's Door" in a live setting, with Mike Peters from The Alarm joining the band on stage.

TORHOUT FESTIVAL, TORHOUT, BELGIUM U2 have played this famous Belgium rock festival on three different occasions. Each Torhout Festival is then followed the next day by the Werchter Festival in another part of Belgium and the artists who play at the Torhout go on to play at the Werchter. U2's first appearance at this festival was on 3rd July 1982 where it is believed Bono's use of the white flag onstage first began. Many people in the audience had white flags and one was eventually passed up to him on the stage. U2 returned to this festival the following year and played here on 2nd July 1983. U2's last appearance here was as the headlining act on 6th July 1985, exactly a week before appearing at Live Aid. U2 dedicated "40" to Joe Cocker, another of the artists on the bill.

See also: Werchter Festival

TOR SLUZEWEKKY HORSE RACE TRACK, WARSAW, POLAND U2's only ever gig in this former communist country took place during the *Pop Mart* tour of Europe on 12th August 1997. Approximately 70,000 fans attended, though there were problems with the massive crowd. Many people got in for free after police tore down security fences shortly before the show began, and about 200 people needed medical treatment after getting crushed when the entrance gate was first opened. During the show, Bono dedicated "New Year's Day" to the audience and when pictures of Lech Walesa were shown on the screen during the song, a large cheer went up.

TOSCA The Dublin restaurant owned by Bono's brother, Norman Hewson. It closed down in August 2000 while Norman concentrated on his cafe next door called "Nude".

See also: Nude

TOTALLY WIRED, DUBLIN, IRELAND This is one of the recording studios in Dublin used for the *All That You Can't Leave Behind* album.

"TOUCH" ("11 O'CLOCK TICK TOCK" SINGLE B-SIDE) This track was the B-side of the single "11 O'clock Tick Tock". It was originally called "Trevor" and sounds rather dated today. It was produced by Martin Hannet and was played live in several shows in 1980 before being dropped.

See also: "Trevor"

TOWN HALL, CHRISTCHURCH, NEW ZEALAND U2's first ever concert in New Zealand (and in the Southern Hemisphere), took place here on 29th August 1984.

It was one of four concerts the band played in New Zealand before moving on to play in Australia.

TRABANT CAR The peculiar East German car that U2 used as a symbol and stage prop during the whole *Zoo TV* era. At the time that U2 were recording *Achtung Baby* in Berlin, just after the fall of the Berlin Wall and East Germany being re-united with the West, hundreds of these cars were being abandoned all over Berlin by drivers who had used them to get to Berlin from the East.

Seen as a symbol of the fall of Communism, these East German cars were neither strong mechanically nor body wise, being made out of compressed cardboard. Anton Corbijn in his photo shoot for the *Achtung Baby* album used several Trabants in his photos. These were included in the album booklet and on covers of several of the *Achtung Baby* singles. He also used them in his promo video of "One" which was filmed in Berlin. *Zoo TV* show designer Willie Williams then had the idea of using Trabants as part of the *Zoo TV* stage set, having them as giant spotlights.

Following a visit to the Trabant factory in Chemnitz by Paul McGuinness, several Trabants were purchased for use on *Zoo TV*. The band then asked Catherine Owens, Rene Castro and Willie Williams to paint designs on them to make them more attractive. One particular Trabant was covered in tiny mirrors and was used as a DJ station by BP Fallon to play records from before U2 arrived on stage. Later on in the show the same Trabant was given a swing by Larry to revolve during "Satellite of Love". You could even win one as a competition prize.

After the *Zoo TV* tour had ended four of the Trabants (or "Trabbies" for short) were donated to the Rock 'n' Roll Hall Of Fame in Cleveland, Ohio, where they now hang in the entrance hall. The four Trabants had the nicknames of "Liberace" (mirrored one), "News Of The World" (newspaper one), "Elec-

Trabants illuminate the stage in London, England.   *Photo: Claire Bolton*

tric Porcupine" (lights one) and "Tigger" (fake fur one).

See also: Rene Castro / Catherine Owens / Rock 'n' Roll Hall of Fame / Willie Williams

THE TRABANT LAND (DOCUMENTARY) A documentary film made by Dreamchaser Productions in May 1992 about the Trabant car and how it came to be used by U2 for the *Zoo TV* tour. In it you see Paul McGuinness at the Trabant factory buying some of the cars, Larry driving one around Berlin and Trabants being decorated by Catherine Owens.

TRANSWORLD DOME, ST LOUIS, MICHIGAN, USA U2 played here on 8th November 1997 as part of the *Pop Mart* tour of North America (third leg). In the audience was a fan dressed up as Macphisto. He was invited up on stage in the middle of "Bullet The Blue Sky" and Bono performed a mock fight with him. They even swapped costumes with Bono taking the horns and jacket off the Macphisto and giving him his hat and sunglasses.

"TRASH OF THE TITANS" See: The Simpsons

"TRASH, TRAMPOLINE AND THE PARTY GIRL" ("A CELEBRATION" SINGLE B-SIDE) (2.33) This studio version of the track is only available on the B-side of the "A Celebration" single (WIP 6770). Its title was soon shortened to "Party Girl" and became

popular with U2 fans from its performance on the "Live At Red Rocks" video. The song was recorded over the Christmas break of 1981 at Dublin's Windmill Lane studios. The band had just finished recording the A-side and had just two hours of studio time left to record the B-side. Each band member (apart from Larry who wasn't there) was allowed just two takes to record their part, whilst Larry's drumming part was a tape of his drum part on "A Celebration" slowed down! The song was first played live at the Caird Hall in Dundee, Scotland on 26th February 1983. The track also appeared on *The B-Sides* CD given away free with early versions of *The Best of 1980-1990* CD.

See also: Party Girl (live)

"TREASURE (WHATEVER HAPPENED TO PETE THE CHOP)" ('NEW YEAR'S DAY' SINGLE B-SIDE) (3.20) This straightforward pop song, featuring the dominant drumming of Larry, was included on the B-side of the "New Year's Day" single released on 7 inch, 12 inch and double 7 inch formats. The "Pete The Chop" in the title refers to a friend of the band's who saw them play in London and asked them to write a song about him. This they did. Island Records thought it could have been U2's first hit single, but the band thought it was too commercial and did not want it released as a single and so re-arranged it. The

Trabants Sydney, Australia. *Photo: Georgia Everett*

line "Whatever happened to Pete The Chop?" came from people at Island Records who from to time to time would ask the question to Paul McGuinness.

"TREVOR" An early U2 song that was later retitled "Touch" and put on the B side of the "11 O'clock Tick Tock" single. It is about a person who smiles all the time because he wants to live forever.

TRIBUTE BANDS Like many big name bands U2 have their fair share of imitators. Tribute bands first started in countries such as Australia and South Africa where some of the big name bands from Britain and America hardly ever played. To compensate for this, local musicians would form a band as a tribute to their particular musical heros, so people would at least be able to see a version of their favourite band playing live in their local pub or club. The idea soon spread to Europe and America, and there is now a thriving industry in tribute bands. Some just play the music of their heroes whilst others also try to dress like them.

The Joshua Trio and The Doppelgangers were probably the first U2 tribute bands. The Doppelgangers were manufactured initially for the promo video shoot of "Even Better Than The Real Thing" in February 1992 where they had to pretend to be U2. They were then used in the TV special of *Zoo TV* in November 1992 and afterwards suggested to Paul McGuinness that they might go full time. The band then set about rehearsing and getting new members before going out on the road in Britain, Ireland and Europe throughout much of the 1990s. Various other U2 tribute bands have formed since then with names taken from U2 songs and albums such as "Achtung Baby", "Rattle and Hum" and "U Zoo". It is believed that there are currently about twenty U2 tribute bands around the world.

Websites: www.tributecity.com
                    www.tributebands.com

See also: The Doppelgangers / The Joshua Trio

TRIMBLE, DAVID The leader of the Democratic Unionist party in Northern Ireland who was awarded the Nobel peace prize in December 1998 along with his political opponent John Hume, for their efforts in bringing peace in Northern Ireland. The two of them appeared on stage with Bono at the concert at the Waterfront Hall in Belfast in May 1998 in support of a "Yes" vote for the Good Friday Peace Agreement. When David Trimble and John Hume were awarded the Nobel Peace Prize in Oslo in December 1998, The Edge and Paul McGuinness attended the ceremony, whilst Bono sent a video message of congratulations.

See also: John Hume / Nobel Peace Prize / Waterfront Hall

TRINITY COLLEGE, DUBLIN, IRELAND U2 first played here on the evening of 3rd February 1979 after playing at McGonagles earlier in the day. They next played here at lunch time on 12th May 1979 during rag week, when they performed a free gig for the students on the steps of the college's Institute of Preventative Medicine. In spite of steady rain, many students stayed to see U2 complete their set – the gig having been publicised by a friend wearing a sandwich board bearing the band's name.

Paul McGuinness was a student here from 1968 to 1971, studying Philosophy and Psychology. The Edge's brother Dik Evans was also a student here, and the band, as well as Lypton Village, would often use his room as a base.

See also: Paul McGuinness

"TRIP THROUGH YOUR WIRES" (*THE JOSHUA TREE* ALBUM TRACK) (3.32) The third track on side two of *The Joshua Tree* album. It features Bono on harmonica and is almost a country song, reflecting the American influence. Like "With Or Without You" it deals with the subject of sexual temptation. The song was premiered on the Irish TV programme "TV Gaga" on 30th January 1986 before *The Joshua Tree* had been recorded. It was first performed in concert at The Summit, Houston, Texas on 7th April 1987.

"TRIUMPH OF THE WILL" This was the title of a 1936 Nazi propaganda film made by Leni Riefenstahl which featured members of the Hitler Youth playing drums at a Nazi rally at the Olympia Stadium in Berlin. This sequence was used in the opening sequences to the *Zoo TV* shows for the *Zooropa* phase of the tour.

See also: Leni Reifenstahl

"TRYING TO THROW YOUR ARMS AROUND THE WORLD" (*ACHTUNG BABY* ALBUM TRACK) (3.53) The third track on side two of the *Achtung Baby* album. Some may have called it one of the weakest tracks on the album, but it was given a new lease of life on the *Zoo TV* tour where it was used as a catwalk song during which Bono would pick a girl out of the crowd and open a bottle of champagne with her. Sometimes he would pick out two girls. It was first played live in concert at the Civic Center, Lakeland, Florida on 29th February 1992 at the first ever *Zoo TV* concert. It was the only song from the show at the Sydney Football Ground which did not make it onto the video, *Zoo TV Live From Sydney*. Amongst the theories about this is that the girl in the film was under-aged or didn't want to be on the film. The more likely explanation is that the whole concert was too long to be included on a 2 hour video tape, so one track had to go and it was this.

TUBE, THE (UK TELEVISION MUSIC SHOW) A famous British music TV programme that went out live on a Friday night for much of the 1980s. It was presented by Jools Holland (formerly of the group Squeeze) and Paula Yates (the then wife of Bob Geldof). Bono made his first appearance when he joined The Police on stage during "Invisible Sun" for the filming of their show at the Gateshead International Stadium which was subsequently broadcast on *The Tube*.

U2 first appeared in their own right on the programme on 16th March 1983. The band played five songs: "Gloria", "New Year's Day", "Sunday Bloody Sunday", "40" and "I Will Follow". The first three were shown live that night whilst "I Will Follow" was broadcast on 24th June and "40" was not broadcast at all.

A few months later *The Tube* sent a crew under director Gavin Taylor out to Red Rocks Amphitheater near Denver, Colorado to film the historic Red Rocks show. Parts of this were broadcast on the *A Midsummer Night's Tube* special a few weeks later. In 1987 U2 were shown singing "The Lost Highway" from their hotel room during the *Joshua Tree* tour of America. This was a special recording by U2 from San Diego, California for the last ever transmission of *The Tube*.

See appendix for a list of TV appearances by U2
See also: Gavin Taylor / Under A Blood Red Sky

TUESDAY BLUE One of the first groups signed to Mother Records. Adam Clayton joined them onstage at the Paradiso, Amsterdam on 9th January 1987.

TURLINGTON, CHRISTY The international supermodel and friend of Naomi Campbell has attended several U2 concerts over the years. She appeared with Bono on the front of the December 1992 edition of *Vogue* magazine. In 1996 and 2000 she took part in fashion shows in Dublin in aid of the Children of Chernobyl charity. In July 2001 Bono was scheduled to give her away at her wedding in America.

See also: Naomi Campbell / Vogue

TURNER, STEVE The Christian poet and music journalist who has written several rock biographies including one on Sir Cliff Richard. In 1987 he was invited by U2 to write their film book *Rattle and Hum* along with Willie Williams.

TV CLUB DUBLIN IRELAND U2's final gig of 1980 took place here on 22nd December.

TV GAGA (RTE TV PROGRAMME) An Irish Television programme in which U2 appeared on 30th January 1986. Both Bono and Larry were interviewed by the presenter and various members of the audience, before they were joined by Adam and The Edge to play some new songs. The first song entitled "Womanfish" has never been performed live since. They also sang a prototype version of "Trip Through Your Wires" as well as the Bob Dylan song "Knocking On Heaven's Door".

"TWILIGHT" (*BOY* ALBUM TRACK) (4.22) The second track on side one of the *Boy* album. It has ambiguous lyrics which could refer to a boy growing up into a man or maybe something more sinister. The song was probably first performed live at the Stardust Club in Dublin on 11th December 1978.

"TWILIGHT" ("ANOTHER DAY" SINGLE B-SIDE) A different version of "Twilight" to the one on the *Boy* album was on the B-side of the "Another Day" single, released only in Ireland. It was recorded at the Eamon Andrews Studio in Dublin in February 1979 and "took four minutes" according to Bono. There was no producer.

See also: Eamon Andrews Studio

TWILIGHT (LIVE) ("SWEETEST THING" SINGLE) This live version was recorded at Red Rocks Amphitheater in June 1983 and included on one of the "Sweetest Thing" singles released in October 1998.

"TWO HEARTS BEAT AS ONE" (*WAR* ALBUM TRACK) (4.00) This was one of two songs that Bono wrote whilst on honeymoon with his wife, Ali, in the Bahamas and is a love song to her. This is a strong pop song, held together by Adam's bass line – it was inevitable that it would be released as a single. It was first performed live at the Caird Hall in Dundee, Scotland on 26th February 1983.

"TWO HEARTS BEAT AS ONE" (SINGLE) (IS 109) (3.52) The single version of "Two Hearts Beat As One" was released in March 1983 at the same time as the *War* album. It only reached number 18 in the UK singles charts despite the fact the fact that the single's B-side "Endless Deep" was not included on the album. It was also released on the B-side of the German only release of "40".

"TWO HEARTS BEAT AS ONE" (REMIX 1) The American DJ Francois Kevorkian was responsible for this first ever remix of a U2 song, that was remixed specially for the disco market at the suggestion of Island Records boss, Chris Blackwell. It was included on a French single release (814 653-7) and a 12 inch UK release (ISD 109) along with another remix by Steve Lillywhite. Its success in Europe prompted Island Records to release a promo version for the US market.

See also: Francois Kevorkian

"TWO HEARTS BEAT AS ONE" (REMIX 2) The second remix of "Two Hearts Beat As One" was remixed by U2 producer Steve Lillywhite and included on the B-side of the 12 inch version.

"TWO HEARTS BEAT AS ONE" (PROMOTIONAL VIDEO) The promotional video of "Two Hearts Beat As One" was filmed in Paris by the side of the Sacre Coeur Cathedral in March 1983. It was a basic film of the band playing the song with the cathedral in the background. Radar, the boy on the cover of *Boy* and *War*, makes a brief appearance, as do fire eaters and acrobats. Meiert Avis was the director, this being his fourth U2 video.

"TWO SHOTS OF HAPPY, ONE SHOT OF SAD" (4.12) The song that Bono had written in a hotel room in Chicago in 1992 especially for Frank Sinatra to sing. The story goes that after the video shoot for the *Duets* song "I've Got You Under My Skin", Bono was invited back to Frank's house. There he was able to sing one verse to Frank but unfortunately that was about as far as it got. He did however get to perform the song with U2 at a specially recorded tribute which was shown at Frank's 80th birthday party in New York on 14th December 1995. The song was then developed with some input from The Edge and U2 recorded it in 1997. It was included as the third track on the single version of "If God Will Send His Angels" and was produced by Nellie Hooper.

See also: Frank Sinatra

"TWO SIDES LIVE" (WBMS) A special radio-only promotional LP transcription disc issued in America by Warner Brothers in the summer of 1981. It contained much of the second show that U2 had performed at the Paradise Theatre in Boston, USA on 6th March 1981. It was issued by Warner Brothers (who distributed Island Records in the USA) as a tool for awakening interest in U2 amongst DJs so that U2 got more airplay on radio stations across the USA. It is now a highly prized collector's item.

"U2-3" (SINGLE) (CBS 7951) The name given to U2's first ever record released in September 1979. It was a single available in both 7 inch and 12 inch formats and was only available in Ireland on CBS Ireland. The A-side was "Out of Control" whilst the B-side contained two tracks, "Stories For Boys" and "Boy-Girl". The 12 inch version was limited to 1,000 hand-numbered copies – the numbering had been done by Jackie Hayden, the marketing director of CBS Records in Ireland. The idea of a 12 inch single release at the time was quite unusual and no doubt helped the single to reach number 1 in the Irish charts. The tracks were recorded at Windmill Lane studios in Dublin in August 1979 and were produced by Chas De Whalley initially as a demo tape. Paul McGuinness then persuaded Jackie Hayden and CBS Ireland to release this as a single in Ireland. The choice of tracks was down to fans, who voted via the Dave Fanning RTE radio programme.

See also: Dave Fanning / Jackie Hayden / Chas De Whalley

U2: A YEAR IN POP (TV DOCUMENTARY) This hour-long programme was screened on ABC-TV in the United States on 26th April 1997. It looked at the band's history and the recording of the *Pop* album, as well as showing highlights from the opening night of the *Pop Mart* tour in Las Vegas just 24 hours ear-

lier. Ratings for the programme were the worst ever for a non-political programme on the Big Three networks of ABC, CBS and NBC. The clip of the band performing "Staring at the Sun" would have been shown, but after the difficulties playing the song at the opening show "Do You Feel Loved" was shown instead.

U2.COM U2's official website first came on-line on 18th July 2000. It was then tested for a few months before being officially opened in October 2000. It was designed by the UK based company Good Technology, and is run jointly by Adam's brother, Sebastian Clayton, Martin Wroe, editor of *Propaganda* Magazine, and Aislin Meehan at Principle Management. In addition to giving up-to-date news about U2, it also has an extensive archive of information on the band as well as providing live webcams from concerts and studios.

Website: www.U2.com

U2 EXCLUSIVE CD! (*THE SUNDAY TIMES* FREE CD) A CD given away free with *The Sunday Times* newspaper on 3rd June 2001. It contained five audio tracks and two video tracks as well as information on Microsoft Office XP (Microsoft had helped with the sponsoring of the CD). The audio tracks were: "Beautiful Day", "The Ground Beneath Her Feet", "I Remember You" (live), "New York" (live) and "I Will Follow" (live). The live tracks had been recorded at the Irving Plaza in New York on 5th December 2000. The video tracks were: "Beautiful Day" and "Don't Take Your Guns To Town" which had been filmed in U2's studios in the South of France and Dublin respectively. Due to its rarity it soon became a highly sought after collector's item amongst U2 fans.

U2 MAGAZINE The official U2 fan club magazine, which was edited by Geoff Parkyn. It started in November 1981 and ran for sixteen issues until the autumn of 1986.

See also: Geoff Parkyn

U2 (ORIGINS OF BAND NAME) **See:** Steve Averill

"U2 2 DATE" (U2 2D 1) A special promotional album for radio stations that was basically a greatest hits album featuring one track from each of U2's album releases from the 1980s. Track listing: I Will Follow, Fire, Two Hearts Beat As One, Sunday Bloody Sunday (live), The Unforgettable Fire, In God's Country, Bad (live), I Still Haven't Found What I'm Looking For (live).

U2 - ZOO TV This was a TV special that was broadcast all around the world on Saturday 29th November 1992. It showed U2 in concert on the recent *Outside Broadcast* tour as well as interviews with the band in

Issues one to four of The U2 Magazine edited by Geoff Parkyn.

a Dublin TV studio and the "surprise" appearance of The Dopplegangers look-a-like U2 group. The whole programme was directed by Kevin Godley.

See also: The Dopplegangers / Kevin Godley / Zoo TV

ULSTER HALL, BELFAST, NORTHERN IRELAND U2 played this venue just once on 17th December 1980 during a short pre-Christmas series of five dates on both sides of the Irish border. They returned to Belfast less than a month later to play at Queen's University for a BBC Northern Ireland TV special.

"ULTRA VIOLET (LIGHT MY WAY)" (*ACHTUNG BABY* ALBUM TRACK) (5.31) The fourth track on side two of the *Achtung Baby* album. The song (like several others on *Achtung Baby*) is about a relationship that has gone horribly wrong – and from which there can be no reconciliation. The chorus sounds like a plea for help, but the help is not there. The song was first performed live at the Civic Centre, Lakeland, Florida on 29th February 1992, the first date of the *Zoo TV* tour. It was played in the encore after "Desire" and before "With Or Without You" and would stay in the *Zoo TV* set for most dates right through to the Dublin RDS show on 28th August 1993.

"UNCHAINED MELODY" ("ALL I WANT IS YOU" SINGLE B-SIDE) (4.52) This song, which had been a number 1 hit for both Jimmy Young and The Righteous Brothers, was recorded by U2 for the B-side of the "All I Want Is You" single. It had been used in the 1988 film *Ghost* and was adapted by Bono as a song to sing at the end of "One" in a live setting. This first happened on the *Zoo TV* tour (first leg) at the Tacoma Dome on 21st April 1992 and would be repeated in many more *Zoo TV* shows. The song was also included on *The B-sides* CD that accompanied *The Best Of 1980-1990* compilation CD.

"UNCHAINED MELODY" (*"LIVE FROM SYDNEY"* VIDEO TRACK) The song "Unchained Melody" was used as a postscript to "One" during several shows on the *Zoo TV* tour. This live version comes from the *Zoo TV Live From Sydney* video filmed on 27th November 1993.

UNDARK 3396 (ALBUM) Ambient album co-ordinated by multimedia artist Russell Mills. The Edge and Eno contributed some ambient music to this project, released in 1996.

UNDER A BLOOD RED SKY (MINI-ALBUM) (IMA3; CID 113) U2's first live album was produced by Jimmy Iovine and released in November 1983. Its budget price reflected the running time of 35 minutes (shorter than a conventional studio album). It was one of the band's biggest selling albums, staying in the UK album charts for over 200 consecutive weeks,

Bono sings on *The Unforgettable Fire* tour.
Photo: Bart Moons

the longest chart reign for any U2 album. Whilst it reached number 1 in the UK album charts, in the USA it was a different story – it could only manage a lowly number 28.

One of the main reasons why this album was released was to counteract the growing number of illegal bootlegs of U2 concerts. If there was an official live U2 album available, it was hoped that the fans would buy that one and not the bootlegs. It was also released to showcase the first phase of U2's career, and as such contained tracks off U2's first three albums, interspersed with non-album single cuts.

Lastly it was used as a vinyl accompaniment to the *Live At Red Rocks* video released at the same time. Although the video contained songs entirely from their Red Rocks, Denver concert of 5th June 1983, the *Live Under a Blood Red Sky* mini-album only contained two tracks from this concert, "Gloria" and "Party Girl". One track, "11 O'clock Tick Tock", came from U2's performance at the Orpheum Theatre in Boston, USA on 6th May 1983. The rest of the tracks, "I Will Follow", "Sunday Bloody Sunday", "The Electric Co.", "New Year's Day" and "40" came from the Lorelei Festival show in Germany on 20th August 1983. The reason for this is that U2 felt that their performances at these two shows had been far more polished than at the Red Rocks show, which had been performed under great pressure. Reviews were mixed. For instance the *NME* said, "as a counter to the bootleggers, it's paltry pickings", yet *Hot Press* was more positive, arguing that it was "the work of a band completely sure about their powers".

Track List: Gloria, 11 O'clock Tick Tock, I Will Follow, Party Girl, Sunday Bloody Sunday, The Electric Co, New Year's Day, 40.

THE UNFORGETTABLE FIRE (ALBUM) (U25; CID 102) U2's fourth studio album was released on 1st October 1984 and, like its predecessor *War*, reached number 1 in the album charts in several countries including the UK. It reached number 12 in the USA, where U2 were still building up their following. The title came from an exhibition of Japanese paintings and drawings by survivors of the first atom bomb blasts on Hiroshima and Nagasaki in August 1945. The exhibition was on loan to the Chicago Peace Museum, which U2 visited in May 1983 during their *War* tour of North America. Four of the album's songs were influenced by the visit to the museum. "A Sort of Homecoming" and "The Unforgettable Fire" were connected with The Unforgettable Fire exhibition, whilst "Pride (In The Name of Love)" and "MLK" were influenced by a section in the museum devoted to Martin Luther King, the black civil rights campaigner.

Brian Eno, former keyboard player with Roxy Music, was brought in as producer. By this time he had gained an excellent reputation as producer of such artists as David Bowie and Talking Heads. Eno brought along with him a young Canadian engineer called Daniel Lanois who would become part of the production team on many more U2 albums.

The album was recorded partly at Dublin's Windmill Lane studios and partly in the ballroom at Slane Castle, situated about 30 miles north of Dublin. The change of producer brought about a change in musical direction in U2. The sound was less rocky and more laid back, with a more European ambient sound, though the American influences were still there in songs like "Elvis Presley And America" and "The 4th Of July".

Critical reaction to the album was mixed to say the least. Adam Sweeting writing in *Melody Maker* wrote, "I like *The Unforgettable Fire* for its clean break with the past... but I find some of the material on it unfinished and well short of inspirational". Like the critics, some U2 fans took a while to acclimatise themselves to the album's new musical direction, especially when the band first played the new songs on tour. The album's highlights included their first top 3 single in the UK, "Pride (In The Name of Love)" and the anti-drugs song "Bad", both of which were destined to become live favourites. Certainly there was more musical diversity on this album when compared to the previous three. As Brian Eno empha-

sized, he and the band were trying to create "musical landscapes" as opposed to straightforward songs.

Track List: 1) A Sort Of Homecoming, 2) Pride (In The Name of Love), 3) Wire, 4) The Unforgettable Fire, 5) Promenade, 6) The 4th Of July, 7) Bad, 8) Indian Summer Sky, 9) Elvis Presley And America, 10) MLK.

See also: Daniel Lanois / Brian Eno / Slane Castle / Windmill Lane studios

"THE UNFORGETTBALE FIRE" (*THE UNFORGET-TABLE FIRE* ALBUM TRACK) (4.55) The fourth track on *The Unforgettable Fire* album and one that shows the new ambient influence of Brian Eno on the group's music. Bono sings in a falsetto voice for the first time on record and sings some very obscure lines to a song dominated by the music as opposed to the lyrics. The music was further heightened by the addition of strings arranged by Noel Kelehan of the RTE Light Orchestra.

"THE UNFORGETTABLE FIRE" (SINGLE) (4.56) The single of the title track of *The Unforgettable Fire* album was quite an unusual choice for a single at the time, reflecting the new ambient style U2 that Brian Eno's production had brought to the band. However it still made number 6 in the UK singles charts, but was not "radio-friendly" enough for the US where it failed to chart. The single was released in a variety of formats with differing tracks to encourage fans to buy each format.

The 7 inch single (IS 220) had a live version of the album track "A Sort of Homecoming" as the B-side. (This had been recorded live at Wembley Arena in London on 15th November 1984.) The 12 inch version (12IS 220) had the extra tracks of "The Three Sunrises", "Love Comes Tumbling" and "Bass Trap". There was also a double 7 inch version released

Aftershow pass from *The Unforgettable Fire* Tour

The *Unforgettable Fire* Tour, Dortmund Germany, 21/11/84. *Photo: Kay Bauersfeld*

for collectors which included all the aforementioned tracks apart from "Bass Trap". This was replaced by "Sixty Seconds In Kingdom Come". "The Unforgettable Fire" was also included on the compilation CD *The Best of 1980-1990*.

"THE UNFORGETTABLE FIRE" (PROMOTIONAL VIDEO) The promo video of "The Unforgettable Fire" was directed by Meiert Avis in January 1985. It was shot mainly in Sweden with scenes of the band walking in the snow interspersed with shots of a fairground swing cleverly juxtaposed with a mushroom cloud from the explosion of a nuclear bomb.

THE UNFORGETTABLE FIRE COLLECTION (VIDEO) (082 974 3) A special video to promote *The Unforgettable Fire* album. Primarily the video shows the band recording the album at both Slane Castle and Windmill Lane studios in the early summer of 1984. This film section was directed by Barry Devlin and produced by James Morris originally for an RTE TV documentary. The video also contains the promo videos of "The Unforgettable Fire", "Bad", "Pride (In The Name of Love)" (versions 1 and 2) and "A Sort of Homecoming". Running Time: 60 minutes
  See also: Barry Devlin

"THE UNFORGETTABLE FIRE" EXHIBITION This was the title of a special exhibition of paintings and drawings made by survivors of the Hiroshima and Nagasaki atom bombings of August 1945. A national treasure in Japan, the exhibition was loaned to the Chicago Peace Museum in 1983. U2 were playing a concert at the Aragon Ballroom in Chicago on 21st May 1983 and decided to visit the museum prior to the evening's concert. The band were suitably inspired by what they saw to write "The Unforgettable Fire" and "A Sort Of Homecoming".
  See also: Chicago Peace Museum

THE UNFORGETTABLE FIRE TOUR The tour to promote *The Unforgettable Fire* album had a false start when several dates in Europe were either postponed

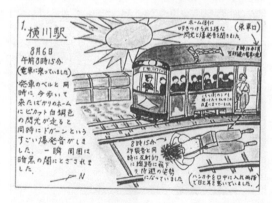

Detail from *The Unforgettable Fire* Exhibition.

or cancelled entirely. The reason for this was that the band needed more time to get used to playing the new material, as well as give their audience time to get into the new songs. U2 had already played several of the *Unforgettable Fire* songs live on their first ever dates in Australia and New Zealand in August and September, but as the tour went on it became increasingly clear that the fans weren't quite ready for the new songs and U2 weren't entirely comfortable playing them live.

So the dates announced for Rotterdam, Copenhagen, Oslo, Stockholm, Hamburg, Dusseldorf, Offenbach, Munich, Bologna, Milan, Lausanne and Paris were all cancelled. Some but not all of these were rescheduled for January 1985. The dates set for Lyon, Marseille, Barcelona, Toulouse, Rennes and Paris remained the same, with the show at the Espace Tony Garnier in Lyon on 18th October 1984 being the opening night of the tour. Unfortunately the majority of the crowd were unfamiliar with the new songs from *The Unforgettable Fire* album and as the concert ended sections of the audience booed, having expected songs from the *War* album.

The first European leg continued with 18 more shows at 13 venues with the two shows at Wembley Arena on 14th and 15th November closing this leg of the tour. A one-off show for German TV was filmed at the Westfalenhalle in Dortmund on 21st November, before the tour moved over to America and Canada for ten dates in December as its second leg.

In January 1985 the third leg of the tour began in Norway for twelve more shows throughout Europe, including Italy for the first time, finishing in Paris on 10th February. The final leg of the tour was once again in North America with 40 dates at 31 venues, finishing in Tampa, Florida on 2nd May 1985. For most of the shows, "The 4th Of July" would be the opening theme music, though for the final few shows this was replaced by "Drowning Man".

Apart from the fact that a member of the audience was brought onto the stage to play guitar on several of the dates, many of the shows were remembered more for crowd problems – people left their seats to get nearer to the stage, with fights sometimes resulting. For the first three legs of the tour a white backdrop was used onto which slides were projected. For the fourth and final stage in North America, these were removed so that the audience could be seated behind the stage giving a 360° view of the stage.

Songs played on the *Unforgettable Fire* tour from: A Day Without Me, A Sort Of Homecoming, Bad, Cry-Electric Company, 11 O'clock Tick Tock, 40, Gloria, I Fall Down, Indian Summer Sky, I Will Follow, Knocking On Heaven's Door, MLK, October, New Year's Day, Party Girl, Pride (In The Name of Love), Seconds, Southern Man, Sunday Bloody Sunday, Surrender, The Unforgettable Fire, Two Hearts Beat As One, Wire

"UNFORGETTABLE FIRE - THE STORY OF U2" OFFICIAL BIOGRAPHY This was the name of the official biography by Eamon Dunphy specially commissioned by U2 and Paul McGuinness in 1987. He was reportedly given a large advance to write the book and free access to all members of U2 and their families, friends and associates. Although the book was a bestseller and included many previously unknown details of the band members' early lives, it contained a fair number of inaccuracies. These were pointed out in a specially written article in *Hot Press* entitled "The Unbelievable Book" by U2 contemporary, Neil McCormick. In 1993 a special epilogue was added to cover the band's career from 1987 to 1993. This was written by Bill Graham.

UNITED CENTER, CHICAGO, ILLINOIS, USA U2 played four sell out concerts here during the *Elevation* tour (first leg) of North America, on 12th, 13th, 15th and 16th May 2001. Many fans who had bought tickets from touts outside on the first night, found that they had brought forgeries once they got to the turnstiles. They were offered the chance to buy tickets for the final two shows but as they had spent their money on the forgeries many were not able to do so. The first night was memorable for the fact that a fan called Jonathan was invited up on stage to play the piano during "Sweetest Thing", which he did perfectly. For several previous shows he had asked to do this, and the band finally relented. On the second night Bono sang to a girl on the stage lying down all through "With Or Without You". On the third night U2 surprised many fans by playing two songs from the very early days – "11 O'clock Tick Tock" and "Out Of Control", the latter not having been played since 1990. On the final night "I Still Haven't Found What I'm Looking For" was played live for the first time on the tour.

"UNITED COLOURS" *(ORIGINAL SOUNDTRACKS 1 ALBUM TRACK)* (5.31) The opening track on the *Original Soundtracks 1* album by Passengers. The music was "used" by Japanese film maker, Tetsuji Kobayshi in his film "United Colours of Plutonium" – a play on words of the fashion giant Benetton's advertising slogan, "United Colours of Benetton".

UNITED NATIONS, NEW YORK CITY, USA On 7th September 2000, Bono as a representative of Jubilee 2000, went to the headquarters of the United Nations to hand over a 21 million signature petition to the United Nations Millennium Summit meeting, seeking debt relief for the world's poorest countries. The petition was signed by people from 150 countries throughout the world and was given by Bono and the President of Nigeria, Olusegun Obasanjo, to the Secretary of the United Nations, Kofi Annan. In a short speech, Bono said, "It's madness that a pop star has to be doing this. Somebody else should be doing this."

See also: Drop The Debt / Jubilee 2000

UNITED STATES OF AMERICA U2 have had a love-hate relationship with the richest and most powerful country in the world over the years. They first visited the US in December 1980 playing a handful of dates on the North Eastern seaboard. Thanks to the help of Frank Barsalona and his Premier Talent agency, they returned in the spring of 1981 to play a mammoth three month tour covering virtually every area of the country from Los Angeles in the west, New Orleans and Miami in the south, through to Chicago in the north and Boston in the east. Even on this tour the band were managing to play to full houses of up to 2,000 capacity. Although the band were starting to receive significant radio airplay, their first two albums were not making much impact on the American album charts – *October* peaked at 104. It was not until the band's third album, *War*, and the well-publicised show at Red Rocks Stadium in Colorado that they began to break America in a big way.

By U2's fourth album, *The Unforgettable Fire*, the American influence in the band's music was becoming more apparent with songs like "The 4th Of July" and "Elvis Presley and America". Also the arrival of MTV in 1981 gradually took the music of U2 into virtually every living room in America through their promotional videos. *The Joshua Tree* album not only broke U2 into the stadium league in America (and Europe) but also gave them three number 1 singles and a number 1 album. Songs such as "Bullet The Blue Sky" and "In God's Country" again reflected the influence of the American dream in the band's songwriting. The album also gave the band their first Grammy awards for Best Album and Best Rock Performance.

The following album, *Rattle & Hum*, was partly recorded on American stages and the studio tracks explored U2's American influences through collaborations with such American musical heroes as Bob Dylan and BB King. The film of *Rattle & Hum* showed the band paying homage to the American dream by visiting Graceland, Elvis's home and laying down tracks at Sun Studios where many say modern rock music first began. However several music critics saw this as U2 saying in effect "we are now on the same level as these heroes" and so the film and album took a critical hammering.

As a result U2 looked back to Europe for inspiration for their next two albums, *Achtung Baby* and *Zooropa*. It was only with *Pop* that the American

feel returned in songs like "Miami" and "The Playboy Mansion". Similarly U2's last album *All That You Can't Leave Behind* pays its respects to the town of "New York". All of U2's major world tours have started in America, and it is the country where they have played the most gigs.

See also: Grammys / New York

UNIVERSAL MUSIC The major record company that bought out Polygram Records in 1999, who in turn had bought out Island Records in 1993. Universal Music is, in effect, U2's record company.

See also: Island Records / Polygram Records

UNIVERSAL STUDIOS LOS ANGELES CALIFORNIA USA U2 played two shows in support of their newly released *All That You Can't Leave Behind* album here on 26th and 27th October 2000. The first night show was for a broadcast by KROQ FM radio station and consisted of four songs: "Elevation", "New York", "Stuck In A Moment" and "Beautiful Day".

The second night show was broadcast for the TV show *Farmclub.com* and consisted of "Elevation", "New York", "Stuck In A Moment", "Beautiful Day" and "Pride". The tracks "Beautiful Day" and "New York" were included on the single releases of "Walk On" and "Stuck In A Moment You Can't Get Out Of".

UNIVERSITY COLLEGE, DUBLIN, IRELAND The university where Bono started as a student in September 1977. He only stayed two weeks though, as he had not passed his Irish Leaving Certificate, so he had to go back to Mount Temple School to study. During a gig by The Alarm here on 23rd October 1983, Bono joined them on stage in a rendition of "Knockin' On Heaven's Door".

UNIVERSITY OF EAST ANGLIA, NORWICH, ENGLAND U2 played two gigs here in 1981. The first was on 28th January during the *Boy* tour of Britain and Europe. The second was on 1st October, the opening date of an 18 date British tour to promote the newly released *October* album.

UNIVERSITY OF EXETER, ENGLAND U2 have played this west of England university twice. The first time was on 7th November 1980 during the *Boy* tour. The second time was on 8th March 1983 during the *War* tour. This particular show was attended by several inmates from a nearby remand centre. This was due to the fact that one of them was so desperate to see U2 play live that he had escaped from the centre the previous day to see U2's show at Bristol Colston Hall. On his return the remand prisoner had managed to persuade the authorities to let his fellow inmates come to the Exeter gig. They were allowed to do this and were introduced to the band afterwards.

UNIVERSITY OF KENT, CANTERBURY, ENGLAND U2 played in this English cathedral city just once, on 11th November 1980. They included "Father Is An Elephant" in their set – a song that has never been released on record.

UNIVERSITY OF LEEDS, ENGLAND U2 played at this venue on 18th March 1983 to a full house of 1,500 students. The venue is famous as the place where The Who recorded their legendary *Live At Leeds* album in 1970.

UNIVERSITY OF SHEFFIELD, ENGLAND This gig on 24th May 1980 was U2's first ever gig in this northern town famous for its own music scene featuring bands such as The Human League, Heaven 17, ABC and Def Leppard. It was also U2's first ever university gig in Britain.

UNIVERSITY OF TENNESSEE, KNOXVILLE, TENNESSEE, USA U2 played here on 10th March 1982 during the tour of America to promote the *October* album. Straight after the show the band went to see Rod Stewart performing at a nearby venue.

"UNTIL THE END OF THE WORLD" (*ACHTUNG BABY* ALBUM TRACK) (4.39) The fourth track on side one of *Achtung Baby*. It tells the story of the betrayal of Jesus by Judas Iscariot through the eyes of Jesus. The song was first played live at the Lakeland Civic Center, Florida on 29th February 1992 and was included in the set for the whole of the *Zoo TV* tour, where Bono would move off the main stage and start walking down the catwalk on his way to the B-stage. He would then reach out to the fans waiting by the B-stage before being pulled back by his minders.

"UNTIL THE END OF THE WORLD" (*UNTIL THE END OF THE WORLD* SOUNDTRACK ALBUM TRACK) The soundtrack album to the film *Until The End Of The World* contains a different version from the one on the *Achtung Baby* album.

"UNTIL THE END OF THE WORLD" (LIVE) (4.57) This rare live version of "Until The End Of The World" can be found on the Greenpeace album *Alternative NRG*. The track was recorded live at the Jack Murphy Stadium, San Diego California USA on 19th November 1992. Bono can be heard shouting the words "Hey Judas!" at the beginning of the song. The song has been played live on all three tours of the last ten years – *Zoo TV*, *Pop Mart* and *Elevation*.
   See also: Alternative NRG

"UNTIL THE END OF THE WORLD" (LIVE) (*ZOO TV LIVE FROM SYDNEY* VIDEO) The live footage of U2 performing "Until The End Of The World" can be seen on the *Zoo TV Live From Sydney* video.

"UNTIL THE END OF THE WORLD" (LIVE) (*POP MART LIVE FROM MEXICO CITY* VIDEO) This live footage of U2 performing "Until The End Of The World" can be seen on the *Pop Mart Live From Mexico City* video.

"UNTIL THE END OF THE WORLD" (LIVE) The film of U2 performing this song live from the Oakland Coliseum California on 18th April 1992 was used at the Freddie Mercury Tribute concert at Wembley Stadium two days later. Although U2 couldn't play live at the Wembley show due to being on tour in America with the *Zoo TV* show, they instead allowed the whole concert to be filmed and footage from that to be shown at Wembley and then beamed all around the world.
   See also: Freddie Mercury / Oakland Coliseum

"UNTIL THE END OF THE WORLD" (PROMOTIONAL VIDEO) (4.38) The video of "Until The End Of The World" was directed by Ritchie Smyth and produced by Ned O'Hanlon. It featured The Edge wrapped up in cling film! It was the final video on the whole collection known as *Achtung Baby – The Videos, The Cameos And A Whole Lot Of Interference From Zoo TV*. The fact that a video was made of this song suggests that at one time it may have been slated for a possible single release, though in the end this did not happen.

UPTOWN THEATER, KANSAS CITY, MISSOURI, USA U2 played a concert here on 25th February 1982 during the *October* promotional tour of the USA. It was at this gig that "A Celebration" was first performed live.

US FESTIVAL, GLEN HELEN REGIONAL PARK, DEVORE, CALIFORNIA, USA U2 took part in this three day festival, appearing here on the 30th May 1983 in the middle of the *War* tour of North America. The audience of around 125,000 was the largest that U2 played to date. U2 appeared on the last day of the festival, which was headlined by David Bowie. Bono peformed two acts to draw attention to U2 from the TV cameras filming the event. The first was falling off the stage into the crowd. The second was climbing up the 120 feet high stage scaffolding to wave to the crowd. The only problem was that the canvas holding him started to rip and Bono had to make an undignified retreat back the way he had come.

VAILLANCOURT, ARMAND The artist who designed the sculpture in San Francisco's Justin Herman Plaza, on which Bono wrote "Rock 'n' Roll Stop the Traffic". As a result of this action Bono was given a misdemeanour charge and summoned to appear at court a few weeks later. A few days later at their concert at Oakland Stadium Vaillancourt appeared on stage and Bono publicly apologised to him. He was then allowed to spray-paint the stage back-drop and wrote, "Stop The Madness!" The charges against Bono were then dropped.

See also: Save The Yuppies concert

VALLE HOVIN STADION, OSLO, NORWAY U2 played to a capacity crowd of 35,000 here on 29th July 1993 during the *Zooropa* tour. Macphisto rang the Norwegian Minister of Fisheries, Jan Henri Olsen, to challenge him over Norway breaking the world ban on whaling. The band also played here during the *Pop Mart* tour on 6th August 1997, finishing with the song they wrote for Roy Orbison, "She's A Mystery To Me". Earlier in the show there was a malfunction of the giant lemon, which failed to open, trapping the four members of U2 for a few minutes, before they escaped out of the back door.

"VAN DIEMEN'S LAND" (*RATTLE & HUM* ALBUM TRACK) (3.06) The second track on the first side of the *Rattle & Hum* album was about John Boyle O'Reilly, one of the leaders of the 1848 uprising in Ireland against the English. The protest took place as a result of the great potato famine and O'Reilly's punishment was transportation from Ireland to Tasmania (a large island south of the Australian mainland). The lyrics were written by The Edge who also sings very creditably on the song, which could have come straight out of the 19th century. The song is used at the beginning of the *Rattle & Hum* film as the credits roll.

See also: John Boyle O'Reilly

VAN DYKE PARKS STRINGS They were responsible for the string arrangements on "All I Want Is You".

STEVIE VAN ZANDT See: Little Steven

VERY SPECIAL ARTS FESTIVAL U2 were one of several acts on this American TV special which was broadcast on 10th September 1989 from the lawn of the White House in Washington DC.

A VERY SPECIAL CHRISTMAS (ALBUM) This 1987 album was conceived and created by Jimmy Iovine, the American producer who had produced the live U2 album *Under A Blood Red Sky*. U2 contributed the Phil Spector penned track "Christmas (Baby Please Come Home)". The album was in aid of the Special Olympics charity and featured Madonna, Bruce Springsteen and Run DMC, as well as U2.

See also: Christmas (Baby Please Come Home)

VILAR DE MOUROS, PORTUGAL U2's first ever concert in Portugal took place here on 3rd August 1982.

VILLAGE, THE See: THE LYPTON VILLAGE

VIPERS, THE A new wave band on the Dublin music scene as the same time as the early U2. One of their members was George Sweeny who had played with Adam Clayton in the Max Quad Band at St Columba's school. U2 appeared on the same bill as The Vipers at the Project Arts Centre in Dublin on 17th February 1979 when both bands took part in the "Dark Space Festival".

VIRGIN PRUNES The Virgin Prunes were formed in 1977 by some of the members of the Lypton Village who had been inspired by the success of the Hype.

The Virgin Prunes were not a conventional rock group. Instead they were more of a performance art/avant garde musical group. The leaders were Gavin Friday (Fionan Hanvey) and Guggi (Derek Rowan) who shared vocals. They were joined by Dave-id (David Watson on vocals), Strongman (Trevor Rowan) on bass, Pod (Anthony Murphy) on drums and Dik Evans (brother of The Edge) on guitar. The early gigs by the Virgin Prunes tended to concentrate on "vibing out" the audience through a confrontational approach they called "Art-Fuck", more often than not creating outrage in the audience. On several occasions they opened as the support act for the early U2 in Dublin.

By 1980 The Virgin Prunes had gained a loyal cult following and signed a recording deal with Rough Trade Records. Their first "album" *New Forms of Beauty* (1981) came out as 7 inch, 10 inch and 12 inch singles, which when put together made up a complete album! After the departure of Pod, who joined U2's road crew, the band were joined by Mary O'Nellon on drums. The band's first complete album was *If I Die... I Die* in 1982.

Later on in the same year a live/studio mix, *Heresie*, was released. In 1984 Guggi called it a day as did Dik Evans. O'Nellon moved to guitar and Pod rejoined on drums for 1986's *The Moon Looked Down and Laughed*. After general disinterest from the public the Virgin Prunes disintegrated with various members trying out solo projects, Gavin Friday having the most success. Three of the former mem-

The Edge, Voorst National, Brussels, 28/10/84 on the *Unforgettable Fire* tour.
Photo: Kay Bauersfeld

bers of the group tried to continue as "The Prunes" but they too broke up a few years later.

Website: www.virginprunes.com

See also: Dave-id / Dik Evans / Gavin Friday / Guggi / The Hype / Pod / Strongman / Lypton Village

VISCONTI, TONY Tony was the renowned producer who had married singer Mary Hopkin (of "Those Were The Days" fame). He had produced Mark Bolan and T.Rex as well as some early David Bowie albums. He was responsible for producing the live version of *The Unforgettable Fire* album track "A Sort of Homecoming" which appeared on the *Wide Awake In America* EP and on the B-side of "The Unforgettable Fire" single.

"VIVA DAVIDOFF" (*MISS SARAJEVO* SINGLE) (4.29) This track taken from the Passengers album session was included on the "Miss Sarajevo" CD single, but was not included on the *Original Soundtracks 1* album.

VOGUE MAGAZINE Bono appeared on the front cover of this prestigious fashion magazine along with Christy Turlington for a "rock meets fashion" special in the December 1992 edition. The pair were photographed with Bono wearing his Fly outfit. It was also a landmark edition of the magazine, as Bono was the first male ever to appear on the front cover of *Vogue* in its history.

For the November 2000 edition Bono again appeared in *Vogue*, this time with Naomi Campbell.

See also: Naomi Campbell / Christy Turlington

VOORST NATIONAL, BRUSSELS, BELGIUM U2 have played this important Belgian venue on three occasions. They first played two nights here during the 1984 *Unforgettable Fire* tour of Europe, on 27th and 28th October 1984. These shows were recorded, but to this day remain unreleased. They then played one date here during the *Joshua Tree* tour, on 8th July 1987.

DE VRIES, MARIUS He played keyboards on "If You Wear That Velvet Dress" on the *Pop* album.

"WAKE UP DEAD MAN" (*POP* ALBUM TRACK) (4.52) The twelfth and final track on the *Pop* album. Preliminarily written during the Dublin *Achtung Baby* sessions it was then recorded more fully in Dublin during the *Zooropa* sessions, but was not included on that album. Some letters of the title are said to be apparent on the cover of *Zooropa*. Parts of the song can be heard on "Salome", which was the B-side for the "Even Better Than The Real Thing" single. A slow song, almost like a prayer from Bono – he addresses Jesus, asking for his help. It was produced by Flood and had an excerpt from "Besronds Nevesta" by Nikolai Iankov Kaoufman in the final mix. It was first performed live at Zeppelinfeld in Nuremberg, Germany on 18th August 1997.

"WAKE UP DEAD MAN" (*POP MART LIVE FROM MEXICO CITY* VIDEO) "Wake Up Dead Man" is the final number of the show and was filmed at the Foro Sol Autodromo, Mexico City, Mexico on 3rd December 1997.

WALDORF ASTORIA HOTEL, NEW YORK CITY, USA This world-famous New York hotel has been the setting for the induction ceremonies of numerous rock artists and groups to The Rock 'n' Roll Hall of Fame since 1987. Although U2 at the time of writing have not been afforded this honour – they will have to wait at least 25 years since their first "commercially released record" – members of the group have been present at the five induction ceremonies. In February 1990 Bono inducted The Who into the Hall, then on 15th January 1992 The Edge helped to induct the Yardbirds, making a speech and playing "Big River" along with Jimmy Page, Neil Young and Keith Richards.

On 19th January 1994, when Bono inducted Bob Marley into the Hall of Fame, the award was accepted by Rita Marley on behalf of her late husband. After making a speech he sang "One Love" with Rita and Ziggy Marley and Whoopi Goldberg. Then on 15th March 1999 Bono inducted Bruce Springsteen into the Hall, quipping that "he was the end of long hair, brown rice and bell bottoms". Finally, Bono inducted Island Records founder, Chris Blackwell, into the Hall on 19th March 2001.

See also: Chris Blackwell / Bob Marley / Keith Richards / Bruce Springsteen / The Yardbirds / The Who

"WALK ON" (*ALL THAT YOU CAN'T LEAVE BEHIND* ALBUM TRACK) (4.55) The fourth track on the *All That You Can't Leave Behind* album. It is a rousing and emotional song, which U2 used to close many of their *Elevation* shows. It was dedicated to 1991 Nobel Peace Prize winner Aung San Suu Kyi who had been under virtual house arrest in her native Burma since 1989. The title of the album came from a line in this song. The song was first performed live at the National Car Rental Center in Fort Lauderdale, Florida on 24th March 2001.

See also: Aung San Suu Kyi

"WALK ON" (SINGLE) (4.23) This *All That You Can't Leave Behind* album track was first released as a single edit in Canada in February 2001 in two formats, reaching number one on the charts. CD1 (3145728192) had the extra tracks of "Beautiful Day" and "New York", both recorded live at Farmclub.com in Universal City on 27th October 2000. CD 2 (3145728202) had the extra tracks of "Big Girls Are Best" and "Beautiful Day" (Quincey And Sonance Remix). (Both sets of extra tracks were identical to the tracks on the UK release of the single "Stuck In A Moment You Can't Get Out Of" which was released concurrently.)

"WALK ON" (PROMOTIONAL VIDEO #1) The first promo video for "Walk On" was directed by Jonas Akerlund who had previously directed the "Beautiful Day" video for U2. It was filmed in Rio de Janeiro, Brazil, in November 2000 and was basically the band performing the song.

"WALK ON" (PROMOTIONAL VIDEO #2) The second promo video for "Walk On" was directed by Liz Friedlander in London in 2000.

WALSTADION, FRANKFURT, GERMANY This was the first of a series of shows that U2 played in Germany during the *Zooropa* tour of 1993. They played here on 2nd June 1993 to a crowd of 50,000. Bono dedicated "One" to a Turkish family who were killed in a firebomb attack on their house in Solingen in Germany a few days earlier.

WALESA, LECH The former President of Poland and, earlier leader of the banned Solidarity Union, which fought for democracy in Poland in the early 1980s. The union at one time boasted a membership of over ten million, but with the onset of martial law, became an illegal organisation. Walesa was arrested and put in jail until November 1982. All these events are said to have influenced the writing of "New Year's Day" which celebrates the struggle of Walesa and the Solidarity movement.

See also: New Year's Day / Solidarity Movement

"WALK TO THE WATER" (*WITH OR WITHOUT* YOU SINGLE B-SIDE) (4.49) This was one of two tracks put on the B-side of the "With Or Without You" single (IS 319), released in March 1987. The other track was "Luminous Times (Hold On To Love)". The song is a slow melodic piece with spoken lyrics. It was also included on *The B-Sides* CD as part of the compilation CD *The Best of 1980-1990*.

WALL, BILLY The DJ from RT 3 Radio. He was one of the judges at the Harp Lager talent contest in Limerick that U2 won in 1978.

"THE WANDERER" (*ZOOROPA* ALBUM TRACK) (4.44) The final track on side two of the *Zooropa* album. It caused a stir amongst U2 fans when the album was released because the vocals were sung by country singer Johnny Cash and not Bono. The music was a curious blend of country and synthesisers. The actual track (along with "The First Time") was written for a Johnny Cash album, but was put on the end of *Zooropa* as a devious conclusion. The lyrics could have come straight from a sci-fi movie, and, as with a lot of U2 songs, a Biblical influence is evident. For instance, the singer was carrying a bible and a gun. Somehow the track would not have worked with Bono singing the vocals. Not surprisingly it has never been performed live.

See also: Johnny Cash

"THE WANDERER" (*FARAWAY, SO CLOSE* SOUNDTRACK ALBUM) The soundtrack album of the Wim Wenders film, *Faraway, So Close* (Island 8 27216 2) also contained a version of "The Wanderer". It was a different version to the *Zooropa* album track, but still featured the vocal by Johnny Cash.

See also: Faraway, So Close! / Stay (Faraway, So Close) / Wim Wenders

WAR (ALBUM) (ILPS9733 / CID112) U2's third album was recorded at Windmill Lane studios, Dublin during the late summer and autumn of 1982, with Steve Lillywhite again producing. Several other producers had been approached and "tried out" including Jimmy Destri, Bill Whelan, Chris Thomas and Sandy Pearlman, but in the end U2 managed to persuade Steve Lillywhite to forgo his "maximum of two albums per band" policy. The title "War" seemed a natural choice. As Bono said at the time: "War seemed to be a motif for 1982 – from the Falklands to the Middle East and South Africa there was war. By calling the album *War*, we're giving people a slap in the face and at the same time getting away from the cosy image a lot of people have of U2".

Certainly this theme of war and fighting could be detected in several of the tracks such as "Sunday Bloody Sunday" and "The Refugee", but the idea of surrender was also in evidence – a concept which Bono said was the main idea behind the album.

Compared to *October*, U2 had more time to prepare and rehearse for the album, before actually getting down to the nitty gritty of recording. They even undertook a "pre-*War*" tour of Britain, Europe and Ireland in December 1982 to try out some of the *War* tracks in a live situation before the final mixing took place in early 1983.

The album was released worldwide on 28th February 1983 going straight into the UK charts at number 1 and remained in the album charts for nearly three years. In America it reached number 12. The cover again featured Peter Rowan (who had been on the cover of the *Boy* album) but this time he was a few years older. His lips were cracked and his hands held back behind his head as though he had been captured by some invading army. It was in his eyes that you could see the greatest change. They were no longer full of innocence, but showed fear, even hatred. This stark black and white cover was juxtaposed with bright red lettering. Despite the fact that the album had gone straight into the charts at number 1, the music press was not unanimous in its praise. For instance, the *NME* said that "*War* was another example of rock music's impotence and decay." *Time Out* however called it "a marvellous third offering from the Dublin-based foursome".

Compared with its predecessor, *October*, *War* has a more commercial sound and embraces a range of musical styles. The production was further enhanced by the addition of several other musicians. Steve Wickham from In Tua Nua played violin on "Sunday Bloody Sunday" and Kid Creole's backing group, the Coconuts, provided backing vocals on some of the tracks. Also, Kenny Fradley played trumpet on "Red Light". Highlights included the opener "Sunday Bloody Sunday", which many said should have been released as a single, "New Year's Day", which gave U2 their first top 10 hit single in the UK, and the closing number "40", which U2 would use to close their shows.

Complete track list: Sunday Bloody Sunday, Seconds, New Years Day, Like A Song, Drowning Man, The Refugee, Two Hearts Beat As One, Red Light, Surrender, 40.

WAR CHILD A charity that was set up in 1993 by film makers Bill Leeson and David Wilson, who saw at first hand children suffering in the war taking place in the former Yugoslavia. The charity grew through the efforts of many musicians and artists including Brian Eno, U2 and Pavarotti. Bono and Pavarotti both donated three dimensional artworks for an exhibition called "Milestones" which were then auctioned off for the charity. Also the proceeds from the "Miss Sarajevo" single and the 1995 Pavarotti and Friends concert were donated to the War Child Charity, specifically to build a music therapy centre in Mostar. This came to fruition in 1997 as the Pavarotti Music Centre. War Child has now spread its work beyond Bosnia to various war zones around the world – such as helping Tibetan refugees in Nepal; street children in central America, South Africa, Rwanda, Ethiopia and Sudan; a food programme in Chechenya; and a school rebuilding project in Azerbaijan.

website: www.warchild.org

See also: Novi Sad Park / Pavarotti / Together For The Children of Bosnia

WAR TOUR Once the *War* album had been completed, U2 undertook a "pre-*War* tour" in December 1982, visiting the UK, Holland, Belgium, Denmark, Sweden, Norway and Ireland. This was to give the band a chance to play some of the tracks they had recorded in a live situation, before the final mix. These were: "New Year's Day", "Sunday Bloody Sunday" and "Surrender". The *War* tour proper started in February 1983, beginning with a British leg of 29 dates, playing mainly city halls and universities. The first date was at The Caird Hall in Dundee, Scotland, where "Two Hearts Beat As One", "Party Girl" and "40" were played live for the first time.

The second leg was a 46 date North American tour running from 23rd April to 29th June 1983, at a mixture of universities and theatres, plus one date at an arena in Los Angeles. It was on this section of the tour that U2 played their famous show at Red Rocks Amphitheater near Denver, Colorado, which resulted in the popular video, *U2 Live At Red Rocks, Under A Blood Red Sky.* After this tour had ended U2 went on to play several large summer festivals in Europe during the summer of 1983 before taking the *War* show to Japan in November, their first ever visit to that country.

The album cover of Radar was used as a stage backdrop and white flags were placed around the stage. Bono would usually take one of these and climb up the lighting rig or onto the balcony during "The Electric Co", a move that backfired on him at the gig at the Sports Arena in Los Angeles. The show would end with "40" with Adam and Edge swapping instruments, as gradually each member of the band left the stage until there was only a single drum beat left. Clannad's "Theme From Harry's Game" was used as the closing music to the whole show.

The *War* tour was the final section of the "first phase" of U2, with the band going away to consider other musical possibilities, which would emerge as their next album, *The Unforgettable Fire.*

Songs performed on the *War* tour: A Celebration, A Day Without Me, An Cat Dubh/Into The Heart, Cry-The Electric Co, 11 O'clock Tick Tock, Fire, 40, Gloria, I Fall Down, I Threw A Brick Through A Window, I Will Follow, Like A Song, New Year's Day, October, Out Of Control, Party Girl, Seconds, Sunday Bloody Sunday, Surrender, Tomorrow, Twilight, Two Hearts Beat As One.

See also: Red Rocks Amphitheater / Sports Arena, Los Angeles / Under A Blood Red Sky / White Flag

WARNER CHAPPEL MUSIC LTD The record company responsible for distributing Island Records in the USA. In the early days their marketing department, and in particular Ellen Darst, made a great effort to help U2 "break through" in America.

See also: Ellen Darst

WASTED TALENT The booking agency responsible for U2's early dates in the UK.

WATERFRONT HALL, BELFAST, NORTHERN IRELAND U2 took part in a special concert here on 19th May 1998, designed to promote a "Yes" vote in the Good Friday agreement referendum. At the end of the concert Bono held aloft the hands of John Hume and David Trimble, the leaders of two opposing political parties who had united in their desire for peace in Northern Ireland. U2 played three songs: "One", "Don't Let Me Down" and "Stand By Me". The Belfast group Ash were also on the bill.

See also: John Hume / David Trimble

WATERS, JOHN The renowned contemporary Irish writer who has written about U2 on several occasions. His essay on U2 "Deus Ex Machina, the Band who Grew to Earth" is one of the postscripts included in *Unforgettable Fire*, the U2 biography by Eamon Dunphy. He also wrote a book on U2 entitled *Race of Angels*, published by Fourth Estate in 1994. It featured some exclusive interviews with the band and concentrated on how the U2 phenomena fitted into Irish history and culture. He also produced the BBC Radio 4 series *Wide Awake In Ireland*.

JULIA WATERS She provided backing vocals on the track "A Room At The Heartbreak Hotel."

WATERS, MAXINE She also provided backing vocals on "A Room At The Heartbreak Hotel".

WAVERLY PARK, MELBOURNE, AUSTRALIA U2 played to 30,000 fans here during the *Pop Mart* tour of the Far East on 21st February 1998. As a mark of respect to the late Michael Hutchence of INXS, the Nick Cave song "Into My Arms" was played over the PA at the end of the concert.

WEIRD AL YANKOVITCH American satirical singer who wrote a parody of the U2 song "Hold Me, Kiss Me, Kill Me" called "Cavity Search.

WEMBLEY ARENA, LONDON, ENGLAND U2 have played this indoor arena next door to Wembley Stadium on three occasions. They first played here on 14th and 15th November 1984 during the *Unforgettable Fire* tour. "A Sort of Homecoming", on the *Wide Awake in America* EP and on the B-side of "The Unforgettable Fire" single, was recorded in the sound check prior to the second show. U2 then returned here again during the *Joshua Tree* tour on 2nd June 1987 despite the fact that they would be playing next door at the larger Wembley stadium two weeks later. This was because the concert was specially arranged for fans who wished to see U2 play live in a smaller venue.

WEMBLEY STADIUM, LONDON, ENGLAND This well-known stadium was built in the 1920s and was used as the venue for the Football FA Cup final from 1923 until 2000. It was also used to host the 1948 Olympic Games and football's 1996 World Cup Finals. In 1972 it was first used as the venue for a rock concert. U2 first played at Wembley Stadium during the *Live Aid* concert on 13th July 1985 (see *Live Aid* entry for more details). They then played two sell out dates here during the *Joshua Tree* tour on 12th and 13th June 1987, where Bono reminded the audience about the band's *Live Aid* appearance: "Two years ago we played on this stage and a great work was done in the name of love."

The Edge phones home from Wembley, 24/8/97.
Photo: Claire Bolton

Next, U2 played four shows here during the 1993 *Zooropa* tour – two dates on 11th and 12th August 1993, followed by two more on 20th and 21st August which were added after the first two dates had sold out. At the show on 11th August, "Babyface" from the *Zooropa* album was played live for the first time, with Bono choosing a girl to come up out of the crowd to video him singing. She was "Linda from Argentina" and ended up sitting on Bono as she filmed him! The satellite link-up with Sarajevo took place as it had done for the past few shows, but many of the British media present were not familiar with it and knocked U2 in their reports for including this section in a rock 'n' roll show. The show was also memorable for the surprise appearance of the writer Salman Rushdie, who Macphisto had rung up from the stage, only to have him appear in person from behind. For the show on 12th August, violinist Jo Shankar played with the group during "Bad".

After shows in Leeds and Cardiff, U2 returned here to play the two added dates. The show on 20th August was not sold out like the other dates, so it was announced that unemployed people could get in free if they presented their UB40 card on entry. At this show, Macphisto rang the Archbishop of Canterbury, George Carey. For the final Wembley show on 21st August, "Trying To Throw Your Arms Around the World" was revived with Bono pulling not one but two girls out of the audience to open his champagne. Many people thought they were twins, but they were in fact sisters, Wiebe and Sieke from Germany. The phone call that night was to Graham Taylor, the then England football team manager, but his answerphone was on, so the crowd sang "You'll Never Walk Alone" into it.

For the *Pop Mart* tour U2 played two sell out shows at Wembley Stadium on 22nd and 23rd August 1997. On the second night Bono's two daughters came out onto the stage to kick the inflatable lemons out into the audience.

WENDERS, WIM The German film director famous for such films as *Paris, Texas* and *Wings of Desire*. The band first met him when he directed their video of "Night & Day" for the *Red Hot and Blue* AIDS project. He also directed the "Stay (Faraway So Close!)" promo video, which was based on his films, *Faraway, So Close* and *Wings Of Desire* (later re-made in Hollywood under the title *City of Angels*). He was also the director of *The Million Dollar Hotel*, finally released in 1999, for which Bono wrote the story. Wenders also directed the promotional video for *The Ground Beneath Her Feet*.

See also: Berlin / Million Dollar Hotel / Night & Day / Stay (Faraway, So Close!) /

Adam Clayton, Werchter Festival, July 3rd, 1983.
Photo: Kay Bauersfeld

WERCHTER FESTIVAL, BELGIUM U2 have played this well-known Belgian music festival on five occasions. This festival has traditionally taken place the day after the Torhout Festival, also in Belgium. U2 first played here on 4th July 1982 and their performance was filmed for Dutch and Belgian TV and radio. "A Day Without Me", "Fire" and "I Threw A Brick Through A Window", recorded that day, were released on the free single that accompanied the limited edition "New Year's Day" double pack single, released in January 1983.

U2 returned to play the festival the following year on 3rd July 1983. Simple Minds were also on the bill and during U2's set, Bono sang some of the Simple Minds song "Someone, Somewhere, In Summertime". Simple Minds vocalist Jim Kerr then came on the stage to sing with Bono, before introducing all the members of U2 to the audience. U2 played here again two years later on 7th July 1985 as headliners above such artists as Paul Young, Depeche Mode and REM. It was a 60,000 sell out and took place less than a week before *Live Aid*. U2 next appeared here on 29th May 1993 with the *Zooropa* show, this concert being added to the tour schedule after their three shows at Rotterdam's Feyonoord stadium had sold

out. The band also played here before 38,000 fans on 25th July 1997 during the *Pop Mart* tour of Europe.

See also: Simple Minds / Torhout Festival

WESERSTADION, BREMEN, GERMANY U2 played to a 45,000 capacity crowd at this German football stadium on 9th June 1993 during the *Zooropa* tour, the first time they had played this German town. Although a second show had been scheduled for the 10th June, this was subsequently cancelled with fans being given refunds or tickets for the other show. The result was an overcrowded stadium with a lot of pushing and shoving.

WESTFALENHALLE, DORTMUND, GERMANY This indoor cycling track with a capacity of 17,000 is Germany's largest indoor stadium. U2 appeared in front of a crowd of 15,000 when they first played here on 21st November 1984, for a German TV special entitled *Rock-pop in Concert*. U2 were third on the bill below Talk Talk and Bryan Adams. The show was broadcast on 12th January 1985. U2 then played three sold out shows here on 14th, 15th and 16th December 1989 during the *Lovetown* tour of Europe. As the three shows progressed, Bono's voice became increasingly strained. As a result, the final show was cut to a mere 75 minutes, provoking anger amongst the crowd.

WESTLAND STUDIOS, DUBLIN, IRELAND The studios where some of the *Zooropa* album was recorded in the first few months of 1993. These are also the studios used for some of the tracks off *All That you Can't Leave Behind*.

See also: All That You Can't Leave Behind / Zooropa

WESTSIDE STUDIOS, LONDON, ENGLAND The studios in London where U2 and Brian Eno, under the pseudonym of "Passengers", spent a week or so experimenting with electronic gadgetry. The resulting sessions came out in the form of the album, *Original Soundtracks 1*.

See also: *Original Soundtracks 1* / Passengers

DE WHALLEY, CHAS The former *Sounds* journalist who produced U2's first single "U2-3" (CBS 7591). He was working for CBS as a talent scout when he was approached by Paul McGuinness about signing U2. He had flown over to Dublin to see the band play live and was impressed, seeing Bono as a potential David Bowie or Alex Harvey. He then produced U2's next demo tape of three tracks – "Out of Control", "Boy/Girl" and "Stories for Boys". The session took place one night in August 1979 at Windmill Lane studios, but apparently didn't go that well, with tension between him and Bono. As Chas admitted, "I learned later that Bono came very close to clocking me that night!"

CBS Ireland executive Jackie Hayden then managed to persuade CBS London to let him release these three tracks as a single in Ireland. This became U2's first number 1 single in Ireland. When U2 played their first London dates in December 1979, a session at CBS's London studios was fitted in with Chas again producing. The only recording from that session that was released on record was the second Ireland single on CBS Ireland, "Another Day" (CBS 8306).

See also: Jackie Hayden / CBS Records / CBS Studios / "U2-3"

"WHATEVER HAPPENED TO YOU" This song by The Call, featured backing vocals from Bono. The track appeared on their 1990 *Red Moon* album.

WHEEL TO REEL (Island ICT 4005 – UK Cassette) A special compilation cassette of tracks by Island Records artists including U2. The U2 track featured was "Gloria". Other artists on this release were Stevie Winwood, Grace Jones and Robert Palmer. It was a notable release for the fact that this compilation album was on one side of the tape, whilst the other side was left blank for the owner to record whatever music he liked. This was a special policy that Island Records followed in the early 1980s – issuing albums on one side of a cassette with a blank tape on the other side. It was part of their "One Plus One" series, which included U2's first two albums. Eventually, due to pressure from other record companies who were actively promoting the "Home Taping Is Killing Music" campaign, this method of cassette production was dropped by Island Records.

WHELAN, BILL Originally a session musician, Bill Whelan went on to become a producer. He is credited as producing one track off the *War* album, "The Refugee". Through his connection with Paul McGuinness - the two of them set up McGuinness-Whelan Publishing. Bill Whelan though will eternally be remembered as the writer of the hugely successful *Riverdance* stage production. As a result of the worldwide success that *Riverdance* brought him, Bill formed the Irish Film Soundtracks company which specialises in producing soundtracks for films.

See also: The Refugee

"WHEN I LOOK AT THE WORLD" (*ALL THAT YOU CAN'T LEAVE BEHIND* ALBUM TRACK) (4.15) The ninth track on the *All That You Can't Leave Behind* album features synthesisers from Brian Eno and additional guitar from Daniel Lanois. The song seems to be looking at how people live their lives and wondering whether one way of dealing with things is necessarily the right way. To date it has not been played live.

"WHEN LOVE COMES TO TOWN" (*RATTLE & HUM* ALBUM TRACK) (4.14) The third track on side three of the *Rattle & Hum* album. It was specially written for BB King by Bono and was recorded at Sun Studios in Memphis, USA, in November 1987, although BB King added his part at a later date. A blues rocker, deliberately in the style of BB King's music, it contains "heavy lyrics" that were deliberately Gospel in flavour, with references to the crucifixion. It was first performed live at the Tarrant County Convention Center in Fort Worth Texas on 24th November 1987, where BB King played his first show supporting U2. Film of the song being rehearsed at the afternoon soundcheck and then performed at the evening's show is included in the film *Rattle & Hum*.

"WHEN LOVE COMES TO TOWN" (SINGLE) (3.31) Naturally such a strong track was the obvious choice for a single, so it was released in a shortened form in April 1989, reaching number 6 in the UK charts, but only 68 in the US chart. It was released in four formats: 7 inch, 12 inch, CD and CD Picture Disc (CIDP 411). The 7 inch B-side included a version of Patti Smith's "Dancing Barefoot", whilst the 12 inch and CD versions contained the "Kingdom Mix" of "When Love Comes to Town" and the "Hard Metal Dance Mix" of "God Part II". The track was included on *The Best of 1980-1990* compilation CD, though it was the album as opposed to the single version that was used.

"WHEN LOVE COMES TO TOWN" (LIVE FROM THE KINGDOM MIX) (B-SIDE OF 'WHEN LOVE COMES TO TOWN' SINGLE) (7.28) This remix of "When Love Comes to Town" was produced by Louil Silas Junior and recorded by David Tickle. It starts off with an excerpt from a sermon by Little Richard in his role of preacher. (He gets a look in at the end as well.) The whole track sounds as if it were recorded live but the audience noise was added into the mix. David Kos played saxophone.

"WHEN LOVE COMES TO TOWN" (*RATTLE & HUM* FILM/VIDEO TRACK) The first rehearsal of this song with U2 and BB King took place at the Tarrant County Convention Centre, Fort Worth, Texas on 24th November 1987 and was included in the film version of *Rattle & Hum*. Some of the actual performance of the song from that night's show was also included.

"WHEN LOVE COMES TO TOWN" (PROMOTIONAL VIDEO) The promotional video of "When Love Comes To Town" was released in March 1989 with Phil Joanou as director. The video contains outtakes from *Rattle & Hum,* including shots from Sun Studios, the gig in Fort Worth on 24th November, as well as some interesting footage of the Dalton Brothers.

It was also included on *The Best of 1980-1990* video collection. At the 1989 MTV Awards, the video won the "Best Video From Film" award.

"WHERE DID IT ALL GO WRONG?" ("EVEN BETTER THAN THE REAL THING" SINGLE) (3.57) This track is actually a demo from a session by U2 at STS Studios in Dublin, hence its roughness. It was only available on the CD version of this single (CID 525). With its harmonies and chord changes it could have been recorded by the Who. It was produced by U2 and Paul Barrett.

"WHERE THE STREETS HAVE NO NAME" (*JOSHUA TREE* ALBUM TRACK) (5.35) This track opens the first side of *The Joshua Tree* album and builds slowly from a quiet start into one of U2's best loved songs. The song is a lament about the way the urban environment is destroying everything created, both on a physical and a spiritual level. As Bono said on his return from Ethiopia where he had seen the relief effort that was going on at first hand: "I came back to this big fat spoilt child of the West and I started to get confused, seeing our cities as wastelands. Even though we aren't physically impoverished I started to see that we're spiritually impoverished." The song was first performed live on the rooftop of the Liquor Store on 7th Avenue and Main Street in Los Angeles, as part of the shoot for the promo video. See below for more details.

"WHERE THE STREETS HAVE NO NAME" (SINGLE) (4.35) The single for "Where The Streets Have No Name" was released in August 1987. It was slightly different to the album version with the start and ending being edited. It also had backing vocals from The Edge added on. It was released in four formats – 7 inch, cassette, 12 inch and CD. The single reached number 13 in the US and number 4 in the British charts. It was included in the compilation CD *The Best of 1980-1990*, though this version is thought to have The Edge's vocals edited out.

"WHERE THE STREETS HAVE NO NAME" (LIVE FROM ROTTERDAM) (*POPHEARTLIVE EP* TRACK) (6.33) Surprisingly the first time a live audio version of this *Joshua Tree* track was released was not until 1997. This version was recorded on the *Pop Mart* tour at the Feyenoord Stadium in Rotterdam, Holland on 18th July 1997.

"WHERE THE STREETS HAVE NO NAME" (LIVE) (*HASTA LA VISTA BABY!* ALBUM TRACK) (6.35) The second official live audio version of this *Joshua Tree* track can be found on the *Propaganda* CD, *Hasta La Vista Baby*, issued in July 2000. It was recorded live at the Foro Sol Autodromo, Mexico City, Mexico on 3rd December 1997.

"WHERE THE STREETS HAVE NO NAME" (LIVE) (*RATTLE & HUM* FILM/VIDEO TRACK) This live version of "Where The Streets Have No Name" was recorded at the Sun Devil Stadium, Tempe, Arizona on 20th December 1987. It was not included on the album of *Rattle & Hum*.

"WHERE THE STREETS HAVE NO NAME" (LIVE) (*ZOO TV LIVE FROM SYDNEY* TRACK) This live version of "Where The Streets Have No Name" was recorded at the Sydney Football Stadium in Australia on 27th November 1993 during the *Zoomerang* tour.

"WHERE THE STREETS HAVE NO NAME" (LIVE) (*POP MART LIVE FROM MEXICO CITY* VIDEO TRACK) This version was recorded at the Foro Sol Autodromo in Mexico City on 3rd December 1997 during the *Pop Mart* tour.

U2 filming "Where The Streets Have No Name"on the roof of an LA liquor store.

"WHERE THE STREETS HAVE NO NAME" (PROMOTIONAL VIDEO) This video is a favourite amongst U2 fans, mainly because of its spontaneity. It was filmed on the roof of the Liquor Store on the corner of 7th Avenue and Main Street, in downtown Los Angeles on 27th March 1987. The video was directed by Meiert Avis and produced by Michael Hamlyn and Ben Dossett. Although it looks as if U2 just played this song and were then told to shut down by the L.A. police, they actually performed it three times, as well as "People Get Ready", "Sunday Bloody Sunday", "In God's Country" and "Pride", the last of these being the one that the police really did stop in mid-flow.

Some critics said that U2 were deliberately copying The Beatles who sang "Get Back" on the roof of the Apple building in London back in 1969. Whether they were or not, the impromptu show not only succeeded in stopping the traffic and drawing a large crowd, but also provided adequate footage for the video. Two versions of the video came to be used: the longer one with the radio commentary including a snatch of "Bullet The Blue Sky" plus all the police action and a shorter version where the band just performed the song.

Various people within the U2 organisation can be seen in the video, including Paul McGuinness, Joe O'Herlihy, Anton Corbijn, producer Michael Hamlyn and the director himself, Meiert Avis. The sign on top of the building is the one for the original Million Dollar Hotel. The video was included in the documentary *Outside It's America* and it won a Grammy at the 1988 Grammy Awards for the Best Performance Video.

See also: Meiert Avis / Michael Hamlyn / Outside It's America

CHARLIE WHISKER He designed the illustration of the baby on the record label of *Achtung Baby*. This was then developed further by Shaughn McGrath for the cover of *Zooropa* into the cigarette smoking "Condom" baby, which became the symbol for the 1993 *Zooropa* tour.

"WHISKEY IN THE JAR" A traditional Irish song that was a top 10 hit in 1973 for the Irish group Thin Lizzy. U2 have performed the song live on several occasions, with Larry taking lead vocals. The song was first played on the *Joshua Tree* tour of North America at the Foxborough Stadium in Massachusetts on 20th August 1987. It was also used as a karaoke number on the *Pop Mart* tour in 1997-8.

WHITE FLAG A feature at U2 concerts from 1982 until the end of the decade. During "Sunday Bloody Sunday" Bono would wave a white flag as though in surrender – the theme of the *War* album. The origin of the white flag is believed to be the Werchter Festival from 1982 where a fan threw a white flag onto the stage for Bono. From then on U2 fans would bring white flags to their concerts.

WHITEWAY, ANDREW U2's tour manager in the very early days. He once accompanied Bono to London in 1979 to drum up support from the music papers for U2.

WHO, THE One of the biggest groups to have come out of Britain in the 1960s after the Beatles and The Rolling Stones. The young U2 were certainly influenced by The Who and had always admired the way they were four individual musicians making their own music. In February 1990 The Who were inducted into the Rock 'n' Roll Hall of Fame at New York's Waldorf Astoria Hotel by Bono, who quipped, that the key to being a great rock 'n' roll band is to "have a great nose!" referring to Pete Townshend. In October 2000 when U2 played a "secret" gig at the Irving

Plaza they chose the Who classic "Won't Get Fooled Again" to finish their set. This is the only time U2 have played a Who song on stage.

"WHO'S GONNA RIDE YOUR WILD HORSES" (*ACHTUNG BABY* ALBUM TRACK) (5.16) The fifth track on the first side of the *Achtung Baby* album. It starts off with some heavy chords from The Edge and moves along slowly until Bono comes in with the chorus line. It would seem to be two separate songs joined together as the producers are credited as being Eno/Lanois and Steve Lillywhite. The song was played live on the 1992 *Zoo TV* tour but had been dropped from the set by 1993. It was first performed live at the Civic Centre in Lakeland, Florida on 29th February 1992.

"WHO'S GONNA RIDE YOUR WILD HORSES" (THE TEMPLE BAR EDIT) (SINGLE) (3.54) This single was a completely different version to the *Achtung Baby* track, being produced by U2 and Paul Barrett and cut down to a more radio-friendly 4 minutes. The song features some pleasant acoustic bass and rhythm guitar, which gives it a lighter feel to the album version. The single was released in November 1992 and reached 14 in the UK charts and 35 in the US charts. The B-side on all four formats was "Paint It Black", whilst the 12 inch and CD had the extra tracks of "Fortunate Son" and the Temple Bar Remix version of the single.

"WHO'S GONNA RIDE YOUR WILD HORSES" (ALTERNATIVE SINGLE) An alternative single, released in the UK, France and Germany in addition to the standard single. This contained the Temple Bar Edit as well as "Paint It Black", "Salome" (Zooromancer Remix) and "Can't Help Falling In Love" (Triple Peaks Remix). The last two tracks had up to that point not been released before. It also contained four black and white CD size prints of each member of U2.

"WHO'S GONNA RIDE YOUR WILD HORSES" (THE TEMPLE BAR REMIX) (4.49) This was the fourth track on the CD and 12 inch versions of the "Who's Gonna Ride Your Wild Horses" single. This remix features piano played by The Edge and Paul Barrett, as well as strings and a Moog organ. It was called the Temple Bar remix after the district of Dublin where STS studios were situated and where the track was remixed.

"WHO'S GONNA RIDE YOUR WILD HORSES" (PROMOTIONAL VIDEO) The promotional video of "Who's Gonna Ride Your Wild Horses" was a collection of concert footage from the 1992 *Zoo TV* tour mixed with Bono singing separately before a white background. It was put together by *Rattle & Hum* director Phil Joanou in November 1992.

WICKHAM, STEVE Steve played violin with occasional U2 support band, In Tua Nua, before going on to find fame with The Waterboys. He added violin on the *War* album track "Sunday Bloody Sunday" giving it an Irish feel. The story goes that The Edge met Steve on the bus one day and that Steve offered his services to The Edge should he ever need them. The Edge took him up on this offer and his contribution to the *War* album was the result. He appeared onstage with U2 at their gig at the Falkoner Teatret in Copenhagen, Denmark on 14th December, 1982. Steve also played with them at their Christmas 1982 concerts at the SFX Centre in Dublin on 22nd, 23rd and 24th December 1982.

WIDE AWAKE IN AMERICA (EP) (CID 113) This four track vinyl EP was released only in America in June 1985. The tracks were two *Unforgettable Fire* outtakes, "Love Comes Tumbling" and "The Three Sunrises" (already available on "The Unforgettable Fire" 12 inch single), plus live versions of "Bad" (Birmingham NEC) and "A Sort of Homecoming" (Wembley Arena). The title came from a line in "Bad" though the two live cuts had been recorded in England rather in America. It entered the US album chart for just one week before being removed as its length was considered too short. It was however reinstated in April 1987 when the CD version reached number 37. The "mini-album", as it was called, was only available as an import in the UK but still entered the UK album chart in the summer of 1985, peaking at number 11.

See also: A Sort of Homecoming / Bad / Love Comes Tumbling / The Three Sunrises / Tony Visconti

WIDE AWAKE IN DUBLIN (RTE TV DOCUMENTARY) A TV documentary about U2 and their "Homecoming" concert at Croke Park in Dublin on 29th June 1985. It also goes behind the scenes at the concert, interviewing such people as Dennis Sheehan, Joe O'Herlihy and Tom Mullally. Apart from film of the Croke Park concert, the documentary also includes footage of the band's groundbreaking concert at Madison Square Gardens in New York and scenes from the *Unforgettable Fire* exhibition that was visiting Dublin at the time.

See also: Croke Park

"WILD HONEY" (*ALL THAT YOU CAN'T LEAVE BEHIND* ALBUM TRACK) (3.45) The fifth track on the album *All That You Can't Leave Behind* is a happy-go-lucky number with acoustic guitar to the fore and a sing along chorus which was included to make the album more upbeat. Daniel Lanois added some extra guitar to the mix.

WILLIS, CAROLYN She provided backing vocals on the *Rattle & Hum* track "Hawkmoon 269".

WILLIAMS, PETER "WILLIE" U2 first met Willie at the Greenbelt Festival in 1981 where Willie was a DJ and U2 were performing. Having previously worked as a lighting designer for Duran Duran, Willie joined the U2 organisation in 1983 and has stayed with them ever since. In 1986 he started the *Propaganda* magazine, which has been published ever since. In 1988 he worked with Steve Turner to co-write the book accompanying the film *Rattle & Hum*. In the 1990s he designed the stage sets for the *Zoo TV* and *Pop Mart* tours. It was his idea to incorporate the Trabants into the backdrop. His diaries of life on the road with U2 have been a popular feature of *Propaganda* magazine and U2.com. Willie has also worked as lighting designer with REM in between touring with U2.

See also: *Propaganda*

WILLIAMS-BRICE STADIUM, COLUMBIA, SOUTH CAROLINA, USA One of U2's *Outside Broadcast* Zoo TV shows took place here on 23rd September 1992. This was the first time that U2 had played in the state of South Carolina and the show had the smallest attendance (28,000) for any of the *Outside Broadcast* shows.

WILNER, HAL The talented producer, arranger, and musician responsible for the *Million Dollar Hotel* soundtrack album.

WILSON, IAN The London based booking agent for the Wasted Talent agency, responsible for booking U2's UK shows in the early 1980s.

Windmill Lane Studios, Dublin. *Photo: Paul Daly*

WINDMILL LANE STUDIOS, DUBLIN, IRELAND The now world-famous studios where U2 have recorded many of their albums. Situated on the south side of the River Liffey which runs through the middle of Dublin, the studios have become a mecca for U2 fans as witnessed by the amount of U2 graffiti on the walls, pavement and even roads around the buildings. U2's management offices were also situated here for several years.

U2 first used Windmill Lane to record their "U2-3" single with Chas de Whalley in August 1979. They would go on to record their first three albums there under the watchful eye of producer Steve Lillywhite. Their fourth album *The Unforgettable Fire* with Eno and Daniel Lanois producing was recorded mainly at Slane Castle in County Meath but the finishing touches were again made at Windmill Lane as seen in *The Making of The Unforgettable Fire* video. Similarly, much of *The Joshua Tree* was recorded here, as was part of *Achtung Baby.* The studios were also host to the frantic sessions of the *Zooropa* album, completed here in between the opening dates of the 1993 *Zooropa* tour.

In 1993 the studios relocated to new premises on the nearby Ringsend Road. It was here that recording sessions for both *Pop* and *All That You Can't Leave Behind* took place. Apart from U2, several major rock artists have recorded albums here, including Bon Jovi.

Website: www.windmill.ie

WINDSOR CASTLE, HARROW ROAD, LONDON, ENGLAND This was the last London date of U2's first mini-tour of London clubs, on 15th December 1979.

"WIRE" (*THE UNFORGETTABLE FIRE* ALBUM TRACK) (4.16) One of the most frenetic pieces of music that U2 have ever produced, from The Edge's frantic opening guitar riff, through Bono's ferocious anti-drug pushing lyrical broadside. It was first performed live in Australia on 17th September 1984 at the Sports and Entertainment Centre in Melbourne and featured on subsequent dates of the *Unforgettable Fire* tour of Europe and the USA.

"WIRE" (DUB MIX) (*NEW MUSICAL EXPRESS* FREE SINGLE) (GIV-1 B) A completely different mix of "Wire" was included on a special four-track EP given away free with the British music paper the *New Musical Express* in June 1985. It was produced by Brian Eno and Daniel Lanois. The other tracks were Bronski Beat – "Hard Rain", Cocteau Twins – "Two", The Smiths – "What She Said" (live). Due to its limited availability, this is now a collectors item.

See also: *New Musical Express*

"THE WIRE" This is an Internet-based newsgroup for U2 fans. The subject matter discussed can be about the latest concert, video or record - or just about anything else connected with U2. Those who join The Wire are called "Wirelings" and wear special tags to U2 concerts so they can meet up with other members.

Website: www.u2wire.com

WISSELOORD STUDIOS, HILVERSUM, HOLLAND U2 used these studios in July 1997 to record a single version of "Please", released in October 1997.

See also: Howie B / Please

"WITH A SHOUT (JERUSALEM)" (*OCTOBER* ALBUM TRACK) (4.02) The third track on the second side of the *October* album is fairly typical of the music that U2 were producing at the time: plenty of echoed guitar from The Edge, a dominant bass from Adam and a heavy drum beat from Larry. As the title indicates, the song is very pro-Christian with references to Jerusalem and the crucifixion. The song is boosted by the addition of horns from the Dublin group, Some Kind of Wonderful.

"WITH OR WITHOUT YOU" (*JOSHUA TREE* ALBUM TRACK) (4.57) For many U2 fans this is the most complete piece of music that U2 have ever composed. It contains all the ingredients of a typical U2 song – a steady rhythm from Larry and Adam that underpins the infinite guitar of The Edge, and a great set of lyrics from Bono. It is believed to have been inspired by Lou Reed who told Bono that he had a great gift and that he should not "give it away". In the lyrics Bono seems to be talking about the way love (in its physical sense) can overpower someone to such an extent that desire for it can hurt or even destroy. The song builds up into a magnificent crescendo and then fades gradually away. Even the contribution of producers Eno and Lanois can be heard with their keyboards and tambourine playing. The song has often been the highlight of U2's live set, being saved as an encore number. It was first performed live at the State University Activity Center in Tempe Arizona on 4th April 1987, the second show of the *Joshua Tree* tour. It has been a regular number in their live shows ever since.

"WITH OR WITHOUT YOU" (SINGLE) (4.55) U2's first ever number 1 single in the United States, staying there for three weeks. This feat unfortunately was not matched in the UK, where it only made number 4. The single was the same version as on the album and was released in March 1987 in four formats: 7 inch, cassette, 12 inch and CD. The B-sides were "Luminous Times (Hold On To Love)" and "Walk to The Water". The cassette single version was deleted in July 1987.

"WITH OR WITHOUT YOU" (LIVE) (*POPHEART LIVE EP* TRACK) (4.38) The first live audio version of "With Or Without You" to be released was this version recorded at the Commonwealth Stadium in Edmonton, Canada on 18th July 1997 during the *Pop Mart* tour. It was the third track on the *Popheart Live EP*, released in October 1997.

"WITH OR WITHOUT YOU" (LIVE) (*HASTA LA VISTA BABY! U2 LIVE FROM MEXICO CITY* ALBUM TRACK) (5.46) This live version of "With Or Without You" was recorded at the Foro Sol Autodromo in Mexico City on 3rd December 1997 during the *Pop Mart* tour. It was on the free CD given away to *Propaganda* readers in July 2000.

"WITH OR WITHOUT YOU" (LIVE) (*RATTLE & HUM* FILM/VIDEO TRACK) The version of "With Or Without You" here was recorded live at the Sun Devil Stadium, Tempe USA on 20th December 1987. It was included in the film, but not on the album. An audio version of this track was included on the promotional EP "Excerpts From *Rattle & Hum*".

"WITH OR WITHOUT YOU" (LIVE) (TRACK ON *ZOO TV LIVE FROM SYDNEY* VIDEO) This film version was recorded live at the Football Ground, Sydney, Australia, on 27th November 1987.

"WITH OR WITHOUT YOU" (LIVE) (*POP MART LIVE FROM MEXICO CITY* VIDEO) This film version was recorded live at the Foro Sol Autodromo in Mexico City on 3rd December 1997 during the *Pop Mart* tour.

"WITH OR WITHOUT YOU" (PROMOTIONAL VIDEO) The promo video for "With or Without You" was shot in both colour and black and white. It was filmed in a studio in County Wickow, Ireland, in February 1987. All through the video Bono has a guitar on his back, though he doesn't actually play it. Meiert Avis was the director and extra footage was provided courtesy of Matt Mahurin. The video won the "Viewers' Choice" award at the 4th annual MTV Awards in Universal City, California, in September 1987.

WOJNAROWICZ, DAVID The American artist whose photograph of buffalo going over the edge of a cliff was used on the cover of the "One" single. All proceeds of the single were donated to AIDS charities as he himself was diagnosed as being HIV positive.

See also: AIDS / One

"WOMANFISH" This was the title of a song that U2 performed on the RTE TV programme, *TV Gaga* on 30th January 1986. According to Bono, the song was about a mermaid he once met in America. This was the only time the song has been performed.

WOMEN'S AID REFUGE CENTRE, DUBLIN The charity that Adam was ordered to pay a donation of £25,000 to after his court case concerning possession of cannabis in 1989.

See also: Adam Clayton

WOOD, RONNIE The Rolling Stones guitarist played guitar on the studio version of "Silver and Gold", which appeared on the *Sun City: Artists Against Apartheid* album, released in 1986. The Edge played guitar on two tracks on Ronnie's 1992 solo album, *Slide on This*.

See also: The Rolling Stones

WORKS ASSOCIATES See: Steve Averill

WORLD MUSIC AMPHITHEATRE, CHICAGO, ILLINOIS, USA U2 played three sell out shows at this 30,000 capacity venue on 15th, 16th and 18th September 1992 on the *Outside Broadcast* leg of the *Zoo TV* tour. During the first show, when two girls were allowed onto the stage for "Trying to Throw Your Arms Around the World", one of them knocked The Edge's hat off exposing his bald head! As a result of the noise from the first show, the mayor of nearby Country Club Hills took U2 and the World Music Amphitheatre to court to try to get them to turn the volume down for the third show. He lost the case, so Bono made several comments during the final show about this, and also rang up the mayor.

WORLD VISION The name of the Christian charity that Bono and his wife Ali did voluntary work for in Ethiopia over a period of five weeks in the autumn of 1985. They were part of an educational relief project where they would use songs and plays to educate people about the need for hygiene to live healthy lives.

"WRECKING BALL" Larry played drums on the title track off the 1995 album by Emmylou Harris.

WRIGHT, EDNA The backing singer on "Hawkmoon 269" and "Desire" (Hollywood Remix).

WROE, MARTIN Martin has been on the editorial team of *Propaganda* ever since it first began in 1986. He is also the site editor of the official U2 website: U2.com. Martin has been involved in the Jubilee 2000 campaign and is on the Board for "Drop The Debt". He is also a freelance writer and has contributed to several UK newspapers including *The Observer* and *The Sunday Times*.

See also: *Propaganda*

WYCLEF JEAN The American singer and rapper, formerly a member of the Fugees, with whom Bono collaborated on "New Day", used as the theme song at the Net Aid concert in October 1999.

See also: Net Aid

XAVIER, FRANCIS was credited as the co-producer with U2 of "Endless Deep", which appeared on the B-side of the single "Two Hearts Beat As One".

XTC The new wave band from Swindon, England, who came to the public's attention with hits such as "Making Plans For Nigel" and "Senses Working Overtime" in the late 1970s and early 1980s. It has been suggested that their use of initial letters to make a phonetic name (XTC – Ecstasy) inspired Steve Averill to suggest the name U2 to Adam as a possible name for his group back in 1979. Certainly the ambiguity of U2, which could mean "you too" or "you two", helped the public remember the name more than the "The Hype".

YALE UNIVERSITY (WOOLSEY HALL), NEW HAVEN, CONNECTICUT, USA U2 played just one gig at this famous American University on 10th May 1983, during the *War* tour of the USA. A special "mini-stage" was built here in front of the main stage, which Bono was able to use to get closer to the audience – an idea that would be used for the *Zoo TV* and *Pop Mart* tours. As this was the occasion of Bono's 23rd birthday, chief roadie Dennis Sheehan came on stage at the end with a large birthday cake and the audience sang "Happy Birthday" to him.

YANKEE STADIUM, NEW YORK CITY, USA U2 did not play a concert at this famous baseball stadium until 1992 – on 29th and 30th August as part of the *Outside Broadcast* leg of the *Zoo TV* tour. Even then this was only because demand for tickets to see U2 in the New York area warranted extra shows. The second show was recorded for transmission all over the world in November 1992 as part of a *Zoo TV* special. The songs performed that night and used in the broadcast were: "Zoo Station", "The Fly", "Even Better Than The Real Thing", "Mysterious Ways", "Until The End Of The World", "Trying To Throw Your Arms Around The World", "When Love Comes To Town", "Satellite Of Love", Bullet The Blue Sky", "Running To Stand Still", "Where The Streets Have No Name" and "Desire". Most of these tracks were also used in the *Zoo Radio* Radio programme.

To date only one of the songs recorded that night, "Love Is Blindness", has appeared on record – on the "Stay" single (live version). The second show is also memorable for showing video footage of Lou Reed singing "Satellite of Love" for the first time at a U2 concert. This was for use in the section of the show when the band sang the song as a duet with Lou Reed from the B-stage. U2 were the second rock act ever to play at this stadium, the first being Billy Joel.

YARDBIRDS, THE This English group, popular in the 1960s, were inducted into the Rock 'n' Roll Hall of Fame by The Edge on 15th January 1993. The band's members have included Eric Clapton, Jimmy Page and Jeff Beck.

YEATS, WB The Irish Poet who Bono has quoted from at U2 concerts. The poem *September 1913* is a particular favourite of his.

"YOU MADE ME THE THIEF OF YOUR HEART" A song performed by Sinead O'Connor for the soundtrack to the movie *In The Name of The Father*, written jointly by Bono, Gavin Friday and Maurice Seezer.

YOUNGLINE (IRISH TV SHOW) U2's first ever TV appearance was on this Irish TV music show in Autumn 1978 where they performed "Street Mission". The announcer even wore a U2 badge.

YOUTH The producer/remix artist (and former bass player of Killing Joke) has been involved with several U2 recordings in the 1990s including "Night & Day" (Steel String Remix), *Achtung Baby*, *Zooropa*, and the single "Hold Me, Thrill Me, Kiss Me, Kill Me".

YOUTH CLUB, HOWTH, DUBLIN, IRELAND U2 played this small youth club twice during the summer of 1979. The first time was on 11th July and the second time was on 11th August. Approximately 250 people attended the second show making it the biggest crowd the band had played to up until that date. U2 played an hour long set which featured "Stories For Boys" as well as a new song, "Silver Lining", which would later become 11 O'clock Tick Tock.

Z

Zoo money, above dollars, below ECUs

ZAAL LUX, HERENTHOUT, BELGIUM U2 appeared here on 25th October 1981 as part of the tour to promote the *October* album. Before this gig the band had appeared on a show called *Generation 80*, which was shown on RTBF 1, a French/Belgian TV station.

ZAPPA, FRANK The famous avantgarde rock artist responsible for many ground-breaking albums from the 1960s through to his death in 1993. During the 1992 Presidential campaign, Zappa had been on TV talking about some of the election issues, including the importance of young people using their vote. As a result of this U2 proclaimed, "Vote for Frank Zappa" on the video screens at the end of their *Outside Broadcast* shows prior to the election.

ZENITH, PARIS, FRANCE U2 played this 7,000 capacity Paris venue during the 1987 *Joshua Tree* tour. As in London with Wembley Arena, U2 had deliberately chosen to play a few smaller venues in contrast to the larger stadium shows on that tour.

ZEPPELINFELD, NUREMBURG, GERMANY U2 played at this former Nazi stadium on 18th August 1997 during the *Pop Mart* tour of Europe. About 35,000 fans attended and during the show Bono spoke to the audience in German suggesting that he should paint some of the concrete grandstand pink. "Wake Up Dead Man" was performed live for the first time here as the final number of the set.

ZOOMERANG The name given to the Australian section of the *Zoo TV* tour. It consisted of six shows in four Australian venues in the towns of Melbourne, Adelaide, Brisbane and Sydney. On the second night of the two Melbourne Cricket Ground shows on 13th November, 1993, Macphisto rang up Dame Edna Everage, the famous Australian entertainer.

The final concert at Sydney on 27th November 1993 was broadcast live to the USA and was shown in 46 other countries over following few weeks. In April 1994, the whole show was released on a video, entitled *Zoo TV Live From Sydney*. The first Sydney show goes down in history as the only time U2 took to the stage without all four members present. This was because Adam was "ill with a virus", so his bass technician, Stuart Morgan, took his place that night to prevent the show being cancelled.

See also: Zoo TV tour

ZOO MONEY The money that Bono used to throw from the stage during the encore number "Desire" on the *Zoo TV* tour. For the *Zooropa* leg of the tour each note had the value of 1 Ecu.

ZOO RADIO The name given to a special radio broadcast that U2 put together with BP Fallon amongst others. The hour long programme was designed to be played on radio stations around the world as a way of publicising the forthcoming *Zoo TV* tour that year. It was broadcast in the UK on 1st January 1993 on BBC Radio 1. It consisted of songs from the *Zoo TV* show, interspersed with interviews, anecdotes, stories and news items. The songs played were live versions, from the *U2-Zoo TV* special, of "The Fly", "Even Better Than The Real Thing", "Mysterious Ways", "Until The End Of The World", "Trying To Throw Your Arms Around The World", "Satellite Of Love", "Bullet The Blue Sky", "Running To Stand Still" and "Where The Streets Have No Name".

There were also previously unreleased live versions of "One" and "Can't Help Falling In Love" plus studio cuts of "Zoo Station" and "Whose Gonna Ride Your Wild Horses". The programme also included contributions from Public Enemy and The Disposable Heroes of Hiphoprisy. In fact it was like the *Zoo TV* shows without the visuals. In the words of Paul McGuinness, "I suppose you just have to close your eyes and imagine what it looks like."

ZOOROPA (ALBUM) (CIDU 29) *Zooropa* was originally going to be released as a single, then an EP, but the whole thing snowballed into an album.

During the first few months of 1993, the band had started recording tracks in the Factory studio in Dublin. Still on a high after the *Outside Broadcast* leg of the *Zoo TV* tour in America (which had finished the previous November) U2 managed to lay down enough tracks for a complete album. Although the *Zooropa* leg of the *Zoo TV* tour started on 9th May, this did not stop the band from putting the finishing touches to the album. So for the early dates of this tour, U2 would do the show, then fly straight back to Dublin to work on the album. The album was produced by Flood, Brian Eno and The Edge, with other recording sessions taking place at Windmill Lane and Westland studios also in Dublin.

The album was released on 5th July 1993 entering the charts at number 1 in nearly every country it was released. Some critics saw it as a "stop-gap" album, in view of its hurried schedule, but most fans were happy with it. One track in particular caused consternation among critics and fans alike, though. This was "The Wanderer", the final track on the album, which had Johnny Cash and not Bono on vocals.

Releasing the album in the middle of the tour meant that the band did not have time to rehearse the songs, so it was not until the show in Rome, Italy on 7th July that the first of the album's songs, "Numb" was played live. As the tour progressed other songs were introduced, so that by the time of the final gig of the *Zoo TV* tour in Tokyo on 10th December 1993, all the tracks on the album had been played live, apart from "Some Days Are Better Than Others" and "The Wanderer".

The album won a Grammy award at the 1994 Awards ceremony for the Best Alternative Album; a nice award to win, but whether it deserved the label "alternative" is open to debate. Certainly the album showed U2 going further along the musical road they had first trodden with *Achtung Baby*, with experimental tracks such as "Numb" and "Daddy's Gonna Pay For Your Crashed Car" tipping a nod in the direction of Bowie's *Low* album. Other tracks like "Stay" and "The First Time" indicated a reaction against the grand industrial sound and a footstep towards simplicity itself. Whilst it may have suffered from the speed of its preparation, *Zooropa* showed that U2 were still capable of producing the goods under pressure.

The CD booklet and cover made it the most colourful U2 album to date with stills from the opening screen footage used and the "Achtung Baby" figure being developed further for the cover.

Zooropa Track List: Zooropa, Babyface, Numb, Lemon, Stay (Faraway So Close), Daddy's Gonna Pay For Your Crashed Car, Some Days Are Better Than Others, The First Time, Dirty Day, The Wanderer.

"ZOOROPA" (*ZOOROPA* ALBUM TRACK) (6.30)
The title track off *Zooropa* was recorded at The Factory in Dublin in February 1993. According to The Edge, the song is about "uncertainty", especially with regard to Europe, which "doesn't seem to know what it is or what it wants to be". The song is split into three parts with the third part stemming from improvisation at a soundcheck. Eno added several layers of keyboards, which helped to give a feeling of uncertainty.

The song was first performed live on the *Zooropa* tour at Glasgow's Celtic Park on 8th August 1993, but was only played for the next two shows at Wembley Stadium, London, before being dropped from the set.

The *Zoomerang* Tour reaches Sydney, Austrailia. *Photo: Georgia Everett.*

ZOOROPA TOUR This was the name given to the 1993 European leg of the *Zoo TV* tour which had started in February 1992 in Florida, USA. This part of the tour began on 9th May in Rotterdam, Holland and finished on 28th August at the RDS Showground in Dublin, Ireland, and consisted of 43 shows at 33 venues, the majority being stadiums. For the first time ever, U2 played in a former Eastern Bloc country – Hungary. Politics was a theme that underlined the tour, especially with the collapse of the communist governments in many Eastern European countries. Using their sophisticated stage technology, U2 were able to set up a live satellite link to war-torn Sarajevo in the former Yugoslavia, and speak directly to some young people there in the middle of a show. Although U2 were heavily criticised by some sections of the music press for doing this, it helped bring the issue to the minds of many young people all over Europe. Most of the set was dominated by songs from the *Achtung Baby* album, but as the tour progressed, more songs were added from the *Zooropa* album (see appendix for complete date list).

Songs performed on the *Zooropa* tour were from: All I Want Is You, Angel Of Harlem, Are You Lonesome Tonight, Babyface, Bad, Bullet The Blue Sky, Can't Help Falling In Love, Dancing Queen, Dear Prudence, Desire, Dirty Old Town, Even Better Than The Real Thing, The First Time, The Fly, Help, I Still Haven't Found What I'm Looking For, I Will Follow, Let It Be, Love Is Blindness, My Girl, Mysterious Ways, New Year's Day, Norwegian Wood, Numb, One, Party Girl, Pride, Rain, Redemption Song, Running To Stand Still, She's A Mystery To Me, Stay (Faraway, So Close), Satellite Of Love, Slow Dancing, So Cruel, Stand By Me, Sunday Bloody Sunday, Trying To Throw Your Arms Around The World, Unchained Melody, Ultra Violet, Until The End Of The World, Van Diemen's Land, When Love Comes To Town, Where The Streets Have No Name, The Wild Rover, With Or Without You, Zooropa, Zoo Station.

"ZOO STATION" (*ACHTUNG BABY* ALBUM TRACK) (4.36) The opening track of the *Achtung Baby* album was used as the opening song for each show of the *Zoo TV* tour. There is actually a "Zoo Station" on the Berlin railway system where passengers alight for the famous Berlin Zoo. When U2 were recording *Achtung Baby* in Berlin in 1991, Bono took the group and the crew to the zoo one day for a break, and it led to the whole concept of *Zoo TV*, with the idea of us all being animals in a zoo. The song was first performed live in Lakeland, Florida, USA, on 29th February 1992, making it the first song on the whole *Zoo TV* tour to be performed live.

See also: Berlin

ZOO TV When U2 played their final concert of the 1980s at the Point Depot in Dublin on 31st December 1989, Bono made a statement that the band "can't go on like this, doing this forever". He later explained that the band needed "to go away for a while and dream it all up again". This is when the seeds for the concept of *Zoo TV* came into being.

The idea was that a U2 show would be like tuning into a TV programme for a couple of hours. Using the latest in hi-tech equipment, huge TV screens at the back of the stage projected multi-media images, as well as thousands of words during "The Fly". Designed by U2's in-house stage manager, Willie Williams, the stage set was at the time one of the largest and most ambitious in rock.

Zoo TV, Wembley, England. *Photo: Claire Bolton*

By the time the show reached the stadia of America, it was even larger, with TV masts and giant screens – including images of the then American President George Bush senior being used. Straight after the *Outside Broadcast* leg of the *Zoo TV* tour had finished, there was a TV special broadcast around the world called *U2 - Zoo TV* which showed concert footage of the show as well as news reports and interviews with the band. On the *Zooropa* section the following year, whole films and images from European history were used, including England's 1966 World Cup soccer victory, and scenes from the Nazi Propaganda film "Triumph of the Will". All this was a precursor to the actual show, which began with Bono rising from the back of the stage to sing "Zoo Station".

As well as all the different images that were shown on the large TV screens, Bono used his remote control to zap the screens to show different channels that were being transmitted in different countries all around the world. At the end of the set, prior to the encore, "confessions" from members of the audience were broadcast – these had been recorded in a special confessional booth in the main arena. *Zoo TV* was very much a first in stadium rock and influenced several other artists ranging from Peter Gabriel to Take That. It was in many ways superseded by the *Pop*

Mart tour in terms of even more advanced technology – such as the world's biggest video wall screen and the revolving lemon. Looking back, *Zoo TV* was a successful period in U2 history, fondly remembered by many fans as a peak in U2's live shows.

See also: Outside Broadcast / TV Drug of The Nation / U2 - Zoo TV programme / Zooropa / Zoo TV tour

ZOO TV LIVE FROM SYDNEY VIDEO (POLYGRAM VIDEO) A full length film of U2's concert at Sydney's football stadium in Australia that took place on 27th November 1993. The show was originally broadcast live to pay per view TV stations in the USA and later broadcast in an edited form to several European satellite TV stations over Christmas 1993. This was U2's final show in Australia for the *Zoomerang* tour and one of the last of the whole *Zoo TV* tour. It was a sell out and the second of two nights that U2 played at the Sydney Football Stadium. The first night was used as a "run through" for the following night's broadcast. The main problem was that Adam didn't play with U2 that night and his place was taken by Stuart Morgan his bass technician. Adam did play on the second night though.

The video was directed by David Mallet and produced by Ned O'Hanlon and Rocky Oldham, and won an award for the Best Music Video (Long Form) at the 1994 Grammy awards. The whole show was featured on the video except for one song, "Trying To Throw Your Arms Around The World". Unlike the summer *Zooropa* dates, there had been changes made to the set to make way for the newer material off the *Zooropa* album. Thus the tracks "Bad", "When Love Comes To Town", "Desire" and "Ultra Violet" had been replaced by "Dirty Day", "Daddy's Gonna Pay For Your Crashed Car" and "Lemon" (which had been released as a single in Australia). The video sold in excess of 3 million copies worldwide and was an excellent visual record of a *Zoo TV* show.

Track listing: Zoo Station, The Fly, Even Better Than The Real Thing, Mysterious Ways, One (Unchained Melody), Until The End Of The World, New Year's Day, Numb, Angel Of Harlem, Stay, Satellite Of Love, Dirty Day, Bullet The Blue Sky, Running To Stand Still, Where The Streets Have No Name, Pride, Daddy's Gonna Pay For Your Crashed Car, Lemon, With Or Without You, Love Is Blindness, Can't Help Falling In Love.

ZOO TV TOUR The *Zoo TV* tour was split up into five main sections and lasted nearly two years. It began at the Civic Centre, Lakeland, Florida on 29th February 1992. The venue is not far from Florida's Disneyland, so it was no coincidence that the last American date of *the* 1992 *Zoo TV* tour took place at California's Anaheim Stadium, not far from Walt Disney World.

As the Florida show was U2's first date in America for five years, press expectations and interest ran very high with extensive media coverage of the event. Two days before the concert, on 27th February, U2 had played "One" live on the stage here during rehearsals for transmission by satellite to *the BBC's Top* of the Pops music programme. This was the first public airing of the song, though its first performance before an audience took place at the Lakeland show. Also at the show itself the following songs were played live for the first time: "Zoo Station", "The Fly", "Even Better Than The Real Thing", "Mysterious Ways", "Until The End Of The World", "Who's Gonna Ride Your Wild Horses", "Trying To Throw Your Arms Around The World", "Satellite Of Love", "Ultra Violet" and "Love Is Blindness". Basically, all of the *tracks on A*chtung Baby were played live for the first time, apart from "So Cruel" and *"Acrob*at".

Zoo TV tour opening night set list: "Zoo Station", "The Fly", "Even Better Than The Real Thing", "Mysterious Ways", "One", "Until The End Of The World", "Who's Gonna Ride Your Wild Horses", "Trying To Throw Your Arms Around The World", "Angel of Harlem", "Satellite Of Love", "Bad", "All I Want Is You", "Bullet The Blue Sky", "Running To Stand Still", "Where The Streets Have No Name", "Pride", "I Still Haven't Found What I'm Looking For", "Desire", "Ultra Violet", "With Or Without You", "Love Is Blindness".

The tour continued in different sections through to the Tokyo Dome, Japan on 10th December 1993. The main sections were:

1) North America: Indoor arenas, 29th February to 23rd April 1992 (32 shows in 30 venues)

2) Europe: Indoor arenas (except Vienna), 7th May to 19th June 1992 (25 shows in 21 venues)

3) *Outside Broadcast*: North American stadia plus four arena shows in Mexico, 7th August to 25th November 1992 (47 shows in 33 venues)

These first three sections grossed a total of $67 million, putting U2 third behind New Kids On The Block and The Rolling Stones in terms of revenue!

4) *Zooropa*: European stadia, 9th May to 28th August 1993 (43 shows at 33 venues)

5) *Zoomerang/New Zooland/Zoo TV Japan*: Australia, New Zealand, Far East stadia, 12th November to 10th December 1993 (10 shows in 7 venues)

Almost five and half million fans saw U2 play a total of 157 concerts over 13 months. The whole tour grossed $155 million.

See also: Outside Broadcast / Zooropa

ZUCCHERO Bono co-wrote the lyrics of "Blue" included on Zucchero's album, *Blue Sugar.*

Appendices

Bibliography

The following publications have all been helpful in the research for this book.

Books

Another Time, Another Place U2 - The Early Days - Bill Graham (Mandarin) 1989

Ballad of the Thin Man - Stuart Bailie

Bono - In His Own Words - Dave Thompson (Omnibus Press) 1989

The Complete Guide To The Music of U2 - Bill Graham (Omnibus) 1995

Hot Press Yearbook 2001

Hungry For Heaven - Steve Turner (Virgin) 1988

Into The Heart - Niall Stokes (Carlton) 1996

The New Rolling Stone Encyclopaedia Of Rock & Roll - Edited by Patricia Romanowski & Holly George-Warren (Fireside) 1995

Outside Is America - Carter Allen (Faber & Faber) 1992

Radio 1's Classic Interviews - Edited by Jeff Simpson (BBC Books) 1992

The Q Encyclopaedia of Rock Stars

Unforgettable Fire - The Story Of U2 - Eamon Dunphy (Viking) 1987

U2 - Mark Taylor (Carlton Books) 1993

U2 A Conspiracy Of Hope - Dave Bowler & Brian Dray (Sidgwick & Jackson) *1993*

U2 At The End Of The World - Bill Flanagan (Bantam Press) 1995

U2 Burning Desire - Sam Goodman (Castle Communications) 1993

U2 Faraway So Close - BP Fallon (Virgin) 1994

The U2 File - A Hot Press History (edited by Niall Stokes) 1985

U2 Live - Pimm Jal de la Parra (Omnibus) 1994

U2 Rattle and Hum - The Official Book Of The U2 Movie - Peter Williams and Steve Turner (Pyramid) 1988

U2 The Rolling Stone Files - Edited by Elysa Gardiner (Sidgwick & Jackson) 1994

U2: Stories For Boys - Dave Thomas (Bobcat) 1987

U2 Three Chords And The Truth -Edited by Niall Stokes (Hot Press) 1989

U2 Touch The Flame - An Illustrated Documentary - Geoff Parkyn (Omnibus) 1987

When The Music's Over (The Story Of Political Pop) - Robin Denselow (Faber & Faber) 1989

Magazines/Newspapers:-

Hot Press, Irish Times, Melody Maker, NME, Rolling Stone, Q, Record Collector, Select, Sounds, Vox.

U2 Tour Programmes:-

The Unforgettable Fire (North America) - 1985, *The Joshua Tree* (North America) - 1987, *Zoo TV* - 1992, *Zooropa* - 1993, *Pop Mart* - 1997, *Elevation* (North America) - 2001

U2 Fanzines and Magazines:-

Acrobat; Collectormania, Eirrin; In The Name of Love; New Zooland; On The Edge of Baldness; Propaganda, Pride; The Real Thing; Silver & Gold; Swagger, No Style; Touch; The Truth, Jokes & Other Stories; What's The Story?, The Zooropean.

U2 Concert Dates

The dates below are all known concerts performed by U2 since March 1978 until 2001. For performances by Feedback and The Hype see main text. The concerts listed here are for performances by U2 before an audience in a music venue open to the general public, as well as a few free ones. For performances by U2 in radio and TV studios see separate section.

1978

March
17th   Harp Lager Contest, Limerick, Ireland
20th   Community Centre, Howth, Ireland

April
11th   McGonagles, Dublin, Ireland

May
     Phibsboro Festival, Dublin, Ireland
25th   Project Arts Centre, Dublin, Ireland

July
31st   McGonagle's, Dublin, Ireland

August
11th   Liberty Hall, Dublin, Ireland
     Arcadia Ballroom, Cork, Ireland

September
9th   Top Hat Ballroom, Dublin, Ireland
18th   Project Arts Centre, Dublin, Ireland

October
     Arcadia Ballrooom, Cork, Ireland

November
     Airport Hotel, Crofton, Ireland

December
11th   The Stardust, Dublin, Ireland

1979

January
3rd   McGonagle's, Dublin, Ireland

February
3rd   McGonagle's, Dublin, Ireland
     Trinity College, Dublin, Ireland
17th   Project Arts Centre, Dublin, Ireland

May
11th   Dandelion Car Park, Dublin, Ireland
12th   Trinity College, Dublin, Ireland

June
3rd   Airport Hotel, Crofton, Ireland
7th   McGonagle's, Dublin, Ireland
10th   Airport Hotel, Crofton, Ireland
14th   McGonagle's, Dublin, Ireland
17th   Airport Hotel, Crofton, Ireland
21st   McGonagle's, Dublin, Ireland
24th   Airport Hotel, Crofton, Ireland
28th   McGonagle's, Dublin, Ireland

July
11th   Youth Club, Howth, Ireland

August
11th   Youth Club Howth, Ireland

12th   Dandelion Car Park, Dublin, Ireland
21st   The Baggot Inn, Dublin, Ireland

September
11th   Project Arts Centre, Dublin, Ireland (Two shows)

October
5th   Opera House, Cork, Ireland

London Club Dates

December
1st   Moonlight Club, West Hampstead, England
2nd   Nashville Rooms, Earl's Court, England
3rd   100 Club, Clapham, England
4th   Hope & Anchor, Islington, England
5th   Rock Garden, Covent Garden, England
7th   Electric Ballroom, Camden Town, England
8th   Electric Ballroom, Camden Town, England
11th   Bridge House, Canning Town, England
12th   Brunel University, Uxbridge, England
14th   Dingwalls, Camden Town, England
15th   Windsor Castle, Harrow Road, London, England

1980

'Come Out To Play' Irish Tour

February
1st   Queen's University, Belfast, Northern Ireland
3rd   Bridge House, Tullamore, Ireland
4th   Country Club, Cork, Ireland
5th   Garden of Eden Club, Tullermeny, Ireland
26th   National Stadium, Dublin, Ireland
27th   Cocovan, Ireland
28th   RTC Waterford
29th   Town Hall, Newry, Northern Ireland

March
1st   Downtown Kampus, Cork, Ireland

The Sounds of Ireland Festival

19th   Acklam Hall, London, England

11 O'clock Tick Tock English Tour

May
22nd   Hope &Anchor, London, England
23rd   Moonlight Club, London, England
24th   Sheffield University, England
26th   New Regent, Brighton, England
27th   Rock Garden, London, England
28th   Trinity Hall, Bristol, England
29th   Cedar Ballroom, Birmingham, England
30th   Nashville, London, England
31st   Polytechnic, Manchester, England

June
2nd   77 Club Nuneaton, England
3rd   Boat Club, Nottingham, England
4th   Beach Club, Manchester, England
5th   Fan Club, Leeds, England
6th   J.B.'s, Dudley, England
7th   Marquee Club, London, England
8th   Half Moon Club, London, England

July
10th   Clarendon Hotel, London, England
11th   Half Moon Club, London, England
12th   Moonlight Club, London, England
13th   Marquee Club, London, England

Irish Summer Festival Dates

27th	Leixlip Castle, Dublin, Ireland
28th	Dalymount Festival, Dublin Ireland

The Boy Tour (1st Leg) UK, Holland, Belgium

September

6th	General Woolfe, Coventry, England
7th	Lyceum Ballroom, London, England
8th	Marquee Club, London, England
9th	Berkeley, Bristol, England
11th	Wellington Club, Hull, England
12th	Taboo Club, Scarborough, England
13th	Queen's Hall, Leeds, England
15th	Marquee Club, London, England
16th	Fiesta Suite, Plymouth, England
17th	Demelzas, Penzance, England
18th	Civic Hall, Totnes, England
19th	Marshall Rooms, Stroud, England
21st	Nag's Head, Woolaston, England
22nd	Marquee Club, London, England
23rd	Limit Club, Sheffield, England
24th	Bogart's, Birmingham, England
25th	Brady's, Liverpool, England
26th	Cedar Ballroom, Birmingham, England
27th	Polytechnic, Coventry, England
29th	Marquee Club, London, England
30th	Polytechnic, Brighton, England

October

2nd	Fan Club, Leeds, England
3rd	Porterhouse, Retford, England
4th	School of Economics, London, England
5th	Half Moon Club, London, England
7th	Boat Club, Nottingham, England
9th	Polytechnic, Manchester, England
11th	Kingston Polytechnic, London
14th	KRO Studios, Hilversum, Holland
15th	The Milkyway, Amsterdam, Holland
16th	Vera, Groningen, Holland
17th	Gigant, Apeldoorn, Holland
18th	Klarick, Brussels, Belgium
19th	Lyceum Ballroom, London England

UK College Tour 1980

November

7th	Exeter University, England
8th	Southampton University, England
9th	Moonlight Club, London, England
11th	Kent University, Canterbury, England
12th	Bradford University, England
13th	Limit Club, Sheffield, England
14th	Town Hall, Kidderminster, England
15th	Polytechnic, Bristol, England
18th	Reading University, England
19th	Polytechnic, Wolverhampton, England
20th	Polytechnic, Blackpool, England
21st	Nite Club, Edinburgh, Scotland
22nd	Brady's, Liverpool, England
24th	Polytechnic, Coventry, England
26th	Marquee Club, London, England
27th	Marquee Club, London, England
28th	Aston University, Birmingham, England
29th	Keele University, Stoke, England
30th	Jenkinson's, Brighton, England

Support To Talking Heads

December

1st	Hammersmith Odeon, London, England

2nd	Hammersmith Odeon, London, England
3rd	Baltard Pavilion, Paris, France

1st American/Canadian Club Dates (N.E.Coast)

6th	The Ritz, New York, NY, USA
7th	Bayou Club, Washington, DC, USA
8th	Stage One, Buffalo, NY, USA
9th	El Mocambo, Toronto, Canada
11th	Mudd Club, New York, NY, USA
12th	Main Event, Providence, RI, USA
13th	Paradise Theater, Boston, MA, USA
14th	Toad's Place, New Haven, CT, USA
15th	Bijou Cafe, Philadelphia, PA, USA

Irish Christmas Tour

17th	Ulster Hall, Belfast, Northern Ireland
18th	Leisureland, Galway, Ireland
19th	Baymount, Sligo, Ireland
20th	Downtown Kampus, Cork, Ireland
22nd	T.V. Club, Dublin, Ireland

1981

UK Winter Tour

January

21st	Queen's University, Belfast, Northern Ireland
24th	Strathclyde University, Glasgow, Scotland
25th	Valentino's Club, Edinburgh, Scotland
26th	York University, England
27th	Polytechnic, Manchester, England
28th	University Of East Anglia, Norwich, England
29th	Iron Horse / Polytechnic, Northampton, England
30th	Loughborough University, England
31st	City Hall, St Albans, England

February

1st	Lyceum Ballroom, London, England

European Winter Tour

9th	Underground, Stockholm, Sweden
10th	Beursschouwburg, Brussels, Belgium
11th	Paradiso, Amsterdam, Holland,
12th	Trojan Horse, The Hague, Holland
13th	De Lantaarn, Rotterdam, Holland
14th	Stadsschouwburg, Sittard, Holland
15th	Onkel Po's, Hamburg, Germany
17th	Kantkino, Berlin, Germany
18th	Sugar Shack, Munich, Germany
19th	Salle du Fauburg, Geneva, Switzerland
20th	Ecole National Travaux, Lyon, France
21st	Le Palace, France, Paris, France

The Boy Tour (2nd Leg) North America

March

3rd	Bayou Club, Washington, DC, USA (Two Shows)
4th	Bijou Cafe, Philadelphia, PA, USA
5th	J.B. Scott's, Albany, NY, USA
6th	Paradise Theatre, Boston, MA, USA (Two Shows)
7th	The Ritz, New York, NY, USA
9th	Le Club, Montreal, Canada
10th	Barrymore's, Ottawa, Canada
11th	Maple Leaf Ballroom, Toronto, Canada
14th	Globe Theater, San Diego, CA, USA
15th	Country Club, Reseda, CA, USA
16th	Woodstock, Anaheim, CA, USA
18th	State College Auditorium, San Jose, CA, USA
19th	The Old Waldolf, San Francisco, CA, USA
20th	The Old Waldolf, San Francisco, CA, USA

22nd   Fog Horn, Portland, OR, USA
23rd   Astor Park, Seattle, WA, USA
24th   Commodore Ballroom, Vancouver, Canada
26th   New Faces Club, Salt Lake City, UT, USA
28th   Rainbow Music Hall, Denver, CO, USA
30th   The Box, Lubbock, TX, USA
31st   The Club Foot, Austin, TX, USA

April
1st   Cardi's, Houston, TX, USA
2nd   Bijou, Dallas, TX, USA
3rd   Quicksilver's, Oklahoma City, OK, USA
4th   Caines Ballroom, Tulsa, OK, USA
6th   Uptown Theater, Kansas City, MO, USA
7th   Washington Uni, Graham Chapel, St Louis, MO, USA
9th   Uncle Sam's, Minneapolis, MN, USA
10th   Fillmore, Ames, IA, USA
11th   University Of Chicago, Chicago, IL, USA
12th   Park West, Chicago, IL, USA
14th   Merling's, Madison, WI, USA
15th   Palm's, Milwaukee, WI, USA
17th   Bogart's Club, Cincinnati, OH, USA
18th   Harpo's, Detroit, MI, USA
19th   The Agora, Columbus, OH, USA
20th   The Agora, Cleveland, OH, USA
21st   The Decade, Pittsburgh, PA, USA

May
2nd   University of Florida, Gainesville, FL, USA
3rd   End Zone, Tampa, FL, USA
4th   The Agora, Hallendale, FL, USA
6th   The Agora, Atlanta, GA, USA
8th   Ol' Man River's, New Orleans, LA, USA
9th   Poets, Memphis, TN, USA
11th   Rainbow Music Hall, Denver, CO, USA
13th   Civic Center, Santa Monica, CA, USA
15th   California Hall, San Francisco, CA, USA
19th   Ryerson Theater, Toronto, Canada, USA
20th   Red Creek, Rochester, NY, USA
21st   Uncle Sam's, Buffalo, NY, USA
22nd   City Limit's, Syracuse, NY, USA
23rd   J.B. Scotts, Albany, NY, USA
24th   Club Casino, Hampton Beach, NH, USA
25th   Center Stage, Providence, RI, USA
27th   Toad's Place, New Haven, CT, USA
28th   Metro, Boston, MA, USA
29th   Palladium, New York, NY, USA
31st   Fast Lane, Asbury Park, NJ, USA

1981 Summer Dates

June
4th   Salford University, England
6th   Friars Club, Aylesbury, England
8th   Pink Pop Festival, Geleen, Holland
9th   Hammersmith Palais, London, England

August
16th   Slane Castle, Dublin, Ireland
24th   Greenbelt Festival, Odel, England
29th   Stadium, Gateshead, England
31st   Coasters, Edinburgh, Scotland

October Tour (1st Leg) UK/Europe

October
1st   University Of East Anglia, England
2nd   Rock City, Nottingham, England
3rd   Salford University, England
4th   Tiffany's, Glasgow, Scotland
6th   Warwick University, Coventry, England
7th   Polytechnic, Leicester, England

8th   Lyceum, Sheffield, England
9th   Mayfair, Newcastle, England
10th   Royal Court Theatre, Liverpool, England
12th   Top Rank, Brighton, England
13th   Locarno, Portsmouth, England
14th   Top Rank, Cardiff, Wales
16th   King's Hall, Stoke, England
17th   Sport's Centre, Bracknell, England
18th   Locarno, Bristol, England
19th   Locarno, Birmingham, England
20th   Tiffany's, Leeds, England
21st   Pavilion, Hemel Hempstead, England
24th   Brielpoort, Deinze, Belgium
25th   Zaal Lux, Herenthout, Belgium
26th   Elysee Montmartre, Paris, France
28th   Stadsgehoorzaal, Leiden, Holland
29th   De Harmonie, Tilburg, Holland
30th   Paradiso, Amsterdam, Holland
31st   Stockvishal, Arnhem, Holland

November
1st   De Lantaarn, Rotterdam, Holland
3rd   Fabrik, Hamburg, Germany
4th   Metropol, Berlin, Germany

October Tour (2nd Leg) USA

13th   J.B. Scott's, Albany, NY, USA
14th   Orpheum Theater, Boston, MA, USA
15th   Toad's Place, New Haven, CT, USA
17th   Center Stage, Providence, RI, USA
18th   Ripley's Music Hall, Philadelphia, PA, USA
20th   The Ritz, New York, NY, USA
21st   The Ritz, New York, NY, USA
22nd   The Ritz, New York, NY, USA
24th   Hitsville North Night Club, Passaic, NJ, USA
25th   Hitsville South Night Club, Asbury Park, NJ, USA
28th   Hollywood Palladium, Los Angeles, CA, USA
29th   Warfield Theater, San Francisco, CA, USA

December
1st   The Agora, Atlanta, GA, USA
2nd   Vanderbilt University, Nashville, TN, USA
4th   Royal Oak Music Theater, Detroit, MI, USA
5th   Fountain St. Church, Grand Rapids, MI, USA
6th   Park West, Chicago, IL, USA
7th   Dooley's, East Lansing, MI, USA
8th   The Agora, Cleveland, OH, USA
10th   Uncle Sam's, Buffalo, NY, USA
11th   Ontario Theater, Washington, DC, USA
12th   Stage West, Hartford, CT, USA
13th   Malibou Beach Club, Long Island, NY, USA

London Christmas Shows
20th   Lyceum Ballroom, London, England
21st   Lyceum Ballroom, London, England

1982

Irish Winter Tour

January
23rd   Leisureland, Galway, Ireland
24th   City Hall, Cork, Ireland
26th   Royal Dublin Society Hall, Dublin, Ireland

October Tour (3rd Leg) USA

February
11th   President Riverboat, New Orleans, LA, USA
13th   Opry House, Austin, TX, USA
14th   Cardi's, San Antonio, TX, USA

15th	Cardi's Houston, TX, USA
16th	Cardi's, Dallas, TX, USA
17th	Jammie's, Oklahoma City, OK, USA
19th	Night Moves, St Louis, MO, USA
21st	First Avenue, Minneapolis, MN, USA
22nd	Headliners, Madison, WI, USA
23rd	University Of Illinois, Champaign, IL, USA
25th	Uptown Theater, Kansas City, MO, USA
27th	Rainbow Music Hall, Denver, CO, USA
28th	Colorado State University, Fort Collins, CO, USA

March

3rd	Lee County Arena, Fort Meyers, FL, USA
4th	Auditorium, West Palm Beach, FL, USA
5th	Curtis Hixon Hall, Tampa, FL, USA
6th	Leon County Arena, Tallahassee, FL, USA
10th	University Of Tennessee, Knoxville, TN, USA
11th	Civic Center, Atlanta, GA, USA
12th	North Hall Auditorium, Memphis, TN, USA
13th	Gardens, Louisville, KY, USA
14th	Convention Center, Indianapolis, IN, USA
16th	University Of Massachusetts, Amerst, MA, USA
17th	The Ritz, New York, NY, USA
18th	The Ritz, New York, USA
19th	Nassau College, Garden city, NY, USA
20th	Brown University, Providence, RI, USA
21st	Nightclub, Phoenix, AZ, USA
25th	Coliseum, Phoenix, AZ, USA
26th	Sports Arena, San Diego, CA, USA
27th	Sports Arena, Los Angeles, CA, USA
29th	Civic Centre, San Francisco, CA, USA
30th	Civic Centre, San Francisco, CA, USA

Summer Dates UK/Europe

May

14th	'Countdown In Concert' 'T Heem, Hattem, Holland

July

1st	Groenoord Hallen, Leiden, Holland
2nd	Roskilde Festival, Denmark
3rd	Tourhout Festival, Belgium
4th	Werchter Festival, Belgium
18th	Punchtown Racecourse, Dublin, Ireland
31st	Stadium, Gateshead, England

August

3rd	Vilar De Mouros, Portugal
7th	Ruisrock Festival, Turku, Finland

'Pre-War' European Tour

December

1st	Tiffany's, Glasgow, Scotland
2nd	Apollo Theatre, Manchester, England
3rd	De Montfort Hall, Leicester, England
4th	Odeon, Birmingham, England
5th	Lyceum Ballroom, London, England
6th	Hammersmith Palais, London England
8th	Muziek Centrum, Utrecht, Holland
8th	Martini Hall, Groningen, Holland
10th	Volksbelang, Mechelen, Belgium
11th	Brielpoort, Deinze, Belgium
12th	Limbughal, Ghent, Belgium
14th	Falkoner Tetret, Copenhagen, Denmark
15th	Konserthuset, Stockholm, Sweden
16th	Oslo, Norway
18th	City Hall, Cork, Ireland
19th	Leisureland, Galway, Ireland
20th	Maysfield Leisure Centre, Belfast
22nd	S.F.X. Centre, Dublin, Ireland
23rd	S.F.X. Centre, Dublin, Ireland

24th	S.F.X Centre, Dublin, Ireland

1983

The War Tour (1st Leg) UK

February

26th	Caird Hall, Dundee, Scotland
27th	Capitol Theatre, Aberdeen, Scotland
28th	Playhouse, Edinburgh, Scotland

March

1st	City Hall, Newcastle, England
2nd	University, Lancaster, England
3rd	Royal Court Theatre, Liverpool, England
4th	Victoria Hall, Hanley, England
6th	Guildhall, Portsmouth, England
7th	Colston Hall, Bristol, England
8th	University, Exeter, England
9th	Arts Centre, Poole, England
10th	Odeon, Birmingham, England
11th	St. David's Hall, Cardiff, Wales
13th	Top Rank, Brighton, England
14th	Hammersmith Odeon, London, England
15th	Gaumont Theatre, Ipswich, England
16th	Tyne Tees TV Studios, Newcastle, England
17th	City Hall, Sheffield, England
18th	University, Leeds, England
19th	Apollo Theatre, Manchester, England
20th	Assembly Rooms, Derby, England
21st	Hammersmith Odeon, London, England
22nd	Hammersmith Palais, London, England
24th	Tiffany's Glasgow, Scotland
25th	Royal Court Theatre, Liverpool, England
26th	City Hall, Newcastle, England
27th	Odeon, Birmingham, England
28th	Royal Centre, Nottingham, England
29th	Hammersmith Palais, London, England

April

3rd	Festival De Printemps, Bourges, France

The War Tour (2nd Leg) North America

23rd	Kenan Stadium, Chapel Hill, NC, USA
24th	Chrysler Hall, Norfolk, VA, USA
25th	Ritchie Coliseum, Coolege Park, VA, USA
27th	Cayhuga Community College, Auburn, NY, USA
28th	Institute Of Technology, Rochester, NY, USA
29th	State University, Dehli, NY, USA
30th	Brown University, Providence, RI, USA

May

1st	Stony Brook, NY, USA
3rd	Fulton Theater, Pittsburgh, PA, USA
5th	Orpheum Theater, Boston, MA, USA
6th	Orpheum Theater, Boston, MA, USA
7th	State University, Albany, NY, USA
8th	Trinity College, Hartford, CT, USA
10th	Yale University, New Haven, CT, USA
11th	Palladium, New York, NY, USA
12th	Capitol Theater, Passaic, NJ, USA
13th	Tower Theater, Philadelphia, PA, USA
14th	Tower Theater, Philadelphia, PA, USA
16th	Shea Center, Buffalo, NY, USA
17th	Massey Hall, Toronto, Canada
19th	Music Hall, Cleveland, OH, USA
20th	Grand Circus Theater, Detroit, MI, USA
21st	Aragon Ballroom, Chicago, IL, USA
22nd	Northrup Auditorium, Minneapolis, MN, USA
25th	Queen Elizabeth Theater, Vancouver, Canada
26th	Paramount Theater, Seattle, WA, USA

27th Paramount Theater, Portland, OR, USA
30th US Festival Glen Helen Regional Park, Devore,CA USA

June
1st Civic Auditorium, San Francisco, CA, USA
3rd Salt Palace Convention Center, Salt Lake City, UT, USA
5th Red Rocks Amphitheater, Denver, CO, USA
6th Colorado State University, Boulder, CO, USA
7th Wichita, KS, USA
8th Memorial Hall, Kansas City, MO, USA
9th The Brady Theater, Tulsa, OK, USA
10th Lloyd Noble Center, Norman, OK, USA
11th The Meadows, Austin, TX, USA
13th Bronco Bowl, Dallas TX, USA
14th Houston TX, USA
17th Sport's Arena, Los Angeles, CA, USA
21st Jai Alai Fronton Hall, Orlando, FL, USA
22nd Curtis Hixon Center, Tampa, FL, USA
23rd Sunrise Musical Theater, Miami, FL, USA
24th Jacksonville, FL, USA
25th Civic Center, Atlanta, GA, USA
27th Coliseum, New Haven, CT, USA
28th Centrum, Worcester, MA, USA
29th Pier 84, New York, NY USA

European Summer Festival Dates

July
2nd Torhout Festival, Belgium
3rd Werchter Festival, Belgium

August
14th Phoenix Park Racecourse, Dublin, Ireland
20th Lorelei Festival, St. Goarshausen, Germany
21st Kalvoya Festival, Oslo, Norway

November
16th NBC Arena, Honolulu, HI, USA

1st Japanese Tour
22nd Festival Hall, Osaka, Japan
23rd Simin Bunka Center, Nagoya, Japan
26th Sun Plaza Hall, Tokyo, Japan
27th Sun Plaza Hall, Tokyo, Japan
28th Sun Plaza Hall, Tokyo, Japan
29th Sun Plaza Hall, Tokyo, Japan

December
18th 'The Big One' Apollo, London, England

1984

First New Zealand Tour

August
29th Town Hall, Christchurch, New Zealand
31st Show Building, Wellington, New Zealand

September
1st Logan Campbell Centre, Auckland, New Zealand
2nd Logan Campbell Centre, Auckland, New Zealand

Under Australian Skies Tour
4th Entertainment Centre, Sydney, Australia
5th Entertainment Centre, Sydney, Australia
6th Entertainment Centre, Sydney, Australia
8th Entertainment Centre, Sydney, Australia
9th Entertainment Centre, Sydney, Australia
11th Festival Hall, Brisbane, Australia
13th Sports & Entertainment Centre, Melbourne, Australia
14th Sports & Entertainment Centre, Melbourne, Australia
15th Sports & Entertainment Centre, Melbourne, Australia
17th Sports & Entertainment Centre, Melbourne, Australia

18th Sports & Entertainment Centre, Melbourne, Australia
20th Apollo Centre, Adelaide, Australia
21st Apollo Centre, Adelaide, Australia
23rd Entertainment Centre, Perth, Australia
24th Entertainment Centre, Perth, Australia

The Unforgettable Fire Tour (1st Leg) Europe

October
18th Espace Tony Garnier/Palais D'Hiver, Lyon, France
19th Stadium, Marseille, France
20th Palais Des Sports, Toulouse, France
22nd Pattinoire, Bordeaux, France
23rd St. Herblain, Nantes, France
25th Espace Ballard, Paris, France
27th Vorst National, Brussels, Belgium
28th Vorst National, Brussels, Belgium
30th Sport Palais Ahoy, Rotterdam, Holland
31st Sport Palais Ahoy, Rotterdam, Holland

The Unforgettable Fire Tour (1st Leg) UK

November
2nd Brixton Academy, London, England
3rd Brixton Academy, London, England
5th Playhouse, Edinburgh, Scotland
6th Barrowlands, Glasgow, Scotland
7th Barrowlands, Glasgow, Scotland
9th Apollo Theatre, Manchester, England
10th Apollo Theatre, Manchester, England
12th NEC, Birmingham, England
14th Wembley Arena, London, England
15th Wembley Arena, London, England
21st Rock Pop In Concert Westfallenhalle Dortmund Germany

The Unforgettable Fire Tour (2nd Leg) North America

December
1st Tower Theatre, Philadelphia, PA, USA
2nd Centrum, Worcester, MA, USA
3rd Radio City Music Hall, New York, NY, USA
5th Constitution Hall, Washington, CD, USA
7th Massey Hall, Toronto, Canada
8th Fox Theater, Detroit, MI, USA
9th Music Hall, Cleveland, OH, USA
11th Aragon Ballroom, Chicago, IL, USA
15th Civic Auditorium, San Francisco, CA, USA
16th Long Bach Arena, Los Angeles, CA, USA

1985

The Unforgettable Fire Tour (3rd Leg) Europe

January
23rd Drammenhalle, Drammen, Norway
25th Isstadion, Stockholm, Sweden
26th Scandanavium, Gothenburg, Sweden
28th Congress Centre, Hamburg, Germany
29th Stadhallem, Offenbach, Germany
31st Sporthalle, Cologne, Germany

February
1st Musensaal, Mannheim, Germany
2nd Rudi-Sedlmeyerhalle, Munich, Germany
4th Palazetto Dello Sport, Milan, Italy
5th Teatro Tenda, Bologna, Italy
6th Teatro Tenda, Bologna, Italy
8th Hellenstadion, Zurich, Switzerland
10th Palais Omnisports, Paris, France

The Unforgettable Fire Tour (4th Leg) North America

25th Reunion Arena, Dallas, TX, USA

26th   Frank Erwin Center, Austin, TX, USA
27th   The Summit, Houston, TX, USA

March
1st   Compton Terrace, Phoenix, AZ, USA
2nd   Sport's Arena, Los Angeles, CA, USA
4th   Sport's Arena, Los Angeles, CA, USA
5th   Sport's Arena, Los Angeles, CA, USA
7th   Cow Palace, San Francisco, CA, USA
8th   Cow Palace, San Francisco, CA, USA
11th   NBC Arena, Honolulu, HI, USA
17th   McNichols Arena, Denver, CO, USA
19th   Auditorium, Minneapolis, MN, USA
21st   Pavilion, Chicago, IL, USA
22nd   Pavilion, Chicago, IL, USA
23rd   Joe Louis Arena, Detroit, MI, USA
25th   Richfield Coliseum, Cleveland, OH, USA
27th   Forum, Montreal, Canada
28th   Maple Leaf Gardens, Toronto, Canada
30th   Civic Center, Ottawa, Canada

April
1st   Madison Square Gardens, New York, NY, USA
2nd   Civic Center, Providence, RI, USA
3rd   Nassau Coliseum, Uniondale, NY, USA
8th   Capitol Center, Landover, MD, USA
9th   Civic Arena, Pittsburgh, PA, USA
10th   Coliseum, Hampton, VA, USA
12th   Meadowlands Arena, East Rutherford, NJ, USA
14th   Meadowlands Arena, East Rutherford, NJ, USA
15th   Meadowlands Arena, East Rutherford, NJ, USA
16th   Centrum, Worcester, MA, USA
18th   Centrum, Worcester, MA, USA
19th   Centrum, Worcester, MA, USA
20th   Civic Center, Hartford, CT, USA
22nd   Spectrum, Philadelphia, PA, USA
23rd   Civic Center, Hartford, CT, USA
24th   Spectrum, Philadelphia, PA, USA
29th   The Omni, Atlanta, GA, USA
30th   Coliseum, Jacksonville, FL, USA

May
2nd   Sun Dome, Tampa, FL, USA
3rd   Sportatorium, Fort Lauderdale, FL, USA
4th   Sportatorium, Fort Lauderdale, FL, USA

1985 European Summer Festival Dates

25th   "Rock Am Ring Festival", Nurburgring, Germany
26th   Neackarstadion, Stuttgart, Germany
27th   Freigelande Halle, Munster, Germany

June
1st   St Jacob's Football Stadium, Basel, Switzerland
22nd   The Longest Day Festival, Milton Keynes Bowl, England
29th   Croke Park, Dublin, Ireland

July
6th   Torhout Festival, Belgium
7th   Werchter Festival, Belgium
13th   "Live Aid", Wembley Stadium, London, England

August
25th   "Lark By The Lee" Festival, Cork, Ireland

1986

May
17th   "Self Aid", RDS Dublin, Ireland

'Conspiracy Of Hope' USA Tour

June

4th   Cow Palace, San Francisco, CA, USA
6th   The Forum, Los Angeles, CA, USA
8th   McNichols Arena, Denver, CO, USA
11th   The Omni, Atlanta, GA, USA
13th   Rosemont Horizon, Chicago, IL, USA
14th   Central Park, New York, NY, USA
15th   Giant's Stadium, East Rutherford, NJ, USA

1987

March
27th   Liquor store rooftop, 7th Av & Main St, Los Angeles, CA, USA ('Where The Streets Have No Name' video shoot)

The Joshua Tree Tour: (1st Leg) North America

April
2nd   Arizona State University, Tempe, AZ, USA
4th   Arizona State University, Tempe, AZ, USA
5th   Community Center, Tucson, AZ, USA
7th   The Summit, Houston, TX, USA
8th   The Summit, Houston, TX, USA
10th   Pan American Center, Las Cruces, NM, USA
12th   Thomas and Mack Arena, Las Vegas, NV, USA
13th   Sport's Arena, San Diego, CA, USA
14th   Sport's Arena, San Diego, CA, USA
17th   Sports Arena, Los Angeles, CA, USA
18th   Sports Arena, Los Angeles, CA, USA
20th   Sports Arena, Los Angeles, CA, USA
21st   Sports Arena, Los Angeles, CA, USA
22nd   Sports Arena, Los Angeles, CA, USA
24th   The Cow Palace, San Francisco, CA, USA
25th   The Cow Palace, San Francisco, CA,USA
29th   Rosemont Horizon, Chicago, IL, USA
30th   Silverdome, Pontiac, MI, USA

May
2nd   Centrum, Worcester, MA, USA
3rd   Centrum, Worcester, MA, USA
4th   Centrum, Worcester, MA, USA
7th   Civic Center, Hartford, CT, USA
8th   Civic Center, Hartford, CT, USA
9th   Civic Center, Hartford, CT, USA
11th   Meadowlands Arena, East Rutherford, NJ, USA
12th   Meadowlands Arena, East Rutherford, NJ, USA
13th   Meadowlands Arena, East Rutherford, NJ, USA
15th   Meadowlands Arena, East Rutherford, NJ, USA
16th   Meadowlands Arena, East Rutherford, NJ, USA

The Joshua Tree Tour (2nd Leg) Europe

27th   Stadio Flaminio, Rome, Italy
29th   Stadio Comunale, Modena, Italy
30th   Stadio Comunale, Modena, Italy

June
2nd   Wembley Arena, London, England
3rd   NEC Birmingham, England
6th   Eriksberg, Gothenburg, Sweden
12th   Wembley Stadium, London, England
13th   Wembley Stadium, London, England
15th   Le Zenith, Paris, France
17th   Mungersdorfer Stadion, Cologne, Germany
21st   St Jacob's Football Stadium, Basel, Switzerland
24th   King's Hall, Belfast, Northern Ireland
27th   Croke Park, Dublin, Ireland
28th   Croke Park, Dublin, Ireland

July
1st   Elland Road Stadium, Leeds, England
4th   Hippodrome de Vincennes, Paris, France
8th   Vorst Nationaal, Brussels, Belgium

10th	Feyenoord Stadium, Rotterdam, Holland
11th	Feyenoord Stadium, Rotterdam, Holland
15th	Estadio Santiago Bernabeu, Madrid, Spain
18th	Espace Richter, Montpellier, France
21st	Olympiahalle, Munich, Germany
22nd	Olympiahalle, Munich, Germany
25th	Arms Park, Cardiff, Wales
29th	SEC, Glasgow, Scotland
30th	SEC, Glasgow, Scotland

August

1st	Murrayfield Stadium, Edinburgh, Scotland
3rd	NEC, Birmingham, England
4th	NEC Birmingham, England
8th	Pairc Ui Chaoimh, Cork, Ireland

The Joshua Tree Tour: (3rd Leg) North America

September

10th	Nassau Coliseum, Uniondale, NY, USA
11th	Nassau Coliscum, Uniondalc, NY, USA
12th	Spectrum Arena, Philadelphia, PA, USA
14th	Giant's Stadium, East Rutherford, NJ, USA
17th	Gardens, Boston, MA, USA
18th	Gardens Boston, MA, USA
20th	Kennedy Stadium, Washington, DC, USA
22nd	Sullivan Stadium, Foxboro, MA, USA
23rd	Coliseum, New Haven, CT, USA
25th	John F. Kennedy Stadium, Philadelphia, PA, USA
28th	Madison Square Gardens, New York, NY, USA
29th	Madison Square Gardens, New York, NY, USA

October

1st	Olympic Stadium, Montreal, Canada
3rd	National Stadium, Toronto, Canada
6th	Municipal Stadium, Cleveland, OH, USA
7th	Memorial Auditorium, Buffalo, NY, USA
9th	Carrier Dome, Syracuse, NY, USA
11th	Silver Stadium, Rochester, NY, USA
13th	Three Rivers Stadium, Pittsburgh, NY, USA
20th	Carver-Hawkeye Arena, Iowa City, IA, USA
22nd	University, Champaign, IL, USA
23rd	Rupp Arena, Lexington, KY, USA
25th	Arena, St Louis, MO, USA
26th	Kemper Arena, Kansas City, MO, USA
28th	Rosemont Horizon, Chicago, IL, USA
29th	Rosemont Horizon, Chicago, IL, USA
30th	Rosemont Horizon, Chicago, IL, USA

November

1st	Hoosier Dome, Indianapolis, IN, USA
3rd	Civic Center, St. Paul, MN, USA
4th	Civic Center, St Paul, MN, USA
7th	McNichols Arena, Denver, CO, USA
8th	McNichols Arena, Denver, CO, USA
11th	'Save The Yuppies' concert, Justin Herman Plaza, San Francisco, CA, USA
12th	B.C. Place Stadium, Vancouver, Canada
14th	Stadium, Oakland, CA, USA
15th	Stadium, Oakland, CA, USA
17th	Memorial Coliseum, Los Angeles, CA, USA
18th	Memorial Coliseum, Los Angeles, CA, USA
22nd	Frank Erwin Center, Austin, TX, USA
23rd	Tarrant County Convention Center, Fort Worth, TX, USA
24th	Tarrant County Convention Center, Fort Worth, TX, USA
26th	Louisiana State University, Baton Rouge, LA, USA
28th	Charles Murphy Athletic Center Murfreesboro, TN, USA

December

3rd	Orange Bowl, Miami, FL, USA
5th	Tampa Stadium, Tampa, FL, USA
8th	The Omni, Atlanta, GA, USA

9th	The Omni, Atlanta, GA, USA
11th	Coliseum, Hampton, VA, USA
12th	Coliseum, Hampton, VA, USA
19th	Sun Devil Stadium, Tempe, AZ, USA
20th	Sun Devil Stadium, Tempe, AZ, USA

1988

October

16th	Smile Jamaica Concert, Dominion Theatre London, England

Rattle & Hum Film Premieres

27th	Savoy Cinema, Dublin, Ireland

November

4th	China Theatre, Los Angeles, CA, USA

1989

The Lovetown Tour: (1st Leg) Australia, New Zealand & Japan

September

21st	Entertainment Centre, Perth, Australia
22nd	Entertainment Centre, Perth, Australia
23rd	Entertainment Centre, Perth, Australia
27th	Entertainment Centre, Sydney, Australia
28th	Entertainment Centre, Sydney, Australia
29th	Entertainment Centre, Sydney, Australia

October

2nd	Entertainment Centre , Brisbane, Australia
3rd	Entertainment Centre , Brisbane, Australia
4th	Entertainment Centre , Brisbane, Australia
7th	National Tennis Centre, Melbourne, Australia
8th	National Tennis Centre, Melbourne, Australia
9th	National Tennis Centre, Melbourne, Australia
12th	National Tennis Centre, Melbourne, Australia
13th	National Tennis Centre, Melbourne, Australia
14th	National Tennis Centre, Melbourne, Australia
16th	National Tennis Centre, Melbourne, Australia
20th	Entertainment Centre, Sydney, Australia
21st	Entertainment Centre, Sydney, Australia
27th	Memorial Drive Stadium, Adelaide, Australia
28th	Memorial Drive Stadium, Adelaide, Australia

November

4th	Lancaster Park, Christchurch, New Zealand
8th	Athletic Park, Wellington, New Zealand
10th	Western Springs Stadium, Auckland, New Zealand
11th	Western Springs Stadium, Auckland, New Zealand
17th	Entertainment Centre, Sydney, Australia
18th	Entertainment Centre, Sydney, Australia
19th	Entertainment Centre, Sydney, Australia
23rd	Sports Arena, Yokohama, Japan
25th	Tokyo Dome, Tokyo, Japan
26th	Tokyo Dome, Tokyo, Japan
28th	Castle Hall, Osaka, Japan
29th	Castle Hall, Osaka, Japan

December

1st	Castle Hall, Osaka, Japan

The Lovetown Tour: (2nd Leg) Europe

11th	Palais Omnisports De Bercy, Paris, France
12th	Palais Omnisports De Bercy, Paris, France
14th	Westfalenhalle, Dortmund, Germany
15th	Westfalenhalle, Dortmund, Germany
16th	Westfalenhalle, Dortmond, Germany
18th	Rai Europa Hal, Amsterdam, Holland (19th & 20th cancelled)

26th   The Point Depot, Dublin, Ireland
27th   The Point Depot, Dublin, Ireland
30th   The Point Depot, Dublin, Ireland
31st   The Point Depot, Dublin, Ireland

1990

January (Rearranged Dutch dates)

5th   Sport Palais Ahoy, Rotterdam, Holland
6th   Sport Palais Ahoy, Rotterdam, Holland
9th   Sport Palais Ahoy, Rotterdam, Holland
10th   Sport Palais Ahoy, Rotterdam, Holland

1992

The Zoo TV Tour: (1st Leg) North America

February
29th   Civic Center, Lakeland, FL, USA

March
1st   Miami Arena, Miami, FL, USA
3rd   Coliseum, Charlotte, NC, USA
5th   The Omni, Atlanta, GA, USA
7th   Coliseum, Hampton, VA, USA
9th   Nassau Coliseum, Uniondale, NY, USA
10th   Spectrum Arena, Philadelphia, PA, USA
12th   Civic Center, Hartford, CT, USA
13th   Centrum, Worcester, MA, USA
15th   Civic Center, Providence, RI, USA
17th   Gardens, Boston, MA, USA
18th   Meadowlands, East Rutherford, NJ, USA
20th   Madison Square Gardens, New York, USA
21st   Knickerbocker Arena, Albany, NY, USA
23rd   Forum, Montreal, Canada
24th   Maple Leaf Gardens, Toronto, Canada
26th   Richfield Coliseum, Cleveland, OH, USA
27th   Palace Of Auburn Hills, Detroit, MI, USA
30th   Target Center, Minneapolis, MN, USA
31st   Rosemont Horizon, Chicago, IL, USA

April
5th   Reunion Arena, Dallas, TX, USA
6th   The Summit, Houston, TX, USA
7th   Frank Erwin Center, Austin, TX, USA
10th   Activity Center, Tempe, AZ, USA
12th   Sport's Arena, Los Angeles, CA, USA
13th   Sport's Arena, Los Angeles, CA, USA
15th   Sport's Arena, San Diego, CA, USA
17th   Arco Arena, Sacramento, CA, USA
18th   Oakland Coliseum, Oakland, CA, USA
20th   Tacoma Dome, Tacoma, WA, USA
21st   Tacoma Dome, Tacoma, WA, USA
23rd   Pacific National Exhibition Coliseum, Vancouver, Canada

The Zoo TV Tour: (2nd Leg): Europe

May
7th   Palais Omnisports De Bercy, Paris, France
9th   Flanders Expo, Ghent, Belgium
11th   Espace Tony Garnier, Lyon, France
12th   Patinoire De Malley, Lausanne, Switzerland
14th   Velodrome, San Sebastian, Spain
16th   Palau Sant Jordi, Barcelona, Spain
18th   Palau Sant Jordi, Barcelona, Spain
21st   Forum Di Assago, Milan, Italy
22nd   Forum Di Assago, Milan, Italy
24th   Donau Insel, Vienna, Austria
25th   Olympiahalle, Munich, Germany
29th   Festhalle, Frankfurt, Germany

31st   Earl's Court Arena, London, England

June
1st   NEC, Birmingham, England
4th   Westfalenhalle, Dortmund, Germany
5th   Westfalenhalle, Dortmund, Germany
8th   Scandanavium, Gothenburg, Sweden
10th   Globen Stockholm, Sweden
11th   Globen, Stockholm, Sweden
13th   Ostseehalle, Keil, Germnany
15th   Sport Palais Ahoy, Rotterdam, Holland
17th   Arena, Sheffield, England
18th   SEC, Glasgow, Scotland
19th   G-Mex Centre, Manchester, England

The Zoo TV Tour (3rd Leg) "Outside Broadcast" North America

August
7th   Hershey Park Stadium, Hershey, PA, USA
12th   Giants' Stadium, East Rutherford, NJ, USA
13th   Giants' Stadium, East Rutherford, NJ, USA
15th   Robert F. Kennedy Stadium, Washington, CD, USA
16th   Robert F. Kennedy Stadium, Washington, DC, USA
18th   Raceway, Saratoga Springs, NY, USA
20th   Foxboro Stadium, Foxboro, MA, USA
22nd   Foxboro Stadium, Foxboro, MA, USA
23rd   Foxboro Stadium, Foxboro, MA, USA
25th   Three Rivers Stadium, Pittsburgh, PA, USA
27th   Olympic Stadium, Montreal, Canada
29th   Yankee Stadium, New York, NY, USA
30th   Yankee Stadium, New York, NY, USA

September
2nd   Veterans Stadium, Philadelphia, PA, USA
3rd   Veteran's Stadium, Philadelphia, PA, USA
5th   National Stadium, Toronto, Canada
6th   National Stadium, Toronto, Canada
9th   Silverdome, Pontiac, MI, USA
11th   Cyclone Stadium, Ames, IA, USA
13th   Camp Randall Stadium, Madison, WI, USA
15th   World Music Amphitheater, Chicago, IL, USA
16th   World Music Amphitheater, Chicago, IL, USA
18th   World Music Amphitheater, Chicago, IL USA
20th   Memorial Stadium, St. Louis, MO, USA
23rd   Williams-Bryce Stadium, Columbia, SC, USA
25th   Georgia Dome, Atlanta, GA, USA

October
3rd   Joe Robbie Stadium, Miami, FL, USA
7th   Legion Field, Birmingham, AL, USA
10th   Tampa Stadium, Tampa, FL, USA
14th   Astrodome, Houston, TX, USA
16th   Texas Stadium, Dallas, TX, USA
18th   Arrowhead Stadium, Kansas City, MO, USA
21st   Mile High Stadium, Denver, CO, USA
24th   Sun Devil Stadium, Tempe, AZ, USA
27th   Sun Bowl, El Paso, TX, USA
30th   Dodger Stadium, Los Angeles, CA, USA
31st   Dodger Stadium, Los Angeles, CA, USA

November
3rd   BC Place Stadium, Vancouver, Canada
4th   BC Place Stadium, Vancouver, Canada
7th   Oakland Stadium, Oakland, CA, USA
10th   Jack Murphy Stadium, San Diego, CA, USA
12th   Sam Boyd Silver Bowl, Las Vegas, NV, USA
14th   Anaheim Stadium, Anaheim, CA, USA
21st   Palacio De Los Deportes, Mexico City, Mexico
22nd   Palacio De Los Deportes, Mexico City, Mexico
24th   Palacio De Los Deportes, Mexico City, Mexico
25th   Palacio De Los Deportes, Mexico City, Mexico

1993

The Zoo TV Tour: (4th Leg) 'Zooropa' Europe

May
9th	Feyenoord Stadium, Rotterdam, Holland
10th	Feyenoord Stadium, Rotterdam, Holland
11th	Feyenoord Stadium, Rotterdam, Holland
15th	Estadio Alvalade, Lisbon, Portugal
19th	Estadio Carlos Tartier, Oviedo, Spain
22nd	Estadio Vicente Calderon, Madrid, Spain
26th	Stade De La Beaujoire, Nantes, France
29th	Werchter Festival, Belgium

June
2nd	Waldstadion, Frankfurt, Germany
4th	Olympiastadion, Munich, Germany
6th	Cannstatter Wiesen, Stuttgart, Germany
9th	Westerstadion, Bremen, Germany
12th	Mungersdorfer Stadion, Cologne, Germany
15th	Olympia Stadion, Berlin, Germany
23rd	Stade De La Meinau, Strasbourg, France
26th	Hippodrome De Vincennes, Paris, France
28th	Stade De La Pontaise, Lausanne, Switzerland
30th	St Jacob's Football Stadium, Basel, Switzerland

July
2nd	Stadio Bentegodi, Verona, Italy
3rd	Stadio Bentegodi, Verona, Italy
6th	Stadio Flamino, Rome, Italy
7th	Stadio Flamino, Rome, Italy
9th	Stadio San Paulo, Naples, Italy
12th	Stadio Delle Alpi, Turin, Italy
14th	Stade Velodrome, Marseille, France
17th	Stadio Comunale, Bologna, Italy
18th	Stadio Comunale, Bologna
23rd	NEP Stadion, Budapest, Hungary
27th	Gentofte Stadion, Copenhagen, Denmark
29th	Valle Hovin Stadion, Oslo, Norway
31st	Stadion, Stockholm, Sweden

August
3rd	Goffert Park, Nijmegen, Holland
7th	Celtic Park, Glasgow, Scotland
8th	Celtic Park, Glasgow, Scotland
11th	Wembley Stadium, London, England
12th	Wembley Stadium, London, England
14th	Roundhay Park, Leeds, England
18th	Arms Park, Cardiff, Wales
20th	Wembley Stadium, London
21st	Wembley Stadium, London
24th	Pairc Ui Chaomh, Cork, Ireland
27th	RDS, Dublin, Ireland
28th	RDS, Dublin, Ireland

The Zoo TV Tour: (5th Leg)

'Zoomerang' Australia

November
12th	Cricket Ground, Melbourne, Australia
13th	Cricket Ground, Melbourne, Australia
16th	Football Park, Adelaide, Australia
20th	ANZ Stadium, Brisbane, Australia
26th	Football Stadium, Sydney, Australia
27th	Football Stadium, Sydney, Australia

'New Zooland' New Zealand

December
1st	Lancaster Park, Christchurch, New Zealand
4th	Western Springs Stadium, Auckland, New Zealand

Zoo TV Japan

9th	Tokyo Dome, Tokyo, Japan
10th	Tokyo Dome, Tokyo, Japan

1997

Pop Mart Tour (1st Leg) North America

April
25th	Sam Boyd Stadium, Las Vegas, NV, USA
28th	Jack Murphy Stadium, San Diego, CA, USA

May
1st	Mile High Stadium, Denver, CO, USA
3rd	Rice Stadium, Salt Lake City, UT, USA
6th	Autzen Stadium, Eugene, OR, USA
9th	Sun Devil Stadium, Tempe, AZ, USA
12th	Cotton Bowl, Dallas, TX, USA
14th	Liberty Bowl, Memphis, TN USA
16th	Death Valley Stadium, Clemson, SC, USA
19th	Arrowhead Stadium, Kansas City, MO, USA
22nd	Three Rivers Stadium, Pittsburgh, PA, USA
24th	The Ohio Stadium, Columbus, OH, USA
26th	R.F.K. Stadium, Washington, D.C., USA
31st	Giants Stadium, East Rutherford, NJ, USA

June
1st	Giants Stadium, East Rutherford, NJ, USA
3rd	Giants Stadium, East Rutherford, NJ, USA
7th	"Tibetan Freedom Concert", Downing Stadium, Randall's Island, New York USA
8th	Franklin Field, Philadelphia PA USA
12th	Winnipeg Stadium, Winnipeg, Canada
14th	Commonwealth Stadium, Edmonton, Canada
15th	Commonwealth Stadium, Edmonton, Canada
18th	Oakland Coliseum, Oakland, CA, USA
19th	Oakland Coliseum, Oakland, CA, USA
21st	L.A. Memorial Coliseum, Los Angeles, CA, USA
25th	Camp Randall Stadium, Madison, WI USA
27th	Soldier Field, Chicago, IL, USA
28th	Soldier Field, Chicago, IL, USA
29th	Soldier Field, Chicago, IL, USA

July
1st	Foxboro Stadium, Boston, MA, USA
2nd	Foxboro Stadium, Boston, MA, USA

Pop Mart Tour (2nd Leg) Europe

18th	Feynoord Stadium, Rotterdam, Holland
19th	Feynoord Stadium, Rotterdam, Holland
25th	Festival site, Werchter, Belgium
27th	Butweizer Hof, Cologne, Germany
29th	Festweise, Leipzig, Germany
31st	Maimankt, Mannheim, Germany

August
2nd	Ullevi, Gothenburg, Sweden
4th	Parken, Copenhagen, Denmark
6th	Vallehovin, Oslo, Norway
9th	Olympic Stadium, Helsinki, Finland
12th	Horse Race Track, Warsaw, Poland
14th	Strahov Stadium, Prague, Czech Republic
16th	Airfield, Wiener Neustadt, Austria
18th	Zeppelinfeld, Nurnberg, Germany
20th	Expo, Hannover, Germany
22nd	Wembley Stadium, London, England
23rd	Wembley Stadium, London, England
26th	Botanic Gardens, Belfast, Northern Ireland
28th	Roundhay Park, Leeds, England
30th	Lansdowne Road, Dublin, Ireland

31st Lansdowne Road, Dublin, Ireland

September
2nd   Murrayfield, Edinburgh, Scotland
6th   Parc des Princes, Paris, France
9th   Estadio Vicente Calderon, Madrid, Spain
11th   Alvalade Stadium, Lisbon, Portugal
13th   Estadi Olimpic De Montjuie, Barcelona, Spain
15th   Espace Grammont, Montpellier, France
18th   Aeroporto Dell' Urbe, Rome, Italy
20th   Festa Dell' Unità, Reggio Emilia, Italy
23rd   Kosevo Stadium, Sarajevo, Bosnia-Herzegovina
26th   Kaftatzoglio, Thessaloniki, Greece
30th   Ramat Gan Stadium, Tel Aviv, Israel

Pop Mart Tour (3rd Leg) North America

October
26th   Skydome, Toronto, Canada
27th   Skydome, Toronto, Canada
29th   Metrodome, Minneapolis, MN, USA
31st   Silverdome, Detroit, MI, USA

November
2nd   Olympic Stadium, Montreal, Canada
8th   Trans World Dome, St. Louis, MO, USA
10th   Tampa Stadium, Tampa, FL, USA
12th   Municipal Stadium, Jacksonville FL, USA
14th   Pro Player Stadium, Miami, FL, USA
21st   Superdome, New Orleans, LA, USA
23rd   Alamodome, San Antonio, TX, USA
26th   Georgia Dome, Atlanta, GA, USA
28th   Astrodome, Houston, TX, USA

December
2nd   Autodromo, Mexico City, Mexico
3rd   Autodromo, Mexico City, Mexico
9th   BC Place Stadium, Vancouver, Canada
12th   Kingdome, Seattle, WA, USA

1998

Pop Mart Tour (4th Leg) South America

January
27th   Nelson Piquet Stadium, Rio De Janeiro, Brazil
30th   Morumbi, Sao Paulo, Brazil
31st   Morumbi, Sao Paulo, Brazil

February
5th   River Plate Stadium, Buenos Aires, Argentina
6th   River Plate Stadium, Buenos Aires, Argentina
7th   River Plate Stadium, Buenos Aires, Argentina
11th   Estadio Nacional, Santiago, Chile

Pop Mart Tour (5th Leg) Australia, Japan, South Africa
17th   Burswood Dome, Perth, Australia
21st   Waverly Park, Melbourne, Australia
25th   ANZ Stadium, Brisbane, Australia
27th   Football Stadium, Sydney, Australia
5th   Tokyo Dome, Tokyo, Japan
11th   Osaka Dome, Osaka, Japan
19th   Cape Town, South Africa
21st   Johannesburg Stadium, Johannesburg, South Africa

May
19th   The Yes Vote, Waterfront Hall, Belfast, N. Ireland

2000

Pre-Elevation Tour Concerts

October
19th   May Ray Club, Paris, France

December
5th   Irving Plaza, New York City, USA

2001

February
7th   Astoria, London, England

Elevation Tour (1st Leg) North America

March
24th   National Car Rental Center, Fort Lauderdale FL, USA
26th   National Car Rental Center, Fort Lauderdale, FL, USA
29th   Charlotte Coliseum, Charlotte, NC, USA
30th   Philips Arena Atlanta, GA, USA

April
2nd   Compaq Center, Houston, TX, USA
3rd   Reunion Arena Dallas, TX, USA
6th   Pepsi Center Denver, CO, USA
9th   Saddledome Calgary, Canada
10th   Saddledome Calgary, Canada
12th   Tacoma Dome, Tacoma, WA, USA
13th   GM Place Vancouver, BC, USA
15th   Rose Garden Portland, OR, USA
17th   Sports Arena San Diego, CA, USA
19th   San Jose Arena San Jose, CA, USA
20th   San Jose Arena San Jose, CA, USA
23rd   Arrowhead Pond Anaheim, CA, USA
24th   Arrowhead Pond Anaheim, CA, USA
28th   America West Arena Phoenix AZ, USA

May
1st   Target Center Minneapolis, MN, USA
3rd   Gund Arena Cleveland, OH, USA
4th   Rupp Arena Lexington, KY, USA
6th   Mellon Arena Pittsburgh PA, USA
7th   Nationwide Arena Columbus, OH USA
9th   Bradley Center Milwaukee, WI, USA
10th   Conseco Fieldhouse Indianapolis, IA, USA
12th   United Center Chicago, MI, USA
13th   United Center Chicago, MI, USA
15th   United Center Chicago, MI, USA
16th   United Center Chicago, MI, USA
24th   Air Canada Center Toronto, Canada
25th   Air Canada Center Toronto, Canada
27th   Molson Center Montreal, Canada
28th   Molson Center Montreal, Canada
30th   The Palace of Auburn Hills Detroit MI USA
31st   HSBC Arena Buffalo NY, USA

June
2nd   Pepsi Center Albany NY, USA
3rd   Hartford Civic Center Hartford CT, USA
5th   Fleet Center Boston, MA, USA
6th   Fleet Center Boston, MA, USA
8th   Fleet Center Boston, MA, USA
9th   Fleet Center Boston, MA, USA
11th   First Union Center Philadelphia, PA, USA
12th   First Union Center Philadelphia, PA, USA
14th   MCI Center Washington, DC, USA
15th   MCI Center Washington, DC, USA

17th	Madison Square Garden New York, USA
19th	Madison Square Garden New York, USA
21st	Continental Arena East Rutherford, NJ, USA
22nd	Continental Arena East Rutherford, NJ, USA

Elevation Tour (2nd Leg) Europe

July

6th	Forum Copenhagen, Denmark
7th	Forum Copenhagen, Denmark
9th	Globe Stockholm, Sweden
10th	Globe Stockholm, Sweden
12th	Arena Cologne, Germany
13th	Arena Cologne, Germany
15th	Olympiahalle Munich, Germany
17th	Palais Omnisports Bercy Paris France
18th	Palais Omnisports Bercy Paris France
21st	Stadio Delle Alpi, Turin, Italy
23rd	Hallenstadion Zurich Swizerland
24th	Hallenstadion Zurich Switerland
26th	Stadhalle Vienna Austria
27th	Stadhalle Vienna Austria
29th	Waldbuhne Berlin Germany
31st	Gelredome Stadium Arnhem Holland

August

1st	Gelredome Stadium Arnhem Holland
3rd	Gelredome Stadium Arnhem Holland
5th	Sportpalais Antwerp Begium
6th	Sportpalais Antwerp Belgium
8th	Paulo St Jordi Barcelona Spain
11th	Evening News Arena Manchester England
12th	Evening News Arena Manchester England
14th	NEC Birmingham England
15th	NEC Birmingham England

18th	Earl's Court London England
19th	Earl's Court London England
21st	Earl's Court London England
22nd	Earl's Court London England
25th	Slane Castle County Meath Ireland
27th	SEC Glasgow, Scotland
28th	SEC Glasgow, Scotland

September

1st	Slane Castle County Meath Ireland

Elevation Tour (3rd Leg) North America (Proposed)

October.

10th	Joyce Center, Notre Dame, IN, USA
12th	Molson Centre, Montreal, PQ, USA
13th	Copps Coliseum, Hamilton, ON, USA
15th	United Center, Chicago, IL, USA
16th	United Center, Chicago, IL, USA
19th	Arena, Baltimore, MD, USA
24th	Madison Square Garden, New York, NY, USA
28th	Continental Airlines Arena, E Rutherford, NJ, USA
30th	Civic Center, Providence, RI, USA

November

2nd	First Union Center, Philadelphia, PA, USA
5th	Frank Erwin Center, Austin, TX, USA
7th	Pepsi Center, Denver, CO, USA
9th	Delta Center, Salt Lake City, UT, USA
12th	Staples Center, Los Angeles, CA, USA
13th	Staples Center, Los Angeles, CA, USA
15th	Arena, Oakland, CA, USA
18th	Thomas & Mack Center, Las Vegas, NV, USA
19th	Staples Center, Los Angeles, CA, USA

Discography

Discography

Below is a full discography of all known official U2 records throughout the world. It is split up into the following sections:- 7 inch single vinyl releases, 12 inch single vinyl releases, vinyl album releases, CD singles, CD albums, cassette singles releases, cassette album releases, radio show vinyl albums and CDs, compilation albums featuring U2 tracks, film sound-track albums featuring U2 tracks, albums and sin-gles by other artists featuring solo appearances from members of U2. Regular releases as well as promo-tional releases and test pressings have been included. As far as possible the country of origin and the cata-alogue number has been included, as well as date of release, though this hasn't been possible in every case. For background information on a particular track see the main section of the book.

A big thank you to the various U2 fans around the world who have provided information for this dis-cography, especially Kay Bauersfeld, Patrice Bruhat and the good folks at Island Records. Although this is probably the most extensive U2 discography ever published, there are still some gaps for certain releases. If anyone has more information to add to this discography for future editions of this book, please contact the author via the publishers.

All U2 releases are on Island Records unless oth-erwise stated

All U2 releases feature a picture sleeve cover unless stated

Key to abbreviations:- AUT = Austria, ARG = Argentina, AUS = Australia, BRA = Brazil, CAN = Canada, COR = Costa Rico, GER = Germany, FRA = France, GU - Guatamela, IRL = Ireland, ISR = Israel, ITA = Italy, JAP = Japan, KOR = South Korea, MAL = Malaysia, MEX = Mexico, MOR = Morocco, NL= Netherlands, NZ = New Zealand, PER = Peru, POR = Portugal, SA = South Africa, SPA = Spain, SWE = Sweden, UK = United Kingdom, UR = Uruguay, USA = United States Of America, VEN = Venezuela, YUG = Yugoslavia, ZIM = Zimbabwe

Vinyl Releases

7 Inch Singles

"U2-3" - Out Of Control / Stories For Boys / Boy-Girl (September 1979)
IRL   CBS 7951

Another Day / Twilight (February 1980)
IRL   CBS 8306   Free postcard included

11 O'clock Tick Tock / Touch (May 1980)
IRL   CBS 8687
UK   WIP 6601
UK   WIP 6601 DJ   Demo copy
UK   One sided test pressing
UK   Two sided test pressing

A Day Without Me / Things To Make And Do   (August 1980)
IRL   CBS 8905
UK   WIP 6630
UK   WIP 6630   1-sided Test pressing
UK   WIP 6630 DJ   1-sided promo (plain sleeve)
UK   WIP 6630 DJ   2 -sided promo
FRA   1 6837 672   no sleeve
NL   IS 102. 657   Different cover - same as *Boy* album cover
GER   IS 102.657   Different cover - same as *Boy* album cover

I Will Follow / Boy-Girl (Live at the Marquee Club - 22nd September 1980) (October 1980)
IRL   CBS 9065
UK   WIP 6656
UK   WIP 6656 DJ   1-sided promo (specially edited ver-sion in black company sleeve)
UK   WIP 6656 DK   2-sided promo
AUS   KISK 8150   (festival sleeve)
NZ   K 8150   Different sleeve

* "4 U2 PLAY" SINGLES SET 1980 The pack contained the four sin-gles below in a plastic wallet. Early issues came in yellow, orange or white vinyl. Later reissues came in black vinyl:-
IRL   CBS 7951   Out Of Control / Stories For Boys / Boy-Girl
IRL   CBS 8306   Another Day / Twilight
IRL   CBS 8687   11 O'clock Tick Tock / Touch
IRL   CBS 9065   I Will Follow / Boy-Girl (Live)

I Will Follow / Out Of Control (Live at the Paradise Theatre, Boston) 1980
USA   IS 49716 Poster-Cover (some copies featured the US *Boy* album stretch face picture sleeve)
USA   IS 49716 Double A-Side Stereo/Mono Promotional Copy
USA   SRC label   One sided test pressing
CAN   IS 49716   with stretch cover

Gloria / Is That All? 1981
ARG   9339   Promotional Copy orange sleeve (edited version)

A Day Without Me / I Will Follow 1981
FRA
GER

Fire / J. Swallo (June 1981)
IRL   CBS 1376
UK   WIP 6679
UK   WIP 6679 DJ   1-sided promotional edited copy
    EP 60417   1-sided test pressing
AUS   K - 8393

Fire / J. Swallo / The Electric Co. (Live) / The Ocean (Live) 1981
UK   UWIP 6679   limited edition double-pack single

Is That All?
ARG   1-sided promotional copy

Gloria / I Will Follow (Live) (October 1981)
IRL   CBS 1718
UK   WIP 6733
UK   WIP 6733 DJ   1-sided promotional edited copy
UK   1-sided test pressing
AUS   K-8510   reissues in blue sleeve
NZ   K-8510   Different sleeve than Australian
cover Gatefold
NL   103-372   Different picture sleeve same as
October

Twilight EP
NL   Unique Dutch only release

A Celebration / Trash, Trampoline & The Party Girl (March 1982)
IRL   CBS 2214
UK   WIP 6670
UK   WIP 6670 A   1-sided test pressing
NL   IS 104 098
GER   IS 104 098
FRA   IS 601 0510   Japanese enlarged design
AUS   K-8716   in blue company sleeve
ITA   WIP 26770
NZ   K 8716

A Celebration / Fire 1982
JAP   7S-69   Cover includes a photo of band (on
Polystar-Island label)
JAP   White label promo

Gloria / I Will Follow (Live) 1982
NL   IS 104.525   B-side was recorded at Veronica's
Countdown, Hattem, Holland and not Boston as with earlier
single

I Will Follow / Gloria 1982
NL   IS 104.525   *Live* - Cover (Werchter 1982)
GER   IS 104.525   *Live* - Cover (Werchter 1982) (grey
label - reissue)

"U2 PAC 2" 1982 (The pack contained the four singles below in a plastic wallet)
IRL   CBS 8905   A Day Without Me / Things To
Make And Do
IRL   CBS 1376   Fire / J. Swallo
IRL   CBS 1718   Gloria / I Will Follow (Live)
IRL   CBS 2214   A Celebration / Trash, Trampoline
And The Party Girl

New Year's Day / Treasure (Whatever Happened To Pete The Chop) (January 1983)
IRL   CBS 3105
UK   WIP 6848
UK   WIP 6848   1-sided test pressing for A and B side
UK   WIP 6848   Miss-pressing on b-side (contains
Martha Reeves - Tamla Motown)
USA   IL7-99915
USA   IL7-99915   Double A-Side White Label Promo-
tional Copy
USA   SRC Label   One sided test pressing
CAN   7999157   promo
GER   IS 105 107
NL   IS 105 000
FRA   IS 811 3237   Red & Purple Label
AUS   K-8983   Festival sleeve
SA
SPA   105 107
SWE   WIP 6848

New Year's Day / Treasure (Whatever Happened To Pete The Chop) / I Threw A Brick Through A Window (Live) / A Day Without Me (Live) / Fire (Live) (Last 3 tracks recorded at Werchter`82) (January 1983)
IRL   CBS A3105
UK   UWIP 6848   Limited edition double-pack single
      EP 600741

New Year's Day / Surrender
MEX   Ariola SP-58 promo with info sheet

New Year's Day / New Year's Day
USA   IL7-99915   promo red paper sleeve

New Year's Day (long version)
JAP   7S-86   Different *Boy* picture sleeve

New Year's Day (short) / Two Hearts Beat As One (short)
USA   7-949751   Yellow label 'Revival of Fittest'
series

Two Hearts Beat As One / Endless Deep (March 1983)
IRL   CBS 3274
UK   IS 109
UK   IS 109   Silver Label
UK   1-sided test pressing for A and B side
USA   IL7-99861
USA   SRC label   One sided test pressing
JAP   7S-101
JAP   7S-101   Promotional Copy has lyric sheet
AUS   K-9098
NZ   K-9098

Two Hearts Beat As One / Endless Deep / New Year's Day (US Remix) / Two Hearts Beat As One (US Remix)
IRL   CBSA 3274
UK   ISD 109   Limited edition double-pack single

Two Hearts Beat As One / Two Hearts Beat As One (US Remix) 1983
FRA   814 653-7   cover has yellow background rather
than red

Two Hearts Beat As One (mono) / Two Hearts Beat As One (stereo)
USA   7-99861   No picture sleeve

Two Hearts Beat As One (remix) / Two Hearts Beat As One (album version) / Two Hearts Beat As One (edit)
USA   DMD 643   No Picture sleeve promo

Sunday Bloody Sunday / Two Hearts Beat As One 1983
GER   IS 105 360

Sunday Bloody Sunday / Red Light 1983
JAP   7S-94   cover features live shot of the band

Sunday Bloody Sunday / Endless Deep 1983
HOL   105 330   Tree label
GER   105 330   Silver label

40 (How Long) (Live)/ Two Hearts Beat As One 1983
GER   105 807 100   Cover-Print says "Die Entdeckung
der Lorelei`83" (The Discovery of Lorelei '83).

I Will Follow (Live Lorelei '83) / I Will Follow (Special Remix for radio) 1984
USA   PR 564   Blue Label Promotional Copy

I Will Follow (Lorelei '83) / Two Hearts Beat As One 1984
USA   IL7-99789   Yellow Label 'Revival of the Fittest
series

Pride (In The Name Of Love) / Boomerang II (September 1984)
IRL   CBS 4727
UK   IS 202

UK   ISP 202   Picture-Disc
USA   IL-99704
GER   106 773 100
FRA   IS 880 236-7
CAN   ISL 97011   No picture sleeve
AUS   K-9502   limited edition picture sleeve
NZ   K-9502   limited edition picture sleeve
JAP   7SI-125
JAP   7SI-125   Promotional Copy
SA
SPA   A 106 773   promo
PER   F-ISL 0106773-4

Pride (In The Name Of Love) / 4th of July / Boomerang I / Boomerang II 1984
IRL   CBSA 4727
UK   ISD 202   Limited edition double-pack single
UK   4 x 1-sided test pressings of each track

Pride (In The Name Of Love) / 4th Of July 1984
USA   IL7-99704
USA   IL7-99704   Double A-Side White Label Promotional Copy

Pride (In The Name Of Love) / The Unforgettable Fire 1985
ARG   White Label Promotional Copy

Pride (In The Name Of Love) 1985
SPA   A 106 773   White label 1-sided promotional copy

Pride (In The Name Of Love) / Pride (In The Name Of Love) 1985
USA   7-99704 promo

The Unforgettable Fire / A Sort Of Homecoming (Live) (April 1985)
IRL   CBS 6185
UK   IS 220
UK   1-side test pressing
UK   ISP 220   Shaped Picture-Disc
GER   IS 107 183
JAP   DO7D-2001   White label promo contains insert
SPA   A 107184

The Unforgettable Fire / A Sort Of Homecoming (Live) / The Three Sunrises / Love Comes Tumbling / 60 Seconds In Kingdom Come 1985
IRL   CBS DA 6185
UK   ISD 220   Limited edition double-pack single

The Unforgettable Fire / MLK 1985
AUS   K-9561
NZ   K-9561   Festival sleeve

The Unforgettable Fire / Pride (In The Name of Love)
ARG   Ariola S-0521 promo

A Sort of Homecoming (Live) / A Sort Of Homecoming (Live) (April 1985)
UK   IS 220   Double A-Side White Label Promotional Copy (plain black sleeve)
USA   SRC label   1-sided test pressing

Gloria / Sunday Bloody Sunday 1985
USA   IL7-94974   Yellow Label `Revival of the Fittest-Series

Two Hearts Beat As One / New Year's Day 1985
USA   IL7-94975   Yellow Label `Revival of the Fittest-Series

Pride (In The Name Of Love) / I Will Follow (Live Lorelei`83) 1985
USA   IL7-94976   Yellow Label `Revival of the Fittest

- Series

Bad / A Sort Of Homecoming 1985
SA   IS WIP 6677   This single was released only in South Africa (no picture sleeve)

"U2 PAC 3" 1985 (Also known as "Arabesque")
(The pack contained the four singles below in a plastic wallet)
Pride (In The Name Of Love) / 4th of July 1985
IRL   CBS 4727   No. 1 of the Singles-Pack

Love Comes Tumbling / 60 Seconds In Kingdom Come / The Three Sunrises 1985
IRL   CBS 7024   No. 2 of the Singles-Pack

Sunday Bloody Sunday / Two Hearts Beat As One 1985
IRL   CBS 7023   No. 3 of the Singles-Pack

Boomerang I / Boomerang II 1985
IRL   CBS 7022   No. 4 of the Singles-Pack

With Or Without You / Luminous Times (Hold On To Love) / Walk To The Water (March 1987)
UK   IS 319
USA   IL7-99469
USA   IL7-99469   Double A-Side White Label Promotional Copy
USA   SRC Label   1-sided test pressing
GER   108 922
JAP   DO7D-2025   One sided promotional copy in different cover with lyric insert
ITA   J.B. 327   Jukebox-Single   B-Side   contains other artist
ITA   15319
CAN   97054
CAN   8703   promo
POR   15319
SPA   1A-108922   promo picture sleeve

With Or Without You / Walk To The Water (March 1987)
UK   IS 319J   Jukebox-Single
USA   IL-799453   Jukebox-Single
SA   ISS 319

With or Without You / Luminous Times 1987
AUS   K-241   Limited picture sleeve with gold sticker
ARG   White Label Promotional Copy

With or Without You / Mothers of the Disappeared
GU   IS I 358

With Or Without You / Gloria / Knockin' On Heavens Door 1987
ITA   Promotional Copy with live tracks

With Or Without You / With Or Without You
USA   7-99469   promo (some in brown vinyl)
USA   ST-IL-51307-SP   promo
USA   PR 1021   promo
ARG   5-0591   promo
MEX   RX 347

With Or Without You
JAP   Polystar RI-2002   1 sided promo

With Or Without You / Simply Red track
BRA   WEA 1112   promo

I Still Haven't Found What I'm Looking For / Spanish Eyes / Deep In The Heart (June 1987)
UK   IS 328
USA   IL7-99430
USA   IL7-99430   Double A-Side White Label Promo-

tional Copy
USA   SRC Label   1-sided test pressing
GER   IS 109 152
SPA   1A 609152   White label promotional copy
JAP   DO7D-2026   with lyrics sheet
MEX   RX 397   Double A-Side White Label Promotional Copy
SWE   IS 328   Test pressing
ITA   IS 328
SA   328

I Still Haven't Found What I'm Looking For / Spanish Eyes (June 1987)
UK   ISJ 328   Jukebox-Single
AUS   K-273   promo with sticker on back cover

I Still Haven't Found What I'm Looking For / I Still Haven't Found What I'm Looking For 1987
USA   7-99431   white label promo
MEX   Ariola RX 397

Where The Streets Have No Name / Silver And Gold / Sweetest Thing (August 1987)
UK   IS 340
USA   IL7-99408
USA   IL7-99408   Double A-Side White Label Promotional Copy
GER   IS 109 382
ITA   IS 340
JAP   DO7D-2027
CAN   IS 97061
MEX   RX 427   Double A-Side White Label Promotional Copy
SA   ISS 13   Double A-Side White Label Promotional Copy
ARG   Promotional Copy No picture sleeve
SPA   1A 109382
SWE   Test pressing

Where The Streets Have No Name / Silver And Gold 1987
UK   ISJB 340   Jukebox-Single
USA   IL7-99407   no picture sleeve
AUS   K-386   Picture sleeve

Where The Streets Have No Name / I Still Haven't Found What I'm Looking For 1987
USA   IL7-94960   Promotional copy

Where The Streets Have No Name
UK   IS340DJ   promo white label
USA   7-99408   promo
SA   15513   promo
MEX   Ariola RX 427 promo

Where The Streets Have No Name / Red Hill Mining Town
UK   promo

Where The Streets Have No Name / Depeche Mode track
ITA   JB 340   Jukebox-Single (also has lyric sheet)

In God's Country / Bullet The blue Sky / Running To Stand Still (November 1987)
USA   IL7-99385
USA   IL7-99385   Double A-Side White Label Promotional Copy
CAN   97066

In God's Country / Bullet The Blue Sky 1987
USA   IL7-99384   Without the official Cover
USA   7-99385   promo

CAN   IS 97064   Double A-Side White Label Promotional Copy

Bullet The Blue Sky / Spanish Eyes / Lucille 1987
UK   Promotional Copy

One Tree Hill / Bullet The Blue Sky / Running To Stand Still 1987
AUS   K-338   with lyric sheet
NZ   8733027   with lyric sheet

I Still Haven't Found What I'm Looking For / Where The Streets Have No Name 1987
USA   IL7-94960   Yellow Label `Revival of the Fittest- Series

With Or Without You / In God's Country 1987
USA   IL7-94961   Yellow Label `Revival of the Fittest´- Series

"The Joshua Tree Collection" 1987
This collection contained the first four of the singles below and was in a PVC case. The Promotional version contained all five of the singles listed below and was in a box. Some promo packs had a miss-pressing of *Red Hill Mining Town* coming out on both sides of the single and the A-side was blacked out by pen. It was limited to just 250 copies.

Where The Streets Have No Name / Red Hill Mining Town
UK   U2 6-1   White Label Promotional Copy
USA

With Or Without You / Running to Still Stand Still
UK   U2 6-2   White Label Promotional Copy
USA

I Still Haven't Found What I'm Looking For / One Tree Hill
UK   U2 6-3   White Label Promotional Copy
USA

Exit / Mothers of the Disappeared
UK   U2 6-4   White Label Promotional Copy

In God's Country / Bullet the Blue Sky
UK   U2 6-5   White Label Promotional Copy
USA

The Joshua Tree Sampler 1987
SWE   A limited edition 7" box set released in Sweden containing the following singles:-

Where The Streets Have No Name / Red Hill Mining Town

Trip Through Your Wires / Silver And Gold

I Still Haven't Found What I'm Looking For / One Tree Hill

Exit / Mothers of the Disappeared

In God's Country / Bullet the Blue Sky
Each Single features a gold printed picture sleeve

Desire / Hallelujah Here She Comes (September 1988)
UK   IS 400
USA   IL7-99250
USA   IL7-99250   Double A-Side White Label Promotional Copy
GER   IS 111 670
JAP   DO7D-2034   Gatefold Cover
AUS   K-616   Limited edition gatefold red vinyl (600 only)
NZ   Red Vinyl
SPA   1A 111670   Gatefold Cover
CAN   IL 97080
FRA   15400
MEX   RX 622   Double A-Side White Label Promotional Copy

BRA 6WP 0051
BRA WEA 47 Double A-Side Promotional Copy
SWE 15400
ITA IS 400

Desire/ track by other artist
ITA JB 346 Jukebox-Single B-Side contains other artist

Desire
USA 7-99250 One sided test pressing
ITA JB 346 juke box promo white label

Desire / Desire
UK ISG 400 test pressing (pink label)
USA 7-99250 promo
BRA WEA 47 promo
MEX Ariola RX 622 promo
ARG RCA 5-0658 promo

Hallelujah Here She Comes/ Hallelujah Here She Comes 1988
USA Double sided promotional copy

Angel of Harlem / A Room At The Heartbreak Hotel (December 1988)
UK IS 402 white label
UK IS 402
USA IL7-99254
USA IL7-99254 Double A-Side White Label Promotional Copy
GER IS 111 920
SPA A 106773 One Sided Promotional Copy
JAP DO7D-2035
CAN 97085
AUS K-704 One sided test pressing
AUS K-704 Turquoise Vinyl (800 only) picture label
ITA 15402
FRA Has a yellow label
SWE Test pressing limited to 10 copies

Angel of Harlem / track by other artist
ITA JB 348 Jukebox-Single B-Side contains other artist

A Room At The Heartbreak Hotel
USA STIL 56341-7 Test pressing

When Love Comes To Town / Dancing Barefoot (April 1989)
UK IS 411
UK 15411A-30 one sided test pressing (pink label)
USA IL7-99225
USA IL7-99225 Double A-Side White Label Promotional Copy
GER IS 112 200
AUS K-781
CAN IL 97094
FRA 112 220

All I Want Is You / Unchained Melody (June 1989)
UK IS 422
UK ISB 422 Limited edition in Tin-box (numbered) (5,000 only)
UK IS 422 two-sided white label test pressing
UK IS 422 A-SU one-sided white label test pressing
USA IL7-99199
USA IL7-99199 Double A-Side White Label Promotional Copy
USA ST-IL-57123-SP promo

GER IS 122 406
AUS K-805
AUS K-805 Purple Vinyl 30 copies only (withdrawn soon after release)
AUS K-805 Limited Edition with free cassingle of *Everlasting love* (Festival/Island k 805)
ITA IS 422

All I Want Is You / Unchained Melody / Desire / Hallelujah Here She Comes 1989
AUS K-805/K-616 Limited edition Double-Single in Bag + Sticker

All I Want Is You / track by other artist
JAP YPS-069 promo

I Still Haven't Found What I'm Looking For (Live New York 1987) 1989
BRA Free Flexi-Disc from the Brazilian Music Magazine *BIZZ*

Alex Descends Into Hell For A Bottle Of Milk/Korova 1 (August 1991)
UK IS 500 B Test Pressing Pink handwritten Label no Picture-Sleeve

The Fly / Alex Descends Into Hell For A Bottle Of Milk/Korova 1 1991
UK IS 500
UK IS 500 Silver Label jukebox promo
GER IS 114 728
FRA IS 868 884-7
FRA IS 868 884-7 Black Promo-Pack incl. 7", CD-Single and Sticker
AUS 868-884-7

The Fly / The Fly
UK IS 500 Test pressing

Mysterious Ways / Mysterious Ways (Solar Plexus Magic Hour Remix) 1991
UK IS 509
UK IS 509 Black Label jukebox promo
UK IS 509 White label test pressing
GER IS 114 930
FRA IS 866 188-7
FRA IS 866 188-7 Brown Promo-Pack incl. 7", CD-Single and a Puzzle of the Cover
AUS IS 866 188-7

One / Lady With The Spinning Head 1992
UK IS 515
UK IS 515 silver label jukebox promo
GER IS 115 164
FRA IS 886 532-7

Even Better Than The Real Thing / Salome 1992
UK IS 525
UK IS 525 Silver label jukebox promo
GER IS 101 887
FRA IS 866976-7 Slightly different cover
SPA IS 74321 10188 7 (1A)

Even Better Than The Real Thing (Perfecto Mix Radio Edit) (July 1992)
UK REAL-2-DJ Double A-Side Promotional Copy

Who's Gonna Ride Your Wild Horses / Paint It Black 1992
UK IS 550
UK IS 550 Silver label jukebox promo
GER IS 120 472
NL IS 112 477

FRA   IS 864 666-7

The Achtung Baby Singles Collection

FRA   The Fly / Alex Descends Into Hell For A Bottle Of Milk/ Korova 1 / Mysterious Ways / Mysterious Ways (Solar Plexus Magic Hour Remix) / One / Lady With The Spinning Head / Even Better Than The Real Thing / Salome / Who's Gonna Ride Your Wild Horses / Paint It Black

Stay (Faraway, So Close!) / I've Got You Under My Skin 1993
UK   IS 578
UK   IS 578   silver label juke box promo
USA   IL-422 858 076 -7

Numb / Numb (July 1993)
UK   NUMJB 1   Black/silver label jukebox single
MEX   Polygram 197-A   promo no picture sleeve

Hold Me, Thrill Me, Kiss Me, Kill Me / Themes From Batman Forever 1995
UK   Island/Atlantic A 7131   Limited edition red vinyl (B-Side is **not** by U2) some miss-pressed in orange vinyl and B-side is credited to U2
UK   A 7131   Juke box promo
FRA   7567   Juke box promo

Miss Sarajevo / One (Live)   1995
UK   IS 625/854 4807   With free poster in a 12" plastic sleeve
UK   ISJB 625   Juke box copy no picture sleeve

Discotheque / Holy Joe (Garage Mix) / Holy Joe (Guilty Mix) 1997
UK   ISJB 649   Juke box promo
USA   422-854 774-7 White paper cover

Discotheque /I Shot The Sheriff (Warren G) 1997
ITA   AS 5001 031   Jukebox promo in Polygram Picture sleeve

Staring At The Sun / North And South Of The River 1997
UK   ISJB658   Jukebox   Promo   (white   custom sleeve)

Last Night On Earth (single version) - Last Night On Earth (First Night In Hell Mix) 1997
UK   ISJB664   Jukebox   promo   (white   custom sleeve) (500 copies)

Please (Strings version) - Where The Streets Have No Name (live from Rotterdam) 1997
UK   ISJB673   Jukebox   promo   (white   custom sleeve)
FRA   PY102   Jukebox promo Note: "Strings version" seems identical to single version

If God Will Send His Angels (single version) - Sunday Bloody Sunday (live from Sarajevo) 1997
UK   ISJB684   jukebox   promo   (white   custom sleeve)

Sweetest Thing (The Single Mix) - Stories For Boys (live from Boston) 1998
UK   ISJB 727   jukebox promo (No picture sleeve)

Acetates

An Cat Dubh
USA   7" acetate

Gloria 1981
UK   Edited Townhouse acetate

Fire (alternative version to single release) 1981

UK   10" acetate

New Year's Day 1983
UK   Double 7" metal acetate

Surrender 1983
JAP   7" acetate

Exit 1987
        7" acetate

Angel Of Harlem 1988
UK   Townhouse Metal acetate

Love Rescue Me 1988
USA   10" acetate

Whose Gonna Ride Your Wild Horses? 1991
UK   10" one sided acetate

Stay (Faraway, So Close!) 1993
UK   10" one sided acetate

The First Time 1993
UK   10" acetate

Hold Me, Thrill Me, Kiss Me, Kill Me 1995
UK   East West 10" gold acetate

Mofo 1997
UK   7"Acetate

12 Inch Singles

"U2-3" Out Of Control / Stories For Boys / Boy-Girl 1979
IRL   CBS 127951   Limited edition of 1.000, each number hand-written by Jackie Hayden of CBS Ireland
IRL   CBS 127951   Reissue of above (both editions came in the CBS plain orange and yellow   sleeve)

I Will Follow / Stevie Winwood - Night train 1980
USA   PRO A1-940   White Label Promotional Copy

Fire / J. Swallow / 11 O'clock Tick Tock (Live) / The Ocean (Live) 1981
GER   IS 600 417
HOL   IS 600 417   also called R.O.K.
SPA   F 600 417

New Year's Day (Long Version) / Treasure / Fire (Live) / I Threw A Brick Through A Window (Live) / A Day Without Me (Live) (Last three tracks recorded live at Werchter '83) 1983
IRL   CBS 12 3105
UK   12WIP 6448
GER   IS 600 741
JAP   18S 183
BRA   21.064   Promotional Copy   incl. other artists
SPA   F 600 780
POR   UWIP 6848-P

New Year's Day (US Remix) / Two Hearts Beat As One (US Remix) 1983
FRA   IS 814 948 1   Different Picture Sleeve
FRA   6863227

New Year's Day / New Year's Day 1983
UK   Set of two 1-sided Test-Pressings green label
USA   DMD 640/604 Promotional Copy

New Year's Day (US Remix)
USA   Promo
BRA   21.080   Promotional Copy including other Artists

Two Hearts Beat As One / New Year's Day (US Remix) / Two Hearts Beat As One (US Remix) 1983

IRL	CBSA 133274	
UK	12 IS 109	
JAP	15S-184/18S 187?	
JAP	15S-184	White Label Promotional Copy
NZ	X-14032	Ltd. Edition of 1.000 !
AUS	X 13112	picture sleeve with giant 12" 45 on cover
AUS	X 53132	no picture sleeve

Two Hearts Beat As One / Two Hearts Beat As One (Remix) / Two Hearts Beat As One (Extended Version) 1983

USA	DMD 643	Promotional Copy Not for sale
JAP	Polystar 155-185	with lyrics

Sunday Bloody Sunday / New Year's Day (US Remix) / Two Hearts Beat As One (US Remix) 1983

GER	600 820
HOL	600 820
BRA	73500

Sunday Bloody Sunday

BRA	73.500	Promotional Copy including other artists
BRA	WEA 21.082	Promo

I Will Follow (Live Lorelei`83) / I Will Follow (Special Remix) 1983

USA	PR 582	Promotional Copy
BRA	WEA 21.090	Promotional copy

Pride (In The Name Of Love) / Boomerang I / Boomerang II / 4th of July 1984

UK	12 IS 202	
UK	1215X 202A-UA	Test pressing (4th July missing)
USA	Promotional Copy	
GER	IS 601 469 - 213	
CAN	IS-1010	
NZ	X 14105	In blue picture sleeve
AUS	IX 14105	White Vinyl
JAP	1851-275	blue picture sleeve
ITA	ISX202	
FRA	880 236-1	
SPA	F-601 469	
POR	12IS 202	

Pride (In The Name Of Love) / Boomerang I / Boomerang II / 11 O'clock Tick Tock (Remix) / Touch 1984

UK	IS X 202	Blue Cover
SPA	F 601 921	
JAP	18SI-275	

Pride (In The Name Of Love) 1984

BRA	WEA PRO 21.049	Promotional Copy - Also contains tracks by other artists

Pride (In The Name Of Love) / Pride (In The Name Of Love) 1984

USA	PR 635	White Label Promotional Copy

The Unforgettable Fire / The Three Sunrises / Bass Trap / A Sort Of Homecoming (Live) / Love Comes Tumbling   1984

IRL	CBS 12 6185	
UK	12 IS 220	
GER	601 759	
CAN	ISM 1026	
AUS	L 18002	Spelling mistake on back-cover. Different version of "Love Comes Tumbling"
AUS	880 716-1	
NZ	L18002	
ITA	12ISX 220	
SPA	F 601-759	
YUG	Yugoton 12IS 220 - MXSI 18003	

Love Comes Tumbling 1984

BRA	WEA 1.002	promo with other artists

"The Unforgettable Fire Sampler" (Wire / Bad / The Unforgettable Fire) (September 1984)

UK	U2-2	3 track Promotional Copy with picture labels

Wire / Wire 1985

USA	PR 675	White Label Promotional Copy
USA	SRC Label	1-sided test pressing

Wire / Bad / The Unforgettable Fire (September 1984)

UK	U2 2-A	Promotional Copy (same tracks on both sides) plain black cover with picture label

A Sort Of Homecoming / A Sort Of Homecoming 1985

USA	PR 701	Whitc Labcl Promotional Copy
USA	1-sided test pressing	

Bad (Live) / Bad (Live) 1985

USA	PR 774	White Label Promotional Copy

Wide Awake In America 1985

UK	With band picture labels	
BRA	WEA PR	Promotional copy

New Year's Day 1985

BRA	WEA 21064	promo with other artists

New Year's Day 1985

BRA	WEA 21080	promo with other artists

With Or Without You / Luminous Times / Walk To The Water 1987

UK	12 IS 319	
USA	0-96786	
USA	PR 1021	Double A-Side Promotional Copy
GER	IS 108 922	
CAN	IS-1130	
AUS	X14480	Festival picture sleeve
SPA	3A 608922	One sided promo
BRA	WEA PRO 1.112	Promotional Copy including other artists
MEX	SL-7172	
ARG	RCA/Ariola TLP-50468	

I Still Haven't Found What I'm Looking For / Spanish Eyes / Deep In The Heart 1987

UK	12 IS 328	
UK	12 IS 328A	one sided white label promo
USA	0-96740	
GER	IS 609 152	
CAN	IS-1135	
USA	IL0-96740	
ARG	TLP-50469	B-side with other artist
SPA	3A 609152	White Label promotional Copy
MEX	SL7173	
BRA	WEA 1127	promo with other artist

Where The Streets Have No Name / Race Against Time / Silver And Gold / Sweetest Thing 1987

UK	12 IS 340	limited edition including lyric-sheet of *Silver and Gold*
USA	IL-0-96740	
GER	IS 609 382	

ARG   RCA/Ariola TLP-5-0469   B-side with other artist
ITA   12 ISX 340

In God's Country / Bullet The Blue Sky / Running To Stand Still 1987
CAN   IS 1167   10,000 only
BRA   WEA 6WP 0008   promo with other artist

Trip Through Your Wires / Luminous Times / Spanish Eyes / Silver And Gold 1987
AUS   SMX 69541   Numbered promotional copy given away free with *Rolling Stone* magazine

Desire (Hollywood Remix) (October 1988)
UK   12 ISX 400   1-Sided Promotional Copy in custom picture sleeve 800 only
GRE   40142   test pressing

Desire / Hallelujah Here She Comes / Desire (Hollywood Remix) 1988
UK   12 IS 400
UK   12 ISG 400   Gatefold Cover
USA   IL0-96600
USA   PR 2499   Double A-Side Promotional Copy in gatefold sleeve
USA   PR 2499   one sided test pressing
USA   DMD 1258   white label promo
GER   IS 611 670
AUS   X 13337   limited edition
CAN   IS-1217
SWE   12 IS 400
BRA   WEA 6 WP.0051   Promotional Copy incl. other Artists
SPA   3A 111670   Gatefold Cover
ITA   ISX 400
GRE   VG 4015Z
COR   Ariola 8005008

Angel Of Harlem / A Room At The Heartbreak Hotel / Love Rescue Me (Live) 1988
UK   12 IS 402
USA   0-96590
USA   DMD 1269   Double A-Side Promotional Copy
GER   IS 611 920
ITA   ISX 402   some promos have different picture sleeves (200 only)
AUS   MX 71509   Red Vinyl 500 copies only
NZ   X 14672
CAN   IS-1218
SWE   12 IS 402
SPA   3A 611920
SPA   A 106773   one sided white label promo
BRA   WEA 6 WP.1005   Promotional Copy with other artist

3-D Dance Mixes   (March 1989)

When Love Comes To Town (Live from the Kingdom Mix) / God Part II (Hard Metal Dance Club Mix) / Desire (Hollywood Remix)
UK   12 ISX 411 Promotional Copy

When Love Comes To Town / God Part II (Hard Metal Mix) / When Love Comes To Town (Live From The Kingdom Mix) / Dancing Barefoot 1988
UK   12 IS 411
UK   12 IS 411A - RE1 -4   2 sided test pressing pink label
USA   ILO-96570
USA   DMD 1310 Double A-Side Promotional Copy

GER   IS 611 200
CAN   IS-1226
AUS   X 14679 paper cover
BRA   WEA 6 WP 1022 Promotional copy with other artist

When Love Comes To Town (Live From The Kingdom Mix) / God Part II (Hard Metal Mix) / Dancing Barefoot   1988
USA   DMD 1324 White Label promotional copy

All I Want Is You / Unchained Melody / Everlasting Love   1989
UK   12 IS 422
UK   12 ISB 422 limited edition box set with 4 photos
USA   IL 0-96550
GER   IS 612 406
ITA   ISX 422
AUS   X 14678
CAN   IS 1243

All I Want Is You / Unchained Melody / Everlasting Love 1989
USA   DMD 1349   White Label Promotional Copy
AUS   X 14678   Ltd. Ed. Green Vinyl

Everlasting Love 1990
BRA   PRO 2801 433 Promotional Copy including other artists

Night & Day (Twilight Mix) / Night & Day (Steel String Remix) (October 1990)
UK   RHB 1   Promotional Copy (4000 only)

The Fly / Alex Descends Into Hell For A Bottle Of Milk/Korova 1 / The Lounge Fly Mix 1991
UK   12 IS 500
USA   IL 422 868 885-1
GER   IS 614 728
GER   IS/BMG 614 728   Promotional pack with picture bag, stickers and BMG promo CD
AUS   IS/PHONOGRAM 868 885-1
SPA   614 728 (3A)
ARG   TLP 00606

The Fly / The Lounge Fly Mix 1991
UK   promo with 16 "Fly" posters
USA   868 - 885 - 1   1 sided test pressing
BRA   2801 531

Mysterious Ways / Mysterious Ways (Solar Plexus Extended Club Mix) / Mysterious Ways (Apollo 440 Magic Hour Remix) / Mysterious Ways (Tabla Motown Remix) / Mysterious Ways (Solar Plexus Club Mix)
UK   12 IS 509
USA   IL 422 866 189-1
USA   PR12-6701   Double A-Side Promotional Copy
GER   IS 614 930
FRA   promo with sticker
AUS   866 189-2   with posters
AUS   white label test pressing

Mysterious Ways (Perfecto Mix) / Mysterious Ways (Ultimatum Mix) / Mysterious Ways (Apollo 440 Magic Hour Remix) / Mysterious Ways (Solar Plexus Extended Club Mix)
UK   12 ISX 509
USA   PR 12-6701   with Tabla Motown Remix

One / Lady With The Spinning Head / Satellite Of Love (February 1992)
UK   12 IS 515
USA   IL 422 866 533-1   promo stamp on front
GER   IS 615 164
FRA   866 533-1
FRA   Blue label test pressing

BRA   promo with different picture sleeve

Lady With The Spinning Head (UVI) / Satellite Of Love (February 1992)
UK   12 IS 515B   White label test pressing with press release

Zoo Station / Lady With The Spinning Head (Extended Dance Mix) / Lady With The Spinning Head 1992
USA PR 12-67151   Promotional Copy Picture Disc (1000 copies only)

Even Better Than The Real Thing / Where Did It All Go Wrong / Salome / Lady With The Spinning Head (Extended Dance Mix) 1992
UK   12 IS 525 with giant poster
USA IL 422 866 977-1
GER IS 601 887
AUS IS 866 977-1   with giant poster

Even Better Than The Real Thing (Perfecto Mix) / Even Better Than The Real Thing / (Trance Mix) / Even Better Than The Real Thing (Sexy Dub Mix) (June 1992)
UK   REAL   white label test pressing promo no picture sleeve
UK   REAL 1   in black die-cut sleeve
UK   REAL U2 /864 197-1
USA AMD J08 0392 promo with black picture sleeve
FRA 864 197-1

Even Better Than The Real Thing (Perfecto Mix) / Even Better Than The Real Thing (Sexy Dub Mix) / Even Better Than The Real Thing (Apollo Stealth Sonic Remix) / Even Better Than The Real Thing (V16 Exit Wound Remix) / Even Better Than The Real Thing (A440 vs. U2 Instrumental Remix) 1992
USA IL 422 862 281-1

Who's Gonna Ride Your Wild Horses (Temple Bar Remix) / Paint It Black / Fortunate Son / Who's Gonna Ride Your Wild Horses (Temple Bar Edit) 1992
UK   12 IS 550
USA IL 422 864 521-1
GER IS 612 472

Salome (Zooromancer Remix) / Can't Help Falling In Love (Mystery Train Dub) (November 1992)
UK   12 IS 550 DJ   Promotional Copy in black die-cut sleeve with picture label (1000 only)

Numb / Numb 1993
USA PR12-6784   White Label Promotional Copy

Lemon (Bad Yard Club) / Lemon (Serious Def Dub) 1993
USA PR12 6804-1   Promotional Copy   10" Yellow Vinyl

Lemon (Bad Yard Club) / Lemon (Version Dub) / Lemon (Momo´s Reprise) / Lemon (Perfecto Mix) / Lemon (Jeep Mix) 1993
USA IL 422 862 957-1   Yellow Vinyl

Lemon (Perfecto Mix) / Lemon (Bad Yard Club) / Lemon (Momo´s Reprise) / Lemon (Serious Def Dub) / Lemon (Version Dub) / Lemon (Trance Mix) (October 1993)
UK   12LEM-DJ-1   Promotional Copy   N u m b e r e d   12" Double-Pack (1000 only)
UK   12LEM-DJ-2   Some with press sheets. Some are in separate sleeves
HOL Same as UK release but not numbered

Lemon (Prefecto Mix) / Lemon (Trance Mix)
UK   IS 12 No picture sleeve

Melon: Salome (Zooromancer Remix) / Lemon (BYC Mix) / Numb (The Soul Assassins Mix) /1 Numb (Gimme Some More Dignity Mix) (February 1995)

UK   12 MELON 1 Promotional Copy (800 only)

Discotheque (DM Deep Club Mix) / Discotheque (Hexidecimal Mix) / Discotheque (DM Deep Instrumental Mix) //Discotheque (Radio Edit) 1997
UK   422-854 789-1 Picture sleeve

Discotheque / Discotheque (David Holmes Mix) / Discotheque (DM Deep Extended Club Mix) / Discotheque (DM Deep Beats Mix) / Discotheque (DM TEC Radio Mix) / Discotheque (DM Deep Instrumental Mix) 1997
UK   12ISD649DJ   Promotional copy

Discotheque / Discotheque (David Holmes Mix) / Discotheque (DM Deep Extended Club Mix) /

Discotheque (DM Deep Beats Mix) / Discotheque (DM TEC Radio Mix) / Discotheque (DM Deep Instrumental Mix) / Discotheque (Howie B, Hairy B Mix) /Discotheque (Hexidecimal Mix) 1997
UK   12IST649   "Discotheque" poster included

Discotheque (Howie B, Hairy B Mix) / Discotheque (Hexidecimal Mix) 1997
UK   12ISX649DJ   Promo

Discotheque (DM Deep Club Mix) / Discotheque (DM Tec Club Mix) 1997
USA PR127398-1   Promo (custom picture sleeve)

Staring At The Sun (Monster Truck Mix) / Staring At The Sun (Lab Rat Mix) / Staring At The Sun (Sad Bastards Mix) 1997
UK   12IS658DJ   Promo
USA PR127463-1   Promo

Last Night On Earth (First Night In Hell Mix) - Happiness Is A Warm Gun (The Gun Mix) - Pop Muzik (Pop Mart Mix) - Happiness Is A Warm Gun (The Danny Saber Mix) 1997
UK   12IS 664DJ   Promo (unique picture sleeve)
USA 12IS 665DJ   Promo (Picture disc)

Mofo (Phunk Phorce Mix) / Mofo (Black Hole Dub) / Mofo (Mother's Mix) / Mofo (House Flavour Mix) / Mofo (Romin Remix) 1997
UK   12 IS684

Mofo (Phunk Phorce Mix) - Mofo (Black Hole Dub) - Mofo (Romin Remix) 1997
UK   12 MOFO 1   Promo (Different Picture Sleeve)

Mofo (Mother's Mix) - Mofo (House Flavour Mix) 1997
UK   12 MOFO 2   Promo (Different Picture Sleeve) (250 copies only)

Mofo (Matthew Roberts Explicit Remix) 1997
UK   12 MOFO 3   one-sided promo (200 copies)
(rubber stamped white label, plain black die-cut sleeve)

Note: rare miss-pressed 2-sided versions exist

Mofo (Mother's Mix) - Mofo (House Flavour mix) - If God Will Send His Angels (Big Yam) 1997
USA PR127822-1   Promo, white cover

Beautiful Day / Beautiful Day 2000
USA Interscope 3145629721

Beautiful Day (Quincey & Sonance remix) 2000
UK   12BEAUT1   1-sided promo
UK   promo CD-R

Beautiful Day (Perfecto vocal mix) - Beautiful Day (Perfecto dub) 2000
UK   white label promo

Beautiful Day (Perfecto vocal mix) - Beautiful Day (Quincey & Sonance remix) 2000
USA Interscope INTR-10254-1 Promo

Vinyl Albums

Boy (October 1980)
IRL   CBS 84658
UK   ILPS 9646
UK   2 x 1-sided test pressings
USA   IL 90040-1   Stretch - Cover
USA   White label 1-sided test pressing
USA   White label double-sided test pressing
GER   IS 202 913
FRA   6313 105   silver label and lyrics
SWE   ILPS 9646   Yellow Vinyl
ITA   ILPS 19646
POR   10.202913.4   with card insert
JAP   Polystar 20S-77
JAP   `EMI´ - Label Not Island (Soon withdrawn after release)
CAN   ISL 9646   Stretch - Cover with promotional sticker on cover
ARG   27544
MEX   LPR 25027

October (October 1981)
IRL   CBS 85369
UK   ILPS 9680
UK   9680A-3U   Two 1-Sided LP Test-Pressings
USA   IL 90092-1
GER   IS 204 185-320
ITA   ILPS 19680
POR   10.204185.48
JAP   25S-44   The track "October" was remixed and shorter than other albums
ARG   TLP-70027
YUG   Jugoton LSI 11007

War (March 1983)
IRL   CBS 25247
UK   ILPS 9733
UK   PILPS 9733   Picture Disc
USA   IL 90067-1
USA   White label test pressing
USA   ILPS 9680   Blue label promotional copy
GER   IS 205 259
FRA   811 148-1
POR   10.205259.40
JAP   25S-156
JAP   R25D-2085   Re-Issue
CAN   ISL 67
ITA   ILPS 19733
ARG   TLP-70046
BRA   610.7049
YUG   Jugoton LSI 11037

Under A Blood Red Sky (November 1983)
IRL   CBS 25801X
UK   IMA 3
UK   2 x 1-sided test pressings
USA   IL 90127-1   "Sunday Bloody Sunday" was longer on early pressings
USA   White label test pressing
GER   IS 205 904
AUS   L-20033   Red Vinyl and sticker
AUS   L-20033   Green/Black Vinyl (There are some miss-pressings in black and green vinyl)
JAP   20S-192

JAP   R20D-2086   Re-Issue
VEN   78002-L
ARG   Ariola TLP-70015
MEX   LPR 25030

The Unforgettable Fire (October 1984)
IRL
UK   U25
UK   2 x 1-sided test pressings
USA   IL 90231-1
GER   IS 206 530
POR   10.206530.50
AUS   RML 53132   Limited edition contained 12" single of "Two Hearts Beat As One" plus sticker
JAP   28SI-252
JAP   R28D-2087   Re-Issue
ARG   TLP-60137
MEX   LPE 25034
UR   212010-1   Red & Yellow Cover
PER   Y-ISL-0206530.2   White Back-Sleeve

Wide Awake In America (1985)
UK   ISSP 220   No official UK-Release
USA   IL7-90279-1
USA   Test pressing
JAP   R15-D-2010

The Joshua Tree   (March 1987)
UK   U26
USA   IL7-90581-1
GER   IS 208 219
SPA   5F 2028219   white label promotional copy with press kit
SWE   Yellow Vinyl
SWE   Red Vinyl
JAP   R28D-2066   Contains gatefold lyric insert and photo
ARG   TLP-90022
BOL   IN/ASL-1075   Black & White Single Cover
ISR   With foldout insert

Swedish Record Club
SWE   5 LP box set contains specially pressed copies of *Boy, October, War, UABRS, TUF, TJT*

Rattle & Hum (November 1988)
UK   U27
UK   Custom label test pressing
UK   2 LP Promotional album with press release, biography and credit listings
USA   IS 9 1003
USA   White label test pressing
GER   IS 303 400
SPA   51303 400   Promotional pack contained sticker, poster, 2 prints and Spanish fan Club   information folder
JAP   R36D-21178
ARG   TLP2-10001   Single Picture-Sleeve
CAN   Brown Vinyl
BRA   2 LP Promotional album
YUG
Also available on CD-Interactive Disc - Baron BM-391

The First Six 1989
ITA   UTWO6   6 LP box set in black and gold lettering with Italian insert

U2 2 Date (December 1989)

UK   U2 2D1   Promotional `Best Of'- Album

Achtung Baby (November 1991)
UK   U28
UK   White Label Test pressing
USA   314-510 347-1
GER   IS 212 110
MEX   Polygram LPE 1250
KOR   RI 3000   Different Back-Sleeve
ARG   TLP 510347-1 Gatefold Picture-Sleeve
FRA   Yellow label test pressing
SPA   212110

Zooropa (July 1993)
UK   U29
USA   314-518 047-1
GER   IS 15371-1
FRA   U29 518047   Pressed in France - Printed in UK
SPA   IS 743 211 537-1   + Inner sleeve + Lyric Sheet
HOL   74321-15371-1
ZIM   2MC STAR 6034

Original Soundtracks 1 (November 1995)
UK   ILPS   8043
USA   314-524 166-1

Pop (March 1997)
UK   U210 534 334-1   limited edition
USA   314-524 334-1
JAP   PHJR 91835

The Best Of 1980-1990 (November 1998)
UK   U2-11
USA   314 572 612-1

All That You Can't Leave Behind (October 2000)
EU   U212/524653-1 no UK or US releases on vinyl, only European Union (EU)

Interview Vinyl Discs

A Dialogue with U2 (November 1983)
UK   U2-1-PR   Interview & Music to *Under A Blood Red Sky* (Some are banded) 1000 only

Newcastle 1983
UK   Interview picture disc

Their Words & Music 1987
USA   PR 2049   Interview & Music to *The Joshua Tree*

The U2 Talkie - A Conversation with Larry, Bono, Adam and The Edge (March 1987)
UK   U2 CLP 1   Interview with RTE Radio 2 DJ, Dave Fanning, plus the following tracks from *The Joshua Tree*:- In God's Country, With Or Without You, I Still Haven't Found What I'm Looking For, Where The Streets Have No Name, Red Hill Mining Town, Mothers Of The Disappeared.

The Joshua Tree   1987
AUS   Same as U2-Talkie but includes a biography and cue sheets

1987 Press Conference (Sweden)
UK   White vinyl demo
UK   Green vinyl shamrock shape / colour photo of Bono
UK   Blue Vinyl, white label 1500 only
UK   Uncut picture disc (250 only)

Tell Tales

UK   Interview Picture Disc

Interview Discs (Baktabak)
UK BAKPAK 1001   Set of four 7 inch interview discs in blue, red, green and yellow vinyl (500 only)

Interview Picture Disc (Baktabak)
UK BAK 2060

Interview Picture Disc (Baktabak)
UK BAK 2142

Philadelphia Interviews Volume 1
UK 6008   On coloured vinyl

Philadelphia Interviews Volume 2
UK 6010   On coloured vinyl

Outside It's America (Press conferences and 1987 interviews)
UK   On green vinyl (1000 only)
UK   White label promo

Compact Discs

Note: All the titles listed below are 5 inch compact discs unless otherwise stated

CD Singles

With Or Without You / Luminous Times / Walk To The Water 1987
UK   CID 319   limited edition in gatefold sleeve
GER   IS 658 922

I Still Haven't Found What I'm Looking For / Spanish Eyes / Deep In The Heart 1987
UK   CID 328
GER   IS 659 152

Where The Streets Have No Name / Race Against Time / Sweetest Thing / Silver & Gold 1987
UK   CID 340
UK   CID 340   promotional disc with sticker
GER   IS 659 382

With Or Without You / Luminous Times (Hold On To Love) / Walk To The Water (CD-video) (1988)
UK   CID 319   This was a specially produced promotional "CD-video" to be played on Phillips' CD-video system. It contained the three tracks as above plus the promotional video for *With Or Without You*.
USA   PR-2104   1-Track Promotional Copy

Excerpts from Rattle And Hum (In God's Country / Bad / With Or Without You / Hawkmoon 269 / God Part II) (October 1988)
UK   U2 V7   Promotional gatefold CD All five tracks live - first three were not included on the album version

Desire / Hallelujah Here She Comes / Desire (Hollywood Remix) 1988
UK   CID 400
UK   CIDP 400   Picture Disc
USA   PR 2500-2   1-Track Promotional Copy
GER   IS 661 670
JAP   P18D-20082   Picture Disc
AUS   D-616   limited edition cardboard sleeve

Desire / Hallelujah Here She Comes (Remix)   1988
JAP   P10D-30006   3" CD-Single

Angel of Harlem / A Room at the Heartbreak Hotel / Love Rescue Me (Live) 1988
UK   CID 402
UK   CIDP 402   Picture Disc
USA   PR 2559-2   1 Track Promotional Copy

USA   2-96590   3" CD-Single
GER   IS 661 920
JAP   P18-20085   Picture Disc

Angel of Harlem / A Room at the Heartbreak Hotel 1988
JAP   P10D-30007   3" CD-Single
USA   IL2-96590   3" CD-Single

When Love Comes To Town / Dancing Barefoot / When Love Comes To Town (Live from the Kingdom Mix) / God Part II (Hard Metal Dance Mix) 1989
UK   CIDP 411
USA   2-96570   3" CD-single in long box
USA   PR 2659-2   1-Track Promotional Copy
GER   IS 662 200
GER   162200   3" CD-single

When Love Comes To Town / Dancing Barefoot 1989
JAP   P09D-31001   3" CD-Single

All I Want Is You (single edit) / Unchained Melody / Everlasting Love / All I Want Is You (album version) 1989
UK   CID 422
USA   PR 2770-2   Promotional Copy
GER   IS 662 406
AUS   D-805
JAP   P19D-10037

All I Want Is You / Unchained Melody 1989
JAP   P09D-31005   3" CD-Single

God Part II (Remix) / Desire (Hollywood Remix) / Hallelujah Here She Comes / A Room at the Heartbreak Hotel / Love Rescue Me (Live) / Dancing Barefoot 1989
USA   PR 2677-2   Promotional Copy

God Part II (EF-X Weapon Mix 8:36) 1989
USA   Promotional Copy   (DJ Remix CD)

The Singles Collection Box 1981- 1989   1989
UK   Ltd. Ed. - contains the following CD´s in a black numbered Box -

Fire / J. Swallo / 11 0´clock Tick Tock (Live) / The Ocean (Live)
AUT   IS 664 972

New Year's Day (Long Version) / Treasure / Fire (Live) / I Threw A Brick Through a Window (Live) / A Day Without Me (Live)
AUT   IS 664 973

Sunday Bloody Sunday / New Year's Day (US Remix) / Two Hearts Beat As One (US Remix)
AUT   IS 664 971

Pride (In The Name Of Love) / Boomerang I / Boomerang II / 4th of July
AUT   IS 664 975

The Unforgettable Fire / The Three Sunrises / A Sort of Homecoming (Live) / Love Comes Tumbling / Bass Trap
AUT   IS 664 974

With or Without You / Luminous Times / Walk to the Water
AUT   IS 664 986

I Still Haven't Found What I'm Looking For / Spanish Eyes / Deep in the Heart
AUT   IS 664 987

Where the Streets Have No Name / Race Against Time / Sweetest Thing / Silver & Gold
AUT   IS 664 988

Desire / Hallelujah Here She Comes / Desire (Hollywood Remix)
GER   IS 661 670   Picture-CD

Angel of Harlem / A Room at the Heartbreak Hotel / Love Rescue Me (Live)
GER   IS 661 920   Picture-CD

When Love Comes to Town / Dancing Barefoot / When Love Comes to Town (live from the Kingdom Mix) / God Part II (Hard Metal Dance Mix)
GER   IS 662 200   Picture-CD

All I Want Is You / Unchained Melody / Everlasting Love / All I Want Is You
GER   IS 662 406   Picture-CD

Island Treasures   1990

In God's Country / 11 O'clock Tick Tock (Live) / With Or Without You
USA   IL 422-878 389-2   USA Only - Release

U2 - October 1991 (October 1991)

I Will Follow, Pride (In The Name Of Love), God Part II, Where The Streets Have No Name
UK   U2 3 Promotional Copy (500 only)

The Fly / Alex Descends Into Hell For A Bottle Of Milk/Korova 1 / The Lounge Fly Mix (October 1991)
UK   CID 500   DIGI-Pack
USA   PRCD 6680-2 1-Track Promotional Copy
GER   IS 664 724
JAP   PSCD-1182

The Fly / Alex Descends Into Hell For A Bottle Of Milk 1991
JAP   PSDD-1102   3" CD-Single

Mysterious Ways / Mysterious Ways (Solar Plexus Extended Mix) / Mysterious Ways (Apollo 440 Magic Hour Remix) / Mysterious Ways (Tabla Motown Remix) / Mysterious Ways (Solar Plexus Club Mix)
UK   CID 509   DIGI-Pack
USA   PRCD 6698-2 1-Track Promotional Copy
GER   IS 664 930
FRA   IS 866 189-2
JAP   PSCD-1188
AUS   866 189-2/1   Double CD-Pack including free black/yellow Remix-CD "U2-Free":-

Mysterious Ways (Ultimatum Mix) / Mysterious Ways (Perfecto Mix) 1991
AUS   U2-FREE   Promotional Copy

Mysterious Ways / Mysterious Ways (Solar Plexus Magic Hour Remix) 1991
JAP   PSDD-3001   3" CD-Single

Mysterious Ways (Perfecto Mix) / Mysterious Ways (Solar Plexus Club Mix) / Mysterious Ways (Ultimatum Mix) 1991
FRA   IS 4214   Promotional Copy

Mysterious Ways (Ultimatum Mix)   1991
USA   PRCD 6701-2 1-Track Promotional Copy

One / Lady With The Spinning Head / Satellite Of Love / Night & Day (Steel String Remix) 1992
UK   CID 515   DIGI-Pack
USA   IL 422 866 533-2
USA   PRCD 6706-2 1-Track Promotional Copy
GER   IS 665 164
FRA   IS 866 533-2
JAP   PHCR-8701

Until The End Of The World   1992
USA   PRCD 6704-2 1-Track Promotional Copy

Even Better Than The Real Thing / Salome / Where Did It All Go Wrong / Lady With The Spinning Head (June 1992)
UK   CID 525   DIGI-Pack
GER   IS 211 018
FRA   IS 866 977-2

USA   PRCD 6723-2   1-Track Promotional Copy

Even Better Than The Real Thing / Salome 1992
FRA   IS 866 976-2   `2-Titres CD´

Even Better Than The Real Thing (Perfecto Mix) / Even Better Than The Real Thing (Sexy Dub Mix) / Even Better Than The Real Thing (Apollo 440 Stealth Sonic Remix) / Even Better Than The Real Thing (V16 Exit Wound Remix) / Even Better Than The Real Thing (A440 vs. U2 Instrumental Remix) (June 1992)
UK   C-REAL-2
USA   PRCD 6735-2   Promotional Copy (+ Perfecto Mix-Radio Edit)
GER   IS 211 0885-2

Even Better Than The Real Thing (Perfecto Mix-7" Edit) 1992
JAP   CDR 83   Recordable Promo-Test pressing

Who's Gonna Ride Your Wild Horses / Paint It Black / Fortunate Son / Who's Gonna Ride Your Wild Horses (Temple Bar Remix) 1992
UK   CID 550   DIGI-Pack
USA   422 864 521-1
USA   PR 6745-2   1-Track Promotional Copy
GER   IS 120 472
FRA   IS 864 667-2
JAP   PHCR-8706

Who's Gonna Ride Your Wild Horses / Paint It Black 1992
FRA   IS 864 666-2   `2-Titres CD´

Who's Gonna Ride Your Wild Horses (Album Version) / Who's Gonna Ride Your Wild Horses (Remix) 1992
USA   PR 6744-2   Promotional Copy

Who's Gonna Ride Your Wild Horses / Paint It Black / Salome (Zooromancer Remix) / Cant Help Falling In Love (Triple Peaks Remix) 1992
UK   CIDX 550   DIGI-Pack   Ltd. ed. incl. 4 Prints
GER   IS 124 512
FRA   IS 864 711-2

ACHTUNG SINGLES-COLLECTION BOX # 1 1992
UK   limited edition red box of only 1000 including 1 original Joshua Tree VIP -Pass + 6 photos from 1986 - contains the following CDs:-

The Fly / Alex Descends Into Hell For A Bottle Of Milk/Korova 1/ The Lounge Fly Mix
USA   IL 422 868 885-2

Mysterious Ways / Mysterious Ways (Solar Plexus Extended Club Mix) / Mysterious

Ways (Apollo 440 Magic Hour Remix) / Mysterious Ways (Tabla Motown Remix) /

Mysterious Ways (Solar Plexus Club Mix)
USA   IL 422 866-189-2

One / Satellite Of Love / Lady With The Spinning Head / Night & Day (Steel String Remix)
USA   IL 422 866 533-2

Who's Gonna Ride Your Wild Horses / Paint It Black / Fortunate Son / Who's Gonna Ride Your Wild Horses (Temple Bar Remix)
USA   IL 422 864 521-2

ACHTUNG SINGLES-COLLECTION BOX # 2 1992
UK   Limited edition red 12" sized box including a certificate and 4 giant photos contains the same CDs as the Achtung Singles #1 box above plus:-

Even Better Than The Real Thing / Salome / Where Did It All Go Wrong / Lady With The Spinning Head (Extended Dance Mix)
USA   IL 422 866 977-2

Numb 1993
UK   NUMCD 1   1-Track Promotional Copy with lyrics (250 only)

Numb / Numb (Perfecto Mix) 1993
USA   PRCD 6785-2   Promotional Copy

Numb (Perfecto Remix) / Numb 1993
USA   PRCD 6795-2   Promotional Copy

Zooropa (Radio Edit) 1993
USA   PRCD 6792-2   Promotional Copy

Lemon (Radio Edit) (September 1993)
UK   LEM-CD-1   Promotional Copy with lyrics

Lemon (Edit) / Lemon (Oakenfold Jeep Mix) / Lemon (Album Version) / Lemon (Morales BYC Version Dub) 1993
AUS   858 15-2
JAP   PHCR-12702

Lemon (LP Edit) / Lemon (Lemonade Mix-Edit) / Lemon (LP Version) / Lemon (Lemonade Mix) 1993
USA   PRCD 6800-2

Stay (Faraway, So Close!) / I've Got You Under My Skin / Lemon (Bad Yard Club Edit) / Lemon (Perfecto Mix) (November 1993) aka "The Swing Format"
UK   CID 578
USA   PRCD 6806-2   1-Track Promotional Copy
GER   IS 74321
AUS   IS 858 077-2
JAP   PHCR-8713

Stay (Faraway, So Close!) (album version) (November 1993)
UK   CIDDJ 578   1-Track Promotional Copy Different Cover to above

Stay (Faraway, So Close!) / I've Got You Under My Skin 1993
USA   IL-422 858 076
FRA   858 076-2   '2-Titres CD'

Stay (Faraway, So Close!) / Slow Dancing / Bullet The Blue Sky (Live) / Love Is Blindness (Live) (November 1993) aka "The Live Format"
UK   CIDX 578   Double CD-Pack incl. CAT-No. 578

Stay (Faraway, So Close!) / I've Got You Under My Skin / Bullet The Blue Sky / Lemon (Bad Yard Edit) / Love Is Blindness (live)
USA   IL 422-858 097-2   5" CD

U2 ZOO TV Tour Zooropa '93 1993

Promo CD contains:- The Fly / Mysterious Ways / One / Even Better Than the Real Thing / Who's Gonna Ride Your Wild Horses
SPA   74321 14504   Promotional Copy (Spain only)

Hold Me, Thrill Me, Kiss Me, Kill Me / Themes from Batman Forever (June 1995)
UK   A7131CD   On Atlantic/Island joint label
GER   7567-85567
AUS   756 787 1312
JAP   AMCY 871

Hold Me, Thrill Me, Kiss Me, Kill Me (Radio Edit) / Hold Me, Thrill Me, Kiss Me, Kill Me (Single Version) 1995
USA   PRCD 62666   Promotional Copy   *Atlantic* - Label
USA   PRCD 6237-2   Promotional Copy
GER   PRCD 31   Promotional Copy

Hold Me, Thrill Me, Kiss Me, Kill Me   1995
UK   East West   CDR (No catalogue number)

Miss Sarajevo / One (Live) / Bottoms (Zoo Station Remix) / Viva Davidoff (October 1995)
UK   CID 625

GER   IS 854 481-2
JAP   PY 940

Miss Sarajevo (Single Version) / Miss Sarajevo (Album Version) 1995
USA   PRCD 7131-2   Promotional Copy

Your Blue Room (edit) 1996
USA   OST 3   Promotional Copy

Discotheque / Holy Joe (Garage Mix) / Holy Joe (Guilty Mix) (February 1997)
UK   CID 649   digipack   (rare issue in slim case)
UK   CIDT 649   cardboard sleeve
UK   ISJB649   Jukebox promo
USA   422-854   white paper cover
USA   422-854 774-2   cardboard sleeve (sleeve #2)
GER   CIDT 649   cardboard sleeve
GER   CID 649   digipack
FRA   CID 649   digipack
FRA   CIDT 649   cardboard sleeve
AUS   854 775-2   digipack
AUS   854 774-2   cardboard sleeve (some were released with free badge)
JAP   PHCR8382   slim case

Discotheque (DM Deep Club Mix) / Discotheque (Howie B, Hairy B Mix) / Discotheque (Hexidecimal Mix) / Discotheque (DM TEC Radio Mix) 1997
UK   CIDX 649/854 877-2
FRA   CIDX 649/854 877-2
GER   CIDX 649/854 877-2
JAP   PHCR8395   "The Club Mixes"
BRA   854 877-2   different back artwork CD
AUS   854 877-2   some were released with a free badge

Discotheque (DM Deep Extended Club Mix) / Discotheque (Hexidecimal Mix) / Discotheque

Holy Joe (Guilty Mix) / Discotheque (Howie B, Hairy B Mix) 1997
USA   422-854 789-2   jewel case

Discotheque (album version) 1997
USA   PRCD7856-2   Promo (unique Picture Sleeve)
BRA   2802 137   Promo

Discotheque (Radio Edit) 1997
UK   DISCO1   Promo (Picture Sleeve)

Discotheque (single version) / Discotheque (Radio edit) 1997
USA   PRCD 7316-2   Promo (Picture Sleeve)

Discotheque (Album version) / Discotheque (Radio edit) 1997
UK   DISCO 2   Promo

Discotheque (Hexidecimal Mix) 1997
UK   CD-R Promo

Staring At The Sun / North And South Of The River (April 1997)
UK   CIDT 658
USA   No picture sleeve
FRA   854 972-2   cardboard sleeve
GER   CIDT658/854 972-2   cardboard sleeve

Staring At The Sun / North And South Of The River / Your Blue Room 1997
UK   CID 658/854 975-2   digipack
USA   422-854 975-2   digipack
FRA   CID 658/854 975-2   digipack
JAP   PHCR-8397   slim case
GER   CID 658/854 975-2   digipack
AUS   854 975-2   digipack

Staring At The Sun (Monster Truck Mix) / Staring At The Sun (Sad Bastards Mix) / North And South Of The River / Staring At The Sun (Lab Rat Mix) 1997
UK   CIDX 658
USA   422-854 973-2   jewel case
FRA   CIDX 658/854 973-2
GER   CIDX 658/854 973-2
JAP
AUS   854 973-2

Staring At The Sun 1997
UK   SUNCD1   One track promo (Different cover)
USA   PRCD 7445-2   One track promo (Different cover)
MEX   CDP 581-2   Promo

Staring At The Sun (Monster Truck Mix) / Staring At The Sun (Lab Rat Mix) / Staring At The Sun (Sad Bastards Mix) 1997
UK   CD-R Promo

Last Night On Earth (single version) / Pop Musik (Pop Mart Mix) 1997
UK   CIDT 664/572 050-2   cardboard sleeve
FRA   CIDT 664/572 050-2   cardboard sleeve
GER   CIDT 664/572 050-2   cardboard sleeve

Last Night On Earth (single version) / Pop Muzik (Pop Mart Mix) / Happiness Is A Warm Gun (The Gun Mix) (August 1997)
UK   CID 664/572 051-2   digipack
AUS   572 051-2   digipack
GER   CID 664/572 051-2   digipack
JAP   PHCR8409   slim case
FRA   CID 664/572 051-2   slim case (some French releases have a mistake on side of the   sleeve: "Happiness Is A Warm Gun (The Mix Mix)")

Last Night On Earth (First Night In Hell Mix) / Numb (The Soul Assassins Mix) / Happiness Is A Warm Gun (The Danny Saber Mix) / Pop Muzik (Pop Mart Mix) 1997
UK   CIDX 664/572 055-2
FRA   CIDX 664/572 055-2
AUS   5720552
GER   CIDX 664/572 055-2

Last Night On Earth (single version) / Pop Musik (Pop Mart Mix) / Happiness Is A Warm Gun (The Gun Mix) / Numb (The Soul Assassins Mix) 1997
USA   572 053-2   jewel case

Last Night On Earth (single version) 1997
UK   NIGHTCD1   one track promo (different Picture Sleeve)
MEX   CDP 634-2   Promo (unique cardboard sleeve)

Last Night On Earth (single version) / Last Night On Earth (album version) 1997
USA   PRCD 7517-2   Promo

Please (single version) / Dirty Day (Junk Day) (October 1997)
UK   CIDT 673/572 128-2   cardboard sleeve
FRA   CIDT 673/572 128-2   cardboard sleeve
GER   CIDT 673/572 128-2   cardboard sleeve

Please (single version) / Dirty Day (Junk Day) / Dirty Day (Bitter Kiss) / I'm Not Your Baby (Skysplitter Dub) 1997
UK   CID 673   digipack
FRA   CID 673/572 129-2
GER   CID 673/572 129-2
AUS   572 129-2   This came with a competition entry form, where winner becomes a   Pop Mart crew member for one of the Australian shows
JAP   PHCR8422

CAN 572 129-2

Please (single edit) / Please (single version) 1997

UK PLEASE CD1 promo (Picture Sleeve, yellow CD) (test pressings also exist)

Please (single edit) 1997

USA PRCD 7679-2 promo (no Picture Sleeve, blue CD)

Please (Single edit) (3:47) / Please (Single version) (5:47) / Please (Song Hook) (0:13) 1997

USA PRCD 7679-2 promo (Picture Sleeve, red CD)

Please (USA edit) (3:47) / Please (Song Hook) (0:10) 1997

UK CIDDJ 673 Promo (Picture Sleeve with sticker, yellow CD)

Note: The "song hook" is just Bono singing "Please... please" for radio production)

Please Pop Heart EP:-

Please (single edit) / Please (live from Rotterdam) / Where The Streets Have No Name (live from Rotterdam) / With Or Without You (live from Edmonton) / Staring At The Sun (live from Rotterdam) 1997

USA 314-572 195-2 Picture Sleeve (jewel case)

Please (live from Rotterdam) / Where The Streets Have No Name (live from Rotterdam) / With Or Without You (live from Edmonton) / Staring At The Sun (live from Rotterdam) 1997

UK CIDX 673/572 133-2

GER CIDX 673

FRA CIDX 673/572 133-2

AUS 572 133-2 came with competition entry form, where winner becomes a Pop Mart crew member for one of the Australian shows

CAN 572 133-2

JAP PHCR8714

JAP PHCR8714 Japanese promo (with back promo sticker and "sample" written in the middle of CD)

If God Will Send His Angels (single version) / Mofo (Romin Remix) (December 1997)

UK CIDT 684/572 190-2

USA 572 190-2

FRA CIDT 684/572 190-2

GER CIDT 684/572 190-2

If God Will Send His Angels (single version) / Slow Dancing / Two Shots Of Happy, One Shot Of Sad / Sunday Bloody Sunday (live from Sarajevo, 23rd Sept. 1997) 1997

UK CID684/572 189

USA 572 189-2 Has "City of Angels" soundtrack sticker on cover

FRA CID684/572 189-2

GER CID684/572 189-2

CAN 572 189-2

If God Will Send His Angels (Single version) 1997

UK ANGELCD1 Different Picture Sleeve, one track promo

MEX CDP 762-2 Promo, cardboard sleeve

If God Will Send His Angels (Single version) (4:32) / If God Will Send His Angels (Research hook) (0:10) 1997

USA PRCD 7749-2 promo, unique "City Of Angels" Picture Sleeve

USA PRCD 7749 promo (has same Picture Sleeve as UK promo)

Note: The "research hook" is just a snippet for radio production

If God Will Send His Angels (single version) 1997

UK Chop Em out UK acetate/ CD-R

Mofo Remixes:-

Mofo (Phunk Phorce Mix) / Mofo (Mother's Mix) / If God Will Send His Angels (The Grand Jury Mix) 1997

UK CIDX 684/572 191-2

FRA CIDX 684/572 191-2

GER CIDX 684/572 191-2

CAN 572 191-2

AUS 572191-2 with Australian tour dates sticker on cover and a 12"x16 1/2" poster

Mofo (Phunk Phorce Mix edit) 1997

UK MOFOCD2 Promo, Different Picture Sleeve

Mofo (Album Version) 1997

UK MOFOCD1 Promo (Pop Mart Mexican Tour dates on back of sleeve, made for export to M e x i c o) (unique Picture Sleeve)

MEX CDP 691-2 Promo cardboard sleeve (unique Picture Sleeve)

Sweetest Thing (The Single Mix) / Stories For Boys (live from Boston) 1998

UK CIDT 727 572 468-2 cardboard sleeve

FRA CIDT 727 572 468-2 cardboard sleeve

Sweetest Thing (single mix) / With Or Without You 1998

JAP PHDR953 3 inch CD snap pack

Sweetest Thing (single mix) / Twilight (live from Red Rocks) / An Cat Dubh (live from Red Rocks) 1998 (Note: An Cat Dubh is followed by Into The Heart)

UK CID 727

GER CID 727 572 466-2

AUS 572 466-2

CAN 314 572 466-2

Sweetest Thing (single mix) / Stories For Boys (live from Boston) / Out Of Control (live from Boston) 1998

UK CIDX 727

GER CIDX 727 572 464-2

AUS 572 464-2

CAN 314 572 464-2

Sweetest Thing (3:00) 1998

UK SWEETCD1 one track promo (picture sleeve)

Note: some without Picture Sleeve but with a promo sticker announcing the release of the Greatest Hits album)

Sweetest Thing (single mix) (3:00) 1998

USA PRCD7961-2 one track promo (picture sleeve)

BRA 2802 306 promo

Sweetest Thing (single mix) / Twilight (live from Red Rocks) / An Cat Dubh (live from Red Rocks) /Stories For Boys (live from Boston) / Out Of Control (live from Boston) 1998

UK CIDDJ 727 Promo (no picture sleeve)

Sweetest Thing 1998

UK promo

SPA promo

The Ground Beneath Her Feet / Million Dollar Hotel trailer (to play on a computer) 2000

UK GROUNDCD1 promo in cardboard sleeve

Note: The sleeve can be placed into a plain blue cardboard with only a hole to see the title

The Ground Beneath Her Feet 2000

UK promo CD-R

USA INTR-10045-2 promo with Picture Sleeve (on Interscope Records)

BRA   2802 447   promo with Picture Sleeve

Beautiful Day / Summer Rain 2000
UK   CIDT 766/562 950-2

Beautiful Day / Summer Rain / Always 2000
UK   CID766/562 945-2
UK   CID766/562 945-2 jewel case with space for 2nd CD
GER   CID766/562 945-2
MEX   562 945-2
CAN   562 945-2
AUS   562 9982   with enhanced "Last Night on Earth" video clip

Beautiful Day / Discotheque (live) / If You Wear That Velvet Dress (live) 2000
UK   CIDX 766/562 946-2
UK   CIDX 766/562 946-2   advance copy with white and blue cover
MEX   562 946-2
CAN   562 946-2
AUS   562 994-2   with "Last Night on Earth (live)"
Note: Live tracks recorded from Mexico, December 1997

Beautiful Day / Summer Rain / Always / Discotheque (live) / If You Wear That Velvet Dress (live) 2000
JAP   UICI 5002

Beautiful Day 2000
UK   BEAUTCD1   promo, slim case with Picture Sleeve
USA   BEAUTCD1   promo, jewel case with Picture sleeve (on Interscope Records)
ARG   PRO1323   promo with Picture Sleeve

'Beautiful Day Remixes' CD:-

Beautiful Day (Radio Edit) / Beautiful Day (Club Mix) / Beautiful Day (Album Version) 2000
MEX   CDP 879-2   promo, no Picture Sleeve
Note: The "Club mix" is the "Quincey & Sonance remix" and the "Radio Edit" is the "Quincey & Sonance radio edit", as found on *Q* magazine CD

Walk On / Beautiful Day (live) / New York (live) 2001
CAN   3145728192   live tracks recorded at the Farmclub

Walk On / Big Girls Are Best / Beautiful Day (Quincey & Sonance mix) 2001
CAN   3145728202

Walk On (radio edit 4:23) / Walk On (album version 4:55) 2001
USA Interscope INTR-10261-2   promo

Stuck In A Moment You Can't Get Out Of / Beautiful Day (live) / New York (live) 2001
UK   CID 770/572778-2
AUS   572 807-2   with bonus track "Beautiful Day (David Holmes Remix)"
Note: live tracks recorded at the Farmclub

Stuck In A Moment You Can't Get Out Of / Big Girls Are Best / Beautiful Day (Quincey & Sonance mix) 2001
UK   CIDX 770/572779-2
AUS   572 806-2   with bonus track "Beautiful Day (The Perfecto Mix)"

Stuck In A Moment You Can't Get Out Of 2001
UK   STUCKCD1   promo

Elevation (Tomb Raider Mix) / Elevation (Escalation Mix) / Elevation(Influx Remix) (June 2001) (CD1)

Elevation (Tomb Raider Mix) / Last Night On Earth (live) / Don't Take Your Guns To Town (June 2001) (CD2)
          includes double sided poster

CD Albums

Boy   1980
UK   CID 110
USA   IL 90040-2   DIGI-Pack
GER   IS 610 561
JAP   PHCR-1701

October 1981
UK   CID 111
USA   IL 90092-2   DIGI-Pack
GER   IS 610 560
JAP   PHCR-1702

War   1983
UK   CID 112
USA   UDCD 571   MFSL Gold-CD
GER   IS 610 5333
JAP   PHCR-1703

Under A Blood Red Sky 1983
UK   CID 113
USA   A2-90127   DIGI-Pack
GER   IS 610 559
JAP   PHCR-1704
CAN   CID-113   different picture sleeve

The Unforgettable Fire 1984
UK   CID 102
UK   Test pressing
GER   IS 610 194
JAP   PHCR-1705
BRA   756.790 2312

Wide Awake In America 1985
UK   CIDU 22

The Joshua Tree 1987
UK   CID U2 6
GER   IS 258 219
JAP   PHCR-1707
KOR   DI 0640

1980-1987 1988
JAP   Polystar Hi 4001   Promotional Copy
(14-Track singles collection)

Rattle & Hum   1988
UK   CID U2 7
USA   2-91003
GER   IS 353 400
JAP   PHCR-1706
BRA   756791 003   Promotional Copy

Achtung Baby 1991
UK   CID U2 8
UK   Black Wooden Box   + Interview CD
USA   IL-314 510 490limited edition in long DIGI-Pack
GER   IS 262 110
GER   IS 262 482   DIGI-Pack
JAP   PHCR-1706
AUS   limited edition for Virgin Megastores only (1 day only sale)

Zoo Radio Transmit 1992
Contains the following tracks:- Until The End Of The World / Even Better Than The Real Thing / Mysterious Ways / The Fly / One / Trying To Throw Your Arms Around The World / Satellite of Love / Bullet The Blue Sky / Where The Streets Have No Name / Running To Stand Still / Can't Help Falling in Love

USA   PRCD 6853-2   Promotional Copy

Zooropa   1993
UK   CID U2 9
GER   IS 153 712
JAP   PHCR-1709
AUS   IS 5180472
AUS   IS 5180472   Limited edition for Virgin Megastores only - 1 Day only sale + Bonus-CD " Mysterious ways"
AUS   IS 5180472   Limited edition for Virgin Megastores only - 1 Day only sale + Bonus-CD "Stay (Faraway, So Close!)"
AUS   ISLAND   Rare metal-tin with Australian pack *Zooropa*-CD & many extras (flag, postcard, sticker) (limited numbered edition of 500)

Melon (Remixes for Propaganda) (January 1995)
MELONCD1 Contains the following tracks:- Lemon (Perfecto Mix) / Salome (Zooromancer Remix) / Numb (Gimme Some More Dignity Mix) / Mysterious Ways (Perfecto Mix) / Stay (Underdog Mix) / Numb (Soul Assassins Mix) / Mysterious Ways (Massive Attack Remix) / Even better Than The Real Thing (Perfecto Mix) / Lemon (Bad Yard Club Mix)
UK   MELONCD 1   9-track Fan Club CD (Limited to 20,000 copies world-wide)

Original Soundtracks 1   1995
UK   CID 0843
UK   OST 1   Promotional Copy with extra track "Bottoms"
USA   314-524 166-2
USA   PRCDMLI   Promo
GER   IS 524 166-2
JAP   PY 811
JAP   PHCR - 1800
AUS   524 166-2
FRA   CID 8043

Pop 1997
UK   CIDU 210 524 334-2
UK   Promo wooden box with CD, certificate, postcard, black T-shirt and 4 beer mats
USA   314 524 334-2
JAP   Nippon Phonogram PHCR 1835   with   "Holy Joe" (Guilty Mix) and booklet
GER   CIDU210 524 334-2
AUS   524 334-2
CAN   314-524 334-2

The Best Of 1980-1990 1998
UK   CIDDU211   with B-sides
USA   314 572 612-2 with B-sides
JAP   PHCR 90715   limited edition with bonus track "Red Hill Mining Town"
CHI   CIDDU 211/524 612-2
SIN   CIDU211 524 613-2   limited edition gold CD with bonus blank gold award CD

Hasta La Vista Baby! U2 Live From Mexico City 2000
HASTA CD 1 Contains the following tracks:- Pop Muzik / Mofo / I Will Follow / Gone / New Year's Day / Staring At The Sun / Bullet The Blue Sky / Please / Where The Streets Have No Name / Lemon (Perfecto Mix), Discotheque / With Or Without You / Hold Me, Thrill Me, Kiss Me, Kill Me / One

All That You Can't Leave Behind 2000
EU   CIDU212/548095-2   with extra track "The Ground Beneath Her Feet"
EU   CIDZU212/548285-2   with lyrics sheet
USA   Interscope 3145483282   with bonus disc containing "Always"
USA   Interscope 3145483292   with bonus disc containing "Summer Rain"
AUS   548085-2   with extra track "The Ground Beneath Her Feet" and slip case
JAP   UICI 1002   with extra track "The Ground Beneath Her Feet"
TAI   5246532
SIN   CIDXU212   limited edition with U2 coffee mug

Interviews On CD

The Conversation Disc Series - U2
UK   ABCD 001   Interview from 1986 from Irish TV with Bono and Larry Picture disc

Outside It's America 1987
UK   Interview Disc (500 only)

Philadelphia Interviews Volume 1
UK   CBAK 4006   Interview Disc

Radio Documentary 1995
UK   OST-2   Promotional Copy   (Double-CD including Music & Interviews)

U2 Interview Disc and Book 1995
UK   SAM 7003   Interview Disc with book and discography

Cassette Tapes

Cassette Singles (AKA Cassingles)

"U2-3" - Out Of Control / Stories For Boys / Boy-Girl 1979
IRL   CBS 40-7951

For You: New Year's Day / Two Hearts Beat As One 1983
JAP   26Y-183

Pride (In The Name Of Love) / Boomerang I / Boomerang II / 4th Of July / A Celebration 1984
UK   CIS 202
AUS   C 14105   Limited edition (without "A Celebration")

Pride (In The Name Of Love) / Boomerang I / Boomerang II / 11 o'clock Tick Tock 1984
CAN   ISC-1035
NZ   C14114

The Three Sunrises / The Unforgettable Fire / A Sort Of Homecoming (Live) / Love Comes Tumbling / Bass Trap 1984
UK   ISPC-1026
AUS   C18002

With or Without You / Luminous Times / Walk To The Water 1987
UK   CIS 319

I Still Haven't Found What I'm Looking For / Spanish Eyes / Deep in the Heart 1987
UK   CIS 328
USA   96786-5

Where The Streets Have No Name / Race Against Time / Silver And Gold / Sweetest Thing 1987
UK   CIS 340
USA   96740-4

In God´s Country / Bullet the Blue Sky / Running to Stand Still 1987
CAN ISC 1167

Desire / Hallelujah Here She Comes 1988
UK   CIS 400
USA ISLC7 7-99250

Desire (Hollywood Remix) 1988
UK   CISX 400   Promotional Copy (in embossed cover)

Angel of Harlem / A Room At The Heartbreak Hotel 1988
UK   CIS 402
AUS C704

When Love Comes To Town / Dancing Barefoot   1989
UK   CIS 411
USA 4-99225
CAN ISLC-97094

All I Want Is You / Unchained Melody 1989
UK   CIS 422
AUS C805

All I Want Is You / Unchained Melody / Everlasting Love 1989
AUS C14678   Same three tracks on both sides

The Fly / Alex Descends Into Hell For A Bottle Of Milk/Korova 1 / 1991
UK   CIS 550
GER IS 412 295
CAN ISLC 868 885-4
USA ISLC 422-868 885-4

Mysterious Ways / Mysterious Ways (Solar Plexus Magic Hour Remix) 1991
UK   CIS 509
USA ISLC 422-866 188-4

Mysterious Ways / Mysterious Ways (Solar Plexus Extended Club Mix) / Mysterious Ways (Apollo 440 Magic Hour Remix) / Mysterious Ways (Tabla Motown Remix) / Mysterious Ways (Solar Plexus Club Mix)
USA ISLC 422-866 189-4

One / Lady With The Spinning Head 1992
UK   CIS 515
USA ISLC 422-866 533-4

Even Better Than The Real Thing / Salome 1992
UK   CIS 525

Who's Gonna Ride Your Wild Horses / Paint It Black 1992
UK   CIS 550

Stay (Faraway, So Close!) / I've Got You Under My Skin 1993
UK   CIS 578
USA 422858 076-4

Hold Me, Thrill Me, Kiss Me, Kill Me 1995

Discotheque / Holy Joe (Garage Mix) / Holy Joe (Guilty Mix) 1997
UK   CIS649
USA 422-854 774-4 cardboard case

Staring At The Sun / North And South Of The River 1997
UK   ISJB658   Jukebox Promo (white custom sleeve)
USA 422-854 972-4
UK   CIS658

Last Night On Earth (single version) / Pop Musik (Pop Mart Mix) 1997
UK   CIS664

Please (single version) / Dirty Day (Junk Day) 1997
UK   CIS 673

If God Will Send His Angels (single version) / Mofo (Romin Remix) 1997
USA 314-572 188-4

If God Will Send His Angels (single version) / Slow Dancing / Two Shots Of Happy, One Shot Of Sad / Sunday Bloody Sunday (live)

Mofo (Romin Remix) / If God Will Send His Angels (Big Yam) / Mofo (Mothers Mix) / Mofo (Phunk Force Mix) 1997
UK   'Chop Em Out'   promo

Sweetest Thing (The Single Mix) / Stories For Boys (live from Boston) 1998
UK   CIS 727

Beautiful Day / Summer Rain 2000
UK   CIS 766/562945-4

Stuck In A Moment You Can't Get Out Of / Big Girls Are Best 2001
UK   CIS 770/572780-4

Cassette Albums

Boy 1980
UK   CIT 9646
UK   CIT 9646   Special Edition has a full side of blank Chrome-Tape
GER IS 402 913
MAL ICT 9646

October 1981
UK   CIT 9680

War 1983
UK   CIT 9733
MAL ICT 9733
MOR ESD 397   Sonya Disque Label

Under A Blood Red Sky 1983
UK   IMC 3
GER IS 405 904
MOR IMC-3

The Unforgettable Fire 1984
UK   UC 2
GER IS 406 530
POR 10.406530.33
CAN different cover and 3 extra tracks

Wide Awake In America 1985
USA ILSC-7 90279-4-A

The Joshua Tree   1987
UK   UC 26
GER IS 408 219
MAL UC 26

Cassette Sampler   1987
UK   BO-U2-1   Promotional Copy featuring 17 tracks

Rattle & Hum 1988
UK   UC 27
USA IS 91003
CAN ISLC2-1204
MAL 842 299-4   2 Cassettes

"U2"
CAN 13 track promotional cassette

Achtung Baby 1991
UK   UC 28
GER IS 412 110

Zooropa   1993
UK   UC 29
MAL UC 29   with *Zooropa* - Stickers
Original Soundtracks 1 1995
The Best of 1980-1990 1998
UK   UC211
USA   314 572 612-4
All That You Can't Leave Behind 2000
EU   UC212 548285-4

Interview Cassettes

The U2 Talkie (1987)
UK   CLP 1   Promotional Interview for *The Joshua Tree* (same as the vinyl version)
The U2 Talkie 1987
UK   U2 CC1   Promotional Copy - Not for sale
The Philadelphia Interviews Volume 1 (Baktabak)
UK   MBAK 6008   Interviews From 1987

Radio Shows

Most of the U2 radio shows that are in circulation come from the USA, where a U2 concert would be recorded by a specialist radio programme maker, like Westwood One. The concert would then be edited, (with commercials and the occasional interview added), and transferred to a normal 12 inch vinyl LP record (or Compact Disc from the 1990's onwards). It would then be sold to other radio stations throughout America for broadcasting on a particular date, often with commercials in between tracks. After the broadcast the disc is meant to be returned to the manufacturer and destroyed! However, quite a few discs seem to end up on the collector's market where there is a big demand for them.

Usually the concert may be unavailable elsewhere in any other format and it will feature unique versions of a particular track. Couple this with the fact that usually less than a hundred of these discs are pressed up, adding to their scarcity, and you can see why they are in such demand with fans. It is not surprising that several of these radio shows have been bootlegged, principally because they have a much better sound quality than a traditional bootleg. Genuine radio shows are usually sent out with a cue-sheet - basically one or two sheets of A4 paper with details of the tracks and commercials and their timings, thus making the DJ's job a little easier. Most come in plain company sleeves, though a recent trend has been to manufacture discs with some distinctive (and often unique) artwork, which only goes to make them more collectable.

Below is a list of almost every known available Radio Show Disc, with details of transmission date, radio company and disc number, concert it was taken from and track listing. If anyone knows of any addi-

tions please contact the author via the publishers of this book.

ABBREVIATIONS:-
DIR = DIR BROADCASTING   WBMS   =   WARNER BROTHERS MUSIC SHOW   WWO = WESTWOOD ONE

Radio Shows On Vinyl

Two Sides Live (15th - 17th May 1981)
The Ocean / 11 O'clock Tick Tock / Touch / An Cat Dubh / Into The Heart / Cry-The Electric Co. / Things To Make And Do / Stories For Boys / Twilight / I Will Follow / Out Of Control / 11 O'clock Tick Tock
USA   WBMS 1-117 Recorded Live at The Paradise Theatre, Boston on 6th March 1981. This was U2's first US radio show concert and has been heavily bootlegged. Original copies have a black and red custom sleeve and the matrix B 15623638

King Biscuit Flower Hour (U2/Devo) (31st January 1982)
U2-Tracks: I Threw A Brick Through A Window / Rejoice / Stories For Boys / I Will Follow / 11 O'clock Tick Tock
USA ABC Radio Network, Show No. 404   2-LP's Recorded live at the Orpheum, Boston 31.01.82. Cue sheets included (1 Side *DEVO)*

In Concert (U2/Bryan Adams) (7th - 9th May 1982)
U2-Tracks: Gloria / Another Time Another Place / I Threw A Brick Through A Window / A Day Without Me / Rejoice / The Cry-The Electric Co. / I Will Follow / Out Of Control
USA   WWO IC 82-9 (2-LP's) Recorded live on the 2nd leg of the *October*-US Tour, late 1981

The Colonies Concert (1982)
USA   Possibly the same as "Two Sides Live" ?

BBC Transcription Disc 295 / In Concert No. 295 (1983)
Surrender / I Threw A Brick Through A Window / A Day Without Me / An Cat Dubh / Into The Heart / Sunday Bloody Sunday / I Fall Down / Cry-The Electric Co. / October / New Year's Day / Gloria / I Will Follow / Fire / A Celebration
UK   CN 4134/5 (1-LP) Recorded live at Hammersmith Palais, London , 6th December 1982. The rarest of U2 radio shows, this has been bootlegged several times. Original copies have a green and white label, whilst bootleg copies have black and white labels.

London Wavelength Show No. 410: BBC Rock Hour (6th March 1983)
USA   1-LP Same as "In Concert No. 295"

King Biscuit Flower Hour (6th March 1983)
USA   2 LP set (possibly the same as London Wavelength Show No. 410?)

London Wavelength: BBC College Concert (27th March 1983)
USA   1-LP Same as "In Concert No. 295"   (without commercials)

In Concert (U2/Berlin) (15th - 17th April 1983)
U2-Tracks: Gloria / Another Time Another Place / I Threw A Brick Through A Window / A Day Without Me / Rejoice / The Cry-The Electric Co. / I Fall Down * / I Will Follow / Stories For Boys * / Twilight * / Out Of Control
USA   WWO IC 83-08 Y   2-LP's Recorded live on the 2nd leg of *October*-US Tour in late 1981 Same show as In Concert (7th-9th May 1982) with 3 extra tracks *

King Biscuit Flower Hour (29th May 1983)
Out Of Control / Two Hearts Beat As One / An Cat Dubh / Into The Heart / Sunday Bloody Sunday / The Electric Co. / October / Gloria / I Threw A Brick Through A Window / A Day Without Me / 11 O'clock Tick Tock / I Will Follow
USA   ABC/DIR No.473   2-LP's Recorded live at the Orpheum Theatre, Boston 6th May 1983

Guest DJ Show (30th May 1983)
USA   Rolling Stone Magazine Show No. 62 RSG 83-62 3-LP-Box Bono and The Edge play their favourite records

Innerview (30th May 1983)
I Will Follow / Surrender / Another Time Another Place / Rejoice / Sunday Bloody Sunday / New Year's Day / Seconds / Two Hearts Beat As One
USA   Series No.25 Show No. 5 1-LP Bono interviewed by Jim Ladd

New Music Profile (June 1983)
USA   NBC Radio 3-LPs U2 have three tracks on this various artists compilation

War Is Declared (8th-10th July 1983)
Out Of Control / Twilight / An Cat Dubh / Into The Heart / Surrender / Two Hearts Beat As One / Seconds / Sunday Bloody Sunday / The Cry-The Electric Co. / I Fall Down / October / New Year's Day / Gloria /
Party Girl / 11 O'clock Tick Tock / I Will Follow / 40.
USA   The Source, NBC 83-27   2-LP's Recorded live at Red Rocks, Denver, 5th June 1983

The U2 Concert (10th July 1983)
USA   The Source 2-LPs same as War Is Declared, but with different cues and commercials

Supergroups - in Concert (U2/Judas Priest) (6th August 1983)
U2-Tracks: Twilight / Two Hearts Beat As One / Sunday Bloody Sunday / An Cat Dubh / Into The Heart / I Threw A Brick Through A Window / A Day Without Me / October / Gloria / 11 O'clock Tick Tock / I Will Follow
USA   DIR SG 28 (3-LP-Box) Recorded live at the Tower Theatre, Philadelphia 13th May 1983

Off the record (week beginning 5th September 1983)
The Electric Co. / Twilight / I Will Follow / Rejoice / Out Of Control / Sunday Bloody Sunday / Like A Song / Seconds / New Year's Day / Gloria / Two Hearts Beat As One / An Cat Dubh / Into The Heart
USA   WWO 83-37 (2-LP's in a picture sleeve) Adam Clayton interviewed by Mary Turner

The Inside Track (U2/Billy Idol) (21st November 1983)
U2-Tracks: Gloria (Live`83) / Stories For Boys / The Electric Co. (Live`83) / New Year's Day / Sunday Bloody Sunday
USA   DIR IT 22 (3-LP-Box (incl. one 1-sided)) Bono interview in New York by Lisa Robinson

Live Cuts (1983)

Off The Record (16th January 1984)
USA   WWO 84-01 (2-LP's) This is a repeat of the "Off The Record" show for w/b 5th September 1983

London Wavelength Show No. 511 (11th March 1984)
USA   (1-LP) Same as In Concert No. 295

The Best Of The Biscuit (3rd June 1984)
USA ABC Network (2-LPs) U2 with other artists. Same material as the King Biscuit Flower Hour show of 29th May 1983, with different cue-sheets and commercials. (Original

labels are black & sky-blue, bootlegs are black & white)

US '83 Festival (26th May 1984)
U2-tracks: Gloria / I Threw A Brick Through A Window / A Day Without Me / An Cat Dubh / Into The Heart / New Year's Day / Surrender / Two hearts Beat As One / Sunday Bloody Sunday / Cry-The Electric Co. / I Will Follow / 40
USA   WWO 84 01US (18-LP box set) A various artists collection of the US Festival which took place on 30th May 1983. One record includes U2's full set. Bono is also interviewed on segments 16 & 17. (With cue sheets and commercials)

Best Of The New Tours (September 1984)
USA   NBC Radio (3-LPs) U2 have three live tracks on this various artists compilation

The Inside Track (U2 / Bryan Adams) (19th November 1984)
USA   DIR IT 38 (3-LP-Box (incl. one 1-sided)) Bono and Adam Clayton interviewed by Lisa Robinson

The Inside Track (U2 / David Byrne) (19th November 1984)
U2-tracks: Pride / I Will Follow / Gloria / Two Hearts Beat As One / Surrender / New Year's Day /Sunday Bloody Sunday
USA   DIR IT 43 (3-LP-Box(incl. one 1-sided)) Bono interviewed by Lisa Robinson about the making of *The Unforgettable Fire*

King Biscuit Flower Hour (December 1984)
USA   2-LP set

Off The Record (28th January 1985)
New Year's Day / I Will Follow / The Unforgettable Fire / Pride (In The Name Of Love) / Gloria (Live) / Party Girl (Live) / Out Of Control / Two Hearts Beat As One / 40. / Sunday Bloody Sunday / Bad
USA   WWO 85-05 (2-LP's) in a picture sleeve Adam Clayton & The Edge interviewed by Mary Turner

King Biscuit Flower Hour (February 1985)
USA   2-LP set

Innerview (1985)
USA   Series 32 Show No.11 (1-LP) The Band's discussing their *Unforgettable Fire Tour*

Superstars Concert Series - The Ultimate Radio Concert (21st September 1985)
Surrender / I Threw A Brick Through A Window / A Day Without Me / An Cat Dubh / Into The Heart / Sunday Bloody Sunday / I Fall Down / The Electric Co. / October / New Year's Day / Gloria / I Will Follow / Fire / A Celebration + Party Girl / 11 O'clock Tick Tock / The Ocean / 40.
USA   Westwood One SS 85-C   3-LP-Box   (same as In Concert No. 295, plus extra 4 tracks at the end)

Live Cuts (1985)

Pioneers In Music (September 1986)
USA   2-LP U2 with Van Morrison and The Boomtown Rats

King Biscuit Flower Hour (2nd November 1986)
USA ABC/DIR No. 652 2 LP set Same as King Biscuit Flower Hour Show No. 473 (29th November 1983) but with different cue sheets and commercials

Radio Show (1986)
USA   U2 with The Rolling Stones

Rockstars (18th - 25th May 1987)
I Still Haven't Found What I'm Looking For / New Year's Day / Sunday Bloody Sunday / In God's Country / A Cel-

ebration / With Or Without You / Gloria / Pride / Out Of Control (Demo & LP Version) / I Will Follow / Bullet The Blue Sky / Where The Streets Have No Name / 40.

USA RTE Show No. 003 (2-LP's) Bono interviewed by Timothy White about U2's history up to *The Joshua Tree*

Isle Of Dreams '87 (1987)

USA WWO 1OCD 87 US   (18 LP set) Features five tracks from *Under A Blood Red Sky*,   including the US censored version of *Cry-The Electric Co.* With cue sheets and commercials

Rock For Amnesty - The Conspiracy Continues (15th June 1987)

U2 tracks:- Sunday Bloody Sunday * / Bad ^ / Maggie's Farm @ / Help @

USA WWO RFA '87 (5 LP set) A various artists collection of artists who took part in the 1986 Conspiracy Of Hope tour of the US. U2 are on side 8 of this set.

@ = recorded live at The Giant's stadium, New York on 15th June 1986. * = from *Under A Blood Red Sky* ^ = from *Wide Awake In America*

Rock Clock (July 1987)

USA 2-LP set U2 with Roxy Music and Foreigner

Radio Show (1987)

USA Bono and Mick Jagger interviewed

Rock On The Road (11th December 1987)

I Will Follow (Live) / Bullet The Blue Sky / Help (Live) / Silver And Gold / New Year's Day + Bono Interview

USA DIR Broadcasting   1-LP   Songs taken from 1986 "Conspiracy Of Hope" and 1987 "Joshua Tree" tours of the US. Total running time is only 23 minutes

The Rise and Rise of U2 (Week beginning 8th August 1988)

Out Of Control / Boy-Girl / Another Day / 11 O'clock Tick Tock / A Day Without Me / Twilight / I Will Follow / Fire / Tomorrow / Gloria / A Celebration / New Year's Day / Sunday Bloody Sunday / Two Hearts Beat As One / 40. / The Unforgettable Fire / A Sort Of Homecoming / Pride / Do They Know It's Christmas Time / Maggie's Farm (Live) / With Or Without You / I Still Haven't Found What I'm Looking For / Where The Streets Have No Name / In God's Country.

USA WWO A 3 LP set, of which the sixth side is blank. The show was a history of U2 and included interviews with the band plus commercials. All the songs were previously released versions except for Maggie's Farm.

Legends of Rock Parts 1 & 2 (Part 1 - 17th-23rd July 1989, Part 2 -- 24th-31st July 1989)

Desire / Where The Streets Have No Name / With Or Without You / Pride* / All Along The Watchtower* / Helter Skelter* / I Will Follow / A Sort Of Homecoming / All I Want Is You / Angel Of Harlem / In God's Country / God Part II / Two Hearts Beat As One / Surrender / Sunday Bloody Sunday / New Year's Day / Gloria ^ / Bad / When Love Comes To Town

* = from *Rattle And Hum*, ^ = from *Under A Blood Red Sky*
USA NBC Radio Entertainment 4-LP-Box (including two 1-sided) A mixture of studio and live tracks and brief interviews

The U2 Story (1989)

USA 2-LPs

NBC (1989)

USA 2-LPs

Other Radio Show LP's (Broadcast dates unknown)

Isle Of Dreams (U2 / Jackson Browne)

Isle Of Dreams (U2 / Don Henley)

Rolling Stone Continuous History Of Rock 'N' Roll

USA 2-LPs U2 with Asia, Soft Cell, etc.

The World Of Rock

USA 4-LPs Various artists compilation including U2

Innerview

Series 34 Show No.8

Radio Shows On Tape

In Concert Nu Rock (20th November 1992)

Zoo Station / The Fly / Mysterious Ways / Until The End Of The World / Trying To Throw Your Arms Around The World / Satellite Of Love / Bullet The Blue Sky / Running To Stand Still / Where The Streets Have No Name / Desire

USA Final broadcast The format is two 10" reel-to-reel tapes. Recorded at various venues on the 1992 Zoo TV "Outside Broadcast" of the US. (Also has interviews with the band and ZOO TV Interference).

Radio Shows On Compact Disc

BBC Transcription Disc (1990)

UK BBC Single CD New Year's Eve 1989 concert from The Point Depot, Dublin ?

BBC Classic Tracks (3rd June 1991)

New Years Day, Sunday Bloody Sunday, October, I Will Follow, Gloria

USA Westwood One Single CD Taken from In Concert No. 295 (with cue sheets and commercials)

British Invasion Volume II (July 1991)

U2 tracks:- *New year's day, I Will Follow, A Celebration*
USA WWO (6 CD set) U2 are just one of 24 groups featured on this compilation

1991: Rock In Review (23rd December 1991 - 1st January 1992)

USA Show # 91-52 (3 CD set) various artists compilation contains the track *Mysterious Ways*

BBC Classic Tracks (1st June 1992)

USA Westwood One #92-93 Single CD Repeat of 3rd June 1991(with cue-sheets and commercials)

On The Radio! Zoo TV (1992)

Mysterious Ways / The Fly / Trying To Throw Your Arms Around The World / Pride (In The Name Of Love) * / Where The Streets Have No Name / Bullet The Blue Sky */ Bad ^/ I Still Haven't Found What I'm Looking For */ Angel Of Harlem / One / With Or Without You / Until The End Of The World / Satellite Of Love / Desire / Love Is Blindness

USA Album network Double-CD Green/Purple Picture-Disc's Conversation with The Edge & Adam Clayton about the Zoo TV Tour and the making of Achtung Baby

* = tracks from *Rattle & Hum* ^ = track from *Wide Awake In America* Rest recorded on Zoo TV tour of US

The U2 Story (4th - 6th September 1992)

New Year's Day / With Or Without You / I Still Haven't Found What I'm Looking For / Where The Streets Have No Name / Desire / Angel Of Harlem / Mysterious Ways / One / Even Better Than The Real Thing

USA Unistar Interview with Bono and The Edge Air date

04/ 06-09-92

Zoo Radio Transmit (25th November 1992)

Until The End Of The World, Even Better Than The Real Thing, Mysterious Ways, The Fly, One, Trying To Throw Your Arms Around The World, Satellite Of Love, Bullet The Blue Sky, Where The Streets Have No Name, Running To Stand Still, Can't Help Falling In Love

USA Album Network Recorded on the Outside Leg tour of US 1992 and includes interviews with each band member , plus support acts, Public Enemy and The Disposable Heroes Of Hiphoprisy This show has come out on bootleg CD.

In the Studio (28th December 1992)

USA Show No. 236-92 Interview with The Edge & Adam Clayton about *Achtung Baby*

Even Better Than the Real Thing / One / Who's Gonna Ride Your Wild Horses /The Fly / Mysterious Ways / Trying To throw Your Arms around The World

BBC Classic Tracks (1st March 1993)

USA Single CD Same as 3rd June 1991, but with different cues and adverts

A Showcase Of Rock - The U2 Story (14th - 15th March 1993)

I Will Follow / October / Gloria / I Fall Down / I Threw A Brick Through A Window / New Year's Day / Like A Song / Two Hearts Beat As One / Sunday Bloody Sunday / 40 / 11 O'clock Tick Tock / Bad / Wire / The Three Sunrises / With Or Without You / Bullet The Blue Sky / I Still Haven't Found / Where The Streets / In God's Country / Helter Skelter / All Along The Watchtower / Desire / Angel Of Harlem / God Part II / When Love Comes To Town / All I Want Is You / The Fly / Mysterious Ways / Until The End Of World

USA Unistar 3-CD Pack Interviews with The Edge, Bono, Adam and Phil Joanou about U2's history

Westwood One presents Zooropa (21st August 1993)

Some Days Are Better Than Others / Zooropa / Numb / Babyface / Mysterious Ways / Even Better Than The Real Thing / Who's Gonna Ride Your Wild Horses / I Will Follow / Desire / A Sort Of Homecoming / One / Until The End Of The World / Ultraviolet / With Or Without You / Stay (Faraway, So Close)

USA WWO Double-CD   Music & Interviews with The Edge, Bono & Adam Clayton about *Zooropa*

Westwood One presents Zoo Radio (21st August 1993)

USA WWO Double-CD   Music & Interviews with The Edge, Bono & Adam Clayton about *Zooropa* Broadcast the same day as above, but does feature different tracks

Westwood One presents Zooropa - Live From Dublin (9th September 1993)

Daddy's Gonna Pay For Your Crashed Car / I Will Follow / Paint It Black / Sunday Bloody Sunday / Salome / Zooropa / Zoo Station / The Fly / Even Better Than The Real Thing / Mysterious Ways / One/Unchained Melody / Until Then End Of The World / New Year's Day / Numb / Trying To Throw Your Arms Around The World / Angel Of Harlem / When Love Comes To Town / Stay / Satellite Of Love / Bad / Bullet The Blue Sky / Running To Stand Still / Where The Streets.../ Pride / Help / Ultraviolet / With Or Without You / Love Is Blindness / I Can't Help Falling In Love

USA WWO 3-CD-Box with cue-sheets. Live concert from Dublin, RDS 28-08-93, the final show of the *Zooropa* tour. First 6 tracks do not come from the concert.

Westwood One presents Zooropa - Live from Sydney (aka Zoo TV Recorded Live In Sydney) (1994)

Zoo Station / The Fly / Even Better Than The Real Thing / Mysterious Ways / One / Unchained Melody / Until The End Of The World / New Year's Day / Numb / Angel Of Harlem / Stay (Faraway, So Close) / Satellite Of Love / Dirty Day / Bullet The Blue Sky / Running To Stand Still / Where The Streets Have No Name / Pride (In The Name Of Love) / Daddy's Gonna Pay For Your Crashed Car / Lemon / With Or Without You / Love Is Blindness / Can't Help Falling In Love

USA WWO # 94-20 Double-CD Live-Transcription from Sydney concert of 27th November 1993

Compilations

Compilations are records that contain tracks by U2 plus other artists. They come in two different types:-Firstly, compilations that contain previously released U2 tracks such as chart singles. Secondly, compilations in aid of a particular charity or cause that contain previously unavailable U2 tracks, either studio or live versions. Below is a list of selected compilations of both types. For more information about particular tracks see the main section of the book.

Compilations 1

Just For Kicks (Irish bands compilation LP) 1980

IRE Kick KK1 Stories for boys

Dancin' Master (Cassette free with New Musical Express) 1981

UK NME 001 An Cat Dubh

Wheel To Reel (Island Records compilation cassette with other artists) 1981

UK   ICT 4005 Gloria (2nd side of the cassette blank for owners own recordings)

Island '81 (Island Records compilation LP of 1981 releases) 1981

UK   RSS 38   Tomorrow & October included

"The Tube" (Selection of groups who had appeared on UK TV programme "The Tube") 1983

UK   New Year's Day

The Island Story 1987

UK   With Or Without You

'Martin' (Martin Hannet Tribute album) (1991)

UK   LP/CD (Factory Records) 11 O'clock Tick Tock

Island Select 1993 (Cassette given away free with Select magazine May 1993)

UK   Cassette Salome (Zooromancer remix)

The Perfecto Remix Album 1994

UK   Even Better Than The Real Thing (Perfecto Remix)

One and Only - 25 Years of Radio One 1996

UK BOJCD25 I Will Follow (in a BBC studio 18th September1980)

VOX Magazine

UK Compilation tape given free contains "Even Better Than The Real Thing" (live) (Dublin, RDS, August 28, 1993)

Special Brew

UK Numb (Gimme Some More Dignity Mix)

Hold On - BBC Radio 1FM Sessions

UK "One" (live at the football stadium Sydney Australia 27/11/1993)

Compilations 2

Wire (Dub Mix) (Free EP single from the New Musical Express)1985
UK   GIV-1B (Also known as the "Celtic Dub Mix") The single also contained tracks by Bronksi Beat, Cocteau Twins and The Smiths (plain cover)

Live For Ireland LP 1986
IRE   Maggie's Farm (live at "Self Aid")

A Very Special Christmas LP 1987
USA   Christmas (Baby, Please Come Home)

Christmas (Baby, Please Come Home) / Madonna: Santa Claus (Promo single from the album) 1987
NZ   Promotional Copy Red Vinyl

Christmas (Baby, Please Come Home) / I Saw Mommy Kissing Santa Claus (J.C. Mellencamp) /

Merry Christmas Baby (Bruce Springsteen) / Back Door Santa (Bon Jovi) (Promo single from the album) 1988
NL   IS 811 169-1/871 169-1   Promotional Copy
AUS A & M 871169-1 Promotional Copy Green Vinyl
AUS A & M 871169-1 Promotional Copy Red Vinyl

Folkways - A Vision Shared (Woody Guthrie / Leadbelly tribute LP) 1988
USA   Jesus Christ (recorded at Sun Studios in 1987)

Jesus Christ / J.C. Mellencamp - Do Re Mi (Promo single from the album) 1988
HOL   CBS PRO 464 Promotional Copy

Rainbow Warriors (Greenpeace Compilation LP & CD) 1989
UK   Pride (In The Name Of Love) (live)
RUS   Melodia A 60 00439 008   Russian version contains free booklet

Earthrise (Greenpeace compilation LP and CD) 1990
UK   I Still Haven't Found What I'm Looking For

Red Hot And Blue (AIDS Awareness Compilation Tribute To Cole Porter LP and CD) 1990
UK   Night & Day
USA   BPM 122 Double 12" Promotional album contained remix of *Night & Day,* plus stickers, information sheet and condom

Peace Together (LP & CD) In aid of the youth of Northern Ireland 1993
UK   CID 8018/518 063-2   Satellite Of Love (Live) with Lou Reed

Alternative NRG (Greenpeace CD) 1994
USA   HR-61449-2 Until The End Of The World (Live)

Earthrise II (Greenpeace CD) 1995
UK   Who's Gonna Ride Your Wild Horses

20 years of resistance to genocide in East Timor 1996
AUS Handsfree Records HANDS20CD Mothers Of The Disappeared

Rock The Planet 1996
UK   533 428 2 Who's Gonna Ride Your Wild Horses

Diana, Princess of Wales 1997
UK   Miss Sarajevo

Tibetan Freedom Concert 1997
USA Grand Royal/Capitol CDP 7243 8 59110 26 One

WBCN Naked Disc 1997

USA   Staring at The Sun (Live)
Across The Bridge of Hope 1998
UK   Please
Forgotten Angels (in aid of the Temple Street Children's Hospital) 1999
IRL   LNCD 7045 If God Will Send His Angels

Soundtrack Albums

This section contains a list of film soundtrack albums that feature one or more songs performed by U2 and the year of their release. Solo performances are in the following section.

They Call It An Accident   1982
        October & October (Instrumental Version)
The Last American Virgin   1982
        I Will Follow
State Of Grace   1987
        Trip Through Your Wires
Blown Away   1987
        With Or Without You
The Courier   1988
        Walk To The Water
Until The End Of The World 1991
        Until The End Of The World
Faraway, So Close!   1993
        Stay (Faraway, So Close!) / The Wanderer
Reality Bites   1994
        All I Want Is You
Pret-a-Porter   1994
        Lemon
Threesome   1994
        Dancing Barefoot
Blown Away   1994
        With or Without You / I Still Haven't Found...
Johnny Mnemonic   1995
        Alex Descends Into Hell For A Bottle of Milk...
Batman Forever   1995
        Hold Me, Thrill Me, Kiss Me, Kill Me
Blackout   1997
        Miami
City Of Angels   1998
        If God Will Send His Angels
Forces of Nature   1999
        Everlasting Love
Runaway Bride   1999
        I Still Haven't Found What I'm Looking For
Three Kings   1999
        In God's Country
The Million Dollar Hotel   2000
        Stateless/Ground Beneath Her Feet/The First Time
The Family Man   2000
        One

Solo Collaborations

Below is a list of all known solo collaborations by the four members of U2 with other artists/groups. The title of the track as well as the album/single it is from, plus its year of release are all listed. For details of each track see main section of the book.

Bono

Bono provides vocals/backing vocals on all tracks below unless otherwise stated

Having A Wonderful Time, Wish You Were Her - from the T-Bone Burnett album, 'Beyond The Trap Door' (1984)

Do They Know It's Christmas / Feed The World - from the Band Aid charity single (1984)

Sun City - single from the 'Artists Against Apartheid' album (1985)

Silver & Gold - From the 'Artists Against Apartheid' album (1985)

In A Lifetime - single from Clannad's 'Macalla' album (1985) (Duet with Maire Ni Bhraonain)

Airwaves - from the Paul Brady album, 'Back to The Centre' (1986)

Purple Heart - from the T-Bone Burnett album, 'Talking Animals' (1988)

She's A Mystery To Me - Bono co-wrote this song from the Roy Orbison album, 'Mystery Girl' (1989)

Royal Station - from the Melissa Etheridge album, 'Brave & Crazy' (1989) (Bono plays harmonica)

A Clockwork Orange - Bono co-wrote the music for this Royal Shakespeare Company stage play with The Edge (1990)

Jah Love - Bono wrote this song from the Neville Brothers album, 'Brother's Keeper' (1990)

Whatever Happened To You? - from The Call album, 'Red Moon' (1990)

My Wild Irish Rose - from the BBC/RTE TV Series, 'Bringing It All Back Home' (1991)

Can't Help Falling In Love - from the soundtrack album of the film, 'Honeymoon In Vegas' (1992)

Misere - Bono wrote this track for Zuccherro (1992)

I've Got You Under My Skin - from the Frank Sinatra album, 'Duets' (1993)

In The Name Of The Father / Billy Boola - from the soundtrack album of the film, 'In The Name Of The Father' (1994)

Thief of Your Heart - from the film 'In The Name of the Father'

The Long Black Veil - from The Chieftans album, 'The Chieftains And Friends' (1994)

Save The Children - from the Marvin Gaye tribute album, 'Inner city Blues' (1995)

Give Me Back My Job - from the album *Go Cat Go Carl Perkins album (1996)*for the World Children's Foundation (1995) (with Johnny Cash and Willie Nelson) (1995)

Little Black Dress -from the Gavin Friday album, 'Shag Tobacco' (1995)

North And South Of The River - single/ track off *Graffiti Tongue* (with Christy Moore and The Edge) (1995)

Let The Good Times Roll - from the Quincy Jones' album, 'Le Q's Jook Joint' (1995) (with Stevie Wonder and Ray Charles)

Hallelujah - from the Leonard Cohen tribute album, 'Tower Of Song' (1995)

Goldeneye - Bono co-wrote the film soundtrack to this James Bond film with The Edge (1995) (song performed by Tina Turner)

Drinking In The Day - Bono wrote this song for the album *Dirty Rotten Shame* by Ronnie Drew *(1995)*

Dreaming With Tears In My Eyes - from *The Songs of*

Jimmy Rodgers - A Tribute album, (1995)

Original Soundtracks 1 - album by Passengers, featuring the four members of U2, Brian Eno and other guests (1995)

Miss Sarajevo (live) / One (live) / Nessum Dorma (live) - from the album/video, 'Pavarotti and Friends Together for The Children Of Bosnia' (1996) (with The Edge, Brian Eno and Pavarotti)

Tomorrow - from the album, 'Common Ground (1996)

Love From A Short Distance Bono co-wrote this poem for the album children of East Timor (1996)

Conversation On A Barstool - written by Bono & Edge for Marianne Faithfull *A Perfect Stranger* (1996)

I'm Not Your Baby with Sinead O'Connor from *The End of Violence* film soundtrack (1997)

Perfect Day from the Children In Need charity single (1997)

A Good Man - track off *Cookies Fortune* soundtrack album (1998)

Lean on Me - from the *Nu Nation Project* album with Kirk Franklin (1998)

Sweet Jane - this live track from Lone Justice album *This World Is Not My Home* (1999)

"The Mothers Of God" (English) / "The Mother Of God" (Spanish) / "Mothers Of The Disappeared"
Bono reads William Butler Yeats poem both in Spanish and English and sing a capela *Mother Of The Disappeared on the album 20 Anos-ni un Paso* (1999)

Blue - lyrics by Bono & Zucchero from Zucchero album and single *Blue Sugar* (1999)

New Day - Net Aid theme song with *Wyclef Jean* (1999)

Slide Away - track from the album *Michael Hutchence* (1999)

Air Suspension album track off *Mocean Worker* (2000)

Never Let Me Go, Falling At Your Feet, Dancin' Shoes Million Dollar Hotel (2000)

The Edge

Snakecharmer - from the Jah Wobble album, 'Snakecharmer' (1983)

Airwaves -from the Paul Brady album, 'Back To The Centre' (1986)

Captive - music for the film soundtrack was written and performed by The Edge (1986)

A Clockwork Orange - The Edge co-wrote the music for this Royal Shakespeare Company stage play with Bono (1990)

My Wild Irish Rose/ April the 3rd - from the BBC/RTE TV Series' 'Bringing It All Back Home' (1991)

Somebody Else / Ain't Rock & Roll - from the Ronnie Wood album, 'Slide On This' (1992)

North & South Of The River - single/track off *Graffiti Tongue* with Christy Moore and Bono (1995)

Goldeneye - The Edge co-wrote the film soundtrack to this James Bond film with Bono (1995) (song performed by Tina Turner)

Little Black Dress - Edge provided backing vocals on this track from *Shag Tobacco* by Gavin Friday (1995)

Original Soundtracks 1 - album by Passengers, featuring the four members of U2, Brian Eno and other guests (1995)

Miss Sarejevo(live) / One (live) / Nessum Dorma (live) - from the album/video, 'Pavarotti and Friends Together For The Children Of Bosnia' (1996)

Rain In Our Room track off the album *Undark* by Russell

Mills (1996)

Conversation On A Barstool - written by Bono & Edge for Marianne Faithfull *A Perfect Stranger* (1996) *Conversation On A Barstool* -written by Bono & Edge for the *"Short Cuts"* soundtrack (1996)

Patrol Car Blues - The Edge plays guitar on this track from *Cookies Fortune* soundtrack (1998)

Island - Edge plays on this track from the album *Ambient Vol. 2 Imaginary Landscapes"* (1999)

Strange Familiar Russell Mills/Undark (2000)

Adam Clayton

Do They Know It's Christmas? - from the Band Aid charity single (1984)

Still Water / Jolie Louise - from the Daniel Lanois album, 'Acadie' (1989)

The Bucks Of Oranmore - from the BBC/RTE TV Series, 'Bringing It All Back Home' (1991) (With The Hughes Band)

On Grafton Street / Don't Forget About Me / These Days In An Open Book / This Heart - from the Nanci Griffiths album, 'Flyer' (1994)

Born Again Savage - track recorded with Little Stephen (1994)

Original Soundtracks 1 - album by Passengers, featuring the four members of U2, Brian Eno and other guests (1995)

Theme From Mission: Impossible / Mission: Impossible Theme (Mission Accomplished) - single (with Larry Mullen Junior) (1996)

One (as a member of Automatic Baby) from the album *Childline* (1996)

Spellbound track from the *Sharon Shannon* album (1999)

Anarchy In The USA track from the *Million Dollar Hotel* sounndtrack album (2000)

Larry Mullen Junior

Airwaves - from the Paul Brady album, 'Back to The Centre' (1986)

Captive - Larry played on the track "Heroine" from this film soundtrack album (1986)

Let's Make It Work - Self Aid single (with Christy Moore) (1986)

Still Water / Jolie Louise - from the Daniel Lanois album, 'Acadie' (1989)

Pet 'Em Under Pressure - Larry wrote and produced this single by the 1990 Ireland World Cup Squad (1990

On Grafton Street / Don't Forget About Me / These Days In An Open Book / This Heart - from the Nanci Griffiths album, 'Flyer' (1994)

Dreaming With Tears In My Eyes - from *The Songs of Jimmy Rodgers - A Tribute* album (1995)

Wrecking Ball from the album *Wrecking Ball* by Emylou Harris (1995)

Original Soundtracks 1 - album by Passengers, featuring all four members of U2, Brian Eno and other guests (1995)

Theme From Mission: Impossible / Mission: Impossible Theme (Mission Accomplished) - single (with Adam Clayton) (1996)

One (as a member of Automatic Baby) from the album *Childline* (1996)

Anarchy In The USA track on the *Million Dollar Hotel* soundtrack album*(2000)*

Videos -

Introducton

Videos which feature U2 come in two categories:- firstly, full length films of the band in concert or in the studio which are sold in music and video shops and secondly, promotional videos which show the band performing one of their songs designed for showing on television. These are listed below, followed by all the promotional videos that have been made of U2, including ones featuring solo appearances by members of U2. For full details of each video see the main text of the book.

Commercially Available U2 Videos

Under A Blood Red Sky (U2 Live At Red Rocks) VHS Video (61 Minutes) Kace/Virgin VVD 045 Director: Gavin Taylor (Certificate E) 1983

The Unforgettable Fire Collection VHS Video (60 Minutes) Island Polygram Video 082 974 3 Director: Barry Devlin (Certificate E) 1985

Rattle & Hum VHS Video CIC Video VHR 2308 (96 Minutes) Director: Phil Joanou (Certificate 15) 1988

Achtung Baby - The Videos, The Cameos & A Whole Lot Of Interference From Zoo TV VHS Video Island/Polygram Video 085 556-3 (65 Minutes) Director: Maurice Linnane (Certificate E) 1992

Numb Video Single. VHS Video Polygram/Island Video 088 162 3 9 (13 Minutes) Directors: Kevin Godley/Matt Mahurin 1993 (No Certificate) 1993

U2 - Zoo TV Live From Sydney VHS Video Polygram/ Island Video 631 150-3 (118 Minutes) Director: David Mallet (Certificate E) 1994

U2 - Pop Mart Live From Mexico City VHS Video Polygram/Island/VVL Video 0958 302-3 (127 Minutes) Director: David Mallet (Certificate E) 1998

U2 - The Best Of 1980-1990 VHS Video Polygram/ Island/VVL Video 0518583 (78 Minutes) Directors Various (Certificate E) 1999

U2 Joshua Tree (Classic Albums) VHS Video Eagle Rock Entertainment/ILC Music ILC 0184 (60 Minutes) Directors: Philip King/Nuala O'Connor (Certificate E) 1999

Note: some of the above are also available in DVD format

Other Commercially Available Videos With Solo Or Group Performances By U2

The World's Greatest Artists Sing: Lennon - A Tribute Pickwick Video PVL 2160 (90 Minutes) Director: Gavin Taylor (Certificate 15) 1991

Contains U2 performing "Help" at the Giant's Stadium, New Jersey, USA 15th June 1986

Bringing It All Back Home BBC Video 1992

A double VHS video of this BBC/RTE documentary series features Bono and The Edge performing the song "Wild Irish Rose". Adam is also featured playing with Steve Wickham and Sinead O'Connor.

Stop Sellafield - The Concert 1993
Contains songs performed by U2 ("The Fly" and "Even Better Than The Real Thing"), Public Enemy, Kraftwerk and BAD II at the G-Mex Centre Manchester, England 19th June 1992

Past Present - Clannad
The greatest hits video by Clannad contains the promo video of the song, "In A Lifetime" on which Bono duetted with Maire ni Brennan from Clannad.

Luciano Pavarotti And Friends: Together For The Children Of Bosnia 1996
Contains film of Bono, The Edge, Brian Eno and Luciano Pavarotti performing "Miss Sarajevo", "One" and "Nessum Dorma" at the Parco Novi Sad, Modena, Italy on 12th September 1995

Promotional Videos Of U2 Songs

Below is a full list of all known U2 promotional videos. Several promo videos are only rumoured to exist. These are marked * Several promo videos have been withdrawn from general release to the media and public. These are marked +. The director's name (where known) is given as well the location and date of its filming or general release.

I Will Follow (London 1980)
I Will Follow (Live in Holland 1982) *
I Will Follow (Live in the USA 1981) *
Gloria (Meiert Avis - Dublin, Ireland October 1981)
A Celebration (Meiert Avis - Kilmainham Jail, Dublin, Ireland April 1982)
New Year's Day (Meiert Avis - Sweden December 1982)
Two Hearts Beat As One (Meiert Avis - Montmartre, Paris, France March 1983)
Sunday Bloody Sunday (live) (Gavin Taylor - Red Rocks, Denver, Colorado, USA, June 1983)
Pride (In The Name Of Love) (Video 1a - sepiatone) (Donald Cammell - St. Francis Xavier Hall, Dublin, Ireland August 1984)
Pride (In The Name Of Love) (Video 1b - colour version) (Donald Cammell - St. Francis Xavier Hall, Dublin, Ireland August 1984]
Pride (In The Name Of Love) (Video 2) (Barry Devlin - Slane Castle, County Meath, Ireland and Windmill Lane studios, Dublin, Ireland July 1984)
Pride (In The Name Of Love) (Video 3) (Anton Corbijn - London, England, August 1984) +
A Sort Of Homecoming (live) (Barry Devlin - Paris; Brussels; Rotterdam; London; Glasgow October/November 1984)
Bad (live) - (Barry Devlin - Paris; Brussels; Rotterdam; London; Glasgow, October/November 1984)
The Unforgettable Fire (Meiert Avis - Sweden January 1985)
With Or Without You (Meiert Avis & Matt Mahurin - Dublin, Ireland February 1987)
Red Hill Mining Town (Neil Jordan - London, England - February 1987) +
I Still Haven't Found What I'm Looking For (Barry Devlin - Las Vegas, Nevada, USA April 1987)
Where The Streets Have No Name (Meiert Avis - 7th & Main, Los Angeles, California, USA April 1987) (short and long versions exist)
In God's Country (Barry Devlin - Arizona, USA, April 1987)
Spanish Eyes (Barry Devlin - Arizona, USA, April 1987)
Christmas (Baby Please Come Home) (Recorded at a soundcheck at LSU Activity Center, Baton Rouge, Louisiana, USA November 1987)
Desire (Richard Lowenstein - Los Angeles, California, USA 1988)
Desire (Hollywood Remix) (Richard Lowenstein - Los Angeles, California, USA 1988)
Angel Of Harlem (Richard Lowenstein - Apollo Theater, New York City/ Los Angeles USA November 1988)
When Love Comes To Town (Phil Joanou - Sun Studios, Memphis/Tarrant County Convention Center, Fort Worth, Texas, USA March 1989)
All I Want Is You (Meiert Avis - Rome, Italy April 1989)
Night & Day (Wim Wenders -Wim Wenders' house, Berlin, Germany October 1990)
The Fly (Ritchie Smyth and Jon Klein - Dublin, London October 1991)
Mysterious Ways (Stephanie Sednaoui - October 1991, Morocco)
One (Version 1) (band in women's clothes, Trabant cars) (Anton Corbijn -Berlin, Germany February 1992)
One (Version 2) (buffalo, flowers) (Mark Pellington - New York City, USA, February 1992) (included in *The Making Of The Other One*)
One (Version 3) (Bono singing at a table) (Philip Joanou - New York City, USA, March 1992)
One (Version 4) (Mark Pellington - New York City, USA March 1992) Same as version 2 but with band shots
One (version 5) (1992) *
Even Better Than The Real Thing (Kevin Godley - Carnaby Street and Pinewood Studios, London, England February 1992)
Even Better Than The Real Thing (concert footage) (Armando Gallo and Kampagh - Los Angeles, USA)
Even Better Than The Real Thing (dance mix) (Ritchie Smyth - Dublin, Ireland July 1992)
Until The End Of The World (Ritchie Smyth November 1991)
Who's Gonna Ride Your Wild Horses (Philip Joanou -Chicago, Illinois, USA, September 1992)
Numb (Kevin Godley - Berlin, Germany June 23, 1993)
Numb (Video Remix) (Josh Pearson and Gardner Post - July 1993)
Love Is Blindness (Matt Mahurin - USA July 1993)
Lemon (Mark Neale - London, England September 1993)
Lemon (Bad Yard Club) (Mark Neale - London, October 1993)
Stay (Faraway, So Close!) (Wim Wenders - Berlin October 1993)
The Wanderer *
Daddy's Gonna Pay For Your Crashed Car *
Zooropa *
Hold Me, Thrill Me, Kiss Me, Kill Me (Kevin Godley & Maurice Linnane - Dublin, June 1995)
Discotheque (Stephane Sednaoui December 1996)
Discotheque (David Morales Mix) (Stephane Sednaoui Miami, Florida, USA January 1997)

Discotheque (Steve Osborne Mix) (Stephane Sednaoui Miami, Florida, USA January 1997)

Staring At The Sun (Version 1) (Jake Scott - New York City, USA (March 1997)

Staring At The Sun (Version 2) (Morleigh Steinberg - Miami, Florida, USA May, 1997)

Last Night On Earth (William Burroughs - Kansas City, Missouri, USA May 1997)

Last Night On Earth (First Night In Hell) (June 1997) *

Please (live) (Maurice Linnane Rotterdam, Holland August 1997)

Please (Anton Corbijn Holland 8th September 1997)

If God Will Send His Angels (Phil Joanou - Detroit, Michigan, USA March 1997)

If God Will Send His Angels (*City of Angels* version) (Phil Joanou - Detroit, Michigan, USA March 1997)

Sweetest Thing (Kevin Godley - Dublin, Ireland September 1998)

Beautiful Day (Version 1) (Jonas Akerlund - Charles De Gaulle Airport, Paris, France, September, 2000)

Beautiful Day (version 2) (Jonas Akerlund - Dublin, Ireland/Paris France September, 2000)

Stuck in a Moment You Can't Get Out Of (Kevin Godley - Los Angeles January, 2001)

Walk On (Version 1) (Jonas Akerlund - Rio De Janeiro, Brazil January 2001)

Walk On (Version 2) (Liz Friedlander - London, England March 2001)

Elevation (Joseph Kahn - Los Angeles, California, USA April 2001)

Promotional Videos Containing Various Members Of U2

Do They Know It's Christmas (Band Aid including Bono and Adam) (London 1984)

Sun City (Artists United Against Apartheid including Bono) (New York November 1985)

In A Lifetime (Clannad and Bono) (Meiert Avis - Gweedore, Donegal, Ireland December 1985)

I've Got You Under My Skin (Bono & Frank Sinatra) (Kevin Godley - Rancho Mirage, California, USA 1993)

In The Name Of The Father (Bono and Gavin Friday) (Jim Sheridan - Dublin, Ireland/London, England 1994)

Save The Children (Bono with Marvin Gaye) (*Inner City Blues* 1995)

Miss Sarajevo (Bono, Edge, Brian Eno, Pavarotti) (Maurice Linnane - Parco Novi Sad, Modena, Italy/Sarajevo, Bosnia September 1995)

Mission: Impossible (Adam and Larry) (Kevin Godley April 1996)

Perfect Day (Bono with various artists) (London, England 1997)

New Day (Wyclef Jean, Bono and others) (New York 1999)

The Ground Beneath Her Feet (Wim Wenders - Cologne, Germany April 2000)

Miscellaneous Videos Featuring U2

Do They Know It's Christmas? (The Story Of The Band Aid)

Includes "Do They Know It's Christmas?" and interviews Release date: December 1984 (Polygram Video 0411212) This is a documentary on the making of the video film

Video Aid - The FEED THE WORLD Compilation

Includes "New Year's Day" and "Do They Know It's Christmas" video clip Release date: 1985 (Virgin Music Video, #0430)

Folkways: A Vision Shared, A Tribute To Woody Guthrie And Leadbelly

Includes: Bono's voice over a shortened version of "Jesus Christ" explaining why U2 chose this song. There is also a video of "This Land Is Your Land" where Bono (vocals) and The Edge (guitar) make two short appearances

A Very Special Christmas

Includes: "Christmas (Baby Please Come Home)" *

Alright Now (Island Records 25th Anniversary)

Includes: "Where The Streets Have No Name" Catalogue number: IVA 007 (1987)

Red Hot and Blue (1990)

Includes: video for "Night & Day"

A Video Postcard From U2

A French promo video promoting *Achtung Baby* limited to 499 copies SECAM format (1991) Contains: excerpts of one video clip from each album

U2 Three

UK/Australian promo video for instore use - 3 video clips on rotation to fill 1 hour Contains: "The Fly" "Mysterious Ways" "One" promo videos **Note:** The Australian release ends with live footage to promote the *Zoomerang* tour

Pop

Contains: *Pop* promo footage with music in background plus excerpts from "Discotheque" and "Wake up Dead Man" Catalogue number: Island PN7-003 US promo (NTSC) Total playing time: 5 min.

Pop Live from Mexico City Preview video

Contains: Pop Musik - Mofo - Please (all tracks live from Rotterdam, July 1997) **Note**: This video was sent by Island records to US TV stations for use in advertisements for the Mexico City Pop Mart broadcast on Showtime & MTV.

Polygram Acoplado sampler

Mexico promo video March 1997 Tracks: Discotheque - Desire - Angel Of Harlem - When Love Comes To Town - Where The Streets Have No Name - One - The Fly - Even Better Than The Real Thing - Numb - Lemon - EPK Discotheque - Popmart Tour Conference (EPK Giveaway Version 2:40 min)

Beautiful Day - The Making Of

Spain - video given free with October 2000 issue of *Rolling Stone* magazine (12min)

U2 Historico

Spanish promo video Tracks: I Will Follow - New Year's Day - Sunday Bloody Sunday (*Red Rocks*) - October (*Red Rocks*) - Pride - Silver & Gold (*Rattle & Hum*) - With or Without You - Desire - Angel of Harlem - Zoo Station - Even Better Than The Real Thing - Satellite of Love (Sydney '93) - Hold Me, Kiss Me, Kill Me - Discotheque - Beautiful Day

TV Appearances

Below is a list of known TV and Radio performances by U2 over the years with details of when and where the show was recorded or broadcast, the name of the TV/Radio show and which TV/Radio station broadcast it. If this is not known the country where it was broadcast is given. See main book for details about individual shows. Special thanks to Kay Bauresfeld and Richard Hare for help in compiling this list.

1978

Autumn - *Youngline* Irish TV performing "Street Mission"

1979

5th October - Cork Opera House (Ireland - RTE)

1980

15th January - *The Late Late Show* (RTE)

1981

9th February - *Mandagsborsen* (Sweden)
12th February - Paard Van Troje, The Hague (Holland)
14th February - *Rock Follies* (Belgium)
28th February - *The Old Grey Whistle Test* (UK - BBC)
30th May - *The Tomorrow Show* (USA)
8th June - Pink Pop Festival (Holland)
June - *Top Of The Pops* (BBC)
12th August - *Rock Goes To College* (Queen's University, Belfast - 21st
January 1981) (BBC)
25th October - *Generation 80* (Belgium/France - RTBF)
4th November - *Rockpalast* (Germany)

1982

14th May - *Countdown In Concert* (Holland)
15th May - *Something Else* (UK - ITV)
May - *Get Set For Summer* (BBC)
2nd July - Roskilde Festival (Denmark)
4th July - Werchter Festival (Belgium - ID-TV)
31st July - *The Tube* (Gateshead) (UK - Channel 4)

1983

January - *Top Of The Pops* (BBC)
16th March - *The Tube* (Channel 4)
31st March - *Top Of The Pops* (BBC)
30th May - US Festival (USA)
21st June - *A Midsummer Night's Tube* (Red Rocks - 5th June 1983) (Channel 4)
29th June - Pier 84 New York (USA)
3rd July - Werchter Festival (Belgium)
July - *Show Time* (Red Rocks - 5th June 1983) (USA)
July - MTV (Red Rocks - 5th June 1983) (USA)
20th August - *Rockpalast* (Lorelei Amphitheatre) (Germany - WDR)
November - Various Japanese TV appearances

1984

21st November - *Rock Pop In Concert* (Germany)
December - *The Old Grey Whistle Test* (BBC)

1985

21st March - University of Illinois, Chicago (USA - CBS)
23rd April - *The Old Grey Whistle Test* (Meadowlands Arena, NJ 12th April 1985) (BBC)
13th July - *Live Aid*, Wembley, London / JFK, Philadelphia (BBC / world-wide)
15th December - *Wide Awake In Dublin* (Croke Park, Dublin - 29th June 1985) (RTE)

1986

30th January - *TV Ga Ga* (RTE)
17th May - *Self Aid*, RDS, Dublin (RTE)
15th June - Giant's Stadium, East Rutherford (MTV)

1987

6th March - *The Tube* (Channel 4)
11th March - *The Old Grey Whistle Test* (BBC)
16th March - *The Late Late Show* (RTE)
24th April - *The Tube* (Channel 4)
May - *Visual Eyes* - Interview with Dave Fanning (RTE)
27th May - *Terramota A Roma* (Stadio Flaminio, Rome) (Italy - RAI)
6th June - *U2 June 6th, 1987* (Eriksberg, Gothenburg) (Sweden)
1st July - Elland Road, Leeds (ITV)
4th July - *Island 25* (Channel 4) / *Les Enfants Du Rock* (France) (Hippodrome De Vincennes, Paris)
8th July - *Brilliant Trees* (Vorst National, Brussels) (Belgium)
10th July - *Countdown* (Feyenoord Stadium, Rotterdam) (Holland)
August - *Anthem For The 80's - World In Action* (Croke Park, Dublin- 27th July) (ITV)
December - *Rock Of Europe - Music Box*
December - *Rockline* (Belgium)
Also: *Visual Eyes* (RTE) / *Much Music* (Canada)

1988

1st January - *Outside It's America - The Old Grey Whistle Test* (BBC)
8th February - 1988 BRIT Awards Ceremony - Royal Albert Hall, London (BBC)
2nd March - 1988 Grammy Awards Ceremony - Radio City Music Hall, NYC (USA)
16th October - *Smile Jamaica* concert, Dominion Theatre, London (ITV)
16th December - *The Late Late Show* (RTE)
Also: *Live Aus Dem Schlachthof* (Germany) / *The Making Of 'Rattle And Hum'*

1989

13th February - 1989 BRIT Awards Ceremony - Royal Albert Hall, London (BBC)
22nd February - 1989 Grammy Awards Ceremony (USA)
10th September - *Very Special Arts Festival* - The White House, Washington DC (NBC)
December - *The Making Of 'All I Want Is You'* (Channel 4)
December - *Lovetown - DEF II* (BBC)
31st December - The Point Depot, Dublin (RTE)
Also: *Fire & Desire* - 1989 (MTV)

1990

1st January - The Point Depot, Dublin (RTE)
6th February - 1990 BRIT Awards ceremony, Dominion Theatre, London (BBC)
Also: *Countdown Revolution* (Australia)

1991

August/September *Bringing It All Back Home* (BBC/RTE)
18th November *The Gay Byrnes Hour* (RTE) (Bono interview)

1992

27th February- *Top of the Pops* (Civic Centre, Lakeland, Florida) (BBC)

20th April - *Freddie Aid*, London (Oakland Coliseum - 18th April) (BBC)

7th May - Palais Omnisports De Bercy, Paris (MTV)

24th May - *120 Minutes* (MTV)

May - *U2 Rockumentary* (MTV)

May - *The Trabant Land* (MTV)

11th June - *Stockholm Weekend - MTV Most Wanted* (Globen, Stockholm) (MTV)

9th September - *MTV Awards Ceremony* (Silverdome, Pontiac) (MTV)

23rd September - *Rock The Vote* (MTV)

26th September - MTV News (Georgia Dome, Atlanta - 25th September) (MTV)

20th November- *Driving Wild Horses* (Channel 4)

28th November - *Zoo TV* documentary (Yankee Stadium, New York - 30th August) (Channel 4/NBC))

9th December - *Billboard Music Awards* ceremony - Universal Amhitheater, Los Angeles (USA)

Also: *Notte Rock* (RAI Italy) / *Zoo York, Zoo York* (USA) / *Pat Kenny Show* (RTE),

Premiere Special / *The Making Of 'One'* (Anton Corbijn version) (MTV) / *The Making of the Other 'One'* (Mark Pellington version) (MTV)

1993

20th January - *MTV 1993 Rock 'n Roll Inaugural Ball* - Washington DC (MTV)

16th February - 1993 BRIT Awards Ceremony - Alexandra Palace, London (ITV)

24th February - 1993 Grammy Awards Ceremony - Shrine Auditorium, Los Angeles (USA)

May - Veronica U2 Special (Feyenoord Stadium, Rotterdam) (Holland - NL 2)

July - *Notte Rock* -Verona Special (Stadio Bentegodi - Verona) (RAI)

Notte Rock - Rome Special (Stadio Flaminio - Rome) (RAI)

August - *Naked City* (Channel 4)

3rd September - MTV Video Music Awards (Edge solo) (MTV)

September - *What's That Noise ?* (Arms Park, Cardiff - 18th August) (BBC)

September- *Music Box* (ITV)

30th November - Football Stadium, Sydney - 27th November (USA/World-wide)

Also: *Station Einer Rock* -Karriere (Germany) / *Zooropa* (France - Canale +) / *Zooropa 1993* Special (MTV) / *Watch More TV* (Italy -TMC) / U2 Weekend (MTV) / Zoo TV Tour Special (RTE)

1994

1st March - 1994 Grammy Awards Ceremony - Radio City Music Hall, New York City (USA)

31st May - World Music Awards ceremony - Monte Carlo (USA - ABC)

24th November - MTV European Music Awards ceremony - Germany (MTV) (Bono accepts the 'Free Your Mind' award for Amnesty International)

1995

12th September - *Pavarotti And Friends* - Novi Parc Sad,

Modena (Italy)

23rd November - MTV European Music Awards - Le Zenith Paris (MTV)

14th December - Frank Sinatra 80th Birthday Tribute (USA) (Bono and Edge sing)

1997

12th February - *Pop Mart* press conference - K Mart Store New York City (world-wide)

26th April - *A Year In Pop* documentary (ABC)

7th June - Tibetan Freedom Concert - New York (world-wide)

18th July - Feyenood Stadium, Rotterdam (BBC / world-wide)

15th August - Comet Awards Ceremony - Cologne (Germany)

4th September - MTV Video Music Awards ceremony - Radio City Music Hall, New York City (MTV)

20th September - Reggio Emilia (Italy)

6th November- MTV European Music Awards ceremony - Ahoy, Rotterdam (MTV)

3rd December - Foro Sol Autodromo, Mexico City (MTV / Showtime)

21st December - opening ceremony of Pavarotti Music Centre, Mostar, Bosnia (world-wide)

Also: *U2 - Their Story In Music* (MTV)

1998

9th February- 1998 BRIT Awards Ceremony (ITV) (accepted from inside the Lemon, Buenos Aires)

26th April *Trash of The Titans* - The Simpsons (USA - Fox TV)

19th May - Yes Vote concert - Waterfront Hall, Belfast (RTE)

15th October - MOBO Awards ceremony London (UK) Edge presents BB King with a lifetime achievement award

20th November - *The Late Late Show* (RTE)

1999

16th February - 1999 BRIT Awards Ceremony - London (ITV)

23rd February - 1999 Grammy Awards Ceremony (USA) (Bono sings)

12th March - *Comic Relief* (BBC) (Bono appears in drag)

6th April - *All Star Tribute To Johnny Cash* (USA - TNT)

22nd April - Bono and Edge perform "The Ground Beneath Her Feet" (BBC)

21st May - *The Late Late Show* (RTE) (Bono and Larry say farewell to Gay Byrne)

9th October - *NetAid* concert - New York (world-wide) (Bono performs solo)

11th November - MTV Europe Music Awards - Dublin (Bono wins the 'Free Your Mind' award)

31st December - America's Millennium Gala - Washington (USA) (Bono performs solo)

2000

5th February - *Saturday Night Live* (RTE) (Bono interviewed by Dave Fanning)

17th March - *TFI Friday* (Channel 4)

September- 'Beautiful Day' video World Premier (VH1)

27th September - *Top of the Pops* - Roof of the Clarence Hotel, Dublin (BBC)

27th October - *Farmclub.com* - Universal Studios, Los Angeles (USA)
30th October - Roof of MTV Studios, New York City (TRL)
October - *Making The Video: Beautiful Day* (MTV)
2nd November- *Top Of The Pops (BBC)*
3rd November - *CD:UK* (ITV)
13th November - Amigo Awards Ceremony - Palacio de Congresos, Madrid (Spain)
16th November - MTV Music Awards Ceremony - Globe Arena, Stockholm (MTV)
23rd November - Globo Studios, Rio De Janeiro (Brazil)
30th November - *My VH-1 Awards* show - Shrine Auditorium, Los Angeles (VH-1)
9th December - *Saturday Night Live* - NBC Studios, New York City (NBC)

2001

21st February - 2001 Grammy Awards Ceremony - Staples Center, Los Angeles (USA)
26th February - 2001 BRIT Awards Ceremony - Earl's Court, London (ITV)
April - *Making The Video: Elevation* (MTV)
6th June - (Fleet Center, Boston)
21st June - *Charlie Rose Show* (USA - PBS) (Bono interviewed)
25th June - *Audio File* (USA - Tech TV)

Radio Programmes
(Including Interviews And Concerts)

1979
5th October - Cork Opera House (RTE)

1980
26th February - National Stadium, Dublin (RTE)
15th September - *Richard Skinner Show* (BBC Radio 1)
22nd September - Mike Read - *The Evening Show* (BBC)
14th October - KRO Radio (Holland)
26th November - *Peter Powell Show* (BBC)
8th December - *Paul Burnett Show* (BBC)

1981
12th February - Paard Van Troje, The Hague (Holland)
6th March - Paradise Theater, Boston (USA)
11th May - Rainbow Music Hall, Denver (USA - KEZY)
8th June - *Pink Pop Festival* (Holland)
23rd August - *In Concert* (BBC)
28th September - *Peter Powell Show* (BBC)
14th October - *Kid Jensen Show* (BBC)
30th October - Paradiso, Amsterdam (Holland)
14th November - Orpheum Theater, Boston (USA - WBCN)
8th December - The Agora, Cleveland (USA - WRUW)
13th December - Malibu Beach Night Club, Lido Beach (USA - WLIR)
Also:- Radio Forth (Scotland) (Bono interview)

1982
14th May - *Countdown In Concert* (Holland)
4th July - Werchter Festival (Belgium - ID-TV)
6th December - Hammersmith Palais, London (UK)

1983
31st January - Kid Jensen Show (BBC)

24th March - Tiffany's, Glasgow (UK - Radio Clyde)
4th May - WBCN Radio, Boston (band interview)
6th May - Orpheum Theater, Boston (USA)
14th May - Tower Theater, Philadelphia (USA)
30th May - *The US Festival* (USA)
5th June - Red Rocks Amphitheater, Denver (USA)
3rd July - Werchter Festival (Belgium)
20th August - Lorely Amphitheatere, St. Goarshausen (Germany - WDR)

1985
13th July - *Live Aid* Wembley, London / JFK, Philadelphia (BBC / world-wide)

1986
17th May - *Self Aid* RDS, Dublin (RTE)
15th June - Giant's Stadium, East Rutherford (USA)

1987
25th June - *Dave Fanning Show* (*In The Nude*) (RTE)
8th September - *Trip Through Your Wires* (USA - DIR Radio Network)
18th December - KUPO Radio, Arizona (USA)
December - *The Rise and Rise Of U2* (BBC)

1988
8th February - 1988 BRIT Awards Ceremony - Royal Albert Hall, London (BBC)
2nd March - 1988 Grammy Awards Ceremony - Radio City Music Hall, NYC (USA)
16th October - *Smile Jamaica* concert (Dominion Theatre, London) (UK)
30th October - *Annie Nightingale Show* (BBC)

1989
13th February - 1989 BRIT Awards Ceremony - Royal Albert Hall, London (BBC)
22nd February - 1989 Grammy Awards Ceremony (USA)
7th June - *Simon Mayo Show* (BBC)
8th July - *Classic Albums - The Joshua Tree* (BBC)
21st October - *The Midnight Show* (Australia - Triple M)
31st December - Point Depot, Dublin (RTE / world-wide)

1990
1st January - Point Depot, Dublin (RTE / world-wide)
6th February - 1990 BRIT Awards ceremony, Dominion Theatre, London (BBC)

1991
14th November - *Achtung Baby Day* (BBC) (every fourth record played was by U2)
18th November - *Dave Fanning Show* HMV Store, Grafton Street, Dublin (RTE)

1992
13th February - *Mark Goodier Show* (interview with U2) (BBC)
28th August - *Rockline* with Dave Herman (USA)
1st October - Interview with The Edge and Adam (UK -XFM)

1993
1st January - *Zoo Radio* (BBC)
16th February - 1993 BRIT Awards Ceremony - Alexandra

Palace, London (ITV)

24th February - 1993 Grammy Awards Ceremony - Shrine Auditorium, Los Angeles (USA)

23rd August - *Gerry Ryan Show* (interview with Bono) (Ireland)

26th August - *Dave Fanning* Show (interview with The Edge) (RTE 2)

28th August - RDS, Dublin (world-wide radio broadcast)

Also: *Network Zoo* (RTE-2FM)

1994

1st March - 1994 Grammy Awards Ceremony - Radio City Music Hall, New York City (USA)

1995

14th December - Frank Sinatra 80th Birthday Tribute (USA) (Bono and Edge sing)

1996

Bono and Edge interview with Simon Mayo (BBC)

1997

12th February - *Pop Mart* press conference - New York City (world-wide)

20th February - *Dave Fanning Show* (2FM)

7th June - *Tibetan Freedom Concert* (world-wide)

20th June - *U2 Takes Over A Radio Station* (USA - KROQ-FM / worldwide)

1998

Worldwide radio interview with U2 (worldwide)

1999

16th February - 1999 BRIT Awards Ceremony - London

23rd February - 1999 Grammy Awards Ceremony (USA) (Bono sings)

9th October - *NetAid* concert - New York (world-wide) (Bono performs solo)

31st December - America's Millennium Gala - Washington (USA) (Bono performs solo)

2000

23rd October - Simon Mayo/Jo Whiley interview (BBC)

26th October - Universal studios, Los Angeles (USA - KROQ)

2001

21st February - 2001 Grammy Awards Ceremony - Staples Center, Los Angeles (USA)

26th February - 2001 BRIT Awards Ceremony - Earl's Court, London

BOOKS

INTRODUCTION

U2 have had many books written on them over the past twenty years, most of them published in the 1990's. Prior to 1987 there had only been a handful, but since the publication of *Unforgettable Fire* by Eamon Dunphy, there has been a whole plethora of titles that have looked at every aspect of their careers. Below is a list of all the known available U2 books in alphabetical order including publisher, year of issue and ISBN number where known. The books are in the English language unless stated otherwise.

U2 BOOKS:-

Another Time, Another Place U2 - The Early Days - Bill Graham (Mandarin) 1989 ISBN 0 7493 0218 6

Achtung Baby - Volume One: The Bootlegs - Sascha Kremer 1994

Bono - In His Own Words - Dave Thompson (Omnibus Press) 1989 ISBN 0 7119 1646 2

Bono: In His Own Words: Susan Black 1998

The Complete Guide To The Music of U2 - Bill Graham (Omnibus) 1995 ISBN 0 7119 4302 8

The Complete Illustrated Guide Through The World Of U2 Bootlegs - Sascha Kremer 1996

A Grand Madness - Ten Years On The Road With U2 - Dianne Ebertt Beeaff (Hawkmoon Publications) 2000 ISBN 0-9656188-1-1

Into The Heart - Niall Stokes 1996 (Carlton) ISBN 0 7119 5569 7

For Love Or Money - J. Gareth Williams

Frank Laufenberg Presents Facts & Platten - Frank Laufenberg (Moewig) 1988 ISBN 3 8118 3347 2

The Legend of U2 (And Other Things Besides) - "Scratch & Kerr" (Anna Livia) 1989

Out Of Control: A Guide To U2 Bootleg CD's - Mark Taylor (Rock Bottom Press)1993

Outside Is America (12 Years With U2 Backstage And Beyond) - Carter Allen (Faber & Faber) 1992 ISBN 1-85283-758-6

Protest (Japanese U2 photo book)

Race of Angels - The Genesis Of U2 - John Waters (4th Estate) 1994 ISBN 1 85702 210 6

The Road To Pop - Carter Allen 1997 (Updated version of "Outside Is America" to Pop)

The Spark That Set The Flame - Marieke Groen 1993

Tempi Lumoinosi - Editor: Niall Stokes (Arcana) 1990 ISBN 88 85859 56 9 (Italian compilation of the two *Hot Press* books, *The U2 File* and *Three Chords And The Truth*).

Tutti I Testi Con Traduzione A Fronte - Riccardo Bertoncelli (Arcana) 1991 ISBN 88 85008 76 3 (Italian translation of the lyrics of all U2 songs from 1980 to 1991, plus discography and videography)

Unforgettable Fire - The Story Of U2 - Eamon Dunphy (Viking) 1987 ISBN 0 670 82104 7

Unforgettable Fire - The Story of U2 (With A New Epilogue) - Eamon Dunphy (Penguin) 1993 ISBN 0 14 023240 0 (A reprint of the original book in paperback form with a brief epilogue about the years 1988 to 1992 by Bill Graham)

U2 - Author Unknown Spanish biography

U2 - Jurgen Seibold (VIP) 1992 A German language book on U2.

U2 - Mark Taylor (Carlton Books) 1993 ISBN 1857995677 (Also in German)

U2 - Mike Nichols (Anabas) 1987 ISBN 1 85099 017 4

U2 - Jackie Shirley (Magna Books) 1993 ISBN 1854225154

U2 A Biography - Winston Brandt (Ballantine) 1986 ISBN 0345 37892 2

U2 A Conspiracy Of Hope - Dave Bowler & Brian Dray

(Sidgwick & Jackson) 1993
ISBN 0 283 06169 3
U2 A Conspiracy Of Hope - Dave Bowler & Brian Dray
(Pan) 1994 ISBN 0 330 33967 2
(Same as above, but in paperback form with a couple of
extra chapters on *Zooropa*).
U2 At The End Of The World - Bill Flanagan (Bantam
Press) 1995 ISBN 0 593 03626 3
U2 Burning Desire - The Complete U2 Story - Sam
Goodman (Castle Communications) 1993 IBN 1 898141 00
2
U2 Fuego Irlandes (Irish Fire) - Lorenzo Alpouente
(Spanish book on the history of U2)
U2 In Quotes (Babylon Books) 1988 ISBN 0907188 392
U2 Faraway So Close - BP Fallon (Virgin) 1994 ISBN 0
86369 885 9
The U2 File - A Hot Press History (edited by Niall
Stokes) 1985
U2 Live - Pimm Jal de la Parra (Omnibus) 1994 ISBN 0
7119 3666 8
U2 Pisando Fuerto (Breaking Through) 1987 (Span-
ish book which quotes U2 from the years 1980 to 1987)
U2 Poster Book - Douglas Jardine (Atlanta Press) 1987
ISBN 1 870049 05 5
**U2 Rattle And Hum - The Official Book Of The U2
Movie** (Pyramid) 1988 ISBN 1871307 414
U2 The Rolling Stone Files - Edited by Elysa Gardiner
(Sidwick & Jackson) 1994 ISBN 0 283 06239 8
U2: Stories For Boys - Dave Thomas (Proteus) 1985
ISBN 08276 3150
U2: Stories For Boys - Dave Thomas (Bobcat) 1987
ISBN 0 7119 1111 8
(A revised edition of above with bits added on to include
The Joshua Tree album and tour).
U2 The Story So Far - Richard Seal (Britannia Press)
1993 ISBN 0 9519937 2 0
U2 Tear Out Photo Book (Oliver Books) 1993 ISBN 1
870049 53 5
U2 Three Chords And The Truth -Edited by Niall
Stokes (Hot Press) 1989
(Published in US by Harmony Books ISBN 0 517 57697)
U2 Touch The Flame - An Illustrated Documentary -
Geoff Parkyn (Omnibus) 1987
ISBN 07119 1233 5
**U2 Wide Awake In America (12 Years With U2
Backstage And Beyond)** - Carter Allen (Boxtree) 1992
ISBN 1 85283 758 6 (English version of *Outside Is Amer-
ica*)
U2 Zoo Book (1992) (A limited edition boxed set of 2000
that contained book, CD, T-shirt and poster

Books With Sections On U2

(not including music encyclopaedias)
Allegro - Anton Corbijn (Shirmers Visual Library) 1991
ISBN 388144 280 (A photographic book by U2's principal
photographer. It contains pictures of Bono and Adam).
A Year With Swollen Appendices - Brian Eno
Bringing It All Back Home (BBC Books) 1991 (The
book of the TV series that looked at the influence and
importance of Irish music. U2 are mentioned).
Cannongate Pocket Book of the Psalms - Introduc-
tion by Bono

**The Complete Guide to Celtic Music: From the
Highland Bagpipe to Riverdance and U2** - June Skin-
ner Sawyers 1999
Hungry For Heaven - Steve Turner (Virgin) 1988 ISBN 0
86369
(By the co-author of the *Rattle And Hum* film book, Steve
Turner looks at how religion has played a part in popular
music. U2 get a whole chapter to themselves in this book)
Idle Worship - Edited by Chris Roberts (Harper Collins)
1994 ISBN 0 00 638266 5
(A book written by musicians and writers about *their*
heroes. It contains a chapter on Frank Sinatra by Bono).
Irish Rock; Roots, Personalities, Directions -
Mark.J.Prendergast 1987 (This book on Irish Rock music
contains forty pages on U2 alone).
**Irish Rock: Where It's Come From; Where It's
Going** - 1992
Radio 1's Classic Interviews - Edited by Jeff Simpson
1992 (BBC Books) ISBN 0 563 36408 4 (In this collection
of BBC Radio 1 interviews, U2 are interviewed about *Rattle
& Hum* in 1988).
Werk - Anton Corbijn 2000 (It contains a whole chapter
devoted to Bono)
**When The Music's Over (The Story Of Political
Pop)** - Robin Denselow 1989 (Faber & Faber) ISBN 0 571
15380 1 (U2 are discussed with regard to Live Aid,
Amnesty International, Central America and Irish Politics
in general).

U2 Songbooks

The U2 Portfolio - Edited by Marc Marot (Blue Mountain
Music) 1985 ISBN 0711907625 This first U2 song book
contained the sheet music and lyrics to the following
songs:- *11 O' Clock Tick Tock, Surrender, Bad, I Will
Follow, New Year's Day, The Unforgettable Fire, Indian
Summer sky, Sunday Bloody Sunday, Stranger In A Strange
Land, Pride (In The Name Of Love), The Electric Co., A
Sort Of Homecoming, Rejoice, October, Drowning Man,
Touch, Gloria.*
The U2 Songbook
The Joshua Tree Songbook - Transcription by Ken
Chipkin (International M.P) 1987 ISBN 0 7119 1315 3 Con-
tains the sheet music for guitar, bass and piano parts to the
songs on *The Joshua Tree,* as well as plenty of Anton Cor-
bijn photos.
U2 Rattle & Hum Songbook - (Wise publications) 1989
ISBN 0 7119 1791 4 Apart from the sheet music for the
guitar and piano parts, this songbook also contains the lyrics
for each song written out separately plus a transcript of
Bono's words in the middle of *Bullet The Blue Sky.*
Achtung Baby Songbook - (International M.P.) 1992
ISBN 0 7119 29112 2 Besides the sheet music for the guitar
and piano parts, this songbook contains a special article on
"The Making Of Achtung Baby" by Brian Eno, a U2 interview with BP Fallon, and many previously unpublished
photos by Anton Corbijn.
The Best Of U2 - Transcription by Andy Aledort (Wise
Publications) ISBN 0 7119 1314 5
The Best Of U2 - Transcription by Wollf Marshal (International M.P.) ISBN 0 86359 501 4 These two books have
the guitar, bass and piano sheet music to the following U2
songs:- *Surrender, Bad, A Sort Of Homecoming, Gloria,*

The Unforgettable Fire, I Will Follow, Sunday Bloody Sunday, October, New year's Day, Pride (In The Name Of Love)

The Best Of U2 - Nouva Carisch 1992 A different set of songs to above:- *I Will Follow, Gloria, October, New year's Day, Surrender, Sunday Bloody Sunday, Pride (In The Name Of Love), A Sort Of Homecoming, Bad, I Still Haven't Found What I'm Looking For, With Or Without You, Where The Streets Have No Name, Angel Of Harlem, Love rescue Me, Desire, One, Mysterious Ways, The Fly.*

The Best Of U2: With Notes and Tablature - Micahel Lefferts 1997

Pop 1997 ISBN 0-7119-6539-0 All the songs from *Pop* with:- *Discotheque, Do You Feel Loved, Mofo, If God will Send His Angels, Staring At The Sun, Last Night On Earth, Gone Miami, The Playboy Mansion, If You Wear That Velvet Dress, Please, Wake Up Dead Man.*

U2 The Complete Songs 1999 (Wise Publications) ISBN 0-7119-7469-1 This book has the sheet music to every U2 song from *Out of Control* to *Pop*. It also has an introduction by Bill Flanagan, a discography, a videography, a gigography, a chronology and many photos from throughout the band's career.

All That You Can't Leave Behind 2000 This contains sheet music to all the songs from the album:- *Beautiful Day, Stuck In A Moment You Can't Get Out Of, Elevation, Walk On, Kite, In A Little While, Wild Honey, Peace On Earth, When I Look At The World, New York, Grace.*

U2 Tour Programmes

War -1983
The Unforgettable Fire (Europe) - 1984
The Unforgettable Fire (North America) - 1985
The Joshua Tree (North America) - 1987
The Joshua Tree (Europe) - 1987
Lovetown Tour - 1989
Zoo TV - 1992
Zoo TV Outside Broadcast - 1992
Zooropa - 1993
Zoomerang - 1993
Pop Mart - 1997
Elevation (North America) - 2001

U2 Fanzines

In the 1990's there were at one time about 100 U2 fanzines being published by U2 fans all over the world, giving the latest news about the band as well as concert and record reviews. Many of them were listed in each issue of *Propaganda* magazine. They ranged from a few type written sheets, hurriedly stapled together to glossy colour magazines, all carefully complied as a labour of love by some dedicated U2 fan. Sadly, with the coming of the Internet, the World Wide Web and Internet chat rooms, U2 fanzines have dwindled to a mere trickle in recent years. The following U2 fanzines are known to be currently available:-

Eirinn - British based English language fanzine
Contact :- Eirinn@btinternet.com
In The Name of Love - Italian based English language fanzine
Contact:- www.geocities.com/inthenameofloveu2fanzine
The Real Thing - British based English language fanzine
Contact:- 14 Corporation Street, Stoke-on-Trent, Staffordshire, ST4 4AU, England

Websites

Over the past ten years the Internet has mushroomed worldwide and websites dedicated to U2 have grown with it. Apart from the official U2 website, U2.com and the other official websites mentioned in the main book, it is estimated that there are now approximately 1,000 U2 websites on the Internet. Below are details of a few selected U2 websites.

General Sites:-
ALL I WANT IS U2: http://www.geocities.com/SunsetStrip/Backstage/7715
AT U2: www.atu2.com
THE THREE SUNRISES: www.threesunrises.com
THE U2 EXPERIENCE: www.angelfire.com/wi/theu2experience
THE U2 ZONE: www.theu2zone.com
U2 INTERFERENCE: www.interference.com
U2 LOG.COM: www.u2log.com
U2 STAR: www.u2star.com/homeame.html
U2 STATION: www.u2station.com
WHERE THE SITE HAS NO NAME: www.wherethesitehasnoname.com

Search engines/links:
THE ALL U2 SEARCH: http://srd.yahoo.com/srst/14281330/u2/29/111/*http://u2search.cjb.net
THE U2 WEB RING: http://srd.yahoo.com/srst/2268585/u2/35/111/*http://www.geocities.com/SunsetStrip/Club/3754
U2 LINKS: www.u2links.com
U2 LINKS 1: http://cx45564-a.chnd1.az.home.com/myweb/u2/u2links.asp

Fan chat:-
FREQUENTLY ASKED QUESTIONS: www.u2faq.com
THE WIRE: www.u2wire.com

Discography:-
FLARE'S U2 COLLECTION: www.users.globalnet.co.uk/~flare/index.html
U2 DISCOGRAPHY: www.geocities.com/Tokyo/Bay/3474/html/u2-aol.html
THE WANDERER: www.u2wanderer.org

Concerts:-
THE UNAFILIATED U2 CONCERT TRANSCRIPTS: http://members.aol.com/reiter/trcript.htm
U2 TOUR.COM: www.u2tour.com
U2 TOURS: www.u2tours.com - detailed log of virtually every U2 concert with set lists

Lyrics:-
MEANING OF U2 LYRICS: www.dtek.chalmers.se/~d4jonas/U2MoL/index.shtml
THE U2 LYRICS ARCHIVE: www.interference.com/u2la
U2*STARING AT THE SUN: www.mindspring.com/~twhite21/U2frame.html

News:-
YOU TWO: www.youtwo.net
U2 NEWS: www.u2news.com

U2 NEWS: www.u2news.de
U2 UNIVERSE: www.u2universe.com

Awards

U2 have won many awards over the years. This list does not include sales awards for records.

Grammy Awards:-

1987:- Album of the Year - *The Joshua Tree*;
Best Rock Performance by a Duo or Group - *Joshua Tree*
1988:- Best Rock Performance by a Duo or Group - "Desire"
Best Performance Music Video (short form) - "Where the Streets Have No Name"
1992:- Best Rock Vocal by a Duo or Group - *Achtung Baby*
1993:- Best Alternative Music Album - *Zooropa*
1994:- Best Music Video (Long Form) - *Zoo TV Live From Sydney*
2000:- Song of the Year - "Beautiful Day"
Record of the Year - "Beautiful Day"
Best Rock Performance by a Duo or Group with Vocal - "Beautiful Day"

BRIT Awards:-

1983:- Best Live Act
1988:- Best International Group
1989:- Best International Group
1990:- Best International Group
1992:- Best Live Act
1998:- Best International Group
2001:- Best International Group / Outstanding Contribution to Music Award

MTV Awards:-

1987:- Viewer's Choice - "With or Without You"
1988:- Best Video From a Film - "When Love Comes to Town"
1992:- Best Group Video / Best Special Effects - "Even Better Than the Real Thing"
1995:- Best Group (MTV Europe)
1997:- Best Live Act (MTV Europe)

Rolling Stone magazine:-

The awards are in two forms - those chose by the readers - "Readers Picks" and those chosen by the editorial staff - "Critics Picks"
1985:- Band of the Year / Best Performance at Live Aid (Readers Picks)
Band of the Year (Critics Picks)
1987:- Artist of the Year / Best Album - *The Joshua Tree* / Best Single - "With or Without You" ("Where The Streets Have No Name" was 2nd and "I Still Haven't Found What I'm Looking For" was 3rd) / Best Band / Best Male Singer - Bono / Best Producer - Daniel Lanois and Brian Eno / Best Songwriter - Bono / Best Video - "Where The Streets Have No Name" ("With or Without You" was 2nd) / Best Album Cover - *The Joshua Tree* / Best Live Performance / Best Guitartist - The Edge / Best Bass Player - Adam Clayton / Best Drummer - Larry Mullen Jr. / Sexiest Male Rock Artist - Bono (Readers Picks)
Artist of the Year / Best Band / Best Producer - Daniel Lanois / Best Guitarist - The Edge (Critics Picks)

1988:- Artist of the Year / Best Album - *Rattle & Hum* / Best Single - "Desire" / Best Band / Best Male Singer - Bono / Best Songwriter - Bono / Best Video - Desire / Best Album Cover - *Rattle & Hum* / Best Bass Player - Adam Clayton / Best Drummer - Larry Mullen Jr. (Readers Picks)
1989:- Best Songwriter - Bono (Readers Picks)
1992:- Comeback of the Year / Best Drummer - Larry Mullen Jr. (Critics Picks)
1993:- Best Single - "One" / Best Band / Best Male Singer / Artist of the Year / Best Album - *Achtung Baby* / Best Songwriter - Bono / Best Album Cover - *Achtung Baby* / Sexiest Male Artist - Bono / Best Tour - ZooTV / Best Drummer - Larry Mullen Jr. / Come back of the Year (Readers Picks)
Best Band (tie with REM) / Best Tour - ZooTV / Worst Tour - ZooTV (Critics Picks)

Billboard:-

1992:- Top Album Rock Tracks Artists / Top Album Rock Tracks / Top Modern Rock Tracks Artits / Top Modern Rock Tracks

Hot Press magazine:-

The Irish Music Journal *Hot Press* magazine has two categories of awards - those chosen by the readers of which U2 have won several categories every year from 1980 onwards, and their own annual awards, The Hot Press Rock Awards held in the autumn, which began in 1996. The second category of award is listed below:-
1998:- Best Band / Best Live Act
1999: - Best Single - "Sweetest Thing"

Other miscellaneous awards:-

1988:- *Sunday Independent*/Irish Life Arts Award
1992:- International Entertainer of the Year - Juno Awards
Best Selling Irish Artist of The Year - World Music Awards
1994:- Best Live Act - Uno Ano De Rock Awards
Best Selling Irish Recording Artists of the Year - World Music Awards
Award For International Achievement - Ivor Novello Awards
1997:- Best International Act - Comet Awards
1999:- "Gig of the Year" from *Oh Yeah!* an Internet website (U2 with Ash at the "Yes vote" concert of 19th May 1998)
2000:- The Freedom of Dublin (with Paul McGuinnness)
2001:- Best Rock Act / "God-like Geniuses" Awards - NME/ Carling "Brats" ceremony
Best International Group - Italian Music Awards

Individual Awards:-

Bono:

1999:- Free Your Mind Award - MTV Europe
2000:- "Man of the Year" Award - NRJ Awards in France

Edge:

1996:- Rory Gallagher Rock Musician Award - Hot Press Rock Awards

Adam:

2000:- "Best Bassist - Male" - Gibson Guitar Awards

Larry:

1997:- Rory Gallagher Rock Musician Award - Hot Press Rock Awards

Buy Online

All SAF and Firefly titles are available from the SAF Publishing website. You can also browse the full range of rock, pop, jazz and experimental music books we have available. You can also keep up with our latest releases and special offers, contact us, and request a catalogue.

www.safpublishing.com

You can also write to us at:

SAF Publishing Ltd, Unit 7, Shaftesbury Centre,

85 Barlby Road, London, W10 6BN. England

Mail Order

All SAF and Firefly titles are also available by mail order from the world famous Helter Skelter bookshop.

You can phone or fax your order to Helter Skelter on these numbers:

Telephone: +44 (0)20 7836 1151 or Fax: +44 (0)20 7240 9880

Office hours: Mon-Fri 10:00am - 7:00pm,

Sat: 10:00am - 6:00pm, Sun: closed.

Helter Skelter Bookshop,

4 Denmark Street, London, WC2H 8LL, United Kingdom.

If you are in London come and visit us, and browse the titles in person!!

Email: helter@skelter.demon.co.uk

Website: http://www.skelter.demon.co.uk

www.safpublishing.com

saf publishing

www.safpublishing.com